INTERPRETING PERSONALITY THEORIES

LEDFORD J. BISCHOF
Professor of Psychology
Northern Illinois University

HARPER & ROW, PUBLISHERS
NEW YORK, EVANSTON, AND LONDON

Dedicated to Betty and Barbara
whose personalities, theoretical or not, continuously fascinate me

And so that we can better understand ourselves, this book is written.

19220

INTERPRETING PERSONALITY THEORIES

D-O

Library of Congress Catalog Card Number: 64-11185

Contents

Preface

The present book is intended to be a textbook on theories of personality for a one-semester course at the undergraduate level. It may also appeal to the fairly sophisticated layman who may find it readable and useable for study groups. Primarily, the book is designed to "stretch the minds" of the undergraduate student. It is hoped that the students who use this as a textbook will be able to expand the understanding and the dimensions of their own personalities and in so doing to gain a deeper understanding of the personality dynamics of their fellow human beings.

The present work grew out of the author's needs in teaching the course Theories of Personality at the undergraduate level. Many excellent works exist in this field but they are primarily source books and not teaching instruments as a textbook should be. In the past the alternative has been to read the works of each individual theorist. This is most difficult, especially at the undergraduate level, since thirty to forty students may be sent to read one or two copies of the work in the library reserve shelves. In some cases the work may exist only in the theorist's original foreign language—a situation which again makes it practically inaccessible to the average undergraduate student. For all these reasons the author has tried to create an undergraduate text in personality theories with a psychological emphasis.

Apropos of the American Psychological Association's Miami meeting in 1958 concerning the undergraduate program in psychology and the lack of recommendation for a unified program, the inclusion of a course in personality theories at the undergraduate level may be somewhat controversial. The author thinks that such a course at the undergraduate level should be mandatory. Personality theories can be (and have been for this writer-teacher) an excellent preparation for education and speech-correction majors interested in more than the techniques inherent in their own disciplines. Psychology majors profit from a theoretical study of personality as a background for later graduate work. As strong a case can be made for this area in the general education sequence as for the traditional basic psychology course. (Personality theory studies *why* man behaves as he does, the dynamics of man's behavior, within a uniquely personal frame of reference; that is, the student involves his own self image with each of the theories. The basic psychology course is usually more concerned with principles of behavior from a nonpersonal frame of reference.) In all, it seems logical to introduce the work of personality theorists to students of human behavior at some point in the undergraduate program rather than to save it for an esoteric approach in the doctoral program. Ideally the undergraduate student should emerge from such a course eager to pursue the ideas of a few theorists on his own. The student usually rejects some theorists and enthusiastically accepts others. This text is an interpretation of the theories designed to help the beginning student of human behavior steer his way through the vast amount of written work. An advanced student of personality theories must read each theorist in the original. It is hoped that this book will help the student as he constructs a personality theory of his own. As the scholar knows, man has always progressed socially and technically through the avenues of theories as directional devices for ongoing work.

The rationale for the sequence of parts and chapters is explained in the introduction and background material for Part I. The manuscript is designed to permit individual instructors to select material to best fit their own syllabuses. Rightly or wrongly, the author's aim is the formulation of a theory of personality by each individual student. This will certainly result if the learning experience in class is worthwhile. The student needs all the help he can get in formulating his own theory of personality. The method the author uses is delineated in Chapter 2, A Point of View. It has proved to be a valuable teaching aid in the interpretation of personality theories. Chapter 2 may be used or ignored with no damage to the continuity of the text. It is recommended, however, as a valuable tool in teaching.

Each textbook is different, or should be, from others of its kind. This work does not attempt to evaluate the separate theories according to any set criteria. This is not an oversight or evasion but a deliberate attempt to bring the student and instructor to a point where they evaluate for themselves the quality of a theory. Too many textbooks attempt to be "all things to all men" and, further, to teach the course for the instructor.

Such is not the intention of this book. As an interpretation it is prone to all the weaknesses inherent in any interpretation: It rephrases, casts a thought in another language, translates, explains, and, in true Webster style, "construe(s) in the light of individual belief, judgment, or interest."

The author has had personal visits with some of the theorists involved in the book. All of the living contributors to the range of personality theories presented in this book have given me their comments, and I have carefully weighed these comments in the preparation of the final version of the book. It is believed, therefore, that no errors of fact are likely to have gone unnoted and that the perspectives are essentially such as the authors would be willing to accept.

With a deep sense of gratitude the author would especially like to thank Miss Anna Freud, Dr. Hilda Himmelweit, Professor Philip Vernon and the staff of the University of London, and Dr. H. J. Eysenck, among many others for their hospitality and guidance while the author was abroad during the academic year 1959–1960. A special note of thanks is directed to Dr. Gordon Allport for his assistance in many things both professional and personal. With affectionate remembrance the author recalls his visit to the late Dr. Carl Jung.

Further thanks go to Mr. J. P. James for research assistance, Miss Joanne Jacobs, Mrs. James Breen, and Mrs. Marvin Sauter Romanski for the typing of the manuscript. To my colleague, friend, and chairman, Dr. A. B. Woodruff, go my thanks for easing the teaching assignments and minimizing the peripheral details of a teaching professor's life while the manuscript was in the final stages. Credit for the clever illustrations go to my friend, Cecil G. Strawn, Jr.

The greatest debt of gratitude, however, is owed to my wife Betty. I should like to acknowledge publicly her infinite patience, meticulous reading of the manuscript, highly intelligent comments, and especially her warm encouragement during the many months the manuscript was in process both here and in Europe.

L. J. B.

PART I

INTRODUCTION AND BACKGROUND

Introduction

Personality theories are the products of man's thinking. They do not exist in nature as do the atoms. Man formulates theories of personality while trying to explain the behavior of his fellow man, particularly the reasons behind the actions that people make. Just as atoms exist and there are theories concerning the reasons for their behavior, so human beings exist, and there are theories concerning the reasons for their behavior.

Oddly enough most people seem to feel more comfortable when a theory or a law becomes identified with the name of the man who originated the idea; or even with the leading exponent of the theory when its origins are confused or lost in antiquity. Thus, men's names are attached to a theoretical position. Examples may be found in theories of learning; of intelligence; of physical laws; and of religious beliefs, such as Christianity, Mohammedanism, Buddhism, and Zoroastrianism. This propensity of man to associate a person's name with a theory holds also for theories of personality.

Each chapter in this book bears the name of the person who originated a major theory of personality. Unfortunately the individual's name in no way identifies the major aspects of the theory. Nevertheless, it is enough to say, "That was a Freudian slip," for instance, in order to express the phenomenon of repression as it is found in Freud's theory. At first, the name identifies the theory, then a turnabout takes place and the theory is identified by the name.

Theories can be studied in many ways. One may organize them historically or heuristically or hierarchically or homogenously or geographically (that is to say, American *vis à vis* European) or haphazardly. The organization of the theorists for study in this book is purely the device of the author: if no serious distortion is done to the theory itself, then the organization is worthwhile. Further explanation of the grouping of theorists into particular sections is presented in the introductory remarks to the section. The strengths and the weaknesses of each theory are also discussed.

Some time ago, in a talk with Gardner Murphy, the suggestion was strongly advanced that the present writer should create a theory of personality of his own for use as a textbook: certain considerations preclude that proposition at this time. The primary task of the present work is to teach others the fundamentals of already existing theories so that they may create their own, rather than to add another theory for the mill. It is more profitable to help others in the groundwork of personality theories than to espouse another.

Parallel to these thoughts is the undergraduate's question, "Why not write a book presenting one large all-inclusive general theory of personality incorporating the best from all of them?" As Maier said: "A general behavior theory is premature at the present time because it (a) discourages exploratory research; (b) emphasizes quantitative measurement at the expense of qualitative analysis; (c) assumes that science develops along deductive logical lines, thereby excluding many other sources of development and kinds of thinking; and (d) is unwilling to entertain concepts which are still vague and in the process of development."[1] And again, "It should be clear . . . that, at best, personality theory may be regarded as in ferment."[2] (For further excellent comment pertinent to creating a single over-all theory of personality see Ammons' discussion of teaching theory-formulation to graduate students in *The Kentucky Symposium*, p. 139–141.)

The theories in the present text have been grouped into the following classifications for ease in studying their relationships to one another:

Part   I: Introduction and Background.
Part   II: Biophysical and Biophilosophical.
Part III: Biosocial and Social Interactions.
Part IV: General and Integrative.
Part   V: Contributions of Other Theories.
Part VI: Final Thoughts and Reconsiderations.

[1] *Learning Theory, Personality Theory, and Clinical Research: The Kentucky Symposium*, Wiley, 1954, p. 64.
[2] C. M. Harsh and H. G. Schrickel, *Personality: Development and Assessment*, 2nd ed., Ronald, 1959, p. 381.

1

Personality Theory:
An Overview

Know then thyself, presume not God to scan
The proper study of mankind is man.

ALEXANDER POPE
Essays on Man, Epistle II, line 1

WHY STUDY PERSONALITY THEORY?

Plato in *The Apology* paraphrases Socrates when he says, "The un-examined life is not worth living." This interesting thought from the ancient Greeks has been carried down through the ages and even today is the rationale for much of man's self-analysis. Personality theories fit within the picture of examining life, because they concern themselves with the general theories of behavior as man lives his life.

Personality theories are functional. By this we mean they are ongoing processes, that they are active and not inactive. "Functional" further means a useful activity, designed to maintain balance between variable parts of a system. Progressing from this we find that personality thories are concerned with the very basis of man's behavior. What we are about to examine, then, are theories which concern themselves with the deepest, innermost determinants of human behavior.

Personality theories are integrative. They attempt to bring together the many facets of man's behavior and to weld these into a meaningful statement which will help to clarify the question of why man behaves as he does. Rather than fractionize man's behavior, personality theorists are interested in unifying the multitude of activities and binding them together into a functioning whole.

The most casual observer of the human scene can find overwhelming evidence that everyone is interested in human behavior. Though not all of us are societally oriented, at least we are extremely interested in ourselves. As outmoded as introspection may be on the current psychological scene, all of us indulge in the phenomenon of self-examination, for we are always held within the walls of our own selves no matter what we do. Personality theorists try to further man's interest in human behavior and to refine the limited knowledge we possess concerning the human animal.

The "What am I?" question is not a new one. Philosophy and religion have for many centuries examined it. Novelists and poets have created literary works directed toward exploring the answers to the question. Personality theory is the psychological attempt to bring more scientific evidence into play in resolving the timeless question of "What am I?"

At times the entire area of personality theory may seem to be best approached from a plain, good, old-fashioned, common-sense point of view. Any student of human behavior, even in the traditional basic psychology class, soon finds that common sense may be indeed common, or general, but its sense is surrounded by prejudice, superstition, and acres of wishful thinking. For example, the common-sense, or popular idea that love will conquer all is neatly handled in Bettelheim's *Love Is Not Enough*. You may love a person with every fiber of your body, but that cannot repair a broken leg or a psychotic ego. Again, personality theory tries to bring fresh insight, and, eventually, predictable patterns into the study of human behavior, strengthened by a growing concern to examine behavior in a research-oriented situation.

One of the universal questions current is that of survival in an age of atomic warfare. Gradually we are beginning to realize the enormity of retaliation leading to annihilation. Out of this framework of fear have come some approaches which suggest possibilities for understanding not hitherto tried. One such approach suggests that modern man must first try to learn to understand himself. With this background of understanding, he may then be better able to understand others, and he will be much better able to cooperate on a more realistic and meaningful level with all peoples. Such an attempt to reanalyze the current international scene was brilliantly made by Jerome Frank (see J. D. Frank, The Great Antagonism: The U.S. Versus the U.S.S.R., *Atlantic*, 202, No. 5, 58-63). Personality theory, then, can be a first step toward the foregoing approach to bettering human relationships on the international scene. It would be intellectual dishonesty to maintain that studying personality theories can bring world peace, but it would also be intellectual evasion to deny the right of self-examination as an avenue toward bettering human relationships on all fronts. If a theory concerning human behavior is universal for all cultures and ethnic groups, it must then be held that to study the theory is to understand all peoples better than has been possible in the past.

Although the reader will realize after some time that this is a book about himself, his personality, his dynamics of behavior, it can never be presented as a book on self-help, or, to use Hilgard's well-chosen words, "a manual on the art of handling people." Study in this field does not replace trained clinical help. Although the text should help students to understand the "why's" of existence, personality theory is not directly concerned with psychiatric therapy.

WHAT CONSTITUTES A THEORY—PERSONALITY OR OTHER?

There is a basic difference between personality theories and theories found in the general area of psychology. In the former case we are concerned with studying the individual in all the facets of his person and determining how these factors explain and predict his behavior. The emphasis is primarily upon normal, everyday behavior. The reasons for man's behavior become the rallying point for personality theory. In the latter case, there are many theories concerning smaller aspects of man's behavior but none concerning the unifying aspects of human behavior. There are theories explaining color combinations, motivation for food rewards, selection and placement of employees in industrial firms, and many others designed to explain behavior in terms of only one direct goal or objective. Many of the valuable theories in psychology try to answer a specific question in a specific field. The work of Roethlisberger, for example, at the Hawthorne Works of the Western Electric Company, revolved around theories of motivation, but these studies used theories designed to improve production and morale *in a specific situation*. Personality theory, on the other hand, concerns itself with motivation as a prime mover in life and throughout life, for both men and women, in all cultural climates: they are designed to grapple with over-all aspects of man's behavior in *all* kinds of situations.

Some confusion may arise from the differences between an hypothesis and a theory. From English and English we find that an hypothesis is an explanation of a complex set of data admittedly tentative and not yet proven, while a theory is a developed hypothesis supported by very substantial evidence.[1] Speculation may lead to an hypothesis, which in turn may lead to a theory, which, if the evidence appears irrefutable, may eventually be established as a law. It is interesting to note that at one time the study of psychology was organized around "laws" of behavior, a term now generally disreputable, although one notes signs of emerging laws of behavior creeping into the literature of behaviorists in psychology. (See especially Brown and Ghiselli, *Scientific Method in Psychology,* p. 161; and for the sophisticated student, see also Egon Brunswik's chapter, "The Conceptual Framework of Psychology," in Vol. I, Pt. 2, of the *International Encyclopedia of Unified Science,* University of Chicago Press, combined edition, 1955.)

As stated previously, we find that a theory is created out of an hypothesis; when the evidence seems overpowering, a theory eventually evolves out of this tested hypothesis. We must now turn our attention to the basic question of what a theory should include. First of all, a theory is a man-made scheme which proceeds from assumptions of hypotheses, having a logical inner consistency which leads to testifiable or empirically oriented reality. The more precisely a theory is constructed, the more fruitful it is in actual use. None of the theories in this book concerning personality fully meets the above definition. However, few theories in any field meet the fullest requirements of optimal definitions. It is not the intent of this work to test each personality theory as to its perfection when held up against the perfection of a definition, but to try to illuminate and educate the reader toward the content of each theory. We are merely interested in formulating a basis for theory construction, so that the reader may better acquaint himself with the rubric of the theoretical approach.

---

[1] H. B. English and A. C. English, *A Comprehensive Dictionary of Psychological and Psychoanalytical Terms,* Longmans, 1958, p. 246. (Courtesy David McKay Co.)

WHAT SHOULD A THEORY DO?

A theory should be simple and forthright enough to make the idea it is trying to present understandable. It should use *clear language* and not be couched in neologisms.

A theory should be *useful* so that it leads to meaningful progress in the evolution of man toward better life goals.

A theory should *bring together* what is known in an orderly manner, incorporating this into a meaningful whole.

A theory should *clarify* man's thinking.

A theory should lead to *accurate prediction* before the fact, not after the fact.

STRUCTURING THE TERM *PERSONALITY*

The reader will notice that there has been a deliberate attempt to avoid the task of defining personality yet. It is not that the word cannot be defined: it can and has been defined by many astute and intelligent writers. There are some objections to defining the term *personality* at this point, however, particularly for the beginning student in the field of personality study. Personality is better defined *after* one has expended considerable effort and energy in studying the concept: it is almost better considered as a concept than as a word. So many phenomena are involved in the term *personality* that clear-cut Websterian definitions are prone to truncate and confuse rather than to expand and clarify.

It is not unknown for man, in his intellectual pursuits, to study a phenomenon without the support of a unanimously accepted definition. Probably outstanding in the field of psychology of this kind is the study of *intelligence*. Many definitions exist for this word, and there is anything but agreement as to what it means, but vast amounts of research, testing, and academic placement are done in the name of intelligence as a behavioral phenomenon.

In essence, the theory of personality to which one subscribes also determines the way in which one will define personality for his own use. This is not to set semantic traps for the novitiate, but to state a truism. Just as one tends to define marriage or religion from the frame of reference of his own marriage or religious beliefs, so one is led to do similarly with personality and the theory he considers the most acceptable. The term *love* is defined in the dictionary, but from those definitions spring so many variations in theme as to make the original definitions an academic question. This does not, we must admit, keep us from trusting that love will operate as each of us conceives it should!

Thus, as we have stated before, one must study personality theories to saturation point before one is capable of defining personality to his own satisfaction. This state of affairs may promote some modicum of motivation: if you wish to be satisfied with a definition of personality, then the path is well marked—study the theories of personality.

All of the above is not intended to beg the question of defining the term *personality* in some measured order. If precise definition seems to be impossible for the moment, let us see what dimensions of personality lend themselves to preparing a definition of the term.

Basically we find that two major areas of consideration are found in personality theory, and though they appear dichotomized, there are common elements between them. Some definitions consider that man's personality is largely biophysical. These definitions concern themselves with what the human being actually is. In contrast to this are the definitions which concern themselves with the effect personalities have upon one another, the biosocial definitions. Under this umbrella of classification most definitions and theories of personality can be fitted without too much effort.

Further attempts to structure the term *personality* and the theories revolving around it may be summarized and outlined as follows:[2]

Nomothetic (largely American) (Methods designed to discover general laws.)	Idiographic (largely European) (Methods designed to understand single and particular individuals.)
1. Study parts or units of personality.	1. Study personality as a unique whole which cannot be analyzed into smaller components.
2. Research designed to find common bonds among all personalities.	2. "Personality cannot be explained but can only be understood."
3. Great emphasis on quantitative efforts.	3. Emphasis on qualitative and unique aspects of personality.

Still further attempts to define *personality* and the theories which sur-

[2] See D. W. MacKinnon, The Structure of Personality, in J. McV. Hunt (ed.), *Personality and the Behavior Disorders,* Ronald, 1944, Vol. I, p. 7.

round it have recently led to advocating the term *personology* as the best approach. Reasons for this grew out of the confusion between character and temperament, both as synonymous terms for personality and as different kinds of personality. Character is now largely treated as the value and ethical norm of an individual. It connotes goodness and badness of content and inner dynamics of the self structure. Temperament is now generally accepted to be only a part of the general term personality and to describe an individual's characteristic emotional states.[3]

Another method which classifies definitions of personality first began with Allport in 1937 (*Personality: A Psychological Interpretation*), and has been utilized by subsequent writers. (An excellent treatment of this approach is to be found in Hall and Lindzey, *Theories of Personality*.) In summary, the definitions seem to be clustered into seven different categories, which Allport drew out after finding some forty-seven distinctive definitions:

1. Biophysical: probably the oldest; defines personality from organic dimensions as well as social characteristics; lends itself to quantification.

2. Biosocial: the reactive stimulus value an individual has to others, who then define or describe in definitive terms the individual's personality for them; his effect upon others.

3. Unique: no two personalities ever the same; each person is different.

4. Integrative: one's personality organizes and integrates the myriad things of which life consists.

5. Adjustment: the homeostatic agent for all of life's problems; the adjudicator of pressures and values.

6. Differential essential: definitions which emphasize the most outstanding feature of the personality, not just uniqueness but the essential features which make each person different in some respect (somewhat allied to typologies).

7. Omnibus: classification that defies categorization; all the other definitions of personality which do not fit into the first six classes.

Trait and type theories and definitions of personality add still another dimension to the field of personality study. Some definitions as they grow out of theoretical considerations cluster about the efforts to identify behavior in accordance with major traits. The term *trait* is greatly overused

[3] *Ibid.*, chap. 1.

as a prefix for too many psychological terms, so that the word has lost much of the power of its meaning. Fundamentally, what is meant by "personality traits" is any enduring and persistent behavioral pattern by which one person can be readily distinguished from others. Thus, we may describe a person's personality as having the trait of honesty, or having the trait of courage. Traits are considered to lie within the individual, whether society gives him credit for the trait or not. They are inner driven ways of behaving. Types, on the other hand, are generally derived from labels which society gives to a personality. Confusion may arise in distinguishing the terms when, at times, the same word is used to describe a trait or a type, such as "One of his strongest traits is honesty," or "He certainly is an honest type of person." The difference then lies not in the behavioral characteristic so much as where the characteristic originates. Traits come from within the individual. Types come from outside of the individual and are designations placed upon the individual for convenience in labelling. At one time it was considered that there could be many traits but that types were restricted in number. However, through the loose use of the terms, especially by lay people, that distinction can scarcely now be made. The average individual is inclined to prefix any convenient adjective to the term *type* and thus describe another's personality.

As a final consideration toward the definition of *personality,* we turn to a pragmatic method, such as that found in Bell, *Projective Techniques* (p. 7). Bell is not trying to define personality nor even to create a personality theory. He attempts to give the underlying assumptions that seem to be involved in creating and using a projective test of personality. From these assumptions students of personality theory may gain a broader insight into the term *personality.*

First, personality is a dynamic and moving force. It is never fixed or rigid. Whatever the personality is, it changes from day to day; whether a person becomes more set in character, or develops in a forward-looking direction. One of the irrefutable facts of life is that daily man grows one day older. So we subscribe to the thesis that personality is not a "cast in the bronze" fact.

Second, personality is of a structured nature. Whatever the dimensions of it may be, it consists of *something.* Beyond the obvious fact of the flesh and blood body, personality may be considered to have inner dynamics, whether they be called drives or dynamisms or forces or id or life style; there is more to man's personality than his body.

Third, personality is a behaving and reacting thing: it does not remain dormant.

Fourth, except possibly for Allport, personality consists of more than what we see on the surface. Whether this is called the unconscious or the persona or the image, the evidence would indicate that not all of what man possesses as a personality is apparent on the surface of his physiognomy or actions.

BIBLIOGRAPHY

PRIMARY SOURCES

BOOKS

Allport, G. W., *Personality: A Psychological Interpretation*, N.Y., Holt, Rinehart and Winston, 1937.

Bell, J. E., *Projective Techniques*, N.Y., Longmans, 1948. (Courtesy David McKay Co.)

Bettelheim, B., *Love Is Not Enough*, N.Y., Free Press, 1950.

Brown, C. W., and E. E. Ghiselli, *Scientific Method in Psychology*, N.Y., McGraw-Hill, 1955.

Brunswik, E., The conceptual framework of psychology, in *International Encyclopedia of Unified Science*, combined edition, *1*, Pt. II, Chicago, Univer. of Chicago Press, 1955, 656–760.

Conant, J. B., *On Understanding Science*, New Haven, Yale Univer. Press, 1947.

English, H. B., and A. C. English, *A Comprehensive Dictionary of Psychological and Psychoanalytical Terms*, N.Y., Longmans, 1958. (Courtesy David McKay Co.)

Hall, C. S., and G. Lindzey, *Theories of Personality*, N.Y., Wiley, 1957.

Hempel, C. G., *Fundamentals of Concept Formation in Empirical Science*, Chicago, Univer. of Chicago Press, 1952.

MacKinnon, D. W., The structure of personality, in J. McV. Hunt (ed.), *Personality and the Behavior Disorders*, *1*, Pt. I, N.Y., Ronald, 1944, 3–48.

PERIODICALS

Frank, J. D., The great antagonism: The U.S. versus the U.S.S.R., *Atlantic*, 202, No. 5, 58–63.

SUGGESTED READINGS

BOOKS

Annual Review of Psychology, Annual Reviews Inc., Cal., Palo Alto.

Sears, R. R., Personality, 1950, *1*, 105–118.

MacKinnon, D. W., Personality, 1951, 2, 113–136.

Eysenck, H. J., Personality, 1952, 3, 155–174.

Bronfenbrenner, U., Personality, 1953, *4*, 157–182.

Child, I. L., Personality, 1954, *5*, 149–170.

Nuttin, J., Personality, 1955, *6*, 161–186.

Personality study becoming a new approach to general psychology of human behavior.

McClelland, D. C., Personality, 1956, 7, 39–62.

Broad review of personality literature to 1955.

Eriksen, C. W., Personality, 1957, 8, 185–210.

Over 500 articles on personality between May, 1955 and April, 1956—author reviews 173 of them.

Jensen, A. R., Personality, 1958, *9*, 295–322.

Review of entire field to April, 1957, extensive bibliography.

Blake, R. R., and Mouton, J. S., Personality, 1959, *10*, 203–232.

Atkinson, J. W., Personality dynamics, 1960, *11*, 255–290.

Messick, S., Personality-structure, 1961, *12*, 93–128.

Jenness, A., Personality Dynamics, 1962, *13*, 479–514.

Barker, S. F., *Induction and Hypothesis: A Study of the Logic of Confirmation,* Ithaca, N.Y., Cornell Univer. Press, 1957.

Eliminative and enumerative induction rejected in favor of competing hypothesis.

Brand, H. (ed.), *The Study of Personality: a book of readings,* N.Y., Wiley, 1954.

David, H. P., and J. C. Brengelmann (eds.), *Perspective in Personality Research,* N.Y., Springer, 1960.

Report of Fifteenth Int. Congress Psychol. Brussels, 1957.

Dreger, R. M., *Fundamentals of Personality,* Philadelphia, Lippincott, 1962.

Experimental approach to major and minor theories.

Lecky, P., *Self-Consistency: A Theory of Personality,* N.Y., Island Press, 1945.

"Personality is the central fact of psychology."

Notcutt, B., *The Psychology of Personality,* N.Y., Philosophical Library, 1953.

Critique of Anglo-American personality theories—attempts to develop a "theory of theories" in personality study.

PERIODICALS

Alexander, P., Theory construction and theory testing, Brit. J. Phil. Sci., 1958, 9, 29–38.

Phenomenology is more than a means of testing a theory—it is something to be explained.

Beck, S. J., The science of personality: nomothetic or idiographic, Psychol. Rev., 1953, 60, 353–359.

Beshers, J. M., Models and theory construction, Amer. Sociol. Rev., 1957, 22, 32–38.

Deemphasize mathematical model in behavioral sciences.

Borgatta, E. F., Toward a methodological codification: the shotgun and the saltshaker, Sociometry, 1961, 24, 432–435.

Theorizing may have to come after the fact.

Dreikurs, R., Are psychological schools of thought outdated?, J. Indiv. Psychol., 1960, 16, 3–10.

Schools of personality theory are needed.

Fisher, M. B., and R. M. Roth, Structure: an essential framework for research, Personnel Guid. J., 1961, 39, 639–644.

Relate research to theory.

Fiske, D. W., Homogeneity and variation in measuring personality, Amer. Psychologist, 1963, 18(10), 643–652.

"Let those of us who are interested in methodology work more closely with personality theorists. . . ."

Grace, H. A., When is science?, Educ. Rev., 1957, 7, 93–101.

Psychology uses 3 techniques: 1. discovery-laboratory experimentation; 2. uncovery-testing or interviewing; 3. recovery-symbol analysis—"An investigation is scientific when the method it employs is appropriate to the problem it seeks to solve." The scientist may choose either but not both.

Lynn, D. B., The organism as a manufacturer of theories, Psychol. Rep., 1957, 3, 353–359.

All men learn by theories.

Morison, R. S., Gradualness, gradualness, gradualness, Amer. Psychologist, 1960, 15, 187–197.

Pavlov's injunction to scientific method and theories—Morison asks for closer relations between theory and practice.

Rokeach, M., and S. H. Bartley, Some pitfalls in psychological theorizing, Amer. Psychologist, 1958, 13, 283–284.

Think before you dream up a new term—is it necessary or does it add to the confusion?

Rosenfeld, L. M., and N. Orlinsky, The effect of research on practice: research and decrease in noncontinuance, Arch. Gen. Psychiat., 1961, 5, 176–182.

Keep a "research diary."

Rosenthal, R., Training students in personality theory, *Amer. Psychologist,* 1958, *13*, 605–606.

Personality theory course is fundamental in training clinical psychologists.

Royce, J. B., Toward the advancement of theoretical psychology, *Psychol. Rep.,* 1957, 3, 401–410.

Desirable to have deducted experimentally verifiable mathematic equations for behavioral phenomena in mid-twentieth century, but present status indicates using inductive rather than deductive, qualitative *vis à vis* quantitative, empirical rather than removed from observations—need low level elementary type of theorizing.

Sanford, N., Personality development during the college years, *Personn. Guid. J.,* 1956, 35, 74–80.

A famous psychologist concludes that the over-all culture of college is important.

Sewell, W. H., Some observations on theory testing, *Rural Sociol.,* 1956, 21, 1–12.

Need for empirical testing of complex behavior theories—Freud is tested and found wanting.

Shapiro, M. B., The single case in fundamental clinical psychology research, *Brit. J. Med. Psychol.,* 1961, 34, 255–262.

Research should center on the individual not groups.

2

A Point of View

When I ran against a Prejudice
That quite cut off the view.

CHARLOTTE GILMAN
An Obstacle, Stanza 1*

INTRODUCTION

The student is asked to give each theory a full hearing free of biases. It is requested that he approach each of the theories as if it would answer all questions regarding the dynamics of man. It will not take long to discover that some theories seem more sensible than others. Let the student withhold judgment, however, until he knows enough about personality theories to exercise the right and *duty* of any learner, which is to challenge the material before him. In keeping with this principle of impartiality the author has tried to withhold his own judgment concerning the theories, and to leave to the reader the pleasure of testing the theory against reality.

SYSTEMS OF THOUGHT

This chapter is a contrivance to help the student arrive at his own theory of personality: He must pick and choose in order to try to formulate a

---

* From Alice Roosevelt (ed.), *Desk Drawer Anthology,* Doubleday & Company, 1938, p. 285.

concept of "why he does the things he does," as explained by personality theorists. Essentially no one else can do this for him. The unsophisticated student frequently demands that the instructor pronounce which theory is the best. To counteract this propensity, the author presents the following section.

Man may go through three stages in formulating opinions about the characteristics of life. Essentially he starts out as a purist, believing that one thing contains all that is worthwhile. This is the initial stage.

Purist

Since he decides he has to believe in something, he accepts with an "all or nothing" vigor the strongest meaningful idea that presents itself to him. Examples: His father is stronger, bigger, better than any other; a certain baseball team is the only one worth supporting; his school is the best in the world.

Before long there is some disillusionment with the puristic position. It becomes harder and harder to fit into all kinds of situations. Attempted defense of it proves many of its weak points. One system just doesn't seem to be applicable to all the varying qualities of life.

If any movement or experience at all has taken place, the student has met and developed other ideas which lead him almost by force to give up all philosophical reference points and start all over again. Most of us profit from experience; however, we may not wish to reject everything, but favor putting more and more of the variable ideas we meet into the framework of our original position. This leads us to synthesize our own ideas. Examples: My father is a wonderful fellow but he does have weak points, and my teacher, coach, scoutmaster, are also fine examples of manhood; the baseball team I so highly prized does lose games and make foolish trades, and other teams afford me equal pleasure; my school, though my very own, does not do or have the fine things I have heard of and seen in other schools. Essentially, the student has now woven together concepts from many sources and has become a synthesist. This is the second stage.

Synthesist

Our "neonatal" theorist has now created a self-devised theory of personality which contains many pieces, scraps, and threads of "why he does what he does." This he has more or less organized within the original framework of his purist position. The relationships between the ideas are loosely formed. The origin and original intent of many of his thoughts have become obscured in the general melée of the system. But his theory can now answer more questions for him. It is a more comfortable position to hold and to defend than was his original position.

As time passes, he may never move beyond his synthesistic position. It may be adequate to bear the weight of all challenges. It is practical until the day he desires to separate one, possibly two, of the threads in this skein for purposes of review and challenge. This he cannot do without pulling apart most of the structure. As with a ball of tangled string, he knows not where he goes next. The trip may be so circuitous that he becomes thoroughly lost within his own system. Our theorist may be ready to abandon his synthesistic system at this point and move on the eclectic approach. This is the third and last stage.

Eclecticist

Let us now look at the individual who has constructed a theory which is eclectic in form. He has selected and put into his theoretical framework ideas that have been examined for their worth. He knows *where* he got the idea, he can *locate* it in the structure, and he can *remove* it for further examination without destroying the whole. Example: My father is a man like all other men with strengths and weaknesses. I know his weaknesses and understand him the better for them. But unlike the purist who, upon finding fault in the figure of father, must accept all or reject all, I can now separate, because I *recognize* them, his noble characteristics from his ignoble ones. And so, unlike the synthesist whose feelings of father are so intertwined that to examine them is literally to destroy them, I can separate the pieces for greater or lesser emphasis in feeling toward the figure of father. Other concepts also receive the same consideration.

SUMMARY

By way of summary, then, let us turn to a diagrammatical device and employ an analogy. Keeping in mind that all analogies are like three-legged stools with one leg missing—they cannot stand by themselves but must be supported—we see that analogies are useful but limited devices. One cannot back off and get another perspective of it but must remain with it for support.

It must be emphasized that man may be a purist in some realms of his life (his politics), a synthesist in others (his choice of fiancée), and an eclecticist in still a third area of life (his choice of architectural design for his house). It seems that the individual is advanced in arriving at some frames of reference and quite far behind in others.

Purist	Example	Analogue
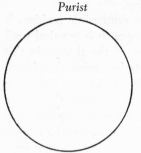	1. An apple is the best and the only kind of fruit worth eating. Eat it and you will need no other.	1. Freud has absolutely all the answers to the dynamics of man. This is the perfect, all-inclusive theory of personality.
		2. May be applied also to concepts of politics, religion, vocational field, etc.
The circle represents the area of totality. It is broken by nothing else. It includes nothing else. It stands pure.		3. The Sunday School level of organized religion.

Dilemma. Here the all or nothing nature of the concept implies that all of its parts are equally good, equally defensible, and equally acceptable.

Synthesist	Example	Analogue
	1. The juice of many fruits (apple, orange, banana, grape, pineapple, etc.) are extracted and served as one liquid. The perfect potable. It contains an admixture of the best fruits all combined into one.	1. Freud, Sheldon, Rogers, Horney, Sullivan are the theorists who make sense. No one of them has the single best answer, but taking the best of these into a unified scheme will tell us "why" man does as as he does.
The circle represents the total frame of reference. The interconnecting lines are the separate ideas interwoven with each other into a unified mass.		2. May be applied also to choice of marriage partner, religion, choice of college, etc.
		3. The adolescent's struggle with the concept of organized religion.

Dilemma. To examine is to destroy. Thus should doubts arise concerning the inclusion of one of the components, one is forced to discard the entire admixture and begin all over again. For example, from the field of qualitative analysis in chemistry, to find the "unknown" we must precipitate, filter, centrifuge, distil, until all the parts are again identified, *but* in so doing we have destroyed the whole. Equally true is the factor of potability. The admixture of fluids may taste flat and without character. There is no central theme to the liquid.

Eclecticist	*Example*	*Analogue*

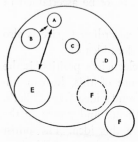

1. A fruit salad consisting of various fruits (apple, orange, banana, grape, pineapple, etc.) is served as a single dish bonded together by a dressing of some kind.

1. I find Freud's concept of dream analysis to be meaningful and useful; it may be included in my theory of personality and is not incompatible with Sheldon's somatotypes. Equally true may be the inclusion of Roger's self-system, Horney's moving away-toward-against people, and Sullivan's stages of development.

The circle again represents the total theory. However, the lettered entities, A, B, C, D, E, and F are most important. They represent the parts (fruits) of the entire system. The distance between them is important. Their varying sizes are important. One component, F, has been removed temporarily for further examination.

2. May apply also to purchase of property, choice of college, increase in products of an industrial firm.

3. The mature concept of organized religion: i.e., there may be value in more than one church form.

Resolution of the Dilemma

1. Continuous evaluation of any one component is possible because it does not destroy the total structure. For instance, the component F has been removed. It will be examined and then the decision to reinsert or eliminate it may be carried out. Let us assume from our example that F

represents pineapple. As we consume the salad, we decide we do not like the acidity of pineapple in conjunction with the other fruits. Now, as not before, we can identify and remove this component to be consumed separately, or returned to the salad because its removal was unsatisfactory to the entire taste sensation. The opportunity for continuous evaluation of separate parts is not possible for the purist or synthesist without destruction of the whole, which, during the period of study, leaves the individual with no system or structure at all.

2. Note the relative distances of A–B and A–E: there is more in common between A and B than A and E, a position that cannot be ascertained in the tangled skein of the synthesist's position.

3. The relative importance of each component according to size is also apparent. Idea D carries much more weight than does idea C.

4. Possibly the most important value to the eclecticist's position is the ability to *identify* the *source* of his ideas; because of this, he can immediately differentiate one fruit from another, Freud's idea from Adler's. With this ability, he can live with his present theory and return to the original source to compare, extend, and evaluate this idea. The purist would have this advantage if he could see in terms other than black or white. The synthesist may return to original sources, but, for the reasons we have mentioned, only after a possibly painful separating-out procedure.

Conclusion

The foregoing section is designed to aid the student in studying the theories of personality so that he may construct a meaningful self-system in regard to the theory of his own personality. "We can put it down as one of the principles learned from the history of science that a theory is only overthrown by a better theory, never merely by contradictory facts."[1]

METHODS OF PROCEDURE

Description

Efforts to study man begin by *describing* accurately and adequately what he is doing. This is not as easy as it sounds: semantic difficulties impede; cultural differences obscure similarities; the field of measurement

[1] J. B. Conant, *On Understanding Science,* Yale Univer. Press, 1947, p. 48.

myriad of industrial endeavors from sales to shipping. Without some hope and plan for predictable results, society would be in a shambles. The field of medicine is perhaps the most sensitive of all fields in trying for predictable results. Error in predicting the results of certain medicines can be deadly!

Hall and Lindzey cogently state the case in the following passages, "The productiveness of the theory is tested *before* the fact not after the fact" (p. 14). "Ideally the theory should lead to accurate predictions . . ." (p. 13).

Control

Not without some danger, however, do we achieve the level of prediction, for if we can predict man's behavior, may we not also control it? Prediction gives us foreknowledge, foreknowledge allows us to prepare, and preparation enables us to meet the future. The future thus known, we may make arrangements, manipulate environment, prepare for known action, and thus control outcome. It was probably no better stated than in the stimulating speech Robert Oppenheimer delivered as guest speaker to the American Psychological Association at its 1955 convention in San Francisco:[3]

The psychologist can hardly do anything without realizing that for him the acquisition of knowledge opens up the most terrifying prospects of controlling what people do and how they feel. This is true for all of you who are engaged in practice, and as the corpus of psychology gains in certitude and subtlety and skill, I can see that the physicist's pleas that what he discovers be used with humanity and be used wisely will seem trivial compared to those pleas which you will have to make and for which you will have to be responsible.

And so, although prediction of human events may lead to the control of human behavior, we must work toward the solving of riddles in man's personality, for to stop short of the predictive level is to lose the *raison d'etre* of study. Man cannot be asked to stop short of a goal because it may be dangerous.

The theories that follow, therefore, have been presented within the general framework of description, explanation, and prediction. It will be obvious to the reader before he proceeds far in his study of the theories that description and explanation are much easier than the goal of predic-

[3] J. R. Oppenheimer, Analogy in Science, *Amer. Psychologist*, 1956, *11*, 127–135.

tion. In fact, almost all of the predictive phases need only be introduced, then left to the reader's introspective powers to determine the efficacy of the theories' predictability. What sparse research we have can only fill out part of the picture.

BIBLIOGRAPHY

PRIMARY SOURCES

BOOKS

Conant, J. B., *On Understanding Science,* New Haven, Yale Univer. Press, 1947.
David, H. P., and H. Von Bracken (eds.), *Perspectives in Personality Theory,* N.Y., Basic Books, 1957.
Hall, C. S., and G. Lindzey, *Theories of Personality,* N.Y., Wiley, 1957.
Kluckhohn, C., and H. A. Murray (eds.), *Personality in Nature, Society, and Culture,* N.Y., Knopf, 1949.

PERIODICALS

Oppenheimer, J., Analogy in science, *Amer. Psychologist,* 1956, *11,* 126–135.

SUGGESTED READINGS

BOOKS

Bronfenbrenner, U., Toward an integrated theory of personality, in R. R. Blake, and G. V. Ramsey (eds.), *Perception: An Approach to Personality,* N.Y., Ronald, 1951.
Newcomb, T. M., *Personality and Social Change: Attitude Formation in a Student Community,* N.Y., Holt, Rinehart and Winston, 1943 (reissue 1957).
  What happens to personality at one eastern girls' college.
Thorpe, L. P., and A. M. Schmuller, *Personality: An Interdisciplinary Approach,* N.Y., Van Nostrand, 1958.
  Eclectic treatment of personality.

PERIODICALS

Fisher, J., The twisted pear and the prediction of behavior, *J. Consult. Psychol.,* 1959, *23,* 400–405.
  Mathematics often inappropriate in predicting human behavior—human beings are too complex.

Henke, M., Some problems of eclecticism, *Psychol. Rev.*, 1957, *64*, 296–305.
  Eclecticism glosses over differences—differences rather than harmonious ideas should be examined more closely.
Kemeny, J. G., and P. Oppenheim, Systematic power, *Phil. Sci.*, 1955, *22*, 27–33.
  The measure of a theory is to explain and predict facts.
Krasner, L., Behavior control and social responsibility, *Amer. Psychologist*, 1962, *17*, 199–203.
  New, important, useful development.
Levy, L. H., Personal constructs and predictive behavior, *J. Abnorm. Soc. Psychol.*, 1956, *53*, 54–58.
  Research on predicting and controlling one's own behavior.
Maslow, A. M., The need to know and the fear of knowing, *J. Gen. Psychol.*, 1963, *68*, 111–125.
  Excellent and readable on why we need to know things. A must for undergraduate psychology majors.
Rescher, N., On prediction and explanation, *Brit. J. Phil. Sci.*, 1958, *8*, 281–290.
  Logically, prediction and explanation are vastly different.
Rogers, C. R., Implications of recent advances in prediction and control of human behavior, *Teachers College Record*, 1956, *57*, 316–322.
Rogers, C. R. and Skinner, B. F., Some issues concerning the control of human behavior: A symposium, *Science*, 1956, *124*, 1057–1066.
  Rogers and Skinner disagree.
Rogers, C. R., The place of the person in the new world of the behavioral sciences, *Personn. Guid. J.*, 1961, *39*, 442–451.
  Control of human behavior.
Rosenthal, R., Training clinical students in personality theory, *Amer. Psychologist*, 1958, *13*, 605–606.
  How one professor has a class construct theories of personality.
Scheffler, I., Explanation, prediction and abstraction, *Brit. J. Phil. Sci.*, 1957, *7*, 293–309.
  Explanation and prediction are distinct from each other.
Stephenson, W., Perspectives in psychology: a note on the methodology of clinical explanation, *Psychol. Rec.*, 1962, *12*, 101–103.
  Clinical research more concerned with explanation than prediction.
Trankell, A., The psychologist as an instrument of prediction, *J. App. Psychol.*, 1959, *43*, 170–175.
  Clinical prediction better than statistical for Swedish air pilots.
Williams, D. C., The new eclecticism, *Canad. J. Psychol.*, 1954, *8*, 113–124.

PART II

BIOPHYSICAL– BIOPHILOSOPHICAL

Fair play is considered a virtue of considerable significance, especially in sports and in dealings with our fellow man. The author suggests that fair play may also be useful in the study of personality theories: again the reader is asked to give each theory a fair and full hearing before any judgment is drawn. It will be obvious from the following pages, as we have said, that not all the theories are equally important or effective in seeking the greater understanding of man.

The writer will not prejudice the reader's mind, but will clarify and interpret the salient features of each theorist. The reader is warned, therefore, that the initial expository treatment may sound as if each theory were absolutely the best one of all. This is a deliberate treatment. Only in the latter portions of the discourse will a criticism be suggested. The ultimate purpose of the book will then be met: to interpret other theories, to make more understandable these theories, and to formulate in the student's mind a self theory based on an analysis of the best theories extant.

This is in contrast to some of the current methods of pedagogy which, to the present author, seem to overuse the "why" approach. Continuously asking a student, "why?", "why?", does not necessarily make him think. He frequently freezes into fright; also, he needs something to think about first; lastly, all learning is based on the appetites created by motivation, and too often the repetitive, "Why?" of the instructor fails to create an appetite for more learning. It creates instead a personal verbal duel between the student and the instructor, who appears either not to know much or to be hiding his knowledge behind a barrage of "whys."

ORGANIZATION OF PART II

This section begins with the work of Sigmund Freud. Any book on personality theory has to start with Freud or end with Freud. Although he is often referred to as the father of Psychoanalysis, he may also be called the father of Personality Theory. Almost all of the other theorists depart from the basic premises of Freud (Jung, Adler, Horney, Sullivan, etc); they can often be best explained by the manner in which they depart from Freud.

Sheldon has been put into the chapter following Freud because Sheldon is closer to the biophysical end than to the other extreme of the biophysical-biophilosophical continuum. Jung ends Part II for the reason that he is more philosophical than physiological. H. A. Murray seems to fit comfortably between the extremes of Freud and Jung.

Again it must be repeated that the order of chapter presentation is a device, not a doctrine.

3

Freud

Amoebas at the start
Were not complex;
They tore themselves apart
And started Sex.

ARTHUR GUITERMAN
Sex, Stanza 1*

SOME BIOGRAPHICAL DATA

Two excellent books among many exist which contain perceptive biographies of Freud. The first is a short autobiography entitled, *An Autobiographical Study*, which Freud wrote in 1935 and others revised in 1946. In this book Freud cleverly interweaves his adult years as a person and the development of his theories. The second book is an outstanding biographical work by one of Freud's closest associates, especially in his later years. Ernest Jones, who died in 1959 and who, some say, kept himself alive long enough to complete a fascinating account of Freud's life, wrote a brilliant and thorough account of Freud's life which was issued in three volumes (1953, 1955, 1958).

In Freud's words, "I was born on May 6th, 1856, at Freiberg in Moravia, a small town in what is now Czechoslovakia. My parents were Jews, and I have remained a Jew myself." (*An Autobiographical Study*.) At the age of four he moved to Vienna. There he eventually became a medical

* From *The Light Guitar*, Harper & Row, 1923, p. 15. Reprinted by permission of Mrs. Guiterman.

student and received his medical degree in 1881. During his student days Freud was to meet severe ostracism as a Jew which, he states, helped him in later years to withstand the gibes of the world because he had learned to inure himself to the displeasure of others. After a short period lacking direction of purpose he became a researcher in the Institute of Cerebral Anatomy and thus became interested in man's mental nature. He left the Institute because his growing family needed more financial support than his assistantship could provide and he went into private practice. Freud's friendship with Joseph Breuer, his year of work with Charcot in France in hypnotic techniques, which he found to be very limited, and his return to develop a cathartic, "talking out" technique with Breuer were all precursors of his psychoanalytic work. From about 1890 to 1900 Freud was a "loner," having broken with Breuer who could not accept Freud's emphasis on sexual factors in the analysis of hysterics. Also as a consequence of his holding stubbornly to his beliefs he was eliminated from the ranking medical organization of his day. These were lonely years for Freud, but in his loneliness and in the work with his patients in private practice he gained the solitude and autonomy of spirit which enabled him to depart from the thinking of the day and create his own theoretical position.

After 1900 Freud began to attract more and more attention, albeit most of it was negative in opinion, from the general populace. His fame, however, brought him the first of the dedicated followers who were to help him inaugurate in 1910 the International Psychoanalytic Association. Early associates with Freud were Carl Jung, assistant to Bleuler at the Burgholzli in Zurich, Switzerland; Alfred Adler of Vienna, who became a favorite with Freud; Brill of New York, Jones of England, and Ferenczi of Budapest. In 1909 Freud and Jung were invited by G. Stanley Hall to attend the twentieth anniversary of Clark University in Worcester, Massachusetts, as guest lecturers. Freud says, "As I stepped on to the platform at Worcester to deliver my 'Five Lectures upon Psycho-Analysis' it seemed like some incredible daydream: psycho-analysis was no longer a product of delusion, it had become a valuable part of reality."

Later Freud was to face the defection of Adler, Jung, Rank, and Stekel from his ranks. The denial of Adler was an especially bitter blow.

World War I made important changes in Freud's thinking as he dealt with the German soldier and began to see a slice of life different from that of his clientele in Vienna. During the postwar years Freud consolidated and revised some of his thinking, which he carefully delineated in his writings of that time.

In 1930 two events occurred which pleased Freud very much. Thomas Mann included him as an acknowledged influence in the history of modern thought. This recognition made Freud feel he was vindicated. The second event Freud describes as follows, "A little later my daughter Anna, acting as my proxy, was given a civic reception in the Rathaus at Frankfort-on-Main on the occasion of my being awarded the Goethe prize for 1930. This was the climax of my life as a citizen." Shortly afterward with the advent of Hitlerian policies in Germany, Freud was forced to curtail his activities and eventually in a regular spy-thriller manner to escape into free country where Jones was so instrumental in bringing him to London for his remaining years. During the period from the middle 1920s Freud was to suffer greatly from an advancing cancerous state of the throat. His last years were spent in considerable pain, but he was uncomplaining. Freud died on September 23, 1939, at 20 Maresfield Gardens, London, in a charming home where his daughter Anna continues to live. A plaque on the side of the home commemorates his residence and death on that site.

INTRODUCTION

There is a unique parallel between the careers of Freud and other intellectual giants. Freud, Darwin, Einstein, Dewey, all pioneered certain aspects of their professional fields, lived rather long and certainly productive lives, lived long enough to explain the "explainers" of their theoretical concepts, and in some instances went through periods of vilification and strong criticism of their then new ideas. There are further parallels between these men. Each attracted to himself a coterie of followers who became so dedicated as to approximate a cult of devotees. True, this was not so apparent in the case of Einstein, except as his followers were more mentally *en rapport* than "worshipers in the temple."

In writing any book on the theories of personality, one would have to use Freud's work either to begin the manuscript or to end it. There could be no place in the middle. It is not only logical, therefore, but mandatory that we should begin the study of man's personality with an interpretation of Freud's psychoanalytic theory.

It should be emphasized again that the following is an interpretation of

Freud's ideas which of course are circumscribed by the present author's viewpoint. It may also seem to the sophisticated reader that many things have been left out of Freud's writings as they are here interpreted. This is certainly true. Any attempt to interpret fully Freud's writings would create a line of books that would make Dr. Eliot's Five Foot Shelf pale by comparison. Almost anyone who writes about Freud becomes an interpreter of him. These writers have been legion, and the end of them is not in sight. This phenomenon attests to the originality and provocativeness of the man with whose ideas we will now deal.

To avoid the distortions of "interpreters of interpreters," the present writer has chosen to utilize the original writings of the theorists where feasible. Interpreting others' interpretations can frequently extend a deviant thread much beyond the original theorist's intent.

The writer has used rough but definable criteria for the extraction of principles from the writings of Freud: (1) Does the theme of the principle actually occur in his writings and not in that of the neo-Freudians who, although they have contributed invaluable help in furthering his work, especially in the area of psychoanalytic practice, can also be classed as interpreters of his writing? (The term *writing* must be used here since that is the medium at the disposal of all of us.) Freud actually collaborated with no one in his work concerning personality theory in the present-day sense of our modern clinics, although he did correspond with and discuss his work quite intimately with a few close associates. (Breuer, Jones, his daughter Anna, to name but a few.) What we know mainly about his work and theoretical position is what he said about them in his writings. Some few writers suggest an intimacy with his thinking which in fact did not exist. They, too, are held to be interpreters of what he wrote despite disclaimers to the contrary. Freud was a "loner" in more ways than one. (2) Does the principle help to weld together the wealth of ideas that he so interestingly presented in his numerous contributions and weld them into a meaningful whole which helps advance the understanding of his theoretical concepts without undue distortion? (All interpreters distort to greater or lesser degree. That is the nature of the beast—one religious sect *vis à vis* another in regard to the Bible, the profuse interpreters of Shakespeare, etc.) (3) Is the principle of large enough proportions to be considered as such and not as simple explanatory material? (4) Does it concern itself primarily with a theory of personality, rather than with a theory of psychoanalytic therapy? (5) Does it meet the basic definition of a principle as traditionally accepted, "a statement of a uniformity in nature. . . . Principle is often used where the uniformity discovered seems for some reason not quite fundamental or not fully established to be called a *law*".[1]

FREUD'S DESCRIPTION OF HUMAN BEHAVIOR

Although Freud did not set down any clear-cut principles in his brilliant and readable writing, the interpreter can deduce certain fundamental concepts so important to his theory as to constitute principles of man's behavior.

Pleasure Principle

Probably foremost of the so-called principles in Freud's approach is that of man as a pleasure-seeking animal. In this we do not use the concept in its hedonistic, philosophical connotation that it is a "duty" to seek pleasure, but rather in the broader psychological connotation that every act is *motivated* by the desire for pleasure and to some degree by the avoidance of pain.

Thus, man's *raison d'etre* in this world is to make and keep things as pleasant as possible. This is not, however, the college sophomore's value system that says, "Let's live it up, for you only live once." Freud would probably eschew the use of pleasure as a principle to excuse man's appetites and gross immorality. For whatever his critics have leveled at Freud, the charge of immorality is a false charge. He was a highly moral individual who considered any use of sex not for procreation as being almost an act of perversion. Consonant with the desire to have as pleasant a life as possible is the underlying theme that man must consequently seek to avoid painful experiences. If he does meet painful experiences, he must solve them or, failing this, avoid meeting them again if this is at all possible.[2]

Being in a pleasant state of existence, then, is a basic principle of

[1] H. B. English and A. C. English, *A Comprehensive Dictionary of Psychological and Psychoanalytical Terms*, Longmans, 1958, p. 407. (Courtesy David McKay Co.)

[2] The treatment of any theory always falls error to overcategorization. This is a pitfall which is inherent in the human inability to see everything at once; one must proceed from step one to step two and so on. This is the learner's problem and dilemma, not the theorist's. Except as he tries, then, to discuss and involve another in his work, Freud was holistic. His theory is of a piece but to discuss it one must take it piece by piece.

Freud's, but this principle describes how man acts and does not necessarily tell us why he chooses to do this. As the reader is aware, we shall attempt to develop the rationale of *why* in a later section devoted to explaining man's behavior. Then in a subsequent section we shall attempt to see if this theory can help us to *predict* man's behavior either through personal experience (introspectively) or through the research which has been done in the behavioral sciences.

Psychologists call being happy a state of *euphoria*. Much has been written about man wanting to be as reasonably happy as possible. This thought occurs even in the Preamble to the United States Constitution in the phrase "the pursuit of happiness." To this we may assume that Freud would have agreed. Freud would possibly have agreed most heartily because of the word *pursuit*, which our early political scientists used. To Freud pleasure or happiness was not a goal so much as it was the motivating force behind man's existence. Without having to look far we find examples in almost every minute of our waking life (and to Freud in our sleeping life, as we shall see later in touching upon dream analysis). All of the advertising efforts surrounding us, our most cherished contacts with family and friends, the television we watch, the movies we see, the sports we indulge in, the books we read, and the avocations we pursue, all seem to center around "having fun." Witness how the average public shuns a losing team, a "sad" play or movie, and pointedly avoids contact with people who "give us a bad time." Personnel psychologists overwhelmingly list as the number one reason for loss of job the inability to get along with people or make them like one.

Thus, to describe man in Freudian terms which accept man as a pleasure-seeking animal wanting to avoid pain does not stretch our imagination greatly. We are to find later in studying Freud's polarity principle that pain itself may be a substitutive form for pleasure. At the moment this may stretch the imagination, but possibly after studying it more carefully and examining illustrations from everyday life, we may be willing to accept this too.

Reality Principle

Not necessarily second in importance but the second to be examined is Freud's later principle that man not only seeks pleasure but is likewise bound by limits of reality which tell him that upon occasion he must postpone an immediate pleasure in favor of a future, more important pleasure. He thus still seeks pleasure but is also realistic and creates an hierarchical form of pleasure: later pleasures judged more important take precedence over current ones deemed less important. For example, take the present moment as you are reading these words. Without stretching the imagination we might assume that you would much prefer being at the student union with your friends, being home and making money, being at the movies, being with your fiancée, being *anywhere* but looking at these words and attempting to read something about Freud because that is the assignment. Why then do you persist? Because, says Freud, you may be described as a reality-principle-motivated human being. You desire a college degree, a passing mark, some goal which keeps you at this page rather than going toward another more immediate and possibly more pleasant objective. We all sense, therefore, that life is bounded by rules which, if followed, will create for us other pleasures.

We shall in subsequent pages introduce and discuss the concepts of instinct and learned behavior. For the present the principle of reality is considered as learned and not inborn or instinctual. Whereas man comes into life already equipped with the pleasure principle, it is only through the lessons of life and the guidance and direction of adults responsible for his upbringing that he acquires the sense of reality in his dealings with self and the environment. It may surprise some readers to discover that Freud did not ignore environment as an influence on human behavior. Thus, the preceding sentence considers both the control of man's inner appetites exclusive of the outer world and those appetites admittedly within himself but fostered and given to him by his environment. By way of illustration: hunger and thirst and sexual appetite may be considered to spring from the inner self. The desire for an automobile, for television, and for myriad other things may be considered to have been brought about by contact with one's environment. Hunger knows no social order or ethical flavor, but automobiles and television are components of one's environment. As any discerning reader may see, however, inner appetites can be and oftentimes are manipulated by outer factors, such as, man's sexual appetites being aroused by sensual stimulae in the environment.

Tension Reduction Principle

Very closely allied with the previous two principles (pleasure and reality) is the principle of *tension reduction*. Its closeness is evident when one realizes that some mechanics must be brought about in going between the extremes of pleasure and reality, especially when, in their most advanced forms, they conflict. Looking to the field of physics and the treatment of material things, we realize that any object when being pulled in two opposite directions will become taut or tense. Metallurgists use the term *tensile strength* in describing this property of steel. Pull a rope or rubber band apart, and you can see the same phenomenon operating more vividly. Consequently the Freudian principle subsumes that man will become tightened up in somewhat the same fashion when he too is being pulled from two diametric fields.[3] In this sense, then, the material, man, is not in a happy state but in an unhappy one because pressure tears him apart. The way to avoid this painful force is to reduce it, remove it, or to become so strong that the pressure becomes relatively weak and tolerable.

Because man cannot ignore that which came to him from birth (pleasure principle) and because man must face reality, both inner and environmental (reality principle) tension becomes a *sine qua non* of his existence. It becomes a governing principle of his life to reduce this tension in the best way he can or succumb to it and be destroyed by it. He may be described as a tension-reducing animal.

Polarity or Duality Principle

At least for the writer this derived principle of Freud's has enormous possibilities for theorizing as well as for speculation about man. This particular principle derived from Freud's writing is not clearly labelled by him or apparent from his work. Rather it is the device of this work in interpreting and attempting to clarify Freud's theories. Weaving in and out of his writings is the concept of two opposing forces forever present in man's life. Everything in life, therefore, is manifest in two dissimilar qualities. For the moment it might be interesting to construct a list of these unlike characteristics that man seems to find in his everyday world:

[3] Some interesting speculations may arise from this simple analogy. Perhaps it is because of the inevitability of this tension that man is interesting and creative and worthwhile. Consider the violin string which is nothing unless it is stretched tight, and produces fine sounds when manipulated properly. Is man and his progress through history the result of being stretched tightly by these two opposing forces? This comes very close to the theorizing of Adler as we shall see in a later chapter (i.e., inferiority feelings, "the great upward drive").

right	wrong
good	bad
up	down
North pole	South pole
man	woman
inside	outside
good god	bad god
Jehovah	Satan
life	death[4]
Eros	Thanatos
cathexis	anticathexis
white	black
positive	negative

No doubt the reader himself could construct a very long list of opposites.

We are surrounded every day with polarities in regard to our actions. Imagine a student's typical day which runs something like this. He begins the day with the fundamental decision to get out of bed or to not get out

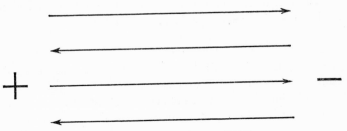

Figure 1. The Polarity of Life.

of bed. "Shall I sleep a little longer because it feels so nice here in bed or shall I get up and make my eight o'clock class?" The decision is either to do it or not to do it. One cannot be half out of bed for very long. One must be either in bed or out of bed. Clothes. "Shall I wear the brown or blue?" No matter how multiple the color choice it eventually descends to a choice of one. "Shall I brush my teeth now or later after breakfast?" "Shall I walk with this person or go along by myself?" "Shall I or shall I not?"

[4] Freud made much of the "Death Instinct" but never described it adequately. Briefly summarized it is man's desire to destroy himself and/or symbolic substances around him. Opposite to this, of course, is the Eros, or love instinct, which is analogous to the pleasure principle as treated in this chapter.

"Should I do it or should I not?" And so through the hours of the day goes life for all of us. We are continuously being confronted with and having to make decisions between doing or not doing certain activities. Decisions, decisions—this is the duality of life, or, its polarity.

Let us assume that the positive and negative figures in the above drawing have the common properties of electrical charges. As we near the positive charge (the good things man does), we acquire its characteristics and become more positively charged or "good" minded. Here, however, we come under the laws of electrical properties; as all physicists know, opposites attract and similar charges repel. We are now in a dilemma. The closer we get to being good, and the more we try to be the best possible person, the more we are repelled. Then we may be heard to say that there are hypocrites in such and such organization, that one must be practical too, for it is not possible to be completely good all the time, everywhere. We finally are repelled by the very characteristics of good and figuratively push away.

What happens then? Being repelled from one polarity, we go in the direction of the other, toward bad, immoral things. Fortunately or unfortunately, depending upon one's value system, we cannot approach this "bad" goal too closely either, for the very same phenomenon operates here to repel us from complete emergence into the bad. The closer we get, the more like the characteristics we become, but this also creates at some point such a sameness that we are finally repelled from this opposing goal. Such is life, or to employ the Freudian phrase, this is the "life cycle."

The sophisticated reader might now ask, "Why not stay in the middle and be neither plus nor minus but neutral?" This is precisely what man does try to do in attempting to maintain some form of homeostasis, but he cannot. In the same sense that he cannot stay neutrally between being hungry and being satiated, he also cannot remain in that stable state of neutrality to all of life's forces. His environment demands that he get off dead center. Pressures are exerted upon him that he cannot ignore. These pressures of his own organic needs or those of society in the form of family demands, occupational demands and mobility, and other environmentally directed pressures keep man, so to speak, on the run. One of the things man cannot do is "freeze" all activity, physical and/or mental, whether it be his own or that of the world surrounding him. It was this concept that made Freud the target for charges of pessimism.

Since we have extended Freud's theoretical position this far, let us move a few steps more in drawing out the life problems which may arise from this dilemma of polarity. To the quality of motion or direction of motion we may add one other dimension, that of *speed*. How fast we travel between these opposite poles may have tremendous bearing on our mental state. This may be modern man's curse. He is required to make so many, many trips back and forth with no chance for a leisurely pace which would help him adjust to change. Concurrently we may assume that the quicker the trip between plus and minus in Figure 1, the quicker the rebound! Thus, the more rapidly we make up our mind about something, the more rapidly we find that we have changed to the other side. Decisions quickly made about religion, jobs, or marriage partners may leave us with decisions to be just as quickly remade.

A reference was made above to "modern man's curse." If the reader wishes, he may now confront man in the historical sense and examine polarity from that point of view. Let us suppose that man in the early centuries of the Christian era was more agricultural than he now is. Historians would not quarrel with this. Let us further suppose that in the pursuance of farming as a way of life things were done more slowly. While the farmer was plowing his field, a task which might take him days on end, he had very little else to think about at that moment than to make straight furrows and possibly to wonder if there were not some faster and less arduous way of plowing. Having to make quick decisions was seldom necessary. All he did was plow all day long. Now we turn our attention to his ancestor who happens to work in an office, in a large metropolis, surrounded by telephones buzzing, voices calling, and all the accoutrements of the commercial world. The higher he progresses in this world of work, the more rapidly do decisions demand his attention. No wonder he becomes bewildered, ulcered, and in need of emotional props. It is not that the twentieth-century man's decisions are necessarily bigger, nor even that failure is more dramatic and painful; it is the fact that the rapidity of decisions is his cross to bear. Death, injuries, loss of loved ones, were all as hard to bear for fourteenth-century man as they are for twentieth-century man. It is the factor of rapidity between the poles of decision which perhaps makes our lives today so emotionally demanding.

Supposing, though, that man through dint of sheer perseverance or through the exigencies of chance manages to approach one of the two poles and to remain there! The explanation for such an unlikely but not impossible phenomenon might be as follows: the human being has now managed to reverse the meaning of the poles for himself. What he has done is to make black white and white black. That which was positive is now negative and vice versa. Is this confusing state of reversal possible for any length of time? In the terminology of psychoanalysis the words *sadism* or *masochism* may help to explain the reversal of poles. Sadism (pleasure from making others suffer) and masochism (pleasure from making self suffer) are not farfetched emotional conditions. Psychoanalytic literature is replete with case histories and accounts of man enjoying another man's being in pain, and certainly of enjoying his own sadness. Looking to our own introspective experience (which often proves very little but is certainly vivid) we see that one may enjoy a sad song. Is it too farfetched to picture the victim of a broken love affair dedicatedly pursuing sad thoughts; of his even enjoying a fantasy of being injured in saving the life of his exsweetheart's little brother and dreaming, as the now grateful girl stands beside the hospital bed, of turning his head to the wall with the murmur, "It was nothing. Really nothing." Hilarious as this sounds, it may not be too far from reality, certainly not as a fictional device of the television program or film screen. Have not some of us enjoyed a gray day and having the blues and resented the intrusion of a boisterous voice that urged us to pep up? In the writer's own clinical experience he has met clients who enjoy attending funerals and getting happiness out of what is unquestionably a sad occasion. Probably the most advanced example of the reversal of poles is the psychotic condition known as the functional psychosis, hebephrenia, where the patient giggles, laughs, and appears to have reached that Valhalla of life: a happy state. Anyone familiar with this emotional disorder will readily testify that this is a very sick and miserable human being despite what may appear as happiness.

In this way, then, man is still caught in a polar condition though he reverses the poles.

Repetition Compulsion Principle

No doubt one may extract from Freud's writing many other principles, depending upon the criteria employed; however, the principle of repetition compulsion will be the last to be treated here.

Somewhat akin to William James whom he met and admired, Freud realized the role of habit in man's behavior. Once the human being has become accustomed to doing an activity in a certain way, he is inclined to repeat this activity in much the same way until he can do it without much conscious thought. Though the similarity between James and Freud is so tenuous as to be almost nonexistent, both men gave to the behavior pattern of habit a major role.

Freud would describe man as a habit-following animal. His extensions of this behavior syndrome are, however, quite interesting to pursue. Since man is inclined to repeat that which is successful, the longer he does so the more fixed this becomes as his *modus operandi* in daily life. Because it is so thoroughly fixed, man follows this method of attacking problems *whether it leads to success or not*. Freud said that the human being was compelled to repeat that activity which once was successful in the past. Unlike James, Freud extended habit far beyond the organic and manipulative functions. In fact, as we shall see at great length later on, he constructed an entire rationale for man's behavior from this proclivity to repeat past experiences. Although this was more fully spelled out by his daughter Anna under the name of *ego defense mechanisms,* it is in essence an extension of the repetition compulsion principle at work.

Dynamics of Behavior

To describe man's personality according to Freud includes much more than the previous principles. In the subsequent text we treat the more prominent dynamics of behavior in Freud's work. After we have described *what* it is that man does in exercising his personality we will attempt in the middle section of the chapter to explain *why* he behaves as he does, using for the most part anecdotal material where applicable. The third function of the chapter is designed to test the predictability of the theory.

Id.   So much has been written concerning Freud's creation of the term *id* that it alone could furnish enough material for a book. After a while any student of psychoanalytical literature finds it difficult to winnow out what it was that Freud said about the id and what the later writers both neo-Freudian and critics of Freud have said.

Freud's approach was not to continue to discuss the id but to utilize its concept in further writings. Since he writes so extremely interestingly, we can almost parrot his words and come out with a fairly easily grasped understanding of the id.

Basic to every living human being, coming with him at the moment of birth and remaining with him throughout life, is the phenomenal energy system called by Freud the *id*. The id knows only the pleasure principle and cares naught for anything else. It is the raw, savage, undisciplined, pleasure-seeking, basic stuff that energizes man throughout life. It knows no laws, follows no rules, and considers only its own appetites. It is the id that gives man his will to continue and sparks all the other energy systems which might be imposed upon it. Contrary to a general opinion of the id that it is all bad and "isn't it a shame that man must have one which has to be held down all the time?", the id performs that invaluable task of keeping man going. Despite the proclivity of the id to go in any direction it wishes, it also must conform to other systems, which conformity produces the need for the polarity and tension reduction principles. It is nonetheless the engine, or the power plant, for man's existence. Although closely allied with the organic systems of man from which it derives its energy, the id is a "true psychic system" and does not have a physical place in the body such as the heart, cerebrum, or other organs. Where does it exist then? It exists probably in the same place that man's sense of love exists, or his feeling for God, or his sense of courage or cowardice.

One can never perceive the id in its raw state. Probably the closest we can come to finding out what the id appears to be is in the study of a small child or in the behavior of a psychotic individual. A child of one squashes bugs, kills things if it so desires, makes entirely selfish demands on others, and in general disports itself in an id-motivated manner. The child apparently follows only the pleasure principle. Or witness the antics of a deeply disturbed psychotic individual who may act in whatever way he chooses. Whether the psychotic flaunts the customs of society is beside the point. He may spit, defecate, use foul language, attempt bodily harm to others, and make every attempt to satisfy only self, a true manifestation of the pleasure principle.

Stripped of controlling devices, or not yet having developed controlling devices, the psychotic and the child may bring us closer to the realization of what Freud meant by the id.

Libido. For many years for the unlearned or undiscriminating reader of Freud's works the libido was considered to be the total contribution of his work; so it is even today. It is true that the layman reader and public in general continue to consider his work as highly sexual in nature. This is only a part of his theoretical formulations; much of the misinformation arose out of the term *libido.*

The libido is that part of the id structure which seeks its gratifications from purely sexual activities. Since sexual appetites are as prevalent in the organic sense as other appetites, although not as strong as the food drive, they are obviously a factor in the psychic makeup of all peoples. Freud was probably the first to emphasize this phenomenon.

Freud wrote also rather pointedly about the libido and in his earlier writings there was much emphasis on the libidinal content of man's personality, not because it was the major part of his personality makeup, but because Freud wrote so extensively concerning the sexual appetites and especially the aberrations of these appetites which he found in his therapy with patients. Freud did not feel he overemphasized the sexual aspects of man's behavior, although many of his professional contemporaries as well as numerous latter day psychoanalysts felt he did so. Freud's split with Adler, the later work of Horney, and many other analysts' writings attest to this schism in emphasis. And, of course, to the general public anything of a sexual nature became overemphasized.

The libido, then, is not the largest part of man's id structure. It is, however, extremely important, for without a driving libidinal desire man would not be as prone to procreate his species. Instead of being something which is shameful, it is a factor in man's being able to continue his species on earth. Freud's contention was that because man enshrouds the sexual aspects of his life with innumerable taboos, man himself has overemphasized the aspects of sexual things in his life. Freud believed that he only explained what it is that man does. Just as the police reporter does not create crime, but only writes of it, Freud felt he did not create the overemphasis on the sexual content of man's life, but only wrote of it.

Ego. We may suppose that if the raw id were left to its own devices it would destroy itself. Something is needed to police its energy and to direct it toward as much fulfillment as can be allowed under the exigencies of life without letting the id destroy itself. Freud said that the ego performs these functions and performs them well. The ego follows the principles of reality. It is the executive with veto powers of all that the id attempts to energize in seeking fulfillment of its desires. The ego makes no ethical value judgments. It is an extension of the id and is never independent of it. The ego is the organized part of the id and merely seeks to find outlets that serve the id's purpose without destroying it. Whereas the id may be considered as the organic part of man's personality, the ego becomes its psychological part. It, the ego, enjoys all of the gratifications that it permits the id to enjoy, but it acts with intelligence in controlling, selecting, and deciding what appetites will be satisfied and just how they are to be satisfied.

As we shall see in a moment, when introduced to the socialized part of the personality, the ego comes under great pressure. In trying to permit the id to express itself and, of course, receiving the benefits of that action and still keeping the action within the bounds of subjective, social reality, the ego is that portion of us which moves back and forth between the polarities mentioned previously. How the ego accomplishes this to the satisfaction of all concerned to a large degree determines our state of emotions. The more it can allow the id to have, within the bounds of reality, the happier we apparently are in life.

Superego. As the reader has undoubtedly anticipated, there is a third component to man's personality, a component which lies at the other end of the continuum from the id. Freud never called this the conscience except "in a whisper," but it comes closer to this than any other term. The superego is the last to develop in Freud's trichotomized picture of the human personality. It must be understood, however, that the superego is internalized. It is within the person's personality and not a set of governmental laws. Only when man develops a superego within himself does he have a fully developed personality. The superego is the ethical-moral arm of the personality. It is idealistic and not realistic. Perfection is its goal rather than pleasure. It makes the decisions whether an activity is good or bad according to the standards of society which it accepts. Societal laws mean nothing to it unless it has accepted them and internalized them.

Although in writing these personality characteristics may be listed and discussed separately, they are not separate entities within the personality. Id, ego, and superego are intrinsically interwoven in all that man does. Each has its separate function but can never exist alone, each being inextricably involved with the other. Only in the case of the undeveloped neonate or in the instance of a psychotic episode do we find one of the elements, usually the ego–superego structure, malfunctioning.

Instinct. Basic to all of Freud's writings and theoretical positions, as well as to the rationale of his psychotherapeutic work, is the concept of instinct. Almost all of what Freud did is predicated on the idea that man came into the world at birth equipped with certain instincts. These Freud did not spell out too definitively as other instincts appear later on in life as new bodily needs develop. It is the latter part of this statement which makes the concept of instinct as most of us know it rather fuzzy. Later developing instincts may be considered to be delayed instincts.

Possibly no other word in the language of the behavioral sciences has caused more unbridled controversy than the term *instinct*. Usually three positions resolve: one denies the term categorically; one is caught in the tendrils of defining the term and levels off at that plane; or one uses the concept as a valuable adjunct to psychoanalytic thought and pays little attention to its precise definition.

In point of fact Freud was more prone to use the concept rather than to expend effort in rounding out a neat and ironclad definition for it. This circumvention is not unusual. Witness the number of things written about personality while as yet no clear-cut definition has emerged for this word. The present text is an example. After more than thirty years of writing, during which time the *idea* of instinct is either directly used or is subsumed in treating of other material, Freud eventually delimited the term *instinct* to cover two phenomena: Eros—love or life instinct, and Thanatos—death or destruction instinct.

In a general way it is assumed that Freud would have accepted the following as a workable definition of *instinct*: "Any set of responses, shown by a great majority of the members of a species, that are associated together in time under specified environmental conditions and specified drive conditions."[5] To this he would add that an instinct is a primary component of man's personality and cannot be reduced to lesser components.

Although Freud did think that instinct is irreducible, to him it did have four features: source, aim, object, and impetus. For example, we may take the incident of a person who is at the moment suffering from a painful toothache. In so doing he is directed by the homeostatic principle of tension reduction as we previously discussed.

1. source: the pain of the aching, throbbing tooth.
2. aim: to remove the painful aching and return to the painfree state which existed prior to the tooth aching.
3. object: arranging for an appointment with the dentist, going to the dentist, sitting in the dentist's chair, gripping the arm of the chair, etc.
4. impetus: how terrible is the ache; as it subsides during the day, the impetus value is lessened; as it grows unbearable during the early hours in bed at night, the impetus value increases tremendously until one swears he will see the dentist the first thing in the morning.

[5] *Ibid.*, p. 265.

To most people interested in the behavioral sciences an instinct to be called such would have to be present in all the species, and there should be no opportunity to learn the characteristic behavior pattern. The toothache example cited above would probably meet some unanimity of agreement if that is what instinct is supposed to be. Obviously Freud, too, had his problems with the term *instinct,* for we see that despite the four-part features of instinct which he posited, he eventually refined his concept to include only two demonstrably clear-cut cases of instinct: the aforementioned life and death instincts. Again we find an example of the polarity or duality principle operating. However, within the polarity of life–death there is an umbrellalike effect. All other instincts may be lumped under either of these two opposing instincts. The crude term *lumped* is probably accurate since the listing of instincts becomes so disparate that any orderly classification is rendered nearly impossible.

In the final analysis we shall proceed as Freud did by using the underlying concept of instinct without defining the term.

Erogenous Zones.   One of the truly original ideas that Freud created in describing our personalities is that of erogenous zones, sometimes called erotogenic zones. An erogenous zone is any part of man's body where the inner and the outer skin meet, an area which may have the potential, when manipulated, of arousing pleasant and sensual feelings. These may be either inborn or developed later in life. In a tangential sense they are all inborn but may be dormant as pleasure feelings if not given the opportunity to be manipulated. Areas of emerging mucous membranes are highly sensitive to irritation. Thus, the lips are much more prone to respond to manipulation than is the small of the back, the point of the elbow, or the calf of the leg, for example. It would seem that the more protruding or outward the mucous membrane, the more highly susceptible it is to becoming an effective erogenous zone.

Naming the zones is a fairly routine organic census technique. They may be considered to be as follows (keeping in mind the closer the mucous membrane to the outer skin the more susceptible it is to sensual gratification): the ears, eyes, mouth (lips), the male and female genitals, and the anal aperture. The eyes and ears are often not considered to be strictly within the scope of erogenous zones; they do, however, meet the criteria of the definition.

If man can produce pleasure by manipulating the erogenous zones, it is not overly difficult to explain his perverted behavior within the Freudian frame of reference. Just how man exploits these zones will be treated in a subsequent section dealing with explaining his behavior. At the moment we will attend to the task of describing his personality.

Developmental Sequence. The term *sequence* is deliberately used to describe how Freud traced the development of man and his personality from birth to adulthood. Sequence connotes that the phenomenon is genetically determined, with the further implication that unless development suffers interference by abnormal conditions, we may expect to find the development progressing exactly alike for all men. Further, the developmental sequence follows quite closely the discovery and utilization of the erogenous zones mentioned in the previous passages.

At this point some digression is in order so as better to explain the basic position of man as he develops in Freud's viewpoint. We will make an analogy of personality as a brick wall versus the concept of a tension system such as a kite. To Freud, "the child was father to the man." As a brick mason slowly constructs a wall of brick, the structure as it grows upward is fixed in relation to the bricks at the bottom or the bricks originally used in construction. The form of the wall, its thickness, all of its characteristics are set. To change them appreciably is to destroy the structure (the personality). The personality, therefore, is set as it goes along. The foundation is unchangeable. Furthermore, it limits and restricts what can be built on top of it. If the bottom of the wall is shaky, poorly constructed, and uneven, the bricks that are placed upon it can only be supported in relation to the strength of the underlying structure. So the child becomes the father (guide, director, chief influence) to the man that eventually emerges in adult life. This does not imply that as the brick wall grows up, it cannot be changed. It is always being changed by newer kinds of brick, by slight alterations to the design, by extra embellishments of the original design, *but* it can never exceed the limits of load bearing as they are set by the underlying structure. Whenever this does happen, and of course it can and does, the structure collapses (a psychotic personality or in the case of a shaky structure, a neurotic personality). Normally most of us continue to vary as we grow up, but sensing the danger of complete collapse or the discomfort of a trembling structure, we are constrained from a departure too far beyond what our substructure will tolerate.

A moment ago mention was made of a *tension system* in contrast to the Freudian "brick-by-brick" analogy. By *tension system* we are referring to the concept of the architect Buckminster Fuller that a structure is best contrived when it is held together by tension and not constructed in a piece by piece method, one brick on top of the other, a method which creates a heavy, inflexible structure. The tension system creates a building which is far easier to manipulate, more economical of material and space, and which can withstand far greater stress and pressure than the heavier, set, inflexible, bulky building of masonry. The newer method of roof construction, where vast areas may be covered without columnar support, the so-called "Dymaxion" house, is a tension system device. A kite such as small boys fly in the air is a tension system. It is held together by the tension of string, strips of wood, and taut paper. It is mobile. It can stand great stresses as the wind buffets it about the sky. This is the opposite to Freud's "brick by brick" concept of man and his developing personality. The controversy rages around these two questions: Is man held from future development by his first few years of life or is he capable of changing as life progresses? The kite may be recovered, strings changed, loosened, retightened and even increased to some slight extent without destroying the kite in process. Equally true, the kite may be destroyed if the environment of wind becomes too strong. But to change its basic features does not automatically bring destruction, the fate of the altered brick wall.

After our sojourn into analogy we may return with possibly a clearer concept of what Freud meant by considering the first five years of life as absolutely essential and decisive in the later formation of the personality. And we have seen what the other side of the door looks like to the deeply dedicated environmentalist who eschews the confinement of the Freudian position. Now we may return to terminology as we describe the sequence of development as Freud saw it.

Oral—The first sequence to develop in the formation of man's personality is related to the erogenous zone of the mouth and more precisely of the lips. Shortly after being born, the human animal uses his lips to ingest food. Food is pleasant (pleasure principle). Whether it be from the mother's breast or from a nippled bottle, the neonate (birth to one month of age) very soon learns (repetition compulsion) that the lips-tongue-oral cavity when manipulated on the mother's breast and/or bottle makes him happy (erogenous zone). Because there are so few conflicting things in his environment, the lesson of lips producing pleasure is quickly and lastingly learned. It is natural for him then to exercise his lips when he wishes to regain a happy state of being. When he is again hungry, the erogenous zone of the mouth comes into play, and he feels happy. Having been reinforced enough times by this particular activity, lips-tongue-oral cavity automatically spell pleasure to his impressionistic state of existence.[6] *Ergo,* if one wants to feel happy, let him use the lips. Being an habituated creature the neonate uses the lips for pleasure no matter what the state of hunger happens to be. Consequently, having trained his lips for pleasure production, he may now stick his fingers, thumb, or any convenient device (toes!) into his mouth and thus receive pleasure whether he is hungry or not (tension reduction). From now on it will be possible to use the lips for pleasure, and food does not have to be a party to the exercise.

Somewhat akin to the generalization that the first things to go into a system are the last to leave (i.e., Jackson's Law), the oral sequence and erogenous zone are the longest and also the strongest of man's stages as he lives out his life. He will always seek his oral zone for pleasure and do so even if such activity is not efficient toward solving the problem and reducing the tension. We will be able to explore this more thoroughly in relation to why man behaves in actual life as he does when we get to the section of the explanation of man's personality. Suffice for the moment to describe what it is that he has as equipment for his personality.

Anal—When enough food waste has accumulated in the lower digestive tract, a tension of the viscera is produced which causes discomfort or pain. When he is older, the human learns that the reality principle operates and that he must not defecate when the pressures become great but must learn to control the eliminative process. As a tiny infant the control of bowel movements is far beyond his sense of reality. The sphincteral muscles of the anal area operate to discharge the feces. With the mass removed and the pressure decreased, the neonate knows pleasure again. In this way the anal area becomes the second sequence to develop. It is likewise the second longest and the second strongest of the erogenous zones.

The unique reciprocity of the zones is apparent since the action of one is allied to the action of another. Thus no erogenous zone in its function or in its development can exist independent from the other. Through a process intercorrelated but not necessarily sympathetic, the erogenous zones in their development become sensitized to each other.

[6] Piaget and his brilliant writing cannot be ignored in the development of the infant mind. The reader is urged to explore his concepts. See especially, Jean Piaget, *The Language and Thought of the Child,* World Publishing (Meridian), 1955.

Phallic—Probably sometime around the age of two the child has passed through the oral and anal stages of development and then proceeds to discover and enjoy the remaining erogenous zones of his body. Primary among these are the sexual organs of penis and vagina although the nostrils and ears and eyes may come to be manipulated for pleasure. Any one familiar with small children is not unaware of the phenomena of placing their fingers in their nostrils to remove encrusted mucous. Clinical cases where small foreign objects are thrust into the nasal passages are not unknown.

From about the beginning of his sixth year until puberty when the endocrine system regenerates an intense period of activity, the child is in a dormant aspect of the sequential development of his personality via the erogenous zones. The first three phenomena discussed are usually called the pregenital stages.

Genital—Reciprocity is the keynote of the genital stage. No new erogenous zones are discovered or employed in this sequence. A synthesis or fusion of the preceding three sequences takes place and instead of directing their force upon the individual, they now become outerdirected, usually toward the opposite sex. The chief physical objective of the genital stage is to indulge in intercourse either for reproduction of the species or for reciprocal pleasure between the partners via use of the erogenous zones. Abortive attempts to consummate the sex act become the mode of behavior where society prohibits full intercourse due to lack of marriage status. Contrary to the belief of many, any sexual act not designed to propagate the species was almost an act of perversion to Freud. He attempted to describe and explain man's sexual behavior but never once condoned extramarital activity.

Love Stages. As an extension of the previous material it is possible and we hope profitable to recast the Freudian material to create sequences in which the erogenous zones play only a background part. This rubric is a rank extension of Freud's work. Nowhere in his writings does he speak of it although others have made similar interpretations.

Consider man as a love-generating animal. Love is to be considered as a reciprocal state of attraction in that to give love one must receive from the love object some source of satisfaction. This would differentiate love from the state of passion (an emotional state so strong as to overrule good judgment) or the state of infatuation (a short erotic attraction which contains no reciprocity, i.e., the love object does nothing of and by itself to foster the relationship toward any one individual). Probably the closest term which we need is the Greek word *agape* which connotes that love goes *between* people. A person cannot love in only one direction but must be loved in return. It is a two-way proposition: I love you, you love me. Anything else would be considered infatuation, passion, or what have you.

Self Love—When the infant comes into life, he knows only one thing: himself. Since we may assume that he is not yet concerned with abstractions about himself, he can only deal with the concrete. There is nothing more concrete than his organic self. His body describes, defines, and circumscribes his total world.[7] He can only know those things that are apparent to his senses. If he cannot touch, taste, see, hear, or smell a person or thing, it does not exist as far as he is concerned. In the beginning his body is the receptor and affector of learned things. Through it he senses and learns pleasure, pain, and some realization of other things.[8] Since his body (himself in the most directive manner) is both a receptor and effector, he, therefore, has a reciprocal situation. Being able to reciprocate with himself, he is now able to make himself a love object because satisfaction and pleasure come from himself. He can suck his toes and fingers; he can find pleasure in his eating and his passing of feces; he can experience pleasure of bodily warmth. In short, he can find himself the most wonderful thing he has known so far in his very short existence. He loves himself because "himself" is the only thing he can know and know how to love. To this stage Freud gave the name autoerotism.

Because he is the first object of his own love and because it is so exclusively his own and because the infant can never be apart from it, this love stage is the longest and strongest of them all. He starts life loving himself and ends life with the feeling of self love being paramount. No other feeling of love will be quite as strong.

Parental Love—Very soon after the infant finds in himself a love object and before he has even formulated self love to a lasting degree, he finds an external object in the form of a mother, father, or some adult figure that does nice things for him. It feeds him, takes wet, uncomfortable clothes off him and replaces them with dry, warm clothes, holds him and comforts him through gastric pains, caresses him, sings to him, plays with him, in short, is a very nice thing to have around. Without much practice on the infant's part he is likely to discover that the ministrations to his needs may also be increased if he too does something like smile, laugh, or

---

[7] See Piaget, *ibid.*

[8] The G. H. Mead concept of the *generalized other* is not intended here.

make responding noises to this adult figure. Consequently a reciprocal relationship is soon established and, as is the case in most infants' lives, it is with the mother, who is usually the purveyor of all these pleasant things. Of course, it also could be any parent surrogate.

The second strongest and longest lasting love stage is related to the parent or parents most concerned with his welfare. To the sophisticated reader familiar with Freudian literature this would seem to be an excellent place to introduce the concept of Oedipus complex and its concomitant operational devices of penis envy and castration complex. If not placed here it might profitably be included in the section on erogenous zones. With this the author does not quarrel. However, dealing with the erogenous zones is complicated enough without adding the exposition necessary to understand the Oedipal complex. Treating Oedipal complex here seems ill-advised because this section is purely an extension and interpretation of Freud's work. Finally, Oedipal complex is a phenomenon of identification, and to Freud a tremendously important one. It has, therefore, been treated in the later section dealing with identification.

Fictional Love—Before life progresses too far, the infant grown into a small child comes to the realization that his present two love objects have certain limits. The insurmountable problem with self is self. One cannot go beyond the limits of what one is. One can only do so much with oneself and then one is circumscribed by the talents and facilities of one's own self. Parents present problems, too. They scold. They also set up what seem to be innumerable rules of conduct such as washing, eating certain foods, conducting self according to the rules of society, and any number of like restrictions. They may even inflict physical punishment in the form of spankings. Now that the child's world is expanding, he can see, and does, that there are other adult figures, and these figures perform magnificent feats like flying through the air, hitting home runs, always winning gun fights with the "bad guy" in a black hat, and, in short, doing so many more exciting things than parent figures ever seem to do. Also, they do not spank or scold. As the child's mental capacity and concurrent fantasy life increase, he becomes more aware of the wonderful world of fictional heroes and what they can do for him. He falls in love, then, with fictional figures—be they real or characters from plays, books, films, television.

Having fictional love is a lasting behavioral pattern. We carry throughout some images of these personality forms which help us to live in fantasy that which we cannot live in reality. Unfortunately, there is a drawback, too, with fictional love objects; the degree of reciprocity is very limited. They can do nothing for us unless we first initiate the action. A book with its hero stays on the library shelf until we make the effort for it to enter our lives. It is the same with the films, television, sports world. The burden of rapport is mainly ours. We find also that in time these love objects become stereotyped and really have very limited use despite the high moments of sharing vicariously their exploits.

Homosexual Love—With a backward glance now to the Freudian sequence we can recapitulate some similarities between this departure from Freud and the extension into love stages that is being proposed.

As the child progresses through the oral, anal, and phallic sequences, he is developing a love for self via the means of his body. The fuller emergence of the phallic period brings forth the fictional stage. Because fantasy is so strongly a part of the phallic period the child casts fictional heroes for his pleasure more easily at this time than in the two previous (oral—anal) periods.

According to Freud, basic to all humans is an inborn bisexuality. All males have some characteristics of the female, and all females have some characteristics of the male. Current endocrine and biochemical research seems to indicate the presence of androgens and estrogens in every living human, the male hormone androgen being predominant in the male and the reverse, a predominance of estrogens being present in the female. Coupling this with the similarity in sexual organs lays the groundwork for the homosexual love stage. It should in no way be interpreted at this age level with any perversion whatsoever.

The young boy of elementary school age becomes enrapt in Cub Scouting and having pals with whom he likes to wrestle and engage in bodily contact activities, and eschews the company of girls. The opposite sex is assigned the role of tolerable nuisance. On the other hand, little girls become members of the Brownies, have slumber parties with one other girl, play happily at dolls, swear life-long allegiance to another girl and then confound parents with a new life-long allegiance the following week, and in general assign to boys the role of "snails and puppy dog tails," accompanied by dirty hands, boisterous behavior, and insensitive manners.

Heterosexual Love—Just as the genital sequence becomes the synthesis of the oral–anal–phallic periods, the heterosexual stage climaxes the four previous stages of self–parental–fictional–homosexual stages. Roughly speaking, the heterosexual and genital phases are comparable.

With the onslaught of puberty and the concomitant functioning of the endocrine system, the young boy or girl finds that there seems to be something deliciously nice in the form of the opposite sex. The first fumbling attempts at rapport are often amusing to the sophisticated adult. The girl or boy does all the wrong things. The girl snatches caps hoping to be chased and tickled and yet protest most vehemently that the "boys are bothering her." The boy acts like a puppy. To get the girl's attention he waits until she is surrounded by friends on the school playground and then he backs off, runs at a galloping pace, plunges right through the middle of the group of girls, upsetting them and, then, stands off with a foolish grin. All this to get the girl's attention! The adult is confused by it all. Very soon the heterosexual byplay takes on more and more sophisticated forms of expression until necking, petting, and deviate forms of physical expression of the sexual appetite are learned and exploited.

As economic and social status increase, the male and female of the species called man have matured through five love stages and have utilized all of them. Life continues through the selection of a marriage partner within the laws of society to the rearing of children who in turn will progress through the love stages that their parents did and thus complete the cycle.

States of Consciousness. One cannot do much with the Freudian approach to personality without incorporating in the descriptive system a treatment of the states of being conscious. It is so very easy to become involved in a semantic squabble about the term *conscious vis à vis unconscious* that one is tempted to invent new terms and try to delimit carefully their use. This is impossible, however, when dealing with a Freudian scheme of things. The entire Freudian position is linked with the belief that something exists in man's mental state which is opposite to the state of being conscious. Rather than belabor the point of whether conscious–unconscious exists and in what manner the terms are abused, we may best bend our efforts to describing what Freud meant by the terms, their characteristics positively basic to his concepts, leaving the verbal in-fighting to the semantically minded.[9]

Conscious—The conscious is that part of man's mental life of which he

[9] See especially the excellent treatment given this confused state by English and English, *op. cit.*

is fully aware. The state of being conscious enables us to know where we are, what is happening around us, who we are, how we are to go about doing what we are presently doing. When something happens, we become aware of it and can purposefully direct our attention to it; our senses tell us things and we can properly interpret their afferent impulses and efferently respond to a demand through them, i.e., winking, blinking, motion of the body; and in short, we are alive in the most acute sense of being. Running, swimming, eating, or any strenuous physical exercise in which mental activity is an integral part is probably the best example of being conscious. The more active we are, the more conscious we seem to be. The end of an exciting basketball game would find us at our highest, mentally conscious self. As you read these words, you may or may not be overtly conscious depending upon the activeness with which you are attending to the task at hand. To Freud, consciousness meant to be vitally and mentally alive and awake.

Preconscious—In descending order (see Figure 2, p. 81) we are next interested in that mental state of being called preconscious, which exists between the mental state of being conscious and the mental state of being unconscious as we shall describe it in a moment. The preconscious is that shadowy land where our memories, for example, grope with a piece of knowledge so readily known in the past but now not immediately in our possession for use. Surely every student who has ever taken an examination has sat groping for a piece of knowledge when he can't quite remember fully the entire fact. When he walked out of the examination room or that evening shortly before falling asleep, it suddenly occurred to him. That piece of information was floating around in the preconscious, almost, but not quite, in the conscious. However, not all things of a mental nature that exist in the preconscious have to be teased out or are coyly unavailable until moments of stress are past. Facts, information, data, feeling tones, emotional states which may lie in the unconscious can be obtained from the preconscious with little or no effort, providing stress is not strongly present. The preconscious acts more as a membrane than a repository. It actually stores very little but utilizes itself as a device to keep the activity of the unconscious from interfering with the work that the conscious must do to keep us alert and attending to the day's activities. All mental content coming from the unconscious to the conscious must pass through the preconscious.

Unconscious—Somewhere in man's mental life, says Freud, there has to be a mental state of being which accounts for things not present to the mind at any given moment but which have occurred to the mind in the past. There must be some storehouse for all that man's mind has gone through. There must also be some mental area in which the mind can play as freely as it wishes in a pure pleasure principle sense without paying obeisance to the rules of the ego–superego. There must be some place in which man can have mental fun without obeying any rules. This area lies in the unconscious aspects of man's mental life. To put it another way, the unconscious is the mental storehouse of man's past and the mental playground of his present pleasures. All that has happened to man in the past is deposited in the mind whether man likes it or not. He may exercise many censoring powers over the contents of the unconscious mental self through the use of the preconscious, but this power of censorship is a continuing process which never stops. When the censorship relaxes, as it may during sleep or moments of stress, the content of the unconscious may come bubbling up through the preconscious and cause emotional pain. This is especially true when the repressed content is largely motivated by the pleasure principle.

Subconscious—The present treatment of the mental phenomenon called the subconscious is another extension of the purely Freudian theory which holds up nonetheless within the general framework of his concepts.

The present author has extracted that activity of man with which he enters life completely equipped and has given to it the term subconscious: that which lies below or outside of consciousness but is not necessarily the opposite of the term conscious. One other distinction applies: whereas everything in the unconscious has to have been at one time in the conscious past, the elements in the subconscious have not been in the mental past but are all present at birth. Man, therefore, comes into the world equipped with a subconscious mental factor. He has also an emerging conscious capacity which may or may not develop adequately (as with idiots and some imbeciles). He accumulates an unconscious mental area only after the conscious mental state has passed along an experience to it.

An illustration which may be helpful in understanding what is meant by subconscious is that state of being which one undergoes during anesthesia. If the reader has experienced the state of suspended mental life that seems to occur with anesthesia, he will find it helpful in comprehending the subconscious. The usual experience is to feel that the anesthetist will not completely do his job prior to the actual surgery, and one has the experience of counting to seven and worrying that the surgeon will cut too soon. This is the last conscious thought, and then, without any seeming passage of time, the surgery is over and the attending nurse or surgeon is cautioning the patient to relax, saying that "it is all over." That period of time during what could possibly be hours of existence with yet no feeling of time experienced was lived in the subconscious. Being in a coma or being unaware of anything takes place in the subconscious.

To the above description must be added the inborn mental processes which accompany man at birth and are largely autonomic in nature but do require some mental effort. Desire for water, hunger for food, attention to breathing, all come out of the subconscious. One does not have to have had these go through the conscious mental process in order for them to operate.

Ego Defense Mechanisms. Although Freud's daughter Anna reconstituted some of her father's work to develop the principle ego defense mechanisms, and many, many neo-Freudians have since expanded and utilized the concept, it was Freud who originated the basic tenets.

All three words in the title are important to an understanding of what is meant by ego defense mechanisms. As we have seen, the ego is a central component of man's personality. We have also seen that man wishes to remain happy even though he realizes that certain realities of life may postpone happiness. In order to meet the vicissitudes of everyday life which care not at all for his ego, man must defend his ego against the outside world, in some cases against himself, too, as we shall see later. This defense becomes mechanical through the repetition compulsion proclivity of man.

One of the chief characteristics of an ego defense mechanism is that it does not enter the conscious state of man's reasoning but that it operates in the unconscious. Hence, the personality is not aware that it is defending its ego. Somewhere in the past it learned this defense technique. Now the personality utilizes the technique even though at times it in no way solves the problem of supporting the ego.

Another chief characteristic of an ego defense mechanism is that it may distort, or even deny reality. It is not outside the realm of possibility that man may lie to himself in order to protect himself from unhappiness. He may also so twist reality without realizing it that any resemblance to what actually happened and how he interprets what happened has disappeared. He may also be so disturbed by an incident which causes him great emotional discomfort as simply to pretend that it did not happen and do such a good job of pretending that he eventually comes to deny what actually existed. The outside world, his friends, and others, stand confused.

The primary ego defense mechanisms are these: repression, regression, reaction formation, projection, and fixation. As previously mentioned these five are primarily the work of Anna Freud who continued to work somewhat in the vein of her father. Other defense mechanisms although not as pointedly described by name in Freud's work are as follows: sublimation, substitution, identification, and displacement. In the recent literature on psychotherapy and allied fields are many other ego defense mechanisms, some of which appear redundant but are possibly useful in describing man's personality.[10] The concept of defense mechanisms apparently intrigues many therapists.

Repression—Repression may be considered as a fundamental defense mechanism, the cornerstone mechanism to many of the others because it comes into play so very early in life and because it influences or causes some of the other ego defenses to be brought into play. In fact, Freud, in his *An Autobiographical Study,* stated, "The theory of repression became the foundation stone of our understanding of the neuroses." And further on, "It is possible to take repression as a centre and to bring all the elements of psychoanalytic theory into relation with it."

Basically, the definition of the word is quite like that in any dictionary. It means to hold back, to prevent from acting, to exclude, or to block. The unique characteristic of the Freudian definition is that *all* of these things are done without the knowledge, in the conscious sense, of the personality. If they are done with the knowledge of the conscious mind, then we may call that *suppression.* Suppression is not a part of the present discussion.

Repression has two factors which must be considered:

1. Content coming up from the id for the first time, not having been previously in the conscious mind and gone back into the id level, is named *primal* repression. By this process certain inborn impulses to act via the pleasure principle are denied first entry into the conscious mind. That is not to say that they are permanently kept out. At the moment in the present consideration of repression they are denied entry, however.
2. *Primary* repression is the denial of a re-entry of some past experience into the conscious mind, especially if the past experience would cause emotional pain.

Repression is an excellent example of the superego structure imposing the reality principle upon the id substructure.

---

[10] See especially Coleman, *Abnormal Psychology and Modern Life,* 2nd ed., Scott, Foresman, 1956, p. 99. Some seventeen defense mechanisms are presented.

Regression—To regress is to go back to a previous state, place, or position. Whereas in the discussion of repression one could repress something which had not existed previously in experience, it is only possible to regress to what has already been experienced. Man cannot *return* to some place he has never been.

Most of Freud's writing about regression concerned his patients' returning to behavior characteristic of their childhood. This became so prevalent in his therapy with patients that the word *infantilism* became almost the synonym of regression. It is possible, however, to regress to an earlier form of behavior which is not of childhood but of later maturity, as we shall see further on.

Regression is a manifestation of the repetition compulsion mentioned previously. The human personality is again inclined to repeat an activity which was once successful or at least pleasant. Since it is a compulsion type of repetition (reasoning plays no part in a compulsion), the activity repeated may in no way solve the present problem and may even worsen it. Usually the regressive form of behavior does not recreate the entire past experience but only portions of it which reinforce the entire past episode. When a personality is frustrated and regresses to an infantile form of behavior, such as pouting, sucking on objects (oral erogenous, pleasure zone), or hitting, he does not also dress, talk, or deport himself completely as a baby. Usually only vestiges of the earlier form of behavior are recreated.

Reaction Formation—This defense mechanism often is one of the hardest concepts to grasp and frequently is rejected vehemently by many beginning students of psychology. In essence, the reaction formation phenomenon is very clearly seen if one remembers the duality or polarity principle. In that principle man was doomed to wander back and forth between two poles of action. The reaction formation mechanism finds man doing just that but in a more subtle way, such that the preconscious keeps him from realizing the true meaning of his behavior.

Shakespeare's oft-quoted line, "The lady doth protest too much, me thinks," fits quite well into the concept of reaction formation. This is akin to the student who is tremendously and everlastingly discussing cheating by other students, or the individual who is so set against something that the listener soon wonders what all the fuss is about. Reaction formation is exhibited by extreme behavior. The individual who appears to be afraid of absolutely nothing gives indications of unconsciously being afraid to such an extent that he must overplay the role of hero. Whereas most people come to a point of fearing some things and avoiding them as best they can, the reactive formation individual continuously seeks out and quite extravagantly enters situations where most of us fear to enter. The American college football player who loudly exhibits aggressiveness may be considered an example.

Projection—The word *projection* receives a great deal of play in the psychological literature. Much of the intent of the word springs from Freud's introduction of it as an ego defense mechanism. Projection means the protection of one's own ego from feelings of guilt by casting them toward another individual and unwittingly blaming him for the very faults that one has himself. We project our anxiety-producing thoughts onto some other person, thereby not having to defend our own thoughts. Thus when the penurious person accuses the world of being stingy, he has unconsciously projected his own feeling of being tightfisted onto all the world, thereby making his own efforts to save a comparatively laudable endeavor. Another example of projection is called "comparing the irregular adjective." "I am thrifty, you are tightfisted, he is stingy"; "I am brave, you take chances, he is foolhardy"; or "I like to relax from studying now and then, you haven't been very busy lately, he is going to flunk out of school if he spends all of his time in the student union." These closely approach the mechanics of projection.

Fixation—Fixation is much like the ego defense mechanism of regression except that the individual who employs this ego defense mechanism does not necessarily go back (regress) to an earlier form of pleasant behavior in order to relieve a present emotional problem. One may fixate or remain at a current pleasurable activity whether or not it solves any problems in the future. The feeling is this one: I like doing this, I do it well, it makes me feel good when I do it, and therefore, why change? To the fixated individual, flexibility leads only to unknown paths, and the unknown may make challenges which cannot be met.

In the usual Freudian sense, the mechanism of fixation describes the holding on to a past idea which was at one time successful in solving emotional problems; consequently, the term is closely allied to regression. One regresses by returning to fixated point. (The following defense mechanisms though not found in Anna Freud's recapitulation are nonetheless integral parts of Freud's concept and writings of the ego defense mechanisms.)

Sublimation—That man has to hold down (repress) his libidinal desires and conform to the reality principle of the ego-superego structure does not necessarily mean that he can do nothing about his desires. Through the unconscious process of sublimation he may direct his thoughts and impulses into fields of expression which afford him some disguised outlet and which, most important, are accepted and at times prized by his fellowmen. Traditionally, the artistic pursuits of sculpturing, painting, dancing, and the like have been assigned this role of release-serving agencies for inhibited sexual desires. It is interesting to speculate on why the general layman has so often accepted this mechanism, all the while indignantly denying most of the other theories of Freud. One may suspect perhaps that individuals who do not create in the artistic sense feel pangs of jealousy about those who do. In addition to the creative arts one must also include physical contact sports such as football, wrestling, and the like as sublimated homosexual tendencies. This revelation is taken as blasphemy by the adherents of bodily contact sports, and tempers explode in indignation. There is, however, no difference between painting and football as sublimatory releases because both fit the criteria.

Substitution—Substitution is closely allied to the defense mechanism of sublimation; both employ efforts toward goals accepted by society instead of goals not acceptable to society (or self). The basic difference lies in the part the conscious *vis à vis* the unconscious plays. Sublimatory activities are not known to the conscious self, whereas substitution may be a conscious process, although frequently it is not. There is also the added difference that the libidinal or sexual repressions are not as prevalent in substitution as they are in sublimation. Agreement with the two preceding statements is not universal by any means. Obviously if the conscious self is operating, i.e., if the self knows what it is doing, then the criteria of a defense mechanism of the ego have not been met. However, the ego defense mechanisms have been expanded greatly by post-Freudians, as was previously mentioned.

Substitution of the conscious type and, hence, not entirely in the Freudian rubric, would be exemplified by the student who indulges in and excels in sports or physical activities for a feeling of success and the pleasure principle because he is unable to gain satisfaction or success in the academic pursuits. The opposite example is a strong and successful emphasis on studying as a substitute for success in athletics. The implied suggestion that highly qualified athletes cannot be successful students or vice versa is obviously sophistry and false.

Identification—In general, we may consider three meanings for the term *identification*. The last of these of these will be treated more fully than the others as it involves a fundamental and complex theory of Freud's which he called the Oedipus complex.

Identification in the first sense means recognition of something, a word, person, place, song. This is possible only if the subject has previously met or learned in the past the characteristics of the object which is recognized. Having once seen the past thing as familiar, one may place it in a serial order (classification or differentiation) or merely accept it.

When we react to a situation which reminds us of a similar situation, but one which we have not experienced directly in the past, we may then be identifying in the secondary sense of this word. Transfer of training comes within the scope of this meaning. Although the various meanings of the word tend to converge, they frequently lose a preciseness in actual usage.

It is in the last definition of the word *identification* that the more accu· rate meaning is conveyed according to the Freudian theory. Whenever one person merges his personality deeply in the personality of another individual, the psychoanalytic definition of *identification* is exhibited. The word means, therefore, more than identifying something from the past or more than employing a past experience which is reminiscent of an analogous experience; it means that one enters directly into the feeling tone of the object toward which one has cathexis. It is more than mere imitation of the other person, more than sympathy for him, and more than a strong empathetic identification with his emotional states; it means feeling one *is* the other person. Obviously, this is not actually possible, for one never loses or supplants one's own ego (except perhaps in the psychotic states).

Oedipus Complex—Using the previous definition of *identification* as a springboard but not a set of semantic rules, we may now consider the theoretical aspects of the Oedipus complex. Incidentally, this theoretical position was responsible for much of the furor and intense indignation that was directed toward Freud by other analysts, the clergy, and laymen in general. Freud himself states that he "stumbled" on the idea and that it took him long hours of consideration to accept it. Prior to his expostulating the theory that children's lives are highly sexually oriented, he accepted and understood in others the historical position that children know nothing about sex and are completely innocent of sexual drives until well after puberty.

When a child is born, the first object it experiences other than itself is its mother. This is the human being who feeds it, clothes it, loves it, and answers to all its needs. If the mother does not perform her tasks in the traditional sense of devoted duty, the child transfers its feeling of love and trust upon the mother surrogate whoever that may be. In most societies it is, of course, a female figure. As the child develops, it identifies strongly with the mother figure. From this dependence for life and identification grows a feeling of love for the mother. Thus both the boy and girl baby begin the earliest years of life with a strong attachment to the mother.

Paralleling the above development of love toward mother is the exploration and discovery by the child of his own body and how it functions. In the course of this learning about one's self the baby notices its sexual organs. At this point the development of the Oedipus process differs for boys and girls, and we must consider them separately. Up to this point the organism has been called "it", but we may now refer to "he" or "she."

In conjunction with loving mother and discovering his own body, the boy also becomes aware of the role his father plays in his life. Father is a stronger, larger, more powerful, less present, and like-sexed creature. Father also shares the mother, her attention, her love, her time, and in fact appears to have some priority for the mother's time and affection. The infant boy becomes aware of this pattern and finds that he and his ego must at times share the mother with the father. The natural outcome of this is a feeling of unexpressed rivalry and concomitant jealousy. In the initial stages of this awareness the infant boy does nothing to curb his feeling of jealousy. However, repression takes place as he develops. He also notices that he is physically more like his father than like his mother, a fact which leads him to identify with the father as well as the mother. Ambivalence (polarity principle) results from this cathexis toward two different individuals, both of whom are so largely instrumental to his well-being. He must share mother with father, which is not to his liking, but he is also more like father than mother, which sense of identification brings him satisfaction. Since, as he develops, the reality principle also develops, he now can fantasize a retribution from his father for usurping some of the father's prerogatives with the mother. Because knowledge of the world was originally confined and continues to be proscribed by his oral–anal–phallic education, it follows that whatever retribution his father will perpetrate upon him will be in this area of the erotogenic zone. The one physical characteristic that definitely makes him different from his mother is his protruding sexual organ, the penis. This, then, becomes the focus of retaliation which he feels his father might make upon him, the removal of the penis, which would make him more femalelike but would also eliminate his one masculine feature. Equally important, the penis as the incestuous organ must be removed in order to eliminate the possibility of an incestuous and competing relationship. This fear Freud referred to as the *castration complex*: the male child fears both the removal of the organ which makes him masculine like father with the consequent loss of his identification with father and also of his continued rivalry with father for mother's love and attention. The polarity principle creates now an anxiety which he is unable to cope with until the reality principle introduces the ego defense mechanism of repression. Now at last he has a method of solving the problem despite its requiring the use symbols and other devious means of gaining expression of the repressed desire for mother. The fictional love stage, later homosexual and heterosexual love stages, and the gradual development of his superego, all help to resolve the polarity.

The boy approximately three to five years of age is generally considered to be in the strongest throes of the polarity of the Oedipal complex. The complex, however, continues to be a vital factor throughout the remainder of his life and has much to do with his adult attitude about the opposite sex, figures of authority, and his relationships with his own wife and the children. No great significance is attached psychoanalytically to the word *Oedipus*. The exploits of the hero Oedipus of Sophocles' tragedy, *Oedipus Rex,* made this an appropriate name to Freud for the complex. Indeed it is, for Oedipus killed his father unknowingly and subsequently married his mother. Since the identities of his parents were unknown to him, the analogy fits well with Freud's theory; all of the above behavior operates in the id (unconscious processes) of the infant boy.

Electra Complex—The Oedipal complex as it operates in the female unconscious is called specifically the *Electra complex* although that term is not too often found in current psychoanalytic literature.

As stated previously, a different set of forces operates for the girl infant. She, too, finds the mother her primary and initial love object after her own oral–anal–phallic narcissistic period, which Freud called autoerotism, has developed. The ministrations of mother and the consequent feeling of love are equally present in her case. However, after this point the similarities between the male and female Oedipal–Electral complexes diverge. Here the steps are much more involuted and complicated. Freud based the Oedipal theory on his investigations and reflections on men and assumed that the female would be a complete parallel, but "this turned out not to hold . . . [and] . . . revealed profound differences between the sexual development of men and women" (An Autobiographical Study, p. 65). It is also true that he first formulated the Oedipal theory from therapy with his adult male patients and only later in life was he able to corroborate the theory to his satisfaction by working with small children as clients [Analysis of a Phobia in a Five-Year-Old Boy (the case of Hans) 1909].

As the small girl becomes familiar with the father, she also notices the relationships between her body and the father's. In conjunction with the feeling of rivalry between the girl and her mother for her father's love, she notices the lack of a male organ in herself. This causes the girl to blame her mother for removing her penis or at least for the lack of a penis for her own body. She attributes this loss to the mother's jealousy which in this way removes the child as a love object with the father. Along with holding her mother responsible for her castrated condition, she identifies quite strongly with the father because he possesses the envied phallic organ. Her envy arises from the obvious comparison of her body which has nothing (or a cavity) to the condition of her father who possesses something neither she nor her mother has. Again the polarity arises. Sharing the lack of something with her mother strengthens her original identification with the mother, and the ambivalence brings emotional anxiety. To this state of anxiety for the girl Freud gave the name penis envy. Dissimilar to the boy's resolvement of his castration complex, the girl does not so readily resolve her polarity, with the result that numerous psychological differences exist between the male and female. The girl continues the rivalry ("Daddy's girl") much longer, represses it less strongly, becomes recalcitrant toward the mother at the onslaught of puberty—approximately at age eleven—and modifies it gradually until she, too, gains a marriage partner and then as a mother displays her ambivalence toward both sexes in her roles as a mother to boys and girls and as a sexual partner to a male.

It must be stressed at this point that all of the foregoing discussion in regard to the Oedipal–Electral complexes are the result of the id operating in the unconscious areas of the psyche. Children are *not* consciously aware of this complex of behavior. This fact is most fundamental to a grasp of Freud's theory.

Displacement—In Freudian terminology *displacement* refers to man's inclination to select an object reminding him of an original object which elicited a strong positive or negative effect, and then to respond to the second object with all the intensity of feeling that the first object created. The use of symbols is almost mandatory in the consideration of displacement. The following incidents may serve as examples:

1. The undergraduate student becomes angry at his professor. Being unable to retaliate against the professor, the angered student "takes it out" on his roommate. The anger is therefore placed against another object even though that object is entirely innocent.
2. The motorist who becomes upset by the driving of sports car enthusiasts. He now displaces his annoyance of sports cars to anything that reminds him of low sweep automobiles. Any object resembling the sports car becomes a symbol of recklessness: berets worn by drivers, fast starts by other automobiles, etc.
3. A widow displaces all of her thwarted love feelings for a lost husband upon the young son who resembles the departed husband.

All of the above examples are indicative of displaced feelings. From displacement spring other types of behavioral patterns such as stereotyping, displaced aggression, scapegoating, etc.

DELIMITATIONS

The foregoing description of Freud's system by no means includes all the many contributions he made to psychoanalytic thinking. Reasons for limiting the material are 1. limitations of space; 2. concern with personality theory rather than with methods of therapy; 3. the fact that no writing explaining another work can be as inclusive as the first; one must go to the original if he is to get the thorough work; 4. the bibliography at the end of the chapter, which indicates many excellent sources for further study. The author urges the student to go as far as he likes, especially in the writings of Freud, who is both interesting and absorbing as an author.

Free association as a therapeutic technique, the analysis of dreams, the phenomenon of forgetting, slips of the tongue during conversation, all of these and many more of Freuds contributions are left to the work of other authors. Freud's *A General Introduction to Psychoanalysis, The Psychopathology of Everyday Life,* and one of his very last, *New Introductory Lectures on Psycho-Analysis,* are highly recommended. The conversational tone of Freud's writings and the flow of style make them usable for the average undergraduate student.

EXPLAINING HUMAN BEHAVIOR VIA FREUD'S PSYCHOANALYTIC THEORY

If the reader has become familiar with Methods of Procedure in Chapter 2, he realizes that each theory will be used also to explain why man does the things he does. The previous section attempted to describe the fundamentals of the theory. We may now profitably see if the theory answers any of the "why" questions for us. The last section puts the test of predictability to each theory.

Students of personality theory may reasonably question the worth of a theory if it does not explain some of man's behavior. To that question this section has been devised primarily. The criteria for the examples in most cases have been the following. As will be seen these do not always fit the theory to the theory's best advantage; in some cases other examples hold.

Criteria for examples:

1. The example should be present in most known cultures or ethnic groups.
2. The examples should be within the actual experience or at least vicarious experience of most people.
3. The example should not necessarily favor the exposition of one theory over another.
4. The example should be useful and as practicable as possible in furthering the explanation of why man behaves as he does.

With the above criteria in mind the following examples are proposed:

1. Marriage: Why does man in most societies go through some kind of formalized ceremony? Why does man select a mate?
2. Perversions: Why does man engage in sexual perversions which in no way are designed to procreate the race? What promotes man's sexual appetites?
3. Suicide: What forces bring man to end his own life? Why does man purposefully and at times painfully put himself to death?
4. Lawbreaking: What causes man to construct laws with other men and then deliberately break some law every day (for example, exceeding speed

limits, throwing debris on the sidewalk, jaywalking, etc.)? The emphasis is all on the *deliberate* flaunting of a law and not on casual or unwitting misdemeanors.

5. Supranatural being: Why do most societies worship a god figure of some kind?

6. Humor: Why does man laugh? What gives him a "sense of humor"?

7. Smoking: Why do most societies who have ever had the opportunity, smoke pipes, cigars, cigarettes, and continue this custom?

8. Play and recreation: Why does man throughout the known world practice some form of participative or spectator recreation?

9. Psychoses–neuroses: Why does man lose his sense of identity and reality and become either psychotic or neurotic? What causes man to have compulsions, obsessions, phobias and the like? (This section considers only the functional disorders, not the organically caused psychoses.)

Admittedly constructing a list such as the above might be a fascinating sort of quiz game, and the endeavor could result in hundreds of "why" questions. (Further examples could be: stuttering, thumbsucking, masochism–sadism, thrift, dreaming, losing one's temper, etc.) Those posed above are intended to draw out of the theory many possibilities for giving us practical information.

Even to the most unsophisticated reader it must be now apparent that any of the theories that could explain adequately all the dynamics underlying the above questions must indeed be the answer to life itself! The questions are not intended to be metaphysical but merely to be a device to bring the reader closer to understanding the practicality of each theory.

Marriage

To explain marriage or the selection of at least one mate with whom to live and share touches some fundamental concepts in the Freudian theory. Man gets married because he seeks pleasure, assuming of course that marriage is considered to be a pleasant state. It is necessary for him to select one wife in most cultures, and in almost all cultures he goes through some sort of ceremony which his society constructs and which delineates the marriage partners as responsible to each other. Also, all of this must be done publicly. Thus the latter part serves the reality principle as well as the pleasure principle. Other reasons under the Freudian system may also be employed in examining the social custom of marriage and why man undergoes this. Through the libidinal appetites which he has now grown to cathecticize toward the opposite sex, he most certainly needs a sexual partner. The erogenous zones have developed, the love stages have matured to the heterosexual stage, and since he wishes to reduce the tension created by unfulfilled wishes, it is a natural behavioral act for him to enter matrimony. The ego and superego structure direct him to a formalized approach to matrimony whenever his background has been such as to develop the concepts handed down by his ethnic group.

Perversions

This particular problem seems almost to be designed for the Freudian theory because there are so many readily available answers to the question of why man commits perverted acts upon himself or with others of his sex or the opposite sex. Probably the main reasons lie in the development of the erogenous zones. As the oral–anal–phallic–genital areas become sensitized, traumatic incidents may prolong or delay the natural sequence. Whatever may be the influence which changes normality, the zone is now ripe for exploitation beyond its normal developmental urgings. Consequently, a child not properly weaned through the phallic–genital period may indulge in masturbatory practices long into adulthood. In fact, much of current psychoanalytic literature devotes itself to explanations of deviant sexual excesses and their effect upon the societal life of man. The temptation in this section is to overexplain rather than underexplain.

Any stimulation of an erogenous zone is considered to be a perverted act in Freudian theory if the stimulation is not in the natural course of marital cohabitation.

Suicide

According to the duality principle man is forever going back and forth between two polarities. In suicide he has gone from Eros (life–love) to its opposite, Thanatos (death), and has managed to remain at the one pole until he has destroyed himself. In his later writings Freud made much of the "Death wish," and later writers have picked this idea up in light of explaining psychoanalytic phenomena. That is to say that man gains satisfaction if not pleasure from destroying things including himself. Suicide epitomizes the greatest destructive act that man can perpetrate.

Lawbreaking

When the pleasure principle under pressure from the id decides to express itself in favor of self at the expense of society, laws may be broken, customs may be flaunted, and the ego may rationalize its behavior in favor of the self. The laws, of course, have been created as a necessity by the collective superegos of men who are guided by the reality principle that man must evolve controls for group behavior if he is not to destroy himself as a group. In fact, Freud, toward the latter part of his work, began to evince a deep interest in social psychology and the use of his theory in explaining collective behavior.

If confronted with his lawbreaking, man makes himself feel better by employing a few of the defense mechanisms, projection, for one. "Other people break far bigger laws than I do; why don't the police catch them and leave me alone?"

Supranatural Being

Freud's explanation of why man worships a god figure went through considerable change between his four essays collected in the volume entitled *Totem and Taboo* (1913), and his further investigations of the origins of religion and morality in the two essays *The Future of an Illusion* (1927) and *Civilization and its Discontents* (1930).[12] The publication of these works brought down the wrath of the current clergy and corroborated for them the concept of Freud as anti-Christ and an evil, sexually obsessed, old man. Beginning in 1907 with a study of the similarity between obsessive acts and religious practices or ritual, especially in relation to "totemism," Oedipus complex, and incestuous repressions, he wrote: "I perceived ever more clearly that the events of human history, the interactions between human nature, cultural development and the precipitates of primeval experiences (the most prominent example of which is religion), are no more than a reflection of the dynamic conflicts between the ego, the id, and the super-ego, which psychoanalysis studies in the individual—are the very same processes repeated on a wider stage" (*An Autobiographical Study*, p. 138).

Humor

By extending some of Freud's theses, we may explain humor as the sudden release of tension which involves the inflation of the ego structure and the enhancement of the ego. This may be brought about by identification with some individual in the humor-producing situation—the Chaplinesque person knocking a top hat off the head of a pompous individual

[12] See Hogarth Standard Edition.

who may be reminiscent of the figure of authority, the father figure, thus revealing some involvement with the Oedipal complex. The obvious principle involved throughout the humor situation is the pleasure principle. (See especially, Jokes and their relation to the unconscious, in the Hogarth Standard Edition, Vol. 8.)

Smoking

The pleasures of smoking, whether it be a pipe, cigarette, cigar, are known throughout the civilized world. This universality of a habit is not difficult for the Freudian theorist to explain. Smoking is a form of tension reduction coupled with repetition compulsion based on the pleasure principle that utilizes the oral erotogenic zone. Aside from the manipulative pleasure of handing the instruments of smoking (the pipe, cigarette, the lighter, tamping the tobacco, turning the cigarette in the corner of the mouth), man regresses to an earlier form of behavior that was pleasant and continues to give him pleasure: the oral cavity. When tensions mount or when one merely behaves repetitively, he reaches for his smoking instruments as a form of oral pleasure sometimes called the "nipple substitute." To the Freudian this is a very natural and easily explained action of man. Picture the modern business executive faced with decisions involving dollars and jobs for his fellowman, caught in a vortex of strong penalties for failure, and surrounded by clattering typewriters and all the cacophony of the commercial world. The Freudian theorist says that there is no surprise that man should seek solace in a cigar which he rolls around in his mouth, sucks, and usually does not smoke to completion. This oral activity returns him to an earlier form of infantile pleasure and thus helps to reduce his inner tensions, despite the fact that it does not help in a direct sense to solve any of his current problems. The college student who is in the midst of a difficult examination will frequently suck or chew the end of a pencil. Thus he seeks the oral zone to relieve his test-produced anxiety although, again, such mouthing of objects gives him no answers for the examination. The childhood propensity for thumbsucking and the almost automatic appeal of bubble gum for children are all part of the return to the oral zone for pleasure.

Play and Recreation

At least six theories about play or combinations of these theories have been formulated by those unconcerned with Freudian theory.

1. Play is a phylogenetic aspect of man's development. Children recapitulate the progress of man's civilization in their play form. Beginning with the infant's nihilistic play where he squashes, kills and plays as he pleases with no thought of consequences to others (doesn't take turns, pushes, hits, bites, etc.,) to the more socialized forms of play in organized sports and games with highly involved sets of rules, the child goes through all the steps that man went through from his caveman savagery to his present mode of living.

2. Play is a preparation for adulthood. The child goes through all the necessary roles he may have to fulfill in later life as he makes believe he is one of his parents, or a hero, or a villain.

3. Play is simply the disposition of excess energy which the child builds up during the confinement of his more societally constricted roles. As children dash out to the playground for recess in a noisy exuberant manner, they are seeking release from pent-up feelings that have arisen out of the formality of a classroom situation. Recess and after-school play provide the chance to explode and do all the things that the teacher could not or would not allow to be done in the classroom.

4. Play is necessary as a change from whatever one has to do in most of one's existence. The academic person indulges in fishing and outdoor activities because it is different from his normal existence and thus adds variety to life.

5. Play and recreation allow man to rest from the vicissitudes of everyday living. This applies especially to the more sedentary recreational forms such as spectator sports, television viewing and the like. Play then is man's chance to rest his body and mind without resorting to sleep.

6. Play is that wonderful medium of life at all ages that allows us to work out our emotional problems under and with the approval of society's codes. If we are angry and disturbed about something in our workaday world, we may strike a golf ball as hard as we can, we may throw a bowling ball with all our might at ten inoffensive pins without retaliation, we may sing or act and take the roles that are not possible for us in regular life. Thus as we play we resolve inner conflicts that make us unhappy.

Freud's theory could accept all of the above possibilities in explaining play and why man seeks recreation no matter what his culture, background, or age. Recasting the preceding theories, the psychoanalytic explanation could be construed as follows.

1. The gradual development of the id structure into the ego and superego superstructures follows man's phylogenetic reasons for play. As he develops, the child indulges in biting (oral, sadistic outlet), pushes or hits other children (pleasure principle predominating), and eventually learns complicated rules for games (reality principle which tells him that by postponing the present

pleasure of retaliation he may gain a more solid and higher pleasure of acceptance and approval from parents and playmates).

2. Many of the child's play and recreation agencies utilize the very developmental stages he is going through. The scouting organizations of Cubs or Brownies help him to express his normal, homosexual appetites. Literature of a make-believe character helps to fulfill the fictional love stage and promote the phantasy level, which he undergoes during the phallic–genitalic ages. His superego is tremendously strengthened during play because of the rules which others construct and which he discovers are useful and necessary.

3. The irrepressible id and libido are frequently allowed to follow the pleasure principle in, at times, thinly disguised recreational activities. The boy may hold a girl's body during dancing and gain some satisfaction for the libidinal appetites.

4. and 5. These non-Freudian theories of play follow the dictates of the duality principle. As he goes from work to its opposite, play, man follows the polarity of interests and living habits.

6. Catharsis and the value of working off emotional problems are highly allied with the therapy for children that is used by both Freudian and non-Freudian therapists. It is one of their chief stocks in trade. Although Freud and, of course, others go far beyond the cathartic aspects and rightfully consider reinterpretation as a *sine qua non* of therapy, much of the technique of free association is involved in his theory of play.

Psychoses–Neuroses

We will make no detailed exposition of explaining why man becomes psychotic or neurotic within the Freudian framework simply because to do so is to summarize at this point the entire theory or to repeat the entire chapter, for Freud's theory concerns itself solely with, grew out of, and was constructed for, the pursuance of the very question: Why does man become so deviant in his emotional behavior as to be psychotic or neurotic? Theorists to be explained in later chapters lend themselves more to this treatment because their theories did not grow from, originally, an explanation of man's deviant behavior. The reader then must content himself with a review of the previous portions of this chapter or a reading of the summary to follow.

PREDICTING HUMAN BEHAVIOR VIA FREUD'S PSYCHOANALYTIC THEORY

Prediction of actions or the *when* question can be directed in two ways: at the single individual, or at a group of individuals. To predict the former is almost impossible; to predict the actions of the latter comes closer to being possible. One person has so many variables floating around his behavior that we may never come to recognize, let alone control, them in order to predict the individual's actions. One would think that the variables would increase in proportion to the size of the group, and they do to some extent. But the individuals contained in a group will tend more and more, as the size of the group increases, to have more and more of the same variables operating. Thus, group prediction becomes somewhat simpler only because the variables become more identifiable. But the true ease in comparing individual with group predictability lies in the factor of deviation from the average. Some individuals will always be at the extremities, but most will tend toward the middle as the size of the group is extended. In dealing with predictability of personality theories for groups, we have size unlimited. We are speaking of all of man, not just a restricted population of college students, agricultural workers, or the like. Our task is now easier, for we want to predict when most of the group will conduct itself in a prescribed manner. The closer we come to increasing the size of "most" of the group, the more successful we are in prediction.

Although prediction of an individual's behavior is complicated by intangible variables, we cannot beg the question. The latter would be the safest thing to do for many reasons. First, the individual is primarily concerned with himself. He will test all theories on the basis of his own experience. Second, meaningful discussion of human behavior always descends to the cliché, "It depends upon the individual." This rejoinder soon becomes habitual and stops any further consideration of one human's behavior. We do not quarrel with the assumption that it is good to know all we can concerning one human being but complete knowledge is never possible, even for ourselves. Another factor arises from the "depends upon the individual" cliché. If each individual is different from all other individuals, which he is, then by the process of *reducto ad absurdum*, we must construct as many laws or theories of behavior as there are people in the world. This, too, is partially true but manifestly absurd when one is trying to promote some definitive considerations of man's behavior. Either we always deal with people in groups, a limited approach, or we are restricted to dealing with each individual in the confines of his individual *gestalt*. But there must be some middle ground in which certain constants are true for most individuals. We have, then, taken out of the group study the largest part of their numbers and looked at them as single people operating under similar responses to life's demands.

Personal Prediction

Two factors are involved in this classification. One factor is the student reader's own introspective feeling regarding prediction of human behavior. The idea either makes sense to him or it does not. The second factor is to consider the evidence as it has been accumulated by investigators, who sometimes call themselves scientists, and their work in a particular theory. Even after weighing the scientific data, the individual alone makes the final decision as to its acceptability as a personality theory leading to prediction.

This first section is concerned primarily with the individual reader's acceptance or rejection of Freud's theory and its worth in predicting human behavior.

If Freud's theory is accurate, we may expect all men, for example, to progress through the erogenous zones of oral–anal–phallic–genital. We may further expect human beings to regress to an oral fixation of sucking or mouthing some object when anxiety and stress are present. Can we predict, for example, that man will always have some supreme being to worship and fear because, as Freud states, man needs some supranatural father figure? Under the psychoanalytic theory man will always be prone to psychotic and neurotic episodes as long as there are pressures in the world and in himself which upset the polarity of his existence. Does it make sense to the reader to accept the thesis that man is forever to go back and forth between two polarities of action or decision and only by being an extreme deviate ever to remain at one of the poles? These are but some of the behaviorisms of man that we may predict if the Freudian theory is correct.

It may be of interest to re-examine some of the defense mechanisms to evaluate their predictability. Suppose, for example, that a child reverses the Oedipal–Electral complex and instead of the boy feeling strong but unconscious rivalry with his father for his mother's love, he feels no rivalry with his father but undergoes an overwhelming attachment and identification with his father, ignoring or even hating his mother. Will this produce a homosexually perverted adult, as Freud stated?

Let us presume that whenever an individual must repress a libidinal desire, he or she will turn to one of the forms of substitution and paint or draw or engage in activities that bring proximity to others' bodies.

Can we accurately say that man, when he is deeply frustrated and cannot retaliate openly to the object of frustration, will displace his anger at a secondary object only remotely akin to the original object?

Is it possible for the reader through introspection to recognize, only tangentially of course, the stirrings and urgings of an id as Freud described it? What proof does one need to find in himself to sense the pulling and tugging of the duality principle of life?

All of the above queries are directed at the individual reader with no attempt to decide scientifically whether they are meaningful or not. The reader either answers them to his satisfaction or he does not, just as he either accepts the reports of research concerning Freud's work or does not accept them.

Scientific or Laboratory Prediction

A concerted effort to continue the work of Freud is now being made by his daughter Anna in the Hampstead Child-Therapy Clinic, Maresfield Gardens, in London. The Hampstead Clinic is primarily devoted to training lay analysts in child therapy and to conducting research. The clinic is well staffed although small in size compared to many American training institutions. Almost all of its output is reported in the annual volumes of *The Psychoanalytic Study of the Child*. Miss Freud is one of the senior editors of this interesting journal. No attempt is made here to evaluate the predictability of their work. The reader is urged to make an independent judgment after having read the journals.

In a straightforward analysis, however, there is almost no research being done which lends itself to testing the predictability of Freud's theory. Much of the work is ex post facto. Case histories are reported, and then the dynamics of the client's background are discussed. Most of the emphasis is directed to the backward view rather than the forward view.

An excellent discussion and summary of psychoanalytic experimentation is contained in G. S. Blum's *Psychoanalytic Theories of Personality* (1953).

Since Freud's inductive–deductive methods were so uniquely personal to him, there is almost no known way to repeat his findings in a controlled experiment. One can only use his basic principles to design other research which may approximate what Freud did. This is no criticism of Freud, since he must be considered in the light of an explorer and discoverer, and a thing may only be discovered once. After that it is merely revisited. But, yet, one has difficulty in revisiting what Freud did. It is obviously not possible to redo the case of little Hans, but one can reexplore the dynamics of incestuous desires and the Oedipal complexes of other children. Having done this, one may further predict that other children will have Oedipal complexes and react in much the same manner as did the boy Hans, whose physician-father treated him under Freud's direction and guidance.

Two excellent works on psychoanalytic theory have posited the same evaluation. Kubie says, ". . . the validity of its [Freud's] predictions are among the basic scientific problems which remain to be solved" (*Psychoanalysis as a Science,* Pumpian-Mindlin (ed.), 1952). Hall and Lindzey in their excellent and definitive book put it cleverly as follows: "It is like betting on a horse after the race has been run. A good theory, on the other hand, is one that enables its user to predict in advance what is going to happen" (*Theories of Personality,* 1957, Wiley, p. 71).

One must pass on, then, the predictability of Freud's work to future investigators whose ingenuity and good luck may produce more than we have at the present time.

———————————◆———————————

SUMMARY

Figure 2 is a diagrammatic attempt to summarize the main features of Freud's theory regarding personality and its formation in man.

The id lies at the bottom, is the largest portion of the personality, and supports the entire structure. Basic to the id is the bottom layer of subconscious processes upon which all of life depends. The physical, sensory, and ongoing organic functions operate out of the subconscious. One does not have to think consciously about breathing, for example, in order to breathe. The id also permeates the unconscious. Only those activities which have been in the conscious and go through the preconscious may be considered in the unconscious. The subconscious, on the other hand, is innate and operates from birth.

The ego, which must deal with reality because it operates in the conscious state, is separated from the id by only the small membrane of the preconscious. The preconscious acts as a doorkeeper rather than as a repository of mental activity. It can only faciliate or limit and restrict passage of mental material from the id to its component, the ego.

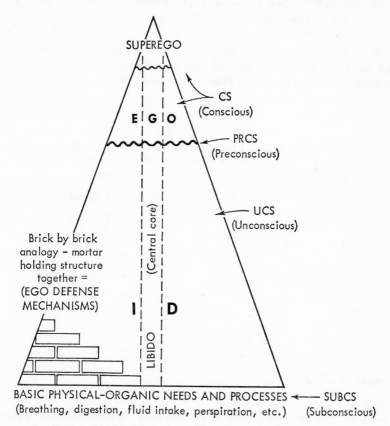

Figure 2. Diagrammatic Summary of Freud's Theory.

The superego, being the last to develop, lies at the top of the structure well within the realm of the conscious. It is the smallest component of the personality structure as well as the latest. If the structure is to collapse, it does so from the top down: the superego defaults first, followed by the ego. The last characteristic of the personality to cease operating is the subconscious level of breathing, digestion, and organic functioning.

Central to the entire structure of the personality (as given in Figure 2) is the core of the libido which runs up right through the middle of the structure to diminish at the apex of the superego and thus be central to, or the core of, much that is within man's personality and is affected by it.

Around the entire structure, protecting it from the pressures and weathering of the outside world, is a brick by brick façade held together by the mortar of the ego defense mechanisms. Consequently, although the ego defense mechanisms may change the outward appearance of the structure, they may never alter the fundamental structure.

Outline

Erogenous Zones	Characteristic Behavior	Love Stages
Oral		Self
Anal		Paternal
Phallic		Fictional
Latent Period		Homosexual
Genital		Heterosexual

BIBLIOGRAPHY

PRIMARY SOURCES

BOOKS

Freud, S., *The Standard Edition of the Complete Psychological Works,* trans. James Strachey, 24 vols., London, Hogarth, 1953–1955.

This is the most complete and definitive compilation of Freud's writings. Because of the immensity of its size—24 volumes—it must usually be read in the reference libraries and hence does not lend itself to browsing at leisure.

Freud, S., *Collected Papers,* Vols. I–V, London, Hogarth, 1925–1950.

Note. No author despite the best of intentions can prepare a full bibliography. The primary purpose of these bibliographies is to present for the student's benefit some current and available sources.

This is a secondary source if the complete volumes are not available.

Freud, S., *Collected Papers*, N.Y., Basic Books, 1959.

First American edition of 5 vols. *Collected Papers*, published in London.

Freud, S., *The Basic Writings of Sigmund Freud*, A. A. Brill (ed.), N.Y., Random House, 1938.

Probably the most available book covering most of his important writings. Also the least expensive.

Freud, S., *A general Selection from the Works of Sigmund Freud*, J. Rickman (ed.), N.Y., Liveright, 1957.

Indicates change and development of Freud's work from 1910–1926.

Freud, S., *The Case of Dora and Other Papers*, N.Y., Norton, 1952.

Nine essays taken from previous writings.

Freud, S., and D. E. Oppenheim, *Dreams in Folklore*, N.Y., Int. Univer. Press, 1958.

Breuer, J., and S. Freud, *Studies on Hysteria*, N.Y., Basic Books, 1957.

Reprint of Vol. XI of Standard Edition.

Freud, S., *The Origin of Psychoanalysis: Letters to Wilhelm Fliess, Drafts and Notes: 1887–1902*, N.Y., Basic Books, 1954.

Also as a paperback published by Doubleday (Anchor), Garden City, N.Y., 1957.

Freud, S., *On Aphasia: A Critical Study* [1891], N.Y., Int. Univer. Press, 1953.

Freud, S., *The Interpretation of Dreams* [1900], London, Hogarth, 1953.

Also as a Basic Book, N.Y., 1955.

Freud, S., *Psychopathology of Everyday Life* [1904], N.Y., New American Library, 1951.

A Mentor Book paperback.

Freud, S., *Leonardo da Vinci: A Study in Psychosexuality* [1910], N.Y., Random House, 1947.

Freud, S., *Totem and Taboo* (1913), N.Y., Random House.

Modern Library paperback with no publication date.

Freud, S., *A General Introduction to Psychoanalysis* [1917], Garden City, N.Y., Doubleday, 1953.

Permabook paperback. Also published Perma Giant in 1949; Garden City Deluxe and Star Editions in 1938, 1943.

Freud, S., *Beyond the Pleasure Principle* [1920], London, Hogarth, 1948.

Freud, S., *Group Psychology and the Analysis of the Ego* [1921], N.Y., Bantam Books, 1960.

Freud, S., *The Ego and the Id* [1923], London, Hogarth, 1947.

Freud, S., *On Creativity and the Unconscious* [1925], N.Y., Harper & Row, 1958.

Freud, S., *Inhibitions, Symptoms and Anxiety* [1926], London, Hogarth, 1936, 1948.

Freud, S., *The Question of Lay Analysis* [1926], N.Y., Norton, 1950.

Freud, S., *Civilization and Its Discontents* [1930], London, Hogarth, 1930.

Freud, S., *New Introductory Lectures on Psychoanalysis* [1933], N.Y., Norton, 1933.

Freud, S., *An Autobiographical Study* [1935], rev. ed. London, Hogarth, 1946.

Freud, S., *An Outline of Psychoanalysis* [1938], N.Y., Norton, 1949.

Freud, S., *Moses and Monotheism* [1939], N.Y., Knopf, 1947.

PERIODICALS

Freud, S., Report on my studies in Paris and Berlin [1886], *Int. J. Psycho. Anal.*, 1956, 37, 2–7.

Breuer, J., and S. Freud, On the psychical mechanism of hysterical phenomena [1893], *Int. J. Psycho. Anal.*, 1956, 37, 8–13.

Freud, S., On the teaching of psychoanalysis in universities [1918], *Int. J. Psycho. Anal.*, 1956, 37, 14–15.

Freud, S., Memorandum on the electrical treatment of war neurotics [1920], *Int. J. Psycho. Anal.*, 1956, 37, 16–18.

Freud, S., An unpublished letter on parapsychology, *Psychoanalysis*, 1954, 4(4), and 5(1), 12–13.

Freud, S., Three letters to America, *Psychoanalysis*, 1952, 1, 5–6.

Freud, S., Four unpublished letters of Freud, *Psychoanal. Quarterly*, 1956, 25, 147–154.

SUGGESTED READINGS

BOOKS

Arlow, J. A., *The Legacy of Sigmund Freud*, N.Y., Int. Univer. Press, 1956.

Bakan, D., *Sigmund Freud and the Jewish Mystical Tradition*, Princeton, N.J., Van Nostrand, 1958.

Blum, G. S., *Psychoanalytic Theories of Personality*, N.Y., McGraw-Hill, 1953.

Brill, A. A., *Basic Principles of PsychoAnalysis* [1921], N.Y., Washington Square Press, 1960.
   Also issued as Garden City ed., 1949, and now reissued as paperback. See especially chap. 5, Wit: Its Technique and Tendencies, an adaption of Freud on wit and humor.

Brill, A. A., *Psychoanalysis, Its Theories and Practical Application*, 3rd ed. Phila., Saunders, 1922.

Brill, A. A., *Freud's Contribution to Psychiatry*, N.Y., Norton, 1944.

Brown, J. A. C., *Freud and the Post-Freudians*, Baltimore, Penguin, 1961.

Horney, Fromm, and Sullivan also included.

Fliess, R., *Erogeneity and Libido: Addenda to the Theory of the Psychosexual Development of the Human*, N.Y., Int. Univer. Press, 1957.

Freud, A., *Psychoanalysis for Teachers and Parents*, N.Y., Emerson, 1935.

Freud, A. (and others, eds.), *The Psychoanalytic Study of the Child*, Vol. 1, 1945 to current Vol. 15, 1960, N.Y., Int. Univer. Press.

A yearly publication—Anna Freud's chief agency for publishing. Reflects thoroughly the new Freudian approach.

Freud, A., *The Ego and the Mechanisms of Defence*, N.Y., Int. Univer. Press, 1946.

Freud, E. L., *Letters of Sigmund Freud*, N.Y., Basic Books, 1961.

His son's collection of 315 letters Freud wrote between 1873 and 1939.

Freud, M., *Sigmund Freud: Man and Father*, N.Y., Vanguard, 1958.

Personal memories of Freud's second child and eldest son.

Fromm, E., *Sigmund Freud's Mission: An Analysis of His Personality and Influence*, N.Y., Harper & Row, 1959.

Glover, E., *Freud or Jung*, N.Y., Norton, 1950.

Compares Freud with Jung—Freud wins. Also as a Meridian Pocketbook, 1956.

Guntrip, H., *Personality Structure and Human Interaction*, N.Y., International Univer. Press, 1961.

Psychoanalysis a true theory of personality.

Hall, C. S., *A Primer of Freudian Psychology*, Cleveland, World Publishing, 1954.

Also published by Mentor Books, 1955.

Hall, C. S., and G. Lindzey, *Theories of Personality*, N.Y., Wiley, 1957, 29–75.

Hilgard, E. R., *Theories of Learning* (2nd ed.), N.Y., Appleton-Century-Crofts, 1956, Chap. 9.

Freud's reality and pleasure principles in the learning theory framework.

Hoffman, F. J., *Freudianism and the Literary Mind* (2nd ed.), Baton Rouge, Louisiana State Univer. Press, 1957.

Also Grove Press, 1959.

Jones, E., *The Life and Work of Sigmund Freud*: Vol. I. (1856–1900): *The Formative Years and the Great Discoveries*, 1953; Vol. II. (1901–1919): *Years of Maturity*, 1955; Vol. III. (1919–1939): *The Last Phase*, 1957, N.Y., Basic Books.

All of the series dedicated to "Anna Freud, True daughter of an immortal sire."

Jones, E., *Sigmund Freud: Four Centenary Addresses*, N.Y., Basic Books, 1956.

Kubie, L. S., Problems and techniques of psychoanalytic validation and progress, in E. Pumpian-Mindlin, (ed.) *Psychoanalysis as Science,* Stanford, Calif., Stanford Univer. Press, 1952, 46–124.

LaPiere, R., *The Freudian Ethic,* N.Y., Duell, Sloan and Pearce, 1959.

Levitt, M., *Freud and Dewey on the Nature of Man,* N.Y., Philosophical Library, 1960.
> They stood "shoulder to shoulder" in some respects.

MacIntyre, A. C., *The Unconscious: A Conceptual Analysis,* N.Y., Humanities Press, 1958.
> Some promise in the unconscious concept but may be more metaphysical than scientific.

Munroe, R. L., *Schools of Psychoanalytic Thought,* N.Y., Holt, Rinehart and Winston, 1955.
> Analysis and integration of Freud, Adler, Jung, Rank, Fromm, Horney, Sullivan, *et. al.*

Nelson, B. (ed.), *Freud and the 20th Century,* N.Y., World Publishing (Meridian), 1957.

Notenberg, M., *The Case History of Sigmund Freud: A Psycho-Biography,* Chicago, Regent Publishing, 1955.

Nunberg, H. and E. Federn (eds.), *Minutes of the Vienna Psychoanalytic Society, Vol. 1, 1906–1908,* N.Y., International Univer. Press, 1962.

Rieff, P., *Freud: The Mind of the Moralist,* N.Y., Viking, 1959.

Roback, A. A., *Freudians: Including unpublished Letters from Freud to Havelock Ellis, Pavlov, Bernard Shaw, Romain Rolland, et al,* Cambridge, Mass., Sci-Art Publishers, 1957.

Roheim, G. (ed.), *Psychoanalysis and the Social Sciences,* N.Y., Int. Univer. Press, 1948.

Schoenwald, R., *Freud: The Man and His Mind, 1856–1956,* N.Y., Knopf, 1956.

Toman, W., *An Introduction to Psychoanalytic Theory of Motivation,* N.Y., Pergamon Press, 1960.
> An attempt to systematize Freudian theory.

Wortis, J., *Fragments of an Analysis with Freud,* N.Y., Simon and Shuster, 1954.
> Diary and notes of former patient analyzed in winter, 1934–35.

PERIODICALS

Adams, L., Sigmund Freud's correct birthday: misunderstanding and solution, *Psychoanal. Rev.,* 1954, *41,* 359–362.

Adelson, J., Freud in America: some observations, *Am. Psychologist,* 1956, *11,* 467–470.

Alexander, F., Unexplored areas in psychoanalytic theory and treatment, *Behav. Sci.,* 1958, *3,* 293–316.

Angel, R. W., Jackson, Freud, and Sherrington on the relation of brain and mind, *Amer. J. Psychiat.*, 1961, *118*, 193–197.

They agreed that mental and physical events were distinct.

Ansbacher, H. L., The significance of the socio-economic status of the patients of Freud and Adler, *Amer. J. Psychother.*, 1959, *13*, 376–382.

Ansbacher, H. L., Was Adler a disciple of Freud? a reply, *J. Ind. Psychol.*, 1962, *18*(2), 126–135.

The answer is no.

Aronoff, J., Freud's conception of the origin of curiosity, *J. Psychol.*, 1962, *54*(1), 39–45.

Curiosity is somatically based during anal-sadistic stage and copes with sibling rivalry.

Atlantic, 208, No. 1, 61–111, special supplement on psychiatry in American life.

Bach, G. R., Freud's time bounded group concepts, *Group Psychotherapy*, 1956, *9*, 301–304.

Bailey, P., Janet, and Freud, *A.M.A. Archives of Neurology and Psychiatry*, 1956, *76*, 76–89.

Bellack, L., Freud and projective techniques, *J. Proj. Tech.*, 1956, *20*, 5–13.

Bernfeld, S., and S. Bernfeld, Freud's first year in practice: 1886–1887, *Bull. Menninger Clinic*, 1952, *16*, 37–49.

Bernfeld, S., Freud's studies on cocaine: 1884–1887, *J. Amer. Psychoan. Ass.*, 1953, *1*, 581–613.

Bonime, W., The psychic energy of Freud and Jung, *Amer. J. Psychiat.*, 1955, *121*, 372–374.

Bruner, J. S., Freud and the image of man, *Amer. Psychologist*, 1956, *11*, 463–466.

Burchard, E. M. L., Mystical and scientific aspects of the psychoanalytic theories of Freud, Adler, and Jung, *Amer. J. Psychother.*, 1960, *15*, 289–307.

Carroll, J. B. and H. Levin, A method for determining the polarity of behavior items, *Child Developm.*, 1956, *27*, 427–438.

Objectivity scoring polarity as love–hate, masculine–feminine, etc.

Colby, K. M., On the disagreement between Freud and Adler, *Amer. Imago*, 1951, *8*, 229–238.

Desmonde, W. H., G. H. Mead, and Freud: American social psychology and psychoanalysis, *Psychoanalysis*, 1957, *4*(4) and *5*(1), 31–50.

Ellenberger, H., The unconscious before Freud, *Bull. Menninger Clinic*, 1957, *21*, 3–15.

The precursors of Freud—Charcot, Bernheim, Janet, and Flournoy.

Eng, E., Freud and the changing present, *Antioch. Rev.*, 1956–57 (winter), 459–468.

Erikson, E. H., Freud's "The origins of psychoanalysis," *Int. J. Psycho. Anal.*, 1955, *36*, 1–15.

Feldman, A. B., Freudian theology, *Psychoanalysis*, 1952, *1*(3), 31–52.

Feldman, B., Sidelights on Freud's *Psychotherapy of Everyday Life, Amer. Imago*, 1960, *17*, 47–60.
  Extending the analysis of Freud's book.

Fizer, J., Errata of Freud, *Amer. J. Psychol.*, 1956, *69*, 309–311.

Fodor, N., Freud and the poltergeist, *Psychoanalysis*, 1955–1956, *4*(2), 22–28.

Fraiberg, L., Freud's writings on art, *Int. J. Psycho. Anal.*, 1956, *37*, 82–96.

Galdston, I., Eros and Thanatos: a critique and elaboration of Freud's death wish, *Amer. J. Psychoanal.*, 1955, *15*, 123–134.

Gervais, T. W., Freud and the culture–psychologists, *Brit. J. Psychol.*, 1955, *46*, 293–305.

Gladston, L., A midcentury assessment of the residuum of Freud's psychoanalytic theory, *Amer. J. Psychother.*, 1957, *11*, 548–559.

Goshen, C. E., The original case material of psychoanalysis, *Amer. J. Psychiat.*, 1952, *108*, 829–834.
  Freud misinterprets because of his own personality.

Hartmann, H., The development of the ego concept in Freud's work, *Int. J. Psycho. Anal.*, 1956, *37*, Pt. VI, 425–437.

Hiltner, S., Freud, psychoanalysis and religion, *Pastoral Psychol.*, 1956, *7*(68), 9–21.

Hitschmann, E., Freud correspondence, *Psychoanal. Quart.*, 1956, *25*, 357–362.

Ichheiser, G., On Freud's blind spots concerning some obvious facts, *J. Ind. Psychol.*, 1960, *16*, 45–55.

Jones, E., Freud's early travels, *Int. J. Psycho. Anal.*, 1954, *35*, 81–84.

Kardiner, A., A. Karush, and L. Ovesey, A methodological study of Freudian theory; Part I. Basic concepts, *J. Nerv. Ment. Dis.*, 1959 (July), *129*, 11–19; Part II. The libido theory, 1959 (Aug), 133–143; Part III. Narcissism, bisexuality and the dual instinct theory, 1959 (Sept.), 207–221; Part IV. The structural hypothesis, the problem of anxiety, and post-Freudian ego psychology, 1959 (Oct.), 341–356.

Kubie, L. S., Pavlov, Freud, and Soviet psychiatry, *Behav. Sci.*, 1959, *4*, 29–34.
  The Russians don't like Freud.

Lewis, N. D. C., and C. Landis, Freud's Library, *Psychoanal. Rev.*, 1957, *44*, 327–354.
  814 titles of 1200 items.

Mann, T., Freud and the future, *Int. J. Psycho. Anal.*, 1956, *37*, 106–115.

Marti-Ibanez, F., A. M. Sackler, M. D. Sackler, and R. R. Sackler, The quest for Freud, *J. Clin. Exp. Psychopatho.*, 1956, *17*, 117–127.

Maslow, A. H., Was Adler a disciple of Freud? A note, *J. Indiv. Psychol.*, 1962, *18*(2), 125.

> Maslow says Adler said no.

Menninger, K., Freud and American psychiatry, *J. Amer. Psychoanal. Ass.*, 1956, *4*, 614–625.

Munsford, R. S., Traditional psychiatry, Freud, and H. S. Sullivan, *Comprehen. Psychiat.*, 1961, *2*, 1–10.

Murphy, G., The current impact of Freud upon psychology, *Amer. Psychologist*, 1956, *11*, 663–672.

Nameche, G. F., Two pictures of man, *J. Humanist. Psychol.*, 1961, *1*(1), 70–88.

> Freud and Rogers on man.

O'Connell, W. E., The adaptive functions of wit and humor, *J. Abnorm. Soc. Psychol.*, 1960, *61*, 263–270.

> Freud on wit and humor differences is valid.

Parsons, T., Social structure and the development of personality: Freud's contribution to the integration of psychology and sociology, *Psychiatry*, 1958, *21*, 321–340.

Racker, H., On Freud's position towards religion, *Amer. Imago*, 1956, *13*, 98–121.

Reik, T., Freud and Jewish wit, *Psychonalysis*, 1954, *2*(3), 12–20.

> Based on Freud's 1905 book, *Wit and Its Relation to the Unconscious*.

Schmid, F., Freud's sociological thinking, *Bull. Menninger Clinic*, 1952, *16*, 1–13.

> Freud was an inadequate sociologist!

Schneck, J. M., Countertransference in Freud's rejection of hypnosis, *Amer. J. Psychiat.*, 1954, *110*, 928–931.

Shor, J., A well-spring of psychoanalysis, *Psychoanalysis*, 1953, *2*(1), 27–33.

Slavson, S. R., Freud's contributions to group psychotherapy, *Int. J. Group Psychother.*, 1956, *6*, 349–357.

Stagner, R., and J. W. Moffitt, A statistical study of Freud's personality types, *J. Clin. Psychol.*, 1956, *12*, 72–74.

> No statistical differences were found.

Starr, A., Psychoanalysis and the fiction of the unconscious, *Sci. and Soc.*, 1951, *15*, 129–143.

Stenzel, E., A reevaluation of Freud's book, *On Aphasia* its significance for psychoanalysis, *Int. J. Psycho. Anal.*, 1954, *35*, 85–89.

Stevenson, I., Is the human personality more plastic in infancy and childhood?, *Amer. J. Psychiat.*, 1957, *114*, 152–161.

> Doubts Freudian theory that childhood is overly formative.

Sulzberger, C. F., Epicurus, Luther, and Freud, *Psychoanalysis*, 1953, *1*(4), 70–72.

Sulzberger, C. F., Two new documents on Freud, *Psychoanalysis*, 1955–1956, 4(2), 9–21.

Swanson, G. E., Mead and Freud: their relevance for social psychology, *Sociometry*, 1961, 24(4), 319–339.

Neither one seems to be relevant.

Trueblood, W. E., The challenge of Freud, *Pastoral Psychol.*, 1958, 9, 37–44.

Tyson, A., and J. Strachey, A chronological hand list of Freud's work, *Int. J. Psycho. Anal.*, 1956, 37, 19–33.

Complete list of all Freud's writings published prior to November, 1955.

Viereck, G. S., An interview with Freud, *Psychoanalysis*, 1957, 4(4) and 5(1), 1–11.

Waelder, R., Freud and the history of science, *J. Amer. Psychoanal. Ass.*, 1956, 4, 602–613.

Walker, N., Science and the Freudian unconscious, *Psychoanalysis*, 1957, 4(4) and 5(1), 117–124.

Freudian unconscious belongs with respectable scientific models.

Wolpe, J., and S. Rachman, Psychoanalytic "evidence": a critique based on Freud's case of little Hans, *J. Nerv. Ment. Dis.*, 1960, 131, 135–148.

Freud was wrong about little Hans.

Zilboorg, G., Freud's fundamental psychiatric orientation, *Int. J. Psycho. Anal.*, 1954, 35, 90–94.

Zilboorg, G., Freud's one hundredth anniversary, *Psychoanal. Quar.*, 1956, 25, 139–146.

Freud was a Lamarkian and prone to forget his sources.

4

Sheldon

. . . the state of the body inevitably
affected the action of the mind . . .

HIPPOLYTE TAINE
The Origins of Contemporary France

It is native personality, and that alone, that endows
a man . . .

WALT WHITMAN
Democratic Vistas

SOME BIOGRAPHICAL DATA

Sheldon is a highly trained investigator with a wide background and interests although his work may seem to give the impression of a scientist with a narrow field. He was born in the United States in Warwick, Rhode Island, in 1899. His Bachelor of Arts degree was granted in 1919 from Brown University. Later he received his M.A. from the University of Colorado, and his Ph.D. from the University of Chicago in 1926, where he majored in psychology. He continued to study at Chicago and obtained an M.D. in 1933. During his training he also taught for two years in the Psychology Department of Chicago (1924–1926) and later at Northwestern University and the University of Wisconsin. One can see that Sheldon was not a regionalist but studied and taught in various parts of the country.

He also served on the medical staff of the Children's Hospital in

Chicago before becoming interested in psychiatry. As a result of this new interest, Sheldon spent the years 1935 and 1936 studying and traveling in Europe. He was particularly interested in the work of Carl Jung in Switzerland and also spent some time with Freud and Kretschmer during his foreign study. When he returned, he again went to the University of Chicago as a full professor of psychology and after two years transferred to Harvard University, Cambridge, Massachusetts. World War II took Sheldon from the Harvard campus where he served as a flight surgeon in the Army Air Force.

Upon his return from service, Sheldon became the Director of the Constitution Laboratory, in the College of Physicians and Surgeons at Columbia University. He is now continuing his work with the Atlas of Women and the Atlas of Children at Columbia as well as retaining interest in clinical disease and the relationship of human constitutional variation to psychiatry.

We are studying, then, the theory of a man who is extremely well trained, with a wide background of teaching and research in leading universities, and who now commands the full resources of an excellent laboratory designed to further the aspects of constitutional psychology.

Demonstrating the breadth of his mind, Sheldon has also written two interesting nonprofessional pieces, one an essay and the other a technical work. His essay written in 1936 concerns the value of religion in modern society and is entitled *Psychology and the Promethean Will*. His technical work is called *Early American Cents, 1793–1814*, written in 1949. Sheldon has by no means a one track mind.

INTRODUCTION

Let us suppose that a theory were constructed, based on research of a quantitative nature, which not only helped to predict man's nature, both as an individual and in groups, but also gave us a checklist to make it easier for the untrained observer to make approximations of a person's personality. This would be a long step in the advancement of personality theory. To some students of personality theory such is the nature of William Sheldon's somatotypic theory.

Sheldon's description of man's behavior is probably the neatest and most compact of all the theories covered in the present text. It has one central theme, a direct approach to the problem, relatively simple language and concepts that come from our everyday life, a degree of repeatability which lends itself to further examination by others, a very high degree of consistency within itself; it permits for continua in human behavior and has the possibility of being practical in studying such deviant groups as psychotics and juvenile delinquents.

In 1934–1935 Sheldon visited Freud, who at that time was still living in Vienna, and, although Sheldon was primarily interested in working with Jung, he undoubtedly felt some of the impact of Freud's ideas upon his own just formulating theories. Sheldon still feels that the psychoanalyst is fumbling with language in trying to describe and understand the unconscious. He feels, for example, that there is no difference between the unconscious and the body—they are the same. He believes that the Freudians are wasting their time in inexactitudinal approaches because they ignore this fact. What the analyst should do, according to Sheldon, is follow a definitive, morphological measuring system which would bring the concept of the unconscious out of the realm of darkness into the light where it could be examined with much more meaning.

William Sheldon is known as a constitutional psychologist. He is interested in studying the "psychological aspects of human behavior as they are related to the morphology [science of bodily form, structure, anatomy] and physiology of the body" (Sheldon, Stevens, and Tucker, *The Varieties of Human Physique: an Introduction to Constitutional Psychology,* 1940). In other words, Sheldon maintains that a relationship exists between the kind of a body man has and his behavior as a human being, and that each has an effect upon the other.

SHELDON'S DESCRIPTION OF HUMAN BEHAVIOR

Body—Temperament Principle

Through long years of research, starting about 1938 and continuing to the present day, Sheldon has espoused a theory which, in its most elementary form, states that there are three primary components of body form and three primary components of temperament that go with the body form. In the following pages we shall examine more closely the derivation of his theory; now we shall look at the kinds of people he defined.

Table 4. 1 is a very short outline of the body types and the corresponding behavior that accompanies each one. The names (body type and behavioral characteristic) have been conjoined for ease in remembering and reference, and may be said to describe a special personality type.

We must now examine the above types of people and describe their behavior, especially the predominant characteristics. For purposes of drawing a clearer picture each one of the types will be described as a *pure* type although it is to be understood that such cases are so exceptional in Sheldon's system as to be practically nonexistent. Almost all people are a combination of all three as we shall see in the subsequent section deal-

Table 4. 1.   Sheldon's Relationship of Body Type to Behavior–Personality

Body Type	Behavior	Personality
Endomorph (tends to be fat)	Viscerotonia (tends to be relaxed)	Endo/viscerotone
Mesomorph (tends to be muscular)	Somatotonia (tends to be assertive)	Meso/somatotone
Ectomorph (tends to be thin)	Cerebrotonia (tends to be restrained)	Ecto/cerebrotone

ing with principles, "Continuous Variables." It is important not to judge Sheldon until one understands that all of us are combinations of the three types mentioned in Table 4. 1.

Endomorph–Viscerotonia—Does the reader know any one who is inclined toward fatness, especially if he does not watch his diet very well? This person has the kind of body which floats high in the water, is inclined to be spherical; although most babies are fat and soft, this individual continues to retain a softness and babylike quality of the skin and flesh. The lips may be inclined to be thicker than those of most people.

The endomorph body and the individual with a viscerotonia temperament, henceforth to be called the endo/viscerotone, is inclined to behave in his everyday life according to the following twenty criteria. (Not all of the behavioral characteristics must be present for one to be classified as an endo/viscerotone, but certainly if one had at least ten of the twenty behavioral characteristics, he should be included in this category.)[1]

[1] The list of twenty characteristics is adapted directly from Sheldon's *The Varieties of Temperament: a Psychology of Constitutional Differences*, 1942, p. 26, although

1. Relaxation in posture and movement. The endo/viscerotone walks with an easy gait. Sometimes he shuffles, most of the time he ambles. He is the kind of soldier who is often hard to train and very hard to keep in step with the marching troops. He opens doors and closes doors sloppily. His lighting a cigarette is a casual kind of manuever, and he can be quite sure to sprinkle ashes around himself and the rug and will not always hit the ash tray even when he tries to use it. The endo/viscerotone is a relaxed guy! When he stands, it is usually to lean against a post, door, or anything that affords support, because essentially he would rather be sitting.

2. Love of physical comfort. Not only does the endo/viscerotone like to sit down, he slouches. If he can do so, he will put his feet up on some convenient object or throw his arm around the back of the chair, sit sideways, anything that makes life easier. His clothes are chosen for comfort. If his wife or friend helps him and wishes him to appear more "smart and well-pressed," it isn't too long until he has the unpressed, slept-in look, and is back in his old comfortable clothes.

3. Slow reaction. The endo/viscerotone is the bane of his roommate because it takes him forever to wake up, get washed, get dressed, or get anywhere. He is inclined to be perpetually late because he does things so slowly. In playing games, he is the slowest of the slow. Tennis is not his game, nor is table tennis, because these games require quick reactive movements, something of which he is incapable. He even plays bridge so slowly that his opponents are inclined to complain. In general, he is inclined to irritate others because he must be waited for, no matter the occasion. He shaves slowly, he walks slowly, he lives slowly.

4. Love of eating. Eating is almost a ritual with the endo/viscerotone. He will eat all day long but not in a refined manner. Crumbs fall while food disappears. Thus eating is more of a vocation than a ritual. He loves to hunt out exotic dining places and will remember enjoyable meals, the place, the menu, and all the trimmings for many months and even years.

5. Socialization of eating. Have you ever sat at a restaurant counter with no one else present when an individual came in and sat right next to you? With all that room, this person sat right next to you! That was an endo/viscerotone, for he intensely dislikes eating alone. In fact, he will postpone or forego a meal if it must be eaten in solitude.

---

the author has extended some of the descriptions to afford a clearer understanding for the student.

6. Pleasure in digestion. The endo/viscerotone likes to pat his stomach after a meal and declare how nice it all was. The satiated feeling is one he likes and cultivates whenever possible. One of his favorite days of the year is Thanksgiving day, especially after the meal.

7. Love of polite ceremony. Introductions all around at a social gathering are his meat. The ritual of lighting candles and the memorizing part of the fraternity initiation all make sense to the endo/viscerotone and he participates with quiet enthusiasm. The church service, the wedding, the receptions, all are part of his repertoire, and he doesn't mind spending time and energy in arranging them properly.

8. Sociophilia. People are the staff of life to the endo/viscerotone. He loves people. This is the individual about whom it was once said, "There are no strangers in his life." He almost feels that it is a challenge to have someone in the group whom he does not know. This is one of his predominant characteristics.

9. Indiscriminate amiability. At a party, Caribbean cruise, social tea, or reception the endo/viscerotone is an inveterate and amiable "table-hopper." It is almost impossible to cut him off or be rude, because he fails to accept it. He may be hurt for the moment but within seconds he's trying with renewed vigor to "win friends and influence people" to the joys of living. Rich or poor, friend or foe, they are all grist for his mill.

10. Greed for affection and approval. (See Horney's "Moving toward people.") This kind of person, when approaching pure viscerotonia, is miserable if he feels you do not like him. He worries about it, mulls it over, and comes to the conclusion that he hasn't tried hard enough to make you like him, because like him you must.

11. Orientation to people. When he visits a scientific exhibit, he is interested in the man who built the machine or the man who operates and demonstrates it, but not the machine. Technical, mechanical, and scientific phenomena bore him or frustrate him because he cannot understand them. If he reads, which he is rather disinterested in doing, it will be to read biographies or fast-moving fiction.

12. Evenness of emotional flow. He is often the envy of his acquaintances. Nothing much seems to bother him as he whistles his way through life. Procrastination comes easy, for there is always another day, and worry solves nothing.

13. Tolerance. He is quite willing to forgive you your errors of omission and commission and will feel grateful to be forgiven his. In the

fraternity or sorority meeting, he can be trusted to introduce the conciliatory motion that is designed to calm ruffled feelings and soothe irritation.

14. Complacency.   Every cloud has a silver lining, and the endo/viscerotone knows this better than any one else.

15. Deep sleep.   This is the roommate who can sleep through anything. Neither storm, voices, nor the blaring radio can disturb his sleep. And in the morning, if an exciting event took place in the dormitory during the night, he will plaintively complain the next morning, "Why didn't you guys wake me up?" For after all there was excitement and people, and he was not of it. The endo/viscerotone sleeps like an exhausted baby, all relaxed and played out.

16. The untempered characteristic.   He is malleable. He feels there are good points to both sides. Any dilemma he wants to resolve by finding out what the others think. With the collaboration of the majority will, he knows that he has made the best decision under the circumstances.

17. Smooth, easy communication of feeling.   This person loves to talk and he is good at it. Writing is painful, partially because one must be alone to write, but also because talking is more direct—and he can do it with ease.

18. Relaxation and sociophilia under alcohol (key characteristic). This is the happy, talkative, singing drunk. While the party continues and the liquor holds out, he is a very happy inebriate. Possibly this feature and the one following (number 19) delineate his personality more accurately than do any others, especially when many of the preceding characteristics are not apparent, or when there is scant time to observe all of them.

19. Need of people when troubled (key characteristic). Do you have someone living in the dormitory whose every problem is known by all the residents of the hall? This is the endo/viscerotone. The "Dear John" letter, the failing grade, the sickness at home, and all the problems of life the endo/viscerotone is ready and eager to communicate. He must do so, for there are no secrets or silent sorrows in the endo/viscerotone's existence. Like a child, he cannot hold the secret but must tell. It does not matter whether help comes from the listener; to share one's problems with one's fellowman is enough to ease the burden.

20. Orientation toward childhood and family relationships.   With all the lovableness, charm, disarming frankness, and zest for living of childhood, the endo/viscerotone lives his life no matter what the chronological

age may be. He loves life and wants to help you enjoy it too. He is not a fool but a sensitive human being with a vast capacity to see, hear, love, and live with clarity and simplicity. He harbors no grudge, and wears his heart on his sleeve.

If any true unadulterated endo/viscerotone lives, the reader must decide. As we shall see, Sheldon believes in the continuous variable, which means that all of us have some of these characteristics in conjunction with those of the next two types. It must be emphasized, however, that some of us are overwhelmingly oriented toward the endo/viscerotonic personality and will be so for the major portion of our lives. Sheldon's theory subsumes a genetic influence and disposition toward being more of one type than the other. The personality with exactly even portions of all three types (endo/viscerotone, meso/somatotone, ecto/cerebrotone) is possibly even more rare than the pure type. In the case of this trichotomized personality, the problems of trivalency may be so overpowering as to eliminate him from the life scene. He must so continuously balance three primary modes of behavior as eventually to break down and reach neurotic or psychotic levels of behavior. The trichotomized type is an interesting subject of conjecture.

Mesomorph–Somatotonia—The meso/somatotone is all muscle, bone, and sinews. He is the individual who is strong of body, much like the professional football player. He has the kind of body that can absorb and administer great physical punishment. His muscles are hard, and his frame is usually big and always strong. Though he may not be overly tall, he has a look of brute strength. Whereas the first type, the endo/viscerotone, had a physique developing primarily out of the endodermal layers of the body, the meso/somatotone is named for the mesodermal, or middle layer, of the human structure. This individual takes pride in his body, for in his body lies his mode of operation. He thinks physically, he acts physically, and he is dominated by his physical existence. To him, all else is soft living or highbrow. He is characterized, then, by the following manifestations of behavior, twenty in number, as was true for the previous type.

1. Assertiveness of posture and movement. Whereas the endo/viscerotone went through a doorway by casually opening and closing it, the meso/somatotone explodes through. He doesn't open doors, he attacks them. He does not walk or amble, he strides. Lighting a cigarette is an act of physical exertion which often causes the match to break. He smokes vigorously with excited inhalation and expulsion of smoke until the

cigarette end glows furiously. If he is standing about, it is nearly impossible for him to be immobile. The meso/somatotone jiggles on his toes, works his fingers, or simply bounces without moving. To be still, unless in a physically challenging soldier's "attention" stance, is most distressing to this type of personality. He wants action.

2. Love of physical adventure.   Instead of wanting to sit after a heavy meal and nod off to sleep as the endo/viscerotone loves to do, this human being gets fretful and restless. He much prefers taking a walk, throwing a ball or football, doing anything rather than just stagnating in inactivity.

3. Energetic characteristic.   Throughout the ages the game of "Follow the leader" has been perpetuated by the meso/somatotone. Whatever he does, he does with the full energy and capacity of his body, from playing cards (all tricks are taken by smashing the card onto the table) to dancing (the rhythm is followed with hand pumping energy, and waltzes are always too slow).

4. Need for, and enjoyment of, exercise.   The meso/somatotone is a miserable patient at home or in the hospital. To be bedridden is the worst of all possible states. To lie in bed on a morning makes him restless to be about the business of the day. He most enjoys games and recreations in which an opponent is involved and the reciprocity of the game is paramount, as in tennis, football, or wrestling, rather than golf or bowling. If he does bowl, he throws the ball down the alley with all his might. He is probably happiest after a hard workout in athletics followed by a shower with a vigorous, cold, stinging spray. Sedentary activities bore him, and thus he finds reading somewhat painful, not for intellectual reasons but because it necessitates keeping in one place. He almost always scans rather than reads.

5. Love of dominating, lust for power. (See Horney's, "Moving against people.")   In addition to liking reciprocal sports because action is involved, he also desires them because they are competitive. It is almost impossible for the meso/somatotone to play anything without a struggle for superiority, even with small children. When chastised for not allowing the little one to win occasionally, he retorts that he is just "Teaching him the game, and you don't want the kid to be a baby all his life, do you?"

6. Love of risk and chance.   Along with "Follow the leader," which gives him exercise and a chance to dominate, the meso/somatotone has an abiding interest in roller-coaster rides and all manner of whirly rides at the amusement park, as well as in driving cars extremely fast in all kinds of

traffic. Water skiing, snow skiing, any type of activity in which danger and possible injury are components, attract him. It is an exhilaration to skirt potential injury and emerge safely, demonstrating to him that he has conquered another facet of life and has emerged triumphant. If another individual duplicates his performance, he must try again and again to win the victory of superior performance. Parroting the musical comedy line, he would say, "Anything you can do, I can do better."

7. Bold directness of manner. Most of his conversation expresses the frontal attack. He approaches his acquaintances with a gibe or critical remark, thus putting them on the immediate defensive and giving himself the upper hand. The first type (endo/viscerotone) makes every effort to have you like him; this type makes every effort to have you notice him and respect his power. His handshake is a bonecrusher, designed to make you at once aware of his superior strength.

8. Physical courage for combat. He makes the ideal soldier in combat, for to attain superiority over his fellowman is a natural goal.

9. Competitive aggressiveness. The smashing volley in table tennis or outdoor tennis, the bone-rattling tackle in football, the vociferous trumping of an opponent's ace, the powerfully smashed golf ball are what the meso/somatotone lives for in his recreational pursuits.

10. Psychological callousness. When his fiancée wishes to indulge in love play and his own sexual appetites are not engaged, he roughly rejects the advances and declares, "It's too hot to be mushy." Sex play for him is for self-gratification and not for demonstration of affection. Poignant death scenes are almost always met with a grimace or unveiled laugh. Sentimentality indicates to the meso/somatotone a weakness in character.

11. Claustrophobia. He never makes a telephone call from a booth with the door closed. He intensely hates to feel "cooped up." He wants the wide open spaces. Small rooms, tight clothing, intimate gatherings are anathema to him.

12. Ruthlessness, freedom from squeamishness. Violent scenes of death do not disturb him. He is more interested in how it happened than in the fact that a victim resulted. Exhibits of medieval tortures fascinate him to the point he cannot pass one up and lingers over the more macabre ones.

13. Unrestrained voice. It is loud, clear, stentorian, with no attempt at modulation. Statements are declared, not uttered, by the meso/somatotone. He finds whispering in the movie theater or library an obnoxious restraint

on his freedom. "A man should stand up and be heard" is his vocal credo.

14. Spartan indifference to pain. The last thing in the world he wants to admit is that the injury hurts; only weaklings admit pain, and he is not a weakling. Only sissies cry.

15. General noisiness. His deportment in the theater or library is matched by the loud muffler on his car and the loud guffaw at anything he considers humorous. (Humor, incidentally, for the meso/somatotone is largely based on man's inhumanity to man.) You can hear him come into the house, close doors, open drawers, and go about the business of the day, for his vigor begets collisions of objects as the lightning begets thunder.

16. Overmaturity of appearance. As a youth, he needs to shave much before his peers. His face and general demeanor frequently make him look older than his years. He uses his body vigorously, and it shows the strain.

17. Horizontal mental cleavage. His mind operates in an across-the-board manner which accepts an idea or rejects it, but is not interested in delving into the background or tangential reasons. This leads to stereotyped thinking, for the meso/somatotone asks only for decisions and not for the philosophy underlying the rationale for a position. A thing is either true or not true, and to entertain too many doubts is to admit that one does not know what he believes in. The meso/somatotone knows what he believes in, and he dislikes contrary evidence.

18. Assertiveness and aggression under alcohol (key characteristic). This is the drunk who likes to fight, pick quarrels, and declare himself, "the best man in the house." Alcohol appears to be a release of pent-up aggressive feelings. Although no actual physical violence may take place, the meso/somatotone, when under the influence of alcohol, will appear loud and boastful. His statements will all be made as a challenge. He defies anyone present to contradict him. Should he meet a like-minded person, there is the challenge to "go outside and settle this thing." He most often, however, selects the "Milquetoast" figure at the bar, walks up to him and states, "I don't like you," possibly, of course, never having seen the meek one before in his life.

As in the case of the previous type, the endo/viscerotone, the meso/somatotone reveals more of his basic personality via alcohol than at other times. During the normal course of each day, he may socialize or minimize his other attributes, but when drinking gets beyond his control he is not able to conceal much of what he really is.

19. Need of action when troubled (key characteristic). Perhaps the

reader knows someone on the college scene who received a lower grade in a course than he thought he was going to get. The endo/viscerotone would tell his friends, write his parents, and seek out other people to commiserate with him in his bad fortune. Not so with the meso/somatotone. He appeals strongly and forcefully to the instructor; failing satisfaction in changing the grade, he proceeds to the departmental chairman, the dean, the president of the university, and to any figure of authority who he feels may redress his wrong. In each case his appeal is made vehemently. He wants action.

20. Orientation toward goals and activities of youth. The muscular individual with the assertive behavior must, when he engages in recreational activities, do so with a purpose. He finds it almost impossible to participate in a game without scoring more points, hitting the ball farther, collecting more specimens than others in like pursuits. His life is goal-directed, usually with the purpose of being the first to reach the goal.

His behavior is remindful of the boastful adolescent who loves activity, who loves to indicate his strength and emergence toward manhood, who directs his energies toward winning. This is the pure type of meso/somatotone.

Ectomorph–Cerebrotonia—The ecto/cerebrotone is usually thin, ascetic appearing, meticulous in dress, and most of the time a lonely "thinker." He finds that the best of all possible worlds lies in the self, his own self. He is rarely heavily muscled, though he may become so through dedicated and solitary, muscle-building exercise in which he engages solely for health reasons. He is inclined toward frailty and angularity of structure, though he is not necessarily tall. He has nervous quick movements.

Again, the reader should keep in mind that the following descriptions are perhaps grossly overdrawn, but do serve to delineate the pure type of ecto/cerebrotone.

1. Restraint in posture and movement. The endo/viscerotone shrugs into a coat, the meso/somatotone muscles his way into a coat, but the ecto/cerebrotone is a symphony of delicate and refined movement as he carefully places each arm into the sleeves of his coat, slowly draws it around his body, and possibly ends with an additional check of his entire attire to see that nothing is out of place. He opens doors with military precision. His every physical act is a discipline of motion. He stands erect, sits erect, sleeps rigidly, and never seems to relax in body.

2. Physiological overresponse. The thin man of the cerebrotonic per-

sonality treats his body like a machine. It must always be "at the ready." He drives an automobile with quick birdlike movements which respond immediately to any suspected danger on the road ahead. He considers the automobile to be an extension of his body, and therefore he must be in possession of its movements at all times. When a nonroutine condition occurs on the road, he immediately decreases speed, applies the brakes, and is alert for an accident.

3. Overly fast reactions. Neurologically the ecto/cerebrotone is like a taut violin string. Whatever physical response he makes is made immediately and with predictable precision. In playing tennis he is light, fast, and accurate, but never powerful. If something spills, he is on his feet instantly. Whereas the endo/viscerotone stumbles up to avoid the spilled soup, and the meso/somatotone roars up, the ecto/cerebrotone dances up lightly and graciously, having sensed the danger of hot soup almost before it landed. Incidentally, the first type would be apologetic and would assume some responsibility for having caused the mishap, he would try to keep the waitress his friend and not have hurt feelings. The second type would demand apologies from the waitress and require redress of some kind for the soiled garments. The third type would brood about the accident, go home immediately to change the garment, and spend the rest of the day wondering, "Why does it always happen to me?"

4. Love of privacy. The ecto/cerebrotone is a loner. He must have some time to himself each day. He enjoys eating alone, listening to records alone, attending the theater alone, and studying alone. Solitude is the staff of life. He is miserable with a roommate. He makes every effort to live in a single room as a college student, where he can control his things and his life even if it means living off campus and traveling inconvenient distances to and from the campus. He regularly plans for a solitary walk in the dark of the night. To be alone for him is to have control of one's environment.

5. Mental overintensity, hyperattention. The ecto/cerebrotone knows how many steps there are up to the library door; he has counted them. During a dull lecture his mind cannot lapse off into reverie or sleep. He continuously must be mentally alert and active. He counts the number of students in the room, the light bulbs in the overhead fixtures, and the number of "uh's" the instructor utters.

6. Secretiveness of feeling, emotional restraint. This type of personality feels that to reveal an emotion is a sign of weakness in control and character. His response to love play is made primarily to satisfy an organic

sexual appetite and does not indicate an emotional feeling on his part. This is the person you may know for years as a working mate or a neighbor and yet feel in twenty years of friendship that you really know nothing about him. A death in his immediate family may not be revealed for months, while the first Sheldonian type will reveal all the details, even the death bed scene.

7. Self-conscious mobility of the eyes and face.   When the ecto/cerebrotone talks to you, he avoids looking directly at you. When he laughs, he does so self-consciously and probably with his hand over his mouth. There appears to be almost a furtiveness about any direct conversational contact with another human being.

8. Sociophobia.   Essentially he dislikes people—especially when he meets them in large groups. He most emphatically dislikes and probably never will give large parties. He prefers small intimate groups whose entertainment centers on passive activities such as listening to symphonic recordings, with talk at a minimum. He avoids to the point of ridicule the meso/somatatone and tolerates only for brief periods of time the happy-go-lucky endo/viscerotone. He literally fears large crowds. He is most uncomfortable sitting in the middle of a mass of people, especially at vociferous gatherings like football games. Such activities seem inane and threatening to him. He much prefers small musicals, art museums, and any type of group activity where the participants are orderly and quietly reserved.

9. Inhibited social address.   It would be interesting to study the three types of Sheldon's as they walk from class to class on a college campus. The first type looks at all the eyes and seeks recognition of any friendly face or gesture. Whether the second type says "Hello" or not depends upon his mood at the moment and the status of the recipient of his potential greeting. The third and present type under discussion looks at the ground, or away, or is deeply involved in thought with no concern for the passing crowd of students. The first type loves to see that all are introduced around the gathering, the second type uses introductions to gain a status position, while the ecto/cerebrotone avoids, to the point of rudeness, introducing people.

10. Resistance to habit and poor routinizing.   With the ecto/cerebrotone there is a tendency to do things differently from day to day and thus resist the monotony of habitual conduct.

11. Agoraphobia.   The ecto/cerebrotone dislikes wide open spaces. He

much prefers the rainy day, the in-front-of-the-fireplace feeling with a good book and solitude, to the wide open spaces of the beach and surf boarding. He likes to feel snug, warm, and cozy no matter the weather. Whereas the meso/somatotone dislikes telephoning from a booth with the door closed, the ecto/cerebrotone always closes the door tightly for reasons of personal privacy as well as for a cozy feeling. He likes clothing to envelope him, eschews shorts and open-throated sports attire, and is inclined to choose apparel that fits tightly.

12. Unpredictability of attitude. Because the ecto/cerebrotone does not reveal the thought processes behind his decisions, he is hard to predict.

13. Vocal restraint and general restraint of noise. He is a quiet person with a well-modulated voice, usually with excellent diction. He does not, however, speak a great deal. In all his actions he is carefully considerate, with the result that doors close quietly, music is muted, automobile gears are engaged smoothly, and life is lived in a low register of sound.

14. Hypersensitivity to pain. Things seem to hurt the ecto/cerebrotone more than they hurt other types. A pain is a deep-seated, shocking, horrible experience to him with lasting effects, while to the muscular meso/somatotone, pain is an enemy to be conquered, and to the roly-poly endo/viscerotone pain is quickly forgotten and rather easily endured. The lingering sting of a severe burn is constantly on the mind of the ecto/cerebrotone. The other two types either become so involved with the outside world as to momentarily forget the burn or accept its nagging pain as a challenge to manhood.

15. Poor sleep habits, chronic fatigue. Because the ecto/cerebrotone never ever really quite relaxes his mental activities, sleep is a difficult state for him to enter. To relax is to lower one's control of self, yet to relax is the *sine qua non* of sleep. Consequently, unable to lose himself, he finds himself tossing at night, thinking through the day's activities, reconstructing the problems of the day, and getting farther and farther from sleep. The entire mental tightrope that he walks keeps him chronically fatigued.

16. Youthful intentness and manner of appearance. This is the person whose age is very difficult to guess from appearance. While the endo/viscerotone is the St. Bernard dog of the species, being easy-going, ambling, friendly, hard to arouse to anger, and the meso/somatotone is the boxer or aggressive German shepherd police dog who bristles with muscle and snarls at threatening overtures, the ecto/cerebrotone is a cross between the

dandied French poodle with high intelligence and the fox terrier with sleek coat and quick movements. The ecto/cerebrotone dresses well, looks young, and stays that way even into advanced age.

17. Vertical mental cleavage, introversion. The third of Sheldon's types likes to think things through to their ultimate sources. Rather than follow the crowd in his avocational pursuits as does the endo/viscerotone, he prefers, for example, to become an expert on fourteenth-century tapestries. He would like most to specialize, for example, in the tapestries of a particular country, or a particular group of weavers. To go deep, be thorough, and by all means to be exhaustive is his way, whether it be his vocation or avocation. For this reason, he often becomes a dedicated researcher or scientist, working away from the mainstream of life, devoting a lifetime to studying the mating habits of the Galapagos turtle or the use of the pronoun in early hieroglyphic tablets. In so doing, he can avoid people, people being unpredictable, demanding, and confusing.

18. Resistance to alcohol (key characteristic). The thin man of the ecto/cerebrotonia personality does not like alcohol, and if he does imbibe, it is only to make a ritual of collecting wines or exotic liquors but hardly for the effect they produce upon consumption. For to the ecto/cerebrotone to be drunk is to lose possession of one's faculties, and to lose control of one's self is the worst of all possible living states. He rejects, resists, and abstains from alcohol, not on moral grounds, but on personal fear of being incapable of controlling his own actions. A "small adequate red wine" is much to be preferred to the grossness of drinks that are usually consumed in quantities. Beer, unless it is a very special imported foreign variety, is vulgar. The delicate aperitif is much to be preferred.

19. Need of solitude when troubled (key characteristic). Perhaps the reader will recall that the endo/viscerotone turned to people when he had problems, and the meso/somatotone turned to action when he had problems. The ecto/cerebrotone just turns away, to be by himself when he has problems. The outside world of acquaintances never knows how deeply or how often the ecto/cerebrotonic personality with the ectomorphic body suffers. He suffers alone. He considers having problems as a sign of weakness. He does not wish to appear weak in front of his fellow man. Since he does not possess the aggressive strength of the meso/somatotone, he withdraws within himself. Such withdrawal obviously removes him from professional counseling help. Thus, he may accentuate his problem as it becomes more and more centripetally directed into himself until complete withdrawal from society results.

20. Orientation toward the later periods of life. Even as an adolescent the ecto/cerebrotone acts older than his contemporaries. He is sedate, they are boisterous; he is polite, they are rough and crude; he appears well dressed, they are sloppy; he likes and prefers to be alone much of the time, they make a cult of doing what the gang does. He, the ecto/cerebrotone, is "old before his time" in the opinion of family and friends.

Those things which elderly people most prefer and enjoy can be said to describe the true ectomorphic body with the ecto/cerebrotonic behavior.

Physique or Body Structure.

Having put together the two primary components of Sheldon's theory, body type and behavior, and having discussed them at some length as they would appear in perfect types, one needs to describe further the development of Sheldon's work as he outlined the three basic types of body, the refinements of his work, and the primary and secondary characteristics of the body types. This will be done in the following section.

Morphogenotype—Fundamentally what Sheldon is interested in is the morphogenotype as it is correlated to man's behavioral self. But the morphogenotype, which is man considered at the very earliest beginning, and on through all stages of his development as an organic structure, is obviously denied as an avenue of research. Implied in such a study are multitudes of variables for each single human being. Further implied in the morphogenotypic type of study are the ramifications of Darwin's work, Mendel's work, and the entire history of man from whatever he once was to his present state of existence physiologically. To study a single human being, then, from this approach, is to trace back his ancestry from the beginning, a manifestly impossible task.

Phenotype—The phenotype is man's body as we see it at the moment. In some degree it is like a photograph. The photograph shows what is, how it looks, the size, the conformation, the present moment of fact. It does not, however, reveal the history of the picture. We do not know what went on in the past other than what we can infer from the present picture, and we are completely unable to predict any of the future, again except by highly conjectural inference.

Therefore, Sheldon felt it was mandatory to construct a third measure of man which would bring together the two ends of the continuous morphogenotype–phenotype.

Somatotype—This is Sheldon's answer to bringing continuity into a consideration of the two aspects of man's organic life: the morphogenotype and the phenotype. The somatotype, then, is man's body in regard to its past, and all the ramifications which that can entail, and an attempt to bring this information together with what we can see of his body in the precise present moment as well as to amalgamate these two factors into what we may expect of the organism in the future. Sheldon cautions that this may be done only if the organism has not undergone violent conditions of injury or disturbing conditions of nutrition; that is to say, that a fairly normal kind of life is being, and will be, led by the organism. He feels that somatotyping as a method is creating a "pathway" which the body will travel "under standard conditions" of existence. The interesting and involved method by which somatotyping is done by Sheldon and his coworkers will be considered in the section following, wherein his objective measurement principle is discussed.

Primary Body Somatotypes

The Endomorph—As we have previously seen, this is the human being who is inclined to be rounded in figure and soft of muscle. Sheldon used the term *endomorph* because the functional characteristics of the endodermal layers of the body most closely describe this type: visceral, digestive, etc. In appearance, the endomorph looks most like the caricaturist's drawing of the roly-poly clown. The fat tends to distribute around the trunk of the body. The breasts are inclined to be heavy and somewhat pendulous. The lips are usually thick. The neck is short. The legs and arms are inclined to be shorter in ratio to the trunk than they are for the other two types.[2]

The Mesomorph—The mesodermal layer of the embryo, the middle layer, eventually gives rise to the muscles that man develops in postnatal life. Because of this, Sheldon gave the name *mesomorph* to the second type he defined, the muscular, athletic person with strong bone structure. The mesomorph usually has wide shoulders, a tapering figure, a strong, wide chest expansion, and he is most often likely to be average-to-tall in height. He is rarely inclined to flabbiness, and his stomach is flat and well held by superb, striated muscles.

The Ectomorph—The brain and central nervous system emanate from the ectodermal layers of the embryo. Sheldon used the term *ectomorph* to name the third type of body build in his somatotypic, classificatory system.

---

[2] This short description in no way takes the place of Sheldon's exactitude in measuring body types. All that is intended is to give the reader some short clues to what Sheldon measures. The reader interested in this technique is urged to consult Sheldon's, *Atlas of Men, A Guide for Somatotyping the Adult Male at All Ages*, Harper & Row, 1954.

The ectomorph has, for his size, the largest central nervous system and brain of all three types. This type is deficient in thickness of the arms, hands, trunk, legs, and neck. He is linear and thin, and his skull is angular. He gives the impression of being delicate; however, his strength may be surprising for its wiriness. The ratio of surface to mass of his body is in favor of the surface of his body, the mass being proportionately much less than the skin surface. In short, he has much more skin in relation to his body mass than does the endomorph (who is just the opposite) or the mesomorph (whose balance is about normal). Having more skin and thus having more afferent nerve receptors in relation to the remainder of his interior mass, the ectomorph is more acutely stimulated by externally derived pain. For him, a sharp blow falls upon less body to absorb shock than it does for the muscular mesomorph or the fatty-tissued endomorph.

Secondary Body Somatotypes.

Sheldon was well aware that there could be and is wide variation within the somatotyping of a single individual. For example, as was stated in describing the "pure" types previously mentioned in the chapter, it is almost impossible to find a pure type of endomorphic body or the pure type of viscerotonic temperament that would correlate with this body type. All of Sheldon's work is based on the relativity of body to temperament for *groups*. He would submit that there are always individual variations from the average, but as he found in his work, the individual variations are very few when all the data are considered. We now turn our attention to the individual variations that occur only in body type without correlating the body to a temperament type. The body-temperament variations will be dealt with in the pages to follow under the heading of Continuous Variables Principle.

Dysplasia—Sheldon discovered inconsistencies, but not many, among the three previous somatotypes as represented in one person's body. That is, a person may have the fleshy trunk of an endomorph and the muscular legs and arms of a mesomorph. Or he discovered a few uneven physiques, for example, who had the angular skull and skin structure of the ectomorph but with the remainder of their physique quite in harmony with the rounded endomorph. Other combinations were also possible. These inconsistencies, then, were termed *dysplasia* or the "d" index in somatotyping. It should be emphasized that there were very few types of these. The term *dysplasia* comes from the work of Kretschmer, an early exponent of the relationship of behavior to physique.

In his initial work, Sheldon found that the ectomorphic body type was more dysplasia prone than were the endomorph or mesomorph, who were inclined to be purer types. He also found in another small study in 1940 that college students when compared, seemed to have more coherent patterns of physique than a psychotic population. Although it is considered a secondary component in his classification system, the "d" index is fundamental to Sheldon's somatotypes.

Pyknic Practical Joke (PPJ)—Though we shall discuss the constancy of the somatotypes later in this chapter, the PPJ type refers to a person who has a muscular mesomorphic body in adolescence but in later life balloons out into obesity to become an endomorph. This type does not have to have eaten large amounts of food in order to change types. The basic type was endomorph in the beginning, but maturity was needed to reveal its truer manifestations. Thus, a secondary factor of somatotyping is sufficient age to get a more accurate picture of the physique. It is not a question of constancy but a question of delayed development. Sheldon feels that at about the age of thirty the true type of body form will emerge regardless of amounts of food consumed. Gross nutritional deficiencies will, of course, alter the physique, but the major relationships of head to trunk, trunk to limbs, and so on, that are used as indices will remain constant even in the face of gross nutritional difficulties.

Textural Aspect—The secondary component called *textural aspect* or "t" index is Sheldon's acknowledgement that some people are more pleasing in appearance to their fellowmen than are others. In some sense, then, it refers to beauty or handsomeness as any culture would define it. Given identical ectomorphic types whose bodies measure similarly, one of them may appear much more handsome to us than the other. One mesomorph may appear gross, the other Adonis-like, one endomorph sleek and well-rounded, the other blubbery, though all would compare in measurements quite identical to the other within their somatotypes. This quality of aesthetic pleasingness, Sheldon felt should be acknowledged, even though it is of secondary importance in the immediate phenotype. The "t" index does, of course, influence how society will react toward the individual, especially if female. The woman with a low "t" index may be called "healthy," while the woman with the high "t" index may be called "beautiful," yet each carries the same bodily proportions.

Gynandromorphy—The "g" index refers to the degree of hermaphroditism that the body possesses. Hermaphroditism is the condition, in this case, of having both kinds of sexual characteristics, not necessarily both kinds of sexual organs. Consequently, a male having a high "g" index is very feminine in appearance though he may not have organically a hermaphroditic structure. The body is soft, the hips wide, the breasts rather fully developed, and there is a fine, feminine texture to the facial skin. This characteristic is, again, a secondary one in Sheldon's system. It does indicate his willingness to broaden the system beyond only three body types. Also, as in the case of the "t" index, this characteristic would have an immediate effect upon society, and the individual's society would consequently in turn affect the individual. The degree would depend upon the societal mores.

Male–Female Aspects—It must be apparent by now even to the most casual reader that Sheldon's theory is essentially a male one, concerned with the study of male physique and its relationship to behavior. This emphasis is accidental on Sheldon's part, nor does he conclude that female somatotyping will necessarily parallel male somatotyping. As we shall see, Sheldon found some fundamental differences. Why then did he specialize in typing men's bodies and build up such a formidable array of statistics regarding only men? The reason is very practical. Somatotyping (as we shall later discuss) requires studying photographs and making measurements of the nude body. Society will hardly tolerate such research on female subjects, but anyone familiar with military procedures will recognize that the nude male is an acceptable phenomenon for study, providing the research is being conducted with discretion. Sheldon is well aware of the one-sidedness of his approach, and one can hardly condemn him for the slant of his work. Lest the reader feel that his theory is to be limited forever to maleness, recent reports indicate that through screening, masking silhouette techniques along with proper and sensible controls, some preliminary somatotyping has been done with females, although the research is hardly of the scope done with male populations.

What, then, do the data indicate in comparing somatotyping of women and men? (This has nothing to do with gynandromorphy which is concerned with the feminine characteristics of men and masculine characteristics of women; here we are comparing men *vis à vis* women.) Sheldon is at present working on a companion book to his *Atlas of Men,* to be entitled *Atlas of Women,* in which he will report his ongoing research with somatotyping females. One wonders if a third work will emerge from this in which the entire picture will be drawn for the total population.

To date, Sheldon reports that women are more prone to the mixing of endomorphic–ectomorphic body types than are men. A consideration of the total population shows women also more inclined toward endomorphy than are men. There is further a smaller range in body types of women than there is in men. Dysplasia is more prevalent among women than men. Despite these differences, however, Shldom feels that his original theory for men will and does hold true for women. In short, there is a unique relationship between a woman's body type and her corresponding behavioral pattern, just as there is for the men he studied. He feels the basis of his theoretical foundation is sound and scientific.

Continuous Variable Principle

In the process of his work, Sheldon felt that a fundamental principle concerning the typing of human bodies was that practically no body is a pure type but always has features of the other two types connected with it. He further maintained that this condition of continuity of bodies holds equally true for temperament. No one appears to be exclusively one kind of body and/or temperament but has within him the physique and behavioral characteristics of all three. He is part endo/viscerone, meso/somatotone, as well as ecto/cerebrotone. *But* he is always more of one type than he is of the other two. To handle this continuous variable of body–body to behavior–behavior, Sheldon constructed a numbering system that is both unique and also a tremendous refinement over the work of his predecessors, both of whom we shall read more about later on.

Table 4.2 is an attempt to explore the multiple variations that one gets when working with six variables: three body types and three behavior types. Sheldon's position is that each individual *has* the components of all three behavior types. It must always be kept in mind, however, that one human being is always more of one type than of the other two.

Sheldon uses a numerical system to indicate the amounts of variation there are in body-behavior types. The numbers range from an absolute minimum, which would be one, to an absolute maximum, which would be seven. The range of one to seven applies for body types as well as behavioral patterns. (As we shall see later in studying his principle that personality can be measured objectively, the body is measured on a one to seven scale as are the behavior patterns, and the total of these is also derived on a one to seven scale.) One can see now by consulting Table 4.2, that a tremendous number of variations in personality can result from using Sheldon's methods. Theoretically, it should be possible to have 343 different somatotypes, but Sheldon found in two studies, one with four thousand college students and the second with forty thousand males, that he was able to define distinctly only 76 in the first study and 88 in the second study.

In the numbering system, the endo/viscerotone figure is always given first, the meso/somatotone figure is always given second, and the ecto/cerebrotone figure is always given last. Thus, the numbers one-one-seven indicate a person who is very low in endo/viscerotonia, very low in meso/somatotonia, and extremely high in ecto/cerebrotonia. To explore further the possibilities, three examples are here given:

(A) 7–1–7: An individual who almost has equal amounts of endo/viscerotonic characteristics along with the same amount of ecto/cerebrotonic characteristics but who is extremely low in meso/somatotonic characteristics. We may suppose that this is an ambivalent person who is torn between liking people and wanting to be alone. He supposedly vacillates between these two extremes and we may further conjecture that he will be inclined to be somewhat unhappy about resolving the ambivalency of his life.

(B) 7–3–1: Here the person is high in endo/viscerotonia with some overtones of the meso/somatotone, but with no feeling of the ecto/cerebrotone. He acts like the ebullient viscerotone, but we may assume that when pushed too far in certain circumstances, he will exhibit the agressiveness of the meso/somatotone. One thing he apparently never does is go off by himself. He either wants people to like him or failing that will consider controlling them.

(C) 1–7–1: Here we have the pure meso/somatotone, who has all the capacities physically and temperamentally of the "pure" type we talked about in the beginning of the chapter.

This analysis of people can become a fascinating game, but the point being made here is that Sheldon's system is highly flexible and does not mold people because of a body type. No one, apparently, fits into any kind of set pattern of behavior. This fact is such an integral part of Sheldon's scheme that the writer has chosen to consider it a fundamental principle of the theory.

Inductive–Empirical Principle

Sheldon came upon his theory not by philosophizing nor by any armchair techniques (as valuable as these may be) but through prodigious

Table 4. 2. Continuous Variables in Sheldon's Theory

1–7–7	1–6–7	1–5–7	1–4–7	1–3–7	1–2–7	1–1–7	
2–7–7	2–6–7	2–5–7	2–4–7	2–3–7	2–2–7	2–1–7	
3–7–7	3–6–7	3–5–7	3–4–7	3–3–7	3–2–7	3–1–7	
4–7–7	4–6–7	4–5–7	4–4–7	4–3–7	4–2–7	4–1–7	
5–7–7	5–6–7	5–5–7	5–4–7	5–3–7	5–2–7	5–1–7	
6–7–7	6–6–7	6–5–7	6–4–7	6–3–7	6–2–7	6–1–7	
7–7–7	7–6–7	7–5–7	7–4–7	7–3–7	7–2–7	7–1–7	49
1–7–6	1–6–6	1–5–6	1–4–6	1–3–6	1–2–6	1–1–6	
2–7–6	2–6–6	2–5–6	2–4–6	2–3–6	2–2–6	2–1–6	
3–7–6	3–6–6	3–5–6	3–4–6	3–3–6	3–2–6	3–1–6	
4–7–6	4–6–6	4–5–6	4–4–6	4–3–6	4–2–6	4–1–6	
5–7–6	5–6–6	5–5–6	5–4–6	5–3–6	5–2–6	5–1–6	
6–7–6	6–6–6	6–5–6	6–4–6	6–3–6	6–2–6	6–1–6	
7–7–6	7–6–6	7–5–6	7–4–6	7–3–6	7–2–6	7–1–6	49
1–7–5	1–6–5	1–5–5	1–4–5	1–3–5	1–2–5	1–1–5	
2–7–5	2–6–5	2–5–5	2–4–5	2–3–5	2–2–5	2–1–5	
3–7–5	3–6–5	3–5–5	3–4–5	3–3–5	3–2–5	3–1–5	
4–7–5	4–6–5	4–5–5	4–4–5	4–3–5	4–2–5	4–1–5	
5–7–5	5–6–5	5–5–5	5–4–5	5–3–5	5–2–5	5–1–5	
6–7–5	6–6–5	6–5–5	6–4–5	6–3–5	6–2–5	6–1–5	
7–7–5	7–6–5	7–5–5	7–4–5	7–3–5	7–2–5	7–1–5	49
1–7–4	1–6–4	1–5–4	1–4–4	1–3–4	1–2–4	1–1–4	
2–7–4	2–6–4	2–5–4	2–4–4	2–3–4	2–2–4	2–1–4	
3–7–4	3–6–4	3–5–4	3–4–4	3–3–4	3–2–4	3–1–4	
4–7–4	4–6–4	4–5–4	4–4–4	4–3–4	4–2–4	4–1–4	
5–7–4	5–6–4	5–5–4	5–4–4	5–3–4	5–2–4	5–1–4	
6–7–4	6–6–4	6–5–4	6–4–4	6–3–4	6–2–4	6–1–4	
7–7–4	7–6–4	7–5–4	7–4–4	7–3–4	7–2–4	7–1–4	49
1–7–3	1–6–3	1–5–3	1–4–3	1–3–3	1–2–3	1–1–3	
2–7–3	2–6–3	2–5–3	2–4–3	2–3–3	2–2–3	2–1–3	
3–7–3	3–6–3	3–5–3	3–4–3	3–3–3	3–2–3	3–1–3	
4–7–3	4–6–3	4–5–3	4–4–3	4–3–3	4–2–3	4–1–3	
5–7–3	5–6–3	5–5–3	5–4–3	5–3–3	5–2–3	5–1–3	
6–7–3	6–6–3	6–5–3	6–4–3	6–3–3	6–2–3	6–1–3	
7–7–3	7–6–3	7–5–3	7–4–3	7–3–3	7–2–3	7–1–3	49
1–7–2	1–6–2	1–5–2	1–4–2	1–3–2	1–2–2	1–1–2	
2–7–2	2–6–2	2–5–2	2–4–2	2–3–2	2–2–2	2–1–2	
3–7–2	3–6–2	3–5–2	3–4–2	3–3–2	3–2–2	3–1–2	

4–7–2	4–6–2	4–5–2	4–4–2	4–3–2	4–2–2	4–1–2	
5–7–2	5–6–2	5–5–2	5–4–2	5–3–2	5–2–2	5–1–2	
6–7–2	6–6–2	6–5–2	6–4–2	6–3–2	6–2–2	6–1–2	
7–7–2	7–6–2	7–5–2	7–4–2	7–3–2	7–2–2	7–1–2	49
1–7–1	1–6–1	1–5–1	1–4–1	1–3–1	1–2–1	1–1–1	
2–7–1	2–6–1	2–5–1	2–4–1	2–3–1	2–2–1	2–1–1	
3–7–1	3–6–1	3–5–1	3–4–1	3–3–1	3–2–1	3–1–1	
4–7–1	4–6–1	4–5–1	4–4–1	4–3–1	4–2–1	4–1–1	
5–7–1	5–6–1	5–5–1	5–4–1	5–3–1	5–2–1	5–1–1	
6–7–1	6–6–1	6–5–1	6–4–1	6–3–1	6–2–1	6–1–1	
7–7–1	7–6–1	7–5–1	7–4–1	7–3–1	7–2–1	7–1–1	49

343

numbers of hours dedicated to the exploration of man and the relationship of his body to his behavior, using the technique he called somatotyping. Sheldon patiently built up his theory, study by study, within a laboratory setting and with full acknowledgement of research controls. In trying to prove that man's genetic past and biological makeup play a crucial part in the development of his personality (morphogenesis) and in being restricted to phenotypic methods, he evolved and is still persistently accruing, via his somatotypic methods, a vast fund of information much clearer and more defensible than that of his predecessors. Sheldon builds up his data in current research form and then draws his conclusions. This is his principle *modus operandi* for all his work. Actually, Sheldon has not himself indicated a theory, nor has he purported to claim one. His main efforts have been to explore the vast empirically derived data he has, with the assumption that there is strong enough evidence to indicate a continuity between body and behavior. Sheldon states no theory as such but subsumes as he must a theoretical rationale; otherwise he would have terminated his work long before this.

Many students are familiar with or will recognize the progenitor of constitutional psychology in the name of Hippocrates. Thus, Sheldon, like many other investigators of man's behavior, has roots that go deeply into the past. Although Sheldon's work owes no direct obeisance to that of Hippocrates (which was more oriented to an endocrine system), there are unique parallels between them. Hippocrates also created a typology of body and a typology of behavior—his being, however, more discrete and with no provision for variable types. Sheldon's interest in constitutional medicine reflects the early belief of Hippocrates that certain types of body were disposed toward certain types of diseases. Hippocrates suggested that there were two kinds of bodies, the first roughly corresponding with Sheldon's ectomorph and the second which would be something of a combination of Sheldon's endomorph and mesomorph, with more emphasis toward endomorphy. Their behavior would also roughly correspond to the Sheldonian descriptions. In addition to the dichotomized types of men, Hippocrates believed that all men could be divided into four behavior patterns, or, as he called them, four humors. The humors, patterned after the fluids of the body, were black bile, yellow bile, red bile, and white bile. Each person was assumed to be predominant in one of the biles and consequently had a temperament that corresponded to that bile.

Later, a French scientist named Rostan began the pattern of actual measurement of body–personality types and became the forerunner of much of the work now being done by the constitutional psychologists. Publishing in 1824, he stated that there were four types of bodies with correlated personalities, which he termed the *digestive, muscular, cerebral,* and *respiratory.* One can see the close affinity in results between the first three types of Rostan's and Sheldon's endomorph, mesomorph, and ectomorph.

In 1909, an Italian anthropologist, Viola, refined the techniques of measurement with much more detailed procedures. He also became convinced that there were three types of bodies, with some secondary qualities to be considered. Viola actually had two separate types called the *microsplanchnic* (small body with long legs and arms) and the *macrosplanchnic* (large body with short legs and arms). His third type, the *normosplanchnic,* was a combination of the previous two types. Viola, however, did little in ascribing behavioral characteristics to the three types. His contribution lay in the refinement of his measuring techniques, which were remarkably good for his day.

Many others come into the picture of constitutional psychology, but perhaps the most advanced theory prior to Sheldon's was the work of Kretschmer, who was a German psychiatrist and whose nomenclature for psychoses will be familiar to students of abnormal psychology. Kretschmer also evolved a trichotomized typology. Kretschmer's three body types were called the *pyknic* (short and plump: Sheldon's endomorph and Rostan's digestive type), the *athletic* (strong and aggressive: Sheldon's mesomorph and Rostan's muscular type), and the *asthenic* (thin and lonely: Sheldon's ectomorph and Rostan's cerebral type). If the reader is enchanted by the discovery that personality types seem to come in threes, he will meet even more of this trichotomized approach in the work of Karen Horney in a subsequent chapter. Kretschmer's interest, gained through work with mentally disturbed people, was primarily directed toward studying the propensity of certain body types to succumb to certain types of mental disorders, especially in regard to the schizophrenics. He was a meticulous researcher, and his work is still worth reading as an approach to the study of body/behavior dynamics in man.

In 1934–1935, Sheldon visited Kretschmer and has since paid tribute to the man who advanced the field of constitutional typology prior to his own investigations. Though Sheldon was undoubtedly influenced and certainly interested in Kretschmer's work, he began afresh to gather his own data, perfect his own techniques, and draw his own conclusions independent of Kretschmer. Sheldon did not copy Kretschmer; he simply noted with deep interest what Kretschmer had done and then proceeded to conduct research along his own lines.

Sheldon felt that he proved that certain body types have an affinity toward specific kinds of mental disorders. He was further convinced that psychosis is but a continuum of normal behavior and *not* a difference in kind of behavior. This was a revolutionary idea for his time as psychotics were considered to be of the "devil" and not human at all.

So we find that Sheldon pays a great deal of attention to the uniqueness of each individual, or what we have chosen to call the continuous variable of man's personality. The pattern of relationships, such as 1–1–7, or 3–4–1, or 2–5–7, or any combination of these as previously discussed, is of much greater interest to Sheldon than is the so-called pure type. To Sheldon, man is a complex creature, and possibly the key to his dynamics lies in the relationship of the body to behavior.

Objective Measurement Principle

There are times in Sheldon's writings when he seems almost obsessed with the objectivity of measurement. He continually cautions against premature judgments concerning typing bodies and behavior and has in his later writings extended the periods of observation almost to the point of utilizing a life-study technique prior to diagnosis. As his work has progressed, the time interval he feels is adequate to study an individual has lengthened.

Interestingly enough, Sheldon and his coworkers approached the problem in two separate but parallel ways: one task group studied the measurement of man's body (the taxonomic approach), while another force of workers initiated and carried on the study of man as he behaves in living his everyday life. Thus, two groups of workers, each doing a different thing, progressed almost simultaneously and eventually were brought together so that their separate work was matched. The results for Sheldon upheld his original hypothesis of a unique relationship between body/behavior, even though he was unable to explore the morphogenetic influences, his primary thesis.

First, we shall very briefly cover some of the interesting approaches he made in studying man's bodily structure.

Body. One of the beginning studies was one of four thousand male college students. Each student was photographed standing in front of the same background. Three photographs were taken, front, back, and side. Using many judges to examine all the variant body forms, and through quite complicated but controlled methods, Sheldon finally satisfied himself that there were three basic body forms: the now familiar endo, ecto, and meso morphs. In addition, he also instituted a tremendous variety of physical measurements which were tried on the same four thousand male college students. Through involved analysis, he reduced these measurements to seventeen. All physical measurements were in relationship to the height of the student–subject. A coworker, S. S. Stevens, invented a machine which, with a relatively untrained operator, could make the same seventeen measurements, but this was discarded eventually, since, in further work, Sheldon discovered that the photographs were as accurate as the actual physical measurement.

As many as forty thousand males have been somatotyped by Sheldon and his coworkers in refining the technique. As his work has progressed, he has strongly advocated a set of photographs taken over a prolonged period (the optimal length of time is not stated because of individual differences) along with as complete a medical history as is possible and as many biological tests as are practical to administer. Failing these optimal conditions, however, one may still utilize his system of somatotyping through the photographic technique.

It is hoped that the reader's curiosity has been sufficiently whetted so that he will examine Sheldon's *Atlas of Men* in which the entire procedure is discussed and illustrated with many photographs for reference and tables to elimimate computation. The measurement method is called the Somatotype Performance Test.

Behavior. Next, Sheldon turned his attention to the measurement of behavior with the same inductive approach. A list of 650 behavioral traits was culled from a study of the vast field of literature concerning personality, behavior, and any type of work which seemed to describe man's behavior. After scrutinizing the list of 650 items, Sheldon and his collaborators reduced the number to 50 by eliminating terms that overlapped, terms that were so nebulous as to defy definition, and those which seemed so insignificant as not to describe behavior at all. A group of thirty-three males were selected as subjects for validating the list of 50 items. Each individual subject was observed and studied through intensive interviews for approximately twelve months. The results of the ratings which Sheldon and his coworkers made (using again a seven-point scale just as they had for studying body types) were correlated with each other. Out of these intercorrelations, Sheldon found certain ratings which seemed to group themselves in clusters of commonality. These clusters were considered to represent the same kind of behavior pattern. For a rating to be included within a cluster, it had to correlate positively at +.60 or higher and had likewise to correlate negatively with the other clusters at −.30. From these data, Sheldon discovered that only 22 of the originally culled 50 items were meaningful, and that these 22 items of behavioral description clustered statistically *into three groups.* So once again the three-ness of things emerged from Sheldon's work just as it had for the body types. Both procedures, of course, were conducted by statistical analysis. The three clusters describing behavior were the aforementioned terms of *viscerotonia, somatotonia,* and *cerebrotonia* with the meanings as we have previously described them.

At this point, it almost seems predestined that Sheldon's work would so neatly resolve into three body types and three behavior types.

Sheldon continued to refine his preliminary results by conducting eight more trial studies. He added, subtracted, and changed the trait descriptions and their combinations, always using his preliminary study criteria: i.e., trait descriptions to be included into a cluster must correlate with each other at +.60 and be mutually exclusive to other clusters at −.30.

By a ninth and final study he had refined his method sufficiently so that with a group of one hundred subjects, which were measured on 78 behavioral trait descriptions, he was able to select twenty traits (all meeting the criteria) for each type (viscerotonia, somatotonia, cerebrotonia) for a total of 60 descriptive terms with which he felt behavior could be sensibly measured. These sixty terms comprise his *Scale for Temperament*. This is the scale which was used in extended form to begin the present chapter. He has since continued to use this temperament scale, virtually unchanged, in all of the subsequent work he has done.

The next logical step, of course, was to select a group of subjects and to investigate the degree of relationship between their behavior and their bodies by measuring both and comparing the results. This he did, as we shall discuss in the following paragraphs.

Body–Behavior Relationships. Now Sheldon turned his research endeavors toward the culmination of investigating the statistical relationship between body and behavior. For this study, which took over five years to conduct, Sheldon and his staff selected two hundred white male subjects who would be willing and capable of participating in the study over so long a period. The subjects were by and large college students (who, of course, are generally available for four years) and professional personnel who would be inclined to maintain rapport with the study. Over an extended period of time, the subjects were observed and interviewed with care through use of the Scale of Temperament. Only after they had been classified by the temperament scale, were they measured for bodily characteristics again by use of the seven point scale that Sheldon had created.

The denouement of Sheldon's work was indeed even more satisfactory than he had hoped, for the relationships between body and behavior were startlingly high. Table 4.3 reveals the basic findings of this study. In Sheldon's words, "These are higher correlations than we expected to find. . . ."

A study of Table 4.3 indicates that viscerotonic behavior correlates with the endomorphic body .79, somatotonic behavior correlates with the mesomorphic body .82, and the cerebrotonic behavior pattern correlates with the ectomorphic body type at .83. All three correlations are significantly high in a statistical sense. Equally of interest is the amount of relationship that does *not* exist between the six components of the matrix.

Sheldon felt that because of the high correlations resulting from this study it was possible that he was measuring "the same thing at different levels of . . . expression." Putting the proposition another way, would it not be possible to measure temperament alone or measure body type alone and thus be able to predict the opposite characteristic without having to measure it? He would, of course, admit that this technique is primarily a group assumption and that any single individual would vary from the mean data. Nevertheless, it appears that Sheldon may have put an extremely valuable tool into the hands of the student of personality.

And so the objective measurement technique of Sheldon, which he so

Table 4. 3. Correlations Between Body and Behavior

Behavior Types	Body Types		
	Endomorph (fat)	Mesomorph (muscular)	Ectomorph (thin)
Viscerotonia (likes people)	.79		
Somatotonia (controls people)	−.29	.82	
Cerebrotonia (avoids people)	−.32	−.58	.83

NOTE. The product moment correlations. Adapted from *The Varieties of Temperament: A Psychology of Constitutional Differences,* 1942, p. 400.

faithfully followed as a principal guide to his work, was for him successful beyond even his expectations.

Constancy of Somatotype Principle

Although Sheldon has advocated more and more in his recent writings that the researcher should take repeated "readings" of the subject's body and conduct exhaustive interviews and observations in somatotyping, he is not suggesting this because the somatotype is likely to change, but because one must arrive at an *accurate* somatotype. To Sheldon, the type does not change, but the investigator may be misled by fragments of information in typing the body and/or behavior. (See, for example, the Pyknic Practical Joke type mentioned previously.)

Sheldon admits that people do grow fatter if they eat too much and that eventually in senility the skeletal structure does decrease slightly, but he stoutly maintains that the *ratio* between the various parts of the body remains constant. In some of the cases which he has studied over a ten-year period the weights of the subjects increased or decreased as much as one hundred pounds without altering the basic characteristics of the somatotype. Apparently the ectomorph may gain weight, but this change does not make him want to be with people any more than he did in the past. He remains a cerebrotone in an ectomorphic body despite his nutritional digressions. Likewise one may starve an endomorph, but he is still inclined to seek people when in trouble and be happy when drunk. As Hall and Lindzey in their classic text state, "Sheldon suggests that as a starved mastiff does not become a poodle, so a starved mesomorph does not become an ectomorph."

What particularly interests Sheldon in his measurements is the ratios of head–neck, chest–trunk, arms, stomach–trunk, and legs, and all of this in relation to the entire skeletal structure. These, he maintains, are constant. What is not constant is the distribution of fatty tissue and, most obviously, the inaccuracies of measurement.

Behavioral Environment Principle

Oddly enough for an investigator who is called a constitutional psychologist and whose efforts have been directed along organic measurement lines, Sheldon is not at all unaware of the environmental influences upon the individual. He does not eschew them as much as he pleads that one always investigate the total field in which the organism operates before he makes even a tentative diagnosis of type. It is important to note, however, that it is *behavior* that Sheldon is talking about primarily, hence his fervent admonition, which has grown more frequent as his work has continued: that the researcher-classifier must take into account all the aspects of the human's behavior via depth interviews and direct observations to be conducted over extended periods of time.

Thus, we have dealt with man's personality as Sheldon, the constitutional psychologist, describes it and as we have interpreted that description. Following, then, we shall see how the Sheldonian approach deals with the problem of explaining why man does the things he does, using the same rubric as the chapter on Freud.

DELIMITATIONS

The author has in no way attempted to be exhaustive in the treatment of Sheldon's work but only to interpret the major aspects of his constitutional psychology.

To get the true flavor of his work, one should read especially Sheldon's second major work, *The Varieties of Temperament: A Psychology of Constitutional Differences* (1942) or his *Atlas of Men, A Guide for Somatotyping the Adult Male at All Ages.* The latter is absolutely necessary if one is to attempt any significant use of his technique. For an extension of his work in two pragmatic areas, delinquency and diagnosing psychotics, read his *Varieties of Delinquent Youth: An Introduction to Constitutional Psychiatry,* and also P. Wittman and C. J. Katz, A Study of the Relationship between Constitutional Variations and Fundamental Psychotic Behavior Reactions, *J. Nerv. Ment. Dis.,* 1948, *108,* 470–476.

EXPLAINING HUMAN BEHAVIOR VIA SHELDON'S
CONSTITUTIONAL PSYCHOLOGY[3]

It may appear that using Sheldon's theory to explain man's behavior would produce a pronounced, singular explanation: the morphogenesis of the body influences man's behavior. Although this may be true to some extent, there are further considerations. For example, which kind of body form typically makes which kind of response to marriage, perversions, and the other seven life situations being used to explain man's behavior? Keeping in mind again that no pure types exist in Sheldon's system, we will deal with explanation as though each body type were involved individually as was done in the fore part of this chapter. Thus, why does the endo/viscerotone get married, the meso/somatotone, the ecto/cerebrotone, and so on?

Marriage

Endo/viscerotone. Marriage is the natural state of being for the endo/viscerone. He can hardly keep from being married, because he likes, needs, and lives for contact with people. Marriage also produces children in the usual course of events, and the endo/viscerotone is a happy man when surrounded by his family. Family means people at all times, throughout the day, for meals, and for life.

Meso/somatotone. Let us assume that the muscular meso/somatotone marries because there is some very attractive girl he would like to possess

---

[3] See Chapter 3 (Freud) where the rationale and criteria for this section are presented.

as his own or because his marriage to a power figure like himself will provide someone who will share his triumphs and contribute strength to his exploits. We may further assume that he will not be an overly affectionate father or husband and that he will push his children into competitive situations and be most anxious that they win prizes. To get married, then, is to show the world what he has created and what he possesses.

Ecto/cerebrotone. Marriage for him is a convenience. It is better than cooking for himself and seeing after his laundry, and less vexing than hiring a domestic for household chores. Probably the marriage partner would have to be a like-minded ecto/cerebrotone because marriage to a meso/somatotone would be threatening, and marriage to the endo/viscerotone would engulf one with people all the time. With an endo/viscerotonic partner there would be parties, people dropping in, attendance at numerous social functions, and never a quiet peaceful moment for oneself.

Perversions

Endo/viscerotone. He is inclined to be the passive member in a perverted act, especially of a homosexual nature. He desperately wants love and affection, and if an act of perversion will gain it for him, he feels justified in such indulgences. He may actively seek opportunities for perverted acts primarily because they bring him into contact with people. Also, the love aspects of perversions are fervently enjoyed. Love rules his world and whatever gains love is justifiable.

Meso/somatotone. The endo/viscerotone sought or accepted perverted acts to be accepted and submissive; the meso/somatotone indulges for opposite reasons: to control by getting pleasure from others. His role in an homosexual incident is the dominant, aggressive, sadistic one. Out of this, he gains his pleasure and continues to repeat homosexual contacts.

Ecto/cerebrotone. Not for moral reasons (as was also the case in drinking alcohol) but because, if one becomes involved emotionally with another, that other gains a grip on the self, the ecto/cerebrotone avoids perverted acts. He may speak of them as disgusting but what he really feels is a sense of weakness and pity toward any human who cannot control himself, especially in relationships with other people. He consequently strongly resists any activity that involves his feelings, and he feels that perversions are high in this classification.

Suicide

Endo/viscerotone. Presumably the endo/viscerotone takes his life because he has become alienated from people; he cannot stand to live a life without people in it who love him and want him. Only through people can one find happiness. Or it may be assumed that his love relationship with one person has been destroyed and that he cannot face life without that person. In either case, alienation from groups or from a single person, the main factor of which he has been deprived is the companionship of other human beings, a situation that is intolerable to further existence.

Meso/somatotone. We may imagine two factors operating in the decision of a meso/somatotone to commit suicide. One, he has lost his strength through illness, poverty, or any circumstance depriving him of control over others. This state of weakness so discourages him that he feels life is not worth living. Second, he has come under the power of others, not through such drastic misfortunes as concentration camp or prisoner of war status, but possibly through imprisonment as a civilian or through his employment by persons stronger than he is, and he is unable to withdraw from the situation.

Ecto/cerebrotone. To some degree, he seems to be the most likely candidate of the three types for suicide. His personality is centripetal. Instead of centrifugally throwing off his problems, he winds them tighter and tighter around himself until they engulf him. He shuns the normal avenues of problem-solving because seeking outside help seems to indicate a weakness in himself. This leaves him with no one but himself as a therapeutic agent. Since it was he himself who got into the difficulty in the first place, he is unable to conduct an "operation boot strap." The knot gets tighter for him as he struggles with it until, as he pulls on it, it chokes him off from life.

Lawbreaking

Endo/viscerotone. Almost every one has heard or used the old cliché, "My son is in trouble because of bad companions." This could be the jolly, fleshy individual's trouble with the law. He is a follower in most circumstances and, thus, where the crowd goes, he goes. If the group indulges in illegal pursuits, he does. To be accepted by the group is more important than to come under the aegis of a law that seems more remote than the companionship and approval of friends. In such a comparison, the law is forced to take a secondary position.

Meso/somatotone. He breaks the law because he wants to. It gets in his way. The ego strength of the meso/somatotone is so great that he can think himself beyond the law. His aim is victory by strength, and if the law intervenes with his objective, it must suffer. That he, too, will suffer if apprehended is considered a piece of bad luck on his part; remorse is lacking. Others break the law every day. It was his foul luck to be caught at the act.

Ecto/cerebrotone. If he breaks the law, which he is unlikely to do, it will be via avenues of quiet crime such as forgery, embezzlement, or solitary forays. Recidivism may be strong because he is, after all, a sociophobe, and society makes the law by the consensus of its social groups in the form of legislatures. He may feel that laws are to govern the weak against themselves. He is outside the general pale of society. Thus, he too feels small remorse and acts aggressively as may the meso/somatotone but as an isolate, outside of, and especially above, the realms of social control.

Supranatural Being

Endo/viscerotone. This individual becomes conditioned to the acceptance of a god figure, and he is likely to perpetuate it in the form of deeply involved service to the church, service that brings the admiration of others. He accepts and even seeks service to the church, for in the church he finds a warm, sensitive air of love and acceptance to all, weak and poor, rich and powerful. He attends regularly because the Sunday service has people in it, and after the service he may visit with his fellow parishioners. To him a god figure is a warm, accepting father figure that will take care of all within the fold. The best part of all to him is the fellowship. His deity is remote but forgiving; his church is a wonderful, open-armed place of fellowship for all, especially himself.

Meso/somatotone. The meso/somatotone is in general inclined to avoid religion because its basis is a hard-to-define, ephemeral something that is supposed to be superior to himself. He finds this idea rather difficult to accept. He may turn his attention to a deity if things go wrong and a figure is needed upon which to place the blame for his illfortune. A supernatural concept then becomes convenient for scapegoating his bad luck. If, however, he does become a member of a religious organization, usually through parental conditioning, he out-Puritans the Puritans. He becomes fervently against sin and any influence which reduces the power of his church to operate. He may be evangelistic in the most remote missionary locations because there is a feeling of power inherent in taking care of the less fortunate. In a sense, he takes the place of an omnipotent deity and does so with a zeal for conformity to his type of religious order. "Fear the Lord" is emblazoned on his armor, and, because he is for the Lord, one must by transferrence fear him too. What he stands for is righteousness of his own brand, and woe to the transgressor who befalls his wrath. Religion means to the meso/somatotone an avenue of power couched in the most noble terms.

Ecto/cerebrotone. He comes to religion slowly, painfully, with great inner struggles that leave him with a deep conviction of a person-to-person relationship. Religion and a superior being are compatible because he treasures superiority. If he is attracted to a form of church worship, it is always to the reflective, quiet type of service. Evangelistic fervor repels him. Even if he worships with others, it matters little to him if their beliefs are at slight variance with his because religion is a deeply personal experience. He rather enjoys the philosphical avenues that lead to the study of a deity. It fills him with a satisfying warmth to achieve by himself, through reflection, a satisfying deity formation. Whereas the endo/viscerotone is confused by too much reflection and by sermons which remonstrate; and the meso/somatotone either immediately joins as one who does not sin, or, if the sermon touches upon a personal activity of his in a critical way, threatens to "quit" the church for a less "blue-nosed" one; the ecto/cerebrotone thoroughly enjoys scholarly sermons whether or not they remonstrate. Religion to him is a solitary way of life to be carried on deeply within one's inner self. He may appear irreligious to some societies because he shuns open display of his beliefs, but they run very deep within him.

Humor

Endo/viscerotone. The endo/viscerotone rather likes to play the clown because it brings laughter and happiness to others who will then like him. He may spend considerable energy seeking ways to create humorous incidents and thus to win the approval of others. He is not bothered if he happens to be the butt of the humor and may even create himself in the image of the jester so long as others laugh and tolerate and like him. He becomes a rather happy companion, always "good for a laugh." The worst thing one can do is ignore his attempts to provide laughs. This he finds intolerable and will go to strange lengths to create attention and force humor upon the unwilling. He likes a happy world and is willing to do more than his share to create it.

Meso/somatotone. "Man's inhumanity to man" is the basis of humor for the muscular meso/somatotone. He finds it funny to see others in predicaments. His own superiority seems manifest when others are in less fortunate roles. Practical jokes where another is made to suffer some embarrassment or inconvenience, seem hilarious to him. To be the receiver of such practical jokes affects him with a destructive wrath that consumes his energy until retribution can be exacted. Humor of this type between two meso/somatotones consists of a series of practical jokes, sometimes building to a crescendo that causes a break between the two practitioners. Humor to the meso/somatotone is a method of displaying superiority in a socially approved way.

Ecto/cerebrotone. As the reader might expect, humor is a minimal feature in the life of the thin ectomorph with the solitary, cerebrotonic behavior. What humor he does find in life falls within the area of the "private joke" between two or three people. He likes his humor privately. He may, however, as his basic rationale is that of the sociophobe, enjoy caustic witticisms that show man up for the fool he is.

Smoking

Endo/viscerotone. He smokes for companionship. Smoking is a pleasant social custom with many, many adherents, and if one is to join the crowd and be where the crowd is, he must indulge in what the crowd does. Smoking is an entree into social groups. There is a belongingness to smoking that he cherishes.

Meso/somatotone. If the somatotone considers smoking effects, he will shun it. In general, he may abstain from tobacco if it appears to impair his physical prowess. If he does smoke, he does it with great vigor and delights in using the stronger forms of tobacco which others avoid, thereby proving his ability to do something harder than others are doing. Smoking, however, has small appeal to him largely because it offers so little opportunity to be active. It is difficult to smoke and play actively in sports or games.

Ecto/cerebrotone. There is a constant struggle between smoking and giving up smoking for the ecto/cerebrotone. He enjoys the reflectiveness of a pipe but dislikes intensely becoming addicted to anything he cannot ultimately reject.

Recreation

Endo/viscerotone. He thoroughly enjoys play situations that are social. Dancing, group games, large parties, all are most happy occasions for him. This is the ideal situation to make friends. He will readily lose to the more aggressive player as long as the opponent continues to play with him. He obviously dislikes solitary sports. Hiking alone in the mountains, playing golf alone, any such activities are not his pleasure. He does enjoy and may make great effort to organize a hunting or fishing trip with the sole purpose of creating a happy and cogenial group of favorite friends. He may do the cooking while the others go off to fish or hunt.

Meso/somatotone. The meso/somatotone thoroughly enjoys sports, games, recreations in which he can excel and which provide competitive situations. Hiking is fine if one is pitting his strength against another hiker. When he plays a game, he must keep score, either against an opponent or against his own past performances, for without a competitive measure of some type a game is worthless. He finds the field of sports especially attractive, for in that he may compete for victory under socially approved rules, and, should he emerge the winner (which is the primary reason for participation), society gives him a prize and public adulation. He feels at this time that this is the best of all possible worlds: he can exercise his superiority drives and receive approval for doing what comes naturally.

Ecto/cerebrotone. The thin-bodied isolate likes cerebration in his games. Solitary sports such as fishing by oneself, golfing by oneself are his favorites. Highly competitive games threaten him to the point where he openly criticizes the game, its players, and all spectators involved. The ecto/cerebrotone considers recreation to be an opportunity to collect things, sort them, and make an exhaustive study of all the ramifications of his collection. Play and recreation are important to the ecto/cerebrotone only as a means of exercising his intellect.

Psychoses–Neuroses[4]

Endo/viscerotone. When he comes to the point that people no longer

[4] In 1948 Wittman in collaboration with Katz and Sheldon constructed a "Check List of Psychotic Behavior" which deals directly with this question of body types and their relationship to psychotic behavior. See Wittman, Sheldon, and Katz, A Study of the Relationship Between Constitutional Variations and Fundamental Psychotic Behavior Reactions, *J. Nerv. Ment. Dis.,* 1948, *108,* 470–476. Some of the findings of his study are incorporated in this material.

will accept him despite his strongest efforts to "win them over," the endo/viscerotone comes close to mental collapse. His psychotic behavior takes the form of bizarre, silly, affective behavior with wide mood swings from happy to sad states. He is both greatly disturbed by the presence of others and ambivalently compelled to seek them.

Meso/somatotone.   This aggressive individual breaks down emotionally for the same reasons that he commits suicide: inability to maintain his ego strength over other human beings either through self-weakness or circumstance. His psychotic behavior takes the form of undifferentiated feelings of being persecuted by others, coupled with the schizoid's inability to control his emotions. His anger is immense although his retribution may be wild and ineffective. He collapses when his strength over others collapses, especially over others whom he considers inferior to himself.

Ecto/cerebrotone.   As one might expect, the isolate from society increases his isolation when psychotically disoriented. The ecto/cerebrotone "thinks" his way into neurotic and psychotic states of emotion. Thinking requires only self, and so, as his mind fails him, he withdraws more and more into catatonic states of complete immobility and rigidity of body.

PREDICTING HUMAN BEHAVIOR VIA SHELDON'S CONSTITUTIONAL THEORY

Sheldon, perhaps more than most of the other theorists, is very concerned about the predictability of man's behavior. Although his interest is mainly in predicting the results he will get from his research, the connection between this and a general prediction of man's behavior is quite direct, for he deals with man as a behaving animal in the total life scene, not with just one aspect of his behavior, such as eye-blink response.

Personal Prediction

Let us first turn our attention to the predicting of human behavior from the reader's own frame of reference. In order to give this some structure, the reader is referred to the list of behavioral characteristics at the beginning of the chapter. A strong note of caution is added: this estimation in no way substitutes for Sheldon's Scale of Temperament although the sixty items he used are involved. It is likewise pure nonsense for the reader to attempt to diagnose his friends for *their* edification with such a crude instrument in the hands of an untrained diagnostician. The method simply adds some grains of objectivity in the evaluation of Sheldon's theory when practiced by the reader.

After the list has been used, the reader may be more objective in deciding the predictability of Sheldon's work strictly from his own experience with the system.

Instructions for Estimating the Somatotypes

1. Select a person for study who has been very well known to you for years, such as a friend or member of the family.

2. Start with the endo/viscerotone and consider each item carefully as to whether it applies *most of the time* to the selected subject. If it seems to describe the individual fairly accurately, make a checkmark for that item. Do not be concerned if it seems to contradict with another item at the moment. If the activity is one which you are unable to observe or judge for the subject, do not mark it.

3. After you have carefully considered and marked the items for all three descriptions, add each in a column separately (one for the endo/viscerotone, one for the meso/somatotone, and one for the ecto/cerebrotone) and write the total at the bottom of the column. The totals give a *rough approximation* of the endo/viscerotonic, meso/somatotonic, and ecto/cerebrotonic characteristics of the subject.

4. To check the accuracy of his rating, the reader may do one of the following: (These do not necessarily evaluate Sheldon's work but rather his method as a predicting agency.)

a. Put the rating aside and attempt another one some months later; compare the results.

b. Have the subject rate himself or herself and then compare the ratings with yours.

c. Reverse the process by having some one rate you; then rate yourself and compare the results.

d. Select a subject well known to you and a group of your acquaintances; have each one rate the person separately; compare your results as to typology.

e. Select a subject sufficiently well known in history and biography, such as Lincoln, Napoleon; rate this person, compare your rating with the general opinion of historians or others who have rated the personage.

f. (This method comes more nearly to the task of prediction.) Have your parents rate you as they knew you ten years ago. Does this rating still hold true in describing you today? Do the same thing yourself by rating a friend or family member as you knew him some years back; does he still behave in this manner?

None of the above methods prove that Sheldon's method can predict human behavior, but they do help the student of personality to apply this theory directly to a life situation and thus to draw some empirical conclusions about it. In this respect a degree of prediction evolves out of agreement with one's own acceptance of this theory. In short, should the ratings equate to one's living experience of another human being, one might further assume that the system has enough merit when applied to others to lead toward prediction.

Scientific or Laboratory Prediction

Once again, as in the previous chapter, the admissibility or inadmissibility of research evidence and personal experience in "proving" a degree of predictability for man's behavior lies largely in the judgment of the individual reader. Sheldon's data have been upheld and attacked. Some say that they do not obtain the same results as he did with body/behavior measurements.[5] Very few (see Wittman's previously mentioned study) appear to defend his work. In general, few corollary studies have taken the time to corroborate Sheldon's work or have used the same methods. Thus, even though somewhat comparable studies exist, the student of personality is left with the major burden of decision. This should not be discouraging to the reader as the same phenomenon applies also to religion, political systems, philosophical beliefs, and even emphasis in nuclear fission, about which experts give conflicting testimony. Eventually the reader must decide for himself the adequacy of the findings and then form an opinion for himself with what evidence he feels is convincing.

What predictability exists, then, within Sheldon's own research? We may consider some of the following as evidence for consideration by the reader.

In a later work (*Atlas of Men*, 1954, p. 19) Sheldon states, "The somatotype is by definition a *prediction* of the future succession of phenotypes which a living person will present, if nutrition remains a constant factor or varies only within normal limits." [Author's italics.]

---

[5] H. J. Eysenck, *Dimensions of Personality*, Routledge, 1947; L. L. Thurstone, Factor Analysis and Body Types, *Psychometrika*, 1946, *11*, 15–21; W. W. Howells, A Factorial Study of Constitutional Type, *Amer. J. Phys. Anthrop.*, 1952, *10*, 91–118; R. W. Newman, Age Changes in Body Build, *Amer. J. Phys. Anthrop.*, 1952, *10*, 75–90.

Again, from the same source (p. 20), "Is there a degree of dependability (predictability) in the somatotype as in practice it is actually gauged?" Sheldon does not answer his own question but feels that further research which emphasizes a longitudinal approach covering the lifetime of a subject or subjects is needed.

In regard to children, Sheldon is presently at work on an atlas of children as well as the atlas of women. Preliminary findings do indicate that women's physiques are somewhat comparable to men in the relationship of body to behavior. He also feels that much could be done in forecasting the future if those responsible for children's development would heed the types of bodies they have and structure their lives enough to keep frustration from occurring; for example, being watchful that the highly evident ectomorphic child is not plunged into situations which call for the mesomorph's muscles or the endomorph's joviality. This is, in a sense, within the realm of predictability, for by such manipulation we may construct either a happy or unhappy future for the child. It will be most interesting to study the forthcoming volumes on women and children which Sheldon and his coworkers are working with now.

As we have said, Sheldon's work has not stimulated many papers or projects from his peers. Perhaps this is a field in which the embryonic psychologist could carve out a niche for himself. This may be especially true in checking the results of Sheldon's work with delinquents (*Varieties of Delinquent Youth; An Introduction to Constitutional Psychiatry*). For example, one might predict results similar to Sheldon's where the majority of his subjects proved to be high in mesomorphy or endomesomorphy and very, very low in ectomorphy. Might one then say that the ectomorphic child is a good risk against delinquency? Questions of this nature lie within the province of predictability in his constitutional psychology theory.

In summarizing, then, the degree of predictability of Sheldon's work according to scientific or laboratory research, we find a high degree within his own system, but, with the exception of Wittman's study, little agreement from research done by others (Eysenck, Howells, Lasker, Newman, Thurstone).

◆

SUMMARY

Sheldon searches for a relationship between the genetic–biological aspects of man, which he calls the *morphogenotypes,* and the behavior of man, which he calls *temperament.* Knowing that morphogenotype research is not possible, he advocates the use of phenotyping. Phenotyping is done through the use of measurement and photographs. This leads to somatotyping, which is the method of evaluating body types and behavioral patterns.

From these data, he has constructed a theory which indicates to him a direct and positive correlation between man's body and his behavior. Certain body types seem to behave in certain ways. Primary body somatotypes with their corresponding behavioral characteristics he named as follows:

Endomorph—Viscerotonia
Mesomorph—Somatotonia
Ectomorph—Cerebrotonia

Secondary body somatotypes he classified as (1) dysplasia—or the "d" index, referring to inconsistencies in the primary types, (2) Pyknic Practical Joke (PPJ)—the late developer who looks like an mesomorph in his youth but turns out to be an endomorph in later years, (3) textural Aspect—the "t" index which referred to handsomeness or beauty of the body, and (4) gynandromorphy—the so-called "g" index measuring female characteristics in the male and vice versa.

Figure 3 is a summary in graphic form, highlighting the main features of Sheldon's constitutional psychology. Starting at the center and reading outward with the endomorph, we find he has a body inclined to fleshiness which correlates +.79 with the viscerotonic temperament. The viscerotonic enjoys being with people, he likes such things as beer and food, and he correlates negatively at −.32 to the cerebrotonic and at −.29 with the somatotonic.

Going clockwise, the next type of body is the muscular mesomorph, who correllates with the somatotonic temperament at +.82. Somatotonia describes the person who prefers to control people, play contact sports like football or boxing. Being very dissimilar to the cerebrotonic, he correlates at −.58 with him.

The thin, asthetic ectomorph correlates +.83 with the counterpart temperament of cerebrotonia. His pleasures are exemplified by Bach and books, while he continues his solitary way in life *sans* people.

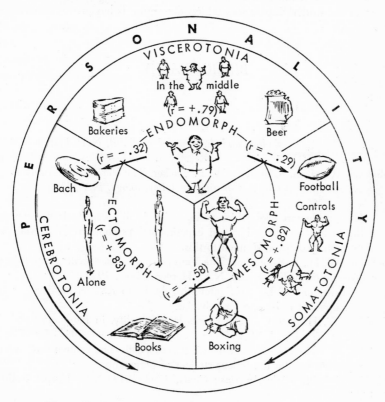

Figure 3. Diagrammatic Summary of Sheldon's Theory.

The outstanding features of Figure 3 are not the types, however; the fundamental fact, according to Sheldon, is that all of us have these components to varying degrees within our personalities. Consequently the entire figure is surrounded by the term personality. We may suppose that in the figure the equal portions of the three types indicates a 4–4–4 distribution; Sheldon used a numerical system to describe the total personality pattern after having measured the body and behavior of an individual. Thus, the three lower figures indicate more or less pure types of endo/viscerotone, meso/somatotone and ecto/cerebrotone.

In final summary, then, Sheldon does not state directly that the body controls behavior but that by studying the body one may receive valuable clues to the underlying factors which determine behavior.

BIBLIOGRAPHY

PRIMARY SOURCES

BOOKS

Sheldon, W. H., *Psychology and the Promethean Will*, N.Y., Harper & Row, 1936.

Sheldon, W. H., S. S. Stevens, W. B. Tucker, *The Varieties of Human Physique: An Introduction to Constitutional Psychology*, N.Y., Harper & Row, 1940.

His introductory book which spells out in detail his methods of measuring the body. Stevens, a Harvard experimental psychologist of considerable talent has contributed much to this.

Sheldon, W. H., S. S. Stevens, *The Varieties of Temperament: A Psychology of Constitutional Differences*, N.Y., Harper & Row, 1942.

Probably one of his most interesting books to read as he develops the measurement technique for behavior.

Sheldon, W. H., Constitutional factors in personality, in *Personality and the Behavior Disorders*, J. McV. Hunt, (ed.), N.Y., Ronald, 1944, 526–549.

Short concise exposition of his work to this date. The volume itself is well worth reading for the serious student of personality.

Sheldon, W. H., *Early American Cents, 1793–1814*, N.Y., Harper & Row, 1949.

Sheldon, W. H., E. M. Hartl, and E. McDermott, *Varieties of Delinquent Youth: An Introduction to Constitutional Psychiatry*, N.Y., Harper & Row, 1949.

Longitudinal study started in 1939 comparing college students with inmates of a rehabilitation home. Consists of many biological sketches.

Sheldon, W. H., C. W. Dupertuis, and E. McDermott, *Atlas of Men: A Guide for Somatotyping the Adult Male of All Ages*, N. Y., Harper & Row, 1954.

Sheldon's *magnus opus* to date. Some of his earlier positions have been modified or refined. If only one source is to be used to study Sheldon this is the best.

PERIODICALS

Child, I. L., and W. H. Sheldon, The correlation between components of physique and scores on certain psychological tests, *Charact. and Pers.*, 1941, *10*, 23–24.

Wittman, P., W. H. Sheldon, and C. J. Katz, A study of the relationship between constitutional variations and fundamental psychotic behavior reactions, *J. Nerv. Ment. Dis.*, 1948, *108*, 470–476.

Sheldon, W. H., Mesomorphs in mischief, *Contemp. Psychol.*, 1957, 2, 125–126.

SUGGESTED READINGS

BOOKS

Eysenck, H. J., *Dimensions of Personality*, London, Routledge, 1947.

Glueck, S., and E. Glueck, *Physique and Delinquency*, N.Y., Harper & Row, 1956.

Glueck, S. (ed.), *The Problem of Delinquency*, Boston, Houghton Mifflin, 1959.
See section on body types and delinquency.

Kretschmer, E., *Physique and Character*, N.Y., Harcourt, Brace & World, 1925. Translation of a 1921 work by W. J. H. Sprott—Kretschmer published in German the twentieth edition of this work in 1951.

Palthe, P. M. W., in *NATO: Agardograph, No. 5, Anthropometry and Human Engineering*, N.Y., Wiley (Interscience), 1955.
Use of Sheldon's methods to measure candidates for pilot training.

Parnell, R. W., *Behavior and Physique: An Introduction to Practical and Applied Somatometry*, Baltimore, Williams & Wilkins, 1958.
Worth reading to compare with Sheldon's methods.

Paterson, D. G., *Physique and Intellect*, N.Y., Appleton-Century-Crofts, 1930.

PERIODICALS

Bernstein, M. E., and G. M. Gustin, Physical and psychological variation and the sex ratio, *J. Hered.*, 1961, *52*, 109–112.
Sheldon's somatotypes and genetic mechanisms.

Brodsky, C. M., A study of norms for body form–behavior relationships, *Anthrop. Quart.*, 1954, *27*, 91–101.
One hundred and twenty-five college students match traits with body forms à la Sheldon—mesomorph most desirable, ectomorph indicates maladjustment, endomorph weak character.

Child, I. L., The relationship of somatotype to self-ratings on Sheldon's temperamental traits, *J. Pers.*, 1950, *18*, 440–453.

Damon, A., Constitution and smoking, *Science*, 1961, *134*, 339–340.
   Lean men smoke more than fat men.

Eysenck, H. J., The Rees-Eysenck body index and Sheldon's somatotype system, *J. Ment. Sci.*, 1959, *105*, 1053–1058.

Fiske, D. W., A study of relationships to somatotype, *J. Appl. Psychol.*, 1944, *28*, 504–519.

Funk, I. C., I. Shatin, E. X. Freed, and L. Rockmore, Somato-psychotherapeutic approach to long-term schizophrenic patients, *J. Nerv. and Ment. Dis.*, 1955, *121*, 423–437.

Glueck, E. T., Body build and the prediction of delinquency, *J. Crim. Law Criminal.*, 1958, *48*, 577–579.

Hood, A. B., A study of the relationship between physique and personality variables as measured by the MMPI, *J. Pers.*, 1963, *31*, 97–107.
   Relationship is very small.

Howells, W. W., A factorial study of constitutional type, *Amer. J. Phys. Anthrop.*, 1952, *10*, 91–118.

Humphreys, L. G., Characteristics of type concepts with special reference to Sheldon's typology, *Psychol. Bull.*, 1957, *54*, 218–228.
   Several limitations in Sheldon's typology.

Janoff, I. Z., L. H. Beck, and I. L. Child, The relation of somatotype to reaction time, resistance to pain, and expressive movement, *J. Pers.*, 1950, *18*, 454–460.

Kline, N. S., and A. M. Tenney, Constitutional factors in prognosis of schizophrenia, *Amer. J. Psychiat.*, 1950, *107*, 432–441.

Kline, N. S., Constitutional factors in the prognosis of schizophrenia: further observations, *Amer. J. Psychiat.*, 1952, *108*, 909–911.

Klineberg, O., S. E. Asch, and H. Block, An experimental study of constitutional types, *Genet. Psychol. Monogr.*, 1934, *16*, No. 3, 139–221.

Lasker, G., The effects of partial starvation on somatotype, *Amer. J. Phys. Anthrop.*, 1947, *5*, 323–341.

Matte-Blanco, I., The constitutional approach to the study of human personality, *Psychiat. Res. Rep.*, 1955, No. 2, 132–154.
   Psychoanalytic concepts related to body constitution, clinically illustrated.

Naccarati, S., The morphologic aspect of intelligence, *Arch. Psychol.*, 1921, No. 45.

Newman, R. W., Age changes in body build, *Amer. J. Phys. Anthrop.*, 1952, *10*, 75–90.

Perbix, S. A., Relationships between somatotype and motor fitness in women, *Res. Quart. Amer. Ass. Hlth. Phys. Educ.*, 1954, *25*, 84–90.
   Physical education majors slightly more mesomorphic.

Seltzer, C. C., The relationship between the masculine component and personality, *Amer. J. Phys. Anthrop.*, 1943, 3, 33–47.

Seltzer, C. C., F. L. Wells, and E. B. McTernon, A relationship between Sheldonian somatotype and psychotype, *J. Pers.*, 1948, 16, 431–436.

Smith, H. C., and S. Boyarsky, The relationship between physique and simple reaction time, *Charact. and Pers.*, 1943, 12, 46–53.

Smith, H. C., Psychometric checks on hypotheses derived from Sheldon's work on physique and temperament, *J. Pers.*, 1949, 17, 310–320.

Sutherland, E. H., Critique of Sheldon's *Varieties of Delinquent Youth*, *Amer. Sociol. Rev.*, 1951, 16, 10–13.

Thurstone, L. L., Factor analysis and body types, *Psychometrika*, 1946, 11, 15–21.

Winthrop, H., The consistency of attitude patterns as a function of body type, *J. Pers.*, 1957, 25, 372–383.

5

Murray

No brain, no personality . . .

Henry A. Murray
article in *Dialectica,* Volume V, page 267

Human hopes and human creeds
Have their roots in human needs.

E. F. Ware
"Ironquill," *The Washerwoman's Song**

SOME BIOGRAPHICAL DATA

The major portion of Murray's life has been involved with the academic life in large universities, either in the eastern United States or abroad. In his roles with these universities he has been a stimulating influence upon many minds. Murray's contribution lies less in the written field than in his capacity to spark the minds of many of his students who have since become well-known names in the psychological world in their own fields. Many owe a debt to his brilliant mind. Though Murray's students have been small in number, they have been great in influence and in volume of research and writing.

Henry Alexander Murray was born on May 13, 1893, in New York City. He acquired all of his education on the eastern seaboard, graduating

* From *Some Rhymes of Ironquill,* copyright 1903 by Putnam & Co. Reprinted by permission of Putnam's & Coward-McCann.

from Harvard in 1915. In 1919, he received his doctorate in medicine from Columbia College of Physicians and Surgeons. During the following seven years he was primarily concerned with research in the areas of chemistry, biology, and of biochemistry. The climax of his professional training came in 1927 when he was awarded a Doctor of Philosophy degree in biochemistry by Cambridge University, England. Thus for approximately twelve years Murray was a student of high standing in the fields of medicine and biology.

It was during his years of European training that Murray first began to be seriously interested in the world of psychological endeavor. Much of this interest Murray attributes to a dramatic effect of the literature of Jung and especially of personal visits with Jung in Zurich. In Murray's words, "The great flood-gates of the wonder-world swung open," through his personal conversations with Jung. After that Murray was a psychologist first and other things second.

From 1927 until 1943, Murray was occupied at Harvard University in roles of ever increasing responsibility and effect. Starting as an instructor in psychology without formal training in the academic psychology of the time, he rose rapidly to become director of the newly created Harvard Psychological Clinic.

In 1943 Murray became an officer in the Army Medical Corps for the purpose of creating screening and selection methods for candidates in the Office of Strategic Services. Much depended upon the correct selection of men to do counterespionage work, and Murray and his coworkers were able to devise ingenious methods for selecting the men. The project was relatively successful. Murray was awarded the Legion of Merit for his work on this project.

Murray returned to Harvard after the war and continued to work at that institution. Dr. Murray retired during the winter of 1962 as a Professor of Clinical Psychology.

In September, 1961, at the American Psychological Association meeting in New York, Dr. Murray was awarded the APA Distinguished Scientific Contribution Award.

INTRODUCTION

If the reader wonders what kind of theory would evolve if a university professor were to construct a theory of personality, perhaps he would find that Henry A. Murray reveals the outcome. Murray has been a university professor most of his professional life with short but interesting digressions during World War II (*Assessment of Men,* Holt, Rinehart, and Winston, 1948); and prior to that, as an intern in surgery for two years; as well as work in biochemistry, practice in psychoanalysis and psychotherapy, and also four years leave of absence to work on the life of Herman Melville. As one also might expect, his theory is quite synthesistic. It incorporates the unconscious, an emphasis on the physiological, and a very great emphasis on naming things; it is always developing, it does not ignore sociological aspects of man, and it covers the full range of human behavior.

Murray's theory could very well be placed in Part IV because of its integrative emphasis. It seems, however, more apt to place his work in this section. The integration is less apparent than is the gathering together of various theoretical positions regarding man's behavior. Across-the-board synthesism seems more indicative of his work than is the integration of ideas into salient features.

Upon examination one finds some close parallels between Sheldon and Murray. Oddly enough, Murray during his medical training days once attempted a cursory study of twenty-five of his fellow medical students in an attempt to correlate anthropometric measures with behavioral traits. However, he pursued the idea no further. Murray also is widely trained and traveled, as was Sheldon, both having earned doctorates in medicine and philosophy and both having studied abroad and come under the influence of such great figures as Jung and Freud. Murray, in a very moving passage, credits Jung with the major emphasis that brought him into the field of psychological study (see What should psychologists do about psychoanalysis?, *J. Abnor. Soc. Psychol.,* 1940, 35, 53). Both men emphasized the unity of experience, but both were willing to "take man apart" in order to study his personality and then reconstruct the pieces into a unified theoretical position. In describing man's behavior Murray and Sheldon have also created long taxonomic lists, Sheldon through his Scale for Temperament and somatotyping and Murray through his needs–press–thema approach.

However, it is not the intent here to link Murray and Sheldon but to introduce Murray to the reader and to justify the inclusion of his work in the section on biophysical–biophilosophical theories of personality.

MURRAY'S DESCRIPTION OF HUMAN BEHAVIOR

Despite the device which this book uses, description–explanation–prediction, Murray strongly denies that personality can be described, especially in a diagnostic sense. To Murray, description connotes a static, immobile, fixed quality which denies the moving, changing, ever-in-flux nature of personality. Murray prefers the term *formulation* in describing personality. However, it is felt by the writer that the devices of his work in no way subverts the work of Murray, and it is hoped that the author's organization will help the reader better to understand the taxonomic nature of Murray's work by emphasizing certain of his primary concepts.

Extracting principles for the reader's edification from Murray's work is somewhat like trying to organize the dictionary into major and minor words, for Murray's penchant for taxonomy has built many terms and phrases which divide and subdivide man's behavior into multiple facets. Once again, as in all the theorists presented here (none of whom created principles *per se*), the salient features of Murray's work have been extracted and labeled *principles* so as to provide a better look at the theory and how it describes man's personality.

Regnancy Principle

At the beginning of this chapter is a noteworthy quotation from an article of Murray's: "No brain, no personality." This theme runs throughout his writings from the earliest to the most current. Fundamentally he is speaking of the basic function of the physiological process which governs and prescribes what the personality can do, but in this section we shall interpret this concept to include also the brain as an administrator of all that the personality does. Thus the brain, and only the brain, gives unity to the behavior of man. The brain is an organic entity, but it must be considered beyond its function as a physiological process of the body. The brain with its most complex and adaptive functions is also the seat of the personality. We must carry some of our interpretations beyond the realm of operant behavior stemming from the locus of the brain.

The question becomes intriguing, for example, if we consider quality. Let us extend and interpret the point involved to consider the differences we might find between the imbecilic and the highly gifted brain. One cannot at this juncture equate Murray's statement with intellectual ability, although that seems a neat and comfortable thing to do. Dr. Murray said to me, " 'No brain' does not mean 'no brains' (no intelligence). It means 'no organ in the cranial capacity', a commonplace to stress the location of processes of personality." Rather we must consider the differences between one brain and the other in all its capacities to adjust and solve problems. Thus the brain of limited ability has less a personality than the brain of high adaptability and power. We may even ponder the statement that "No brain" in the sense that the lowest idiot would beget such a marginal personality would seem no personality at all. Were one to observe the idiot in a number of conditions calling for response of some kind by the personality (brain), he would perforce agree that "No brain, no personality" appears as a fruitful contribution to the world of personality study. Again it must be emphasized that quality of brain is *not* concomitant with intelligence as measured by the usual intelligence test. What is connoted is the aptitudinal approach: that the brain with the greatest amount of skill in many areas is the brain likely to be adjoined to the best personality. Interpretations such as the above immediately bring forth the rebuttal that "brainy" people many times are duds in life situations. Therefore, "No brain, no personality" is a false concept. Again, what is meant is total brain strength, not popularity. The wider, the stronger, the more penetrating, the more adaptable, and the more spontaneous the brain is in handling problems which arise in *all* functions of life, the greater the personality. This is but one interpretation that can be deduced from Murray's statement, "No brain, no personality."

Two other points which are less interpretive of Murray's words must also be considered: the interdependence of physiological and neurological processes and the factor of constitutional types somewhat as Sheldon approached them. To Murray any ongoing behavioral process must have in the brain an ongoing neural excitation which has hierarchical dimensions. It is the brain which "rules," or is regnant of the needs and demands of the moment. The demands may be mainly organic (hunger), mainly symbolic (reading), or may be any of the multiple combinations of both (continuing to read an assignment although the reader is quite bothered by a taste and hunger for some food). Again it is the brain which rules and makes the decisions regarding the subsequent action to be taken. The hierarchy of alternative actions to be taken is determined by the brain. These single units of experience come so rapidly and in such uninterrupted succession that a regnancy is considered to be in multiples. A single unit happens so quickly as to defy examination. We shall see more of this in the future study of serials.

Also involved in regnancy as a concept of personality and its behavior is Murray's acceptance of constitutional types as having differing modes of regnancy in responding to situations. This concept has not been spelled out in his writings, but it is fundamental in much of his description of the regnant process.

In summary, all behavioral processes of a strictly organic type, or of a psychological nature, or both, are processes of a functioning brain. One final word: a regnant process may be conscious or unconscious. We shall deal with Murray's concept of the unconscious in a further section.

Motivation Principle

Perhaps the most important feature of Murray's theory is his intense interest and development of motivation and how it affects human behavior. Above all Murray is a motivational psychologist, by which one means a psychologist who studies the *direction* of man's endeavors in the mental, physical, or verbal realm. As we shall see, his taxonomic bent is given full rein in the development of this aspect of his theory. Murray has not, as yet, taken the one step back, to study where the motivation originates. In his system the "motivator" is met as if it came full blown into man's existence.

Within the concept of motivation principle we shall deal with five components of his system: 1. tension reduction, 2. needs, 3. press, 4. vector–value, 5. thema.

Tension Reduction. Like many other theorists Murray does not consider man to be living in a tensionless state, but both biologically and psychologically Murray finds room for tension reduction. Homeostasis (maintaining an equilibrium between body states) is a true biological phenomenon, and Murray uses it in his theory to explain his first position in regard to tension reduction. Man desires to avoid pain and get pleasure as a mode of existence; therefore, hunger states, organic disunity, and all other biological conditions of imbalance man desires to correct that he may return to a state of no tension or no pain. Thus, as he is hungry, he eats food and dissipates the feeling of discomfort that comes from hunger. This is, incidentally, the position of Freud and, of course, others. But, to Murray the organic homestatic state is but half of the picture describing tension reduction states. From the subsequent section on needs, presses, etc., we shall see that neither does man care for a *completely* tensionless state. As a completely tensionless organism, man would progress not at all. Thus, Murray feels that while homeostasis of the organism leads to conservation of its properties, it in no way brings the organisms to construct anything. Homeostasis alone leads to a vegetablelike existence. Man is, then, possessed by the "divine discontent." He feels that progress is a natural state of existence. The desire for better living, more material property, and all of the motivations for going beyond the present state of existence are also of major importance in reducing tension.

To the formula of tension ⸺→ reduction of tension, which he would refer to as the traditional homeostatic condition of man, Murray adds the valuable concept that is expressed in the formula: *generation* of tension ⸺→ reduction of tension. Man has a need for positive thrust, for excitement, for movement even though it may not evolve into forward progress and success, for zest, appetite, and desire for being with his fellowmen. The constructive need-systems lead to advancement in the total scene of life, while the conservative need-systems lead to maintaining the status quo of our existence.

We may now consider the avenues by which man is motivated. In his theoretical system, tension reduction, need, press, and the other factors in the motivational scheme are not independent of each other but are highly coordinated complexes which become inseparable in action. It is only in the studying of these phenomena that we are able to pull them apart for more intensive understanding of their importance.

Need. By a very close scrutiny of a small number of subjects and by his intensive study of their needs Murray has developed a rather involved taxonomy of *needs*. Much of his need theory emerged early in the total construction of the theory. Although he has since redeveloped and reemphasized the fundamental concept of need in his theory, probably still the best source for his rationale is his first major text, *Explorations in Personality*, which he published in 1938.

Criteria: In studying the need structure of man, Murray found that he required criteria in order to establish that a need existed. This was, of course, an inference on his part because he was not studying his own needs via introspection but was attempting to study and later to classify the needs of his subjects. The criteria he established were as follows: 1. response to a particular object or to a series of like objects which seemed to serve as stimuli; 2. kind of behavior involved; 3. consequences or end result of that behavior; 4. amount and kind of emotional response connected with the behavior; 5. amount of satisfaction or dissatisfaction when the total response is achieved. Having thus established the necessary criteria for recognizing a need in others, Murray also provided a definition for need. Defining terms is a task not very often done by theorists of personality, as we have stated in Chapter 1.

Definition: Inherent in Murray's definition are at least six major points, accompanied by corollary actions (from *Explorations in Personality,* 1938, p. 123).

1. "A need is a construct," i.e., a term made by man,
2. "which stands for a force," i.e., there is power and strength within the person,
3. "in the brain region," i.e., the regnancy idea that personality stems from the brain,
4. "which organizes . . . action," i.e., it is more than just haphazard activity
5. "so as to transform in a certain direction," i.e., the person is going to be different as the result of a need,
6. "an existing, unsatisfying situation," i.e., need grows out of dissatisfaction to lead to a goal of satisfaction.

Corollaries on a minor level are as follows:

1. The need may be "provoked by internal processes" or "more frequently by . . . environmental forces."
2. "Need is accompanied by a particular feeling or emotion."
3. "It may be weak or intense."
4. It may be "momentary or enduring."
5. It "usually persists and gives rise to a certain course of overt behavior or fantasy."

Number: With the criteria that Murray set up, and with his definition and its major and minor factors in mind, we may study the taxonomic efforts of Murray as he considered the number and types of needs that motivates man. The present list has been modified in his later work and also modified by others interested in his theoretical concepts of need. The original list of twenty terms holds the basic components of Murray's need concept.

The needs are listed in alphabetical order (as adopted from Murray's *Explorations in Personality*, 1938, pp. 152–226); Murray originally gave no emphasis or priority for one need over the other as man uses them.

1. abasement: be resigned to fate; seek and enjoy pain, illness, misfortune; blame or belittle self; confess and atone; surrender, admit inferiority.

2. achievement: overcome obstacles; rival and surpass others; accomplish something difficult; master, manipulate or organize physical objects, human beings, or ideas; increase self-regard by successful exercise of talent.

3. affiliation: please and win affection; approach, enjoy, and reciprocate with like persons; adhere and remain loyal to a friend.

4. aggression: overcome opposition forcefully; oppose forcefully or punish another; revenge an injury.

5. autonomy: avoid or quit activities prescribed by domineering authorities; resist coercion and restriction; be independent and free to act according to impulse; defy convention.

6. counteraction: overcome weakness; repress fear; efface a dishonor by action; maintain self-respect and pride on a high level; search for obstacles and difficulties to overcome.

7. defendance: defend the self against assault, criticism and blame; vindicate the ego.

8. deference: emulate an exemplar; conform to custom; admire and support a superior.

9. dominance: influence or direct the behavior of others by suggestion, seduction, persuasion, or command; control one's human environment.

10. exhibition: make an impression; be seen and heard.

11. harmavoidance: take precautionary measures; escape from a dangerous situation; avoid pain, physical injury, illness, and death.

12. infavoidance: refrain from action because of the fear of failure; avoid humiliation.

13. nurturance: give sympathy and gratify the needs of a helpless object; assist an object in danger; feed or help or support or console or protect or comfort or nurse or heal others.

14. order: achieve cleanliness, arrangement, organization, balance, neatness, tidiness, and precision.

15. play:	seek enjoyable relaxation of stress; act for "fun" without further purpose.
16. rejection:	exclude, abandon, expel, or remain indifferent to an inferior object.
17. sentience:	seek and enjoy sensuous impressions.
18. sex:	form and further an erotic relationship; have sexual intercourse.
19. succorance:	remain close to a devoted protector; always have a supporter; have one's needs gratified by the sympathetic aid of an allied object.
20. understanding:	be interested in theory; speculate, formulate, analyse, and generalize.

As man is motivated by the needs we have seen, he uses them in accordance with certain methodology. Some of the ways in which man considers and uses the needs are discussed below.

Prepotency—When two or more needs demand satisfaction at the same time by the same person, a priority for action must occur. Some needs are of more urgent character, or, as Murray states, there is a prepotency factor inherent in the need itself which mandates that it receive first attention by the subject. Hunger, for example, in extreme cases, which is a primary or viscerogenic need, has a built-in prepotency which allows it to be satisfied before such a need as play. Thus, there is an hierarchy of needs, and the level is ordered less by the subject than by the need itself.

Fusion—Not all needs contradict themselves or come into conflict. Needs which are complementary become fused as motivating devices. Although the needs themselves are not identical, they may be satisfied by a single course of action. Thus, one may satisfy his need for protection and dominance by the same course of action. It is the behavior which is fused although the two needs are not similar in basic character.

Subsidiation—Some needs may be met only through the steps of meeting the demands of lesser but necessary waystep needs. For example, to meet the need for achievement one may first have to meet the need for deference. The college student may wish to achieve a certain degree of success on his campus. In order to achieve achievement he must also as a step along the way exercise deference by adopting and conforming to the customs of the local campus in his manners, speech, forms of recreation, and general demeanor.

Conflict—The last special consideration of the list of needs is the obvious fact that needs may often be in conflict. As we have seen, man is a tension-reducing animal. When he comes upon two, or possibly three, needs which conflict with each other, he produces tension. Murray feels that if one is to know more about the human being, he must know specifically what needs the person has that are in direct conflict. This idea resembles the Freudian polarity or duality principle. Most often conflict needs are dichotomized, with only two being involved, and no third or fourth needs in chainlike conflict. Such a complex of more than two conflicting characters is not at present under discussion.

Murray feels that not all of the twenty needs listed are present in all people. Some of us may never experience certain of these needs in our lifetimes, while others of us may run the gamut of the entire list and do so in a relatively short period of days or weeks. Still others of us may have favorite needs to which we pay attention rather constantly, employing other needs only occasionally. To understand how we use these needs one may find the following section useful.

Types—There is a distinction between the needs man uses according to Murray. These distinctions are listed under five different types of needs:

> primary and secondary,
> proactive and reactive,
> overt and covert,
> focal and diffuse,
> effect and modal—with process activity.

Oddly enough, types of needs, as Murray deals with them, seem to be dichotomized, and one wonders what effect the Freudian duality principle has had upon the typology which deals with apposites.

Primary and secondary types of needs—The primary needs of man, sometimes called the *viscerogenic needs,* are those of an organic–biologic nature such as food, water, air, elimination of bodily wastes, and, as Murray feels, the sexual needs of man, which are primarily organic in nature for both sexes.

In apposition to the primary needs are the secondary or *psychogenic needs* which come from the basis of the primary needs but in a diffuse and indirect manner. Many of the needs listed would be properly considered as secondary needs; for example, achievement, affiliation. These needs are not to be considered as unimportant because they are called secondary. The term refers rather to states of development. Primary needs develop first, followed by the secondary or psychogenic needs. The latter, as we shall see, may become quite important and even take precedence over the primary, or organic, needs in times of great stress. The nomenclature refers, then, to sequence rather than to dominance.

Proactive and reactive types of needs—Once again the word *apposites* describes Murray's need types as they, the terms, are not distinctly in opposition to each other, but exist in an interrelated, side-by-side relationship.

In some sense this distinction between types of needs seems redundant to the primary–secondary classification since the proactive need means that need which originates within the person, while the reactive need means that which originates outside of the person. Acting under the proactive need the person merely reacts to the stimulus. However, Murray is speaking here of relationships between people and not just processes. Thus, in dealing with a group of two or more people, the individual may begin the action of the group through some need within himself. If he does, then this is the proactive need which is being met. On the other hand there is the need of the proactor for someone to react to his stimulus, which situation Murray called the *reactive need*. Both needs are intricately interwoven with each other, in something of a cause–effect relationship. In clapping hands one cannot produce an effect with only one component, i.e., with only one hand.

Overt and covert types of needs—Again referring to the list of needs, we find that some needs can be openly expressed. Society will sanction them and even give prizes of one kind or another for successfully meeting these needs. Such needs would be called the overt or open, needs. They are openly expressed and openly met. Examples are achievement, defendance, and counteraction. A study of the list of needs also brings out those which must be fantasized or dealt with in a dream stage or obtained through devious means. These are called the covert, or secret, hidden, needs. Examples (depending upon the society in which one were operating) might be aggression, sentience, and succorance. To meet these needs, one might perforce be quite secretive about his activities or achieve the need fulfillment through day dreaming.

Focal and diffuse types of needs—As we shall see in a later section which considers Murray's longitudinal principles with their proceedings and serials, there are types of needs which can be satisfactorily met by closeness to an environmental object. These needs are *focal*. The focal needs can be met by only one object, or, in a few cases, by very few objects. Thus, in the need for deference one might want only to admire and support one person. This is a focal need. On the other hand in the need for harmavoidance he wishes and needs to avoid *all* kinds of pain. Pain has a universal quality of hurt that everyone wishes to avoid. True, one may construct a high and low order of pain-reducing stimuli, but past a certain point of excitation, pain is pain and our subject needs to avoid all of it. A toothache in full, throbbing state brings the need of harmavoidance. At the moment, it might seem that a burned finger would be much the easier pain to bear, but once the burned finger were to hurt, it would have the value of the aching tooth. One has the diffuse need to avoid pain, be it in any part of his body or even in his societal contacts.

Effect and modal types of needs—The fifth and last type of need that Murray outlined is called *effect* and *modal*. An effect need is one that leads to a direct and identifiable goal object. In an automobile trip we have the need to arrive at a definite goal. We depart from one place and drive in the most direct and practicable route to our destination. There is a direct need involved. In the process of driving, however, Murray acknowledges the joy of manipulating the automobile. The sheer pleasure of physically operating the car is what he called a *process activity*. Murray calls this the *sheer function pleasure*. Out of this grows the need to function with a high degree of excellence. The expert manner in which we operate the automobile goes beyond the pleasure of operating it, and this is what Murray called the *modal need*. In short, the mode of operation in which we satisfy need may be as important as the goal we strive for.

Press.   Still within the concept of motivation principle, we find Murray's corollary term of *press*, which he applied to the external factors of man's life. The term *press*, which applies to an object or to a person, means that attribute which either gets in the way of or aids a person in satisfying his needs. It presses him into one form of action or another. *Press potency* is "what can be done ' . . . to the subject or for the subject—the power it has to affect the well-being of the subject in one way or another' " (*Explorations in Personality*, p. 121). The press comes from the environment, while the need comes from within the person.

A typical list of press concepts follows. The press itself is of no value in an understanding of the personality of the subject. The subject's subjective view and impression of the press makes it significant in further understanding the human personality.

Murray, in *Explorations in Personality*, presents long lists of press terms which he has evolved from working with a selected group of subjects. The terms may be applicable to an explanation of the dynamics of behavior for an individual through techniques Murray has developed, or may, as well, give a measure of the relative importance or quantitative characteristics in the study of an individual:

1. **p** Family insupport
    a. Cultural discord
    b. Family discord
    c. Capricious discipline
    d. Parental separation
    e. Absence of parent:
        Father
        Mother
    f. Parental illness:
        Father
        Mother
    g. Death of parent:
        Father
        Mother
    h. Inferior parent:
        Father
        Mother
    i. Dissimilar parent:
        Father
        Mother
    j. Poverty
    k. Unsettled home
2. **p** Danger or Misfortune
    a. Physical insupport, Height
    b. Water
    c. Aloneness, darkness
    d. Inclement weather, Lightning
    e. Fire
    f. Accident
    g. Animal
3. **p** Lack or Loss
    a. of Nourishment
    b. of Possessions
    c. of Companionship
    d. of Variety

4. **p** Retention, Withholding Objects
5. **p** Rejection, Unconcern and Scorn
6. **p** Rival, competing contemporary
7. **p** Birth of sibling
8. **p** Aggression
    a. Maltreatment by elder male, Elder female
    b. Maltreatment by contemporaries
    c. Quarrelsome contemporaries
9. **Fp** Aggression–Dominance, Punishment
10. **p** Dominance, coercion and prohibition
11. **Fp** Dominance–nurturance
    a. Parental Ego idealism:
        Mother
        Father
        Physical
        Econ, Vocation
        Caste
        Intellectual
    b. Possessive parent:
        Mother
        Father
    c. Oversolicitous parent
        Fears: accident-illness-bad influences.

Murray shows two ways for considering the press quality of persons or objects: *Alpha press* is the objective and real characteristic of the press. In this there is no distortion or subjective interpretation of the press. It is what the outside observer not involved in the ramifications of the press object would consider it to be. *Beta press* is the subjective personal interpretation the individual makes of those objects which influence him. Obviously his behavior is most influenced by the beta aspect of the press since that is what he sees and feels and responds to. There may be, of course, a wide disparity between the alpha and beta aspects of the same press concept.

In addition to alpha and beta aspects of press Murray describes the capacity of the press object to attract or repel the individual, using Freud's term *cathexis* for this. Cathexis may be described as the emotional charge which can attract or repel and which is within the object itself. Contrary to this is the sentiment of the person toward the press object, the sentiment being, according to Murray, negative or positive, short or long term but usually long term, and always conditioned by the capacity within the person rather than within the object.

Vector–Value.   Murray as well as many others interested in his theoretical work have been aware of the inadequacy of the need concept to explain fundamentally why man behaves as he does. The need, according to some observers of his theoretical system, seems to appear full blown and with little to help one understand where it comes from. The significance of what need does is what Murray has most adequately dealt with, according to these observers. What is lacking is the origins of these needs. As has been stated, Murray is aware of this problem. The lack is not a weakness in his theory but rather a sign that his is a developing theory, with the aspect of primary and original sources as yet undeveloped. To complete the picture, Murray has in writings subsequent to his original thesis of 1938 (*Explorations in Personality*), expanded the need–press idea to include the vector–value theme.

The word *vector* has long had psychological respectability, especially in the work of Lewin (see Chapter 14). Murray uses this term, which means *a force going in a defined direction.* The force may be weak or strong. The direction is prescribed by the other variables which impinge on the one vector force. Although the term is probably most widely used in the field of statistics, it has been used by others than Murray to connote an emotional charge directed toward some given object. *Value* bears the usual meaning: that of "the worth or price or power inherent in an article," a price which is determined by man. That is, the article has the value but does not declare its own value: man sets the price.

Again preoccupied with taxonomic efforts to better understand man, Murray has begun to create a list of values and vectors which he feels help us to understand the need concept and in totality the entire motivational life of man.

The basis (values) for man's needs which help bring about the direction and strength of desire (vector) that he will utilize to achieve tension reduction and to explain his motivational existence *in toto* are incoporated in a matrix which Murray hopes to use further in laboratory work and experimentation.

In addition to the above reason for the use of value–vector (to get deeper into fundamental causes) Murray is primarily interested in the *interaction* between factors which create behavior patterns in man. Thus, if a man has a need to do a certain thing, he will, or can be expected to, behave in a somewhat circumscribed way. In practice this interactional study of behavior is beginning to emerge from Murray's laboratory work. As yet it is not refined.[1]

What follows is his tentative list of vectors and values as he has worked them out to date:

Vectors (how you do it, activity, etc.)	Value (why you do it, worthwhileness, etc.)
acquisition	aesthetic value
avoidance	affiliation
conservation	authority
construction	body
defendance	ideology
destruction	knowledge
expression	property
expulsion	
reception	
rejection	
transmission	

Thema. One further idea remains to be presented in Murray's motiva-

[1] The interested reader will find this emerging concept of Murray's in the periodical, *Dialectica*, 1951, 5, pp. 266–292. The use of value–vector is more a technical method in studying personalities than a basic tenet of Murray. Hence it is not presented here in its entirety.

tional principle. The idea of *thema* refers to the totality of the sequence from press to need. This may be a simple one-to-one relationship: a singular press which leads to a singular need. Murray finds, however, that the theme, or plot, or sequence, of presses and needs is chiefly plural. Thus, one may discover themes which are in serial order. One may lead to another which leads still to another, all of them of a complex nature. *Thema* is Murray's method of handling more than one need press relationship but not in as direct a manner as he has attempted recently with the value–vector method, which he feels is more definite in ordering behavior along dynamic and descriptive lines.

Thus we find the major components of the principles which underlie motivation, according to Murray, to be tension reduction, needs, press, vector–value, and thema.

Longitudinal Principle

Although short in length this is also one of the primary components of Murray's theory of personality. In Murray's frequently quoted passage, "the history of the personality *is* the personality," we have the key thought to the longitudinal principle. Like many psychoanalysts, Murray believes that the "child is father to the man," but not perhaps in the inflexible way that many of the neo-Freudian analysts have interpreted the statement. (See Freud—Summary, Chapter 3.) Murray feels with many other personality theorists that much of what man does is recurrent and that many of his behavior patterns are enduring. Man operates out of habits he forms as he goes along in life. Expressed in still another way, man's life consists of a series of events which he follows from day to day. With the statement, "The trouble with life is that it is so daily," Murray would agree and would add that if one is to study what a person is and how he became that way, he must examine past daily experiences. Murray feels that the ideal case study would begin at birth and include all of an individual's experiences up to the present moment of study.

Complexes. As part of the study of the development of man, Murray has paid strong attention to the erotogenic zones emphasized by Freud; Murray, however, considers them in a somewhat different rationale from Freud. Taking them as complexes to be adjusted to and worked through, Murray finds five of these complexes to operate in the developmental process of man. He describes them as enjoyable conditions, all of which are roughly and rudely interrupted by external forces beyond the control of the child. The first is the feeling of safety and dependent existence within the womb, a state which is rudely interrupted by the act of birth. The second is the sucking activity as food is ingested from the mother's breast or the bottle, with all that accompanies this process in the warm and loving ministrations of the mother or nurse; this labial pleasure, too, is halted by the adults' persistent efforts to wean the child. The third is the exercising of the anal muscles in the free and pleasurable sensation of defecation and consequent release of visceral pressure. As everyone is aware, this pleasure is also delimited by persistent toilet training. The fourth pleasant sensation is that of urination which also comes within the same pleasure sense and curbing sense as defecation. The fifth complex of pleasure which the child enjoys, and which is denied him, is the genital friction of the penis or vagina, with much the same explanation from Murray that Freud gave to the phallic period of development. Murray names the complexes in order: *claustral*—passive feeling of warmth and protection in the womb; *oral*—enjoyment of taking in food; *anal*—the pleasure of bowel and tension release with concomitant pleasure of the exercise of sphincteral muscles; *urethral*—the feeling corresponding to the anal complex, and castration, which he expands beyond the Freud-ian approach. All of these complexes play a large part in the longitudinal development of the child, as he is denied each of these pleasures by society for reasons which he may not support.

Those developmental aspects which revolve around the erogenous zones Murray has evolved and expanded beyond the work of Freud, or some of the neo-Freudians like Rank, into a rich and meaningful description which can be found in his first major work on personality, *Explorations in Personality*. Much of what he wrote then still has a strong influence on his present work in evaluation of personality. The entire longitudinal work of Murray gives much emphasis to his thesis that the child is father to the man and that those who would study the personality at any given period must perforce study the background of the individual, a thesis which is not unpopular with most of the current personality theorists.

Proceedings and Serials. In addition to the infantile complexes in-troduced in the previous section, Murray has added to the longitudinal picture of man the concept of *serials* and *proceedings*. He uses the term *proceedings* to indicate that man is forever moving in his life, that man is dynamic and not static, that whatever man does must be considered in a sequence of actions. Proceedings, therefore, are those activities of man by which he interacts with another object (an automobile that refuses to start, for example) or with another human being (asking a girl for a date). Both examples indicate an interaction between the subject (man) and an object (car) or another subject (girl). Proceedings help Murray to cast man in a time sequence rather than in a frozen, snapshot description of his behavior.

Proceedings may be internalized: the subject reasons through a problem within his own mind; or externalized: the subject talks with a companion, sells an article, or engages in any other external activity in which overt action takes place.

Proceedings may also be of short or long duration. Short proceedings are exemplified by a momentary conversation or an activity such as a social gathering of an evening's length. The *durance* (the term Murray uses of a proceeding longer than a conversation) may be illustrated by an individual's service in the armed forces, a four-year college period, the total event of being a teen-ager, and the like.

In addition to interior–exterior and length aspects of proceedings, Murray also recently has presented the possibility that proceedings may conflict, or more accurately overlap, in their functions. Mealtime for a husband or wife who also function as the mother or father of a small child is an excellent example of overlapping proceedings. While they are eating and attempting to talk to each other, the child may be demanding immediate and continual attention. Thus the proceeding is both overlapping and conflicting for the parents.

Serials are, in a sense, the accumulated proceedings of man with the additional provision that a serial has a history behind it; it has a goal of finite or indefinite characteristic to be met; in other words, the entire serial is purposive. The three aspects of a serial are ordination, programs, and schedules. By *ordination* is meant the establishment of programs and schedules in an hierarchical form to give greater or less importance to them. Hence a priority or order is given to the establishing of serial activity. *Programs* are the attempts of man to create subgoals which help him to arrive eventually at the total goal. *Schedules* help him to avoid or at least to minimize conflicting programs. In effect, all three aspects of serials are tightly interwoven in many of man's activities, and cannot be considered apart from each other. For example, the student who wishes to make his living eventually as a medical doctor is in the process of creating a serial. Through the process of ordination, he selects an undergraduate course of studies designed toward obtaining admission to a medical school. In doing this he must bear in mind the type and location of the medical school he hopes to enter. At this point, he considers the past in relation to what he must do at the present in order to regulate the future. Having once made an orderly serial of activities for himself, the student must follow a program which is designed to bring about the desired end. He thus studies a program of courses and arranges subgoals within the major goal structure. As he proceeds in his program, he will quite likely encounter conflicts such as lack of money, or a deep interest in getting married. He might then, via the schedules he creates or which have been created for him by outside pressures, decide to drop from school until he has accumulated enough money to continue his premedical education. Or he might make the decision and schedule events so that he does or does not get married as a result of his need–press–thema demands. If he gets married, he brings certain consequences and changes to his life. If he decides against marriage, that decision minimizes the schedule changes he must make toward fulfilling his total goal structure.

In all, the entire aspect of the longitudinal principles of man's life are of utmost importance to the basic cloth of Murray's system.

Physiological Processes Principle

Deeply imbedded in Murray's entire theoretical scheme is the dedication to the idea that man is an animal and controlled and motivated by animal needs. This is not intended to mean that man is coarse or rough or crude in his behavior but that man is foremost a biologically functioning organism. His need structure is founded first upon his physiological appetites. After these are met, he becomes more than an existing organism: he becomes a societal creature.

First, it is necessary to repeat the primary or viscerogenic needs that Murray found essential to the motivational structure of man. Why does man do the things he does? Much of the answer to this question, for Murray, is found in the fact that man is an organic entity. He does what he does for air, water, food, eliminative pressures, etc.

Second, we find that in some of his definitions for personality is this statement concerning man's organic self: "Personality may be biologically defined as the governing organ, or superordinate institution of the body. As such it is located in the brain." (*Dialectica*, 1951, 5, p. 267.)

Third, his entire concept of tension reduction is predicated in the organic, biological field.

Fourth, the idea of priority of needs and a hierarchy of motivators is spelled out in his concept of prepotency, as discussed earlier in this chapter.

Fifth, there is, in the contribution of the regnant processes principle, the basic foundation that the physiological and neurological processes are first. Stated in other terms: there is no personality if the fundamental stuff which makes up personality is reduced or affected in some way. In its widest application of the term *regnant processes* the idiot, the person existing in complete coma, or the deceased have no personality.

Finally, Murray does not deny in any of his writings, and even openly supports at times, the value of Sheldonian approach. Murray feels that one's constitutional type may indeed have much to do with the formation and future functioning of his total personality. For to Murray, a synthesistically oriented theorist, it is ill advised to deny another theory that may be valuable in helping to explain man's diffuse nature.

Abstract Principle

Murray has been heavily influenced by the psychoanalytically oriented theorists, but in an unorthodoxy of his own he has created, in some respects, a parallel system; in other respects a contradictory system. Equally as basic to Murray's system as the physiological processes is the undertone of the unconscious operating. Personality is of an abstract nature just as much as it is of an observable organic nature. Murray first recognized the defense mechanisms of repression and reaction formation in 1938, some time before it was fashionable for orthodox psychologists to maintain a position of acceptance towards Freud's psychoanalytic theories of personality. Although some clinicians had accepted and used his therapeutic techniques as the *modus operandi* of their work, the background of Freud's theory as it applied to personality dynamics was not as readily accepted. Murray accepted it as meaningful, and he further incorporated it into his own system of personality theory.

Roughly two areas of acceptance can be found in Murray's use of psychoanalytic theory: the levels of unconscious, preconscious, conscious and a deep and elaborated acceptance of the id–ego–superego structure of personality.

In a magazine article published in 1936 (Basic Concepts for a Psychology of Personality, *J. Gen. Psychol.*, 1936, *15*, 241–268), Murray acknowledged that all of man's behavior is *not* on the surface. At that time, he was uncertain (and in good professional company) as to where the unconscious determinants of personality lie within the lower regions of man's unseen behavior, but he was nonetheless convinced that the regnant processes are not all in man's awareness. Thus an individual may not only be a mystery to others, but he may also be a mystery to himself because he cannot find logical reasons for his own behavior. The claustral, oral, anal, urethral, and castration complexes mentioned earlier are based on the abstract nature of man. Murray further accepted the idea that man as a being with hidden motives and unconscious drives and needs is man in the natural state, and not a deviant explanation of man founded on psychotic behavior. All men operate partially under unconscious motivators.

In extending the abstract nature of man, Murray uses the Freudian *id, ego,* and *superego* concepts but introduces refinements of his own. Murray's chief departure from the Freudian id is to give it the capacity for good as well as for evil. Man's id motivation can as well be acceptable to the child, as he develops, as it can be to his parents and society. The energy, ebullience, and playfulness which a child displays and that both please himself and endear him to his parents all come out of the id structure, an id structure which also creates in him the undesirable and unacceptable behaviorisms which disturb the self and the exterior world. Murray further feels that the id content differs in humans. One person has a larger id than does another person, and, because of this, his problems, and strengths for energizing action are greater. How an individual adjusts to life is partially determined by the amount of id he has to motivate him and that he likewise has to learn to control. The smaller the id, then, the less the person can accomplish. The larger the id the more he may accomplish providing he is able to channel the id strength into acceptable goals.

The ego is also considered to be more than a police force which forever controls the raw id impulses. Murray feels that the ego as it organizes, tests, and seeks opportunities for id expression can and does find exhilaration from goals which self and society approve. Rather than cast the ego in an ever-repressant role, Murray chooses to consider the ego as a wise and many times benevolent administrator. With id strength behind it, the ego creates as much pleasure for the id as it represses pleasure for the id. In essence, Murray's contribution to psychoanalytic theory (not unlike that of other neo-Freudians) is more encouraging than depressing.

In addition to the regular concept of the superego as a conscience system imposed by parents and figures of authority for the child, Murray feels that symbolic figures from literature and other forms of nonhuman contact are equally affective in creating the superego structure for the child. In addition to this are the child's friends and acquaintances who can and do help to create the superego for each other. Parallel to the superego, Murray feels, is the ego-ideal which is Murray's device for adding a goal for the superego. The superego does not try merely to adjust to society in a day-to-day way but it also has long-time goals to strive for. It is man's way of arriving "at his future best."

It can be seen then that Murray is guided by a principle that man is an abstract entity not entirely controlled by surface phenomena but much motivated by inner dynamics, dynamics not always understood by himself or by the society in which he operates.

Uniqueness Principle

Briefly stated, Murray feels that each human being is an individual like no other human being who ever was or who could ever be. His strong conviction of the individuality of man is highly accepted by most current personality theorists. This conviction of Murray's is a foundation stone to much of the research he has done. He prefers to work intensively with small groups in order best to discover the complex and different nature of each subject in the study.

In addition to the uniqueness principle and as part of it, Murray has paid strong attention to the varying aptitudes and achievements of his subjects in research. He feels a strong disposition toward the aptitudinal picture of man's intellectual, physical, and social abilities. Murray supports the contention that man has not one area of general ability in the Spearman sense but that he is composed of abilities such as physical agility, memory factors, spatial factors, and the like.

Role Concept Principle

The last of the principles which we shall attribute to Murray (though certainly others not as central as those mentioned could be extracted) is man's need to assume a role in society. He speaks of this need to achieve status and definition in the society in which he operates as a necessary component of man's existence. It is further necessary for an individual to be able to define all the roles he is placed in, and in some sense to be able to accept at least most of the roleship requirements as his society defines them.

Murray has continued to rethink and bring forward his theory, as this statement indicates (personal communication, April 4, 1962):

The emphasis on need is OK, but without the idea of cathexis one doesn't arrive at a formulation of the particular aims towards which the needs are oriented. I think at the time *Explorations* was written I was stressing needs, any one of which might manifest itself in a great variety of ways. But now I am more inclined to put the emphasis on aim (or goal) which may serve as a fulfilment of several needs. An individual is usually aware of his aim but not of all the needs that might be satisfied by the realization of that aim. Also, the means or mode of progress towards the aim is a decisive component of the individual's endeavor.

EXPLAINING HUMAN BEHAVIOR VIA MURRAY'S PERSONOLOGY THEORY[2]

Henry A. Murray's theory, which he called *personology*, lends itself well to the format of this book as it attempts to explain why man does the things he does. Part of the strength of Murray's work in this kind of application lies in the breadth of his theory. Murray is essentially a synthesist. He has tried to bring some order into what can be described as a loose and amorphous direction of effort. With his penchant for organizing and highlighting data under a taxonomic system, Murray produces work which is useful in the effort to explain man's behavior.

In application, one weakness of the present work emerges. The need concept of Murray's is so convenient and meaningful that one is tempted to overuse it and to overexplain man's behavior, using only this portion of his theory. The following text suffers from this overemphasis.

Marriage

As marriage is a unique relationship between two people, we may assume that Murray's list of needs would explain marriage through the need for affiliation (please and win affection) and possibly in some cases through the need of deference (conform to custom). It is quite possible that one of the marriage partners has the need for dominance and thus seeks a partner less strong and hence submissive to his will. We may also find persons whose need for nurturing (to assist, feed, help) could motivate a marriage. The need for sensuous expressions, the need for sex (form and further an erotic relationship), and the need for succor (remain

[2] See Chapter 3 on Freud for criteria.

close to a devoted protector) could all help to explain marriage. It is hard to single out any one need factor as primary by means of Murray's system. This is to be expected, for Murray explains that men are complex and unique, and therefore there can be no universal explanation for marriage. In addition, one individual may be using all of the above reasons either as he decides to become engaged and then married or as his marriage proceeds through the years. As it does, one need may become more important as others lose their motivating power. This explanation would be covered by Murray's qualifiers in the need structure: prepotency, fusion, proactive–reactive, and subsidiation factors, for example.

Equally important in the explanation of man marrying are his press factors (external forces) such as affiliation, friendships, and sex. Since the needs–press concept is like the mirror image of the other, the ensuing explanations will emphasize the needs concept at the expense of the press concepts. Each being complementary to the other, redundancy may be avoided and understanding brought into sharper focus by emphasizing only the needs while yet understanding that the press is equally present and effective.

Perversions

First basing the practice of perverted acts upon Murray's adaption of the Freudian erogenous zones in the development of the child (see Longitudinal Principles, complexes)—in that these areas are conditioned as pleasure-producing zones only to be made restricted in use by others—we further find the needs for abasement (seek and enjoy pain), aggression (oppose forcefully or punish another), dominance (influence or direct behavior of others by seduction), play (act for fun without further purpose), sentience, and sex, all or some of them operating in a perverted act. Conflict and fusion may be present as the perverted individual attempts to fulfill needs which run counter to society's and his own acceptance of behavior.

Suicide

The need for abasement (surrender) may be operating here within a true conflict situation. On the other hand, the failure to satisfy almost all of the other needs is as potent in producing a suicide as is the need for abasement. The latter may be only the triggering device, set off by rank failure in the more positive aspects of need.

Lawbreaking

Let us assume, as an example, that an individual has just committed the crime of entering and unlawfully removing property from a home—in short, burglary. Why did he commit an illegal act? We may assume that the burglar is motivated either by only one major need, or by many needs. Going down the alphabetical list of Murray's needs, one finds many of them which might operate in the act of the burglar. He might, for example, be motivated by the need of abasement. The burglar feels resigned to his fate of being an outcast from the major portion of society. He may have been convicted many times before for other illegal acts until now he feels that the only way to gain a living in his world is to take it. Since he has already been labeled a criminal, he might as well make a living being a criminal. We may also find that our burglar has a strong desire to achieve by overcoming the obstacles involved in stealthily entering a home. He accomplishes something difficult which most people could not or would not do. He is, at the moment and in his frame of reference, a successful man; particulary so if his acquaintances in the field of crime feel that he has pulled off a major coup in the size of the "take" and in the difficulties involved in breaking and entering a home. Achievement then becomes an explanation for burglary. Assuming the burglar has been imprisoned before because of his activities, he may also be motivated by the need for aggression—to punish or get revenge on a society which has deprived him, in his frame of reference, of freedom in the past. The need for autonomy may be present. By burglarizing a home, he can defy convention, be independent from working for others, and be free to act according to his own impulses. Especially this may be true if he has no real need for the profits of the theft. The burglar "can be his own boss" with a complete feeling of autonomy. Counteraction, in the sense of searching for obstacles and difficulties to overcome, may take place (as in the Raffles type of criminal). If the burglar happens to be an adolescent, the act of stealing something of value from a private home may be a vindication of his ego and thus may satisfy the need for defendance. Likewise, he may exercise the need for deference in conforming to custom, gaining the admiration and respect of older boys whom he considers superior by committing a particularly spectacular and daring burglary. Social workers with young people in large cities have more than once posed this explanation of burglaries by adolescent youth.

So many of these need factors seem to operate in our burglary case that we may summarize as follows:

Dominance. Through the use of the burglary profits he may influence, command, or control the behavior of others. Certainly he has influenced and controlled the behavior of the victims by depriving them of their lawful property. They must now go about the business of catching him, of repossessing their own property, in short, of being controlled by his activities.

Exhibition. Most authorities on juvenile behavior have voluminous records of the adolescent burglar who commits the act to show off to his friends. The author has heard about high school "fraternities" in which the initiate must perform an act of burglary in a local store in order to be accepted into the private club. This type of act is a combination of some of the other needs also, namely deference, affiliation, etc.

Thus we may continue with the list of Murray's needs, although not such a strong case may be made for the remaining terms in the list. Sentience, for example, may be a factor in the case of emotionally disturbed individuals who steal for the sensuous thrill involved in the act of stealing, while the value and use of the object stolen is of no consequence. Kleptomania and the stealing of women's underclothing by emotionally disturbed males are also examples. However, these do bring into play vast complexes of interwoven needs and consequently do not serve well as examples for the present text.

Supranatural Being

Probably foremost in Murray's list of needs in explaining why man worships and believes in a supranatural being are deference (emulate an exemplar), succorance (remain close to a devoted protector and always have a supporter), and understanding (be interested in theory, speculate, formulate, and generalize). In the practice of his religious feelings, man may also exercise needs for abasement (confess and atone), affiliation (please and win affection), dominance (influence and direct behavior of others—example: strongly evangelistic and fervently puritanical churches), and nurturing (support, console, or comfort others). Believing in and supporting a religious group seems quite natural according to the needs expressed by Murray.

Humor

Except as humor is used to motivate the behavior of others, the rubric of Murray's needs does not neatly answer the question of why man has a sense of humor. It is easier to answer the question of why he uses humor in life than question of why he has it. Man may laugh at situations in which he is himself the goat or object of the humor and thus hope to win affection and approval of himself, much as did the medieval court jester. He may likewise laugh in derision at something else, attempting to increase his own importance and thus achieve the need for aggression and dominance. Jokes pointed toward minority groups may fall within this classification. He may also laugh for the obvious need to relax from stress (play) and thus relieve tension, and also to seek enjoyment of sensuous impressions (sentience). For all or one of these reasons may man laugh and enjoy humor as we use the need list of Murray.

Smoking

Much like the reasons for humor, the reasons for smoking are not clear cut in intrapersonal needs. Using the concept of need for explanations brings one closer to interpersonal or societal reasons for smoking than to personal needs. Man smokes tobacco because other men do. The question arises, would man continue to smoke tobacco, having learned from other men, if in the future he were not to be surrounded by tobacco users? Is there a need within man for the use of tobacco? Using Murray's list, we may posit the need for sentience (seek and enjoy sensuous impressions) as a possible answer. Other than the need for play (relaxation of stress and acting for "fun" without further purpose) all the remaining needs appear to be associated with societal factors. The need for sentience in the Murray sense subsumes his treatment of the longitudinal principle with special reference to the section on complexes. If the complexes are considered as basic to man's development in the Freudian sense, (as utilized by Murray), a clearer explanation is obtained for man's use of tobacco. Without this foundation, smoking appears to be a primarily social act.

Play and Recreation

The explanation of man's reasons for playing seem so directly connected to a Murray explanation, using the needs theory, that the question might almost have been chosen expressly for this theory. Such is not the case. Murray's work is so broad and inclusive that he provides answers to questions in many areas.

Through his efforts in research, Murray finds that man has a direct need within the self to play (seek enjoyable relaxation of stress, act for "fun" without further purpose). Of course, man may also play for secondary reasons if the play activity gives him such need fulfillment as achievement (rival and surpass others) and dominance (influence the behavior of others), to cite two of the possible explanations. Play, then, to Murray is a natural state of existence for man. He needs it.

Psychoses—Neuroses

Presumably all of the needs that Murray sees in man operate either singly or in groups when man, unable to maintain a somewhat stabilized emotional equilibrium, falls into a psychotic or neurotic episode, of short or long duration. Apparently what takes place is best explained by phenomena which operate under the need structure.

From the statement, "No brain, no personality," we may assume that the personality will disintegrate if the brain disintegrates. In the first place the disintegration may be a purely organic malfunctioning of the neural system. Paresis, Korsakoff's syndrome, and many other organic disabilities may be taken as examples. The etiology of this type of brain function collapse is simpler (though possibly not simpler in therapy) than in functional psychoses and neuroses. Here, using Murray's system, we have a fairly clear picture of what happens.

Fundamentally what may occur in an emotional breakdown is an inability to operate the tension reduction aspects of man's life. In Murray's terms a man is either unable to reduce the tensions in his life and create for himself the tensionless state or, more pertinent to his theory, unable to reduce the tensions which he himself has created. It must be remembered that to Murray, tension reduction is more than simple conservation; it is uniquely a construction of images to be pursued and conquered.

Prepotency, fusion, subsidiation, and conflict become the *modus operandi* of emotional breakdowns. Needs clash, come into conflict, refuse to be superseded by other needs, or fail to be arrangeable in proper sequence. Thus, failure to meet the needs of man is basic to all psychotic and neurotic episodes. Although the needs are the basic stuff of man's existence, the emotional disorder lies not in the needs themselves but in man's inability to handle them. Needs, in this sense, are not good or bad *per se;* ineptitude in using them creates tense emotional states. Like fire, they are necessary to life. Like fire, they must be handled intelligently if one is to avoid pain.

In summary, then, man becomes psychotic or neurotic because he is unable to reduce the tensions in his life.

PREDICTING HUMAN BEHAVIOR VIA MURRAY'S PERSONOLOGY THEORY

Murray feels that fundamentally, predicting human behavior is an impossible task. Yet one finds a remarkable degree of success in predicting human behavior from Murray's own work. All prediction needs a full set of underlying facts, and one's knowledge of facts is always incomplete or fragmentary, a statement that few psychologists or laymen would deny. To claim to depict completely all human behavior at all times is absurd. Nothing could chill life more completely than to know one's future irrevocably. Predicting, however, the *tendency* to act in certain ways in selected situations is well within the partial scope of the psychological world. Some aspects of the commercial world (advertising, purchasing materials, etc.), most efforts of the psychological therapist, and indeed the normal hopes and dreams of the lay world are predicated on some educated hunches for the future. In brief all the world continues its life on the prediction that the future is sufficiently worthwhile to continue the efforts of today. Not to do so would be to cease today's efforts.

Personal Prediction

Once again it is the reader who makes the primary decision as to the predictability of life according to Murray's contribution. After examining Murray's list of needs, the reader may or may not agree that these needs reflect his own. If the majority of the items do coincide, we may expect, then, that the reader's needs will continue to function much as they did in the past. Following Murray's suggestion that man is an habituated animal, we find that the needs of the past may be expected to continue in the future. This will be especially true if the needs have been satisfactorily met often enough for the establishing of a pattern of behavior. Needs, important in the past and satisfactorily met, may be expected to be important in the life of the future.

The reader may further assume for himself that certain needs have a higher priority than others. Some needs may have conflicted with others; these, too, may be expected to conflict in the future. Some conflicts may have been allayed by fusing them into another avenue of approach; we may assume that the individual successful in this will continue to be so, and hence be able to predict some success in the fusion of needs for the future.

From a personal frame of reference, then, the reader decides the predictability of needs as Murray proposes them. We shall assess in the next section to what extent the evidence of research indicates predictability.

Scientific or Laboratory Prediction

As previously indicated, Murray has found some degree of success in predicting human behavior within a prescribed area of operations. Two of his major activities attest to this success: the Thematic Apperception Test and his fascinating work with the Office of Strategic Services in World War II.

In *Explorations in Personality* (1938) he and his collaborators presented a then unique method of assessing and studying personality via a projective type device. This "test" has become widely popular and ranks a close second to the ubiquitous Rorschach ink blot test in psychological circles for both research and therapeutic work. While looking at twenty vaguely familiar pictures, the subject is asked to use his imagination and create stories or incidents relevant to the pictures. The account should reflect the past, present, and future as the subject sees them in his stories about the pictures. From the subject's interpretation, the psychometrist attempts to create an understanding of the inner dynamics of the subject's life. Any reference to *Psychological Abstracts* will attest to the wide use of this instrument in predicting future behavior of patients and subjects in psychological work. Although the TAT is used primarily for diagnostic purposes, one finds a high degree of prediction of patient behavior involved in the actual use of the instrument, a predictability often much above what chance would indicate.

More closely allied to predictability of human behavior is the work that Murray and others did in selecting candidates for espionage work for the military forces in World War II. Under the title, *Assessment of Men,* some highly ingenious methods were reported in choosing candidates to be parachuted into northern Italy for espionage work; the selection had a relatively high degree of success. In this work, Murray and many others employed multiple kinds of selection devices, many of which were well within the scope of his theories. Murray has always been a strong advocate of the interdisciplinary approach to behavioral studies. The OSS project employed sociologists, psychiatrists, and educators, as well as psychologists, and was, therefore, the truly interdisciplinary approach which Murray has advocated for many years.

In contrast to some theorists, Murray has not confined his research efforts to proving his theory. His interests range widely. Two of his atypical but indicative efforts concerned themselves with studying the clairvoyant efficacy of dreams during the Lindberg baby kidnapping of the 1930s (see H. A. Murray and D. R. Wheeler, A Note on the Possible Clairvoyance of Dreams, *J. Psychol.*, 1937, 3, pp. 309–313), and his unique analysis of the psychological content in Herman Melville's classic, *Moby Dick* (see H. A. Murray, *In Nomine Diaboli, New England Quarterly*, 1951, 24, pp. 435–452). These two studies attest the wide interests of Murray beyond the formulation of theoretical concepts concerning personality.

———————————————◆———————————————

SUMMARY

The major part of Murray's theory of personality is based on man as a motivated animal. The author has extracted seven principles from Murray's theory which seem to highlight its major factors. The seven principles are these:

1. Regnancy principle: highlighted by Murray's statement, "No brain, no personality."

2. Motivations principle: based on man's making a continuous effort to reduce the tensions in his life which are caused by the needs he feels from within and the press of society from without. The amalgamation of this needs–press phenomena does more than reestablish status quo; it also creates newer tension areas to be reduced, so that man moves forward toward constructive goals rather than merely conserving goals. The methods by which man handles his need–press life may lead to conflict or fusion of needs or to subsidiating

them into an hierarchal structure. Needs may have characteristics within themselves. They may be primary or secondary, originate within the self or be brought into the personality from society, openly expressed (overt) or disguised in expression (covert), directed toward one object (focal) or toward many objects (diffused). Finally, needs may be exercised for an immediate purpose (effect) or purely for enjoyment of the process of the activity with no goal object in mind (modal). Murray has recently attempted to classify needs into vectors (how you do it) and value (why you do it).

3. Longitudinal principle: characterized by his statement, "The history of the personality is the personality." One cannot study personality and ignore the past life of the personality. Involved in the developmental aspects of man is the emergence of the erotogenic zones and their effect on man's future behavior, the zones being much the same as those Freud suggested, but interpreted somewhat differently by Murray. The zones are the claustral, oral, anal, and urethral; in addition there is a castration complex revolving around the Freudian phallic theory. Longitudinally speaking, man also arranges his life along short time goals (proceedings) which may be overtly or covertly expressed and along long time goals (serials) in which the activities or proceedings must progress along orderly lines in order to achieve the end goal.

4. Physiological process principle: much allied to the regnancy principle but with the additional emphasis that man is first and foremost an organic being.

5. Abstract principle: approaches the neo-Freudians in accepting the id, ego, superego structure as Freud introduced it, but with important deviations of his own similar to those of all the neo-Freudians. Murray is convinced that not all behavior is surface phenomenon.

6. Uniqueness principle: typified by the expression, "No man is like any other man in some respects and is like all other men in other respects." Each man is unique.

7. Role concept principle: one of Murray's newer incorporations in his theory of personality, possibly influenced by his work with Kluckhohn. Illustrated by the oft-quoted line from Shakespeare's *As You Like It*, "All the world's a stage,/And all the men and women merely players:/They have their exits and their entrances;/And one man in his time plays many parts. "

Figure 4 summarizes the effects of the needs and press on the personality. Needs, coming partially from within the conscious and partially from without, attempt to keep the personality in formation with the help, but sometimes hindrance, of the press (environment). The structure is always and recurrently lopsided to the right. This affords motion off dead center and connates tension reduction as more than a state of equilibrium, as a

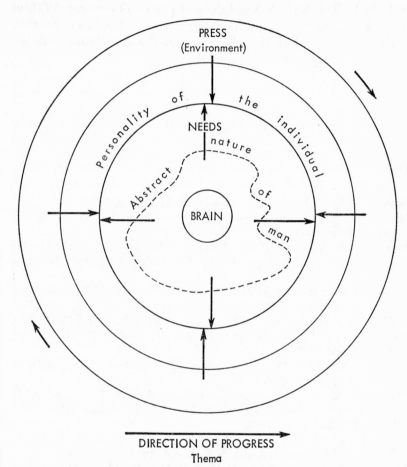

Figure 4. Diagrammatic Summary of Murray's Theory.

force for movement. As the wheel that is always slightly off center and retains its new off-center position with each turn of the wheel, the personality is nevertheless always moving in only one direction, the future. The conflicts and victories of the past have either weakened or strengthened it: their necessity as a foundation cannot be denied (Longitudinal) principle).

Central to the entire structure of man's personality, the very core of it, is the brain. This is the hub and the center of man's existence. Without that hub, the structure collapses or disintegrates, and thus fails to function.

The route over which the wheel has passed and its future route are described as themas, proceedings, and serials.

BIBLIOGRAPHY

PRIMARY SOURCES

BOOKS

Murray, H. A., *Explorations in Personality*, N.Y., Oxford, 1938.

Murray, H. A., *Thematic Apperception Test*, Cambridge, Mass., Harvard Univer. Press, 1943.

Murray, H. A., Assessment of the whole person, in *Proceedings of the Meeting of Military Psychologists and Psychiatrists*, College Park, Md., Maryland Univer. Press, 1945.

Murray, H. A., *Assessment of Men*, N.Y., Holt, Rinehart and Winston, 1948.

Murray, H. A. Research planning: a few proposals, in S. S. Sargent, and M. W. Smith, (eds.), *Culture and Personality*, Beloit, Wis., Viking Fund, 1949.

Murray, H. A. (ed.), Introduction in H. Melville, *Pierre or The Ambiguities*, N.Y., Hendricks House, 1949.

Kluckhohn, C. and H. A. Murray, *Personality in Nature, Society, and Culture*, N.Y., Knopf, 1950.

Murray, H. A., Toward a classification of interactions, in T. Parsons, and E. A. Shils, (eds.), *Toward a General Theory of Action*, Cambridge, Mass., Harvard Univer. Press, 1951.

Kluckhohn, C., H. A. Murray, and D. M. Schneider, *Personality in Nature, Society, and Culture* (2nd ed.), N.Y., Knopf, 1953.

Murray, H. A., Versions of man, in *Man's Right to Knowledge*, N.Y., Columbia Univer. Press, 1955.

Murray, H. A., Introduction to *Clinical Studies of Personality*, 1-2, A. Burton, and R. E. Harris, N.Y., Harper & Row, 1955.

Murray, H. A., Introduction to Methods in *Personality Assessment*, G. G. Stern, M. I. Stein, and B. S. Bloom, N.Y. Free Press, 1956.

Murray, H. A., Drive, time, strategy, measurement, and our way of life, in G. Lindzey, (ed.), *Assessment of Human Motives*, N.Y., Holt, Rinehart and Winston, 1958.

Murray, H. A., Introduction to the issue "Myth and mythmaking," Boston, *Daedalus*, American Academy of Arts and Sciences, 1959.

Murray, H. A., Vicissitudes of creativity, in H. H. Anderson, (ed.), *Creativity and its Cultivation*, N.Y., Harper & Row, 1959.

Murray, H. A., Preparations for the scaffold of a comprehensive system, in S. Koch, (ed.), *Psychology: A Study of a Science*, 3, N.Y., McGraw-Hill, 1959.

Murray, H. A., Two versions of man, in H. Shapley, (ed.), *Science Ponders Religion*, N.Y., Appleton-Century-Crofts, 1960.

Murray, H. A., Historical trends in personality research, in H. P. David, and J. C. Brengelmann, (eds.), *Perspectives in Personality Research*, N.Y., Springer, 1960.

Murray, H. A., The possible nature of a "mythology" to come, in *Myth and Mythmaking*, N.Y., G. Braziller, 1960.

Murray, H. A., Beyond yesterday's idealisms, in *The Fate of Man*, N.Y., G. Braziller, 1961.

Murray, H. A., Prospect for psychology, in G. Nielson (ed.), *Proceedings of the Fourteenth International Congress of Applied Psychology, Vol. 1, Psychology and International Affairs*, Copenhagen, Denmark, Munksgaard, 1962.

PERIODICALS

Murray, H. A., Ten publications on research on physiological ontogeny. Summarized in: (with A. E. Cohn,) Physiological ontogeny: Vol. I, the present status of the problem, *Quart. Rev. Biol.*, 1925–1927, 2, 469–493.

Murray, H. A., A case of pinealoma with symptoms suggestive of compulsion neurosis, *Arch. Neurol. Psychiat., Chicago*, 1928, 19, 932–945.

Murray, H. A., H. Barry, Jr. and D. W. MacKinnon, Hypnotizability as a personality trait, *Hum. Biol.*, 1931, 3, 1–36.

Murray, H. A., The effect of fear upon estimates of the maliciousness of other personalities, *J. Soc. Psychol.*, 1933, 4, 310–329.

Murray, H. A., H. A. Wolff, and C. E. Smith, The psychology of humor, *J. Abnorm. Soc. Psychol.*, 1934, 28, 341–365.

Murray, H. A., The psychology of humor: Vol. II. Mirth responses to disparagement jokes as a manifestation of an aggressive disposition, *J. Abnorm. Soc. Psychol.*, 1934, 29, 66–81.

Morgan, C. D. and H. A. Murray, A method of investigating fantasies, *Arch. Neurol. Psychiat., Chicago*, 1935, 34, 289–306.

Murray, H. A., Psychology and the university, *Arch. Neurol. Psychiat., Chicago*, 1935, 34, 803–897.

Murray, H. A., The Harvard Psychological Clinic, *Harv. Alumni Bull.*, Oct. 25, 1935.

Murray, H. A., Facts which support the concept of need or drive, *J. Psychol.*, 1936, 3, 27–42.

Murray, H. A., Techniques for systematic investigation of fantasy, *J. Psychol.*, 1936, *3*, 115–143.

Murray, H. A., Some concepts for a psychology of personality, *J. Gen. Psychol.*, 1936, *15*, 240–268.

Murray, H. A. and D. R. Wheeler, A note on the possible clairvoyance of dreams, *J. Psychol.*, 1936, *3*, 309–313.

Wolf, R. and H. A. Murray, An experiment in judging personalities, *J. Psychol.*, 1936, *3*, 345–365.

Murray, H. A., Visceral manifestations of personality, *J. Abnorm. Soc. Psychol.*, 1937, *32*, 161–184.

Murray, H. A., Sigmund Freud: 1856–1939, *Amer. J. Psychol.*, 1940, *53*, 134–138.

Murray, H. A., What should psychologists do about psychoanalysis?, *J. Abnorm. Soc. Psychol.*, 1940, *35*, 150–175.

Murray, H. A. and M. Stein, Note on the selection of combat officers, *Psychosom. Med.*, 1943, *5*, 386–391.

Murray, H. A. and C. D. Morgan, A clinical study of sentiments, *Genet. Psychol. Monogr.*, 1945, *32*, 3–311.

Murray, H. A. and D. W. MacKinnon, Assessment of OSS personnel, *J. Consult. Psychol.*, 1946, *10*, 76–80.

Murray, H. A., Proposals for research in clinical psychology, *J. Orthopsychiat.*, 1947, *17*, 203–210.

Murray, H. A., Time for a positive morality, *Surv. Graphic*, 1947, *36*, 195 ff.

Murray, H. A., America's mission, *Surv. Graphic*, 1948, 37, 411–415.

Murray, H. A., Uses of the TAT, *Amer. J. Psychiat.*, 1951, *107*, 8.

Murray, H. A., Thematic Apperception Test, *Milit. Clin. Psychol.*, 1951, *45*, 54–71.

Murray, H. A., *In nomine diaboli*, *New England Quart.*, 1951, 24, 435–452.

Murray, H. A., Some basic psychological assumptions and conception, *Dialectica*, 1951, *5*, 266–292.

Murray, H. A., Poet of creative dissolution (Conrad Aiken), *Wake*, 1952, *11*, 95–106.

Murray, H. A., Science in two societies, in *The Contemporary Scene*, Metropolitan Museum of Art, N.Y., 1954.

Davids, A. and H. A. Murray, Preliminary appraisal of an auditory projective technique for studying personality and cognition, *Amer. J. Orthopsychiat.*, 1955, *25*, 543–554.

Murray, H. A., Religion in an age of science, *Christian Reg.*, 1956, *135*.

Murray, H. A., Morton Prince: Sketch of his life and work, *J. Abnorm. Soc. Psychol.*, 1956, *52*, 291–295.

Murray, H. A., Individuality: The meaning and content of individuality in contemporary America, *Daedalus*, 1958, *87*, 25–47.

Murray, H. A., H. Cantril, and M. May, Some glimpses of Soviet psychology, *Amer. Psychologist*, 1959, *14*, 303–307.

Murray, H. A., Myth and mythmaking, *Daedulus*, 1959, 88(2), 211–380.

Murray, H. A., Unprecedented evolutions, *Daedalus*, 1961, *90*, 547–570.

Murray, H. A., Prospect for psychology, *Science*, 1962, *136*, 483–488.

One encounter with a hallucinogenic drug.

SUGGESTED READINGS

BOOKS

Hall, C. S., and G. Lindzey, *Theories of Personality*, N.Y., Wiley, 1957, 157–205.

White, R. W. (ed.), *The Study of Lives: essays on personality in honor of Henry A. Murray*, N.Y., Atherton Press, 1963.

Eighteen essays on personality reflecting Murray's influence as teacher and friend.

PERIODICALS

Bellak, L. and H. A. Murray, an appreciation, *J. Proj. Tech.*, 1958, *22*, 143–144.

Special TAT issue of the Journal.

Chambers, I. L., and L. J. Broussard, The role of need-attitudes in adjustment, *J. Clin. Psychol.*, 1960, *16*(4), 383–387.

Using the Murray need system to evaluate attitudes.

Edwards, A. L., *Edward's Personal Preference Schedule*, Psychol. Corp., N.Y., 1953.

Two hundred and twenty-five paired comparisons based on 15 of Murray's needs.

Faith, H. W. Jr., The discrepancy between self-ideal self concepts as needs projected to thematic apperception test pictures, *Dissertation Abstract*, 1961, *21*, 1999–2000.

McClenahan, M.L.P., The relationship of test-defined needs to illuminance matches of need-related pictures, *Dissert. Abstr.*, 1961, *21*(12), 3862–3863.

McCreary, J. K., The problem of personality definition, *J. Gen. Psychol.*, 1960, *63*, 107–111.

Reviews definitions by Allport, Lewin, Murray, and Murphy.

6

Jung

Every cradle asks us, "whence?" and every coffin, "whither?"
The poor barbarian weeping above his dead can answer these questions
as intelligently as the robed priest of the most authentic creed.

ROBERT G. INGERSOLL
Address at a Little Boy's Grave

SOME BIOGRAPHICAL DATA

Carl Gustav Jung was born in Kesswyl, on the shores of Lake Constance in Switzerland, on July 26, 1875. He continued to reside in Switzerland, where he maintained a residence and clinical practice in the small town of Küsnacht, south of Zurich, along the shores of Lake Zurich.[1] Jung obtained a Doctor of Medicine degree from the University of Basel in Switzerland. He began his psychiatric work as an assistant in the famed Burghölzli Mental Hospital in Zurich. Through his work and contacts at the mental hospital he later worked with Eugen Bleuler and also Pierre Janet in Paris. Prior to World War I he gave up his teaching and research posts, first at the Burghölzli Mental Hospital and in 1913 at the University of Zurich, in order to devote full time to his then large private practice. He also conducted training seminars for many years and, of course, continued to write voluminously about his theoretical system and

---

[1] The author is indebted to the late Dr. Jung for his hospitality and guidance during a visit to his home in Küsnacht in the spring of 1960. In response to this chapter he said, "I don't believe a word of it, but I can't disagree with anything you have said." Then he laughed merrily. He was a delightful conversationalist and host.

case studies. Shortly after his semiretirement in the immediate post-World War II years, he accepted a created chair of medical psychology for him at the University of Basel. Prior to his semiretirement Jung traveled extensively throughout the world in pursuance of the history of man as he found it in Oriental and Occidental cultures.

Jung's association with Freud started in 1906 through correspondence concerning the validity Jung found for Freud's dream analysis techniques. At the founding of the association in 1910 Jung had been elected its first president. So close was the relationship between the two men, that Freud considered him to be his successor and, in fact, they traveled amicably together to give the famous Clark University lectures at the twentieth anniversary celebration in Worcester, Massachusetts, arranged by G. Stanley Hall. The friendship lasted until 1914 when Jung withdrew from the International Psychoanalytic Association and further contacts with the then Freud-dominated organization. Many accounts have been written of their disaffection with each other. Probably the most complete, though likely to be one-sided, is that of Ernest Jones in his three-volume series on Freud (*The Life and Work of Sigmund Freud,* N.Y., Basic Books, 1953, 1955, 1958). Other accounts by Freud, "The History of the Psychoanalytic Movement," *The Basic Writings of Sigmund Freud,* A. A. Brill, (ed.), Random House, 1938; and Jung, *Analytical Psychology,* Moffat-Yard, 1916, may also be valuable to the student interested in this aspect of Jung's and Freud's lives. For a more straightforward account of Jung's life, the reader may wish to see *Current Biography,* 1943, or the two issues of *Time* magazine, 1952, 60, p. 37, "Biographical Sketch of Carl Gustav Jung," and 1955, 65, pp. 62–70, "The Old Wise Man."

On June 6, 1961, Dr. Jung died at his home in Küsnacht, Switzerland, an occasion noted by the whole intellectual world with deep regret.

INTRODUCTION

In many ways Carl Gustav Jung was the "grand old man" of personality theorists. He lived through the earliest era of personality theory, wrote voluminously, gathered many honors, and continued until his death to write, treat a few patients, and excite the psychological world with his work. Jung's influence on the psychological world has been unique. His theories are not popular in the sense that many papers at the psychological meetings are oriented toward his work. Most psychologists are bothered by Jung. They cannot ignore him. The usual reaction toward Jung is an attack on his theory, then, with a satisfied feeling that all has been put in its proper place, the psychologist continues with his main thesis. But to ignore Jung does not seem to satisfy psychologists. Jung irritated them because he was different, mystical, circuitous in writing style, provocative. He led one to accept vigorously or totally reject his theories on personality. There seems to be little room for half-hearted measures. Although Jung was quite aware of the world of psychologists, his position in it left him quite unimpressed, as he continued to feel that truth is truth whether it happens to be popular or not.

Perhaps one clue to the influence of Jung was his deep, and among psychologists, rarely duplicated erudition in fields far beyond the usually cultivated areas of psychology. He went back to the historical aspects of man's existence in both written and artifactual records in an attempt to provide clearer answers to the ubiquitous question of why man does the things he does. Jung delved deeply into alchemy, mythology, religion, archeology, rituals, symbols, Sanskrit, and other forgotten languages, as well as into the newer attempts in psychoanalysis, all in a dedicated attempt to learn more of the personality of man as he exists today. If a new language had to be learned to trace a remote source of information, Jung learned it rather than attempt translations or ignore the thread he felt to be a promising lead. Jung's learning and erudition were impressive and honest.

None of Jung's positive influence appears to be direct, although in the writings of Allport, Rogers, Murphy, and Maslow, as well as in the writings of the nonpsychologists, Arnold Toynbee and Philip Wylie, one finds oblique references to, and a strong influence of, the Jungian point of view.

Jung's theory is different from others in that it is shadowy, metaphysical, of a nature almost impossible to test in a laboratory situation, and appears to reverse the current trend for statistical treatment of data of a psychological nature.

Jung's theory is a hopeful one: man is gradually emerging through the ages into a better and more civilized human being, operating within better and better frames of reference. His theory also gives encouragement to the middle and later years of life, an attitude which runs counter to the modern trend of emphasis on child psychology. Although Jung was originally attracted to Freud and his work to the extent of being Freud's announced successor, as we have seen, he broke sharply with Freud in 1914. Freud's theory is inclined to emphasize the dreary inescapable polarity of life; Jung treated the improving aspect of man's existence.

As is the case with many original and provocative writers, Jung at times was accused of supporting a position when in fact he was attempting to explain it. This, Jung felt, led to unfairness in the evaluation of his own work and was the obstacle to objective reporting.

JUNG'S DESCRIPTION OF HUMAN BEHAVIOR

In describing Jung's work, one finds it easy to oversimplify his theoretical position into principles, although he speaks of only two principles as such, using terms which he borrowed from the field of physics: *entropy* and *equivalence*. The temptation to discern more is strong, because of the great volume of his written work. Jung felt that his work was not theoretical but based on observable and identifiable facts that are evident to all who take the time to discover them in the world of today, and in what we know of the world of yesterday.

The author presents Jung's work by means of four principles, which seem to help the undergraduate student digest the written work and apparently do no great injustice to the central core of his ideas. To gain a greater grasp of all that is Jungian, one must read Jung for years, preferably in the original German text. Such an endeavor obviously removes a study of Jung from all but a few undergraduates; it is hoped this work may help the student to greater understanding.

The four principles mentioned above are: polarity, self-actualization, unconscious states, and teleology. The order is unimportant. All four principles as used in this text apply equally well to Jungian psychology. Because they apply more to psychoanalysis as a technique than to understanding the basics of personality, no treatment is given to Jung's analytic methods, such as sentence completion or dream analysis, even though these are basic to his work and are of interest. They do, however, concern themselves more with operational factors than with systems of thought.

Polarity Principle

Probably one of the most universal ideas extant among personality theorists is the concept of polarity. Jung is no exception, and much of what his theory contains has been grouped within the principle of polarity in this text. Also, as with so many other theories, discussing and emphasizing one idea at a time creates the impression that these are singular factors in the theory with no relationship to other factors. This is not true; almost all of the polarity principles discussed herein are directly related to some other aspect of Jung's work. But, as always, they must be discussed singly, so that they may be better understood. Relationships will be developed as the text continues.

After many years of study, concentration, and reflection Jung became convinced that all the world and perhaps the universe, animate and inanimate, exists because of opposition. There is and always must be opposites, and opposites beget conflict. Without conflict, life is nothing. Conflict is the basic stuff of life. Conflict begets progress. Without conflict nothing happens because only through conflict can one thing or another emerge beyond the point at which conflict began. Progress, movement, change of position, therefore, are only possible under conditions of stress. Wishing to remove the stress of conflict with an opponent causes the original object to be motivated into action. Opposition, conflict, resultant stress, and the removal of stress are the *sine qua non* of the world we live in. In a rather metaphysical way Jung said that whatever exists has an opposite even if that opposite is the lack of existence of the original condition: life–no life, hunger–no hunger, love–no love, house–no house, clothes–no clothes. In most cases what exists has a counterpart whose existence is equally as real as the first entity. However, in the case of life–no life, for example, one can only assume that the opposite of life is no life, a state called death. Other oppositions, such as water eroding rock, two nations at war, or two automobiles in collision obviously indicate factually real quantities in opposition.

In contrast to the Freudian position that life consists of the eternal going back and forth *of one object* between two poles, and thus the evolution of a perpetually frustrated, vacillating object, never able to settle at any point, Jung suggested a happier ending to the story of opposition and its resolution into equilibrium. True equilibrium is of short duration, but it is a sign of progress. All is not a "vale of tears" for Jung. Opposition not only moves the object off dead center, which results in prolongation of existence, but it may be resolved into progress within itself by three actions. The actions are *compensation, union,* and the aforementioned *opposition.*

When the personality feels that it is in conflict because it cannot accomplish a desired goal, it may seek another goal equally attractive and in so doing remove the conflict. This form of compensation moves the personality forward toward a new position, even though the advanced position may not be in the direction of the original goal. The important factor to Jung was that the personality has done something to move itself from its original position. Symbolic action is not as important as physical action in a compensatory move. Simply dreaming about conquering an objective (although dreaming was most important as a behavioral phenomenon to Jung) is not a true compensatory action. For example, think of the student who desires athletic recognition but cannot "make" the team and who, therefore, redoubles his efforts in the classroom and achieves scholastic recognition instead of athletic recognition. The unfortunate connotations of this oft-repeated example are that all good students are assumed to be compensating for failure in athletics, their real goal. It ignores the fact that some students study and expend effort in study because they want to learn. The opposite is equally as fallacious when misused: athletes are athletes because they cannot be scholars. A more meaningful example may be found in the case of a student who uses color and design to compensate in dress for a deformity in stature and figure. But to Jung compensation which grows out of conflict is a favorable factor for man's personality. It helps him go forward.

In the second type of action, opposing forces may unite in seeking a resolution satisfactory to both forces. Once again, progress has been made, and again the value of opposition in life is demonstrated. Although this appears paradoxical, the following example may help to give it clarity. Have you ever witnessed or been involved in a fight with two members of the same family? Frequently one finds that interference in this type of battle only brings the wrath of both opponents directed against the peacemaker. Thus, the conflict of the brothers is united against another object, the peacemaker, a result which leads to a mutual feeling between the kin toward a third object. Peace reigns, amicability between brothers is reestablished, the frustrated energy has been expended on a third force, and some progress in relationships in the family results. It is true that the resolution of conflict may not always be morally correct, as we see in the case of two nations who loathe and suspect each other, but are quite willing to unite against a third nation which seeks to attack them both. The union of opposing forces, then, according to Jung, may be a way of merely resolving opposition.

The third type of action, in which opposition leads to movement and possible progress is best typified by the rivalry of two students for grades or scholastic status. Spurred on by their conflict with each other, both extend themselves far beyond the limits of learning the subject matter. Much of the commercial world refines its product, price, and service because of the impetus of opposing commercial rivals.

To Jung opposition was good. Only by action can man possibly make forward steps.

With the above as a general introduction to Jung's concept of polarity as exemplified by opposition in life, we may now examine more closely the specific polarities that he felt exist in man's personality.

Principle of Equivalence

As was stated previously, the use of the term *principles* was only used twice by Jung and then in a borrowed sense. The inclusion of the polarity aspects of Jung's work at this point in this text connotes not so much that they are opposing forces, but that they represent opposite ends of a scale of behavior.

The principle of equivalence comes from the field of physics, the first law of thermodynamics. Sometimes called the *conservation of energy principle,* it means that energy used to change the condition of some object is not lost, but will reappear in another form in another object. For instance, the energy used in the burning of an object is not lost but transformed into the energy of heat. Jung uses this principle to apply to man's personality dynamics. As the desire for one object diminishes, an equal amount of desire may be directed toward another object. The principal feature regarding man's behavior is that desire is not lost entirely; it is merely diverted to another objective. Desire remains constant if it is present at all; the goals change. The student who desires a social life in college does not lose the desire when he ceases to date one coed; he seeks another coed as his dating partner. Athletically motivated students who desire the outlet of sports may transfer their activities from football to basketball to baseball as the academic year progresses. Students who engage in only one sport and come to the end of that season must use the energy and time formerly expended in long practice sessions in moving toward fresh goals. Desire shifted from one activity may be directed toward diverse activities, such as more time for studying, socializing with friends, and trips home, all of which were not possible during the season when energy was expended only in playing on a varsity team.

What happens when a desire is repressed? This question was most important to Jung, for out of it comes the symbolic life of man through which he must dream or fantasize his activities toward the desired goal. The answer is that the energy conserved is redirected toward the desired object through the dream world, whether it be by diurnal or nocturnal dreaming. Much of what man is, Jung stated, he is because he can dream his way toward the resolution of a conflict.

Principle of Entropy

The principle of entropy, which is the second law of thermodynamics, states that the properties of one body when placed in juxtaposition to another that is similar in kind, but different in degree will tend to assume the characteristics of the most highly charged body. It is important to note that the bodies must be of the same species or type. Man to man or animal to animal fits this specification. When the bodies are in contact, the most highly charged body loses some of its charge, until the two are equal in respect to the exchanged characteristic. Two bodies of water of different levels, when connected, will eventually be equal in level. The state that results from this phenomenon is a loss of energy as the two bodies reach a state of equilibrium. As Jung applied this law of physics to the dynamics of personality, certain extensions of the theory also apply. Since the personality is not a closed system, it is never possible to achieve a true state of balance or equilibrium between two people or within one person concerning two activities. Society and inner changes create constantly changing conditions, and feed energy into the dynamics of personality, all of which tend to keep the person's behavior off balance while he continuously attempts to keep himself in balance. However, in spite of the fact that man can never win the battle of balancing his conflicts, the nearer he comes to achieving this, the nearer he comes to peace and tranquility. This state of true harmony, however, does not necessarily accomplish anything, as we will recall from the previous discussion on the value of conflict. To illustrate: it is only because one body of water is placed higher than a second receiving body of water that power can be produced through a hydroelectric dynamo system. Two lakes of equal altitude produce no power or movement between their respective waters.

We shall see more of these two systems as they operate within the personality in the following sections of the chapter. To repeat: all of Jung's system is highly interrelated.

Regression vs. *Progression.* As Jung believed, the personality either goes forward or goes backward. It is not possible to stay happily but unproductively in the middle. Progression obviously connotes movement forward, and such movement further connotes some kind of change which is beneficial to the personality. In the meantime, what good can come out of regression, or backward movement, according to Jung? Much, he said, because not all that man accomplishes is done in a direct to-the-target manner. More times than man realizes he attains goals by returning to a previous position, reorienting himself, and possibly finding a better pathway than the first to attain the hoped-for goal. The strategic withdrawal is often the wisest maneuver. As we shall see, this withdrawal is sometimes made through symbols and in the unconscious areas of the personality, but the value of regression in not to be minimized. Again, this is in contrast to the Freudian doctrine which holds that the personality forever vacillates between two polarities but does not necessarily move forward or learn new methods of approach.

Personal Unconscious vs. *Collective Unconscious.* The full treatment of this concept is given later in the chapter, but at the moment it is deemed important to introduce the concept briefly because of the polar nature of Jung's two states of unconsciousness: *personal* and *collective.*

The *personal unconscious,* somewhat akin to Freud's unconscious, is the storehouse of all that has happened to the individual. All previous, conscious material which is now not available to the conscious mind because it has been forgotten, repressed, or was not strong originally in a subliminal sense, resides in the personal unconscious.

The collective unconscious is one of Jung's most controversial contributions to the field of personality theory. Essentially, what Jung suggested is that man is born with a predisposition through his racial past to act in certain ways. As man has evolved through the centuries, he has accumulated knowledge and feelings. These, plus the accumulated predispositions of the present generation, do not disappear but are handed down via inheritance to each succeeding generation. All of this storehouse of knowledge, feelings, superstitions, may never be triggered to action if no opportunity presents itself as a stimulus. Certain seemingly universal fears known to all men—feelings about mother, aspirations toward a supernatural figure, worship of gods and deities—all are examples of the collective unconscious. It is as if man through the ages shares an increasingly complex repository of memories collectively passed down from one generation to the next. This phenomenon, stated Jung, has continued to be active for all the centuries of man's existence. Jung gave various names to the collective unconscious, sometimes calling it primordial images, imagos, behavior patterns, but most often he referred to the collective unconscious as archetypes.

The personal *vis à vis* the collective unconscious states of man's personality operates sometimes independently and sometimes in coordination with the other, but always is a different phenomenon within the personality. At times, when the personal unconscious is incapable of reducing pressures for man, the collective unconscious through the richness of its accumulated past can solve man's present problems. Conversely, as men acquire rich experiences in the present life, these are then passed on to future generations in the form of predispositions to act in prescribed ways found to be useful, or strong enough not to be ignored.

Conscious vs. *Unconscious*. A polarity also exists between the conscious and the unconscious aspects of man's behavior. The latter, despite its being of two kinds (personal and collective), is different from the state of awareness or consciousness of the world. The conscious has as its central core the ego. The ego is that part of man's personality which has feelings, perceptions, and thought processes which help the personality to attend to the business of everyday living. However, it never operates alone, for there is much by-play between it and the two areas of the unconscious. To the ego falls the task of directing life's processes. The direction is always a vacillating proposition between the ego in the conscious, and the tug and pull and influence of the unconscious. Much of what goes on in this process is governed by the principles of entropy and equivalence. Thus, what conflicts the conscious mind cannot resolve are often resolved by the unconscious impinging subtly upon the conscious. The total effect again creates a polarity in life which does not always connote direct struggle between the two forces, but which may aid the ongoing life of the personality. Progress results eventually through the by-play of the two states of being.

Extraversion vs. *Introversion*. Very few original concepts of Jung have been adapted by the modern psychological world, but his suggestion that the personality moves in two different directions, either extroverted or introverted, is one of those few. The extraverted personality moves in the direction of people, toward the objective, nonreflective world, and a life centered on action. The introverted personality moves in the opposite direction, where his world is quiet, free from people, and centers on subjective experiences which are quite personal. Although current psychological research has discovered a third position of ambiversion, many lay people still adhere to the extraversion–introversion description of personality. Where the conscious self or ego is oriented toward extraverted behavior, the principle of polarity causes the unconscious realism of the personality to be oriented toward introversion. The individual who is brash, bold, and direct in behavior utilizes dreams and fantasies which make him into the image of the quiet, reflective scholar, the opposite of his known personality to the world. The opposite, of course, applies to the introverted personality. His dreams and aspirations in fantasy-form are desires to be more forthright and direct in contacts with people. By the reciprocity of these two forces, said Jung, the total personality comes nearer the middle of the two polarities than the external personality would suggest. Perhaps, after all, Jung was not so much in disagreement with the research which indicates a middle point called *ambivert,* although he did not create or use the term.

Superior Functions vs. *Inferior Functions.*   In a following section on the self-actualization principle more will be said about the four functions. At the moment we may consider these functions as being of superior or inferior strength. The four functions are as follows:

> Intuition: why it is (theory)
> Sensation: what it is (recognition)
> Feeling: what it is worth (value)
> Thinking: what it means (understanding)

Most personalities utilize one function more comfortably and continuously than the other three. This becomes the superior function. A person may be looking at an oil painting and see it primarily for its value or worth. His superior function in reacting to oil paintings is what Jung called the *feeling* or *value* of the painting. It is, or is not, valuable. The other three functions at this time will be inferior, although one of the three may act in an auxiliary or supportive capacity. For example, besides his feeling for the painting, a man may consider oil paintings also through his sensation function. The sensation function tells him that he recognizes it as a painting of the sea shore. Assuming that the painting is an *avant garde* work and he can sensate nothing because he can recognize nothing in the picture, the auxiliary aspect of the sensation function influences his feelings. The primary feeling function now places a lower value on the picture as far as he, the viewer, is concerned because he cannot recognize or receive an identifiable sensation from the painting. The other two functions in this situation (thinking and intuition) are inferior. Inferior functions usually express themselves via symbols in dreams and fantasies. In our example above, the viewer may express via the unconscious a feeling of rejection and disturbance about the painting because he cannot understand it. He is unable to think about it or know what it means. This causes him to be irritated and angry about such pictures, but he cannot express this feeling well because he cannot understand the picture.

Again, the aspects of polarity, so important to the basics of Jung's system, are illustrated by the superior and inferior functions of the personality.

Physical Energy vs. *Psychic Energy.* From the libido comes all energy for the individual. Although the term *libido* is at times used in a confused sense by Jung, we may assume that, as in the Freudian system, this is a wellspring for energy. Jung did not consider the term to mean primarily sexual energy. (It was partially on the accusation of Jung, that Freud's work overemphasized the sexual content in the personality, that they parted ways.) From the libido emerges two types of energy: psychic and physical. Since these both use the same source of energy, there may at times be conflict in their demands upon the source of energy. The polarity of physical energy (walking, muscular working, etc.) to psychic energy (thinking, feeling, perceiving, etc.) creates a reciprocity which keeps the individual somewhat in balance between the poles.

Organic Needs vs. *Cultural Needs.* Somewhat similar to the previous polarity is Jung's suggestion that organic needs and cultural needs are in conflict for the basic energy provided by the libido. A priority system exists here, so that the organic needs take precedence in obtaining the libidinal (psychic) energy first. After the organic needs have been satisfied, the psychic needs may use whatever energy remains. The primary demands to maintain life (eating, sleeping, eliminating, etc.) must be met before the person can hope to pursue the cultural needs (reading, creating art forms, pursuing hobbies, worship, etc.). Jung pointed out that man is progressing as a living thing, because, as he better meets his organic needs, he spends less and less energy and time on these needs; therefore, man is able to create higher and better forms of culture. Jung is saying that bread comes first; then man may have Bach, Beethoven, and books.

Anima vs. *Animus.* It will be recalled from the previous discussion regarding the collective unconscious that all individuals inherit a characteristic from their ancestors which is universal. This archetype, when referring to man's bisexuality, is called the *anima* or the *animus*. In males the feminine characteristic is called the anima. In females the masculine characteristic is called the animus, revealing Jung's feeling that there is something of the opposite sex in each of the sexes. Although this concept has wide acceptance in the present day, Jung boldly annouced his concept much before it was totally accepted. He departed, however, from the generally approved biological theory of androgens and estrogens. Jung credited the bisexuality of man to primordial influences. He admitted the influence of the sex chromosomes but insisted that these are the result of racial experience and not of genetically organic evolution as such. He stated, "the whole nature of man presupposes woman . . . " and, of course, the reverse would be equally true. By this archetype, which has accumulated over the ages, man and woman are able to appreciate and understand each other's role. We may assume further that under the structure of progress, as Jung believed, man and woman are progressively becoming more and more in tune with the sex roles of each other. The ultimate of this trend was not discussed by Jung directly.

Sublimation vs. *Repression.*　The reader will remember that, according to the principles of entropy and equivalency, energy does not just disappear but goes into another form of expression. Jung felt that this is definitely important when psychic energy from the libidinal source is not permitted full expression. As usual in his system there seem to be only two directions or polarities in which the frustrated psychic energy can move: It may move upward into fields of expression which are socially acceptable and can be pursued openly, or it may move downward into hidden avenues of expression which are not always acceptable to society. The former method is called *sublimation,* while the latter is called *repression.*

In sublimation the personality moves forward because the outside world encourages its motives. Being given encouragement, the sublimated psychic energy can act in a rational manner and coordinate its strength to bring about the desired goal. The energy is there because of the principles of entropy and equivalence. The only real factor which has changed is the nature of the goal. Unmarried women may, for example, sublimate their very understandable desire for children and the role of motherhood into most valuable roles in society by being teachers of the young. Through this avenue they may "mother" children, be kind to them, be responsive, warm, all of which society holds in high esteem. This is not to say that all unmarried teachers are using sublimated psychic energies. The reasons for entering and remaining in an occupation are varied. In this example we are merely trying to point out a method of sublimation which transplants the energy directed toward one goal, motherhood, to that of another, entering the teaching field, although this may not be directly within the conscious reasoning of the teacher. Sublimation often hides its real reasons from the sublimator.

Repression is disturbing. The psychic energy is blocked. It cannot disappear, according to the principles of entropy and equivalency. Therefore, the psychic energy descends into the deepest recesses of the unconscious to boil and roil about, creating tighter tensions the more it is repressed. Having no place to go but into the ego forms of consciousness to which it is denied access, the repressed feeling causes pain and irrational behavior. Not being coordinated, because its goal is unobtainable, the repressed psychic energy can only create pressure. This causes the personality to behave in odd and neurotic ways. Sudden mood shifts, headaches, irritability, lack of concentration, all or any of these may be the result of repressed psychic energy. In most cases the individual is largely unaware of what is happening. Usually only through deep insight and psychotherapy is the individual able to uncover the dynamics of repressed psychic energy. All is not hopeless, however, according to Jung, because, as we have discussed in the section on regression vs. progression, the "strategic withdrawal" may be the wisest move. By allowing the personality to move backward, it may be possible to find other goal structures, or an acceptable sublimatory action. If the pain of repression is high enough, the psychic energy may perforce do something about relieving the situation. The deepest forms of repressed behavior may eventuate into psychotic behavior, a poor adjustment according to society, but one which may satisfy the personality because no other method of solving the problem has occurred. The catatonic in deep, trancelike state has "solved" his problem to some degree by complete withdrawal.

Causality vs. *Teleology.* The term *teleology* is important enough in Jung's work to be considered a principle later in these pages, but for the present it represents such an important polarity (with causality at the other pole) that we have included it here.

Although almost all personality theorists do not deny that man is a goal-seeking creature of some kind, few place the emphasis on the distant future as Jung did. *Teleology,* a term more often encountered in philosophy and theology than in psychology, means essentially "that the present can be *explained* in terms of the future." This carries it beyond the concept that man goes along seeking immediate goals, to the aspect of man as seeking and being strongly influenced by goals and aspirations in the very far future.

In contrast to the teleological viewpoint as an explanatory factor for man's dynamics of behavior is the currently popular mode of explaining man's behavior by what he has been in the past. His past is irrevocable. It has happened and one cannot undo the past. If you wish to know why a person behaves as he does now, you must explore and examine his past for the answers.

Jung did not deny the causality of the past as a determiner of the present, but he accepted causality as only a part of the picture for describing present behavior. Aside from the fact that he felt that concentration on one's past only leads to discouragement (you are stuck with your irrevocable past), Jung felt strongly that all people conduct themselves in the present by a forward-looking philosophy. The college student, for example, works and dreams and plans for the day when he will graduate, get a job, get married, and achieve wealth and success. This dream of the future, stated Jung, explains better why he studies and remains in college in the present than describing him as such and such a student because he came from such and such a background. Jung was willing to admit that man's progress may be curtailed by his habits of the past, but insisted also that man has his eye to the future.

Thus, to Jung a polarity exists between what a person has been and what he is trying to become. Only by the interplay between these two factors can we explain why he acts as he does in the present. The past is prologue, the present is action, while the future determines behavior.

Process of Individuation. In summary, all of the previous personality factors and others we shall write about must be balanced in equality if a true self is to emerge. Governed by the principles of entropy and equivalency, the system cannot be in a state of equilibrium while one factor is greater than the other. Tension and conflict result. These allow man to be unhappy and frustrated. The true goal in life is to seek a full state of development for all of the component parts, be they psychic or organic, conscious or unconscious. However, Jung declared, such a perfect state of affairs is impossible, as man is not a closed system existing only within himself. The human being cannot avoid the storms and stresses of the exterior world any more than he can keep his interior organic self in a balanced state between hunger and satiation or sleep and wakefulness. The demands of society, friends and foe, also continuously tip the balances. Only because man has to keep working continuously to equate the polarities in his life does he move forward and progress, although progress may not be easy.

Self-Actualization Principle

Jung was an optimist about man and his future. Although he read and studied extensively the unwritten and written past of man, his main interest was in the future of man. He found the future good. It is good because it is better than the past, and all indications are that it will continue to improve just as it has in the past. Modern man, he felt, is an improvement over primodial primitive man. There is no reason to suspect that with all the past vicissitudes of life, famine, pestilence, disease, methods of warfare which man was able to surmount, that progress will cease. The very struggle that man must go through to survive strengthens him and assures that the race will continue. The polarity of man's existence guarantees struggle, out of which comes progress.

Man's gradual improvement does not come out of a mass effort, but only through individuals. Individuation within the self (seeing that all parts of the self attempt equalization) and also individuals as single identities are the keystones of progress for man as a whole. Man acts in concert with other men primarily for reasons of well-being and mutual aid, but any group improvement is only the accumulation of its variegated parts, the part being the individual.

The emphasis, then, for Jung was the single personality. How does the personality of man reach its highest level of self-actualization? What are the basic components of the personality system he has to use, and how does he go about using them?

The Components of Self-actualization. The personality consists of various parts or systems, some of which are the ego, the self, the states of conscious and unconscious, the functions, the persona, the attitudes of introversion and extraversion, the psychic and physical energy systems, and the culmination of all of these into the *self*, as it is fully actualized through the polar quality of existence. Synonymously with the term *per-*

sonality Jung uses the term *psyche,* although at times in a confused way. The highest level of interaction within the psyche is the *self.*

Ego.   As Jung developed his theory of personality through the years, he refined and confined the concept of ego to include only the conscious mental activities of man. The ego structures the external and, in part, the internal world for the individual. Through the ego he knows himself. The ego attends to the conscious processes of thinking, perceiving, and identifying sensations in the world in which he lives. It is the ego which man knows best and at whose level he operates in his daily world. It gets him up, dresses him, remembers for him the things he must do, and makes his primary decisions of the day. To Jung the ego exists in the center of man's conscious world. However, because it is in the center of his conscious world it must, therefore, be in conflict with the unconscious world. People who live primarily at the ego-conscious level sometimes resent and become angry at the suggestion that a part of their personality or psyche may exist at a level outside of the conscious. This is defensible, according to the Jungian theory. The conscious and the unconscious are in opposition. The primarily consciously oriented individual resents the intrusion of the unconscious. He feels it is a sign of weakness or witchcraft, lacking any proof in substance or fact as he knows them in his conscious world. There is, however, said Jung, an attempt by the unconscious to manifest itself through dreams, autistic thinking, and heavy dependence upon symbols in life. Ritual and fantasy in personal life or a strong reaction amounting to reaction formation absorb the doubter of the unconscious. In this way the psyche is attempting to bring balance to the ego through pressure created by the unacknowledged unconscious. The more strongly the consciously oriented ego denies and vehemently scoffs at the idea of an unconscious, the more the unconscious is proving its existence. Eventually the ego gives way (usually in life after the forties) to the self. In the self we have the full acknowledgement and use of both conscious and unconscious states of being. The self inherits the role of the old ego.

Self.   The self, lying "midway between the conscious and the unconscious," is able to give equilibrium to the total personality: the psyche. It does more than balance the psyche; it also keeps the psyche in a relatively stable position. Man achieves this stability only, in most cases, in later life after he has emerged from the brashness of adolescence and the worldly orientation of the early adult. The attitudes of extraversion gradually are replaced by the attitudes of introversion as the individual lives through middle age. During this period the middle-aged person no longer needs the physical energy he once used to make a start in life, and thus, following the precepts of entropy and equivalency, he displaces physical energy with psychic energy to balance out the life picture. Likewise, the organic needs become less important, especially if he has managed to accrue some wealth and position, thus freeing more of his mental and physical energy. To take the place of organic needs, he may pursue and enjoy the cultural needs of later life. (At this time the individual may wish that he had pursued more education and had acquired college degrees and the like while he was younger. This he could never have done unless his earlier years were saturated with a physical energy which more than fulfilled his organic needs. If it were possible to reverse this individual's life, the chances are strong that he would repeat the same pattern.) The total result of these readjustments is a balanced psyche, due to the ability of the self to change from one pole to another, arriving at the midpoint if the self is actualized in most of its potential. As we have seen, the personality never fully achieves a state of balance and fulfillment because of the outer and unpredictable influences of life.

Jung felt that only in very rare instances, in some religious figures, such as that of Jesus of Nazareth and some religious men of the Orient, has a psyche come near to being in perfect harmony. Jung's interest in religion and in rituals and the theory of Nirvana resulted in much of his writing about the balanced psyche.

Conscious and Unconscious State. These two states of being are primary components of man's existence. When his psyche is able to use and live in both states to the profit of the psyche, then it is in equilibrium. So many of the observable characteristics of man are in the conscious state, for that is what we see and feel both in ourselves and others, that Jung spent relatively little time in discussing it as a single entity. Most of his writings deal with the reciprocity of the conscious to the unconscious. The unconscious is divided into two parts: the personal unconscious and the collective unconscious. The personal unconscious contains such phenomena as the persona and the complexes. The collective unconscious contains the concepts of archetypes, shadow, and synchronicity. The line between conscious and unconscious behavior by the psyche is amorphous and there is much free flow between the two states of being in daily life. A more complete exposition of these two states follows later in the chapter. At this point it is necessary to note that they are the chief components of the psyche. Because they constitute a major contribution in themselves, they are treated separately, as fundamental principles of Jungian psychology.

Functions.   One of the few articles of Jung's theory that does not lend itself readily to polarities is his four fundamental, mental functions. Although the functions were employed to illustrate superior and inferior functions, it is only by extension that the four activities align themselves into opposing groups. Here again we see the polarity or dualism of Jung's ideas.

The chief objective of the functions is to develop equally well so that the psyche may be in full balance, as was previously described in the discussion on polarity. When the functions do not array themselves equally within the system, superior and inferior functions result. Usually each of the superior and inferior functions is supported by an auxiliary function. The personality is rarely able to create a state of equal power between the functions although this is the end goal for their existing. Jung mentioned precisely four functions and firmly held to the view that these four, and no more, exist in man's psyche. Whenever the superior function is in full sway, it is always in the conscious realm, while its counterpart, the inferior one, is in the unconscious, where it has a highly disturbing effect on the mental processes. As man develops in all his potential and as he gets older and more mature, two, three, or rarely all four functions perform with equal efficiency.

The illogical and nonrational mental functions are intuition and sensation. The logical and rational functions are feeling and thinking. All four are necessary for man's mind to perform if he is to know and live in this world.

Intuition—When a student, confronted with a decision which must be made, is unable to give his reasons for the decision, he may often be said to have acted intuitively. Intuition goes beyond the senses of sight, hearing, and so on, to lower levels of consciousness. Thinking is not a part of intuition. We come upon our decision without any conscious activity of which we are aware. Obviously, subliminal cues are used, but because they are subliminal, we cannot reconstruct our thought processes.

Jung felt that intuition is as important to man's mental life as is any of the other three functions. Only by intuition is man able to solve some of his problems. Sensating, feeling, and thinking may bring him no nearer to a solution, because the facts do not lend themselves to the five senses, to a personal commitment of emotion, or to the orderly arrangement of facts. Man then may be able to arrive profitably at some sort of conclusion by intuition, which employs none of these mental functions. But intuition, like sensation, knows no orderly rules of logic. The answers come from the inner recesses of the unconscious through patterns and processes that cannot be traced.

Sensation—Although this term has been a point of contention and discourse in the field of philosophy to the detriment of its psychological meaning, Jung felt no confusion in its use as one of the nonrational, mental functions. Sensation "establishes what is actually given." Sensation is seeing, hearing, smelling, tasting, and feeling.

Through the avenue of our senses we know about the world around us. It tells us what is. The fact that the sensor does not have to think through his reaction to color, flavor, painful touches, and so on makes this mental function a nonrational one. He may have to think through whether he recognizes a certain fruit taste and then further think through whether he likes it or not, but he does not have to think about whether he is tasting the substance. He is stimulated either to taste or not taste. This phenomenon requires no thought but only a substance strong enough to excite the taste buds.

Feeling—To most semanticists and psychologists, *feeling* is a term with multiple meanings, most of them not clearly defined. In addition to the multiplicity of definitions psychologists in general consider feeling to be a nonrational, emotional state. That is, if one judges situations by his feelings, it is assumed that his judgment is based primarily on emotions and can be influenced by emotions contrary to what wisdom and facts would indicate. To Jung the term *feeling* is a subjective concept which connotes "the value an individual places upon a person, place, or event." How he feels about something tells us how important it is to him. If the individual states he feels strongly about an object, he is indicating that the object is of great importance to him. Weak feeling indicates passivity or almost complete lack of interest and, hence, value. Rarely do two persons have an identical value of feeling toward the same object because feeling arises from the self's inner, individualistic judgment. Feeling is one of the most subjective experiences of man.

Jung considered feeling to be a rational state of mind—an unusual attitude in comparison with other professional and/or lay interpretations. However, his position was that feeling tells us the value of an object. One cannot place value upon an object without comparing the original with one or more other objects. The moment a conparison is made, the thought processes growing out of the emotions involved are employed. Thought processes, or the use of mental energy, are forms of rational behavior. Therefore, accepted or not by others, to Jung "feeling" is a rational type of function of the mind. The mind has to make judgments. No matter if the basis for judging is the emotions, the values which derive from judgment are as rational as any other form of evaluation made by an individual.

Feeling as a mental function is an essential to man's existence. Through feeling man derives the goals he strives for. Feeling helps man to raise or lower himself depending on the total benefit of the value-goal. However, all of this, because man has feeling, helps man to move away from dead center.

Thinking—Thinking is the fourth of the functions as proposed by Jung. Thinking is also rational. When man thinks, he makes an orderly arrangement of facts as he knows them. His senses may not necessarily come into play. Relationships are especially important to man in his thinking because thinking requires an orderly array and establishment of order for more than one set of propositions. Thus, to Jung, thinking neatly fills out the roster of the four mental functions which are so important to man's existence.

Persona. Jung adapted the Greek term *persona*, which means mask, to describe the "face" man presents to society. This face may be quite alien to his real feelings and intentions. Man derives his persona partially from the roles that society decides for him and partially by his own acceptance, creation, and change of society's concept of his role. The individual who lives primarily behind a public mask is called the *personal man*. He may deviate so widely from his own personal feelings as to become alienated from them. Such action destroys the individual's ability to reach a true self-actualization. Jung believed this is one of the major causes of man's becoming emotionally distraught in the modern day. The personal man lives by false aims and purposes. His real self and his public self become so widely separated that it becomes impossible for him to create a genuine self, true to his own ideals. The further man deviates from his true self-actualization, the more mentally sick he becomes. When the persona is minimized by man and he comes closer to genuine self-actualization, Jung called him the *individual man*. Life is a struggle between the polarities of personal man and individual man as characters within the same personality.

Extraversion–Introversion. The self contains within it both factors of extraversion and introversion. As discussed in the polarities, the extrovert aspect of the self is oriented toward people. The extravert displays emotion, is inclined to be volatile, and favors action over contemplative thought. The introvert reverses the process by hiding feelings and seeking solutions to life's problems through passivity. To achieve true self-actualization, man must bring both introvertive and extravertive characteristics into proper and lasting balance. Although this is never totally possible because the personality is not a closed system, Jung felt that the struggle for this goal is worthwhile, for it gives man a more interesting facet both to himself and to others.

The Mechanics of Self-Actualization. Man achieves self-actualization by various methods, some incompatible with each other, some complementary to each other.

1. Primary to all of the mechanisms of self-actualization are the factors of polarity: regression *vs.* progression, personal unconscious *vs.* collective unconscious, conscious *vs.* unconscious, extraversion *vs.* introversion (carried into action), superior functions *vs.* inferior functions, physical energy *vs.* psychic energy, organic needs *vs.* cultural needs, anima *vs.* animus, sublimation *vs.* repression, and causality *vs.* teleology. All of these, of course, operate within the principles of equivalence and entropy.

2. Basic to the methods by which man gains a more complete self is the machinery he inherits in the form of his body and all of its mammalian characteristics. Through heredity man inherits two valuable factors which, as life progresses, enable him better to achieve self-actualization than can the lower forms of animal life. He inherits a biological system fully equipped with instincts. The main function of his instincts is to preserve life and to reproduce his own kind. Man also inherits the potentiality of racial experiences, which Jung called *primordial images,* or *archetypes,* or *imagos,* or *behavioral patterns.* This controversial contribution of Jung's states that the human being does not lose all of the knowledge and experiences that it took his ancestors so long and so painfully to learn. Man inherits a potential fear of harmful animals and frightening natural phenomena, such as lightning and thunder, for example.

3. Man is more than an accumulation of his past experiences. He is also a collection of dreams and hopes for the future. Through the dynamics of the present life and the effect of his past he fashions a plan of some sort for the future. By this method man becomes a forward-looking creature, a fact which Jung considered to be of primary importance in achieving

self-actualization. Man can never become fully self-actualized without purposive behavior.

4. It is very rare in the Jungian theory for an adolescent or young adult to achieve full self-actualization. As the individual develops through his span of years, his primary energy source is organic and exists at the vulnerable, conscious level. It is not until he develops the counterpart of organic energy (psychic energy) that man can come near to a true self. The extroverted, impulsive behavior of children and youth must make room for the spiritual, more introverted behavior of adults, with their accumulated wisdom and value systems based on deeper philosophical grounds. Actual chronological years are not the most important factors in this type of self-actualization through stages of development, but Jung considered most people in our civilization to reach this revaluation of values around the ages of forty or fifty. The age may vary through differing cultures and civilizations. This aspect of Jung's personality theory can hardly be expected to appeal to younger people.

5. In some sense the more experience the personality gains, the better able it is to broaden and gain full selfhood. Jung felt that only as the various components of the personality are developed can the personality obtain self-actualization. Since development grows out of profitable experience, the human who has the most experiences in life and who can make them profitable is the human who can come the closest to achieving selfhood or self-actualization. This process called *individuation* is the one by which the personality reaches the highest level of development of all its parts. All of the polarities come near to balancing each other. When this level has been approached, Jung felt that man has developed into the best person he can possibly become. Through the transcendent function all spiritual systems comes to the flowering which is man's goal of life.

6. Symbols are basic to Jung's theory of personality. Man is fortunate in that he can operate in life with symbols, whereas lower forms of animal life must conduct all of their operations through concrete facts. Much of man can exist at the symbolic level through pictures, words, dreams, music, and art forms, the symbolism of clothing and speech, while animals must live off actual flesh and food and actual physical contact with the earth's goods. Symbolism helps man to achieve a higher and more differentiated self than that possible for animals. In a general way, as man descends in behavior, he loses more and more of his capacity to operate with symbols. The gross human being is one who has very few symbols in his existence.

Symbols perform two basic functions for man. The first function is that of a repository for all of his ancestors' experiences. Here the symbol helps him to overcome instinctual behavior which he cannot express openly. The second function represents the aspirational levels of man as he progresses through the ages. Here man develops through higher and higher forms of symbols, never fully aware of the symbol's full meaning as he uses it. Jung felt that there is tremendous importance in the hidden meanings of the symbols man uses. Much of his writing has delved deeply, and at times esoterically, into the symbology of man's existence throughout recorded history.

If man is to use symbols wisely, he should attempt to find symbols which help him to discharge repressed desires in more and more productive ways. Progress in a civilization may be partially marked by that civilization's capacity to create and maintain symbols which help it to release overpowering libidinal drives, drives which would harm its constituents.

Unconscious States Principle

Like Freud, Jung placed great emphasis on the power and effect of the unconscious upon man's behavior. To ignore the unconscious is to invite mental and emotional trouble through delusions, compulsions, and phobic difficulties. The unconscious part of man's psyche will not be ignored, even though one may deny that such an amorphously described state exists in man's personality makeup.

Unlike Freud, however, Jung divided the state of the unconscious into two categories, each most important to the behavior of man. He did not include the preconscious or subconscious states in his theory. Below the level of the ego which lies in the conscious state of being are the personal unconscious and the collective unconscious. Both personal and collective states may operate singly or in harmony with each other. Some parts of the collective unconscious have been so well identified and studied by Jung that these are discussed as separate systems: anima and animus, persona, symbols, and the shadow.

Personal Unconscious. All experiences which man undergoes as he lives through life are not forgotten, nor do they disappear. They become instead part of the personal unconscious. This region of the mind is the storehouse of experience. Each individual, therefore, has a different personal unconscious than has any other individual. Material may get into the unconscious because it is forgotten or was of such a subliminal nature as not to be noticed in the first place, or it may be deliberately suppressed because it is a painful and disturbing memory of a past experience. There is always much reciprocity between the ego in the conscious state and the material in the personal unconcious. In living each day, man uses much of the material from the unconscious, which he deliberately brings up from that region to aid him in the problems of the day. As with Freud's treatment of repression, here, too, man may be unable to bring out a repressed thought or piece of information because it is associated with a painful past experience. However, the flow is usually quite free between the conscious and the personal unconscious. Jung felt that man does not fully appreciate the value of the personal unconscious in his daily life.

Complexes—As man proceeds through life and gathers experiences in many areas, he begins to build cores of memories, emotions, and residual feelings around certain phenomena. These central cores of experience are called *complexes*. One may have, for example, a mother complex, a father complex, a power complex, a complex dominated by an overpowering desire to live in a meticulously kept home, or any kind of complex which has a central core of experiences powerful enough to remain in the ego field. As these complexes evolve out of repetitive experience which is both satisfying and strong enough to have residuals in the ego, they also perform another function of attracting and interpreting new experiences around the former complex. This is called the *constellating power* of a complex. To some degree and dependent upon the drive of the complex's constellating power, almost any experience can be interpreted and gathered into the complex as being appropriate to it. For example, people with complexes centered around outdoor life and primitive living may twist and turn any experience to interpret it around the complex of the value of outdoor living. Musical artists, painters, professional athletes, and the like are possible examples of the constellating power of a complex. Mothers with a strong complex regarding their mother role are frequently seen.

Most of the time the complex and its central core operate in the personal unconscious. The individual is not totally aware that he interprets and utilizes so many extraneous phenomena in the service of his complex. The complex may, however, merge into the ego conscious level. Frequently, at such a time, the individual will rationalize his stereotyped interpretation of all events in the light of his complex, especially if it is pointed out to him by others not so complex minded. By and large however, the complex will make use of similar experiences, rather than dissimilar ones. Individuals whose complexes are directed by the same type of constellating power frequently band together in organizations.

The personal unconscious and the collective unconscious may also aid each other in regard to man's use of complexes. Not infrequently the personal unconscious has reawakened some past archetype in man's primordial past which belongs to the collective unconscious. Camping and the outdoor life, for example, may be derivatives of man's early existence on this planet. In reciprocation, the camping and outdoor life of fishing and hunting may reinforce this archetype as it has been handed down through the ages through the collective unconscious. One gives the complex a background of inherited potentials, while the other advances and enriches the background for future generations which may inherit the archetype. It should be remembered that the personal unconscious is man's past as he has actually lived and experienced it in his lifetime. Should there be no opportunity to experience, for example, outdoor life, then it is hardly possible to reawaken the primordial experiences of outdoor living even though these experiences may lurk in the collective uncon-scious as archetypes.

Jung suggested three ways of studying the constellating power of a complex: 1. by assessing the degree of emotional expression displayed by the individual when in pursuit of or engaged in a complex; 2. by observing the behavior of the individual directly and indirectly (indirect observation Jung called *analytical deduction,* by which he meant that the observer must infer from peripheral data the power of the complex); and 3. by noting any behavioral disturbances such as forgetfulness, or strong emotional reactions, when something (a word, gesture, article of clothing, etc.) is presented to the individual's attention. The incitor is called a *complex indicator.*

Collective Unconscious. It seemed as logical to Jung to attribute an accumulated past of experiences for all men collectively as it did to attribute the same phenomenon for a single individual, as he did in the personal unconscious. If one man can accumulate experiences out of his past personal life and have them stored in the unconscious, why, then, cannot man, as a generic total, accumulate and hand down to his progeny all of the collected experiences of man as he has lived and learned them through the ages? To Jung the answer was that man does, both singularly and collectively, accumulate experiences which are not lost but retained and are available for further use, should the opportunity arise. Because man does not change radically (i.e., he keeps the same cerebral system,—does not have two heads, breathes air, does not revert to gills, continues to procreate in the same manner, does not lay eggs), it stands to reason that most of his experiences are going to be repetitive. As generation after generation, over the thousands of years man has existed in his present state, goes through similar experiences of eating, sleeping, obtaining food, procreating, defending itself from harm, the generations store up valuable experiences which they have kept extant.

It was obvious to Jung that man transmits and communicates skills, attitudes, and customs to his children, who in turn transmit them to their children. But, it did not answer for him the tremendous potency and staying power of certain concepts found in almost all civilizations. Surely, Jung felt, some of these ideas would have died out generations ago had they been restricted to only direct communication of generation to generation. There must be more than the direct mouth to mouth, ritual to ritual, and symbol to symbol transmitting of man's past. Through Jung's tremendous digging into the lore of the past and through his dedicated study of many, many cultures, he became convinced that man through his cerebral system inherits the richness of his ancestors' past experiences. The inheritance as such is not direct. The tendency or predisposition is always inherited with the brain, but if no event occurs which can reinforce the predisposition, it may never occur in the lifetime of any single individual.

The collective unconscious includes all of man's accumulated experience back through his prehuman existence, providing that experience has been repeated often enough to leave memory traces in the brain. Consequently, the collective unconscious is universal. Some cultures in the present day may have less opportunity to release the memory than do other cultures because of variant conditions. The collective unconscious is the fundamental base for all of man's psyche or personality. All that man is, in the present day, is built upon the collective unconscious. Whatever the individual does in his modern world is founded upon his primordial past. This gives to man many commonalities,—fear of the dark, worship of power and status, such as emerge between nations at war, the worship of some sort of deity figure, and especially the care and nurture of one's offspring. Jung reasoned that such universal phenomena cannot have been transmitted down through each generation by custom and law alone. He suggests that man inherits these behavior patterns through his brain. The universality of some collective unconscious patterns is the result of repeated reinforcements in the past from animal life on up to present man. The relatively few deviates from the collective unconscious pattern are pathological cases whose ego in the conscious, and more often, whose personal unconscious run counter to the strengths of the collective unconscious. Because the collective unconscious is so powerful and omnipresent, any gross deviation from it is bound to cause abnormalities in the present psyche. Child abandonment, for example, is a personality deviation not because the law says it is but because it is against man's collective unconscious. To defy too strongly the collective unconscious is to invite into one's present day personality strife and unhappiness. Mother love, to illustrate, is not taught by example but is inherited from one's past through the collective unconscious. Animals do not care for their young out of a sense of duty and societal pressure but out of their own forms of collective unconscious. Man is a higher form of life than are animals, and he, too, inherits the same tendency. Again, when he ignores this tendency or has not had it reinforced into his own personal unconscious, he will be the victim of emotional stress.

Archetypes—Archetype is the name usually given to the kinds of images from his collective unconscious that man uses most frequently. Other names used have been *behavior patterns, imagos,* or *primordial images.* An archetype always carries great emotion with it. Jung and some of his coworkers named a few of the archetypes and suggested that there are many more as yet unidentified and unnamed, that are equally forceful in man's personality makeup. A few named are these: God, Devil, mother and father figures, the child, birth, death, reincarnation or life after death, world's end, and the hero and villain figures.

Many archetypes often become interwoven with each other as illustrated by the Christian phrase, "God the Father." Crime movies and western films, as well as many sporting events, are following archetypal patterns by which the audience constructs a "good" guy and a "bad" guy within the situation. A hero without the counterpoint of a villain is unpalatable, fictional fare for most people. Each complements the other in the welding of archetypal figures. As an example, there is the spectator to an athletic contest, who begins the game with a completely nonpartisan viewpoint, but soon succumbs to the archetypal images of a hero team and a villain team. He wishes one team to win, despite the fact that at the beginning of the contest he had not felt partisan. "May the best team win" is a cliché which means "I" shall pick the best team as the contest develops. Man is unable to keep from identifying with an athletic team if his emotions are involved. (It must be remembered that all archetypes are charged with emotion.)

In place of the Freudian id or libidinal forces in the unconscious, Jung proposed the term *shadow* to represent the raw, savage, animal instincts in man. Morally bad, reprehensible conduct comes out of the vestigial collective unconscious that man inherits from his animal ancestry. However, differing from Freud, Jung felt that this shadow, the animalistic side of man, helps him to develop the polarities so necessary to man's existence and so necessary to his eventual progress. Only through bad does man get to know good and try to achieve the good life.

Another kind of phenomenon which Jung called *synchronicity* applies to archetypes. A thought and event may occur simultaneously without the one being caused by the other. Most of our present-day thinking holds that for every event there must be a corresponding cause. Jung went beyond the causal relationship in the world and suggested that a different plane of relationships may exist. Stemming from his exhaustive study of the field of parapsychology and its manifestations in poltergeists, clairvoyance, and mental telepathy, he felt that something operates in the universe beyond the probability of chance. Actions which we do not fully understand but can only observe may take place at the same period of time in which we are thinking about them, but neither has caused the other to happen. Dreaming of a death and then discovering later that the death actually occurred is an illustration of synchronicity. The dream did not cause the death. The death, since it was not communicated to the dreamer at the time of the dream, did not cause the dream.

As synchronicity applies to archetypes, we may find one archetype emerging simultaneously in two different parts of the world. Occidental and Oriental cultures may evolve the same archetype at the same time in history with no communication of the archetype from one to the other. Sun worship, reincarnation, and similar archetypes may be considered as examples. In addition to the cultural occurrence of archetypes, synchronicity may also occur within a single personality. One individual may dream of his own death (an archetype) and experience that death just as it was dreamed.

Teleology Principle

Originally, the term *teleology* came from the field of philosophical theology, where it comprises a considerable body of study concerned with the doctrine that "a universal purpose pervades all reality and that all events tend to its ultimate fulfillment."[2] As Jung used the term, the meaning varies to include a number of things. Basically, it means that man is improving all the time and will eventually have achieved true self-actualization. Admittedly, this path of improvement must take thousands upon thousands of years, but Jung felt, without being facetious, that man has the time. As discussed in the previous pages, man has already made steps toward selfhood. Man already has the necessary equipment in the polarities, brain structure, and the life energy eventually to reach self-actualization. However, the progress of man seems so slow that modern man feels defeated when considering his teleological end. Hence, to hasten the process, he assumes a life after death and/or a resurrection process at the end of the world which could achieve perfect selfhood in a heaven to come constructed by forces other than man. Jung felt that man constructs his own Nirvana, has already made initial steps, and will eventually achieve it, but that the longevity of the process depresses and frustrates our present day minds. All lives, then, which are lived to the nearest point of achieving selfhood, help to advance the cause through the inheritance of the archetypes.

How does man achieve this state of Valhalla or heaven on earth? Obviously, thought Jung, he reaches it only through the passage of thousands of years, because of man's unequal polarities—not only within each psyche itself, but between psyches. Since man's psyche is not a closed system but is influenced by other psyches, true selfhood cannot come to any one psyche until the other psyches have reached selfhood. Man attempts to create short cuts to selfhood. He is irritated and frustrated by results which are not immediately present to his knowledge. Many of the short cuts may be in the forms of religious beliefs and practices. By utilizing better balancing and loftier symbols, man has invaluable tools, with which to achieve ultimate self-actualization. In the final summation, what man considers as a form of perfect life, a Valhalla, a heavenly form of life, is to be reached by the efforts of each individual psyche first bringing

[2] See English and English, *A Comprehensive Dictionary of Psychological and Psychoanalytical Terms*, Longmans, 1958, p. 544. (Courtesy David McKay Co.)

itself into perfect and harmonious balance and then by repeating somewhat the same process in its interpersonal dealings with the psyches of others. Nothing can be achieved without the initial efforts of the singular personality, Jung felt. Individuation starts from self and moves to others. From the polarities principle, true harmony in self and others would bring no progress because progress is achieved through the balancing of all forces. Harmony, in some degree, is the cessation of all movement, the resolvement of all action-producing imbalance.

The end result of man's teleological frame of reference is to give him purpose and plans for the future. Man is guided by more than the immediate goals of day-to-day and year-to-year living; he is guided also by a sense of responsibility to future generations and to mankind as a whole. To deny this, Jung felt, is to deny the existence of man through the past ages of fire, famine, pestilence, war, and all the vicissitudes of living. Man would have given up ages ago were it not for his teleological frame of reference. The present concern to keep the world alive despite nuclear warfare is an example of man's teleological thinking.

DELIMITATIONS

This chapter has not covered the work Jung has done with sentence completion tests or with his work in serial dream analysis. These seem more fitted to a text on therapeutic and analytic techniques. Much of Jung's work on mythology, the occult sciences, religion, and symbology in literature has also been omitted for the same reasons. A complete discussion of his vast amount of written work would require at least a two-volume work.

EXPLAINING HUMAN BEHAVIOR VIA JUNG'S ANALYTIC THEORY[3]

Jung's theory has the capacity of either explaining the behavior of man totally or of being completely incapable of explaining some facets of it. The usual behavioral activities of man's life are used as indexes to test the theory's applicability. These nine activities are as follows: marriage, perversions, suicide, lawbreaking, supranatural being, humor, smoking, play and recreation, and psychoses–neuroses.

[3] See Chapter 3 (Freud) for comparison.

Marriage

Presumably man gets married because marriage is an archetype which he inherits. Marriage has been practiced as a custom for ages. Marriage started as a custom before the laws for marriage were instituted. Man and woman selected each other for mates following the constellating power of the mother and father complexes. Man had to be born from a mother. He continues the complex implanted in his personal unconscious by selecting a mother figure of his own. He cannot share his own mother for reasons of age-differential; menopause before long removes the mother from procreating. His father's priority with the mother also interferes with taking the mother as a wife figure. Taboos against incest are created and passed down through the generations by the collective unconscious through an archetype. The taboo is created by a male–father dominated society which resists and resents the competition of the male offspring. Incest is a male–father instigated taboo. Mothers may discharge through cuddling and loving the infant their own unconscious incestuous drives. However, man's collective unconscious had its beginnings in the animal forebearers of man, and he continues to need and want some contact both sexually and affectionately with a mother figure. Thus he can weld a number of archetypes together in the form of a wife who satisfies his inherited collective unconscious need for a mother figure. Even in societies practicing polygamy the tendency is to select a favorite wife figure. Children reared by multiple mother figures (nurses, nannies, etc.) are inclined to be *less satisfied* by a single wife figure although societal pressure may insist upon retaining a single wife during marriage. Such cases are prone to ambivalence and emotional strife, within the psyche, between the ego in the conscious and the archetype of the single mother within the collective unconscious.

Wives operate out of a differing set of circumstances in regard to marriage. Although the female also inherits archetypes in the collective unconscious from her animal forebearers, her avenues of expression are somewhat different. Even in the prelude stages to marriage of courtship, her desire for children is strong. Children help her to identify with and fulfill the archetype of mother. Males in courtship rarely plan or anticipate or strongly desire children. The desire of the male for children comes after the fact of birth not before the fact of birth. The female's mother archetype has a reinforcing effect during the difficulties of the nine month gestation period. Marriage, then, to the female is an avenue to satisfying the mother archetype, but as in many archetypes there is interplay and reinforcement between them. Thus, she also satisfied the hero archetype by selecting and entering into marriage. Whether or not society had laws to enforce marriage, man and woman would continue to become married because the archetype is so strongly implanted through the ages by the collective unconscious.

Other factors also operate in the state of being married. The anima and the animus are tremendously important in marriage and especially in a successful marriage. Man understands woman better because of his anima, and woman understands man better because of her animus archetype. Following Jung's teleological idea that the world gradually gets better and better, the male and female anima and animus archetypes are continuing to increase and become more potent. The more man becomes like woman and the more woman becomes like man, the more will they have sympathy and understanding of the roles each other plays in life. The greater the empathy for the marriage partner, the less friction and the more happiness one finds in the relationship. Jung feels that the nature of man's married state has changed considerably over the past hundreds of years. This change he attributes to the increase of inherited anima–animus archetypes.

Perversions

Acts of perversion may grow out of the shadow content of man's collective unconscious. Since man inherits all that has happened to his race, even the animal past, we then assume that the animal content of his primordial past could account for perverted activities.

Acts of homosexuality also may be considered as a confusion of the anima in the male and the animus in the female. The polarities of these characteristics may become so repressed as to take precedence over the true sex role of the conscious ego. This may be particularly true where the male has had difficulty in identifying and reinforcing his anima with his mother. The opposite may occur for the female toward the father.

In essence, a perversion is a regressive displacement of energy. Because of the principle of equivalency the repressed physical–psychical energy system reverts to an animal form of behavior because through repression the energy has no other place to exhibit itself. Physical–psychical energy which cannot be displayed in a normal way toward another human (male or female) must be displayed in some manner. It does not just disappear.

The principle of equivalency infers that energy lost to one outlet is transferred to another outlet. The thwarted, repressed energy then regresses to perversion.

Suicide

To the suicide the archetype of death has become an answer to the person's inability to balance the polarities of life. The ego in the conscious completely crumbles and is taken over by the combined forces of the personal and collective unconscious states. Death becomes a complex indicator, and all thoughts, plans, and ideation become constellated around the death archetype. The complete collapse of the present teleological frame of reference causes the person to seek death by his own hands as a form of rebirth, which permits a fresh start in another type of world. The polarity of life *vs.* death becomes unbalanced in favor of death as a form of regression. If there is no life after death to look forward to, then the life preceding birth is to be preferred by the suicide over the imbalance so unresolvable in the present life. The suicide reaches the ultimate in repression until he achieves complete regression to nonlife.

Lawbreaking

It is rather difficult to see any primary causes for lawbreaking in Jung's system. It is possible to attribute deliberate illegal action against one's fellow man to the shadow archetype. This seems almost too easy an explanation. The persona may be useful in hiding the true ego feelings from the psyche. Repression may further cause the criminal to repress feelings into the personal unconscious. Together these two phenomena may operate in such harmony as to convince the ego and self that lawbreaking is a proper type of behavior.

One might expect under Jung's matrix that theft and major forms of crime would be perpetrated by younger people whose physical energy systems and whose physical appetites are in ascendance over the psychical energy systems. By this reasoning we may assume that thieving in the general population would be perpetrated infrequently by older persons. Their value systems are replaced by wiser and more sagacious behavior as against the previous physical appetites of youth and young adulthood. Essentially the thief lacks a higher basis of symbols and uses primarily self-indulgent symbols of money, wealth, power, and any illegal gains that he can get without working for them.

Supranatural Being

Jung spent a great deal of time studying and writing about the religions of man, including the rites of worship, the symbols attached to the religious beliefs, and also the representations of the central figure of authority, or the god figure. Some of his writing brought him the criticism of being antireligious or irreligious. Jung felt these critics to be unfair. He felt that his studying and writing objectively about all religions as he found them caused others to assume his objectivity to be a form of irreligion. For example, he was unwilling to state whether God exists in the Christian frame of reference. He was further unwilling to state that God does not exist. He did state unequivocally, however, that man throughout the ages has believed in a god of some sort. This, he felt, is the crux of the matter. Christian man believes in God, has believed in Him for ages, and will continue to believe in Him. That belief, to Jung, is the most important thing for a psychologist to work on. Jung's next interest was in *why* man believes in a god figure no matter what age, race, or circumstance he is in.

Man, in his earliest form of existence as an animal, did not believe in a supreme being. Gradually as man emerged into higher and higher forms of chordate life and eventually emerged with the physical form that he now possesses, he accrued archetypes of power, omnipresence, and omniscience. The primary archetype for these qualities was the sun. The sun seemed to primordial man to possess all the necessary attributes of power (only sunlight could grow crops, give heat, etc.), and seemed to be a convenient object as a repository of knowledge. Gradually as man lived further through the ages, he developed men of great stature, knowledge, power, but all of these men had the weakness of being mortal. They died. The repetition of dead heroes becomes confusing, and they become unsatisfactory as objects of worship. Kings, potentates, and war figures during their lives can exert tremendous influence but upon death become mere symbols. Large and elaborate temples of death were constructed for the dead heroes either by themselves or by their families. Gradually, as man passed through the ages, he merged the memories of the hero figures into a composite figure with supernatural abilities. The construction of a god figure created the continuity which the human gods could not give. Thus, man passed from recognition of power and knowledge in any form, to sun worship, to human figure worship via ancestors and living heroes, to worship of the supernatural in the form of the human figure. The Greek gods in human form with human passions and the ancient Roman form of worshipping the living emperor were logical steps in developing the pattern of supreme being for man in the present century. All of this was passed on from generation to generation over the hundreds of centuries through the inheritance of the archetypes of power and knowledge, until these archetypes merged into a unitary factor called a god.

Humor

Not much can be found in Jung's theory to explain definitively the reasons for man's laughter or his sense of humor. There are, however, some meaningful extensions of the theory that are quite applicable to an explanation of humor.

Ostensibly, man laughs because he has found a unity with self. For periods of his life he finds a genuine self-actualization amid a weltering world of indecision, strife, and struggle. The keynote of humor, apparently, is the sudden release of tension, the emphasis being on the suddenness of release. In addition to the suddenness is the unexpected character of the tension released. The more unexpected is the new triumph over tension, the more intense the humor. If one knows the resolvement of a joke, it is not as funny as if one meets the resolvement suddenly and unexpectedly. Comedians whose humor is expected and anticipated are never as stimulating as those whose stories and antics are unexpected. The entire laugh-producing situation must, however, resolve a tension within man. Frequently his tension release is in the form of symbols. Thus, man laughs at the symbol of the wealthy and pompous top-hatted figure being humiliated because part of his tension in life may be created by figures of authority. The top-hatted aristocrat is a symbol of all authority over the individual. To see this symbol demeaned is to achieve symbolic equilibrium. We do not laugh at man's inhumanity to man so much as we laugh at man's ability (symbolic or actual) to achieve equality with other men who are tension-producing. We do not laugh at the blind, crippled child falling down, for he produces no tension in our lives. We laugh at the fallen, pompous aristocrat who owns more than we do and who controls our lives. The more unexpected, the funnier it is.

The identification with symbols may be a reawakened vestige of an archetype or a repressed image in the personal unconscious.

The entire process of humor probably comes within the scope of the feeling function of the mind. It has to be built upon subjective experiences. Things not known to us cannot be mirth-producing phenomena no matter how vigorously others may be laughing or enjoying the joke. The Englishman's humor, the American's humor, the Oriental's humor may be expected to operate through differing symbols and situations.

In summary, using Jung's system to explain humor, we see it as the resolvement of tension—a leveling of polarities—with no real expended energy on the part of the person enjoying the humor. To work for tension reduction is not funny. The end result here may be an absorbing feeling of well-being and deep satisfaction rather than of humor. To achieve the same end with no effort except to pay attention apparently is very funny. One further thought should be explored. The rich man must be brought to the same level and yet not allowed to grovel. A balance produces tension-release. To see the aristocrat in abject misery is to unbalance the scales again, and humor does not result. We don't want the rich man to break his leg: we only want him to fall down.

Smoking

Again, no clear-cut answers come from Jung's work to explain why some men persist in smoking tobacco. That smoking is fairly universal seems to be manifest. Once the habit is introduced to any culture, it seems to spread rapidly and be maintained despite laws (England's post-Raleigh period) and medical advice (the current lung cancer emphasis) to the contrary. Possibly smoking tobacco with its inhaling-exhaling of smoke may reawaken an archetype directly, or through symbology, of past smoke-producing phenomena. If one is not introduced to using tobacco the archetype cannot be released. However, the addiction seems to be fairly universal once the individual pursues the use of tobacco for any appreciable period of time.

Play and Recreation

Play and forms of recreation probably begin as the use of sheer physical energy by the infant, and the child and adolescent. Later this is replaced by psychical energy during the ages of forty to fifty as man balances his dual forms of energies and transforms his psyche from outer-driven to inner-driven. Essentially because man is a polar-driven animal and must work to maintain life (clothe, feed, and shelter himself), he must also balance the work forces in his life with its opposite, play and recreation.

Equally important is the effect of the principle of equivalence as it applies to this question. According to this law of forces seeking a common level, energy (both physical and psychical) which is not used in work becomes available for play and recreation. The forces attempt to reach a state of equilibrium. The principle of entropy states in effect, "All work and no play makes Jack a dull boy." In order to balance the personality so that it may more closely achieve self-actualization through the energy available to the system, one allows the energy to transmit itself from its original position of work (which is necessary) to the secondary position, which does not have the original energy, play, (is not necessary to maintain life).

Symbols may exercise a large role in man's many forms of recreation. Hunting, fishing, photography, music, ballet, whether they are participative or spectator activities, have tremendous potentiality to recreate archetypal symbols in man's past. Playing chess, for example, may give satisfaction through the manipulation of the symbols that each chess piece represents. Collecting antiques may represent the symbology of the past both in the personal and the collective unconscious.

Probably the best example of symbols and archetypes is in the children's fascination with masks and costumes at Hallowe'en. Children take so readily to this custom that one would think it seemed to be developed almost full blown shortly after birth. Pre-Lenten costume balls and Mardi Gras activities are an expression of the same thing at the adult level.

Play and recreation may also be explained by some or all of the following reasons: when the human being is repressed, thwarted, and unable to reach his goal, he may be able to gain the goal by sublimatory activities. Certain roles in lodges and secret societies may help the thwarted personality achieve a role of leadership not otherwise available to him in everyday life.

The polarity of the organic versus the cultural aspects of man's life may be involved in play. As the antidote to work man must engage in recreational activities of some sort. Obviously what may be play and recreation to some may be hard work to others.

Through play, man "rounds out" his personality. This entire process is what Jung called *individuation*. Play, therefore, is part of the process of growing up and of relieving in maturity the tension of earning a living and attending to the serious and unavoidable aspects of adult life.

Psychoses—Neuroses

Basically, psychoses and neuroses represent man's inability to maintain a balanced or equated polarity in conducting his life. The ego becomes exclusively or decidedly one-sided. In psychoses there is a complete collapse of the ego back into the inner recesses of the personal and collective unconsciouses. When he is repressed toward fulfilling some life goal and where he is further unable to sublimate himself toward another goal, man regresses into goal structures not actually acceptable to himself or to society. Strong emotional sickness of the psychotic type is like having the shadow run wild. The entire psyche regresses to archaic, animal forms of behavior. In less severe forms of emotional sickness there may be an accentuated and overpowering use of one of the four mental functions at the expense of the other three. Either thinking, feeling, intuiting, or sensing may assume such a superior role as to render the other three inoperative. The persona (mask) may become so dominant as to create a totally one-sided ego, as in some forms of neurotic behavior. All in all, whatever the type or severity of the emotional disorder, it can be taken as a failure of the psyche to maintain a proper balance between the polarities of life according to interpretation through Jung's theories.

Essentially, psychoses and neuroses are an alienation of the self from its true goal of self-actualization. In this sense the culture is of no consequence. Emotional disorder is not a question of being out of tune with one's culture so much as it is of being out of tune with one's real self. Consequently, neurosis is more than bizarre behavior, especially as it may be interpreted by contemporaries in the culture. This interpretation avoids the sociological question of what is a mental disorder, since a form of behavior which is acceptable in one culture may be considered neurotic in another culture. To Jung, the deviation from cultural norms is not the point. The inability to balance out personal polarities is.

As the principle of equivalence operates in a mental disorder, the ego is unable to use the energy available to it. Since this is contrary to the equating properties of energy according to the principle, the entire energy load is blocked within the personal and collective unconscious systems. The resulting imbalance can only create tremendous tension and unrest in the entire system of the psyche. The principle of entropy may be unable to operate because the two systems of conscious and unconscious are out of contact with each other. Being out of contact they cannot influence or exchange energy. The cleavage between them eliminates any chance for the exchange of energy.

In the psychotic and neurotic personality causality and teleology become confused. At times the sick psyche uses the future to explain the past rather than using and interpreting the past to explain the future. Since the future is unknown, it can be of little value in explaining that which has already happened. In effect, the psychotic states, "My personal world is getting worse and worse, and that is why I have never been able to be happy in the past."

Failure to balance the polar forces of life, Jung felt, comes frequently in the mid-forties when the psyche makes the transition from the over-emphasis on physical energy to a greater emphasis upon psychic energy. At this critical and hazardous period man may be unable to make the shift in emphasis. Many forms of neuroses and some syndromes, such as involutional melancholia, may result. The idiosyncrasies and pecadillos of the "fair, fat, and forty" group may be manifestations of this failure in shifting emphasis from physical to psychic energy systems.

Probably more true for the neurotic than the psychotic is the confusion and adoption of mistaken, erroneous, and erratic symbols. The mysophobic's obsessions about germs, the megalomaniac's overevaluation of self, and the frequently seen phenomenon of the neurotic's absorption in religion and its symbols may be considered to be examples of symbol misuse. The use of wrong symbols may also be found in nations which pursue, to the exclusion of most other things, a symbol of power, or in smaller ethnic groups where the symbols of materialism and "Keeping up with the Joneses" may be expressions of false goals. Jung felt very strongly the effect and power of symbols in man's individual and collective life. When man follows symbols which are alien to helping him fulfill true self-actualization, whether it be as a person or group of persons, a sickness of psyche, individual or group, must necessarily follow. Mental sickness is always associated with symbols inappropriate to man's true self-actualization.

PREDICTING HUMAN BEHAVIOR VIA JUNG'S ANALYTIC THEORY

As one considers Jung's thoughts on teleology, one sees that much of his system concerns itself with prediction. Jung predicted that man is going to be a better and better species. He predicted that man will increase in his potentialities for improvement just as man has done in the past. However, as far as definitive prediction is concerned there is very little in his system that comes near to establishing any kind or type of predictability except on the broadest of bases.

Personal Prediction

There is little in Jung's theory upon which the individual can make any predictive efforts. Much of his theory concerns broad, metaphysical aspects of man's behavior over thousands of years of time. Little of it concerns the day-to-day problems with which the student reader can involve himself. Essentially, again, only the reader in his own personal way can make the decisions that will convince him of the value of Jung's theory for prediction.

As a point of departure, it is interesting to speculate on the predictability of the things that man will fear. Consider, for example, the archetypes of things man fears. If it were possible to raise at least two generations of children with no knowledge of snakes, would they continue to hold the snake in derision and to fear it universally? Any reader of a basic psychology book knows that some children have been reared to love and fondle snakes. Jung's point is that this is so unusual that it becomes a *cause celèbre*. He considers the snake as an inherited archetype. The imago snake is so firmly implanted in man's background that it takes very little experience to recreate the imago. The experience may be actually physical, or it may be symbolic through contacts with the printed page and the spoken word. Jung further postulated that the snake universally represents evil and becomes an object of revulsion and scorn by most people in most cultures. Even the small snake bears the brunt of being a snake. This is not true of the puppy dog, fawn, or bear cub, all of whom may become objects of fear and distrust as they grow older, stronger, and more threatening. The snake, he felt, inherits antipathy even as a small snake because man through the imagos gives the snake this role. Fear of the dark, fear of thunder, fear of lightning also are imagos which man inherits from his past. All it takes for these phenomena to become fears is a slight contact, physically or symbolically. Fears of dogs, water, high places have to be learned through more prolonged experiences because they apparently are not imagos from man's past to be freed at the slightest contact with them. Such fears as mentioned above were questions of susceptibility to Jung. He asked, for example, why man seems so universally to fear a "bogie-man" if the susceptibility to it is not inherited. Parents of small children who stringently rear their children to have no contact with "spooks" or similar imaginary creatures often complain that their child seems to create the imaginary characters by himself with absolutely no reinforcement or with only the slightest shred of experience. Cursory experiences with other phenomena which later produce fear do not seem to "take" so immediately. Many fears have to be learned. Fear of the supernatural seems to be ready, full-blown and available, to control behavior with only the slightest symbolical reinforcement. This, said Jung, is because of the difficult-to-explain archetype which the child inherits. Now it is the task of the reader to determine whether it can be predicted that man will continue to harbor certain archetypes such as fear of snakes or fear of a supernatural figure, as found in the child's "bogie-man."

Scientific or Laboratory Prediction

Although Jung felt he was dealing with factual materials, and he felt this strongly, there are an extremely small number of studies designed around the material of Jung's work. Most of the current reactions, as stated in the beginning of the chapter, are strong rebuttals of Jung's work and understandably so, as little of his theory lends itself to experimentation of a statistical or laboratory nature. Although many heuristically oriented theories lend themselves to research design as we know it now, Jung's does not.

Jung's one work of a research nature revolved around the study of the serial nature of dreams. Much of his later work was concerned with this. He did not devalue the importance of the single dream but felt rather that only through an exhaustive study of dreams as they occur over prolonged periods can one get at the underlying nature of man. An extremely involved and prolonged dream series is analyzed in his book *Psychology and Alchemy*. One finds also in this book a somewhat belabored but extensive discussion of the proof of archetypes.

Jung's earliest research work, preceding and during World War I, concerned itself with the relationship to be found between the free association test (now generally referred to as the word association test) and the concomitant organic responses. Jung may be considered as a precursor of the lie detector devices now used in many psychological and police laboratories, though he was by no means directly responsible for its current development. The free association method itself, however, preceded Jung by many years with the work of Wundt in Liepzig and of Galton in England. Jung also predated some of the work of Murray and his Thematic Apperception Test. Again we do not know the direct influence Jung had upon Murray and his coworkers in their TAT work, although Murray expresses a tremendous admiration for Jung and acknowledges the influence Jung had upon his own entry into psychological work. The association of the TAT and Jung's work comes about through the method Jung used, and which he originated, of having the patient use what he called "active imagination" in describing all of his responses to a dream image or self-created visual image. In the beginning Jung worked carefully in noting the responses and changes in respiration and perspiration as measured by the pneumograph and galvanometer that come from the patient's subconscious during the process. He later became extremely intuitive and untangled complex cases through the method of "active imagination," without the use of apparatus.

Probably the most imitative and productive research that has come out of Jung's work has been through the emphasis upon the extravertive–introvertive natures of man. Although this research was heavy in volume during the 1920s and 1930s, very little is going on now in this field, with the possible exception of Eysenck (see Chapter 14). Most investigators since have been unable to produce pure polarities of the extravert or the introvert, but most of the research seems to indicate a strong ambiverted nature with occasional overtones of one or the other extremes. Predicting behavior was not a result of any of these studies on introversion–extraversion.

The case study methods of Jung were much the same as those of Freud. Both men made innovations and refinements in methods as they proceeded to work with larger and more varied case loads, but this is a method of therapy and, as such, has not been well researched except possibly for the later work of Carl Rogers.

Self-actualization as a concept was first fully expounded by Jung. Many, many others have since written and designed research around this concept although no direct evidence seems to be present that the researchers and writers were following leads that Jung gave. Allport, Angyal, Maslow, Murphy, and especially Rogers have made self-actualization a major part of their theories.

H. Gray, for a very short period in the late 1940s, was one of the most directly involved current investigators of Jungian psychology. Gray's main emphasis was on the psychological types as he interpreted them in Jung's writings. Other writers, namely Frieda and M. S. Fordham, have been fairly thorough in investigating the development of personality and the emergence of archetypes through case study material. None of the above, however, have conducted appreciable research within the framework of Jung's position but rather have cast themselves into the role of interpreters.[4]

In the final analysis, therefore, almost nothing exists of a scientific or laboratory nature which helps to interpret Jung's theory in the light of its capacity to make any meaningful predictions about man's behavior. In reading Jung's work one gains the impression that most of his work is "after the fact." This is especially true because so much of his studying has been of historical and archaic behavior patterns of mankind.

◆

SUMMARY

The author has chosen to interpret Dr. Jung's theories about personality on a polar basis. Using this approach, one can assume all of Jung's work to be a struggle between two opposing forces that man has gone through since time began. The tensions arising from the struggle, the resolvement of these tensions, the new strength and direction that result from successful resolvement of polarities, and the immense effect of man's past as he inherits behavioral traits have all been discussed in this chapter.

Once again a diagram has been constructed to help highlight the major features of Jungs system concerning personality. The diagram shown in Figure 5 is only a means of thinking about Jung's system and is not to be taken too literally.

The main feature of the diagram in Figure 5 represents the process of balancing that the ego-self structures must maintain, despite the constant

---

[4] See especially H. Gray, Jung's psychological types, *J. Gen. Psychol.*, 1947, 37, 177–185; H. Gray, Jung's psychological types, *Ibid.*, 1949, 40, 63–88; F. Fordham, *An Introduction to Jung's Psychology*, Penguin Books, 1953; M. S. Fordham, *The Life of Childhood*, Routledge, 1947; M. S. Fordham, A Discussion of Archetypes and Internal Objects, *Brit. J. Med. Psychol.*, 1949, 22, 3–7.

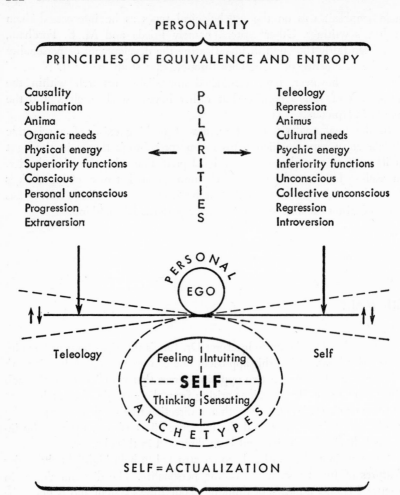

Figure 5. Diagrammatic Summary of Jung's Theory.

downward pressures exerted by the polarities. The full state of equilibrium shown is called self-actualization. The self operates as a fulcrum in the process, bearing all of the weight of the polar factors and making the adjustments to keep the entire structure in balance. The ego lying above the self and covered by the façade of the persona (which is all that other men see) is more prone to move back and forth quickly when the polarities exert undue pressure. The width of the horizontal line can be interpreted as the individual differences found from man to man. Some personalities have "wider" personalities than do others, and thus are easier to stabilize. In the act of balancing or achieving equilibrium both the ego and self must be in direct alignment above and below each other. Any other position produces an imbalance. The persona, by taking precedence over the true ego, may so alter the structure as to produce an imbalance. Further imbalance may result if one or more of the four mental functions (feeling, intuition, etc.) becomes superior at the expense of the others. All four mental functions should be in equal parts, as shown in the diagram, if one is to achieve full self-actualization. The archetypes surrounding the self structure are also important to the stability of the entire process. As life progresses, the size of the self and ego circumferences should grow larger. The larger and more experienced the four mental functions become, the easier it is to keep the system in balance. Differing polarities shown above may be emphasized at different times in life. Some polarities, hardly ever being of unequal weights, rarely cause a lack of balance, while others may be continuously out of proper proportion to each other, thus causing the ego and self to move constantly back and forth in an attempt to compensate for the unequal pressures from above. Through the ages man has teleologically been able to smooth the exterior structure of the self. The smoother this surface, of course, the easier it is to bring about movement and to achieve balance when difficulties arise between the polarities. Regression is any downward or upward movement which disturbs equilibrium of the life plank. Progression is the levelling out of the life plank. It should appear obvious that true balance for any appreciable length of time would be quite rare because of the tremendous number of variable conditions which must be met to bring it about. Neuroses and psychoses result when any of the numerous factors become more permanently out of balance. Life ceases, supposedly, when the ego-self structures are deflated to nothing.

BIBLIOGRAPHY

PRIMARY SOURCES

BOOKS

The works of Jung may be found in two major sources: his own and those of other authors edited and published through the Bollingen Foundation established in 1941. (Bollingen is the name of his home in Küsnacht on the shores of Lake Zurich.) The foundation publishes through Pantheon Press.

Jung, C. G., *The Collected Works of C. G. Jung*, Bollingen Series, H. Read, M. Fordham and G. Adler, (eds.): Vol. I. *Psychiatric Studies*, 1957; Vol. 3. *The Psychogenesis of Mental Disease*, 1960; Vol. 4. *Freud and Psychoanalysis*, 1961; Vol. 5. *Symbols of Transformation*, 1956; Vol. 7. *Two Essays on Analytical Psychology*, 1953.
    Also published as Meridian paperback, 1956.
    Vol. 8. *The Structure and Dynamics of the Psyche*, 1960; Vol. 9. Part I, *The Archetypes and the Collective Unconscious*, 1959; Vol. 9. Part II, *Aion: Researches into the Phenomenology of the Self*, 1959; Vol. 11. *Psychology and Religion: West and East*, 1958.
    Also published as a paperback by Yale Univer. Press, New Haven, 1960 —based on Terry Lectures given at Yale in 1937.
    Vol. 12. *Psychology and Alchemy*, 1953; Vol. 16. *The Practice of Psychotherapy*, 1954; Vol. 17. *The Development of Personality*, 1954.
Jung, C. G., *The Theory of Psychoanalysis*, N.Y., Nervous and Mental Disease Pub. Co., 1915.
Jung, C. G., *Analytical Psychology*, N.Y., Moffat-Yard, 1916.
Jung, C. G., *Collected Papers on Analytical Psychology*, N.Y., Moffat-Yard, 1917.
Jung, C. G., *Studies in Word Association*, London, Heinemann, 1918.
Jung, C. G., *Psychology of the Unconscious*, N.Y., Dodd, Mead, 1925.
Jung, C. G., *Contributions to Analytical Psychology*, N.Y., Harcourt, Brace & World, 1928.
Wilhelm, R., and C. G. Jung, *The Secret of the Golden Flower*, N.Y., Harcourt, Brace & World, 1931.
Jung, C. G., *Modern Man in Search of a Soul*, N.Y., Harcourt, Brace & World, 1933.
    Also as Harvest Book paperback.
Jung, C. G., *Psychological Types*, N.Y., Harcourt, Brace & World, 1933.

Also published as a Pantheon Book—the 1923 translation by H. G. Baynes.

Jung, C. G., *Psychology and Religion*, New Haven, Conn. Yale Univer. Press, 1938.
Also published in Bollingen Series, No. 11.

Jung, C. G., *The Integration of Personality*, N.Y., Holt, Rinehart and Winston, 1939.

Jung, C. G., and C. Kerenyi, *Essays on a Science of Mythology*, N.Y., Pantheon, 1949.

Jung, C. G., *Psychological Reflections: An Anthology from the Writings of C. G. Jung*, N.Y., Pantheon, 1953.
Selected and edited by J. Jacobi—thirty-first in Bollingen Series.

Jung, C. G., *Answer to Job*, London, Routledge, 1954.

Jung, C. G. and W. Pauli, *The Interpretation of Nature and the Psyche*, N.Y., Pantheon, 1955.
Fifty-first publication in Bollingen Series: translated from 1952 German edition. Jung on synchronicity and physicist, Pauli on Kepler's theories.

Jung, C. G., *Two Essays on Analytical Psychology*, N.Y., World Pub. (Meridian), 1956.
Two essays "On the psychology of the unconscious" and "The relations between the ego and the unconscious," first published in 1912 and 1916 —Also appear as Vol. 7 in Bollingen Series.

Jung, C. G., *The Undiscovered Self*, Little, Brown, Boston, 1958.

Jung, C. G., *Psyche and Symbol*, V. de Laszlo, (ed.), Garden City, N.Y., Doubleday (Anchor), 1958.
Contains commentary on "The Secret of the Golden Flower."

Jung, C. G., *The Basic Writings of C. G. Jung*, V. de Laszlo (ed.), N.Y., Random House, 1959.

Jung, C. G., *Symbols of Transformation: An Analysis of the Prelude to a Case of Schizophrenia* (trans. by R. F. C. Hull), N.Y., Harper & Row, 1962.
Original version published in 1912.

PERIODICALS

Jung, C. G., Psychotherapists or the clergy, *Pastoral Psychol.*, 1956, 7(63), 27–44.

SUGGESTED READINGS

BOOKS

Adler, G., *Studies in Analytical Psychology*, N.Y., Norton, 1948.

Clark, R. A., *Six Talks on Jung's Psychology*, Pittsburgh, Boxwood Press, 1953.

Cox, D., *Jung and St. Paul: A Study of the Doctrine of Justification by Faith and Its Relation to the Concept of Individuation*, N.Y., Association Press, 1959.

Dry, A. M., *The Psychology of Jung: a Critical Interpretation*, N.Y., Wiley, 1961.

Eisler, R., *Man Into Wolf: An Anthropological Interpretation of Sadism, Masochism, and Lycanthropy*, N.Y., Philosophical Library, 1952.
    Based on Jung's archetypal ideas.

Fordham, F., *An Introduction to Jung's Psychology*, Baltimore, Penguin, 1953.

Fordham, M., *The Life of Childhood*, London, Routledge, 1947.

Freud, S., *An Autobiographical Study*, London, Hogarth, 1935.

Freud, S., The history of the psychoanalytic movement, in *The Basic Writings of Sigmund Freud*, A. A. Brill, (ed.), N.Y., Random House, 1938.

Glover, E., *Freud or Jung?*, N.Y., Norton, 1950.
    Compare Freud to Jung—Freud wins. Also as a Meridian Pocketbook, 1956.

Goldbrunner, J., *Individuation: A Study of the Depth Psychology of Carl Gustav Jung*, N.Y., Pantheon, 1956.

Hostie, R., *Religion and the Psychology of Jung*, N.Y., Sheed and Ward, 1957.

Jacobi, J., *The Psychology of C. G. Jung* (rev. ed.), New Haven, Conn., Yale Univer. Press, 1951.

Jacobi, J., *Complex/Archetype/Symbol in the Psychology of C. G. Jung*, N.Y., Pantheon, 1959.

Jones, E., *The Life and Work of Sigmund Freud*: Vol. I. (1856–1900) The formative years and the great discoveries, 1953; Vol. II. (1901–1919) Years of maturity, 1955; Vol. III. (1919–1939) The last phase, 1957, N.Y. Basic Books.
    See especially vol. II.

Martin, P. W., *Experiment in Depth: A Study of the Work of Jung, Eliot, and Toynbee*, N.Y., Pantheon, 1955.

Munroe, R. L., *Schools of Psychoanalytic Thought*, N.Y., Dryden, 1955.
    Analysis and integration of Freud, Adler, Jung, Rank, Fromm, Horney, Sullivan, *et al*.

Pollard, W. G., *Physicist and Christianity*, N.Y., Seabury Press, 1961.
    Tridimensional life and heaven as possibilities of synchronicity.

Progoff, I., *Jung's Psychology and Its Social Meaning*, N.Y., Grove Press, 1953.
    A paperback edition.

Progoff, I., *The Death and Rebirth of Psychology: An Integrative Evaluation of Freud, Adler, Jung, and Rank and the Impact of Their Culminating Insights on Modern Man*, N.Y., Julian Press, 1956.

PERIODICALS

Adler, G., A discussion on archetypes and internal objects: III, a contribution of clinical material, *Brit. J. Med. Psychol.*, 1949, 22, 16–22.

Arluck, E. W., Training facilities of the C. G. Jung Institute, Zurich, *Amer. Psychologist*, 1960, 15, 626–629.

Bash, J. W., Einstellungstypus and Erlebnistypus: C. G. Jung and Herman Rorschach, *J. Proj. Tech.*, 1955, 19, 236–242.

Bonime, W., The psychic energy of Freud and Jung, *Amer. J. Psychiat.*, 1955, 121, 372–374.

Burchard, E. W. L., Mystical and scientific aspects of the psychoanalytic theories of Freud, Adler, and Jung, *Amer. J. Psychother.*, 1960, 15, 289–307.

Clark, R. A., Jung and Freud: a chapter in psychoanalytic history, *Amer. J. Psychother.*, 1955, 9, 605–611.

Douglas, W., Carl Gustav Jung: 1875–1961, *Am. J. Psychol.*, 1961, 74, 639–641.

Fordham, M., A discussion on archetypes and internal objects: on the reality of archetypes, *Brit. J. Med. Psychol.*, 1949, 22, 3–7.

Fordham, M., The concept of the objective psyche, *Brit. J. Med. Psychol.*, 1951, 24, 221–231.

Fordham, M., On Jung's contribution to social psychiatry, *Int. J. Soc. Psychiat.*, 1955, 1(1), 14–21.

Fordham, M., Symposium on Jung's contributions to analytical thought and practice: 1. The evolution of Jung's researches, 3–8; 2. On Jung's concept of the symbols (by R. Moody, 9–14); 3. The transference in analytical psychology (by A. Plant, 15–19), *Brit. J. Med. Psychol.*, 1956, 29.

Gray, H., Jung's psychological types: meaning and consistency of the questionnaire, *J. Gen. Psychol.*, 1947, 37, 177–185.

Gray, H., Jung's psychological types in men and women, *Stanford Med. Bull.*, 1948, 6, 29–36.

Gray, H., Jung's psychological types: ambiguous scores and their interpretations, *J. Gen. Psychol.*, 1949, 40, 63–88.

Gray, H., Freud and Jung: their contrasting psychological types, *Psychoanal. Rev.*, 1949, 36, 22–44.

Harms, E., Carl Gustav Jung—defender of Freud and the Jews, *Psychiat. Quart.*, 1946, 20, 199–230.

Harms, E., Carl Gustav Jung, *Amer. J. Psychiat.*, 1962, 118, 728–732. Obituary.

Hawkey, M. L., The witch and the bogey: archetypes in the case study of a child, *Brit. J. Med. Psychol.*, 1947, 21, 12–29.

Henderson, J. L., Jung and education, *Educ. Psychol. Baroda*, 1954, 11, 196–202.

Illing, H. A., C. G. Jung on the present trends in psychotherapy, *Human Relations*, 1957, *10*, 77–83.

Jackson, M., Jung's "archetypes" and psychiatry, *J. Ment. Sci.*, 1960, *106*, 1518–1526.

Jacobi, J., Pictures from the unconscious, *J. Proj. Tech.*, 1955, *19*, 264–270.

Jaeger, M., Reflection on the work of Jung and Rank, *J. Psychother. Relig. Proc.*, 1955, *2*, 47–57.

Lewis, A. Jung's early works, *J. Analyt. Psychol.*, 1957, *2*, 119–136.

Mace, C. A., On the eightieth birthday of C. G. Jung, *J. Analyt. Psychol.*, 1956, *1*, 189–192.

Mac Lead, R. B., Teleology and theory of human behavior, *Science*, 1957, *125*, 477–480.

> Social sciences should think teleologically and in more global terms.

Mindess, H., Analytical psychology and the Rorschach test, *J. Proj. Tech.*, 1955, *19*, 243–252.

Spiegelman, M., Jungian theory and the analysis of thematic tests, *J. Proj. Tech.*, 1955, *19*, 253–263.

Stein, L., Analytical psychology: a "modern science," *J. Analyt. Psychol.*, 1958, *3*, 43–50.

Strauss, F. H., Interpretation of thematic test material: a Jungian approach, *Bull. Brit. Psychol. Soc.*, 1954, *23*, 12–13.

Strunk, O., Psychology, religion, and C. G. Jung: a review of periodical literature, *J. Bible and Relig.*, 1956, *24*, 106–113.

Time, Biographical sketch of Carl Gustav Jung, 1952, *60*, 37.

Time, The old wise man, 1955, *65*, 62–70.

Toynbee, A., The value of C. G. Jung's work for historians, *J. Analyt. Psychol.*, 1956, *1*, 193–194.

Valett, R. E., Jung's effect on psychology, *Bull. Brit. Psychol. Soc.*, 1962, *46*, 58–66.

> Possibilities of research by the analytic procedure.

Weigert, E. V., Dissent in the early history of psychoanalysis, *Psychiatry*, 1942, *5*, 349–359.

PART III

BIOSOCIAL–SOCIAL INTERACTION

Most of the theories in this third part reflect a strong American influence, an influence which is quite natural, for all of the theorists whose work is discussed in this section have either taught or worked in this country although only one (Sullivan) is a native American.

The orientation of the biosocial and social interaction theories is toward the outside world rather than toward the inner man, as in the theories discussed in Part II. Following the Lockean tradition, strong, almost exclusive environmentalistic leaning appears in the social psychological work of Adler. This societal influence reaches probably its strongest effect in the work of Fromm.

In the main, the biosocial theorists conceive of man as a reactive animal rather than a self-active one.

In contrast to the Freudian prognosis of continuous strife these theorists emphasize the meliorative and optimistic approaches to man's dynamics. Life can become better and better, has been getting that way through the ages, and will continue to improve rather than repeat itself, as in the Freudian framework.

The primary emphasis, then, of the four theorists included in Part III (Adler, Sullivan, Horney, Moreno) is that personality is social rather than biological. Man's personality is a product of the society in which he lives.

7

Adler

*Men's weaknesses are often necessary to the
purposes of life.*

Maurice Maeterlinck
Joyselle, Act II

SOME BIOGRAPHICAL DATA

In 1870, when Freud was fourteen years old, Alfred Adler was born in Vienna, Austria. The two men were destined to meet and for a short time work closely together. Adler graduated from the same medical school as had Freud. Freud received his doctorate in medicine in 1881 from the University of Vienna, Adler in 1895 the same degree.

For a time after receiving his degree, Adler specialized in eye diseases but soon went into the practice of general medicine. Like Freud, Adler became interested in the mental aspects of his generalized practice. Before long he, too, went into the practice of psychiatry. The two men were attracted to each other and joined forces with others through the founding of the Vienna Psychoanalytic Society, of which Adler later became the president. Jung parted company with Freud in 1914, while Adler had already cooled toward Freud's pansexualism and had left the Freudian group in 1911.

Both Freud and Adler served as physicians in the Austrian Army during World War I. Their experiences in the war, although they were not associated with each other at that time, had a pronounced effect upon the formulation of their theories. Adler continued to practice psychotherapy and develop his own concepts and techniques on an individual basis. Gradually there also grew around him a coterie of followers and believers in his system, which he named *individual psychology*, in contrast to Freud's psychoanalysis. During the 1920s and 1930s neither man had much to do with the other professionally, although they both practiced in Vienna. Their split in 1911 was never healed.

Adler left Vienna in 1935 during the regime of the Nazis, while Freud left in 1938. Adler came to the United States, where he continued his private practice as a psychiatrist and attracted many wealthy and influential clients. During this time, he also accepted the position of Professor of Medical Psychology at the Long Island College of Medicine, where he continued to attract many followers and devotees.

Alfred Adler died suddenly at the age of 67 while he was on a tour and lecturing in Aberdeen, Scotland, in 1937.

INTRODUCTION

Alfred Adler was and considered himself to be a neo-Freudian somewhat in the mold of Jung and Karen Horney. He, like them, rejected the pansexualism of Freud. He, too, was a close friend and professional associate of Freud. And, he, too, left the Vienna group of psychoanalysts to form his own personal psychoanalytic approach.

One of the chief characteristics of Adler has been his capacity to change. From the time he first began to formulate theories about human behavior until his death in 1937, Adler exhibited a continued evolution of his ideas which has been interesting and in many cases quite logical. Though he never contradicted his previous work, Adler showed the metamorphosis of his thinking from an original idea to ideas more complex and inclusive of more complete behavioral phenomena. This strengthened his theoretical position considerably.

The evolution in Adler's thinking is reflected by some of the following changes he made in the theoretical structure of human behavior. Beginning with an increased absorption in man as an aggressive animal, a concept which gradually weaned him away from sex as the prime mover of man, he moved to considering man as a complex of characteristics seeking power as the prime mover in life. Finally, Adler came to the conclusion that the true motivator in man was his seeking to be superior.

In the same vein, Adler changed his ideas from man as a lustful animal, driven by opportunities to express his lustful desires, to what amounts to almost a complete reversal: man as a socially responsible animal. He believed that man is imbued at birth with social awareness and only needs to be awakened to his responsibilities to other men for their welfare as well as to his own personal welfare. In the end, Adler was convinced that the human animal had a deeply imbedded social interest in his fellow human animals.

Other changes are reflected in his development of the organ inferiority complex to the broader and more comprehensive theory that man is essentially governed by a feeling of inferiority, and thus moves forward in life to achieve new and finer things motivated by the desire to overcome his basic weakness. Organ inferiority means that man is born with a basically inferior organ in his body. This organ's being weaker than the other parts of his body serves as a compensation device for overcoming obstacles. More important is the role of the weaker organ in providing a rationalization for failure to perform difficult or onerous tasks. Migraine headaches, asthma, weak eyes, ulcers, and the like may be evidences of organs of inferiority.

Adler did not conceive a theory and spend the remainder of his professional life defending his original position. He continued to refine his work before criticism demanded it. Adler was an excellent example of his own theory. He continuously strove for superiority in his work, being motivated by a feeling that his present position was inferior to what he could eventually reach by more work and effort. In essence, this behavior epitomizes the hard core of Alfred Adler's personality theory. This is in deep contrast to the impression one frequently receives in studying the personalities of personality theorists. What the theorist does as a personality at times seems to be in direct contradiction to what the theorist states as a theory.

There is a nucleus of his followers whose work centers mainly on New York, Chicago, and Los Angeles, where branches exist of the American Society of Individual Psychology. The term *individual psychology* is one that Adler used; it has become identified with his work especially through the title of his most definitive book, *The Practice and Theory of Individual Psychology* published in 1927. At the time of this writing, probably the best and most devoted work being done in the Adlerian field is by the gifted team of Rowena and Heinz Ansbacher whose book, *The Individual-Psychology of Alfred Adler* (Basic Books, New York, 1956), is a compendium and excellent collection of Adler's writings.

ADLER'S DESCRIPTION OF HUMAN BEHAVIOR

Not many of the theories discussed in this book lend themselves as readily as does Adler's to a description of human behavior. Many of his ideas are clear cut and describe well what it is that man does as he pursues a life pattern. Part of the ease in using Adlerian psychology in descriptive ways lies in his few well-defined concepts. Unlike Jung, or particularly Freud, both of whom spun out multiple variations on a theme, Adler was economical in the same sense as Sheldon: a few well-formulated and basic unitary concepts sufficed.

Adler was a master at separating the meaningful from the trivial in reporting his case studies. Not infrequently the reader has the feeling of knowing almost at first hand the case being studied. He wrote voluminously and those of his writings translated thus far display this facility of description.

The reader will note that Adler was a humanist in the tradition of Jung. Later theorists, such as Carl Rogers and Gordon Allport fall within the same camp. Unlike Freud, Adler felt that man has a chance to be better and move upward in life, to reduce his problems and eventually (though not as distinctly and teleologically as Jung puts it) to arrive at a nearly perfect adjustment to the life process.

The author has abstracted seven principles of human behavior, as he interprets them, from Adler's work. Some interpreters may find fewer, some more. These seven seem to represent accurately the salient features of Adler's work. They are the principles of 1. inferiority; 2. superiority; 3. style of life; 4. creative self; 5. conscious self; 6. fictional goals; and 7. social interest. Upon these seven hooks the author hangs the cloth of Adler's theoretical work on man's personality.

Inferiority Principle

Adler believed that man is born into the world feeling incomplete and unfulfilled, with a deep sense of inferiority. Everything that lies before the newborn babe is better, bigger, larger, and more competent than he. To a neonate, this state of affairs hardly makes any difference in his struggle for existence. As he continues to live, however, his perceptive system makes him aware of his inferior role in society. As man moves through the first, second, third, and fourth years of his life, he is continuously reminded that most of the world surrounding him can reach things, throw things, prepare things, and control things much better than he can. Feeling inferior makes him wish to emulate the strengths and capacities of others around him. In some few abnormal cases, the child may remain at an inferior level, be unable to try anything new, or may revert to an even more inferior role. These three abnormalities are rare, however. Most of humanity wants to go beyond where it is, as does the child who desires to be more complete than he is at any given moment in his early development. Plateaus in development, although quite natural, do not last very long. Once having attained a plateau in his development toward more and better skills and powers, one has only a temporary feeling of satisfaction and success. The moment the human being can see something bigger and better beyond where he is at the moment, he again feels inferior, unfulfilled, or incomplete. The entire process starts again, the process which leads from inferiority to efforts for new attainments, to achievement of the new level (either symbolically or actually), to recognition of a newer and higher level, and then to the inevitable feeling of inferiority once again. This, said Adler, is the stuff of life. This feeling of inferiority introduced at birth is what keeps man living through the ages. Man biologically and psychologically inherits the feeling of inferiority.

The idea of man as an inferiority-driven being first came to Adler when he was practicing general medicine in Vienna early in this century. At that time, Adler noticed that many of his patients seemed to localize their complaints and illnesses toward specific regions of the body. In a time which preceded psychosomatic medicine, Adler discovered, too, that man turns to illness to solve many of his nonphysical problems. Frequently, the complaints and syndromes which Adler studied were not associated with the actual condition of the organic system of the patients he was seeing. Out of these experiences, Adler evolved a theory which he referred to as *organ inferiority*. At that time (though he was later to expand the concept), Adler felt that man is born into the world with a potentially weak organ in his body. Stress, the natural course of events in life, or any multiple of causes could create a breakdown in the potentially weak organ. The total result of the inferior organ was to make man compensate for its weakness by trying all the harder to succeed. Compensation for an inferior organ frequently determined the style of life and the manner in which the human would strive for superiority in life: individuals with weak bodies in childhood who would exercise prodigiously to build stronger bodies, and then become professional athletes; Demosthenes and his pebbles to cure stuttering; Franklin Delano Roosevelt's political career after his attack of poliomyelitis—all these can be considered examples of this inferiority-motivated phenomenon.

Organ inferiority also became interpreted later as a device used to evade painful and insurmountable tasks as the individual conceived them within his personal frame of reference. Under this interpretation also, man was born with a potentially weak organ which would come to his rescue whenever the pressures of life became too strong for him to surmount. If the striving for superiority became blocked or totally inaccessible to the individual, he could seek solace and excuse his inferiority by claiming sickness of the weak organ. Thus, some business men in highly competitive and pressure-wracked occupations may develop ulcers, while others in the same field may develop migraine headaches, and still others may find solace in sinus difficulties or asthmatic problems, or any type of organic breakdown which allows them to rationalize failure or withdraw from failure-producing situations. The inferior organ, of course, varies from individual to individual.

Having associated inferiority with organic conditions, Adler then created what he called the *masculine protest*. By a somewhat devious route in his thinking, Adler grouped being inferior with weakness and femininity. Inferiority, then, was akin to femininity. Both males and females were considered to be in protest against weakness, women because of their inherent weakness as the female of the species and males for the association with femaleness which connoted inferiority. Adler himself was dissatisfied with this truncated concept. Gradually he widened and strengthened the concept to include the generalized idea that all mankind is inferior at birth and that the inferiority has nothing to do with femininity, but is the result of an hereditary condition, followed after birth by a feeling of being incomplete.

In summary, then, Adler's concept of the inferiority principle developed through the years from 1897 to 1911, when he left the Freudian group under protest, and even strong criticism from the Vienna Psychoanalytic Society, of which he was president at the time. His ideas on inferiority feelings developed through organic inferiority to masculine protest to the generalized concept that all men are inferior and weak at birth and thus begin a lifelong struggle to elevate themselves from their present levels.

Superiority Principle

To treat this principle as an entity separate from the principle of inferiority feelings would be wrong, since both are so entwined that to speak of one immediately brings the other into play: they are mutual and highly complementary principles. However, because the development in Adler's thinking on *superiority* as a principle was somewhat different from his thinking on *inferiority*, we shall separate these principles. As they operate in man's life, the semantic separation is not possible.

After starting with an acceptance of Freud's emphasis on sexuality as a prime motivator in life, Adler soon became disenchanted with the monotony of the approach. As he defended his ideas before the Vienna Psychoanalytic Society, he stressed that man is an aggressive animal and must be so in order to survive. During the "masculine protest" phase, he gradually evolved through his therapy with clients a belief in man as more than an aggressive animal, as one who seeks power in the physical and/or symbolic sense in order to survive. Too many patients he was seeing then appeared to lack totally aggressive qualities and might be described as power-less human beings. By a reverse process, Adler reasoned that the opposite of power-lessness is power. Therefore, what man wants is power. This idea, too, had a short life with Adler. Soon he came to the concept which he continued to develop throughout the remainder of his professional life, the concept that man simply wishes to be superior and that this superiority wish grows out of feelings of being inadequate or inferior. With the newer concept of *superiority*, Adler continued to feel that wanting to be superior is a universal and timeless property of man's personality.

The softening of Adler's approach through the sequence of sexuality–aggressiveness–power and superiority is interesting to note. Running parallel to this, as we shall see later in the chapter, is his emerging concept of man's social interest.

To Adler, there are no separate drives or needs such as those Murray incorporated in his theory. There is only one drive, and that is the desire for superiority, which Adler felt grows out of feelings of inferiority. The two principles are inseparable. It should be noted that superiority does not mean power over other men. It does not mean that one human is necessarily more gifted than another (though Adler readily admitted and strongly advocated the uniqueness of persons), but that each human is striving to be superior within *himself* and not necessarily in competition with other men. *Superiority* means, to the Adlerian, "superiority over self." The prime mover in life, the dynamic that describes why man does the things he does, is man's striving for superiority.

Style of Life Principle

In order for man to achieve superiority out of his feelings of inferiority, it is necessary for him to conduct his life in a certain prescribed way. This way of conducting his life Adler called the *style of life*. The style of life that each human being pursues is a combination of two things: his inner self-driven and dictated direction of behavior, and the forces from his environment which aid, interfere, or reshape the direction which the inner self wishes to take. The most important part of this two-way system is the inner self of each human. A singular event may produce an entirely different reaction within the inner selves of two humans. The important feature is that behavior is caused primarily within the self but always in counter play with the environment. Adler did not feel that man is a free floating chip on the waters of life, rising and falling, advancing and retreating according to the dictates of other forces. Man has and always will have the capacity to interpret exterior forces for himself. He further has the capacity to avoid, attack, or be defeated by outside forces. Defeat may call for new directions. Direct attack upon outside forces may strengthen or weaken his inner structure. Avoidance may call for entirely new directions of his effort. The salient feature of any of the variables which man may endure from outside forces is, however, man's own ability to conduct his own affairs. To Adler, man has enough will power, not always fully free, to make and arrange a life of his own. Adler, although one of the very first to acknowledge the effects of environmental forces and thus aid the struggling field of social psychology at that time, could not accept the purely environmentalistic viewpoint that man is solely a product of his environment. To Adler there is too much material born and developed within man. This self-operated system he called the *style of life*.

Each human being's style of life is unique unto himself. Probably, thought Adler, no two human beings ever lived who have, or could have, identical styles of life. At least two forces demand a unique style of life for each individual human being. The first force comes from the individual's hereditary past with all of the variable components inherent in the system at birth. The second force comes from the variant environment that each human being undergoes immediately upon being born. Since no two human beings can occupy the same space at the same time, the environment for each must, therefore, be different. Even Siamese twins do not look at themselves from the viewpoint of the other. With different environments and different inherited systems, no two human beings can be expected to behave in the same way. To the Freudian, sex is the *sine qua non* of all men's behavior. To the Adlerian, sex may or may not be the *sine qua non* of any man's behavior. It would depend upon his individual style of life.

Despite the fact that each life is unique, Adler felt that there are certain strong threads which are common to people. Just as each human being requires the organic functions of heart, lungs, and liver, he also has a feeling of inferiority, superiority, and a unique life style.

Each person has the same goals which he hopes to reach through his creative self, but the paths to these goals are always different. The universality of the goals are the same. His behavior on the way to these goals is always dissimilar; however, of course, the mainsprings of action are always feelings of inferiority and superiority.

Just as there is consistency in everyone's feelings of inferiority and superiority, so there is a tremendous amount of consistency within one person's style of life. The style of life frequently prescribes a singular interpretive quality for all of the experiences that a human being may encounter. The individual whose style of life revolves around feelings of neglect and being unloved interprets all of the experiences of life from that singular frame of reference. Those activities which are not applicable to such interpretation are ignored or twisted into forms appropriate to the desired interpretation. The unloved child feels that all human contacts substantiate his role of being unloved; contacts with human beings who do give him love prove that that is what life might be for him if he were not unloved. The individual whose style of life centers on feelings of aggression and power considers any display of counter power to be a challenge to self, while displays of cooperation or weakness indicate his own strength. Most human beings, however, do not have styles of life in such strong tones of black and white. As we shall see later, the style of life is ameliorated by the creative self and particularly by social interest. The majority of people follow a style of life that is tempered by broader goals than the examples cited above. The basic style of life, however, is not an amorphous thing centering on vague concepts, such as wanting, in a nebulous way, to be a good fellow. The style of life is a strongly interpretive and bonding agent: It controls all actions of life in a determined way. It continues to operate throughout life, and remains constant to its central core. It is the sole unifying force in life.

From birth to about the age of five or six, the style of life is becoming fixed. Based on the inherited capacities of the child and, equally important, on the child's use and interpretation of these capacities, the style of life is being formed during these years—and, according to Adler, it rarely changes. What may and frequently does change is the form of expression the individual utilizes to bring about his desired ends. To change deliberately another's style of life is well nigh impossible. To change one's own style of life (which is essentially the only way it can change) is painful, since for the moment of change one has no style of life—an intolerable situation. Adler feels the most practical way of change is to divert the basic style towards ends that meet with less and less frustration. Basically, then, the style of life remains constant throughout life. What changes are the ways of achieving goals and the interpretation machinery which the individual uses to satisfy the style of life. Thus, to the unloved child whose style of life is being unloved, it is more practical to form fictional goals where love is not so important than it is to attempt to convince him that the past of being unloved is not important and that the possibilities for love in the future will make up for the past. It is possible to change the basic style of life, Adler felt, but the cost in emotions and the effort in energy frequently rule against it. Besides, the successes that accrue to even a faulty style of life make change a hazardous risk. It is far easier to continue on the old and known style, which becomes more mechanical and fixed as life progresses through the years, than it is to change. Adler felt so strongly about the formative years in man's childhood that he wrote volumes about educational methods. He was one of the very first to establish child guidance clinics. He directed a great deal of energy also to improving schools and in particular to educating parents to the risks involved in faulty early childhood training.

Precisely how does one develop a style of life? What forces create an almost immutable way of living? Why are there so many differing styles of life in the children of the same family where their environment may be so parallel? The answer might lie in the universal feeling of inferiority with which all men are born and in the ensuing striving for superiority. However, since these are universal characteristics, the individual shadings must come from other sources. These sources, which Adler felt account for the uniqueness in men's personalities, grow out of the different physical, psychological, and sociological conditions for each human. In trying to overcome a differing set of these three influences, man emerges as different from all other men. Some specific factors which lead to a faulty style of life causing men to differ are childhood experiences; the number of brothers and sisters one has, as well as one's order of birth in the family—this status being called *positional psychology*.

Through his work with individuals in therapy, Adler felt there are three factors which, unless checked or compensated for, will create styles of life which are inoperable in society and make for the individual and others a lifetime of unhappiness and grief. These three factors are inferiorities of an organic or mental nature, pampered and indulged childhood, and neglect in childhood.

The physically impaired child may understandably have much greater feelings of inferiority than the able bodied child. Whether he fails to achieve superiority or achieves it with resounding success, the fact remains that his physical disability is highly instrumental in formulating his style of life. Some children with organic weaknesses never surmount their inferiority feelings and succumb to a style of life defeated and subjected to all the perils of existence. Other children (and many biographies remind us of this) compensate so strongly for an inferior organic weakness that they achieve a degree of superiority far beyond what one might expect from their otherwise normal talents. Examples may be found everywhere. Small-statured people who themselves consider this an inferior organic structure, although society may not, can be found to have gained outstanding success whether the field be athletics, the arts, or the industrial world. Chronically ill children have been known to strive valiantly to compensate for their bodies and thus possibly become more successful than they would have been, had they possessed physically normal bodies in childhood. Obviously the compensation of the organically weak does not lead automatically to success. The pathways from inferiority to superiority may bring them only to the level of normal bodied human beings. The gradient of improvement itself, however, may be quite unusual. The outstanding feature, to Adler, of these cases was that the style of life becomes formulated through the organic weakness of the individual. In some cases, a faulty life pattern results from an organic inferiority that is too restricting or confining to overcome. In other cases, the organic inferiority gives added strength and compensatory goal activity, resulting in superiority within self.

Mental impairment as an inferiority feeling source operates somewhat more severely in our society for several reasons. One, compensation is far more difficult to attain by a limited brain than by a normal one, because of difficulty in understanding. Two, the variety of avenues for compensation is more limited for mental activities than it is for physical activities. Three, modern society operates more on brain power than it does on muscular power. Four, society understands less and tolerates less the compensatory activities of the mentally inferior than of the physically (but mentally normal) inferior. (A child on crutches presents a far more sympathetic picture than does a moron.) The end result is that one might expect to find, and does find, more faulty life styles from the mentally impaired than from the physically impaired. But, whatever he does, the mentally impaired personality sets his life style by the incapacities he inherits and the strivings toward superiority he makes from them.

The degree to which both types (physically and mentally impaired) may achieve superiority, according to Adler, is the amount of encouragement and realistic guidance the child receives from his parents or other adult parent figures. Adler felt it to be particularly important that the parents serve as excellent models. It is not so much in the techniques they use as in the parents' own style of life that the child who is physically or mentally impaired gains his greatest strength toward achieving superiority over the self's inferiorities. Because each child has a different style of life anyway, the techniques are as varied as the number of children they are applied to. Consequently Adler stressed the parental model as the basic feature for the child's superiority strivings.

Passing from the physical to the psychological conditions which create uniqueness in the style of life, we find a more fundamental environmental force operating, although Adler never denied the basic instinctual predispositions to act that we find in Freud's and Jung's work. Still keeping within the rubric of childhood experiences, we see that a faulty life style may result from the behavioral patterns which the child forms in his early years. Adler felt very strongly that the pampered and indulged child is a psychological cripple headed for a life utterly lacking in true superiority of self. He was vehement in his feelings toward parents or any figures of authority over children who allow the child to be petted and pampered. Yielding too often to the wishes of the child, he felt, deprives the child of the invaluable opportunity to exercise and develop a feeling of superiority within self. Having been sufficiently deprived of the one challenge which could bring him growth, the child becomes saddled with a style of life that is good for nothing. The child is now of no real value to himself and of less value to the world at large. Adler's condemnation was directed towards the parents. The child, he felt, can in no way develop a life style of his own, completely independent of those who care for him. When a human being has nothing to struggle for because all hurdles have been removed or minimized, he can in no way learn how to surmount the hurdles he is forced to meet later in life. The essential relationship between inferiority–superiority is subverted by the artificial superiority supplied by the well-meaning parents. Adler considered the pampered personality to be the scourge of society. Innumerable times he spoke out against the egocentric demands of the pampered person whose style of life revolves around taking from others to achieve a false superiority rather than developing within himself the great struggle to emerge from inferiority to superiority. Out of this group in society, came many of the potentially dangerous individuals whose demands upon others do not cease at adulthood. It will be remembered that the style of life is continuous throughout life and that the longer the style continues, the more deeply imbedded it becomes.

The neglected child suffers equally in developing a style of life. Although his faulty life style is as harmful and painful to himself as the pampered personality, he acts with less friction toward society. His contribution to society is less, but the real loss comes with the lack of triumph he obtains in life. Neglect commits him to having only himself as a model. The trial and error of self-direction may be so costly to his strivings that he ultimately ceases to struggle upward. Even the successes he manages to achieve do not seem to be reinforced by others. The end result is a lackadaisical style of life which brings neither joy to himself nor pleasure to other persons.

Sociological conditions also may operate with equal force in molding a defective style of life despite the normality of the physical and psychological conditions. As an example, stultifying poverty may form and shape the style of life so severely as to deprive it completely of any enrichment and opportunities for growth. Conversely, an enriched and stimulating early environment may foster the style of life adaptable to multiples of conditions in later life. The reciprocity between self and social forces is a never ending one, Adler stated.

In summary, then, man creates a style of life out of the physical, psychological, and social conditions within which his life develops. The previous passages used the criteria of faulty development to illustrate the three conditions. In addition, the factors of mental–physical inferiorities, pampering, and neglect were employed to bring out the affect of creating the life style. The subsequent passages concern positional psychology, which Adler considered could bring additional insight into how a style of life comes into being.

Positional psychology has not met with great acceptance as a fruitful avenue of research, although many employers, lay people, and psychological clinics often give thoughtful consideration to the order in which one has been born into the family. Only children, children coming from very large families, and children who have many siblings not of their sex are considered in light of these familial facts. The value of positional psychology is not under consideration here. The following material is presented in an interpretive sense to promote further understanding of how a style of life may be created out of the psychological and social forces surrounding the human at birth. Interpretive liberties have been taken with Adler's original theme in order to demonstrate fully the positional phenomena.[1] The writing style is deliberately journalistic and novel-like.

Mr. and Mrs. Jones have three boys. Their names are John, Harry, and Larry. All three boys are now well advanced into their adult years. Each son is married. John is the oldest son, Harry was born four years later, and Larry, the youngest in the family, was born four years after Harry. The spread in ages, then, is eight years between John, the oldest, and Larry, the youngest, with Harry in the middle.

The Joneses can still remember John's birth. They lived at that time in a small flat and had been married about a year and a half. The birth was a thrilling event. Both sets of grandparents were deeply involved, for this was the first time that they were grandparents. John came into life to face six grown adults: a set of parents completely unlearned in the role of parenthood, and two sets of grandparents also uninitiated in grandparentry, but with definite ideas learned from their own children on just how a baby should be reared. Some rivalry existed between the two grandmothers about the best methods to be used. At times the rivalry became more than subtle. John gradually became aware of this and made good use of it, too. What one grandma might refuse could often be wheedled out of the other one, who was inclined (in a nice way, of course) to take an opposite view to the first.

John's biggest problems were with his parents, however. They never seemed

---

[1] No family such as that described here actually exists. The illustration is a montage drawn from the author's clinical experience with clients mainly in therapy. No professional confidences are violated.

to know exactly how to act. Both Mom and Dad seemed to be learning from him about how to be parents. Every single little thing he did got noticed. They always seemed to overdo or underdo everything. Life got to be a series of stresses, but a fellow learned how to manipulate Mom and Dad fairly soon. There was always plenty of practice, too, because if you couldn't work on the folks, there was usually at least one grandparent visiting the house and being proud and contradictory. John got very good at manipulating human beings who were adults. Children were different. There were none in the house at all, and the kids in the neighborhood were either too big or too selfish or too little to be interesting.

But life to John was wonderful. Dad took him everywhere and promised he would be famous some day. They took hundreds and hundreds of pictures of him, even to buying an expensive movie camera and a tape recorder which he broke. Every one of the toys in the house was his. It was lonesome many times but make-believe can create a pal out of any teddy bear. It was lonesome, that is, until Harry, his brother, came into the house.

John will never forget the day Harry came home. Things were very mixed up then. His mom's grandma and his dad argued once about the way he should eat. It was absolutely wonderful to have Mom home again, and it was even better than before because now it wouldn't be lonesome at all with a baby brother to play with. But, he should have known better. The first time John met Harry, he got scolded and yelled at. Naturally he had to see if Harry was built as well as his teddy bear, so when he pushed Harry's eye in to see if the other one popped out as it did in his teddy bear and when he wanted to see if Harry's leg would turn completely around, too, everyone yelled. His father said, "What are you trying to do?" Harry wasn't very satisfactory as a playmate, and Harry was very, very selfish about his mother and wouldn't share her at all.

Now, Harry always said he lived in a world of "hand-me-downs." Even his parents at times seemed secondhand. It seemed that he got things like bicycles and ice skates only after John had thoroughly wrecked them. Then John would get new bikes and new skates, and Harry would have to do with the old ones. Even his bed and most of his clothes at first were John's old things. His folks didn't take so many pictures of him as they did of John. They didn't even telephone long distance to Grandma and Grandpa when he said his first words the way they did for John. One time, Grandma even forgot his birthday. She said there were beginning to be so many grandchildren that, "My goodness, it was hard to keep up with them all." The biggest fights came with John, who wouldn't share anything. All the old toys Harry now had John still felt were his, and John would get the new ones, too. Mom kept saying over and over to his brother John, "Remember he's smaller than you are," as if being small were a penalty. But the kids in the neighborhood were wonderful. John would never let Harry play with his friends, but there were plenty of kids the right size who didn't keep on bossing him around the way a bigger brother did.

Larry, right from the start was called "Lovable." There were some fights in the beginning between John and Harry as to who was going to take care of Larry. He was cute, like a real doll. John usually won, of course, and would get to change Larry and do other things so that Harry went out to play. Larry loved life. There was always someone to play with in the house and give him extra turns at bat and chase for him and stick up for him in fights, and there were new things to play with (the old bike had worn out, and Dad had done well in business, and they had moved to a nice big house). Mom and Dad let him do lots of things John and Harry never, never got to do. They always told him so, too. Mom was very sentimental. She aways called him her "Baby."

John married a local girl he had met at the church fellowship groups. He went to junior college for two years and then decided not to go on to state university because his part-time work at the shoe store brought good money, and his dad at that time couldn't help very much with two other brothers to feed and clothe. John married a girl very much like himself, a solid person. She had helped raise her brothers and sisters, too, after her mother had died, so she knew what life was about. She often helped John with the accounting for the shoe store he now owned for himself. John never moved away and he still sees a lot of the folks. Almost every weekend or Sundays they spend together. He's the treasurer of the church, and lots of people call him, "good, solid, conservative stuff."

The folks haven't seen Harry for two years now. He's a real go-getter. He not only finished college with a tremendous reputation as an athlete and student, too, but he went on for a law degree. He did it all himself with practically no help from his dad. Dad would have been glad to help, but Harry moved fast and never seemed to confide in Dad what he was doing. It seemed to be done by the time the folks knew of it. He even eloped with a girl they say is brilliant but somewhat erratic. She was an actress. Actually Mom was hurt about Harry running away like that, but all things work out. His old room fit nicely for the sewing room she had always wanted, and she was terribly proud of his business success. Some say that he could buy and sell his brothers.

Poor Larry has had a hard time of it. He's been divorced once, and his present marriage doesn't seem to make either of them very happy. His mother still calls him her "Baby" and this infuriates Larry. At his wedding she cried and cried all the way through. In college, Larry was tremendously popular and got to be the fraternity president two years in a row, something which had never happened before. It took him a little longer to graduate because he transferred colleges twice and he changed his major many times. His first wife was a "Homecoming Queen" and very popular. She was an only child, and her folks spent a lot of money on her. People liked her a lot even though she seemed awfully contradictory at times. She's remarried now to a widower with two children, and the marriage is a model of marital happiness. Larry remarried shortly after the divorce to an older friend of his first wife. He has been a salesman for some time but keeps changing companies. Larry has many friends and has been quite famous in a way because he has won the state amateur golf title for three times. His mother keeps the cup because his present wife makes caustic comments about the cup being worth a hundred customers for each year. Most people like Larry at parties but he hasn't seemed to keep many friends over the years.

This fictional account of the three boys in the Jones family serves as a demonstration of the forces which may occur in constructing a style of life out of the common fabric of a single family. Each son grew to pursue a unique style of life, possibly out of the inferiorities which he surmounted from early childhood. John perhaps developed his conservative style of life partially out of experiences in an adult world in childhood. Harry turned to the outside world from the home; in the outside world, he learned to be aggressive and to fend for himself. Larry was never given a true chance to develop a style of life and thus emerged with a faulty one based on strong relationships with people but with an incapacity to struggle for himself toward a superiority based on his own achievements.

Adler, however, felt dissatisfied with the mechanistic aspects of the style of life approach for man's pathway from inferiority to superiority. Returning to some of the earlier threads of ideas of man as a dynamic, *unifying*, highly interpretive, self-structure, Adler went a step further and evolved the concept of the creative self.

Creative Self Principle

Man is more than a product of his environment. Man is more than a totally predisposed animal confined by his instinctual inherited past. Man is an interpreter of life. By this Adler meant that the human animal creates a self structure out of his inherited past, interprets the impressions he receives from his ongoing life, searches for new experiences to fulfill his desires for superiority, and puts these all together to create a self that is different from any other self and which describes his own peculiar style of life. The creative self is an additional step beyond the style of life. The latter is reactive and mechanical. The creative self, however, is more than that. It is original, inventive, and makes something that never existed before: a new personality. It creates a self. To Adler, the term was very accurate in all its connotations. Adler felt that this concept was the cap-stone to his career. For his remaining days, he subordinated all other concepts within his theoretical system to the power and unifying force of the creative self. It was as if Adler himself toward the end of his life had created his own personal creative self. The concept left him satisfied and contented with his own work.

Conscious Self Principle

Adler in his work never openly expressed in any long discourses his belief that man is a conscious, aware animal, but the belief is evident through all of his work. He felt that man is aware of everything he is doing and upon self-examination can deduce why he has acted in certain prescribed ways. Consciousness is the core of personality. The human animal is fully aware of what he is doing every day, and nothing like the unconscious, preconscious, or subconscious lurks beneath his personality ready to erupt at any given moment. The fact that man may not attend at any given moment to a memory of the past did not mean to Adler that the unnoticed past is buried in a sea of repressed vestigial forces.

The human animal with his type of brain can perform only so many mental processes at one time. Those things which are not in a state of awareness at any given moment may become so at the will of man. Memory is a mechanism of the mind, and, like all processes, it may not operate efficiently. Inefficiency of the mind or forgetfulness is a product of the lack of organic well-being, coupled with poor training, or lack of training, of the memory functions of the brain. Individual differences also come into play. Consequently, that which man is not aware of can be brought into awareness if the mental functions are efficient.

Adler did not accept the Freudian preconscious and unconscious areas of man's life. As a social psychologist, Adler thought this seemed akin to mysticism. He felt that man knows quite consciously what he is doing; he knows where he is going; he has the ability to plan and direct his own behavior toward goals he consciously selects. This is in such direct contra-diction to Freud's theory that it is understandable that the two men parted and never reestablished a professional relationship.

Fictional Goals Principle

Although Adler felt that the past is tremendously important, since out of it grows man's style of life and his creative self, it is the future which shapes what man will do with his creative self at any given moment.

The past may set the stage and thus limit the actions of the actors, but the future determines what the players will do. The past is prologue, but the future is the scene. Adler says, "The final goal alone can explain man's behavior." For example, the undergraduate student is not motivated by his record, good or bad, in elementary school. He is not in college to perpetuate that record if it is good or to correct the record if it is bad. He is, paraphrasing Adler, in college to get a degree. This motivates him to study to remain in college, and to pursue all of the necessary tasks that college life demands. The undergraduate is not necessarily motivated by the subject matter of the day as much as he is by the final grade in the course.

To continue with the college student as an example, his grade and his degree are creations of fiction. Grades and degrees do not represent anything material or concrete. They are semantic devices or fictions representing a larger composite of future goals. Although man is motivated by organic needs such as food, clothing, and shelter, these basic needs become represented in fictional ways. An automobile to the adolescent means more than transportation. It means the symbols of prestige, equality with other adult motorists, freedom, and possibly many symbolic or fictional goals far beyond the simple process of being transported from one place to another by the automobile.

In quite another sense, the goal may be a fiction because it is fabricated as an ideal to strive for. The goal is a fiction because it is removed from reality and will be unattainable to the creative self striving for superiority. One may find examples of this in the phrases, "perfect husband" and "always tell the truth." Noteworthy phrases that they are, the individual may find it impossible to reach them as the fictional goals of life.

Fictional goals are inseparable from the style of life and the creative self. Man moves forward toward superiority via his style of life and creative self out of feelings of inferiority always pulled and attracted by his fictional goals.

Fictional finalism, as Adler sometimes termed *fictional goals*, is an operating force in man's day to day behavior. It is not an ideal floating way out beyond his reach, as a star in the sky. Man through his creative self makes his own fictional goal from native ability and self-experiences. The human personality is fully aware of his fictional goal and will continuously interpret the daily happenings of life into the perspective of his fictional goal.

Social Interest Principle

This final principle extracted from Adler's work gives further light to the developmental growth in Adler's thinking. Starting from his initial interest in the aggressive characteristics of man, passing through his theory that man is a power-hungry animal to his final principles of the human being as an inferiority-to-superiority-driven personality exhibiting a style of life and creative self progression, Adler expanded his theory in 1929 to proclaim that man is also a socially interested human being. He reasoned that man is born with an interest in social beings. This interest in similar creatures is universal. Like all instincts, it needs a contact to bring it into action. This contact with other human beings, Adler stated, is an automatic condition. Man has to be brought up by man just as definitely as he has to be born out of man. To start with, a human being is predisposed to be interested in like appearing human creatures. The interest is in the societal environment surrounding him; it is not yet social interest as it later develops. The child notices a mother, a father, other similar appearing human beings surrounding him, and also the important fact that they do things for him. They (people in general) feed him, bathe him, clothe him, give him solace when pain interferes with his normal state of existence. Adler reasoned that this care of the child must make an impression upon him and that this impression is most logically one that the world is good and that one helps one's fellowman. Gradually, as the child is reared from his animal state, the predisposition toward other persons is educated into a concern for the welfare of other persons. Being reared by socialized animals turns the baby into a socialized animal.

The process of socialization takes a great deal of time and continuous effort. Taking turns on slides, helping mother with the housework, receiving high praise for ineffective efforts, sharing with siblings the food and comforts of the common home, all have their effect upon the child's natural bent to grow from natural feelings of inferiority to greater heights of superiority. The aggressive qualities of superiority become socialized through the efforts of the surrounding environment.

After the formative years to four or five, and continuing through the elementary school experiences, the child begins to identify with social groups of his own. Much of the world at that time is designed to help him. Schools have been constructed and operated, toys have been purchased, opportunities for recreation are provided, all of which maintain and strengthen the feeling of social interest and concern for fellow man. The child enters the world inadequate to cope with his needs. He notices other inadequate characteristics in his peers. Through a process of empathy, he learns what it feels like to be weak and have others help him. He in turn wishes to exercise his emerging feelings of superiority so that when the opportunities arise he, too, turns back to help the less fortunate. The process both enriches his own feelings of superiority and strengthens the social interest he is beginning to develop. Through the processes of identification, empathy, and cooperation, the child learns that a unique reciprocity exists within the world: help others as you may need help yourself in achieving superiority.

Because man never fully achieves superiority (as soon as one goal is reached the next one beckons), he retains a feeling of inadequacy. The feeling is universal and thus becomes a common bond between men. Held to others by common bonds of inadequacy, man feels that a strong and perfect society may help him achieve for himself a fuller feeling of superiority. Possibly the perfect society will lift him along with it and through association fulfill his inner desire for superiority. The style of life and its more encompassing creative self now incorporate a principle of social interest that permeates his behavior throughout life.

Adler in his own life was a strong believer in social causes and democratic principles, indicating again a theorist who appears to have lived much more closely by his theory than have some of the others.

To summarize, we have discussed Alfred Adler's theory of personality by using the device of seven principles; each principle is entwined with another, and all operate within the dynamics of man's personality. The seven principles used are these: 1. inferiority; 2. superiority; 3. style of life; 4. creative self; 5. conscious self; 6. fictional goals; and 7. social interest. The next section attempts to use Adler's theory to explain *why* man indulges in certain prescribed sets of behavior.

EXPLAINING HUMAN BEHAVIOR VIA ADLER'S INDIVIDUAL PSYCHOLOGY THEORY

Possibly the answers to this section can be briefly and succinctly stated by Adler's own statement: "The final goal alone can *explain* man's behavior" (in Murchison's *Psychologies of 1930*, p. 400; italics mine). The prospect to expand tempts, nevertheless; there are extrapolations one may make from his theory which come close to explaining the dynamics of man's behavior in certain functions. In other cases, the theory is found wanting as an explanatory tool. Let the reader supply the above quotation as a preface to the following eight sections while reserving the right to challenge or accept. The nine activities used by the author to present Adler's work as an explanatory device are as follows: marriage, perversions, suicide, lawbreaking, supranatural being, humor, smoking, play and recreation, and psychoses–neuroses.

Marriage

It may be assumed, from the Adlerian viewpoint, that man enters into marriage for at least two reasons: it fits his style of life, and it satisfies his sense of social interest. In the former case, he has been reared by a set of parents whose husband and wife roles he has witnessed for many years. Obviously children in institutions do not have parents and do not see the full play of husband and wife roles, but it may be assumed that they are not raised in a vacuum, so can see these familial roles operating in the lives of others. In the case of social interest, the person may feel it is now his turn to fulfill his creative self by assuming the role of marriage and in so doing to perpetuate the race. Possibly it is universal that each set of parents wants a better world for its children than they had. Through fostering children in marriage, man has the opportunity to bring the world closer to a state of perfection by passing his experiences on to his children, who in turn may be able to achieve a higher state of superiority than he. The preceding explanation presupposes that children are a natural concomitant of marriage. Fictional goals may also be a part of the marriage picture. Having a home, having a partner for life, and paralleling the fictional goals of most other human beings who are also married may all serve as additional answers to the question of why man does get married.

Perversions

It is practically impossible to pull out of Adler's work enough data to examine the reasons for man's perverted acts. Primarily this is so because Adler early in his career departed from the Freudian sexualism that so readily lends itself to a discussion of perversion. Adler, in his refutation of Freud's emphasis on sex as a motivator in man's life, thought that sexualism grows out of one's style of life, not that the style of life grows out of sexualism. Progressing from this explanation as a base, we may find further motives in the lives of pampered or neglected children. Both have faulty styles of life. The pampered child may later in life indulge in perversions because his entire style of life is faulty. We may further assume that his acts of expression in matters sexual may also be faulty. Being inclined to follow rules of conduct designed primarily for his self pleasure, the indulged personality may further indulge himself by deviate sexual behavior. On the other hand, the neglected personality may have no decent models of acceptable behavior to follow. Consequently, he practices sexual acts that, once established and proved satisfying to him, are continued because no elevating forces are present to realign his sexual behavior.

Suicide

In some ways, one may draw interesting explanations for suicide from Adler's work:

Suicide may be caused by the oddity of having the feeling of inferiority completely inverted. If the human being's feeling of inferiority gets turned about, he can see no superiority level whatsoever. All that can appear to him is a downward path of regression instead of progression from inferior levels. The lowest degree of inferiority would be cessation of life. It may appear very logical, then, to the individual with inverted feelings of inferiority to descend into death as the only practical direction to go. Consequently he commits suicide as the necessary next step from his present level of inferiority.

Another explanation centers more meaningfully on the complete frustration of superiority strivings. Here, we must assume that the frustration has been extremely severe and of a very long duration with no alternatives being apparent to the suicidal person. The result of such conditions could be a total collapse of creative self and all of its underpinnings gained from the style of life. With no fictional goals to follow, the pampered individual with a totally blocked superiority striving may kill himself. Death with all of its uncertainties may by chance appear to give the superiority which the human being has craved for a long time. This factor may especially operate for the harrassed human who believes in a life in the hereafter. The mental machinations may be so construed as to make him feel he can hardly wait to enter a better world where superiority is practically guaranteed by mere presence in the heavenly state.

Lawbreaking

Adler's work fits readily into an explanation of those who deliberately flaunt the laws of men. He wrote and spoke many times about the pampered child who grows up with an utter disregard for the social welfare of other men. Being accustomed to having things without working for them and constructing a style of life around this custom, he logically continues to feel that the "world owes him a living." How and in what manner he perpetuates his faulty life style depends upon the opportunities and peculiarities of his environment. The neglected child may also develop a faulty life style in which he must take for himself those gifts that others seem to get by merely existing. Since he, too, has a striving for superiority, he can satisfy his goal structure only by taking what he wants when he wants it. Others appear to get it for nothing. Why should not he have the same privileges? Once the pampered or neglected personality has met success in satisfying the superiority cravings, he begins to add to his already faulty style of life a new facet of disregard for the laws of man. In his mind "nothing succeeds like success," and he is now very successful in meeting the demands of his superiority feelings. Unless other methods equally efficient are introduced, change seems a foolhardy thing for him to attempt.

Supranatural Being

Probably the concept of fictional goals comes the closest to providing some rationale for explaining this facet of man's behavior according to Adler. Coupled with this may be a god figure as an extension of man's creative self. Whatever the basic causes for creating and believing in a supernatural being, Adler felt this belief contributed greatly to man's style of life. Whatever man's belief may be (Christian or Hebrew or Mohammedan or sunworship), Adler considered religion to have a strong effect on the day-to-day operation of man's style of life.

As we have seen, man operates toward ever higher fictional goals. Fictional goals have the same properties for the mechanics of superiority strivings as do other goals. As man builds higher and higher goal structures, he ultimately wants to construct a goal figure which can do all things, know all things, and be the ultimate of all things. The result is a fictional goal of the supranatural being. In societies where the creative self has emerged as a strong influence, man is inclined to posses a singular supranatural figure which approximates, looks like, and has somewhat the same properties as his own creative self figure. In some cases, he may have intermediary supranatural figures with somewhat the same properties as the primary figure, either through being in proximity to the figure, or through possession of some of the supernatural powers. Whatever the explanation for man's belief in a supranatural being, Adler never doubted the significant part it has upon man's conduct and strivings for superiority.

Humor

Although not a humorless man, Adler created work which lends itself poorly to explaining why man laughs except, again, by nebulous extensions. We may assume that man has humor because he has emerged from inferiority to superiority in a delightfully pleasant way. Possibly, the emergence may have a suddenness and unexpected quality which produces laughter, the Jungian explanation for humor. The sweetness of triumph over inferiority gives man the full measure of happiness. Lack of effort on the part of the superiority striving human may make the victory all the sweeter. Symbols, too, may be involved in achieving superiority over inferiority. Pushed by inferiority feelings and pulled by superiority strivings, man may momentarily achieve his desired state of a higher level of being. This unexpected bonus gives him an exhilarated sense of pleasure which, although it does not last long, for its duration is heady to the senses.

Smoking

This facet of man's behavior finds no direct connection with the works of Adler. One explanation may be that man indulges in smoking because he wants to incorporate it into his style of life. Possibly he may feel inferior when surrounded by others who give the appearance of pleasure when smoking. Because this pleasure is something he does not have and which, therefore, makes him feel inferior, he, too, begins the practice of using tobacco. He may now identify with others in a social interest. Once having established the habit, he incorporates it in his style of life. Eliminating the practice of using tobacco becomes more difficult if one is surrounded by other fellow beings who continue to smoke. The feeling of social interest in his fellowmen welds him to their patterns of behavior. Other human beings do not smoke because it satisfies their feelings for superiority not to practice an activity which they consider to be inferior and degrading. By refusing to conform to a social habit which one may interpret even as odious, he fulfills his sense of superiority. The decision to smoke or not to smoke illustrates the uniqueness of man's personality and the individuality of his style of life. There appears to be no organic explanation in Adler's theory as convenient to use as the one in Freud's.

Play and Recreation

The style of life may be considered a possible reason for man's capacity to play and enjoy forms of recreation. When man begins life as a baby, he is not saddled with work. His early life consists of random activities which are designed to satisfy only himself. As a small baby and later as a child, he is not obligated or accountable for any productive activity. He simply plays and is often encouraged to do so by his parents and peers. As Adler has stated, the first four or five years are crucial to establishing a style of life. It would seem natural, then, for man to continue these strongly imbued play habits throughout the remainder of his life within the matrix of his own unique style of life. Consequently, he is inclined to perpetuate those habits of play which he found most satisfying to his style of life early in his babyhood and childhood. In addition, we may further assume that children who have had little opportunity for play and can therefore not incorporate a strong thread of play into their life styles will continue into adulthood to minimize play as an activity. Work and serious endeavors have a stronger place in their adult style of life than does play.

Psychoses—Neuroses

Psychotic behavior might be construed in Adlerian terms as the complete collapse of a style of life. The broken personality of the psychotic has lost its way in life: it is styleless. Perhaps this came about because there were too many continuous failures to enable one to emerge from high pressure feelings of inferiority toward unobtainable superiority. Faced with repeated failures to emerge from inferiority, the personality retreats to repetitive small steps of continuing past triumphs. Thus we may expect behavior from the psychotic which is childish and infantile, for in that past climate of smaller steps the personality had once known achievement in going from inferior to superior levels of behavior. The style of life becomes a false imitative repetition of old successful habits. The longer the psychotic continues to reinforce the past infantile behavior, the longer and deeper the false style of life becomes ingrained into the personality. Therapy, consequently, is made more difficult according to the length of time of the psychotic state. At times, in many psychotics one may notice an absorption in a deity or god figure. This may be construed under the Adler frame of reference as the perpetuation of a fictional goal which will bring about the resolving of all the failures to achieve superiority.

The neurotic operating under some of the above conditions does not, however, often lose his style of life but continues to bend and twist it into a false style of life. As we recall, Adler felt that pampered or neglected children are unable to create a normalized style of life. With this artficial style of life as a background, the neurotic unless helped, may continue to conduct his life along paths which bring him and society unhappiness. The neurotic does not lose his style of life as does the psychotic; he operates under a crippled and ineffective one. His creative self is unfulfilled, and his fictional goal system is confused.

PREDICTING HUMAN BEHAVIOR VIA ADLER'S INDIVIDUAL PSYCHOLOGY

Predictability is not the strength of Adler's theory. Two reasons for this seem evident from the core of his system. On the one hand, the Adlerian system is built around the uniqueness of man, and on the other hand the emphasis is with man not only as highly individual and personalized, but as a being in a highly therapeutic climate.

Although it is almost impossible to draw out prediction from Adler's theories because of the personalized style of life, it is easy to make one solid prediction: every individual will continue to be different from every other individual that has ever lived or is now living.

Adler worked and did research in a clinical setting. He did not work in a laboratory. He was a highly individual worker like Freud, and continued to be the solitary worker with small collaborative efforts with others. He worked with few subjects, although some of his later work in therapy was done with larger groups in order to conserve time and to operate more efficiently.

Personal Prediction

The judge of any theory is the reader and student of the theory. As such, the student must weigh the theory for himself and accept or reject whatever evidence seems meaningful to him. Perhaps it may be possible for the student to accept Adler's ideas about the patterns of behavior which emerge into the style of life, especially those concerning the influence of one's position in the family. It is possible that Adler could anticipate certain behavior patterns from an only child in the family. Possibly the youngest of three sons will turn out to be a rather soft, easy going, socialized human with not too much striving for superiority. Perhaps the reader has known in others, or himself feels addicted to, some kind of organic inferiority to which he can ascribe a will to succeed that might not have otherwise been present. Equally true may be the phenomenon of behavior which seeks and uses an organic weakness to evade pressure points in life. These are the things which the student of a theory ultimately decides for himself, contrary to or in substantiation of evidence gathered in life.

Scientific or Laboratory Prediction

As previously stated, Alfred Adler was not a laboratory research psychologist. He felt that in his daily contacts with human beings as therapeutic subjects, he had opportunity to sample the behavior of man and to draw further conclusions from this selected audience. Many other theorists have a similar attitude.

Since his time, many of those who subscribe to the basic tenets of Adler also work in a therapeutic situation. Much of the research mentioned in the psychological journals of today centers on the reporting of a single case in process of therapy and the parallels between the case and Adler's theories. This again is not unusual, for followers of Jung, Freud, Rogers, and many others exchange and refine their techniques via this method.

Probably the closest single source that one may find centering itself on the Adlerian reference is the *American Journal of Individual Psychology* (later changed to *Journal of Individual Psychology*) so ably edited by Heinz and Rowena Ansbacher. The present emphasis upon psychosomatic medicine may be attributed by some to be an extension of Adler's earlier work in organ inferiority. However, most of those working in the psychosomatic field today rarely discuss the relationship of their work with Adler's earlier work on the mind–body paradigm.

That man can be assumed to have fictional goals, feelings of inferiority leading to superiority, a style of life emerging into a creative self, and a universal social sense is evidence yet to be drawn out of the scientific or laboratory type of research.

SUMMARY

The grand staircase of life in Figure 6 represents a diagrammatical attempt to summarize the personality theory of Alfred Adler as the author interprets it.

It seems to the author that Adler's main rationale is man's lifelong struggle to emerge from inferiority feelings to superiority feelings, only to find himself repeating the entire process all over again because there is always another step above his present level to which man aspires.

Many figures are represented on the staircase in an attempt to portray the versatility and uniqueness of each individual's style of life. The path of progress for most figures is upward from one level of inferiority to the next higher level of superiority. At the very top of the long climb upward is the fictional finalism that man continuously aspires to. The course of one's life may be thought of as the long climb up the staircase.

Certain figures have been drawn to show the versatility of man's approaches. Starting on the right side top of the drawing a figure is shown in the act of suicide. The struggle has been too difficult, and this personality is destroying his life by leaping off. Below it are shown psychotics and neurotics who are unable to advance because of faulty styles or because of a complete inability to move to the next higher step. In the center of the staircase are shown the social interest aspects of man's behavior with three figures climbing together. Each one helps and gives comfort to the other. Also shown in the drawing are the neglected child, the child whose parents help him in his initial steps, and the pampered child on his father's shoulders. The pampered child is thus unable to learn how to climb because he rides freely on the efforts of someone else. The legend below the drawing indicates further aspects of man's behavior via the Adlerian approach.

Other factors, of course, enter the picture. Some individuals may excuse their inability to go upward because of an organic inferiority. This disability may moderate their gait. It may cause them to strive harder and thereby develop faster and easier ways of achieving the next rungs of superiority. Positional psychology may also give more aid to certain children born first or last in the family. The firstborn may have a difficult time. His parents have to learn how to help him. They may overdo or underdo

Figure 6. Diagrammatic Summary of Adler's Theory.

their roles. As more and more children enter the family, the parents have to divide their time between the many children for whom they are responsible. An only child may have a difficult time trying new steps and new ways for himself. His parents overemphasize everything he does.

Life, therefore, as summarized here by Adler's theory, is a struggle upward from life to death, each traveler using his own method, each traveler aware of others, each traveler pulled by many common goals, and each traveler prone to all the vicissitudes of the trip.

BIBLIOGRAPHY

Primary Sources

BOOKS

Adler, A., *The Neurotic Constitution*, N.Y., Moffat, 1917.

Adler, A., *Study of Organ Inferiority and Its Psychical Compensation*, N.Y., Nervous and Mental Diseases Publishing Co., 1917.

Adler, A., *Practice and Theory of Individual Psychology*, N.Y., Harcourt, Brace & World, 1927.

Adler, A., *Understanding Human Nature*, N.Y., Chilton, 1927.

Adler, A., *Problems of Neurosis*, London, Routledge, 1929.

Adler, A., *The Science of Living*, N.Y., Chilton, 1929.

Adler, A., Individual psychology, in C. Murchison (ed.), *Psychologies of 1930*, Worcester, Mass., Clark Univer. Press, 1930, 395–405.

Adler, A., *The Pattern of Life*, N.Y., Holt, Rinehart and Winston, 1930.

Adler, A., *The Education of the Individual* [1930], N.Y., Philosophical Library, 1958.

Adler, A., *What Life Should Mean to You*, Boston, Little, Brown, 1931.

Adler, A., *Social Interest*, N.Y., Putnam, 1939.

PERIODICALS

Adler, A., The fundamental views of individual psychology, *Int. J. Indiv. Psychol.*, 1935, *1*, 5–8.

Adler, A., Physical manifestations of psychic disturbances, *Indiv. Psychol. Bull.*, 1944, *4*, 3–8.

Adler, A., The progress of mankind, *J. Indiv. Psychol.*, 1957, *13*, 9–13.
    Originally published in 1937—first English translation.

Adler, A., Suicide (1937), *J. Indiv. Psychol.*, 1958, *14*, 57–61.
    You hurt others by hurting yourself.

Suggested Readings

BOOKS

Adler, K., and D. Deutsch (eds.), *Essays in Individual Psychology*, N.Y., Grove Press, 1959.

A paperback, but also in two other editions.

Ansbacher, H. L., and R. R. Ansbacher, *The Individual Psychology of Alfred Adler,* N.Y., Basic Books, 1956.
> The complete and thorough word on Alfred Adler.

Bottome, P., *Alfred Adler: A Portrait from Life,* N.Y., Vanguard, 1957.
> Originally published in England, 1939—very thorough and devoted biography.

Dreikurs, R., *Manual of Child Guidance,* Ann Arbor, Mich., Edwards, 1946.
> Represents Adler's positional psychology.

Dreikurs, R., *Fundamentals of Adlerian Psychology,* N.Y., Chilton, 1950.
> Excellent source and equal to Ansbacher's tome.

Dreikurs, R., Individual psychology, in A. A. Roback (ed.), *Present Day Psychology,* N.Y., Philosophical Library, 1955.

Ganz, M., *The Psychology of Alfred Adler and the Development of the Child,* N.Y., Humanities Press, 1953.

Hoff, H., and W. Ringel, A Modern Psychosomatic View of the Theory of Organ Inferiority by Alfred Adler, in A. Jores, and H. Freyberger (eds.), *Advances in Psychosomatic Medicine,* N.Y., Brunner, Inc., 1961.

Jones, E., *The Life and Work of Sigmund Freud: Vol. II, Years of Maturity (1901–1919),* N.Y., Basic Books, 1955.
> The Adler–Freud split from the Freudian viewpoint.

Jones, H. E., Order of birth in relation to the development of the child, in C. Murchison (ed.), *Handbook of Social Psychology,* Worcester, Mass., Clark Univer. Press, 1931, 204–241.

Munroe, R. L., *Schools of Psychoanalytic Thought,* N.Y., Holt, Rinehart and Winston, 1955.
> Analysis and integration of Freud, Adler, Jung, Rank, Fromm, Horney, Sullivan, *et al.*

Ray, M. B., *The Importance of Feeling Inferior,* N.Y., Harper & Row, 1957.
> Wonderful imaginary conversation between Adler and Freud—also utilizes Adlerian concepts.

Shafer, V. W., A construct validation of Adler's social interest, *Dissertation Abstracts,* 1959, *19,* Ohio State Univer., 3374–3375.

Way, L., *Adler's Place in Psychology,* N.Y., Macmillan, 1950.

PERIODICALS

Adler, A., Historical review, *Amer. J. Indiv. Psychol.,* 1952, *10,* 80–82.
> Alexandria Adler, president of the American Society of Adlerian Psychology describes its beginning.

Adler, A., The concept of compensation and overcompensation in Alfred Adler's and Kurt Goldstein's theories, *J. Indiv. Psychol.,* 1959, *15,* 79–82.

Angers, W. P., Achievement motivation: an Adlerian approach, *Psychol. Rec.,* 1960, *10,* 179–186.

The private intelligence of bank robbers: two anonymous self accounts, *J. Indiv. Psychol.*, 1962, *18*, 77–88.

Adler's descriptions of criminals fit these two.

Ansbacher, H. L., Causality and indeterminism according to Alfred Adler, and some current American personality theories, *Indiv. Psychol. Bull.*, 1951, *9*, 96–107.

Ansbacher, H. L., Purcell's "memory and psychological security" and Adlerian theory, *J. Abnorm. Soc. Psychol.*, 1953, *48*, 596–597.

Ansbacher, H. L., The alienation syndrome "and Adler's concept of distance".

Also, A. Davids, some comments on Ansbacher's note on the "alienation syndrome" and Adler's concept of "distance," *J. Consult. Psychol.*, 1956, *20*, 483–486.

Ansbacher, H. L., Anomie: the sociologists conception of lack of social interest, *J. Indiv. Psychol.*, 1959, *15*, 212–214.

Adler and Durkheim compared.

Ansbacher, H. L., Rudolf Hildebrand: a forerunner of Alfred Adler, *J. Indiv. Psychol.*, 1962, *18*(1), 12–17.

Ansbacher, H. L., Was Adler a disciple of Freud? a reply, *J. Ind. Psychol.*, 1962, *18*(2), 126–135.

The answer is no.

Arnold, N., An Adlerian evaluation of methods and techniques in psychotherapy of adults, *Amer. J. Indiv. Psychol.*, 1954, *11*, 34–46.

Arnold, N., What is an Adlerian?, *Indiv. Psychol. Bull.*, 1951, *9*, 146–148.

Baldwin, A. L., Differences in parent behavior toward three- and nine-year-old children, *J. Person.*, 1947–1948, *16*, 143–165.

The differences are pronounced.

Beecher, W., and M. Beecher, What makes an Adlerian?, *Indiv. Psychol. Bull.*, 1951, *9*, 146–148.

Burchard, E. W. L., Mystical and scientific aspects of the psychoanalytic theories of Freud, Adler, and Jung, *Amer. J. Psychother.*, 1960, *15*, 289–307.

Cohen, F., Psychological characteristics of the second child as compared with the first, *Indiv. J. Psychol.*, 1951, *26*, 79–84.

Second-born more intelligent, humorous, and less neurotic than first-born.

Colby, K. M., On the disagreement between Freud and Adler, *Amer. Imago*, 1951, *8*, 229–238.

Colver, T., and D. F. Kerridge, Birth order in epileptic children, *Neurol. Neurosurg. Psychiat.*, 1962, *25*, 59–62.

Epilepsy more frequent in first born than second born.

Connors, C. K., Birth order and needs for affiliation, *J. Pers.*, 1963, *31*(3), 408–416.

First born have less expectancy of affiliative reward.

Deutsch, D., An instance of Adlerian psychotherapy, *Case Reports, Clin. Psychol.*, 1956, 3, 113–130.

DeVries, S. J., Some basic principles of Adlerian psychology, *Indiv. Psychol. Bull.*, 1951, 9, 149–151.

Dreikurs, R., The international picture of individual psychology, *Indiv. Psychol. Bull.*, 1951, 9, 1–3.

Dreikurs, R., Adler's contribution to medicine, psychology, education, *Amer. J. Indiv. Psychol.*, 1952–53, 10, 83–86.

Dreikurs, R., Adlerian analysis of interaction, *Group Psychother.*, 1955, 8, 298–307.

Dreikurs, R., What is psychotherapy: the Adlerian viewpoint, *Amer. Psychother. Monograph* No. 1, 1959, 16–22.

Faron, A., The influence of Alfred Adler on current psychology, *Amer. J. Indiv. Psychol.*, 1952–53, 10, 59–76.

Federn, E., Was Adler a disciple of Freud?: a Freudian view, *J. Indiv. Psychol.*, 1963, 19(1), 80–82.
   The issue is an historical one.

Gelfand, S., The relation of birth order to pain tolerance, *J. Clin. Psychol.*, 1963, 19(4), 406.
   No relationship was found.

Glass, D. C., M. Horwitz, I. Firestone, and J. Grinker, Birth order and reactions to frustration, *J. Abnorm. and Soc. Psychol.*, 1963, 66(2), 192–194.
   Contradictory findings from previous studies suggests birth order is ecological not psychological.

Greenberg, H., R. Guerino, M. Lasken, D. Mayer, and D. Piskowski, Order of birth as a determinent of personality and attitudinal characteristics, *J. Soc. Psychol.*, 1963, 60, 221–230.
   Some slight difference primarily affecting the youngest child.

Grey, L., A comparison of the educational philosophy of John Dewey and Alfred Adler, *Amer. J. Indiv. Psychol.*, 1954, 11, 71–80.

Grunwald, B., The application of Adlerian principles in the classroom, *Amer. J. Indiv. Psychol.*, 1955, 11, 131–141.

Hoch, P., Influence of Alfred Adler on psychoanalysis, *Amer. J. Indiv. Psychol.*, 1952–53, 10, 54–58.

James, W. T., K. Horney, and E. Fromm, In relation to Alfred Adler, *Indiv. Psychol. Bull.*, 1947, 6, 105–116.

Koch, H. L., Some personality correlates of sex, sibling position, and sex of sibling among five- and six-year-old children, *Genet. Psychol. Monogr.*, 1955, 52, 3–50.

Krishman, B., Order of birth and temperament, *Indiv. J. Psychol.*, 1951, 26, 85–87.

Langman, L., Adlerian thought in Asch's social psychology, *J. Indiv. Psychol.*, 1960, *16*, 137–145.

Parallels between Adler and Asch.

Ledermann, E. K., A review of the principles of Adlerian psychology, *Int. J. Soc. Psychiat.*, 1956, *2*, 172–184.

Differences between Freud, Jung, and Adler.

Lilienfeld, A. M., and B. Pasamanick, 1. The association of maternal and fetal factors with the development of mental deficiency. 2. Relationship of maternal age, birth order, previous reproductive loss and degree of mental deficiency, *Amer. J. Ment. Defic.*, 1956, *60*, 557–569.

Long, L. M. K., Alfred Adler and Gordon W. Allport: a comparison on certain topics in personality theory, *Amer. J. Indiv. Psychol.*, 1952–53, *10*, 43–53.

Long, L. M. K., Alfred Adler and the problem of the unconscious, *Amer. J. Indiv. Psychol.*, 1955, *11*, 163–166.

Maslow, A. H., Was Adler a disciple of Freud? A note, *J. Indiv. Psychol.*, 1962, *18*(2), 125.

Maslow says Adler said no.

McArthur, C., Personalities of first and second children, *Psychiatry*, 1956, *19*, 47–54.

First child serious and adult-oriented. Second, peer-oriented with laziness and friendliness.

McKeown, T., and R. G. Record, Maternal age and birth order as indices of environmental influence, *Amer. J. Human Genetics*, 1956, *8*, 8–23.

Must be taken with clinical and other evidence to be useful.

Montagu, M. F. A., Sex order of birth, *Amer. J. Orthopsychiat.*, 1948, *18*, 351–353.

Order of birth and sex of child both important.

Moore, M., Alfred Adler—creative personality, *Amer. J. Indiv. Psychol.*, 1954, *11*, 1–8.

Orr, J. K., and F. Risch, Is the order of birth a factor in epilepsy?, *Neurology*, 1953, *3*, 679–683.

Overton, R. K., Experimental studies of organ inferiority, *J. Indiv. Psychol.*, 1958, *14*, 62–63.

Direct and indirect support of Adler's concept.

Papanek, H. and E. Papanek, Individual psychology today, *Amer. J. Psychother.*, 1961, *15*, 4–26.

Peller, L. E., Character development in nursery school, *Mental Hygiene*, 1948, *32*, 177–202.

The oldest child takes care of the youngest.

Phillips, E. L., Cultural vs. intropsychic factors in childhood behavior problem referrals, *J. Clin. Psychol.*, 1956, *12*, 400–401.

First born referred more often for psychological help.

Raychaudhuri, A. K., Are the first born more susceptible to functional mental diseases?, *J. Nerv. Ment. Dis.*, 1956, *124*, 478–486.

Heredity does not affect first born but physical and socio/familial conditions may.

Rayner, O., Adler and his psychology, *Men. Health, London*, 1957, *16*, 58–62.

Rotter, J. B., An analysis of Adlerian psychology from a research orientation, *J. Indiv. Psychol.*, 1962, *18*(1), 3–11.

Some limitations of individual psychology and suggestions for research.

Shoobs, N. E., Individual psychology and psychodrama, *Amer. J. Indiv. Psychol.*, 1956, *12*, 46–52.

How to be an Adlerian and still use psychodrama.

Shulman, B. H., Adler's place in psychology, *Indiv. Psychol. Bull.*, 1951, *9*, 31–35.

Shulman, B. H., The family constellation in personality diagnosis, *J. Indiv. Psychol.*, 1962, *18*, 35–47.

A guide expedites measuring the style of life.

Stern, A., Existential psychology and individual psychology, *J. Indiv. Psychol.*, 1958, *14*, 38–50.

Sartre and Adler are more alike than we may realize.

Stotland, E., and J. A. Walsh, Birth order and an experimental study of empathy, *J. Abnorm. Soc. Psychol.*, 1963, *66*(6), 610–614.

Later born children more sympathetic.

Stotland, E., and R. E. Dunn, Empathy, self esteem, and birth order, *J. Soc. Abnorm. Psychol.*, 1963, *66*(6), 532–540.

Tendency for later borns to empathize more readily.

Thorne, G. L., Conforming behavior as related to birth order, anxiety, and rejection, *Dissert. Abstr.*, 1962, *22*(9), 3280.

Ullman, M., Dreaming, life style, and physiology: a comment on Adler's view of the dream, *J. Indiv. Psychol.*, 1962, *18*, 18–25.

Von Dusen, W., Adler and existence analysis, *J. Indiv. Psychol.*, 1959, *15*, 100–111.

Adler and phenomenology complement each other.

8

Sullivan

No man is an island, entire of itself—

John Donne
Devotions XVII

SOME BIOGRAPHICAL DATA

Harry Stack Sullivan was born and educated in America and always remained dedicated to his country. He was born in New York State on February 21, 1892 of farm parents. Like many other personality theorists, he first trained as a medical doctor and was graduated from the Chicago College of Medicine and Surgery in 1917, just in time to enter World War I as a medical officer. After being demobilized, and until 1922, he worked for the federal government, first as a medical officer in the Federal Board of Vocational Education and later with the Public Health Service. In 1923 he went to St. Elizabeth Hospital in Washington, D.C. for a year and the following year joined the staff of the medical school at the University of Maryland, where he remained until 1930. During this period his affiliation with the Pratt Hospital in Towson, Maryland, gave him his opportunity to conduct research concerning schizophrenia. His close contact with William Alanson White and the strong influence White gave to his work brought Sullivan the presidency of the William Alanson White Foundation in 1933. Sullivan continued in the presidency until 1943.

Sullivan served in many capacities during the later years of his professional life. He helped found, and, until his death, was a director of the Washington School of Psychiatry; he became editor of the journal *Psychiatry* which advanced his public recognition, served as consultant for the Selective Service Board in the early years of World War II, acted as consultant to the United Nations UNESCO project on tensions. He was returning from an Executive Board meeting of the World Federation for Mental Health held in Amsterdam when, on January 14, 1949, he died suddenly in Paris, France.

During his lifetime many people influenced Sullivan. Other than White, Sigmund Freud, George Herbert Mead, Adolph Meyer, Leonard Cotrell, Ruth Benedict, and especially Edward Sapir, all had some influence on the formulation of Sullivan's work and theory on man's personality. The lives Sullivan influenced have in turn created many valuable concepts beyond his own valuable work. Through his editorship of the journal, *Psychiatry*, the Washington School of Psychiatry, his innumerable consultancies for federal and international agencies, and his students in the medical school of the University of Maryland, Sullivan's impact on the world of psychiatry and the field of human behavior has been extremely valuable. His untimely death cut too short a productive life dedicated to making the human race run an easier and less anxious course.

INTRODUCTION

Harry Stack Sullivan's theory is much easier to categorize than that of other theorists, according to the organization of this text. Whereas other theorists' works, such as Freud's, are vast and encyclopedic, Sullivan's is neater, more orderly in arrangement. Another feature lending itself to the treatment of this text is the high sense of prediction that arises from Sullivan's work. Sullivan's work is not as fully spelled out as some other theorists' (he died at the age of 56), nor is it as fully developed as a completed system of thought. However, others attracted to his work have continued to develop Sullivan's work to a high and more inclusive degree. Sullivan's theories have made a definite impact and a moving contribution to the further understanding of man's behavior.

With no levity or disrespect intended, Sullivan could be called the "anxious" theorist. As will be discussed later, a great central theme of his theory revolves around anxiety in man: anxiety as a prime mover, as the builder of a self-system, and as the great educator in life. The word *anxiety* itself has become popular coinage in the writings of many psychologists and psychiatrists. Anxiety has been given many variant meanings. Sullivan's emphasis on anxiety also has some wide variations in theme as he uses the term in describing man's behavior.

Sullivan began his professional work as a somewhat Freudian-oriented psychiatrist. However, where others such as Fromm and Horney are considered to be renovators of Freudian theory, Sullivan is often credited with being a highly original innovator of Freudian theory. As a psychiatrist Sullivan worked primarily with emotionally disturbed people. His theory, then, is based, as were so many others, on the deviant type of personality as the raw material for theorization. Out of his early beginnings as a Freudian-flavored psychiatrist into his highly original and valuable work with schizophrenics, Sullivan evolved a theory which he called the *interpersonal theory of psychiatry*. It has been allied, therefore, to the field of psychiatry, but psychologists, and especially sociologists as well, have made heavy use of his work. Out of all this came a further impetus for the field of social psychology. The end result of Sullivan's work is far removed from its earlier flavor of Freudianism.

Sullivan, like Adler, followed the precepts of his own theory in his personal way of living. He felt, because man was a socially created animal and society was doing a poor job of creating, that society as it exists today was in dire need of help. He was a strong critic of modern society and its effect upon man's development. As a consequence he spent time, energy, and money in working toward the betterment of world peace causes. His contribution was immense to these organizations.

Part of Sullivan's appeal to the field of sociology has been the emphasis he placed on society as the creator of man's personality. Another attraction of the interpersonal theory has been the tenet that man can change, that man does change, and even that man *has* to change in his basic personality pattern as he grows to and through maturity. This has helped other societally oriented theorists to substantiate their belief in the forces of the environment as a molder of man. Part of Sullivan's theory states that man lives in a tension system. There exists a state of tension within himself as a single individual and a further tension state that exists between himself and all other individuals. These forces of tension within self and between selves make man what he is. In addition, life itself is a tension system, according to Sullivan. The analogy of Freud's work was that of a building constructed brick by brick and quite unchangeable after the primary foundation is constructed. The analogy of the interpersonal theory of Sullivan's is that of a kite, or structure, which is held together by the tension between its parts. The entire structure, although retaining a basic shape, may be altered and changed, depending upon the tensions within the system.

Harry Stack Sullivan was not a prolific writer. He did not have to be in promulgating his theories. Although in his lifetime he wrote one full treatise on his theory, *Conceptions of Modern Psychiatry* (1947), his main influence came through his work in UNESCO, his vivid lectures, his devoted students, and the many highly competent professional friends he made by his own pleasant personality.[1]

In addition to his brilliant intellect and his influence on the psychiatric and psychological world, Sullivan had a high degree of empathy for his fellowman. He felt many times so keenly attuned to the sufferings and tribulations of his patients that he incorporated part of these feelings of sympathy into his techniques of psychiatric interviewing. Sullivan was no passive student of humanity. He was a dedicated student of life as it is lived by all types of people. He felt a responsibility toward man.

Sullivan considered his theory (as a good environmentalist should) to be a product of the society that he, Sullivan, knew. He acknowledged that it was unique to the western world and might be altered by being applied in other cultures. He felt this to be particularly true regarding the stages of development.

SULLIVAN'S DESCRIPTION OF HUMAN BEHAVIOR

Personality was a word to Sullivan rather than an entity for study. His theory stressed the relationships between personalities and not the study of the single personality. The human being does not exist as a single personality. His personality can only exist as it is related to others.

Sullivan does not deny the influence of man's biological system. In fact he begins his theory on the basis of man as an operating organic system. Man's body does condition his personality but only to the extent that the

[1] To date two other books containing lectures which Sullivan gave have been collected, edited, and published by others. In 1944 and 1945 he gave a series of lectures now published as *The Psychiatric Interview* (1954). His lecture series of 1946 and 1947, along with excerpts from some of his notebooks, are brought together in *The Interpersonal Theory of Psychiatry*. The latter work contains the most recent data on his interpersonal theory.

body is necessary to life. At times, man may even subvert his biological needs to the more powerful needs of his social system. He may diet, or end his life, or overcome tremendous physical obstacles if the pressures and tensions of society demand it.

Of primary importance to the interpersonal theory of personality is the way in which the human being develops in his early years of infancy, childhood, and adolescence. This is not to be interpreted as saying that the early formative years permanently stamp the personality. It does indicate that the interpersonal patterns of early life are extremely important to the personality. These patterns continue to exert the most important influence on man's behavior. They do not, however, mandate the elimination of current social determiners of personality. If one lives in a stable environment, his personality is stable. If one lives in an unstable environment, his personality will be unstable. This effect continues throughout life.

In the author's treatment of Harry Stack Sullivan's work six principles have been extracted, around which the major features of his theory have been grouped. At the moment these six principles seem to cover adequately the salient features of his theory. They are these: 1. interpersonal relations; 2. tension system; 3. anxiety; 4. dynamisms; 5. personifications; and 6. cognitive experiences.

Interpersonal Relations Principle

It is pointless, Sullivan declares, to discuss or even think about one human personality by itself. It must always be considered and studied and seen in relationship to one, two, or more other personalities. No one can have a personality all by himself exclusive of the world about him. Sullivan believes this interpersonal relationship is the foundation of personality. The moment man is born into the world he is in contact with at least one other personality who sees that he stays alive. This contact with other personalities persists throughout his life, either in actual contact or in vestigial forms.

The single human personality can display itself only in relationship to other personalities. The reciprocity of human beings to one another is a key structure in the theories of Sullivan. Not all contacts have to be between living beings. The interaction may take place between a living person and a fictional character. Santa Claus, children's cowboy television heroes, and other nonexisting human prototypes may serve as the other interacting personality. In such cases the fictional figure is based upon the personification of a live human being who strengthens the fictional image. In every case where personality is concerned, it is meaningless to discuss one personality apart from others, and even in the case of nonliving personalities, an interaction exists. The fictional figure affects in some degree the behavior of the living personality. The living personality creates and changes the fictional personality as time goes on. Once having constructed a fictional personality, man finds it has the power to affect his own behavior. Pygmalion-like, the interaction takes place. Santa Claus may be Kris Kringle or St. Nicholas or Father Christmas, depending upon the ethnic group. Each group, having started essentially with the same figure, has modified it further to suit its needs and in turn has been affected to some degree by the now self-created image.

In addition to legendary images conceived as personalities with an interactive effect, there may also be an interacting dream image which bears no direct relationship to any known human being. The principle of interpersonality relationships still operates even in dreams, and analogously, in this case, to the created image.

Even basic psychological mental activities are considered by Sullivan to be involved in interpersonal relationships. For example, the mental activities of imagining, perceiving, remembering, and thinking are connected with other personalities and are not exclusively inner dynamics of behavior void of influence from other personalities. Everything we do, Sullivan feels, is the result of the social order in which we live. Other personalities have made some effect upon our behavior no matter how intrapersonal it seems to be. In imagination we have dreams and images that revolve about other people. We dream of success, not over trees, but what we can do to trees that will impress other people. The astronaut imagines himself in outer space with all of its unknown qualities and apparently nonhuman features but the culmination of his imagination in stellar space is his coming back. He wants to come back not only for life's sake but also because that is where people are. His outer space behavior will be partially determined by what other personalities did to him before he went aloft. It can further be assumed that his behavior in space will be affected by concern for the opinions of others upon his return. Perception is highly involved in interpersonal relationships. The personality reared in circumstances of wealth walks through a smart shopping district and perceives the expensive displays as obtainable merchandise fitting his interests and desires. The personality reared in poverty walks along the same street, sees the same glittering displays, and is bound to perceive them in a different light. He either covets, resents, or plans some day to achieve these symbols of wealth. In any case, his perceptive system is different from that of the wealthy individual. Perception differs in this case because of one's background and training, gained through life with other personalities.

Remembering is influenced by other personalities, too. That which is important or nonimportant to remember is influenced by our parents, friends, and other personalities whom we deem to be worthy of imitation. Whether one remembers baseball scores or musical scores and considers either one or the other to be worth remembering is the product of our contact with other personalities. Even the methods and mnemonic devices we wish to employ are the result of influence from teachers, parents, or friends. And lastly, our thinking becomes oriented along the lines of those personalities among whom we live. Personalities living in subtropical climates, personalities from Oriental or Occidental cultures are inclined to think differently from each other. The human neural systems (ganglia, dendrites, neurones, synaptic gaps, etc.) may be identical, but the end products of the thinking process may be opposite to each other.

All of the preceding discourse does not say that for Sullivan one is categorically denied the opportunity to study the individual personalities. Such later principles in this chapter as dynamisms, personifications, and cognitive experiences are studies of the individual personality. Such study is necessary, Sullivan feels, if one is to comprehend the nature of man, but it is equally necessary that one does not lose sight of the interactive systems which always operate within and around the single personality.

Tension System Principle

Like numerous other theorists, Sullivan feels that man strives to reduce the tensions in his life. From the level of complete lack of tension, which he calls *euphoria* (a psychiatric term generally used to describe delusional feelings of well-being), to the state of excessive tension akin to psychoses, Sullivan considers an important aspect of man's personality to be the reduction of tensions which threaten man's security.

Tension arises from two sources: organic needs and social insecurity which leads to feelings of anxiety. Organic needs which are basic to all personalities are both general and specific. Instances of general organic needs may be air and water. Specific organic needs may be pine-scented, perfumed, or at least nonobnoxious air, or fluids such as coffee, soft drinks, or alcoholic drinks. The general need is often satisfied and tension reduced by satisfying the socially indoctrinated, specific need. Hunger, for example, may be assuaged by sucking, smoking, or using the lips and mouth as one would in eating. In addition to the categories of general and specific organic needs, these needs may also be arranged in hierarchical order from most important in reducing tension to least important. Illustrations of the subordination of one biological need to another may be found in our habit of eating a sweet dessert after the main meal instead of before. Or we may wish for pure sweet air to breathe before we wish for scented air. One need must be met before the other becomes important.

Reducing the social tensions of life within this principle of tension systems is a process so important to Sullivan's system that it has been treated largely as a singular principle under the rubric of the anxiety principle. Much can be said concerning the reduction of tensions from man's social behavior. For the present we find that man is surrounded by feelings of anxiety which he meets upon entering life. From his mother's anxious intent that he survive and be fed and clothed properly, on to the precautions that society takes to keep its constituents safe from injury, pain, or death (polio drives, heart disease campaigns, auto-safety measures, etc.) the individual prolongs and develops the feelings of anxiety he first met at birth. These threats to his security may be either real or imagined. In either case, anxiety situations may be met by similar tension reducing behavior. Whether he has actually had a serious automobile accident on a frantic metropolitan throughway or whether he has only seen pictures and heard accounts of accidents on the same throughway, we may expect the driver in traffic to be anxious about avoiding a similar accident. Similarly, lightning may never have struck the individual, but he exercises caution on the golf course in a thunderstorm, and his behavior is anxiety-centered. In all cases, his behavior of anxiety may be mollified and disguised by the presence of other personalities with him. Further feelings of anxiety may also accrue from real or imagined social rebuffs. The college freshman may hesitate to ask for a dancing partner at his first college mixer because of the imagined threat of refusal. He may never have been refused before and may be an accomplished social dancer, but the imagined threat of refusal is stultifying enough to keep him on the sidelines, wistfully eyeing the proceedings and possible dance partners for the entire evening. He gives all the manifestations of being anxious to guard his ego from blunt refusal. Tension and ambivalence ensue as he neither wants to deny himself the pleasures of college social life, nor undergo the threat to his ego. He may avoid further similar social occasions until he possesses a coed friend who gives him the security he has learned from his early infancy to need.

The following is a marked departure from the express meaning of Sullivan's tension reduction systems but seems particularly appropriate to a further understanding of the interpersonal theory of behavior. It also strikingly illustrates the pattern of man's changeable behavior as he progresses through life. The interpretation as such does not exist in Sullivan's works.

An Adaptation of the Tension System. Freud considered the personality to be primarily set in a definable mold after the first five or six years. Previously the analogy was drawn that man's personality is like a brick structure which once formed can only be altered slightly and that to change it completely is to destroy the structure. In Sullivan's tension system we find a very different analogy to the structuring of man's personality from birth to burial.

Using the tension principle from the work of Buckminster Fuller, a renowned architect whose Dymaxion house is built on the principle of tension, we find that a structure may exist which is held together by tension. Previously most architectural structures have been constructed from the bottom up, with the material at the foundation responsible for the stability of the entire super-structure. From Fuller's work we find that an immensely strong structure may be built which holds itself together. It is not dependent upon the bottommost parts but is dependent upon each of its integral parts. A box kite is an excellent example of the tension system. It is held together by the tension of all its component parts. Each piece of the kite plays an equally important role in the rigidity of the device. The box kite may be transported through various kinds of air turbulence, it may bear stress and strain which is equally divided between its parts, and it may be altered without the collapse of the entire structure. In such a device as the box kite, which exemplifies Buckminster Fuller's tension system, we may find a unique example to apply to Sullivan's theories on personality.

According to Sullivan, man has a personality which strives to equalize the tensions between its various parts. When a state of complete tension equality is achieved, the personality is happy and anxiety free. However, the personality is rendered tensionless only to the degree that no outward forces play upon it. The moment any exterior force disturbs its own unique balancing of tensions, extra stress is brought to bear upon the entire structure to equalize the pressures of one of its members against the other. Fortunately for the personality the entire structure must bear the burden of the exterior forces. Since man during his lifetime forever floats in the environment of other personality structures, he can never avoid the unequal stresses placed on his own structure by others. The result is a personality built upon the tension system of self and affected daily by the tension systems of other personalities. Unfortunately, however, the strength of having the entire structure bear the burden of exterior forces also is an outstanding weakness of the personality tension system. When the exterior forces are too strong too long the entire personality structure becomes twisted and misshapen into a state of psychoses. Thus, man pursues an existence bound together by his own tension system, quite capable of mobility into variant climates, a mobility of which a brick structure is incapable, but all the while prey to the influences of all other similar personality structures.

By this extension of Sullivan's theory on tension systems it is hoped that a greater degree of understanding has been achieved. Further analogies could be drawn from the Buckminster Fuller idea, but the present treatment seems adequate.

Anxiety Principle

General Conditions. Harry Stack Sullivan placed a great deal of emphasis upon the anxiety that man feels. Man is an anxious animal. Although anxiety is so closely associated with the tension system principle as actually to be a part of it, anxiety is also more than an adjunct of another system. It is one of the prime motivators in life, according to Sullivan. Anxiety is both productive and destructive. Slight anxiety is good for man. It moves him off dead center. Total anxiety leads man to utter confusion and renders him incapable of intelligent action. Anxiety, therefore, varies in intensity, sometimes causing the personality to make greater effort to keep his tensions in hand, and at other times causing him to behave in a psychotic or neurotic fashion, as he attempts to straighten out the twisted strands of his existence. Sullivan believed that tension systems are similar among men, but that each man has his own peculiar method of handling them. Individuality is manifested in the way men meet their stresses.

In the beginning of his life, man's first educative experience comes out of his feelings of anxiety transmitted by his mother. Her behavior, looks, and general demeanor center on anxious moments in the child's care and welfare. The infant soon notices that he is worried about and that he is cautioned about the dangers of fire, high places, and all of the other dangers for which precautions must be taken in raising a child. Through empathy and emulation the infant takes to himself the feelings of anxiety concerning health and safety which he first noticed in the mother. In the beginning he knew only pain and pleasure. Something hurt or it felt good. Gradually as he received sympathy and ministrations for his cuts and bruises, he began to exercise caution, and with caution grew the feeling that he is surrounded by a world which can hurt or harm him. Through the cognitive experience of parataxical thinking he associates many activities not necessarily anxiety-producing with what he considers an anxiety-packed situation. Some anxiety helps him to learn what is good and what is harmful. Too much anxiety makes him withdraw into a shell of security.

Out of early life experiences, the personality constructs the self system, creates personifications, and maintains a tension system.

Self System. One of the results growing out of the anxious human being in childhood is the creation of the self system. Emerging from the mother-fed feelings of anxiety regarding himself and later trying to construct a system which will secure him from tension, the human personality gradually builds a self system to do these things for him. Conforming to the social rules of his parents avoids anxiety: being a good little boy brings praise; being a bad little boy brings punishment. The good me-bad me dichotomy has opposite rewards. Conformity avoids anxiety; nonconformity produces anxiety. Anxiety begets tension. Tension is painful. By the process of evolutionary development, the child can create a system of doing things according to conformity, but this self system does not often represent his true self. Once the self system proves its worth in avoiding anxiety ("Do what you are told and never mind how you feel"), it is apt to become isolated from the real self, which often feels contrary to what the self system is doing to conform.

Having once been instituted in childhood, a self system tends to persist and be reinforced as life progresses, even though conformity not in tune with the real self is demanded. The personality considers the self system to be highly valuable in reducing anxiety. Any valuable item is guarded and held in high esteem. The personality continues to use the self system especially to protect it from criticism by its real self. The wider the gulf and the greater the use of the self system, the more complex and independent it becomes. A schizoid situation develops if the distance between the self system and the true self continues to widen. It is possible, therefore, for the true self to be unable ultimately to control the self system with its devious ways.

Sullivan felt, however, that some self system was essential to avoid or at least reduce anxiety in the modern world. One of the problems in life, then, is to use but control one's self system. Frank analyses and criticism of the self system by the real self may help in providing controls to a schizoid situation.

Seven Life Periods. Table 8. 1 is designed to help the student to make a short survey of Sullivan's contribution to developmental psychology through the avenue of anxiety periods. Sullivan proposed seven states. He felt that these were possibly more applicable to western European cultures, which he knew best, than they might be to other cultures. The period of adolescence was of such importance to Sullivan that he preferred to make three groupings within it rather than one single grouping entitled *adolescence.* This omission may seem strange to some readers familiar with the more traditional groupings of life stages. (See Gesell, Hurlock, Erikson, etc.)

Dynamism Principle

The following three principles (dynamisms, personifications, and cognitive experiences) are similar in that they are processes by which the personality achieves interaction with other personalities. They are being treated separately in this work, however, to enable the student of personality better to study them and to keep them from being confused. Actually, the three processes are one and the same operation. They are developed within the personality in the same order as they are presented here with the exception of prototaxic experiences, which run parallel with the development of dynamisms.

A dynamism is any recurring, habitual action, attitude, or feeling that one person has about one or more other persons. It is the smallest unit of human behavior that can be analyzed and studied profitably by another human. It is a relatively enduring behavior pattern. It can be closely associated with habit.

Dynamisms accumulate throughout life as the human being experiences more and more social contacts. The wider the variety of experiences one has, the greater the number of dynamisms he will possess. The total group of dynamisms may become so complex as to constitute a particular style of living. The self system previously mentioned is a complex of dynamisms built around the potent energizing emotion of anxiety.

Dynamisms change only when there has been an accumulation of different dynamisms crowding upon it. The ancient problem of differences in degree and differences in kind is involved in changing a dynamism. Differences of degree do not change the basic properties of a dynamism, whereas differences in kind do change the dynamism. Just exactly what constitutes a difference in degree and a difference in kind is most troublesome to define. Apparently, and in some manner not explicitly stated by Sullivan, the difference of kind is decided by the self. What may appear as a difference of degree to some personalities will be construed as a difference of kind by other personalities. However it may be, only the differences in kind of dynamisms may alter preceding and currently operating dynamisms. We may further assume that the trick in therapy, in kind, if we are to change the basic behavior pattern of the client, is to make him accept dynamisms which are different.

Dynamisms may be openly expressed (overt) or secretly practiced within the self system (covert). Such activities as laughing, talking, and dancing may be examples of the former, while autistic thinking and reasoning may be examples of covert dynamisms.

Most dynamisms serve a basic need of the body, however remote that may seem as the dynamisms operate. Sullivan reveals his early Freudian influence by associating many of the dynamisms with the erotogenic zones of the body. The mouth, anus, genitals are involved at times with dynamisms, although other parts of the body, too, such as the hands, feet, and back may be involved.

Some examples of dynamisms may be as follows: the dynamism of lust would be indicated by excessive gambling; dreading new situations would be considered the dynamism of fear; and the dynamism of aggression would reveal itself in fighting or strongly exerting the self at the expense of others.

Personification Principle

Personifications are the images one has first of self and then of others. In a sense they represent a stereotype of self. Personifications shared by

Table 8. 1. Seven Life Periods According to Sullivan's Theory

Period	Approximate Ages	Body Zone	Self System	Cognitive Experiences	Pertinent Interpersonal Experiences
Infancy	0–18 mo. (Birth to articulate speech)	Oral	Barely emerging	Largely prototaxic	1. Nursing–breast or bottle; great stress on nipple orientation 2. Fearing the good-bad mother 3. Occasional success at satisfying self independent of mother 4. Completely dependent on paternal-maternal care
Childhood	18–20 mo. to age 4–5 (speech to needing playmates)		Sex role recognition	Largely parataxic emerging to syntaxic	1. Personifications 2. Dramatizations–plays at being adult 3. Possible "malevolent transformations"–feeling the world is against you–create isolation 4. Dependent
Juvenile	5–6 to 11 (Elementary School)	Dormant genital	Integrating needs–internal controls	Syntaxic most of the time, fascination with symbols	1. Socialization–cooperation and competition 2. Learning controls 3. Orientation in how to live 4. Dependent

Table 8. 1. (*Continued*)

Pre-adolescence	11–13 (Jr. High School)	Emerging genital	Somewhat stabilized	Syntaxic	1. Outstanding need for peer of same sex 2. Begins genuine human relationships 3. Needs opportunity for equality—mutuality and particularly reciprocity in interpersonal relationships 4. Emerging and confusing independence
Early adolescence	12–17 (High School)	Fully genital	Confused, but continuingly stabilized	Syntaxic (highly sexually oriented)	1. Strongly lustful 2. Double social needs: erotic for opposite sex and intimacy for like-sexed peer. (confusion leads to homosexuality) 3. Highly independent
Late adolescence	17–19 to early 20s (College)	Fully matured	Integrated and stabilized	Fully syntaxic	1. Strong security against anxiety 2. Prolonged period 3. Full member of social group 4. Fully independent
Adulthood	20–30 etc. (Parenthood)	Completely heterosexual	Completely stabilized	Syntaxic and completely symbolic	1. Society has now created a fully social animal from a human animal 2. Completely independent of paternal control

many others become the stereotype as it is generally known. In the main, however, personifications are the pictures of others which the person carries in his own mind. Accuracy is not necessarily involved in a personification of someone else. "Love is blind," "My child can do no wrong; he must be understood first" are examples of the prejudicial characteristics of a personification.

As the child develops, he first gains an impression of the thing he knows best: himself. From the good–bad nature of himself he notices and empathizes with the good–bad nature of others as he interprets their behavior. These impressions grow into a complicated personification of many persons. Each person then is a composite, or complex personification, of the previous experiences the child has had with similar personalities. By adopting personifications of others, the self hopes to protect itself from anxiety. On the prejudged basis that some people are harmful and thus to be avoided or controlled, the personification serves as a tool to decrease the tensions in life. Any person resembling the original personified concept gains the reputation, good or bad, of the original personification. Consequently, although personifications are highly instrumental in interpersonal processes, they may not be accurate estimations of another's qualities.

Cognitive Experiences Principle

The third interpersonal process which Sullivan incorporated in his theory of personality refers to the development patterns in human thinking. By these mental processes man interrelates with other men, and thus the processes become important to Sullivan's theory. The cognitive experiences principle consists of three hierarchical forms of thinking which relate oneself to other human beings. The lowest level is the prototaxic experience. The next higher and more involved experience is parataxic. The highest mental experience man attains is the syntaxic mode of interacting with others.

Prototaxic. In the beginning, man's conscious mental processes consist of raw sensations of a momentary nature. Fleeting through the infantile mind, Sullivan believes, are sensations, feelings, and fragmentary images, none of which are of long duration. Prototaxic experiences of a mental nature (it can hardly be called thinking in the popular sense) are rarely, if ever, connected with each other. They occur at random, are vivid experiences during their duration, leave vestiges of memory traces, and are a necessary prelude to the next two modes of mental processes. No logical behavior ensues from the impact of prototaxic mental experiences. The baby follows one clue to another with apparently completely random responses. The important factor is that in this manner he gradually becomes aware of his surroundings, and particularly of the human beings who constitute his environment. In a haphazard way, then, man begins to get some fleeting impressions of the world beyond his own physical and mental self.

Parataxic. Parataxic thinking sees causal relationships between two simultaneous phenomena whether there is really a degree of causality or not. The parataxically oriented mind confuses correlation with causation. Because two things happen at the same time, he is inclined to believe that one activity created or caused the other activity. The author recalls an intriguingly titled paper, "Superstition in the Pigeon," which was presented at a Midwestern Psychological Association meeting. The paper clearly indicated that a pigeon had made a random movement at the exact moment that a food pellet was introduced into the cage. The pigeon "thought" that his queer sideways gesture of the head had caused the food pellet to be introduced into the cage. The one reinforcement was sufficient to perpetuate the head jerk in the pigeon which always assumed that food would be gained by the movement. This is a perfect example of parataxic thinking. Another and oft-told example from basic psychology classes serves well to illustrate parataxic thinking: A certain gentleman stated that every time he heard the fire engine there also happened to be a fire; *Ergo;* fire engines cause fires!

This type of thinking may do a disservice to the child's sense of interpersonal relations, and hence it becomes important to Sullivan's theory. Part of the self system, as well as personifications, may be formed by the child's inability to separate two concurrent factors. He may feel, for example, that wherever there is a police officer there is crime or trouble. Failing to make the proper association between the officr's function and the occurrence of trouble, he may attribute the trouble to the police. In his childish mind police officers cause trouble. Unfortunately, this type of parataxical thinking is frequently the foundation for adult prejudices and superstitious beliefs. Sullivan felt that too much of modern man's thinking does not progress beyond parataxic thinking. It must be admitted that there is strong evidence to substantiate his claim.

Syntaxic. This is the highest of the three types of thinking as Sullivan incorporated them into his theoretical system. Syntaxic thinking uses symbols as its basis. These symbols may be verbal or numerical, but they must have been accepted by enough people for them to have an agreed-upon meaning. Private symbols convey nothing to the uninitiated, as witness the rituals of a fraternity or sorority. Public symbols, Sullivan felt, are absolutely necessary for man to carry on an interpersonal relationship with other men. The complexities of society remove the ancient possibility of human contact by gestures or even rudimentary speech. In a sense, man can only progress in his relationships with other men as he creates and employs more meaningful symbols.

The value of syntaxic thinking based upon symbology is further increased by its aiding man to a greater degree of logical quality in his personal thinking, as well as by the invaluable avenue it gives him for communication with others.

EXPLAINING HUMAN BEHAVIOR VIA SULLIVAN'S INTERPERSONAL THEORY

Explaining human behavior via Sullivan's theory would be quite simple if one were to state only that man does what he does because of interpersonal ralationships. Whatever he does is done because another human being taught him to do it or because he imitated the behavior of another person. However, Sullivan's theory has many more ramifications than a unitary thought pervading all of man's activities. Nine of man's activities are employed in using the current theory to explain why man does the things he does: marriage, perversions, suicide, lawbreaking, supranatural being, humor, smoking, play and recreation, and psychoses–neuroses.

Marriage

It would seem that man enters matrimony and all the preliminary functions of courtship primarily because he lives in a society that uses that system to propagate the race and rear its families. This answer does not, however, explain why man began the custom. To seek answers for this we must examine Sullivan's concepts of the tension system, personifications, the seven life periods, as well as the underlying strata of human interaction.

Anxious to protect himself from threats to ego and feelings of insecurity man seeks an alter ego that will help to maintain and fix the tensions within his life. On previous pages we discussed the feeling of security the college student can obtain by attending dances with a fiancee. The social evening is much more predictable if one can be assured of attention and participation in dancing with a social partner. Even if the "date" leaves much to be desired in appearance and poise, the terrible insecurities of acceptance and rejection from others has been removed. At least the social partner (good or bad) pays attention to the "date." Many people may even tolerate friction or lassitude from the social partner as long as the roles for the evening are understood and support the feeling of participation in the social event. To be abandoned at a college social is the most grievous of social dilemmas. To be slightly bored is a regrettable but tolerable situation providing one can have some participation in the event and can be relieved of the uncertainties that foster his sense of insecurity. It is better to know what you have, even though it may not be exactly what you want, than to suffer the pangs of insecurity. Excluding for the moment the developmental phase of man's erotogenic system, we can see that much of dating and courtship is built around the feeling of security it gives to the two persons involved in the burgeoning romance.

Biologically, man is also in the throes of the dynamisms of his erotic needs as he emerges through adolescence. The strong biological urges within his physical system now transfer their once dormant energies to new, invigorated energies, from feelings of intimacy to desires for erotic expression. He dreams, thinks, fantasizes, and fumblingly attempts socialized opportunities with the opposite sex. Coupled with the desire must be some opportunity to support a romance according to the social customs of the day. Continuous solitary walks in the woods are of limited social value if all of one's peers are engaged in group activities. Without at least a minimum of economic support (the boy for dating expenses, the girl for clothes and smart appearance) the social partnership may never be aligned. The adolescents of both sexes are keenly aware of what the social group is doing. The insecurities of the female, for example, in not knowing whether she is to be invited to the prom, are excruciating, as any parent of a teen-age daughter knows. Equally true is the befuddlement of the male, hesitating to ask for a date for fear of refusal or a half-hearted acceptance. Both incidents indicate the fear of insecurity which Sullivan felt to be so powerful in the lives of man. A final consideration in the early times of heterosexual contacts is the number of dynamisms which gradually evolve out of dating contacts. The unique person-to-person contacts that illustrate dynamisms are strengthened toward heterosexual growth by the accumulation of the experiences one gets through continued dating. The more dates, the more dynamisms one has toward the opposite sex.

Personalities enter into the choice of social partner but appear to be more acutely involved in the actual selection of a marriage partner at the time "engagements" are to be expected. When queried, many young men or young women can give only evasive reasons for becoming engaged or for dating steadily with the same person. ("I don't know, we just seem to have fun together and enjoy each other.") The effect of personifications may be seen in this situation. Personifications grow out of parataxical experiences of the past and are not always accurate. When shared they become stereotypes. Consequently, the boy, for example, may bring into his selection of a marriage partner vestiges of the personifications he has of his mother. He may want to marry a girl who fits the stereotype of his social group. Some girls just simply won't do as possibilities for wives, but may be eligible for casual dates. Common religion, equivalent socio-economic backgrounds, and the like enter into the group personifications called stereotypes which the male uses in selecting a future wife.

Finally, it can also be stated that man gets married because that is the prevailing custom in his social climate. The rituals of marriage, the manner in which the marriage is arranged (self-selected dating or parentally arranged), and even how the marriage will continue into the years of adulthood and parenthood become intricately involved in the social climate of the times. Some ethnic or professional groups may consider divorce as a normal course of events. Other groups may consider divorce as an evil of close to satanic depths. Some religions condone divorce, others do not. Some environments may consider the children resulting from a marriage as things to be schooled and trained by others, while the opposite can be found in societies whose family ties are tightly bound throughout life. The ultimate effect, according to Sullivan's interpersonal theory of personality, is that marriage is another example of social interactive forces that play upon a man's life all of his days.

Perversions

One explanation of this aspect of man's possible behavior has already emerged in the discussion of the life stages during the early adolescent years. At this level of development, the adolescent may confuse the need for intimacy with like-sexed peers that he has carried over from his preadolescent period into the early adolescent period with the strongly emergent erotic need for the opposite sex. Such confusion of needs may result in an overt or latent homosexuality. The strong lusts that come with early adolescence may also be subverted by interpersonal contacts with already practicing homosexuals or sexual inverts of other types. Presumably some vestiges of dynamisms carried over from infancy and childhood have an effect upon perverted acts. Each of these dynamisms, of course, has been the result of repeated contacts with one or more other human beings. The Sullivanian rationale is that perversions can come only from contacts with other human beings since interpersonal contact is the keystone of his system. Ostensibly, two people, neither of whom has ever had a perverted experience, coming into contact with each other, will probably not be led to commit a perverted act. There has been no one from whom they could learn it. It would be possible, one might surmise, that the uninitiated perverted partners might learn their deviate sexual activity through trial-and-error sex play. Symbols, however, may be as potent in inducing perversions as actual previous physical contacts. Pornographic jokes, pictures, and the like, have their effect on human behavior. Personifications of a deviant nature may also influence the sexual behavior of the adolescent. (It is presumed here that man does not first begin perverted sexual behavior, particularly of a homosexual nature, in his adult years.)

In summary, whatever deviant and nonproductive sexual behavior the human being indulges in is probably learned and reinforced from interpersonal contacts with other humans.

Suicide

It is possible in explaining suicide via Sullivan's theory to incorporate a number of factors. We may assume, for example, that the self system becomes completely alienated from the true self. The anxieties of life become so overwhelming that the self system develops wider and wider façades to reduce anxiety, but the attempts are ineffectual. Gradually, as the distance between true self and self system increases, the true self can no longer control its self system. As a result, the self system may decide to stop living, and a suicide results.

It may also follow that the tension system which holds the personality together and yet creates demands upon the personality may become so tight that the pressure becomes intolerable. If the tension system is unable to distribute equally throughout the system the forces that bear upon it, the breakdown of the system may be further advanced. Certain parts of the system may have to endure greater stresses than do others. Inequality of the burden of exterior pressures throughout the system eventually causes the most involved parts to collapse. As they collapse, they bring the entire personality structure into ruin. The twisted remains may then find nonexistence to be a more favorable solution than is continuation in a misshapen, painful condition. In this analysis we are faced with the greatest strength and also the greatest weakness of a tension system: when operating as a true tension system, it distributes equally throughout its structure the strains of any one of its parts; but if any one of its member parts breaks, the entire structure collapses. Whatever happens to one facet of the personality happens to all facets of the personality. Whenever one portion of the personality totally disintegrates, all portions of the personality disintegrate.

Still a third factor must be considered in suicide. The two above explanations stress the intrapersonal aspects of taking one's life. The major emphasis, however, in Sullivan's theory is the effect and power of the interpersonal aspects of man's life. We may find an explanation from the interpersonal viewpoint by examining the behavior of the much publicized Kamikaze pilots of Japan in World War II. Here we had a group of able-bodied, highly trained individuals in an exclusive organization. The fighter pilots, having gone through the highly selective training process, became closely knit as a homogeneous and compatible group. The peer structure of the group was unique. What indoctrination was brought to bear upon a few was quickly adopted by the remaining members of the group. Consequently, if some of the group were inculcated with the chauvinistic pleasures of dying to protect an even larger group made up of mothers, fathers, families, he had not far to go to convince the remaining members of the group that death with a great purpose was an ennobling experience. The task of accepting suicide might have been even simpler if the pilots came, as they did, from an ethnic group which had in its own past accepted suicide as a natural concomitant to thwarted hopes. The total result is an explanation of suicide built around interpersonal relationships. As a counter example one did not find large groups of American pilots accepting suicide as a natural counterpart of military behavior. The ethnic climate was wrong for this; the peer group relationships were not as tightly interwoven, and the course of the war appeared to them in a different light than it did to the Japanese pilots at the time of Kamikaze attacks. An outstanding point to remember is that the Japanese pilots were not mentally deranged in the true sense of psychotic behavior, but were more closely following the dictates of interpersonal relationships. No doubt to the Japanese pilots, personifications of previous suicidal heroes also were a potent motivating factor.

Lawbreaking

Four factors emerge as possible explanations for man's deliberately breaking the major laws of his fellow man: a faulty self system; faulty personifications; erroneous cognitive experiences as to cause and effect; and, in many cases, an illegal attempt to reduce the tensions in life to more acceptable dimensions, only to find that one has created an entirely new structure of tensions in the criminal world of law avoidance.

Once again the self system may, in its attempts to protect the real self from anxiety, perpetrate crimes which the real self would not tolerate. An ambivalence results from the schizoid behavior of the entire personality. Crimes of passion and emotional outbursts resulting in illegal behavior may be explained as follows by using the Sullivanian system.

As the child grows and matures, he may set up for himself personifications which he admires for their audacious and action-packed lives. These figures whom he deeply admires and wishes to emulate may be criminals of the lowest order, but the child sees them as living dangerous and exciting lives. The personifications may even represent to the child submerged desires to flaunt the world of authority and the constricted life that he feels is unfair. Basing his own self system on the admired criminal figures, the child may pattern his behavior after personifications which are largely criminal. This may be true especially when the dynamisms of everyday life keep being reinforced by criminal figures cast in heroic roles, by way of Robin Hood legends, or sayings such as, "There is honor among thieves."

Occasionally one finds in correctional institutions for adolescents a type of parataxic thinking which rationalizes illegal behavior. There are inmates who excuse stealing on the grounds that stolen property indicates wealth to one's contemporaries, when in fact the peer world is aware that the stolen property so flamboyantly displayed is illgotten, and the result is a still further lowering in peer prestige rather than the opposite desired effect. Other examples stated previously are: because policemen are always present where there is trouble, policemen cause trouble; criminals live well with fine automobiles and large houses—therefore, crime pays. The end results of crime are rarely thought through by the individual prone to live his life according to parataxical cognitive processes.

The fourth explanation of criminal behavior may be found in crimes which are perpetrated to alleviate obvious distress of an economic or physical nature. Social distress may be equally as potent as organic distress. Stealing to provide medical services and greater comfort for one's family is also familiar to legal authorities. Stealing for prestige, however, and particularly at certain developmental stages, may be far more prevalent than either of the above examples. Authorities in juvenile delinquency will often state that this is the prime rationale for most youthful auto thefts. The anxiety and tensions of a "have-not" adolescent who is gifted in no particular manner may seem to be resolved by illegal behavior. That this illegal behavior creates further and more drastic anxieties is considered only infrequently by the adolescent. The prototaxic thinking of sensation rules for the moment of theft. Cause and effect, or the symbolic consequences of one's acts, are not present at the moment of decision to commit an illegal act. Successful and role-satisfied adolescents rarely steal property. It is the adolescent who lacks the satisfactions of life, with the anxiety that this lack brings, who breaks laws.

Supranatural Being

Sullivan's interpersonal theory does not have much to say in explaining why man worships deity figures. It may be assumed that a god figure is a highly idealized personification. Man creates a composite of all the good and great things he sees in adult figures. This composite becomes a deity to him. When the group creates a deity figure acceptable to the majority in the group, the figure becomes a stereotype and possesses the composite personifications of most of the group. This figure is then worshipped as a god. What kind of god it becomes depends, of course, on the stereotypic personification of the cultural group. In some cultures it is conceived as a representative figure of the culture. Oriental gods resemble and represent the Oriental appearance. Occidental gods are presumed to look like an adult in the western world. It is hardly likely that the western world would worship a god figure that looked like an Oriental, for example. The major thesis à la Sullivan remains that the creation of a god figure is part and parcel of interpersonal relationships. Man learns from others what kind of god to expect and in what ways he may consider the god to act upon his life. Through parents, other adults, and through church forms, he receives his own image of a god.

Under the interpersonal theory of Sullivan, the act of worshipping is more easily explained than is the object of worship. Worship, whether it be in a temple, synagogue, cathedral, or church, is an interpersonal group activity. Few religions, though there are some, worship as solitary individuals. Most forms of worship incorporate groups of people. The conduct of the worshippers during the service of worship is a highly ritualistic and orderly type of behavior. The group determines the mode of worship, with only small deviations permitted by the congregation. The entire effort of worship becomes highly organized. The order of service, the emphasis of worship, and the place of worship are group determined, either through elected officials or by consensus of the group. So influential is the group upon the act of worship that the size of the group becomes an indication of success or failure in the act of worship. Rivalry between groups is indicated by the open or subtle forms of missionary work undertaken to convert other groups to accept one's own group as a more pure form of worship. The interpersonal effect of worshipping may go beyond the singular act of worshipping a deity. The individual may attend church because it is expected of him in his station in life, or because of the impression he wishes to create. He may attend church because at the service he meets people he likes; here the process of socialization is important, with little thought given to worshipping a deity. Such a person may request the rites of christening, marriage and burial, not for reasons of conviction, but because it is expected of him in his society. The combined effort of his group may go beyond the process of worship to indulge in greater and greater social reforms in the community and in the world, efforts which have only tenuous threads to the acts of worshipping a deity.

In short, one may consider religion as a highly organized interpersonal activity in which one's personality may be deeply affected.

Humor

Why man has a sense of humor and what use he makes of it are not readily drawn out of Sullivan's interpersonal theory of personality. The writer has had to be highly inventive at times in composing these sections, and explaining humor presents a vexing challenge. Saying that man laughs because other men laugh is truly begging the question. Perhaps we may posit the following two explanations for humor under the interpersonal theory: man has a sense of humor which is a vestige of prototaxic cognitive processes begun in infancy, and/or, man has a sense of humor because it is a unique and successful means of releasing tension and anxiety.

Even the most unsophisticated and disinterested student of human behavior is aware that small infants will smile and gurgle happily with no apparent reinforcement from other human beings in the beginning. The baby can be observed smiling and making happy noises even when no other person is present to the infant's senses. Later, but not much later, the infant responds to the tickling and playful proddings of his parents. Still later he may be found to respond sensitively to known figures like his parents or older siblings but to be indifferent or even frightened at the attempts of strangers to make him laugh or smile. What may happen, then, is that a natural state of well-being is educated into a response of pleasure accompanied with appropriate gestures and sounds as the infant associates well-being with attentive parents. Through the accumulations of dynamisms he gradually reinforces smiling and laughing as an interpersonal activity. One laughs when he is stimulated by other people who are acceptable to self. Much later in adult life man does not laugh at his avowed enemy, even though the enemy may do something that would normally be acceptable as funny. Interpersonally we laugh only at the tolerably acceptable figures. We laugh at the rich man losing his high silk hat not because we hate him as an enemy but because we envy him as a figure with higher authority. On the other hand the American public could not laugh at or be amused by the stereotype of the Japanese soldier shortly after Pearl Harbor. Any figure which threatens man cannot produce humor. In any case we may assume humor is directly connected with the interhuman situations in which man finds himself. Trees, no matter how grotesque, are not funny. Animals, on the other hand, may be hilariously funny but only when we see anthropomorphically many human traits in their behavior. The bear in the zoo begging for peanuts is highly humorous because he is acting like a human being. The wild bear seen in the woods, but not threateningly met, is exciting and dangerous but not humorous. The closer animals come to human behavior, the more humorous we find them. Man, therefore, laughs at man, not nature. Humor is the result of the interplay between human beings. The previous explanation may show how man came to have a sense of humor, but it suffers in trying to explain when and for what reasons man exposes his sense of humor. Perhaps the next paragraph may help in this.

According to Sullivan, life is a tight, tensioned world of many anxieties, real or fancied. It is possible that man has a sense of humor and uses it for no more involved reason than to release the tensions in his life caused by the myriad anxieties that he feels surround him. A sudden laugh, a high feeling of exhilaration caused by a humorous incident, a seeking of the ridiculous in a situation which is compounded of frustrations, may all be ascribed to man's reducing tension by using humor. The tension reduction mechanism of humor may in no way solve the real problem, but it well serves its purpose if the individual feels the reduction of tension. The world of the individual may be as black as ever, but if he can laugh about his problems, he has gone a long way toward reducing the anxiety caused by the problem. Once the tension has become manageable, he may be in a better state to achieve a genuine resolution of what was once insoluble. Perhaps this latter is the most meaningful explanation of man's sense of humor.

Smoking

Two explanations of smoking as an aspect of man's behavior seem possible. One explanation presumes that smoking is a social custom; the other explanation presumes that smoking is a regressive type of behavior based on the early dynamisms of man's life.

In the very earliest years of man's life, he utilizes certain areas of the body by which he begins to interact with his environment. The mouth, for example, plays a crucial role in helping the child know his mother, or mother surrogate. The infant uses the mouth, tongue and lips. From organic contact with the nipple the child learns to know a good nipple, a bad nipple, and all the variations of sucking behavior associated with ingesting food. Since this type of contact is essentially basic for all human beings, the dynamism of oral orientation is universal. Dynamisms are early forms of habit associations with other humans. The dynamisms of contact with other human beings orally is one of the earliest dynamisms to be habitually reinforced. Contact with others, particularly with those who connote pleasant relationships, becomes associated with the oral zone of the body. Such behavioral illustrations as sucking the thumb, chewing gum, nail biting, and, of course, smoking a pipe or cigarettes may be regressive attempts to recapture the pleasant rapport one once associated with a warm, acceptant, nuturing mother figure. The basis for regression is not to exercise a portion of the body but to renew symbolically through the oral cavity a former pleasant interpersonal relationship. The oral zone is merely the *modus operandi*. The basic rationale is the recapture of former dynamisms built around pleasant associations since as one learns to smoke, the experience is rarely pleasant. The smoke is acrid, burns the tongue, irritates the eyes, and leaves a dry sensation in the mouth. Despite the initial discomforts of learning to smoke, the individual persists because the dynamism associated with oral contacts and pleasant interhuman feelings is stronger than the initial unpleasantness of smoking. Dynamisms, being like habit, continue to reinforce the pleasures of smoking as long as one continues to smoke. A stage is reached where the habituation quality of a dynamism makes it practically impossible for the individual to give up this form of behavior. Furthermore, dynamisms reinforce each other, as we shall see in the next paragraph. After a while the act of smoking becomes an intricate complex of regressive oral dynamisms, social contact, and manipulative dynamisms. To cease smoking, then, is to create tremendous anxieties and tension as one attempts to destroy reinforced dynamisms that have long been valuable to the self as anxiety reducing habits. For the habitual smoker, smoking reduces tension, and to destroy willfully a satisfactory tension reduction device is to court strong anxiety states to achieve a goal which seems nebulous.

One may also suggest that smoking is primarily an imitative dynamism founded on social contacts. A man smokes because other men smoke. Through smoking he can find companionship and a feeling of oneness with his fellow man. Smoking may be considered "smart," the "vogue," the "fad," but the genuine basis for it is the interpersonal effect upon the single individual's behavior. Smoking is an act perpetrated and continued as a social response to others. Interlinked with the social imitativeness of smoking are the dynamisms described in the preceding paragraph. The entire process is a developmental one as man progresses through the age groups until he, too, can acquire the habit within the accepted social rules of his society.

Play and Recreation

Probably the most acceptable reason for man's play is the obvious one of tension reduction in his every day world. In this sense play and recreation do not have to be easy and nonstrenuous. The activity itself may be extremely hazardous, such as mountain climbing, or very strenuous, such as tennis and water skiing, but the activity must bring some change of pace and a certain tension reduction in return for his troubles. Thus the bookkeeper may enjoy swimming underwater with an aqua lung because this is different from his job and takes him from the cares of the sedentary task of working with figures all day long. On the other hand, the pilot of a jet craft may enjoy raising prize roses because it removes him from the disciplined rigors of piloting jet planes. Under this explanation, therefore, the very wealthy man who chooses not to be employed in a daily task can get very little recreation from the normal avenues of sports and hobbies because these things are like what he does all the time. In order for him to enjoy an activity as play or recreation, he must deviate from the ordinary course of his daily tension-producing activity. Hence, when the very wealthy seek recreational possibilities, they may often be led to deviant ways of behaving as they quickly use up the ordinary avenues of recreation enjoyed by the average working man. They will range farther and farther and seek more and more sensational methods of play, having become saturated with normal recreations. It may be harder for the very wealthy to receive any tension-reducing benefits from recreation than it is for the poor, whose one Sunday at the beach is relished and relived with much pleasure.

Tension reduction through play may also be highly symbolic. Plays, movies, television, sports, and variety programs may symbolize many things to the viewer to whom the activity becomes a true tension reducing device. Empathetically one may soar to the heights and descend to sorrow through the medium of drama in its many forms, knowing at the end that it was all "make believe" and that one must again see to the mundane activities of normal living. We may expect, then, the person whose sedentary life produces the tension of stifling boredom to enjoy the sensational in drama. Whatever the rationale for passively witnessing a dramatic or athletic production for its symbolism, the total effect is to reduce the tensions in life through the symbolism represented.

Another approach to man's play, according to Sullivan, is to examine his concepts of personifications and dynamisms. This method determines *what kind* of play and recreation the individual chooses for himself while the tension-reduction explanation determines *why* man plays. In the beginning of his life man indulges in generalized random activity designed to give pleasure to himself alone. He sucks on things for an oral pleasure, he enjoys random muscular movements, he vocalizes and enjoys the sounds he can create with his own voice box, and he deports himself in a purely prototaxical relationship to his exterior world. After he emerges from infancy and reaches the nursery and kindergarten age, his play is still highly individual, but he is placed in situations where parallel play is encouraged. The usual frictions develop through rivalry for toys and equipment until he is taught by his society to cooperate and especially to enjoy reciprocal play with others. This lesson is repeated over and over again until the multiple dynamisms of the lessons are developed into a truly socialized, reciprocal play situation. All of this is part of the socialization treatment he receives from his elders. Nonconformity to the pattern of play is punished and discouraged by all possible means. Play becomes a training situation and laboratory for later adult life. One learns roles, reciprocal pleasures for ego strength, and multiple other benefits from play. But play from early schooling on is designed primarily as a social enterprise. The withdrawn individual, the shy child, and the wallflower are all recipients of pity, as well as of renewed efforts to make them become part of the group. Recreation of an individualized nature is given tacit approval but in no way seems to be encouraged, as is socialized play. The usual parental and teacher attitude toward hobbies appears to be that they cannot be forced, whereas the attitude toward group play situations seems to be that they must be enforced, even though subtly. The wallflower is considered a social loss and by implication an emotional problem. Before long, even individual hobbies become socialized, and clubs are formed to make a group effort out of an individual pursuit. Things are collected or made, not for their intrinsic value to the person for reasons of beauty or pride, but to be displayed and entered into competition with other personal hobbies of others. Stamps are collected, not because the person enjoys looking at the color and beauty of the stamps, but because he wants to have a bigger or better stamp collection than the other collectors. Both individual and social recreational activities come within the pattern of the society within which one operates. We play because play is a social activity built upon the dynamisms of past experiences.

Personifications enter into play and recreation as the objects toward which the person may direct his play efforts. An instance of this is the father who envisions his son as a professional baseball player. Either openly or covertly he encourages his son to emulate his own concept of the successful athlete. Although the son may never achieve professional status, the personification, nevertheless, has been cast for the son to follow. Personifications in play may have nothing to do with a parentally involved image. The popular "cops and robbers" or "cowboys and Indians" become personifications in play which the adult will later follow through the symbology of the "western" movie or the crime and detective play or book. The symbology may also hold true for the child whose early personification was the professional baseball player. In this case, the later personification is realized through the passive role of spectator, statistician, or historian of baseball records. The role of spectator is further enhanced by the belongingness one feels in the social group while attending a baseball game surrounded by other avid followers of the local team and its baseball heroes. The entire procedure is one of social participation stemming out of personifications. Popular heroes like Babe Ruth drew large crowds to the baseball parks, while teams with few hero figures did not.

One final consideration can be made regarding the role of interpersonal relationships in play and recreation. Taking, for example, the recreations of bridge for women and bowling for men, we may find that they owe their popularity to the social aspects of the activity rather than to the personal involvement inherent in the game. Admittedly the physical pleasure of throwing the bowling ball and knocking down some pins is a very real function of the game. Men, however, rarely bowl alone just to experience this pleasure, although this is possible within the rules of the game. One player may compete against all other players by bowling alone when he has time for it, posting his scores and so be in competition with all other bowlers competing at that place. But although scores are posted, one rarely bowls alone for the sheer pleasure of knocking pins down at the end of the alley. This denies the bowler that ecstatic pleasure of achieving a "strike" and then turning about to face the spectators with the look of Caesar after Gaul. The kidding banter, the competitive pressure, and the team spirit are as much an integral part of bowling as is the physical involvement of the sport. In the same sense playing golf alone (what good is a hole-in-one if no one knows about it?) and fishing alone (what good is a catch of phenomenal size if it cannot be displayed to others?) are not as acceptable as playing golf with a foursome or going up north with a party of men to rough it in a shack. Again, man plays because of the social aspects of play and recreation.

As suggested previously, it is possible that women play bridge (and men, poker) because of the socialization possible in the game. Some observers of women's bridge clubs may even suggest that the game is incidental to the pleasant talk and socialization that it affords. Few players of either sex appear to spend as much time studying the game as their scores would indicate that they need. Bridge is merely the *modus operandi* for a social situation.

In summary, man indulges in play and recreation to ease tension, to emulate personifications either actively or symbolically, and primarily to be an active part of a social situation, either directly or as a spectator to the activity. Man with his personality is a socially interactive animal, even in play.

Psychoses—Neuroses

According to Sullivan, man is surrounded by feelings of anxiety and a resultant tension that grows out of these feelings. To protect himself from the debilitating effects of these forces, he creates a self system which has the power to deceive, twist, or ameliorate the anxiety-producing world about him. Unless man controls his self system (which has only one aim: to reduce tension and anxiety), the self system will eventually control his genuine self of reality. We may assume, under the interpersonal theory of Sullivan, that psychosis or neurosis results when the true self and the self-system become thoroughly dichotomized. With the self-system in the driver's seat there can be no true insight into one's behavior, but only a stylized dedication to removing anxiety even though, because of lack of insight, behavior directed by the self-system may produce anxieties and pressures beyond the original field. The individual's behavior is then out of the field of reality, a situation which creates a collapse in the interpersonal behavior patterns which he has been using and evolving since infancy. It is, therefore, extremely rare for a young child to become psychotic, although he may possibly become neurotic, because he does not yet have a fully developed self system which is strong enough to split from his real self. The child lives chiefly in a world of reality because his senses and his physical world are more fully developed than are his mental and social world. The psychotic adult, on the other hand, becomes the slave of his dynamically oriented self system. The stronger the self system, the greater is the chance for psychotic behavior. Yet, as we have seen, the self system is the *sine qua non* of public life. Without some kind of self system to screen the anxieties of life, we are unable to operate in a world of reality.

It is further possible that when a psychotic attack occurs, there has been a collapse in the syntaxic way of thinking and a regression to the prototaxic way of thinking. Life becomes as it was in the infantile world of sensual impressions and raw feelings, unaccompanied by reasoned behavior. The human personality becomes a flow of external conscious experiences with little or no attempt at cognitive relationships. Realization of self injury, injury to others, other peoples' feelings of pity or revulsion are all now beyond the realm of the psychotic's prototaxical oriented mind. Life to the psychotic consists of raw sensations, and out of this maelstrom of sounds and impressions he attempts to reduce anxiety and produce quietude, only to be faced with more anxiety as his attempts fail, until complete withdrawl or agitated conflict result.

The childhood process which Sullivan called *malevolent transformation,* by which the child feels he is surrounded by enemies, may become foremost in the psychotic's mind. By regression to malevolent transformation the psychotic may revert to paranoid behavior, looking for enemies wherever he encounters people. According to his unique personal capacities, he may then become a confused paranoid of the schizophrenic type or a wily paranoiac.

Some differentiation may be found in the patterns of behavior between the psychotic and the neurotic. The neurotic may alleviate his anxiety and hope to reduce tension by utilizing the processes of sublimations and substitutions; the psychotic does not. Consequently, the neurotic may operate in the exterior world of society while the psychotic is almost always confined to an environment away from contact with the world at large.

The main thesis, however, in using Sullivan's interpersonal theory to explain psychoses and neuroses lies in the simple fact that both are produced by uncontrollable anxiety which grows out of an overpowering and prolonged state of tension with other human beings. Trees, clouds, fruit, any phenomenon of nature cannot be the casual factor in mental illness. Man's emotional problems are created by man's contact with man. All other phenomena are ancillary to the primal factor of interpersonal relationships.

PREDICTING HUMAN BEHAVIOR VIA SULLIVAN'S INTERPERSONAL THEORY

Harry Stack Sullivan was less concerned with predicting human behavior than he was with helping humans to behave better. During all of his professional life Sullivan was more than a cloistered observer of the human scene. He was actively engaged both in a clinical, and later on, in an international way, in trying to help man reduce the anxieties of modern life. His work has overtones of prediction within it. Most of the threads of evidence for predicting man's behavior come out of his therapeutic methods rather than in the basic postulations of his theory on personality. Unfortunately Sullivan did not live long enough to give him time to study man further in a prognostic sense. His brilliance and compassion for his fellowmen utilized his energy to the fullest. Oddly enough his work with the Selective Service System in 1940 and 1941, as well as his later work (1948) with UNESCO, had connotations of predicting human behavior although possibly the ongoing problems of the time screened the end results.

Personal Prediction

As a student of Sullivan's theory one must decide for himself whether he lives in an anxious world and whether he predicts that man's behavior will be circumscribed by anxiety and the tensions it produces. Essentially one may ask whether the world of man will ever be free from anxiety or whether anxiety is inescapable in human life. If it is, then we may predict for the future certain aspects of man's communal existence. If tension is to be always with us, we may expect the products of this tension to bear upon man's future existence. Beginning with the basic tensions of an organic biological system and continuing through to such mass phenomena as racial problems and socio-economic inequalities—all anxiety-producing —we may accept the hypothesis that man lives and will continue to live in an anxious world. Thus, from these postulations we may predict some patterns of man's behavior. At the time of this writing and, it would seem, for a depressingly long time in the future, the possibilities of nuclear warfare produce an anxious world fraught with the haunting fear that political situations and pressures will trigger warfare and annihilate the human race. Obvious anxieties arise from this situation. Whether one may predict a resolution of the present-day anxieties, or whether anxiety has been and and will continue to be woven through the fabric of life, is in the final analysis the task of the individual. No theory can hope or be expected to bear the weight of such considerations. First the individual must decide whether life is lived in an anxiety state of varying degrees and then proceed to the ultimate question: will life continue to be lived in a world of anxiety and the tension it brings about? It would seem that these are questions of individual faith based on an adequate theoretical position, and no cleverly devised scientific data or statistical treatment can be expected to predict the future of man's behavior, either individually or collectively.

Sullivan's theory has a popular appeal to the student of personality in regard to predicting that man does have the capacity to change. Most students of personality reject the thesis that the personality is formed at or around the age of six to such an extent that change is practically impossible. The inflexibility of the personality according to other theorists, such as Freud, seems to offend the democratic ideals of many students. Sullivan offers the thesis that man does and will change because what he is has been created by the society in which he operates. If that society changes, he too will change. Within a narrow band of personal freedom, man is free to become what he will. However, the choices are restricted to such an overpowering degree by his environment that we must almost conclude within Sullivan's frame of reference that man *has* to change. After all man has a personality only in relation to other men. Personality as such in the individual is a hypothetical construct. In a sense each one of us does not have a personality of his own but receives a personality from all other personalities. Any change in others changes ourselves. If this theoretical position is accepted, then we may predict personally that all personalities, our own included, will and must change in the course of life.

A third consideration arises when one deals with prediction as the single individual accepts or rejects evidence from Sullivan's work. Deciding for himself, the individual must determine whether it is predictable that all men in a given culture will proceed through the stages of life as Sullivan describes them. Keeping in mind that Sullivan presented the stages of life only for western European cultures, the individual in this culture must decide whether he has himself proceeded from infancy, childhood, the various stages of adolescence and then into adulthood as they are described in the interpersonal theory. One may further predict that all men will progress through the three levels of cognitive experiences: prototaxic, parataxic, and syntaxic.

Scientific or Laboratory Prediction

Probably Sullivan's greatest success has been through the impact he has made upon the practicing clinician, who in psychiatric treatments has the grave responsibility of changing sick human emotional behavior to something better. Sullivan worked in the world of reality, and his work has stimulated many gifted followers to carry on his original theses. Much of the aftereffect of Sullivan's teaching and writing lies however, in the field of psychiatric practice, rather than in the realm of theoretical testing. Much of the research he has stimulated has been designed to aid psychiatric counseling, and only by inference has his theory been involved. One text stands out as a direct effort to advance his interpersonal theory, Ruesch and Bateson's *Communication, the Social Matrix of Psychiatry*, Norton, 1951, in which the authors investigate the interpersonal relationships between culture and personalities.

The excellent journal, *Psychiatry*, continues to carry on the work of Sullivan's interpersonal theory in many realms of research. The William Alanson White Psychiatric Foundation has undertaken the major contribution furthering the empirical work of Harry Stack Sullivan.

―――――――◆―――――――

SUMMARY

The six principles of Sullivan's work as used in this text are interpersonal relations, tension system, anxiety, dynamisms, personifications, and cognitive experience. No single diagrammatic device lends itself to summarizing his theory as some of the other theories have been depicted.

Interpersonal relations is the basic core of Sullivan's theory. He believed that the human personality is never separate from all other human personalities. All that the individual's personality has been, is, and will be is the product of the interpersonal contacts he makes through life. One may study a single personality as an object of study just as one may study the human heart separately from the body only if one keeps always in mind that the heart or the personality cannot exist alone. Even man's innermost thoughts and mental processes are products of the interhuman environment. Dreams, thinking, remembering, and other introspective processes are couched in terms of interpersonal experiences and forces. The reciprocity of personalities is a key theme in Sullivan's theory.

Life consists of a series of interwoven and sequential tensions for the human animal. The tensions may be of the basic, organic, biological type and may later incorporate the tremendous tensions of societal living. To reduce tension is a primary task of living. At no time in his life is man free for any appreciable time from the pressures of tension. Tension may be considered in two ways: as an interior system which holds man together to face the struggles of life, and externally as man is the recipient of pressures from the world outside himself.

Figure 7 illustrates, by the use of a box kite, the interior type of tension system.

After the theme of Buckminster Fuller we may extend Sullivan's work to consider man as being held together by tension within the structure.

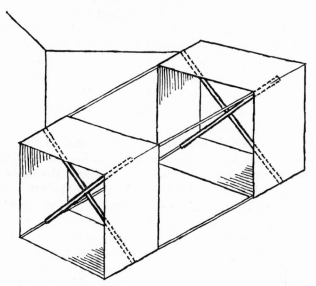

Figure 7. Diagrammatic Summary of Sullivan's Theory.

This permits man to face the pressures of an outside world by distributing the force among all the interior parts. Whatever forces come to bear upon one part of the structure are divided amongst all its parts. The structure is consequently a free floating object, subject to all the exterior forces which play upon it. Change may be incorporated to a limited extent by adding new appurtenances or by gradual and painful stresses within the structure which form a new shape.

The essential connotation of tension, however, as employed by Sullivan is that man comes into a world of tension at birth and soon learns to adopt to the conditions of this state of existence. As he develops, he learns through dynamisms to reduce the tensions of life. The mechanics he may use for this are the self-system, personifications, dramatizations, and cognitive experiences.

To Sullivan the world is an anxious place in which to live. Anxiety and tension are so uniquely interwoven in his theory that at times cause and effect are not readily distinguishable. Fundamentally, the world of anxiety causes tension, although it also seems that tension creates anxiety.

Out of anxiety grows much of the formulation of the basic fabric of man's personality. The self system is a cardinal feature of the personality and one which Sullivan utilized heavily in studying schizophrenic behavior. Man creates a self system which is a false portion of his personality in that it exists only to protect the real self from anxiety. Because the self system knows no true insight, it contains no self-corrective powers and at times may take control of the true self. The result is a split personality dominated by a system concerned only with the preservation of self.

The seven life periods have already been treated in summary form. To summarize them further may truncate them beyond recognition. The major point to remember is that Sullivan considered the stages to adulthood to be crucial times for developing the personality. His work in this field has been widely adapted by others interested in the developmental aspects of man.

A dynamism is the smallest unit of human contact with another human being. It is cumulative and can be considered much like a habit formation. Dynamisms are difficult to change. They may be expressed overtly or covertly. Sullivan feels that most dynamisms are associated with various parts of the body. Dynamisms related to the oral zone are created early in life and tend to persist strongly throughout the remainder of life.

Personifications are the images one has first of the self and later other human beings. A personification shared by a majority of people in an environment becomes a stereotype. One does not necessarily create accurate pictures of others through personifications.

The three levels of cognitive experiences are prototaxic, parataxic, and syntaxic. The first is a form of mental reaction to stimuli which is primarily sensory in nature. The second form sees causal relationships between simultaneous phenomena whether there is a degree of causality or not. The third and the highest form of cognitive experience employs symbols to express relationships and to retain the knowledge gained from this type of thinking.

BIBLIOGRAPHY

PRIMARY SOURCES

BOOKS

Sullivan, H. S., Tensions interpersonal and international: a psychiatrist's view, in H. Cantril (ed.), *Tensions That Cause War*, Urbana, Ill. Univer. of Illinois Press, 1950, 79–138.

Sullivan, H. S., *Conceptions of Modern Psychiatry*, N.Y., Norton, 1953.
Based on W. A. White lectures on five essays of 1940.

Sullivan, H. S., *The Interpersonal Theory of Psychiatry*, N.Y., Norton, 1953.
Primarily from lectures given in the winter of 1946–1947.

Sullivan, H. S., *The Psychiatric Interview*, N.Y., Norton, 1954.
Based on two lecture series given in 1944–1945.

Sullivan, H. S., *Clinical Studies in Psychiatry*, N.Y., Norton, 1956.
Published posthumously—based on 1943 lectures.

Sullivan, H. S., H. S. Perry (ed.), *Schizophrenia as a Human Process*, N.Y., Norton, 1962.
Covers all his major articles from 1924–1935.

PERIODICALS

Sullivan, H. S., The psychiatric interview, *Psychiatry*, 1952, *15*, 127–141.

SUGGESTED READINGS

BOOKS

Blitsten, D. R., *The Social Theories of Harry Stack Sullivan*, N.Y., William-Frederick, 1953.
Selection of his papers from 1892–1949.

Brown, I. A. C., *Freud and the Post-Freudians*, Baltimore, Penguin, 1961.
Horney, Fromm, and Sullivan also included.

Deutsch, F. and W. F. Murphy, *The Clinical Interview*, N.Y., International Univer. Press, 1955.

Maccoby, E. E., and N. Maccoby, The interview: a tool of social science, in G. Lindzey (ed.), *Handbook of Social Psychology*, Vol. I, Cambridge, Mass., Addison-Wesley, 1954, 449–487.

Munroe, R. L., *Schools of Psychoanalytic Thought*, N.Y., Holt, Rinehart and Winston, 1955.
Analysis and integration of Freud, Adler, Jung, Rank, Fromm, Horney, Sullivan, *et al.*

Mullahy, P., *Oedipus—Myth and Complex*, N.Y., Hermitage House, 1948.

Mullahy, P. (ed.), *A Study of Interpersonal Relations*, N.Y., Hermitage House, 1949.

Mullahy, P. (ed.), *The Contributions of Harry Stack Sullivan: A Symposium on Interpersonal Theory in Psychiatry and Social Science*, N.Y., Hermitage House, 1952.

Seven articles appraising Sullivan's contributions plus a photograph and full bibliography of his writings.

Ruesch, J., and G. Bateson, *Communication: The Social Matrix of Society*, N.Y., Norton, 1951.

Saltzman, L., *Developments in Psychoanalysis*, N.Y., Grune and Stratton, 1962.

The innovations of Horney and Sullivan.

PERIODICALS

Arieti, D., The double methodology in the study of personality and its disorders, *Amer. J. Psychother.*, 1957, *11*, 532–547.

Fromm and Sullivan on the idiographic—historical and nomothetic-scientific approaches to personality study.

Blitsten, D. R., Harry Stack Sullivan's suggestions concerning the place of small groups in personality development, *Autonomous Groups Bull.*, 1954, *9*(4), 3–12.

Chrzanowski, G., What is psychotherapy? the viewpoint of the Sullivanian school, *Ann. Psychother. Monogr.*, No. 1, 1959, 31–36.

Goldman, G. D., Group psychotherapy from the point of view of various schools of psychology: III some applications of Harry Stack Sullivan's theories to group psychotherapy, *Int. J. Group Psychother.*, 1957, *7*, 385–391.

Use of parataxis in group work.

Green, M. R., Prelogical processes and participant communication, *Psychiat. Quart.*, 1961, *35*, 726–740.

Sullivan on prelogical processes.

Harris, C., Sullivan's concept of scientific method as applied to psychiatry, *Phil. Sci.*, 1954, *21*, 33–43.

A critique of Sullivan.

Kates, S. L., First-impression formation and authoritarianism, *Human Relat.*, 1959, *12*, 277–286.

One aspect of Sullivan's concept of perceiving others in terms of self proves to be correct.

Mumford, R. S., Traditional psychiatry, Freud, and H. S. Sullivan, *Comprehen. Psychiat.*, 1961, *2*, 1–10.

Nydes, J., Interpersonal relations: personal and depersonalized, *Psychoanalysis,* 1952, *1,* 36–47.

A critique of Sullivan's theory as being very limited.

Siberman, H. L., The psychology and psychiatry of Harry Stack Sullivan, *Psychiat. Quart. Suppl.,* 1955, *29,* 7–22.

Smith, D. E. P., Interdisciplinary approach to the genesis of anxiety, *Educ. Theory,* 1956, *6,* 222–231.

Compares Freud, Rank, Mowrer, Angyal, Goldstein, Lewin, Rogers, Kierkegaard, and Sullivan on theories of anxiety.

Strupp, H. H., Infantile sexuality in the theories of Freud and Sullivan, *Complex,* 1952, *7,* 51–62.

Thompson, C., Concepts of the self in interpersonal theory, *Amer. J. Psychother.,* 1958, *12,* 5–17.

Examines confusion of self-system and concept of self in Sullivanian terms.

9

Horney

Love Conquers all.

VIRGIL
Eclogues, X, line 69

This is the Law of the Yukon,
that only the strong shall thrive.

ROBERT SERVICE
*The Law of the Yukon**

I never found the companion that
was so companionable as solitude.

HENRY THOREAU
Walden, Chapter V, Solitude

SOME BIOGRAPHICAL DATA

Like many of the theorists represented in this book, Karen Horney was German-born. On September 16, 1885, she was born in the city of Hamburg in the northern part of Germany, of a Norwegian father and a Dutch mother. She attended medical school at the University of Berlin and while there became interested in psychoanalysis. She was a resident physician at a Berlin psychiatric hospital for four years, and then became

* From *The Law of the Yukon,* in *The Complete Poems of Robert Service.* With the permission of Dodd Mead & Company, Inc.

a practicing analyst in Berlin, as well as a teacher for two years in the Berlin Psychoanalytic Institute.

In 1932 she was invited to Chicago to become assistant director of the Institute for Psychoanalysis there. In 1934 Dr. Horney went to New York where she for a time trained analysts at the New York Psychoanalytic Institute. She also gave lectures at the New School for Social Research, practiced as an analyst and did extensive writing. Later she became Dean of the American Institute of Psychoanalysis, a position she held until her death December 4, 1952.

She was deeply influenced by Freud, having studied with Dr. Karl Abraham, a well-known pupil of Freud. However, Horney found herself unable to accept all Freudian tenets and considered Freud's work a foundation upon which could be built further concepts. Unlike Freud, Horney emphasized cultural factors as an influence on personality and contended further that man is essentially a constructive creature rather than one ridden by the destructive drives posited by Freud.

Karen Horney reflected in her own life, the constructive attitude she proclaimed. In addition to her extremely heavy professional obligations, she maintained a balanced personal life. In 1909 she was married to Oscar Horney, a lawyer. They had three daughters.

INTRODUCTION

Karen Horney is the only woman theorist in the present text. She has overtones of feminine protest in her theoretical concepts, but these are, however, protests against Freud's concepts of the female role rather than protests against being a female herself.

Horney was, and readily admitted to it, a neo-Freudian in her approach to the dynamics of man's behavior. There is much in Freud's work to which she subscribed. Her early training and the analysis she underwent were strongly in the Freudian tradition. In her later years, however, as a practicing psychoanalyst and then as a writer and theorist, she desexed Freud's theory. The denial of pansexualism as she interpreted Freud's work developed from her experiences in the United States as a therapist and her deep conviction that man and his personality are derivatives of the culture.

Beyond her professional contacts she gained popular attention through the publishing of five books: *Neurotic Personality of Our Times,*

1937; *New Ways in Psychoanalysis*, 1939; *Self-analysis*, 1942; *Our Inner Conflict*, 1945; and, her last book, published in 1950, *Neurosis and Human Growth*.

Karen Horney had the deep conviction that mankind not only has the capacity for change but that this change in man's behavior both singularly and collectively is for the better. She felt that man has a positive nature. Her last statement in her last book is indicative of hope for the future: "Our [meaning her philosophy], with all its cognizance of the tragic element in neurosis, is an optimistic one." (*Neurosis and Human Growth*, p. 378.)

Besides the early, strong influence of Freud upon her thinking, Horney also had a deep appreciation for the ideology of Erich Fromm, whom she quoted frequently in her last two books and for whom she expressed a profound respect. She also quoted liberally from the writings of the Danish philosopher and theologian, Sören Kierkegaard, whose writings appear to have had an effect on her theorizing.

Like many other theorists Horney improved and added to her theory, never being quite satisfied with her position. As one reads her books, starting with her publication of 1937, one is impressed with the progression of her ideas. Each book builds upon the material of the previous ones until a clear picture of evolutionary thinking becomes apparent. The progression of her ideas, however, seems not to emerge as clearly in her last book, *Neurosis and Human Growth*, as in the previous books. Here she presented a recapitulation of the total theory rather than a progressive step from the previous works.

The author recalls with pleasure hearing Dr. Horney as a platform speaker describe the disillusionment she felt in her initial attempts at psychoanalysis shortly after arriving in this country from Berlin in 1932. In a somewhat humorous vein she related in detail the inital interviews she had had with her cleints. Having been trained as a Freudian, she naturally expected and tried to elicit responses which would bring out the psychosexual problems of the client. Time after time the client appeared confused or irritated when questioned about sexual problems. He felt fine about his sexual life. Things were going great between him and his wife. No, he didn't hate his mother when he was a baby, and his dad was a pretty good pal of his until the day he died. What was he worried about? Then Horney discovered that her clients were understandably worried and troubled and sick about "losing my job" or

"I hate my foreman," "I have no money to pay the rent and my kid has tuberculosis." Suddenly, Horney stated in her talk, she discovered that in the Depression years in the United States people were not worried about sex. If anything, sex was helping them and was not a source of deep-seated neurosis. Her clients were behaving neurotically because of societal pressures, economic inadequacies, or occupational pressures. She related that the disenchantment she felt, and which led to a reorientation in her thinking, was one of the first steps toward departing from the traditional Freudian approach in psychoanalysis, an approach that she was to reexamine and restructure for the rest of her professional career.

It should be noted that Horney at no time wrote about personality theories. She wrote and taught and worked on the neurotic aspects of man's behavior. However, in so doing she successfully developed a rationale for man's behavior that helps to explain why man does the things he does. It is only by attenuating Horney's theories on neuroses, however, that others, including the author, have been able to construct a theory of personality from a theory designed to explain neurotic behavior. It is for the reader to decide how closely a general theory of behavior has been created out of a specific theory of neurotic behavior.

HORNEY'S DESCRIPTION OF HUMAN BEHAVIOR

A reader of the literature of Karen Horney may be impressed with the similarity between the three kinds of behavior that Sheldon discovered through research and the three methods of reacting to people, moving toward, against, or away from people that Horney posited. To the writer's knowledge there was no direct influence of one upon the other. One can only conjecture reasons for the similarity between the two systems of thought. Even the descriptions of behavior in the Sheldon and Horney typologies, as we shall see in subsequent sections, appear to be quite similar. (Horney, however, eschewed the typology approach.) One possible reason for this resemblance of theories may be attributed to the strong inclination that Horney had for trichotomizing her concepts. Even the most cursory reading of her material brings out the remarkable number of times she chose to phrase her ideas in three forms.[1]

---

[1] The presenting of ideas and material in triadic form is widely employed. The author explores this phenomena in a forthcoming book, *The Triads in Life*. The reader is urged to notice the frequency in which things come in threes: Examples

Again in order to distill Horney's work into some form of principles for the purposes of this book, one needs to examine the amount of agreement and disagreement between her concepts and those of Freud. This approach is logical in that Horney is, and wanted to be, considered a neo-Freudian. It is also to be understood, that since she based her work on that of Freud, we must examine those Freudian concepts which lie at the bottom of her own theoretical position. The following schematic presentation highlights the basic agreements and disagreements she had with the work of Freud.

Agreement with Freud

1. Psychic determinism—The cause and effect of man's behavior is primary to understanding the dynamics of man. For every action there must be a preceding causal reason. Behavior does not happen haphazardly; lying beneath behavioral acts are precursors of a causal nature.
2. Unconscious motivation—At one point Horney claimed that this takes first place as a contribution of Freud.
3. Emotional drives—Emotions are the primary driving mechanisms of man's behavior. Man is a nonrational animal.
4. Ego defense mechanisms—Though she added her own particular flavor in using the ego defenses, Horney, after extending their meanings in her own terms considered them an invaluable tool to therapy.
5. Therapeutic techniques—Although this is a book on theories,

Disagreement with Freud

1. Id, ego, superego—The disagreement is not so pronounced as are the extensions she makes to his primary mechanisms.
2. Repetition complex—Man does not repeat infantile behavior in a blind fashion but rather reacts to situations of anxiety out of a character structure which he derives from all of his earlier life. (See the principle, Character Structure.)
3. Oedipal complex—This is not an exclusively sex oriented behaviorism but a parentally induced anxiety wrought from feelings of punishment, indulgence, or rejection that are a part of the child's environment but which does not necessarily develop in all children.
4. Penis envy—The same disagreement holds true as for the above. Horney says it is just as sensible to say that the boy child envies his mother's capacity to "make

---

abound in all areas, from the theological Father, Son, and Holy Ghost, the philosophical thesis, antithesis, synthesis, to the children's game of animal-vegetable-mineral.

not techniques, one should note that Horney "value(d) most highly" the instruments of therapy such as transference, free association, dream analysis, which Freud introduced.

babies" and thus feel envy as to say that the girl child envies her father's penis and thus becomes involved with rejection of mother.

5. Libido—Horney preferred to consider libido as an emotional drive rather than an animalistic sex impulse that forever plagues man. "All is not gold that glitters, all is not sexuality that looks it." (*Neurotic Personality of Our Time*, p. 157.) She further felt that sexual problems are the effect, *not* the cause of anxiety. Man turns to sexual behavior as a method of reassurance for insecure feelings.

A summary, then, of Horney's appreciation and depreciation of Freud's work is that she felt that his real contribution was not that he solved problems but that he, "made them accessible to understanding." This contribution she prized highly and credited him richly for it. While her debt to Freud was openly expressed and warmly given, she further felt that, "We find what we may expect to find" when reading Freud. Freud is a very persuasive writer, and one must be vigilant in avoiding the acceptance of the first basic assumptions, for when one does accept, one becomes swept along in the development of Freud's ideas until the basic assumptions are being used as irrefutable proof of further assumptions. She felt Freud to be guilty of circular reasoning, a feat in which he was brilliant. Her final judgment was that Freud studied only two cultures and that each was false in regard to the pursuits of the normal man for frictionless existence. Had Freud analyzed American or British patients, he would not have evolved his theories in so culturally bound a manner. She pointed out that Freud's patients were largely from the rich, pampered, overindulged and thrill-seeking Viennese society. The second large group of patients he met were the German Soldiers of World War I. Neither group, she suggested, was composed of normal, everyday people from all walks of life.

It is not the intent here, however, to criticize the work of Freud, but to advance the ideas of Horney. It is only because Horney based her work on that of Freud that we must know her appraisal of his work. It is obvious that the reader must have some basic knowledge of Freud's fundamental position in order to understand fully Horney's theory. No attempt is made here to recapitulate his work for that purpose, but the reader is urged to "know" Freud well enough so that Horney's theory emerges more clearly.

A brief review of her publications is helpful not only in tracing the changing concepts she followed but in advancing the basic assumptions of her theory.

The Neurotic Personality of Our Time (1937). Here the main contention is that neuroses are brought about by cultural factors, a contention which more specifically meant that neuroses are generated by disturbances in human relationships. Horney felt that compulsive drives are specifically neurotic, born out of feelings of isolation, helplessness, fear, and hostility, and specifically that man aims at safety more than sexual satisfaction.

New Ways in Psychoanalysis (1939). Whereas the first book was primarily intended for the educated lay person as well as for the professional therapist, the second book, "is not to show what is wrong with psychoanalysis, but, through eliminating the debatable elements, to enable psychoanalysis to develop to the height of its potentialities." She followed with a reappraisal built around Freud's terminology; each concept was examined with the result that none was rejected outright, but some were rephrased to include her ideas regarding sex as other than a prime motivator of human behavior; the cultural effect upon man's behavior; the character structure rather than infantile repetitions of adults; and the spontaneity that the normal person must possess in order to handle the cause and effect aspects of his development.

Self-Analysis (1942). This became a controversial book in some circles where it was interpreted as a "self-help do-it-yourself book" for neurotics. Horney rejected this criticism by stating that man had to solve his problems for himself. The analyst was only a highly skilled professional who could help but never, by his own efforts, without the cooperation of the patient, resolve conflict. She felt that psychoanalysis was not the only cure, but that "Life itself is the most effective help for our development."

Our Inner Conflicts (1945). This is considered by many, including the author, to be her magnum opus. It was in this book that she summarized her development and came to the conclusion that there are three ways of responding to life situations—moving toward people, or moving against people, or moving away from people—and that most of us utilize all three. The response depends upon the situation that confronts us, and as we develop from infancy into adulthood, we grow through the manifestations of all three interpersonal methods.

Neurosis and Human Growth (1950). This book concerns itself with man's striving to be his idealized self, a condition which, of course, man cannot sustain at all times in all places. Horney thought that "it involves a fundamental problem of morality—that of man's desire, drive, or religious obligation to attain perfection."

The following six principles extracted from her writings are pertinent to an understanding of Horney's social psychological theory of personality: optimism–positivism; society–culture; character structure; self–concept; complementation–conflict; and self analysis. The order in no way indicates the degree of importance as this interpreter sees it but provides a sequential treatment necessary for better understanding.

Optimism—Positivism Principle

Karen Horney had faith in the changeable nature of mankind for the better. She was optimistic about the evolution of the human being from the levels of the past. She was encouraged by the positive qualities in mankind and felt her theory was a constructive one because eventually it might lead to resolving neuroticism. Since in all her thinking, neurotic behavior is central, she felt that the resolution of neurotic behavior would lead to a happier and healthier society.

Two quotations from *Our Inner Conflicts* attest to this optimism. The first is from the beginning of the book and the last from one of the final statements. In between the two statements is repeated, with equal emphasis, the same theme of optimistic positivism.

My own belief is that man has the capacity as well as the desire to develop his potentialities and become a decent human being, and that these deteriorate if his relationship to others and hence to himself is, and continues to be, disturbed. I believe that man can change and go on changing as long as he lives. And this belief has grown with deeper understanding [p. 19].

Our daring to name such high goals rests upon the belief that the human personality can change. It is not only the child who is pliable. All of us retain the capacity to change, even to change in fundamental ways, as long as we live. This belief is supported by experience [p. 242].

In a slightly different vein Horney approached the problem of human growth and its striving for perfection via the idealized image with a reference to the Christian injunction, "Be ye perfect." Her point was not that man should be "goody-goody" but that he must strive for perfection if happiness is to be attained, and neurotic behavior brought into controllable dimensions. Her feeling was that without this approach man's existence would be a shambles and, indeed, that man would probably long ago have ceased to exist. "Would it not be hazardous, indeed ruinous, to man's moral and social life to dispense with such dictates?" (*Neurosis and Human Growth,* p. 14). Horney was far from naive, and she realized the impact of life's problems upon man as he strives for perfection. This causal factor to neurotic behavior is discussed in the principle entitled self-concept. We wish merely to introduce the idea here because it does deal with the positive aspects of man's behavior as Horney sees it.

Society–Culture Principle

To Horney man is more than a product of this interactions with other men in a social order; he is also refined and molded by the particular mores, customs, and roles that his particular culture impresses upon him. Thus the principle here emphasizes more than interpersonal relationships, incorporating as well the *rules* by which man plays the game of life. How man employs methods to achieve the end of a better and more productive life will be further explored in the complementation–conflict principle. For the present it is the formulative effect of the interaction of man to man and the general and specific rules by which he interacts that concern us.

The reader may recall the effect of American culture and particularly of the Depression of the early thirties that so impressed Karen Horney when she first began to practice psychoanalysis in Chicago. In her second published work after this experience, *New Ways in Psychoanalysis,* she characterized the change from Freudianism to social–cultural thinking by stating, ". . . the entire emphasis falls on the life conditions molding the character," and later, "A prevailingly sociological orientation then takes the place of a prevailingly anatomical-physiological one" (p. 9). With statements such as these Horney departed from the dedicated Freudian camp and set out in new directions with her own interpretations.

Horney felt that our present culture generates a great deal of anxiety in the individuals living in it. She felt that neuroses are a natural concomitant of man living under the industrialism of today. With the influence of Fromm upon her thinking she also thought that man's loss of security when he left the medieval system gave rise to a struggle for status and the longing to be "somebody." This cultural attitude surrounded by a western civilization that was built upon individual competitiveness (and one might assume group competitiveness) ranked first in her thinking as a causal factor for neuroses. Almost the entire theme of her first book, *Neurotic Personality of Our Time,* is dedicated to the conflict in culture, the struggle in society, and the tremendous amounts of endeavor one must face in adjusting to life conditions.

So deep was Horney's feeling toward the imprint of society and culture upon man that she agreed with some sociologists that no such thing as normal psychology existed for all of mankind. One could only define psychological principles from the frame of reference of the culture within which the human operated. In the same sense she felt that "Thus, the term neurotic, while originally medical, cannot be used now without its cultural implications" (*The Neurotic Personality of Our Time,* p. 14). In dealing with aspects of normality, she later states, "The conception of what is normal varies not only with the culture but also within the same culture, in the course of time." So, as cultures changed within themselves, did the concept of normality. All of the above, of course, is to be found repeatedly in the literature of sociology.

It is obvious that Karen Horney was speaking primarily of anxiety as it manifests itself in neurotic behavior and not directly about character formulation as it is seen in personality theory. Without being guilty of any attenuations, however, one sees that she also spoke of an underlying basic personality formation beneath the syndromes of neuroses. Again, although she was not writing directly about personality theory, she continuously subsumed and created a basic set of motives *which, when disturbed,* create neuroses. It is out of this phenomenon that most writers find a personality theory in the work of Karen Horney.

Character-Structure Principle

A third major theme which departs from Freud but which is also important to the full development of her own theoretical position may be found in Horney's work. Horney began the formulation by denying the pervasive effect of the repetition compulsion motive by which man is sub-consciously driven to repeat earlier infantilisms throughout his life in a hopeful effort to recreate the pleasures that the behavior once gave to him. The fallacy of this position, she felt, is that one might just as well call anxiety in the child, for example, a precocious grown up attitude, as to call anxiety in the adult an infantile reaction. In no way does Horney ignore the experiences of early childhood. To her, "Genetic understanding is useful only as long as it helps the functional under-standing" (*The Neurotic Personality of Our Time*, p. 33). Although she admitted that a complete understanding of human behavior in the pres-ent is not possible without tracing behavior back to infantile conditions, she strongly believed the genetic approach confused the issue rather than clarified it. This she felt is particularly true of the purist Freudian approach which leads the analyst to neglect existing conditions of society and culture which she felt should be so prevailing and forceful in analysis.

Horney preferred to consider that ". . . the entirety of infantile experiences combines to form a certain *character structure*." (My italics.) *Character structure* means the total experiences the adult accumulates during his lifetime, experiences which in turn circumscribe his capacities. The character structure not only limits his abilities; but it may also increase his potentialities, effects which depend upon the experiences he accumulates as life progresses. Her idea is that the personality is not set by early infantile experiences, but that these experiences are only a part of the always ongoing structuring of the personality. Events may happen in the years one is twenty or thirty, for example, which are as crucial to the individual's welfare as any earlier experience. Man is a product of his environment; and as his environment is always with him, the self-same environment continues to change him. Life conditions mold the character. While one is alive, they will always continue to mold the character. The crux of all character structure is human relationships. As we shall see later, man does not have his character molded by natural phenomena such as stars, storms, or sea water. Other people, and only other people, are instrumental in creating a human personality out of the stuff with which man enters the world at birth.

Man, however, does have the capacity for inner directedness. He is more than a chip floating freely on the sea of life. In her final book, *Neurosis and Human Growth*, Horney deliberately phrased the term *neurosis* in the singular, for here she was concerned about what the analyst can do to help the single individual to grow and develop. "Self knowledge, then, is not an aim in itself, but a means of liberating the forces of spontaneous growth." Spontaneity is an inner personal characteristic and not a societally derived force. Self-knowledge is supremely important in the formulation of the personality which she termed character structure. This is something which no society can build for one but which one can only build for himself. Man has a moral obligation and a moral privilege to seek self-knowledge. She chose to call this striving the *morality of evolution*. This means that man has the evolutionary forces within him to realize his greatest potential. Evolution comes from within and not from society.

Self-Concept Principle

The following main theme from Horney's work is highly involved. The convolutions of the theme of the self-concept are woven throughout her writings and although unclear they, nevertheless, constitute a major aspect of her theory. The word *self* is most difficult to define technically. The Englishes in their extremely competent dictionary give the word *self* an extensive treatment and mention that there must be nearly one thousand combination forms of *self*.[2] Consequently, because of the divergent general usage of the word and because of Horney's gradual development of the concept of self throughout her work, the ideas do not always emerge as clearly as one would wish.

The following diagram traces the self-concept principle of Horney in its major aspects only. The ramifications of the concept must be left to the reader of her original work.

Starting with the real or actual self, man hopes to achieve a full realization of all his potentialities and to reach the maximum of highest development. This dynamic, Horney, feels, is universal. However, in order to achieve self-realization man must have, or feels he must have, an idealized self before him to follow as a model. In doing this he too frequently by-passes the genuine goal of self-realization and constructs behavioral activities patterned after the idealized self. When man does this, he is seeking an unobtainable goal and is certain to evolve neuroticisms in his behavior. The idealized self (the perfect person) is never

[2] H. B. English, and A. C. English, *A Comprehensive Dictionary of Psychological and Psychoanalytical Terms*, Longmans, 1958, pp. 484–485. (Courtesy David McKay Co.)

possible. Instead of returning to the "spontaneity" of the real self, man continues to drift away from what he actually is and to follow the further removed image of what he would like to be. An image is false, illusory, and never true to reality. The further man drifts toward an illusory goal, the more alienated he becomes from his actual self. The result is inner conflict, which leads to neurotic behavior through a person's vain attempt to resolve the inner conflict. Somewhat akin to the Freudian superego, which tells man he must be the best possible person he can be, is the self-abnegation to which the neurotic turns, self-abnegation

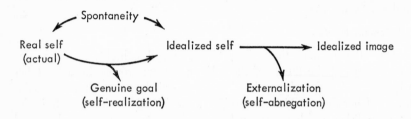

which makes him feel he "should" be doing this or he "should not" have done that. One of the mechanisms the neurotic employs in his futile attempt to be like his idealized image is the mechanism of externalization. There are other mechanisms which we shall study in the principle of complementation–conflict, but for the moment we follow Horney's emphasis of the major mechanism called *externalization*. Externalization means more than projection (the process of ascribing to others one's own unacknowledged desires or faults). The externalizing individual not only shifts the responsibility toward some other object but he actually *feels* that all of these things take place outside of himself. He has become so alienated from his actual self by trying to live in his idealized image that all of his failures may be blamed upon outside forces. Horney saw the process of externalization in many of man's neurotic manifestations.

Horney's self-concept principle states that unless man "retains his spontaneity" or holds to being the "spontaneous individual" his real self then becomes alienated and emotionally sick. Her plea was that through analysis, either by self and/or by the professional analyst, the individual regains his will power and objective judgment, so that decisions he makes for himself will be reinstated in all their dignity.

Finally, as was stated previously in the character-structure principle, a morality of evolution helps man to realize his true potentials and freely plays upon the constructive evolutionary forces with which he is endowed in life. Horney rejected the Freudian belief in the necessity of taming the *status naturae* in seeking the real self. The second alternative of employing supernatural aids or of resorting to the strenuous ideal of reason and will she felt is the proper endeavor of theology and philosophy, but not of herself, since she was unqualified to speak in these areas. The third possibility of moral evolution was the one which she advocated— finding and using the real self as a directing force in life. This she felt is not only a moral privilege for man but also is a moral obligation for himself and posterity.

Complementation—Conflict Principle

We come now to what the author considers to be the most original and strongest theme that Horney created in her theoretical work on personality. It is also the most renowned of her contributions to the field of personality theory. This major theme appears in her fourth book, *Our Inner Conflicts,* 1945.

Although it may seem to the reader that the three types of reactions to life situations are typologies, Horney denied being a typologist. "I definitely do not intend in this chapter or the following to establish a new typology. A typology is certainly desirable but must be established on a much broader basis" (p. 48). Her advice is well taken. Her position was that all of us use all three methods of reacting to people. Only the highly neurotic individual utilizes one method to the exclusion of the other two. We (are we not all normal?) play all three melodies, our choice depending upon the situation and upon our individual talents; we slide from one effort to another in response to our fellow man. Horney, too, felt that it would be convenient to have a typology. It makes things so much easier to understand. Behavior can be categorized and, following that, be readily identified for therapy and also for the reactions necessary to everyday living. However, she felt that a broader base is necessary, a base which incorporates more than neurotic actions. A true typology would mean that each of the ways of reacting to people, moving toward, against, or away from people, would represent true types who react in this manner as their normal everyday way of doing things. Since there are no normal people who use one of these reactions exclusively, a typology is not possible. The broad base is missing.

Major Adjustment Techniques. The schematic presentation that follows is highly economical, verbally. Each word represents an involved extension of meaning that we now hope to portray.

(helpless)	moving	toward	people	(infant)
(hostile)	moving	against	people	(adolescent)
(isolate)	moving	away from	people	(adult)

Originally Horney became interested in the neurotic's inclination to be either helpless or hostile in conflict situations. This is the theme, somewhat, of her first three books. In the fourth book, *Our Inner Conflicts,* she developed a third type of reaction: isolation from self and from others. The first type said, "If you love me, you won't hurt me." By accepting his helplessness to resolve conflict, he hopes desperately to win the affection of others and by doing this have them resolve conflicts for him. The second type states, "If I have power, no one can hurt me." He assumes that the world around him is hostile; therefore, the best way to reduce conflict and tension is to control the hostile elements of life. The third type has as his slogan, "If I withdraw, nothing can hurt me." His resolution of conflict is to isolate himself from it both physically and mentally. Thus, we have the three types of neurotic behavior as Horney saw them: the helpless, the hostile, and the isolate.

The next term to consider is the word *moving* in the schematic presentation above. Horney considered life to be always moving, never static. Everything about life moves. Living things change, grow, develop, mature, get older, get bigger, and never remain the same. Specifically, Horney felt this way about the human being. In the very few seconds, for example, that it has taken the reader to read these few sentences he has aged and therefore changed, imperceptibly, but nonetheless changed. Expanding this minute example to all the aspects of life, Horney felt that movement is a vital criterion of life. An assumption might be, therefore, that a definition of death is the cessation of movement. Consequently the living human personality must always be considered in the terms of movement. Man's personality is forever in a state of flux. The motion may not be, and rarely is, a continuous flowing motion toward any specific goal. Possibly the motion may be considered like that of the water fly skittering about the surface of a pond. The peripatetic motions of a hummingbird in flight may be an even more accurate example for the motion that Horney considered, for the human personality is multidirectional. Whatever he does, Horney felt, man is never still. He cannot be. To live is to be in motion physically, mentally, emotionally, socially, or in any combinations of these.

Since man's personality is constantly in motion, Horney identified three general directions toward which the personality moves. However, the directions of toward, against, and away from, will not be discussed at the moment but developed more fully in a later section. The goal of movement, then, is in the direction of people. The trouble with man is man. The conflicts, anxieties, worries, neuroses that plague man's existence have their roots in his fellowmen. Man's deepest concern revolves around his relationships with all the fellow human beings that surround his life. It matters not whether he knows them personally. It may be a matter of his reputation with the public at large that causes him anxiety. The few worries man may have about lightning, tornadoes, and extremely violent physical forces are transitory. The importance of external violence may be the impression his conduct leaves upon others during the frightening experience. He may be terribly concerned about an act of nature, but in the end it is his reputation for bravery or cowardice that may mandate his behavior. The human being does not worry about trees or grass or houses. He worries about what others may say about his Dutch Elm disease, his weedy and crabgrassed lawn, and his seedy and unpainted house. Weather doesn't worry man. Weather either promotes or delays his social outdoor contacts, such as swimming, golfing, or picnicking. Horney's entire rationale is pointed toward the only goal that man could possibly have: his fellowman.

Chronologically, the human personality goes through the three types of adjustive techniques as they are listed in the schematic presentation from infancy through adolescence to end with adulthood, each age level being oriented toward the corresponding method as shown. As an infant the human is more inclined to win with love, "If you love me, you won't hurt me," than to try hostility or isolation. The reason seems obvious. The young of any species (with possibly the exception of snakes!) is generally considered to be cute, cuddly, and attractive. Puppies, kittens, lion cubs, and so on appear to be lovable objects, and so, we may presume, does the young of man's own species: the baby. It is natural for the baby to use his strongest asset: his lovableness. It is unnatural for the baby to be hostile simply because he is so very dependent upon others for food and sustenance. For the same reason it is also unnatural for the baby to attempt to isolate himself.

Upon reaching adolescence the human may seem to act aggressively. He may become hostile toward the very parents who nurtured him and found him so lovable in his babyhood. Being neither man nor child, the adolescent may move against people as he searches for the role he wishes to fulfill in adulthood.

Especially in the later years of adulthood we may find the adjustment technique of moving away from people much more prominent than it has ever before. The older citizen feels he does not need to circulate in society as freely as he once did. A few good friends and quiet pastimes are preferable to the old noisy country club parties. He reasons that since he has lived this long in life and not been able to change the world dramatically, there is no use now trying to change it by participating in drives, and clubs, and movements of an uplifting nature. He will let the younger men with more energy do those things he once so actively did. As a result we find that the general pattern of behavior for the later adult follows the lines of withdrawal or isolation.

In summary, then, we may extend Horney's three types of neurotic adjustment techniques to follow a chronological pattern from moving toward people to moving against people to the isolationist desire to move away from people.

Before beginning a detailed analysis of the three types of neuroses, we do well to remind ourselves again that most people utilize all three techniques in moving through the vicissitudes of everyday living. And we must also always keep in mind that no human is entirely free from irregular behavior which is either neurotic or bordering upon the neurotic. Thus, each of us singles out one of the following three modes of behavior whenever our conflicts become too difficult to resolve in an ordinary way. Supplementary methods of resolving conflicts are discussed in the following section "Minor Adjustment Techniques." However, it must be emphasized again that even though most of us employ all three techniques, we are always inclined to utilize one more than the other two when anxiety becomes overpowering, a situation which occurs more often than we would wish.

We shall now examine the dynamics of neurotics who either move toward, against, or away from people, keeping in mind that we are also looking at ourselves when we are in deep stress. We complement the aspects of our personalities by the judicious use of the adjustment techniques. Conflict arises immediately when we descend too deeply into the exclusive use of any one of the techniques. Our real self becomes unable to use spontaneously the most comfortable method based on our strongest assets. Conflict within ourselves (which grows out of conflict with our fellowman) may also arise when each of the three methods is so equal in strength that a trivalence emerges. The result is a stalemate of action. This latter conflict is rare and is a neurotic trait rather than a behavioral pattern.

Complementation and conflict of the trichotomized adjustment techniques that follow occupy a major position in the principles of Horney's work.

Moving Toward People (Helplessness). The slogan that best identifies this person is "If you love me, you will not hurt me. If I give in, I shall not be hurt." Beginning with the premise that we do not hurt the things we love, the first type makes supreme efforts to win the affection of all who surround him. Love protects. He concludes that if he cannot beat them, it is best to join them. The following points summarize his behavior when inner conflicts upset the equilibrium of life.

1. He has tried and tried to be superior. All of the methods he has used have seemed to bring unsatisfactory results and to leave him dissatisfied. At length he accepts his own helplessness to cope with conflict within himself and conflict as it has developed toward others. By accepting helplessness he can use it as a device to win the approval of others. He is the "nice guy," the one we all love. We enjoy his company because, always affable, he makes every effort to win us over. His own vanity is subjugated to the will and pleasure of his friends, for he must have friends. "Love conquers all."

2. Once he has accepted his helplessness to cope with figures stronger than himself, the person who moves toward people makes a strong effort to feel safe by attaching himself to the strongest person and/or group that will accept him. Because of the feeling of belonging and support which the group gives him actually or vicariously, he feels stronger and more capable of confronting life.

3. If he fails, others in the group will come to his rescue. Even if no particularly identifiable group will accept him and protect him, this individual still persists in making supreme efforts to gain favor with all. He suffers bitterly if rejected. His psyche cannot stand lack of love and affection. Almost nothing is too much to ask of him. He will do favors, lend or give his property, slavishly be attentive to the desires and wants

of others, always be alert to kindnesses he may perform, and will never lose sight of the objective for which he seeks: to make others obligated to him through what he does for them. That he does this in so dedicated a manner is unknown to him. The Golden Rule precept is his meat and drink, for by following this laudable concept he not only gets credit for being a "good guy" but he buys affection by making people indebted to him for past favors. "Do unto others as you would have them do unto you" is his way to win friends and influence people.

4. Failure to achieve his goal of winning affection frequently turns him into a hypochondriac or a victim of multiple psychosomatic complaints. He reasons that society always commiserates with an invalid. He realizes that society frowns upon kicking an underdog. He finds comfort in the phrase, "poor little ol' me."

5. When he marries or seeks a dating partner, he overwhelms his loved one with dedicated affection. The relationship is based upon long selfless service to win the affection of the affianced. He is inclined to date and marry a stronger individual than himself because such a one can give him strength and protection. Relationships with others as weak as he is soon collapse. How can one lean on a reed? He finds it impossible to do for another what he himself wants done for him. Each one in this situation clings to the other, but the relationship cannot sustain itself; the one who moves towards people consumes them with his love. Two such people simply cancel each other out. If such a marriage does come about (mainly through the efforts of others), it may end in divorce. This causes their friends to be highly confused for "they both seem to be such nice people." As a slogan to describe the love-seeker the reader may pick one of the following song titles: "All of me, why not take all of me," or, "I can't give you anything but love, Baby."

6. We may assume that the helpless individual with the preemptive desire for affection developed in somewhat the following manner. One day when he was a small child, the ice-cream truck with its tinkling bell came past his home on a warm Sunday afternoon. At the moment his father was recovering from a heavy Sunday dinner by lying half-asleep on the livingroom sofa listening to the baseball broadcast. Suddenly the father is awakened by the child's insistent coaxing for an ice-cream cone. The child continues aggressively to demand a treat. The father refuses. The child repeats his demands, howling louder and louder. The father is thoroughly irritated. The child gets a slap on his bottom. The next

attempt to get ice cream is to sulk and withdraw. The results of that isolating approach are even less successful than the first aggressive maneuver. This time his father goes back to sleep. Finally, the youngster tiptoes up to his daddy and gives him a big kiss. "Shucks," says the father. "What a sweet kid. Why not let him have some ice cream right after dinner? After all you're only young once!" Using love and affection wins the prize of ice cream. Having tried all three methods, the child may eventually perfect the love approach. "I get a lot of ice cream that way." Obviously the above anecdote is imaginary, but it may serve to illustrate how one becomes successful in using one adjustment technique, after having tried all three. The motto is "You can catch more flies with sugar than you can with vinegar."

Moving Against People (*Hostility*). This individual says, "If I have power, no one can hurt me." Although, according to Horney, all of us use this technique at times when we feel it is appropriate to the situation, this type of neurotic overemphasizes the use of aggressiveness in contacts with people. The following summary brings out the most salient rationale of his behavior.

1. He accepts and takes for granted that he lives in a hostile world. Consciously or subconsciously, he is determined to fight and resist the hostility around him. To the personalities who move against people, "It's a dog eat dog world."

2. The primary feeling here is a desire to be strong and defeat the opposition whoever and wherever they may be. Because there is an implicit distrust of others—"What's their angle?"—the defenses are always up. All human motives are suspect. "What's in it for him?" The desire, then, to protect oneself at all times and to come out fighting overemphasizes power and strength in all situations. The wisest philosophy is, "Might makes right."

3. Not all aggressive actions are overt, however. The hostile individual may make great efforts to help others by the most humanitarian methods, but implicit in the help he gives to others is an unacknowledged gift to himself of power and control over others. This individual may be attracted to social welfare work without realizing that it is the feeling of superiority and control of welfare patients which gives him job satisfaction. Ministers and teachers and doctors may be following this dynamic of feeling superior by helping others less fortunate than themselves. It is possible that these neurotically motivated individuals may be quite

unaware of the inner motivations of their actions. In other instances the seeking of power may be less subtly felt by the personality as it moves against people. By appearing to help others he may be quite openly striving for superiority against a world weaker than himself. Serving on club committees to win the approval of others may serve him well until he can be elected to the top office in the organization and *then* change things to the way they ought to be for his own satisfaction. The lures, devices, and gimmicks he uses to win and influence people may have as their slogan, "Never give a sucker an even break."

4. His regard for the first type who strives to move toward people and be loved by them is touched with a mixture of contempt and amusement. The affectionate one is so soft and vulnerable. He typifies him as a "sloppy sentimentalist."

5. His behavior in dating and in marriage have much the same characterstics. He dates only the best on the campus. For his social partner he wants either the beauty queen or the girl with money, privileges, and a convertible. Again, his method of obtaining these may be to use subtle flattery, but the end in view is to become associated with someone who will enhance *his* status with others. In marriage he also seeks a partner who has beauty, brains, charm, or money, all of which reflect *his* good taste in a wife and who will bring to the marriage more than a fair share of success. He eschews the weak and clinging partner who longs to be protected, unless she has money or prestige which he can share. Although the masculine pronoun is used it is to be understood that this kind of neuroticism applies to women as well as to men. All in all, "It costs so little more to go first class" in love and marriage.

6. In reviewing the development pattern of this type we refer again to the small child desiring ice cream. This time he raises so much furor with his father that the father finally digs into his pocket for the necessary money just to, "Keep the kid quiet for a minute and get a little peace around here." Enough successes with the aggressive method may gradually develop this type of technique in dealing with people. Thus the child reasons knowingly or unknowingly to himself, "You may as well get your fair share of things. Everybody else does, so why not watch out for number one?"

Moving Away from People (Isolation). The isolation for this individual may be either physical, or mental, or both. According to Horney and others, one does not have to be removed physically in order to be isolated from a group of people. Isolation of a mental nature is probably most pronounced in the schizophrenic, catatonic type. The individual who isolates himself to the point of neurotic behavior to solve his problems says, "If I withdraw, nothing can hurt me."

1. The individual who has the tendency to withdraw or the neurotic who follows this pattern exclusively wants neither to belong nor to fight. His strongest wish is to remain apart. Because people are the main sources of unhappiness and conflict, his overwhelming desire is to be completely free of entanglements. Complete independence guarantees for him no heartbreaking involvements. If he can establish that he is not dependent upon others and especially that others may not look to him for support, he keeps trouble out of his life. He lives for himself and by himself. He feels that he has not much in common with others and that they do not understand him anyway. If questioned about his aloofness and his general pattern of nonparticipation in society, he responds with, "Am I my brother's keeper?" His answer is, "No."

2. Lacking the normal amount of social participation, the isolationist looks to books, dreams, fantasies, and art forms for recreation and relaxation. Thus he builds up a world of his own, and because it is his exclusive property, he can do with it what he wants. He can change it, expand it, or destroy it and build another. The democratic process or the fight for survival he can ignore. What he has is his alone because he made it that way. Consequently, much of his manipulation must come through vicarious means. He writes, he dreams, he reads literature for the stuff with which to make his world immune from others. His slogan: "There's nothing so companionable as a good book."

3. In order to exist apart from others either mentally or geographically one must be strong enough to support one's own demands. The weak and those who bore themselves, therefore, cannot adopt this mode of adjustment. The isolationist is self-sufficient. He has to be. There is no one else to fall back upon in time of need or crisis. If he cannot be proficient in many things, he restricts his existence to the few things he can do well. It may be gardening, or the hermit existence of caretaker, or any type of occupation and avocation which he can hold for himself, though it may be limited in scope. Whether his strengths are broad or narrow, he becomes an expert for his own pleasure, contrary to what the crowd may be doing. He feels popularity is a fool's game. Popularity is given by others, and they can take it away any time they want to.

His response is, "Only the strong can stand being unpopular."

4. To perpetuate the role of individuality he becomes an extreme individualist. The moment the crowd discovers his private hideaways, he deserts them for even more remote places. It matters not that his "Shangri-La" is very inconvenient and inaccessible. He wants to be out of season all year long. To be different is to harbor jealously one's own uniqueness. To follow the crowd is anathema to him. "The public be damned."

5. Dating is a matter of convenience. He dates because that is the only way he will be admitted to certain activities he might enjoy. In dating he seeks a partner very much like himself who can also withdraw into silence for the evening's engagement. He avoids the affectionate type who moves toward people as an incessant talker and table hopper. Under no circumstance does he care to date an aggressive individual, even if it means missing the event. The first type as a date may make strong overtures toward getting involved as a steady companion, a situation which would threaten his control of life. The second type is the very kind of companion he hates, for by that person he is controlled and manipulated. Marriage is postponed until the late twenties or thirties if marriage occurs at all. The single life is much to be preferred, but he may chance upon another companion who also treasures solitude and withdrawal from people. For them the sexual aspects of marriage are transitory and solely for the satisfaction of a physical appetite. Intimacy in the sex act requires a state of emotion impossible for them to give or sustain. Marriage is a contractual agreement to live together, arrived at because living together is convenient. The long-time single male reasons that restaurant food is monotonous and expensive. Laundries are costly and bothersome. The regimentation of daily living bores him and creates inconveniences which keep him from enjoying other things. The services he now needs, if his parents are no longer living and he has to fend for himself, become a burden. Thus, if he can find someone who does not make too strong a demand upon his emotions, he is inclined to marry as a convenient means toward easier living. On the opposite side the female who is an isolate by choice, be it conscious or subconscious, arrives at a marriage through somewhat similar circumstances. For one thing, marriage would eliminate her having to work for a living in a world of people. Perhaps she may reason that a husband is away most of the day in his occupation, a fact which gives her even more time than

before to enjoy her own solitary pursuits. If the right, nondemanding male comes along, she might be very attracted to marriage. Being supported, having a secure economic future, and having fine things of her very own which she does not have to share with a mother or roommate appeal to her very much. Or perhaps the marriage may not interfere with her chosen occupation, since her husband, too, is willing to make it a working partnership, much in the form of a business agreement. Each, by their pooling resources, can have and enjoy fine records, furniture, books, paintings, and the artforms they both enjoy so much. Children happening to such a marriage are upsetting. If children do result, they are quickly channelled into proper slots, with a minimum of affection afforded them. Isolation-driven people usually utilize contraceptive devices with practiced regularity.

6. The rigidity of isolating one's feelings from the control of others may have had its source in the following: In his very earliest years the child gives his love unstintingly to a mother, father, or some other person. In the person he loves are all the virtues and sustenance he needs for love and understanding. Perhaps he loves not wisely but too well. In the course of events the object of his love may at some time deny him. In his own mind the denial is brutal and open. Perhaps he finds that his favorite love object—Mommy, Daddy, or both, also love his little baby brother or sister. They may have divorced and in the proceedings bandied him about like a piece of property. Whatever the cause, he discovers that his emotions, his trust, his faith, his hopes, his objects of unquestioning love are now denied him. We may assume that the experience is so terrifyingly traumatic that he vows never again to give his heart to another person, never again to lose control over his feelings. Having once been caused pain by having another in possession of his emotions, he insulates himself from further harm. Perhaps as he pursues an isolated pathway from people, he discovers that loneliness is preferable to heartache. The result is a determination not to have a hasty heart for any one, and to "never wear your heart on your sleeve."

In the preceding discussion of Horney's three types of adjustment techniques the illustrations have been overdrawn to highlight the deeper neurotic kinds of behavior. Overemphasis of neurotic reaction in moving toward, against, or away from people may make easier an understanding of some of the basic concepts of Horney's theory of neuroses from which we have drawn a general theory of personality.

The conflict that arises out of inability to utilize the three types of adjustment techniques originally was presented as ten neurotic needs in her 1942 publication, *Self-Analysis*. The difference between the ability of the normal person to integrate these needs and avoid conflict, and the lack of ability of the neurotic to do the same, is a matter of degree. Even though the normal personality is able to complement one or more of the following ten needs with others of the ten needs, he has more success with some of them than with others. The deeply involved neurotic fails with most of them in trying to integrate them into a life pattern (character structure) and consequently drifts further and further toward an unrealistic, idealized image. Despite his many failures with the ten needs the neurotic, too, has better success with some than with others. As a final result, for both the neurotic and the normal individual, adjustment is a matter of degree: variable degrees of the needs and variable degrees of success in complementation between the normal and neurotic.

Ten Neurotic Needs. Following are the ten needs from which Horney evolved her three basic types of adjustment techniques, moving toward, against, and away from people. All personalities have these needs to some degree. The neurotic has them to an overpowering degree. Most of us complement these needs. The neurotic cannot.

Neurotic Need	Salient Feature	Tendency of Moving in Relation to People
1. affection and approval	live to please others and win love	toward
2. dominant partner in life	give in and be protected by strong mate in exchange for pervasive love	toward
3. narrowly confined limits of life	to be ultra reactionary, conservative, retain *status quo,* retire to background	away from
4. power	glorify power and strength, despise weakness	against
5. exploitation of others	win at games, always be dominant	against
6. prestige	have name in the newspapers, be recognized	against (?)

7. personal admiration	have others see you as your idealized image	against
8. ambition in personal achievement	have a consuming desire to be rich, famous, important regardless of cost to self and others	against
9. self-sufficiency and independence	go to extreme lengths to avoid being obligated to anyone	away from
10. perfection and unassailability	be flawless because of hypersensitivity to criticism	away from (?)

Thus, out of her rich background of experience in psychoanalysis and using the above ten neurotic needs, Karen Horney drew out the three types of reactions toward people which man may use as he lives his life.

Minor Adjustment Techniques, Auxiliary Approaches to Artificial Harmony. In addition to the trichotomized approach discussed previously Horney also suggested a lower level of effort which man employs to bring into his life integration of all of the opposing forces he meets in dealing with people. Although the following techniques are false efforts to reduce conflict, Horney felt that they are more common than the deeper neurotic levels of moving toward, against, or away from people. To some extent, then, more of us use the following auxiliary approaches to artificial harmony in life than use the ten neurotic methods and the three subsequent techniques.

Karen Horney did not deny Freud's ego defense mechanisms, and her approaches are supplementary to Freud's contribution. Horney called the seven approaches that follow, the *protective structure,* which the personality erects to ease the basic conflicts of man as he relates to self and others.

1. *Blind spots*—When a basic inner conflict becomes unmanageable, we may be inclined to ignore the conflicting force. Disregard of behavior which does not fit the picture of our idealized self is an artificial attempt to bring balance into life. Because the self is oblivious to the true situation, there is no direct solution to the problem. Because the attempted solution is artificial, it cannot be expected to last very long. Conflict once again emerges. Blind spots occur, for example, when a mother is unable to tolerate the thought of being a poor mother. By ignoring the reports she hears of her son's poor behavior, she spares herself, for the moment at least, the revealing truth of her own inadequacies as a mother. Students who ignore the devastating effect that not studying can have upon grades

may be practicing the use of blind spots. The utilization of this particular protective structure is generally a matter of degree. Depending on the amount of conflict involved, we may develop within ourselves stronger blind spots for some phenomena than for others. Between individuals there may also be differing degrees of blind spots. False though the success of the method may be, by simply ignoring an unhappy fact, we are temporarily persuaded that it does not exist.

2. *Compartments*—Compartmenting different aspects of our life is, according to Horney, the result of inability to integrate the different roles we must sustain in life, so that one has two or more sets of rules which are contradictory. The professor who is adamantly opposed to cheating by the students in his classroom, and yet cheats at golf or bridge, is guilty of compartmentalizing his values about honesty. The ruthless business man who is in turn a devoted religious worker, espousing the highest Christian principles on Sunday, is also guilty of making compartments in his life. Because it is difficult to follow a clear-cut policy in all of life's aspects, individuals may turn to acting one way in one kind of situation and to a reverse way in another kind of situation. This Horney called *compartmenting*.

3. *Rationalization*—Similar to the definitions given this word by many writers is Horney's definition, which states *rationalization* to be "giving *good* reasons to excuse conduct, rather than giving the *real* reason" to explain conduct. She felt that rationalization, as somewhat an extension of externalization, is a low form of self-deception based upon erroneous reasoning processes. Its damage to the personality's ability to complement the forces of life is not to be underestimated, she felt, because of the pervasive use of this artificial approach to harmony. Horney saw a wide range in what is rationalized as well as a wide range in the methods employed. The breadth of the technique and its adaptability make it one of the most popularly used of all seven protective structures. Also, because it requires a conscious mental process akin to reasoning, the practitioner feels he is fully justified in its use and hence it becomes difficult to control. Rationalization is one of the primary methods by which the personality tries to eliminate the discrepancy between the actual (real) self and the sought-after, idealized self. Examples from the activities of everyday life are numerous. The football team that lost because it rained (failing to realize that it also rained on the opponent), the student who fails examinations because he gets "nervous" (failing to realize that practically no serious

student takes an examination calmly), the housewife whose home is a shambles and attributes this to the fact she has children (failing to realize that some control can be exercised over children and that millions of housewives who also have children manage to keep some semblance of order in the home) are some of the many examples that may be cited to illustrate the phenomenon of rationalization.

4. *Excessive Self-Control*—Originally Horney was so impressed with the power of this auxiliary device to achieve artificial harmony that it was included as a part of the ten neurotic needs. The openness of the technique and the tremendous will power needed to sustain excessive self-control have, however, brought it into the realm of an artificial device. Horney is not speaking against the value of will power and control of self in a civilized society. She is concened with slavish rigidity, whether it be conscious or subconscious, of excessive self-control which grows out of the feeling of panic the personality may have if he lets himself go even once. Most of us must in the ordinary course of living control our appetites and desires. When we lapse from this control of self, we do not lose all self-control. In many cases we gain a renewed and more successful control of self for use in the future. Moreover, the punishment following lack of self-control frequently teaches us the value of control. Not so, however, for the individual who practices rigid, compulsive self-control, for the fear of one failure is so truly frightening to him that he must at all costs maintain excessive self-control or collapse completely.

5. *Arbitrary Rightness*—To the person utilizing this device the worst of all possible worlds is to be indecisive about something. By settling an issue once and for all he gives himself a double-barrelled protection of being entirely free from doubt and being free from outside influences. Once he has made the decision that something is wrong, for example, he no longer must worry about that. It is wrong. It will always be wrong. To him, equivocation is a sign of weak, vacillating, simple minds. To be doubt-free is to be strong. Reopening a question is the surest road to conflict. Conflict leads to unhappiness, and with his fear of losing his idealized image, he cannot tolerate conflict. Positiveness is synonymous with purity. Horney feels that this state of being arbitrarily right grows stronger with each apparent success the personality feels it has obtained by refusal to entertain doubts. If uninfluenced by others, the person becomes more and more positive about everything until no doubts remain about anything —anything, that is, which has been "reasonably" thought out. She further

suggests that where the personality has an equal desire to move against people and to move away from people, we may expect the minor adjustment technique of arbitrary rightness to emerge. To have opinions one must necessarily be strong enough to come to conclusions and to hold them regardless of the opinions of opposing forces. This is a characteristic of moving against people. Likewise to avoid conflicting data one must remove himself from the influences of others. This is a characteristic of moving away from people. Both types of behavior assure a protection for the response of arbitrary rightness, such as we may find in an aged male adult who comes from a foreign background where males are strong and unquestioned. Being in a strange country he retires from its invidious influences and develops stronger and stronger opinions, substantiated by the conflicting dynamics of his background.

6. *Elusiveness*—Opposite to the above protective structure is the defense of never making up one's mind about anything, simple or complex. As an artificial device the value in this method is that if one never commits himself to anything, he can never be wrong. If he is never wrong, he can never be criticized for being wrong. When one is faced with decisions, the obvious diversion is to reexamine the past, discuss the enormous variations which may be drawn from any set of circumstances, and postpone a decision until all the facts are in. Since it may be impossible to gather all available data, a decision is therefore unwarranted and impossible to make at this time. By being elusive one may subvert any and all decisions for which one may eventually be held to account. The extension of elusiveness operates in the following manner: A student will say, "I could get good grades *if* I studied." The student will not, however, study. By studying the student makes a commitment which, once made, identifies him as taking a position. Once he has taken a position to study and does so, he no longer can be elusive. If he should fail *now*, there is no one to blame but himself! The criticism that may follow concerns his lack of mental ability. Prior to this one might criticize him for being lazy, which he considers in a quasihumorous way to be regrettable, but all too human. The criticism now maligns his intelligence. His ego may not be able to accept this. Thus the student may be elusive about trying in college. If he tries and fails, he has no excuse. If he never commits himself to study, he always has the excuse that he could get good grades if he tried. In the end he fails college anyway but *not* on the grounds of his lack of mental ability. Horney feels evasion is the dullard's device.

7. *Cynicism*—The last protective structure in Horney's treatment of the auxiliary approaches to artificial harmony as a minor adjustment technique deals with the denial of moral reality. The cynic plays it safe by not believing in anything with an ethical or moral structure. If he follows a pattern of total disbelief, he may then be disappointed in nothing. Because he believes in nothing, he avoids the heartaches that come from having believed in something that ends in failure. The device he uses is to deprecate any value which seems to hold forth hope. Probably growing from a background of repeated failure, his decision is never to believe in a value system again. In this way he avoids the failures of the past. By denying and deriding man's pet goals he relieves himself of the tortuous task of deciding what he believes in himself. Better be sneering than sorry.

Summary. All of the preceding methods come within the framework of man's attempt to integrate the complementary forces in his life in order to achieve the actualization of a real self and in so doing to avoid the pain of conflict. Horney sees most of these devices as neuroses, but the line between normality and neuroses is variable. The neuroses may exist within the self or may be existent within interpersonal relationships. The result of using protective devices is a reduction of the inner conflicts that beset man. We may now examine the final principle of self-analysis as the author perceives it in Horney's work.

Self-Analysis Principle

Karen Horney believed that life itself gives balance to man's existence. Although this idea appears to be an off-theme to the dynamics of man, it was not so to Horney. Adjustment to life's problems is as much a part of the core of man's existence as are the deeper inner dynamics he may possess. All of the above are part of her answer to the question of why man behaves the way he does and as such belong in the framework of a general theory of behavior.

Horney asked the provocative question, how did man ever solve his emotional problems before psychiatry and psychology came onto the scene? In no way did she demean the role of these two, but she did hold to the proposition that man must have had some success is solving his own problems before the refinements of psychiatry and psychology developed. If man had had no successes, it is likely that he would have perished. Using the premise that the human race has built within it certain alleviating factors, Horney proposed that we not lose sight of the tremendous value of self-analysis as an aid to emotional problem solving. Although she did not deny the extra benefits which may come from professional help through the efforts of psychiatrists and psychologists, her primary thesis was that we must hold to the value of past benefits while we continue to improve the current practices. In order to clarify her position as well as to aid those interested in self-analysis, she brought out her third book in 1942, *Self-Analysis*.

In support of her thesis, Horney felt that all of us who are not psychotically involved do some elementary analysis of our own behavior, possibly every day. Rather than to ignore this prevalent phenomenon she advocated training it so that it may operate more efficiently and with greater insight.

Ultimately, Horney suggested that all therapy involves self-analysis and that the true role of the therapist is to make analysis and manipulation of self easier and more profitable. No therapist can change human behavior without the involvement of the client. Just as no one can learn for another (teaching is basically preparing the ground), neither can a therapist take the client's place in analysis. Ultimately the client analyzes himself.

Horney was prompt in admitting that extreme neurotics and psychotics are unable to help themselves in the initial stages of therapy. Operation "boot strap" is not possible for those deeply involved in emotional problems. What she hoped to do with her severest cases was to bring them up to a point where they might take the responsibility for their own therapy through insight into their own dynamics. But, although severe neuroses should be in the hands of experts, man can go a long way in disentangling his own conflicts.

In some ways self-analysis may be less dangerous to the patient's welfare than an analysis controlled exclusively by the therapist. There may be times when the client wishes to avoid painful references to past injuries. If the therapist can do no more than uncover old scar tissues with no improvement in their condition, Horney felt the client's wisdom might be the better guide. Not all problems which the therapist may uncover are amenable to therapy. The very act of digging around in the client's past may bring out more problems than the therapist can possibly solve. For reasons such as these Horney felt a tremendous value should be placed on helping the client develop his own capacities for self-analysis.

Horney further felt that a valuable advantage might be gained for future problem areas if the client were led to develop his own techniques of analysis. Patients who become deeply dependent upon their therapist because of prolonged leaning upon him are poor prognostic risks. The moment a new problem arises, they can hardly wait to get back to their therapist for more help. Karen Horney felt that the client is much farther along the road toward emancipation from the therapist if he is given the skills to analyze his own behavior.

In a final note it should be added that Horney was discussing analysis of one's own development, conduct in daily life, resolvement of restrictive problem areas, and skills necessary to live in concert with fellow man. The practice of deep therapy she reserved for the professionally trained expert. The crucial point of her position is that living in this world as we know it contains factors which build man up, as well as tear him down. A loving spouse, children laughing, a lovely fall day, all are factors in bringing therapy to man's problems without recourse to psychiatric help. By analyzing our dynamics, she felt, we can go a long, long way toward keeping emotionally intact and toward solving minor emotional problems. This she felt we have done in the past; to lose its benefits would serve man poorly.

EXPLAINING HUMAN BEHAVIOR VIA HORNEY'S SOCIAL PSYCHOLOGICAL THEORY

The following discourse attempts to use Horney's theory to explain human behavior in marriage, perversions, suicide, lawbreaking, belief in a supranatural being, humor, smoking, play and recreation, psychoses–neuroses. Three different explanations for specific behavior may arise, corresponding to the three directions of movement in people suggested by Horney.

Marriage

Apparently the helpless person marries for love; the hostile person for prestige and enhancement to self; and the isolate for convenience in living arrangements.

Perversions

No clear reasons for perverted acts emerge from the theoretical position of Horney. As an analyst Horney was not unaware of perverted acts. However, perversions are sexual abnormalities and, in rejecting the pan-sexualism of Freud, Horney spent little time in discussing sexual behavior.

The dynamics of sexual behavior are, therefore minimized in the work of Horney, probably not because she felt them unimportant but because she felt the interrelationships of man were more important.

Two fundamental reasons for perversions may be considered, however: character structure and masochism. Horney thought that perversion cannot explain character but that the character structure can explain the perversion. Under this circumstance it would seem that all perversions are the result of masochisms. With this as a background we may now briefly examine how adherents of the three major adustment techniques arrive at pervertive activities.

The personality who moves toward people in a neurotically driven desire to win affection may become perverted as a result of the conflict caused by failure to win affection. Horney felt that the neurotic wishes to suffer as little as anyone else but that he may submit to the degrading activities of perversion in order to have a modicum of attention from others. The conflict between the desire for affection and failure to satisfy this desire may be artificially satisfied by masochistic suffering. In suffering the pervert may be saying that he has failed and that this is his just punishment in atonement for failure. Or he may feel that by submitting to perverted acts, he is winning the approval of another human being despite the degradation of the contact.

The hostile individual may have varying reasons for perverted acts. On the one hand his behavior may be an unconscious attempt to reverse his role of moving against people continuously. In the breakdown of this hostile role he may turn to its opposite by submitting to the humiliation of perversion. Because he is unable to sustain the activities of hostility, he breaks down occasionally. The conflict in emotions which accompanies the breakdown causes him to swing to the role of permitting others to torture him. The conflict, of course, increases rather than decreases. The pervert is a neurotic, and thus his basic character structure is founded on his neurosis. On the other hand an equally acceptable causal explanation may lie at a relatively more simple level. The hostile personality is perverted only as an overt, aggressive practitioner of perversion. He never submits to perversion but drives and lures others into degrading themselves for his pleasure. It may be the crowning triumph of his driving anxiety to control other human beings. He, too, demonstrates that perversion is an overpowering neurotic act.

When the individual who moves away from people commits perverted acts, a different set of circumstances may be assumed to be responsible. It will be remembered that the isolate became an isolate because of an early experience of having his love crushed by another human being. His primary wish now is to avoid the pain of conflict arising from wanting to be loved yet being denied love. The resolution of the conflict lies in retention within self of all emotionally charged feelings. The rationale is that only self can protect self. Revolving around the same framework of masochism, the isolate goes to extremes. The extreme of being independent of people is to be subjectively dependent upon them. Horney reasons that by intensifying the contradictory feeling the personality "narcotizes" the original feeling into a state of nonfeeling. If the isolate intensifies his dependence upon others, the original conflict of being hurt by rejected love may be alleviated. Much of the perverted activity of the isolate is indulged through fantasy and rarely through personal contact.

Suicide

In some ways it is easier, according to Horney's theory, to determine why man wants to commit suicide than it is to explain why man wants to stay alive! Perhaps this is true because Horney was interested in the deviant personality and wrote more concerning him than she did of the basic dynamics of man.

Horney considered suicide to be the phenomenon which occurs when the idealized self and idealized image become completely alienated from the true or actual self. The conflict rising from failure to reach the idealized goal causes man to destroy himself. As we shall see in a moment, he may have to destroy himself if his neurotic urges to destroy others become impossible to control.

Horney began with Freud's concept of the "death" wish. She felt the reality of Freud's death wish to be highly speculative, but the dynamics of it made analytical sense to her, if one always remembers the powerful effect of society upon *how* one deals with the death wish. Horney followed then the matrix of his reasoning that the death wish is instinctual. Continuing with the basic premise of duality and the subsequent reaction of regression in all of its manifestations, man comes into life wishing to regress into nonlife or death. Because he enters life with this desire it may be termed an instinct. Opposing the death wish (Freud has said "The goal of life is death") is, of course, the life wish. However, when man becomes unable to support the life wish (Eros), he succumbs to the death wish

(Thanatos). This leads to the desire to destroy life whether it be his own or others! Out of the death instinct comes the desire to destroy, and out of the desire to destroy comes homicide or suicide. In this particular section we are only interested in suicide. To discuss it further we must now turn to the trichotomized personality structure as Horney phrased it, keeping in mind her highly critical attitude of the Freudian death wish as an instinct only.

It may be assumed that the hostile and isolate personalities operate under somewhat the same set of conditions in regard to suicide. The hostile individual wishes to destroy others for various reasons: he cannot control them; he has become weak and is thus threatened by being controlled by others; or his overwhelming desire to manipulate gets out of hand. However, there are laws and customs and strong deterrent reasons against putting others to death. Through the confusion of his own neurotic emotional sickness, he sees that the only plausible alternative to destroying others is to destroy himself. Suicide then follows as an answer to his overwhelming urge for destruction rising from the power of the death wish.

The isolate individual also wishes to destroy those who have hurt him terribly. He also operates under the influence of the death wish. He also has the same deterrent factors restraining his bringing death to others that operated for the hostile neurotic. The further he isolates himself from fellow human beings, the further he detaches himself from his real self toward the idealized image, the closer he comes to destroying himself. He does not have the power of the hostile personality. The only one left to destroy is himself. He gains an added advantage in his deviant reasoning: death will surely take him as far away as possible from the influence and heartbreaks that others have caused him. By committing suicide he even has the added advantage of not having to trust others to his destruction. In a macabre, do-it-yourself manner he can make his final gesture all by himself and be independent of any one for the service. Death is a complete isolation which he feels he has never known before. Perhaps the suicidal senile psychotic now feels he has not been a bother to anyone in his old age.

The helpless (moving toward people) neurotic may possibly operate under the following dynamics within the frame of reference of Horney's work. If and when he does commit suicide, he may do so out of the complete failure to win the love of anyone. Because no one seems to care, he may be driven to making the complete masochistic sacrifice of himself on the altar of martyrdom. Horney feels that he does not consider suicide in a realistic sense. What he really wants is to have people feel sorry for him and thus he can be loved and protected again. Suicide, however, removes him from the benefits of being a martyr. Providing warm human contacts are completely denied him, he may "die on the doorstep" of those who fail to appreciate his winning ways. If he does, they will be sorry. Under these pressures the potential suicide plays and dreams with the idea of the world's renewed sense of devotion to him now that he is gone. Horney's feeling was that the helpless personality may try suicide but almost always is an ineffectual way. He really doesn't want to die. He only wants the benefits of the eulogies at his funeral. Horney expressed quaintly his infrequent success: "It often depends on accidental factors whether or not such [suicidal] attempts succeed. If I may be allowed the anomaly, nobody would be more astonished to find him actually dead than he himself" (*Neurosis and Human Growth,* p. 149).

Lawbreaking

We may assume that there are at least three reasons for explaining the breaking of laws by man if we use Horney's system. Again, these reasons are extensions of her theory; there are no direct references in her work to the following behavioral patterns.

When he consciously and deliberately breaks a law, the person who moves toward people probably does so to earn the approval of his fellow peers. Either the activity itself wins him the approval of others, or the material things which accrue from the illegal act are used to win favor and friends. Such societal pressures as "keeping up with the Joneses", or the petty shoplifting of teenagers, or going along with the gang in burglaring property could be considered examples of the essentially helpless neurotic who wants desperately to have people like him.

The strong, aggressive, hostile individual probably steals because in his thinking the following clichés are sufficient justification for his illegal behavior: "The Lord helps those who help themselves"; "Possession is nine-tenths of the law"; "A fool and his money are soon parted"; "Help yourself, everybody else does." His illegal behavior may be far from subtle because he feels justified under the circumstances of his own lack of goods to mug, slug, or beat his victim in order to gain their property. The first individual may steal out of a philanthropic Robin Hood motive; this second type steals for the good of one person only: himself. In point of fact, illegal activities may be the favorite gambit of the hostile individual who has neither the talent nor the power to gain his end of control of people through legitimate means. Lawbreaking then becomes a major avenue for his neurotic hostility rather than a means to an economic end.

It is more difficult to explain lawbreaking in terms of the isolate's frame of reference. Explanations here are more nebulous than for other types and other theories. We may assume either that he breaks laws which will help in some way to insulate him from annoying human contact or that the ill-gotten gains help him to withdraw from the contacts usually necessary in getting and maintaining a job in the social order in which he lives. By and large we may assume that the isolate resists temptations to break laws because the penalty may be too harsh for his ego. To be apprehended and convicted throws him into repulsive contact with other humanity. Occasionally, however, we may assume that he commits a crime which has no direct remunerative value but has a punitive effect toward some individual he feels has wronged him. Thus the "loner" in elementary school may steal indiscriminately from any and all classmates, with the value of the articles being incidental. His prime objective is to harass and punish those who will not accept him and who he feels have denied his pathetically advanced love in the past. The thefts are probably senseless and petty.

Supranatural Being

Horney says little in her work about religion or a god figure except tangentially. It is also difficult to ascertain through Horney where the concept of the supranatural came from. One finds it much easier to explain how man worships than why he worships. For the moment we may assume that a supranatural figure is an extension of man's idealized image. All that man ever hopes to be and all the virtues, powers, and love he would like to possess he finds in a god figure. Because his actual self can never attain the ultimate ideal which he feels would resolve all of his conflicts he turns to a god figure imbued with all the properties he would like to have within himself. Through social interaction with other men he constructs or accepts a somewhat commonly defined supranatural figure. The figure always reflects his cultural pattern, because man is a cultural product. So, although we find it difficult to find where man gets his idea of a god, we find it easier to see how he uses this idea for his own purposes. Again we may find that the three types of reaction to people within the neurotic framework may approach religion with differing purposes.

The helpless person who determinedly moves toward people, as well as all of us who have tendencies in that direction, may emphasize a god figure who is compassionate and loving toward us. Not being able to win much affection from his fellowman, the helpless personality may gain great strength and comfort in his belief of a god who loves and protects him *always*. Probably he likes best those parts of the Christian religion, for example, which emphasize the Christmas story and the baby figure of Jesus. Much of his emphasis is upon the figure of Jesus of Nazareth. He feels that God is love. To him religion is love and service to others.

The personality who moves against people and also all of us with inclinations toward that frame of reference may emphasize the omnipotence of a god figure. To the hostile person the emphasis should be upon the rightness and wrongness of sin. Because he allies himself with rightness, all those who do not believe as he does have thereby allied themselves with sin and irreligion. That being the case, he feels no compunction in using any means in correcting the sins of his fellow man. Convinced that he is on god's side, he now has *carte blanche* to persecute and punish the unbeliever. Perhaps he likes best those parts of the Christian religion, for example, which emphasize that the Lord is a jealous god who brings his wrath down upon the infidel. Much of his emphasis is upon the figure of the god itself. He feels that a god is the all powerful ruler of everything, a position he himself would like to fill. To him religion is a system of rightness and wrongness which he must enforce upon others who disbelieve.

The isolate, and all of us who have tendencies in that direction, may find in religion the solace and comfort of the spiritual nature of a religious figure. The monastic life, the withdrawn pursuits, and the rejection of emotional evangelism are the important factors for the personality who desires to move away from people. That which he can do in worshipping he would like to do alone. Perhaps he likes best those parts of the Christian religion which emphasize the Holy Ghost. Much of his emphasis is upon solitary worship. He feels that God is a spirit. To him religion is a direct one-to-one relationship between himself and his deity with no emphasis upon fellowship or stewardship.

Humor

Humor may have three explanations within Horney's theoretical structure.

The helpless one *produces* humor and seeks situations where he may be the clown, the buffoon, the jester. He uses humor as a tool to amuse others and make them laugh. If you laugh at him, you will like him. If he makes you happy, you will be on his side. He is willing to go to extreme lengths to get a laugh.

The hostile person *uses* humor. He demonstrates superiority by psuedo-humorous situations. He appreciates most the jokes which are at the expense of someone else, practical jokes which place other persons in embarrassing predicaments. Through this he gains a false sense of superiority. An example: by hiding another's clothing he can watch him frantically search for it. This makes him feel he is controlling behavior because *he* knows where the clothing is. His humor is probably based on man's inhumanity to man.

The isolate *collects* or *avoids* humor and may feel that life is serious and not very funny at all. He may collect for his own use humorous incidents which demonstrate the fallibility of man. His humor consists of private jokes for his own amusement. The highest kind of humor to him is that which portrays man as a slavish follower of customs.

Smoking

Nothing that one may find in Horney's work helps to explain directly why man indulges in the use of tobacco. One is forced to draw far-reaching extensions from her work in attempting to explain this phenomenon of man's behavior.

We may, therefore, hazard the guess that the helpless individual smokes to be a part of the crowd. Smoking is for him a part of togetherness. He smokes, or does not smoke, depending on the customs of his gang. The personality that strives to move against people uses tobacco primarily to demonstrate his leadership. He is inclined to be ahead of the crowd by excessive addiction or to go in the opposite direction by giving up smoking, but only after he announces how strong he is in ceasing a behavior which his peers are too weak to quit.

Play and Recreation

Horney does not speak specifically of play or recreation as part of the dynamics of man, but we may assume some or all of the following forces to be a part of the explanation of why man indulges in games or other types of play and recreation. Foremost of the explanatory factors is probably the interrelationship of man. Man learns to play from his fellow-man. Play, in whatever forms it takes, is a part of the custom of society. We may further assume that play is one of man's finest devices to reduce anxiety and the conflict that grows out of anxiety. It will be remembered

that Horney felt life itself with all of its variant activities is a strong therapeutic agent for man.

Play and recreation may also be man's attempt to get nearer to his
idealized image. Because recreational activities may be apart from the
general rules of society (the hunter can kill, the boxer can deliver a blow,
the actor can say lines unacceptable to parlor etiquette), the participant in
play may fulfill desires for the idealized person that he would like to be
without paying the penalty of breaking a social law. In play he can be all
the things required by the image of his idealized self.

Finally, we may find that an individual's play pattern follows along the
lines of his character structure with its possibilities for going in three interpersonal ways. The helpless person may find that play is a way of life for
him. He likes play. When people play, they are generally happy. If he can
promote play and live in a recreationally oriented world, he may be able
to surround himself with happy people all of whom are potential friends.
The hostile personality may use play as he used humor: to gain either
momentarily or symbolically those advantages over others which he is
unable to gain in normal living. Play for him is a means to an end. It
can be a substitute form of showing his mastery and superiority over others.
He may not be an executive in real life but on the playing fields he can
excel in hitting or running or throwing or the smashing tennis volley. Play
is a way to win victories over fellow man. Again, we may find that as the
isolate withdraws from people because he does not want the pain of being
hurt and denied, the need for affiliation is still strong. Possibly by the
avenues of recreation he may fill the gap of missing human relationships
which he can trust and control. If his recreation is reading, he may choose
his literary friends at his own pleasure and drop them just as neatly, if
they do not serve him well. Probably, to the isolationist, play is developed
in its highest symbolical form.

Psychoses—Neuroses

As stated previously, Horney's entire theory is drawn from her
contributions to the field of neuroses. Consequently, to explain fully this
deviation in man's behavior is to recapitulate all of her five books almost in
their totality. Since this obviously is not possible, only a few pertinent
features will be discussed herein. Actually turnabout is more in order here.
One studies Horney to study neuroses, not how the neurotic becomes
normal but how the normal man becomes neurotic.

Much of Horney's writing, of course, concerned itself with psychoanalytic techniques and procedures, in addition to the basic dynamics of neuroses. In some cases it is not possible from her writings to tell where neuroses end and psychoses begin, but primarily Horney was developing the concept of neuroses. Organic psychoses are not a subject of her writings.

Some of the salient features of her theory of neuroses (and only tangentially to psychoses) are listed below.

1. Because man changes and is constantly in change as he attempts to adjust to his environment, Horney preferred to use the term *trends* for behavior problems. Thus the three trends of movement concerning people may bring conflict and anxiety which lead to neurosis when man cannot balance the three trends in his normal living pattern. Rigidity is the keynote to neurotic patterns of behavior. Conflict is caused by failure to coordinate the trichotomized trends in human relationships. In turn conflict arising out of anxiety and fear causes neuroses.

2. A second causal factor, particularly in western civilization, is the competitive, choatic, and commercial emphasis of the modern culture pattern. Horney feels strongly that modern man lives in a culture that practically guarantees conflict in the normal persuance of life. She would subscribe to the term, *anxious age,* and credit it for much of human suffering.

3. Also contributing to the development of neuroses is the faulty character structure man may receive from his parents' poor enactment of their roles. If the child is ignored or overindulged or pressured too greatly, these factors promulgated by his parents may eventuate in a character structure which the individual is unable to change basically to avoid neurotic behavior in life.

4. Much of a neurosis, as we shall see more specifically in the next paragraph, grows out of man's alienation from his actual self as he strives toward the idealized image. The further he drifts away from the real person he is, the more and more neurotic man is inclined to become. Eventually he may be so far removed from actuality in self as to be psychotic. Most of the time, we assume, he limps back to reality as life forces bring him back to his real self. However, the structure of normality grows weaker and less resilient if he persists in striving for an idealized image, an image that is never obtainable.

5. We may finally assume that complete rigidity, when continued for too great a time with no therapy either from life or professionals to alleviate the condition, could result in specific psychotic reactions as follows: moving toward people may lead to manic-depressive behavior with the emphasis on manic-euphoric behavior; moving against people may lead to paranoiac behavior where the person is filled with suspicions and accusations that others try to

control him; and moving away from people may lead to schizoid reactions, especially of the completely withdrawn catatonic type.

PREDICTING HUMAN BEHAVIOR VIA HORNEY'S SOCIAL PSYCHOLOGICAL THEORY

Like most other theories, Horney's work does not lend itself to predictions that one can make either personally or objectively through scientific and laboratory work. There is an undercurrent of prognostic feeling running beneath the statements of her published work which are of a predictive nature. The general tone is that we may expect neurotic behavior from individuals who behave in ways which Horney discusses. One may assume that in the ongoing daily therapy of their profession all psychoanalysts must perforce proceed on some basis of better-than-guessing what the future holds for their clients. Just as the medical practitioner conducts his practice along lines of predictable (within limits) patient behavior under the influence of prescribed medicines, the psychoanalyst presumes through diagnosis that certain therapeutic approaches will bring forth desired and predictable patient behavior. However, these are pragmatic facets of clinical insight coming out of the practice of therapy, and, consequently, one does not find such predictions in the published work of a therapist although it is a part of his practice of therapy.

Personal Prediction

The reader must ask for himself whether man goes through helplessness, hostility, and isolation as he lives through infancy, adolescence, and through the middle and later years of adulthood. May we assume that this is a predictable course of an individual's life? This question and others to follow may have for the individual reader in his own personal prediction a modicum of face validity although no evidence may exist from directed research toward these phenomena.

We as individuals interested in our own personalities may predict that some or all of the following will occur in our lives:

1. The seven auxiliary approaches to artificial harmony such as blind spots, compartments, rationalization, excessive control, arbitrary rightness, elusiveness, and cynicism to operate and will continue to operate.

2. The historical evidence of the past is that humanity is getting better and will continue to improve in the future.

3. All of us strive to create an idealization of ourselves which, if over-

emphasized, may become too illusory and lead us to follow an image of what we think our idealized selves may be.

4. When we are in deep stress and have exhausted the usual means of resolving our conflicts, we ultimately move toward people, or against them, or away from them.

5. Man will continue to solve many of his emotional problems and thus avoid deeper neuroses by self-analysis and by his own capacity to change his behavior.

Scientific or Laboratory Prediction

The direct influence of the work of many outstanding theorists upon scientifically rigorous research is not easily determined. There appear to be no conspicuous studies of the three types of neurotic behavior, yet one must believe that Horney's influence has been strong among psycho-analysts nonetheless. Perhaps her strength may be in operational factors during therapy.

Whatever the predictive success of Horney's work, the results are prob-ably buried in the success she and her students have had in the ongoing business of improving behavior through psychoanalysis.

◆

SUMMARY

Departing from its original content as Freudian indoctrinated psycho-analysis, Karen Horney's work can probably be best summarized by re-ferring to the previous six principles extracted from her work, with special emphasis upon the three types of neurotic maneuvers that are possible when man fails to integrate the conflicting forces in his society.

Optimism–Positivism Principle. Mankind has the capacity to change. The human personality is not rigidly held to the formations of early child-hood.

Society–Culture Principle. Man's personality is a product of his inter-actions with other men. These interactions are bounded by the society in which he lives, as well as the past societies in which he lived, and the cultural rules he has had to follow.

Character-Structure Principle. Throughout his life man creates a structured character. This character structure may be changed. In general it remains constant within any given environment and is also inclined to remain constant through life. Rather than prescribing how an individual will behave, it circumscribes the limits within which he has free choice to behave.

Self-Concept Principle. *Self-Concept* means first, "an awareness of oneself as a human being," and secondly, the "importance or significance of oneself in the roles of life." It also distinguishes the person's self from all other selves he sees around him. The actual or real self is all that we have to operate with in life. Because we would like to be better than we are, or more important than we are, we may construct idealized pictures of ourselves. If these pictures become more important than the real self, we may depart too widely from the real self and idealize ourselves into an unobtainable image. Inability to reach the idealized image may cause us to blame others by the process of externalization.

Complementation–Conflict Principle. The writer considers this to be the major theme and contribution of Horney's theory. There are two divisions: the major adjustment techniques and the minor adjustment techniques. The prominent features of the major adjustment techniques are highlighted in Figure 8.

"Wait for me"

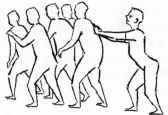

"C'mon get going"

"Leave me alone, I'm thinking"

Figure 8. Diagrammatic Summary of Horney's Theory.

Out of the following ten neurotic needs Horney felt that the individual tends to respond in one of three ways towards other individuals—toward, against, and away from other people. The ten neurotic needs are these:

affection and approval, dominant partner in life, confined limits of life, power, exploitation of others, prestige, personal admiration, ambition in personal achievement, self sufficiency and independence, and perfection and unassailability.

Figure 8 indicates the three types of reactions to people that all of us may have a tendency to duplicate. When we are unable to complement their forces to ease the conflicts in life, we become fixed at one of the three types into a neurotic pattern.

The minor adjustment techniques call for auxiliary approaches to artificial harmony used in striving to complement the conflicting forces of life. Horney discusses seven of these: blind spot, compartments, rationalization, excessive self-control, arbitrary rightness, elusiveness, and cynicism.

Self-Analysis Principle. Horney feels that man has the capacity to analyze his own dynamics with enough skill and success to solve many, but not all, of his own problems. She feels that man has always done this with some measure of success and that he will continue to do so in the future. Life itself has many curative powers. Man must learn to use these through developing the ability to analyze his own role in life.

BIBLIOGRAPHY

PRIMARY SOURCES

BOOKS

Horney, K., *Neurotic Personality of Our Times*, N.Y., Norton, 1937.
Horney, K., *New Ways in Psychoanalysis*, N.Y., Norton, 1939.
Horney, K., *Self-Analysis*, N.Y., Norton, 1942.
Horney, K., *Our Inner Conflicts*, N.Y., Norton, 1945.
Horney, K., *Neurosis and Human Growth*, N.Y., Norton, 1950.
Horney, K., *Are You Considering Psychoanalysis?* N.Y., Norton, 1962.
   Paperback of original 1946 paper.

PERIODICALS

Kelman, H. (chairman), F. A. Weiss, P. Tillich, and K. Horney, Human nature can change: a symposium, *Amer. J. Psychoanal.*, 1952, 12, 62–68.
Horney, K., Values and Problems, *Amer. J. Psychoanal.*, 1952, 12, 80–81, (abstract).

Horney, K. (moderator), Constructive forces in the therapeutic process: a round table discussion, *Amer. J. Psychoanal.*, 1953, *13*, 14–19.

Horney, K., Culture and aggression: some considerations and objections to Freud's theory of instinctual drives toward death and destruction, *Amer. J. Psychoanal.*, 1960, *20*, 130–138.

TAPE RECORDINGS

Horney, K., *Can Human Nature Change?*, (G. W. Kisker, ed.) No. 101, Cincinnati, Ohio, Sound Seminars.

SUGGESTED READINGS

BOOKS

Brown, I. A. C., *Freud and the Post-Freudians*, Baltimore, Penguin, 1961.
Horney, Fromm, and Sullivan also included.

Munroe, R. L., *Schools of Psychoanalytic Thought*, N.Y., Holt, Rinehart and Winston, 1955.
Analysis and integration of Freud, Adler, Jung, Rank, Fromm, Horney, Sullivan, *et al*.

Saltzman, L., *Developments in Psychoanalysis*, N.Y., Grune & Stratton, 1962.
The innovations of Horney and Sullivan.

PERIODICALS

Cameron, D. E., Karen Horney: a pioneer in the science of human relations, *Amer. J. Psychoanal.*, 1954, *14*, 19–29.

James, W. T., K. Horney, and E. Fromm, In relation to Alfred Adler, *Indiv. Psychol. Bull.*, 1947, *6*, 105–116.

Kelman, N., Karen Horney, M.D., 1885–1952, *Psychoanal. Rev.*, 1953, *40*, 191–193.

Kelman, N., In memorium: Karen Horney, M.D., 1885–1952, *Amer. J. Psychoanal.*, 1954, *14*, 5–7.

Kelman, N., What is psychotherapy? The viewpoint of the Karen Horney group, *Ann. Psychother. Monogr.*, 1959, No. 1, 37–43.
The goal is a full personal life.

Lussheimer, P., N. Kelman, E. Kilpatrick, H. Gershman, E. A. Gutheil, and C. Oberndorf, Tributes to Karen Horney, *Amer. J. Psychoanal.*, 1954, *14*, 8–13.

Oberndorf, C. P., Dr. Karen Horney, *Int. J. Psycho. Anal.*, 1953, *34*, 154–155.

Robbins, I., An analysis of Horney's concept of the real self, *Educational Theory*, 1958, *8*, 162–168.

Rose, D., Application of Karen Horney's theories to group analysis, *Int. J. Group Psychother.*, 1953, *3*, 270–279.

Tillich, P., Karen Horney: a funeral address, *Pastoral Psychol.*, 1953, 4(34), 11–13.

Vollmerhausen, J. W., Alienation in the light of Karen Horney's theory of neurosis, *Amer. J. Psychoanal.*, 1961, *21*, 144–155.
Conflict in self-alienation.

Weiss, F. A., Karen Horney: a bibliography, *Amer. J. Psychoanal.*, 1954, *14*, 15–18.
Contains all known published writings of Horney.

Weiss, F. A., Karen Horney: her early papers, *Amer. J. Psychoanal.*, 1954, *14*, 55–64.

Wilkins, J. W., Jr., An experimental investigation of certain aspects of the personality theory of Karen Horney, *Dissertation Abstracts*, 1959, *19*, 3359, Michigan State Univer.

Wolman, B., Psychoanalysis without libido: an analysis of Karen Horney's contribution to psychoanalytic theory, *Amer. J. Psychother.*, 1954, *8*, 21–31.

10

Moreno

All the world's a stage,
And all the men and women merely players:
They have their exits and their entrances:
And one man in his time plays many parts . . .

WILLIAM SHAKESPEARE
As You Like It, II, 7.

SOME BIOGRAPHICAL DATA

Jacob L. Moreno was born in Bucharest, Rumania, in 1892.[1] He was first a student at the University of Vienna, later a member of the philosophy faculty, and still later a medical student. He received his M.D. from this institution in 1917. After this time he was successively the Superintendent, Mittendorf State Hospital near Vienna and health officer of Voslau, Austria, and concurrently with the latter post, a psychiatrist in private practice. During his professional life in Vienna he displayed a deep interest in psychodrama, founding *Das Stegreiftheater* (The Spontaniety Theatre), even developing in 1922 a stage especially adapted to spontaneity work. The dates for his beginning work in these areas were actually: Group psychotherapy, 1913 (Spittelberg, Vienna), Sociometry, 1915–1916

[1] In preparing the manuscript, I sent the present chapter to Dr. Moreno for his comments. I am extremely grateful to him for his suggestions. The present treatment does not incorporate all of his remarks although he found, "It is fascinating reading and it documents that you have a high spontaneity quotient." His other comments follow in the chapter where appropriate.

(Mittendorf, near Vienna), Role playing, 1909–1911 (Viennese Gardens).

In 1925 he came to the United States where he was licensed as a physician in New York in 1927. He became a naturalized citizen of the United States in 1935. His years since then in this country have been filled with an increasing interest in psychodrama, sociometry, and group psychotherapy. His efforts and accomplishments in these areas can be only partially recounted here. He has engaged in private psychiatric work since 1928. This same year he began psychodramatic work with children at the Plymouth Institute in Brooklyn, Mt. Sinai Hospital, New York City, and later did the same type of work at Grosvenor Neighborhood House and Hunter College. In 1931–1932 Moreno made sociometric studies at Sing Sing Prison, Public School 181, Brooklyn, New York, and from 1932–1938 did the first long term sociometric work at the New York Training School for Girls in Hudson, New York. The Moreno Sanitarium, formerly known as Beacon Hill, was founded by him in 1936. He has taught at the New School of Social Research, at Teachers College, Columbia University, and has been on the faculty of New York University since 1951.

Moreno has, throughout his professional life, been a prolific writer of articles, many of them appearing in *Sociometry*. He has written a number of books, edited others, and has even made a film on psychodrama. Altogether, Moreno has led a prodigiously full and fruitful professional life.

Moreno was married in 1949 to Zerka Toeman. He has two children, Regina and Jonathan. The Morenos reside at Beacon, New York.

INTRODUCTION

The figure of Jacob L. Moreno as a personality theorist is not as clear as that of some of the previous theorists in the present text.[2] Most students of the field of personality have emphasized Moreno's techniques of socio-

---

[2] Moreno himself says: "I question the first statement, and wish to refer you to my major work on personality development, Spontaneity Theory of Child Development, especially the Introduction, pp. 89–90, *Sociometry*, Vol. VII, 1944, first paragraph from which I quote herewith: 'The theoretical structure of every empirical science needs from time to time a thorough overhauling. New findings, and perhaps, still more than this, new dimensions of investigation require and demand new supporting hypotheses. A *theory of personality*, for instance, is needed, especially a theory of child development, which is in better accord with the dimensions of study in which an increasingly large number of child psychologists, social psychologists, analysts, and therapists are engaged. They still carry on with antiquated concepts which do not quite meet new situations. The theories of child

drama, psychodrama, and the related sociometric devices which he has so cleverly created as a major contribution to the psychological world. Others have felt that he is primarily a sociological thinker, dealing chiefly in the field of group behavior with little or no relevance to the psychological manifestations of man's behavior. Still others consider Moreno as a practitioner of the art of therapy in his role as the guiding light of the theater for role playing at Beacon, New York. To many educators he is the originator of the sociogram which was introduced to them through the publication, by the Horace-Mann-Lincoln Institute, of the pamphlet "How to Construct a Sociogram" (1947, Teachers College, Columbia University). Some know Moreno as the originator and long-time editor (1937, Vol. I, No. 1, to 1956, Vol. XVIII, No. 4) of the periodical *Sociometry*. Moreno is all these things and a good bit more.[3]

Moreno began his professional life as a medical doctor in Vienna. His dynamic and forceful personality soon led him into greater concerns for the welfare of his fellowmen, concerns that go beyond the realm of the medical sciences. Feeling that "No [science] is an island of itself," Moreno turned his fertile mind in any direction that to him appeared a fruitful avenue for a wider understanding of the dynamics of man's behavior. Moreno admits to having a strong ego, and many who have met him speak of the impact of his personality. The author recalls vividly an encounter with Moreno in an unstructured situation (a publisher's exhibition) at

---

development, as evolved by behaviorism, the Gestalt School, and psychoanalysis have lost their magnetism in some quarters, probably because they have lost their usefulness in empirical and experimental study. The appeal of concepts such as spontaneity, warming-up process, spontaneity training, auxiliary ego, role-playing, and tele (mental distance-receptors) is growing in momentum.'

"Indeed, my ambition was to construct 1. a *personality theory* which is superior to that of Freud—psychodrama, 2. a *social theory* which is superior to that of Marx—sociometry, and 3. a cosmic theory which is superior to that of the Old and the New Testament, the Koran and the Speeches of Buddha—The Words of the Father, published in 1920 in German as 'Das Testament des Vaters,' in English as 'The Words of the Father' in 1941."

[3] Moreno states, "He [Moreno] introduced the first systematic *theory of interpersonal relations*, see *Sociometry*, Vol. I, No. 1, 1937, pp. 1–74—one year before H. S. Sullivan who duplicated it in his *Psychiatry*, Vol. I, No. 1, 1938. He introduced the concept of "The Encounter" ten years before Martin Buber, in 1914. He created the scientific foundations of group psychotherapy and coined all the terms pertinent to it: group therapy, group psychotherapy, group cohesiveness, group catharsis, acting out and the concept of self realization which, as an 'actual' process comes to life in psychodramatic presentation."

which time Moreno corralled the spectators for an impromptu demonstration of spontaneity, to the mixed bewilderment of the participants. Moreno's adventurous and creative imagination has caused Read Bain to state, "Moreno is always the actor" (*Sociometry and the Science of Man*, p. 41).[4]

Moreno is a prodigious writer. Starting in 1914 in Austria, he has continued to the present day to be a prolific and highly inventive author of many, many, many articles. Some of his articles have been in joint authorship with members of his family: Florence B., Zerka T., or Jonathan Moreno. Other articles were collaborative efforts with members of his staff at his institute in Beacon, New York. Most of his written work, however, has been the singular effort of Moreno. The primary source of Moreno's written work may be found in the issues of *Sociometry* especially during the years of his editorship, 1937–1956. Frequently one finds reprints of these articles as monographs of his institute's publishing house, Beacon House. Currently Moreno has found a major outlet for his work in the issues of *Group Psychotherapy* which has inherited the mantle of *Sociometry* but with an avowed international flavor. Besides his one major volume, *Who Shall Survive?*, and his last editorship of the voluminous eighteenth volume of *Sociometry* (published as a book under the title *Sociometry and the Science of Man*), and recently *The Sociometry Reader,* Moreno has also created one motion picture on the practice and techniques of his work, *Introduction to Psychodrama.*

Since approximately 1937 the wide expansion and adaptation of Moreno's basic tenets have had an intriguing, cumulative effect on the minds of sociologists, psychiatrists and psychologists alike. Moreno himself has broadened the application of his concepts, but the basic tenets of his original work remain essentially unchanged. For example, Moreno frequently states that everything in life is in the "here and now." His is the psychology of the moment, the present moment in any human being's life. This and the concepts of spontaneity–creativity–cultural conserve, tele, warming up, role playing, the social atom, and sociogenetic laws have remained essentially as Moreno first conceived them. The applications of Moreno's theories widen with each new devotee, but the basic theory continues to hold.

[4] The reader-researcher should note that *Sociometry and the Science of Man* has double pagination: one for the book itself and the other for the continuous issue pagination of the periodical *Sociometry*. References in this text (*Interpreting Personality Theories*) refer to the single volume pagination as found in the upper right hand corner of Moreno's *Sociometry and the Science of Man.*

Since the earliest germ of an idea about role playing which he first attempted in the Komoedian Haus in Vienna on April 1, 1921, Moreno has continued to expand his concepts into sociodrama, psychodrama, sociometry, group psychotherapy, and the theoretical framework of the trichotomized idea of spontaneity–creativity–cultural conserve. Gardner Murphy, himself one of the world's reknowned personality theoreticians, has called Moreno's work more than a technical trick or device, ". . . the beginning of a new way of viewing human relationships," and a social theory in its own right (*Sociometry and the Science of Man*, p. 37). Probably one of the most unique and powerfully dramatic descriptions of role playing, particularly role reversal, is Moreno's quotation from his earliest work, *Einladung zu einer Begegnung* (1914), in which he states, "A meeting of two: eye to eye, face to face, and when you are near I will tear your eyes out and place them instead of mine, and you will tear my eyes out and will place them instead of yours, then I will look at you with your eyes and you will look at me with mine" (p. 3).

Although Moreno eulogized Freud on the occasion of the hundredth anniversary of Freud's birth in 1956, he felt that his own techniques were far more advanced than Freud's because at last they freed the therapist from the couch and the chair. Through the spontaneity of psychodrama both the client and the therapist could actively participate in lifelike situations that revealed real advances in changing human behavior *in situ*. Also Moreno felt that the heavy emphasis which Freud placed upon the unconscious states of man was in error. Moreno preferred to consider the formulations of spontaneity–creativity as being the root-form of all behavior and, indeed, of the entire behavior of the universe itself. "Spontaneity–creativity is *the* problem of psychology." In comparing his theory with those of the big three—Freud, Jung, and Adler—Moreno found his system superior. He rejected Freud's repetition–compulsion principle on the grounds that man does not continue slavishly to repeat infantile behavior but rather that man always builds his roles on the success or failure of past roles. He felt the "big three" neither had a theoretical foundation based on a logical approach nor that their clinical methods went much beyond the understanding of the one person being analyzed, whereas Moreno's own treatment of interpersonal groups was wider and more inclusive of the total understanding of human behavior. Moreno also felt that it is far more efficient of time and effort to deal with groups in sociodrama situations than to spend time in the one-to-one relationship that individual psychotherapy demands. Moreno was a precursor to Lewin in regard to the positional diagrams which Lewin so brilliantly espoused. As far back as 1916 Moreno used diagrams to indicate the space and movements between the psychodrama actors, much in the same way that Lewin was to adopt them in 1936. Moreno published these diagrams in his first book on the theater for spontaneity (Stegreiftheater) in Berlin, Germany, 1923.

One author, Jiri Nehnevajsa, in *Sociometry and the Science of Man* (p. 49), feels with many others, including Gardner Murphy, that Moreno has created a "theory of human behavior." Moreno's work includes a combination of theory, therapy, and research.[5] This text makes no attempt to deal with the "how to do it" aspects of psychodrama or sociometry. It is the intent here to treat only the theoretical aspects of Moreno's work as they apply to the dynamics of man's personality. In short, *why* does man do the things he does?

MORENO'S DESCRIPTION OF HUMAN BEHAVIOR

In searching for the main themes or principles involved in Moreno's work, one is tempted to incorporate his personality theory into three main groups: spontaneity, creativity, and cultural conserves. There are, however, as we shall see, many concepts of his that do not fit comfortably in any of these three groups. Contrary to almost all of the other theorists considered in the present book, Moreno does consider himself to be a personality theorist. In many ways he considers himself to be primarily concerned with "social reconditioning." His work revolves around this central core. In keeping with others (Murphy, Nehnevajsa, *et al.*) the author feels that the breadth and depth of Moreno's work are admirably adapted to a theory about why man behaves as he does. In short: a theory of personality is involved in Jacob Moreno's writings.

As the present author interprets the contributions of Moreno, at least ten major themes, concepts, or principles appear. The order of their presentation in the present chapter has no special significance. Other interpreters may, of course, be more comfortable with more, others with fewer than ten principles. For the present it is felt that the ten that follow adequately

---

[5] Any serious student of Carl Roger's work will see a high degree of comparison in the theory, therapy, research approach of the two, but, of course, not in the essence of their theories. (See Chapter 11).

cover the primary basic structure of Moreno and his theoretical considerations of man's complex personality. Admittedly some of the principles are more important than others, but the reader may best make this value judgment for himself. The ten principles are: social atom; tele; warming up; role playing; spontaneity; creativity; cultural conserves; group development; sociogenetic law; and measurement.

Social Atom Principle

The first time that Moreno used the term *social atom* in any specific connotation was in a 1932 publication, *Group Method and Group Psychotherapy*, although tangential references had been made to this concept prior to that time. By definition, the social atom is the "smallest living social unit," one which cannot be further subdivided. The relationship between the social atom and tele is very close as we shall see later in this chapter. Social atoms, when reduced to their basic nature in man's behavior, are the mastic that holds society together. Although tele has characteristics of positive and negative human relationships, the social atom is neither positive nor negative. It is a state of relationship between one human being and another. Beneath the tele relationship is the social atom. The key word in regard to social atoms is *reciprocity*. Thus, there may be an attraction or repulsion in any reciprocal relationship between two people, but the social atom itself does not lend itself to negative or positive relationships. The attraction and repulsion comes from the feeling-tone of the reciprocating human beings, not from the social atomic structure. The social atom describes the structure; the human beings involved bring into the structure their feelings of attraction or repulsion to each other. The concept of tele is reserved for describing the action involved in the reciprocity of human to human. Little of man's personality in actual behavioral examples is explained thus far. We must proceed further with the concept of the social atom.

The social atom has two distinct perspectives as it operates in human behavior: psychological and collective. The social atom in the former case refers to one person and his relationship with others. Thus, the one-to-one relationship of a husband to his wife is a form of the psychological social atom. In the collective perspective the social atom is viewed as the smallest part of human society. An example for this may be found in the casual encounter of a customer with a sales clerk. This relationship between two people cannot be further reduced. From the viewpoint of the psychological social atom there is implied a previous feeling tone between the two reciprocating human beings. Collective social atoms imply no previous condition of feeling tone between the individuals involved. Psychological social atoms, therefore, have longer histories and more definable reciprocal relationships. Collective social atoms are generally of short duration with little or no previous history, and the reciprocity in relationships is more difficult to define. Putting it another way, we may better predict what a husband and wife will do than what a salesclerk and customer will do.

Social atoms do not exist in isolation from all other types of human behavior. In a sense, social atoms are the building bricks of all human encounter. As the child continues to grow into adulthood, the social atomic structure also continues to grow, and with growth it changes. The roles each human must play and the roles each human chooses to emphasize require stronger or weaker social atomic structuring. Individuals who are unable to handle their roles in a manner satisfactory to themselves and to society have an unbalanced social structure. Neurotics, for example, may be considered to have an unbalanced social structure.

A further distinction is made between the social atoms and the cultural atom. Just as personality disorders may occur due to an unbalanced social atom formation, such disorders also may be caused by a poor adjustment between the cultural atom and the social atom of an individual. Cultural atoms are formed by the irreducible role that one receives in the culture within which he operates. The difficult role of the Negro in contemporary American society may serve as an illustration. Although the man with colored skin may have a strong affective social atomic structure with an individual whose skin is white, the culture in which they both operate restricts the cultural atomic structure to such a stringent degree that personality disorders may result. The culture restricts whom they may marry, with whom they may attend church or enter a business relationship, as well as multiple other cultural atomic relationships. World War II gave examples of the difficulties of adjustment for the social atom versus cultural atom: one brother might be an officer while another brother was an enlisted man; or two friends would find their social atom structure restricted by the culture atom structure of officer to enlisted man. We may see from the above that neither the social atom or the cultural atom may be further reduced. In the military services an officer is an officer, not just part officer and part enlisted man. Likewise in cultures which assign a colored person the irreducible role of being colored, there are no halfway points.

The cultural atom like the social atom is irreducible. What the individual does with his role and how he reacts to it is, of course, a matter of individual difference. This we shall study more explicitly in the following sections on role playing.

When two or more social atoms combine, the combination results in what Moreno calls *social molecules*. As two or more social molecules combine and become more complex, the result is a classoid or a socoid. The entire structure is now the psychosocial network. These networks may further have sympathetic relationships with other networks in other communities; even throughout the world. So far the previous discourse appears to be a matter of words combined into a large definition, but with little practical significance. For better understanding an example of gossip on a college campus may be used. Let us assume that two fraternity brothers or two sorority sisters (social atoms) whisper an item of gossip that they have heard or read about. The rumor, in this case, concerns the annual trek many college students make during the Easter vacation to Ft. Lauderdale or similar places in Florida. It is rumored that the white students will attempt to stage sit-in strikes at various places during the vacation week as a supportive measure condemning segregation of colored and white in the South. As many rumors do, this rumor soon spreads throughout the Greek letter organization (social molecule). Before long the rumor permeates the entire campus, both to other organized fraternities and sororities and also to those students who do not belong to fraternities or sororities. The Greek letter organizations might be termed classoids while the nonmember students might be termed socoids. As the rumor gains force and wider circulation on other college campuses (psychosocial network), it may even be publicized throughout the world by newspapers and television. Thus we may have an example of the development of the progress from social atom through all the stages to psychosocial network.

Tele Principle

It is not possible to deal with Moreno's works without coming repeatedly upon the concept of tele, or "t," or telic sensitivity. Even a reader who scans his writings will have his eye caught by the term *tele*. The concept tele is basic to Moreno's theory of personality. It is one of the central themes in sociometry. A true grasp of the meaning of tele helps to explain the social atom, because tele is a part of the social atom. Whereas the social atom is considered to be the smallest indivisible unit of action between humans, tele is the *process* of action between individuals. Therefore, to get a deeper understanding of the social atom one must also study the process of tele in the structure of the social atom.

Moreno feels that man does more than act: he does not act in a vacuum, he coacts. This coaction between individuals is called the *tele factor*. By definition *tele* means, ". . . the simplest unit of feeling transmitted from one individual towards another . . ." (*Who Shall Survive?*, p. 159). And as Moreno wrote to me:

> . . . it represents a two-way process, a process of the reciprocation. In contrast empathy has been defined by Lipps as a 'one-way nonreciprocal feeling into an esthetic object'; transference, according to Freud, is a 'one-way projection,' from one individual to another, a delusionary process. Tele is responsible for the two-way and multiple feelings of several individuals into each others private worlds and the socio-emotional structure resulting from them. Tele is a binder; transference is a disintegrater. A transference relation eventually either vanishes or changes into a tele relation. Therefore tele is conceived as the main stem with two branches, transference and empathy.

Tele is the true basis of interaction between humans. It represents a two-way process, a process of reciprocation. As we shall see in later paragraphs, Moreno speaks of "t" as having some sort of physiological basis between two human beings. Out of the primordial basis of acting toward other humans in an organic or biological manner, as do animals who do not communicate with involved symbolic speech patterns, man has evolved a similar basis of acting toward individuals beyond the human physiological systems. Man has a physiological system that can function without outside stimulation (feeling, hunger, breathing, elimination of body wastes, etc.), and because these functions are the forerunners of telic sensitivity, tele is more than reacting to other people. Tele has a built-in self starter. The self-energizing characteristics of tele may, therefore, initiate a feeling tone within the individual, even before anything has happened to cause a reaction to another person. Man's personality is more than a reactive agent like the surface of a body of water when a pebble strikes it. Man has the capacity to create his own waves. In this sense, then, man coacts with other human beings as well as reacts to them.

Just as man has an aversion–affection continuum of biological feeling within himself (he likes or dislikes certain foods, likes or dislikes certain odors, etc.), he also has a flow of affection and disaffection between himself and others, be they single persons or groups. Thus tele becomes the, ". . . flow—to and fro—of affectivity between individuals" (*Sociometry and the Science of Man*, p. 62). This like–dislike emotional tone is no respecter of bi-variant groups. White may like black, male female, Republican Democrat, German French, and vice versa. There is, of course, always the reactive factor in tele. The essential feature of tele is that an emotional feeling tone exists in almost all human relationships. The exceptions are so few as to be insignificant.

In using the Greek word *tele*, meaning *far* or *far off*, Moreno intends the word to mean "distance." This meaning holds for him more than time and space connotations; etymologically it carries a further connotation of "emotional tone between two human objects." The origin of the word is *telencephalon* or endbrain, the neurological term meaning "the anterior subdivision of the embryonic brain in which are developed the olfactory lobes, the cerebral hemispheres, and the corpora striata." Moreno felt that tele begins as the infant gradually develops ideas of nearness and distance, both within and without himself. The physical distance receptors of the visual and auditory senses gradually help the infant to differentiate objects from persons. This leads further to the infant's liking and disliking objects and persons, a reaction called *positive* or *negative tele*. Tele also develops into a sensitivity for real objects and for imagined objects. When tele begins in the human system, it is a psycho-organic level of expression of feeling and is inarticulate. Gradually as the human mechanisms mature, the tele sensitivity becomes psycho-social and develops to a highly articulate level.

Other attributes of tele follow.

Intensity. The intensity of accepting or rejecting another human being is variable within the single human subject. At times he may have a strong feeling of tele toward another human whether it be a feeling of acceptance or rejection; at other times, the intensity of his feeling may be quite low.

Sensitivity. The degree of sensitivity also varies considerably between two individuals. A telic relationship implies more than empathy or counterempathy. The ability to "penetrate and understand" another individual is implied in telic sensitivity. A therapist and his client will be operating at a loss if there is no high degree of telic sensitivity. In like manner a marriage may be only a formal agreement if the marriage relationship lacks a high degree of telic sensitivity.

Simple tele. This results when both the subject and the object of the tele relationship have an unimpeded flow of emotional tone toward each other.

Infra tele. The imcompatability of two related individuals who have contrary feelings for each other.

Ambivalent tele. Two related individuals have simultaneously ambivalent feelings for each other.

Projective. This is an aspect of tele not entirely clear but apparently it signifies that one individual in the tele relationship "projects" a stronger feeling tone than does the other individual. One may further make the assumption that some aspect of the future in telic relationships is also intended by the term.

Retrojective. This is a perplexing concept of tele which means that one individual takes unto himself the feeling tones of other individuals "and infuses them with new intensity, throwing them back upon the others, a telic feedback."

Tele for persons, objects, and symbols. These represent a trichotomy of tele affectivity within the individual that has developmental and societal overtones. As man develops and matures from infancy to adulthood, the sensitivity and intenseness of his tele relationships may proceed from persons to objects to symbols in that order. A truly matured adult, we may further assume, has all three tele feelings developed to such a degree that they complement each other within the individual's personality. The child is more successful with people as he begins life than he is with objects or symbols. Gradually, as he grows through the periods of childhood and adolescence into adulthood, he also becomes skilled in tele for things such as bicycles and toys; later for the printed word, spoken word, and all other forms of symbolic tele relationships. Because tele is affected by its six previously named attributes (intensity, sensitivity, simple and infra tele, projective, and retrojective) it may be possible that an individual or group of individuals become more successful and more oriented toward one of these three forms of tele. Something like the following would then be expected to happen: societies which overemphasize tele for persons evolve a high degree of emotionality in their relationships; object tele in its extreme forms creates a technologically oriented society which has little sympathy for people or symbolic ideation; and overtly symbolic tele societies become withdrawn in a contemplative Buddha-like organization with little or no thought of the people in the society or of the use of objects such as food, clothing, and shelter in making comfortable its every day existence. Presumably one aspect of therapy is to help the client to bring all three aspects of tele into complementary order.

Negative, neutral, positive. These are attributes of tele which denote pretty much what the terms mean. One may have a negative tele operating toward persons, objects or things; he would dislike people in general or be bored with objects such as automobiles or dislike reading and other forms of symbolic behavior. Neutral tele indicates a feeling of apathy toward any of the three referrant qualities. Positive tele obviously conveys the idea of an enthusiastic devotee of persons or objects or symbols. Within the same frame of reference the individual may have negative or neutral or positive tele feelings toward different persons without a comparison toward objects or symbols. The reverse would hold true for objects or for symbols. In short, the comparison is not always between persons versus objects or symbols. The comparison may be between persons, objects, or symbols.

"*Tele—Transference—Empathy.* Tele is the binding, constant, integrating forces of reciprocation with two branches: transference, the pathological dissociating aspect, and empathy, the esthetic one-way aspect. As a construct they are separated from tele but *in vivo* they are interwoven."[6]

Telic sensitivity is the smallest unit of feeling that can be measured by a sociometric device (sociogram). However, just as is true in measuring intelligence, tele cannot be measured directly. The sociometrist can measure only the manifestations of telic sensitivity. Moreno feels that by itself tele has no social existence. It is an abstraction. To be understood tele must be considered always as a process within the social atom. "Tele is the fundamental factor underlying our perception of others. We see them, not as they are; nor yet as we are; but as they are in relation to ourselves" (*Sociometry and the Science of Man,* p. 275).

Warming Up Principle

It would be difficult to find an adult who has not witnessed at some time or other an act of warming up. One can find many examples such as an automobile engine being warmed up, track athletes warming up prior to racing, individuals who make circular motions before signing an important document, and singers who vocalize before singing a solo. The business of living is full of examples of the warming up process. As we shall see Moreno attaches great importance to the activity known as *warming up.* It is essential to his theory of man's behavior exemplified in the personality structure.

General Importance. Almost every act of man begins with the act of warming up. Man begins his day by emerging from a state of sleep in a gradual way, warming up for the process of leaving his bed and assuming the state of wakefulness. Even after he gets out of bed, he may need a prolonged period of warming up to the activities and demands of the

[6] Personal communication to the author, May 15, 1962.

coming day. He yawns, he stretches, he scratches himself, and he ponders the immediate problems which have to be met and solved, such as the choice of clothing and the consuming of breakfast. All of this activity can be called a *warming up* for the business of conducting life through one day. At the end of each day man operates in somewhat a reverse order. Then he begins to unwind from the multitude of activities which have absorbed his mind and made demands upon his body. In order to prepare for the cessation of mental and organic activity, he must reverse the process he went through that morning and begin to warm up for sleep. His program of settling down for the night may incorporate certain techniques. Prior to getting into the bed he may snack, or smoke, or read, or watch television, or deliberately turn his mind to the habitual orderly habits of "putting the house to bed" by locking doors, adjusting the thermostat, and the like. Whatever he does and how ever he does it, the activities are designed to be a warming up preliminary to sleep. In between the warming up processes of waking from sleep and putting himself to sleep, man has a day full of activities almost all of which must be preceded by warming up procedures.

There is a circular quality in the relationship of warming up and spontaneity. Warming up creates spontaneity. Spontaneity in turn shortens the period of warming up. Moreno feels that at times he does not know which comes first, warming up or spontaneity, because each is so entwined with the other as to seem to be both cause and effect. Moreno likens this to the ancient paradox of the chicken and the egg.

The usual definition of warming up does not, however, include the many ramifications of its effect upon man's personality.[7] In a sense the shorter and more controlled the process of warming up becomes, the greater the degree of spontaneity which results. Also the shorter the period of warming up, the more efficient the personality becomes in meeting the situations of life. The more quickly one can make preliminary adjustments prior to beginning a task, the less trial and error is involved in "shifting gears," especially in proceeding from one task to another. Consequently one of life's goals in creating a good personality is to be aware of and to appreciate the effect of the warming up period. Efficient warming up pro-

[7] "A brief time at the beginning of a task during which preliminary adjustments are made," H. B. English and A. C. English, *A Comprehensive Dictionary of Psychological and Psychoanalytical Terms*, Longmans, 1958, p. 587. (Courtesy David McKay Co.).

cedures may also reduce emotional anxiety. Take, for example, the ubiquitous intrusion of the telephone call. Answering a telephone permits very little opportunity for warming up to the voice on the other end of the line. The usual reinforcement clues such as the speaker's appearance, the location of the conversation (one expects to talk of bowling in a bowling alley) are absent; the abrupt interrupting ring of the telephone, the voice not always clear and the face unseen, and the disruption of the activity prior to the telephone ringing are not designed to aid the answering party in warming up to the conversation. Emotional anxiety may result, therefore, if the individual does not possess adequate spontaneity and an efficient warming up technique suited to telephone conversations.

Warming up exists before and *in* the course of any act whether the act is creative or not. As we have seen in the previous paragraphs, warming up and spontaneity have a circular effect (one reinforces the other). In later paragraphs we shall see the high degree of reciprocity that exists in the triad of spontaneity–creativity–cultural conserve. Consequently, warming up does not mean the same thing as conditioning. Conditioning implies a set relationship between a stimulus and a response. Although the term *conditioning* has been so widely stretched in usage that it approaches ambiguity, it is not synonymous with our present term *warming up*. To use the previous telephone example, it is true that an individual may become conditioned to respond to the telephone's ringing by arising and answering the call with little or no thought immediately apparent. However automatic that response becomes, he is still confronted with a warming up task the moment he picks up the receiver. From then on the telephone conversation demonstrates that in the act of conversation the individual makes preliminary adjustments and that the manner in which he makes them produces reciprocal adjustments from the respondent. Thus, both prior to the call, and during the call, the warming up process is operating. A conditioned response would produce only a singular behavior pattern. The warming up procedure both prepares the subject for the act and is highly involved in structuring the act as it proceeds from singular act to singular act. As the individual warms up to the telephone conversation, he becomes more spontaneous. As he becomes more spontaneous, he increases to warm up to the situation. In summary, therefore, warming up exists before and in the course of any act whether the act is creative or not, and it is not synonymous with conditioning.

Purely as a sidelight to Moreno's theory it is interesting to note that the current well-publicized high speed electric computers do not possess this fundamental concept of personality which Moreno calls warming up, nor its corollary, spontaneity. The gigantic electric brains possess phenomenal conditioned responses but lack the ingenuity of man's reciprocity to situations.

The Development of Warming Up. How does man gain this capacity for warming up? Moreno feels that the infant, in a developmental sense, is an actor who does not "know his lines." He further feels that one of the miracles of life is how the new-born baby enters life with so little warming up time other than the nine-month gestation period. From the dark, quiet, wet world of the womb, protected by constant temperature and assured of a continuous flow of nourishment, the tiny infant is plunged into a bright, dry, noisy, hot and cold world where he must adjust to irregular feedings regulated by outside forces. Moreno feels the infant needs immediately all the help he can get in developing a minimum of warming up procedures. At best the neonate has only imperfect physical self-starters. In the birth act itself the beginning movements for freedom from the uterus are initiated by the infant, but they must always be aided by others, primarily the mother, the midwife, or the attending physician. The very first warming up procedures that the human being attempts in life are inadequate for the occasion: he must be helped to be born. Life begins with the physical self-starters such as breathing (though the neonate may need help in this by a slap on the bottom), elimination, pulse, and first sucking motions. These soon grow into the realm of interpersonal relations. In a sense all of childhood and adolescence is a warming up period just as is the intrauterine life. What Moreno calls the mental and interpersonal starters (mother, obstetrician, nurses) come to the rescue of the physical starters (sucking, eating, passing gas, breathing, etc.). Mental starters aid the neonate in developing a level of mentation, or the mental processes which actually go along with the significant physical starters. Soon, therefore, the neonate recognizes outside forces which aid his own physical self-starters.

Mentation leads to the development of an auxiliary ego which is an extension of the self, or a substitute person for the self. The persons who feed, clothe, and minister to the neonate become identified as auxiliary egos. The human being retains these auxiliary egos throughout the remainder of his life in the form of husband or wife, mothers and fathers, friends, teachers, leaders, employers, governments, and the like. Parallel with the development and retention for life of one or more auxiliary egos is the development and lifetime retention of auxiliary objects. The bottle which replaces the mother's breast, the thumb which may replace the bottle, the blanket which may replace the uteral warmth, the doll which may replace the past period of protected infancy and so become a pseudo auxiliary ego, and the toy which recaptures uncomplicated childhood may all become auxiliary objects in one form or another for the remainder of life. The importance of auxiliary egos and objects lies in their capacity to shorten the warming up period. If one is dealing with the familiar or its symbol, one does not need to go through a bothersome warming up period for the new and unknown.

Adult Implications. According to Moreno each warming up process has an organic locus of greatest strength. He differs from Freud in his concept of the erogenous zones, because to Moreno the locus is more than the skin itself. As an illustration, the oral zone or locus represents also the condition or type of nipple (mother's breast or rubber nipple), the condition of the milk, the air, and proximity of the infant to the source of milk, all of which are contributing factors to the locus. In like manner hands, feet, and other areas of the body may coact or interact with the original oral zone. The final result is that the location of a warming up process may lie well outside the body itself and be oriented to places, objects, or other human beings.

The warming up process as it strives towards an act may express itself in three ways.

1. Somatic: in which the preliminary steps to adjustment are basically organic, with little or no relationship to the next two methods of expression. There is, however, usually a relationship involved between the methods of expression, although it may be operating covertly. (A miler in a track meet may appear to be jogging around the track merely as a somatic warming up process, but we may presume he is also concerned with the psychological and sociological ramifications of winning or losing the race.)
2. Psychological: which is a warming up time to prepare for the question, "What does it mean to me?". In the above example, a win or a loss in the mile event must be prepared for, along with the physical behavior of the miler during the event.
3. Social: which attempts to prepare for the question, "How does it affect others?".

Moreno distinguishes five types of warming up: undirected, directed, general state, immediate, and chain. The undirected type is vague, chaotic, and confused in its direction. It may involve individuals or groups. A college student called before the dean for reasons not known goes through the process of undirected warming up. There is an alertness to action or response, but the reason and direction for the action are obscure or unknown. The result is a feeling of tenseness with highly undifferentiated behavior.

The directed type of warming up may also be of an individual or group, but the entire action moves toward a specific goal. There is little or no deviation in the progress of the warming up act. Football teams suited up and waiting in the dressing room for the game to begin demonstrate the directed type of warming up. The coach's preliminary remarks, the previous week's practice, the pep rally, the scouting reports are all designed toward the undeviating goal of victory. What the team is warming up for is no mystery. The efficiency of the warming up process may lead to perceptual spontaneity. For example, films of the opponent's team may lead to discovering new ways of meeting the situation by developing counter plays and counter defensive measures.

In the general state of warming up, the person knows that a novel response will be required, but the specific goal is lacking or unclear. A young coed who is about to embark on an arranged blind date may be expected to exhibit the general state type of warming up. She knows something about what is going to happen and dresses and prepares herself cosmetically for a social engagement, but the reciprocity and further warming up that depend upon her date are unknown.

Any kind of emergency situation usually gives rise to the immediate type of warming up. Because there is little or no warming up possible in this situation, the individual must warm up at once with whatever residual capacity he brings from similar situations. If there have been no previous experiences comparable to the emergency situation, the individual will probably utilize a symbolic approach. Failing to have any past experiences similar to the present emergency situation, he may warm up in an entirely inappropriate way to the situation. For example, being told that a person you love dearly has just died calls for an immediate warm up to what the news means and how one is to adjust to it. If one has had past experience in losing a friend, the warm up to the news probably will follow the last pattern. However, because the event is fortunately a rare one, the announcement of a sudden death usually leaves one unprepared. Probably small children give the best examples of the inappropriate response in warming up to the expected social reaction. Their questions may be irrelevant or even crude.

The last type of warming up period that Moreno mentions is the chain. The response of an audience to a comedian can be used for an example. As the comedian tells his jokes to a new audience he gradually builds up laughter as one person after another gets warmed up to this particular comedian's type of humor until finally there is an accumulative effect of one audience member upon the other. Actors in a play may also have the same chain warming up process in regard to each other as they proceed from the first to the last act.

Moreno speaks of some things such as the conceptual trichotomy of truth–beauty–love which do not require a warming up process. In a metaphysical way he feels that whatever is good has beauty and truth in it. Similarly, truth is both beautiful and good, and finally beauty contains truth and goodness; hence the spontaneity and creativity which follow these stimuli do not need a warming up period.

In the final analysis, life cannot be played without one's warming up to all of its endeavors. The warming up process is significant in the roles we play in our every day living as well as in the roles that are played in Moreno's therapeutic techniques of psychodrama.

Role Playing Principle

Moreno's name has become highly identified with the term *role playing*, primarily as a psychotherapeutic technique. As we shall see, however, the theoretical aspects of role playing in the life of man have contributed much to personality theory. To Moreno the roles that man plays and must play in life are more than artificially staged psychodrama, they are attempts at self-realization, but are often frustrated. In addition to the kind of roles that human personalities play, there is an equal emphasis upon other aspects of role taking: how we get our roles and how we feel about them. This idea goes beyond the idea of what our roles in life are.

Actors in early Greek drama literally read their lines from scrolls or rolls. From this has come the extension of meaning and change in the spelling of the word to indicate that one who takes a role is an actor. We now define role almost synonymously with role playing as "the characteristic function and contribution of an individual in a group, as well as the expected behavior and position defined by the group for the individual." Because everyone is expected to live up to his official role in society, conflict may arise between the self and the roles man has to play in society. Adolescents, for example, can be expected to have role confusion and contradiction in their behavior as they are trying to learn their roles. At other times a half-learned or poorly learned role may cause one to have anxiety. Viewing the human personality from the role playing frame of reference, we may say that man strives for sociostasis (to maintain his status in the group) rather than homeostasis (maintaining his status within himself as a person).

In the Morenian sense role playing is a subform of psychodrama and sociodrama. Although the terms *psychodrama* and *sociodrama* are frequently used interchangeably, Read Bain even coined the term *psychosociodrama,* there are implied some subtle and not so subtle differences between the terms. Generally speaking, psychodrama implies a deeper level of therapy than does sociodrama. In methodology there is not quite the same pronounced difference. Other differences may be roughly summarized as follows: psychodrama may concern itself with an individual's depth diagnosis and therapy, while sociodrama may concern itself more often with group diagnosis and therapy; psychodrama emphasizes the individual, while sociodrama emphasizes the group and the individual's place in the group. *Psychodrama* is an older word than *sociodrama;* psychodrama primarily attempts to change individual behavior while sociodrama primarily attempts to change group behavior; the concern in the former is, "Individual, heal thyself," in the latter, "Community, heal thyself." Psychodrama is a measure of the individual while sociodrama is a measure of the group; in psychodrama the actors represent individual personalities while in sociodrama the actors represent the group. And in the final analysis, all depends upon one's viewpoint: one may look at a group interacting and interpret it as a psychodramatic event while another viewing the same scene may interpret it as an example of sociodrama. The writer does not wish to convey the thought, "You pays your money and takes your choice," but often in usage the terms do become confused.

Historical Background. Jacob Moreno was not the first writer to employ the concept of role or role playing, although the term has been tightly associated with his name. The Shakespearean quotation which introduces this chapter indicates a prior use of the concept of role playing in life. George Herbert Mead, of the University of Chicago, was much concerned with the roles man takes. During the period 1911 to 1925 Mead lectured often and eloquently on the structure of society as seen from the role-taking process of man. Mead's book, *Mind, Self, and Society,* published posthumously (Univer. Chicago Press, 1934), finally spelled out his explanation of how societies are constructed through the roles its constituents must take.

Moreno wrote to me concerning Mead: "Mead was an excellent theoretician and observer but to our knowledge he never carried out a single experiment in role playing and did not formulate any design for role research. It is a long step from observing and analyzing role taking as found in society to experimenting with role playing and developing a first body of empirical research as Moreno has done. Eleven years before Mead's book was published, Moreno published his book *Das Stegreiftheater* which appeared in 1923. It already contained such terms and concepts as role player and role playing. It was he who later introduced most of the current concepts and terms—role practice, role research, role reversal, role perception, role enactment, role expectancy, etc."

In the meantime, Moreno was passing from his medical work to a greater and absorbing interest in role playing as an activity, but not as a description of society as in the case of Mead. Starting around 1911 Moreno began to experiment and work out his theoretical ideas on role playing and allied concepts. The first sessions were conducted in the gardens of Vienna in a highly informal atmosphere. These sessions culminated in the first structured performance which took place on April 1, 1921, at the Komoedian Haus, a theater for drama in Vienna. During the period 1911 to 1924 Moreno was also involved in other activities which had strong sociodramatic overtones, such as the vast effort, in 1916, to relocate southern Tyrol natives who were being displaced from their mountain homes by the threat of advancing Italian troops during World War I. How Moreno and others attempted to reform these people in Mittendorf, a settlement adjacent to Vienna, makes a fascinating account and one which helped him further to formulate his theories. Finally, role playing through the avenue of psychodrama and sociodrama found a home in the Stegreiftheater of Vienna in 1923. Moreno's work with role playing was continued in the United States with the establishment of The Impromptu Group Theatre, performing at Carnegie Hall, New York City, 1923–1931, and the first theater for psychodrama, in Beacon, New York, 1935.

General Theorems. None of the following general theorems is stated directly by Moreno although he does refer to general theorems. The following have been culled out of his writings in order to present a clearer position of the "role" of role playing in his work.

1. Roles may be imaginary or real, based on fantasy or fact.
2. Through the medium of play one may personify other forms of life by taking and acting out roles.
3. The personality can be taught to expand itself and to explore the unknown through the avenue of role playing.
4. Role playing can change personality as well as study personality.
5. Role playing may bolster the individual's ego.
6. Role playing, especially through the method of sociodrama, can be an effective technique for reducing the distance between two variant ethnic groups.
7. The more roles one learns to play the greater flexibility one has in dealing with the problems of life.
8. Roles which are learned efficiently reduce the warming up period necessary to changing life conditions. (Note Polonius's advice to Laertes, "To thine own self be true . . .")
9. The individual learns about society primarily through the roles he plays.

Development. With a rather sophisticated phrase Moreno described the child as, *"Megalomania 'Normalis'—Dosim Repetatur."* Thus, using his previous training as a medical doctor, Moreno diagnosed the child's first role as a megalomaniac and then stated that the prescription to retain this inner core of the first role is to repeat it. Out of this super self-centered role that the infant first plays, he must gradually and at times painfully learn all the new roles that society demands of him as well as learning the new roles he desires for himself. The latter roles of self-choice may defy society's demands, or they may be ignored by society, especially when they are roles played at the fantasy level. (Perhaps James Thurber's "The Secret Life of Walter Mitty" exemplifies fantasy at the adult level.) Through all of the developmental process of role playing runs the central theme of the infant and his normal megalomania. The core of his personality is supported by referring continuously in life to his own self, or by "repeated doses," as Moreno phrases it. All other roles revolve around this central core, and all other roles are subordinate to the core of self. The *modus operandi,* as we shall see in the next section, by which man learns to expand his roles, is the technique of role reversal.

Role Reversal. Moreno places a heavy emphasis on role reversal. Role reversal is important both as a learning technique for children and adults and as a method of therapy for individuals and social groups. To a pointed degree role reversal is the heart of role playing theory as demonstrated in psychodrama and sociodrama. Role reversal is the foundation of a balanced personality, although, as we shall see later, the individual can never completely reverse a role. By being able to see the world through other eyes through role reversal, one can, for limited times, break the terrible trap of always being one's self. We get bored with ourselves. We are very limited in our self-perceptual systems. We need the viewpoint of others to correct our own myopia concerning the world. In a larger sense, Moreno feels that man may be able to achieve a lasting peace between nations if he can cultivate and maintain the capacity to reverse roles with the peoples of all nations. Thus, role reversal may also be the *sine qua non* of a balanced society on earth.

Moreno poses some hypotheses regarding the indispensable nature of role reversal. Some of these grew out of his experience with his son Jonathan when the son was between the ages of two to three. Other hypotheses are extracted from his work in psychodrama and sociodrama both in the United States and in Europe. The following listing of role reversal hypotheses is only partial and the order of presentation is not significant.

1. Role reversal is a technique of socialization and self-integration.
2. Role reversal is an indispensable requirement for establishing a psychodramatic community.
3. Role reversal may be a corrective method for unsocial behavior.
4. Role reversal is an invaluable teaching and learning device.
5. Role reversal may go through three critical stages: (1) inferior subhuman beings such as animals or insects, (2) nonhuman objects such as machines, trees, stones, water, automobiles, and (3) superior and powerful beings like parents, teachers, God, or a devil.
6. Role reversal tends to decrease the dependency of a child towards his parents.
7. Role reversal is most effective when the psychological distance between the two individuals is small.
8. Role reversal increases role perception.
9. The more roles the individual plays in life the greater his capacity to reverse roles.
10. Children use their parents as a natural untrained auxiliary ego object in role reversals.
11. Role reversal requires specific techniques which must be mastered in order to benefit from the viewpoint of the other person.

Moreno concedes that complete role reversal is not possible in practicality. Reciprocity is a necessary function of role reversal (that is, the other object must give some response in turn), so that in no. 5 of the above hypotheses, for example, the child has trouble getting a stone, dog, or authority figure to respond to its efforts.

Role Playing Relationship to Spontaneity and Creativity. There is a close reciprocal relationship between role playing and spontaneity–creativity. Role playing is the avenue to the making of a truly spontaneous individual. Out of spontaneity comes the creativity that man needs to exist in this world. However, if an individual tightly structures his role, he creates one form of the phenomenon that Moreno calls *cultural conserve.* By "storing up" his capacity to play a role in which the individual does not deviate from a set pattern of behavior, he loses the advantage of further spontaneity–creativity.

According to Moreno, the past structures man's roles, the present governs the action of these roles, and the future sets the goals for his roles. If spontaneity and the resultant creativity are allowed to be an integral part of all roles man plays, he may automatically play each role in full concert with the past, present, and future. Without spontaneity–creativity a role may be frozen into the past, the present, or the future. Roles which are structured in the past emphasize regressive infantile behavior, while roles structured only in the present lack a central core of behavior and vacillate wildly according to the stimuli present at the moment. Roles cast in the future are inclined to remain at the phantasy level with little or no application to problems of the moment. Therefore, without spontaneity which helps create new roles, man is unable to develop through life a personality suited to his highest potential.

Kinds of Roles. Moreno differentiates three kinds of roles: psychosomatic, social, and psychodramatic. Psychosomatic role taking emerges out of the functions of reality and the functions of fantasy that the infant copes with from birth. If he merges his reality and fantasy roles successfully, the child is able to accept and use the one set of roles Moreno calls *psychosomatic roles.* Once this is done successfully, the individual may orient himself toward persons, things, and goals that actually exist outside of himself. This orientation is called the *social role.* Psychodramatic roles grow out of orientation towards persons, things, and goals which the individual imagines are outside of himself. "They are called respectively *social roles* (the parent) and *psychodramatic roles* (the god)" (*Sociometry and the Science of Man,* p. 152).

Abuses of Role Playing. Moreno condemns the practice of collecting

various people into a situation where they are encouraged to start a conversation about anything they want in the hopes that something significant
will emerge from just talking. The assumption is that if enough people
talk about enough things, an idea will result beneficial to all, merely
through statistical probability. He terms this practice the *role playing
fallacy*. It may occur in a social setting, in an educational classroom as a
teaching technique, or in an advertising agency as a method called
brainstorming. Wherever it occurs, Moreno feels it cannot achieve its
objective of creativity because an adequate warming up period is assumed
to exist in the operation itself. Without an adequate warm up the spontaneity which should follow is lacking, and without spontaneity one cannot hope for creative results. What usually results in free play discussion
is a pot pourri of words leading to confusion and a resultant feeling of
disenchantment among the participants.

Spontaneity Principle

If man is ever to move beyond his present position, Moreno feels, he
must act spontaneously toward the problems of life. Acknowledging Berg-
son's contribution of the *élan vital*, Moreno has moved far beyond the
concept of a vital and creative force which is in all living things and has
been the root of all evolutionary progress. Beginning with this Bergsonian
concept, Moreno has evolved a dynamic design to describe the human
personality.

Spontaneity may be described as "the self-initiated behavior of man."
Moreno calls it a hypothesis, an entity that no one actually sees. Difficulty
in defining *spontaneity* does not relieve the personality theorist of asking
its meaning. Spontaneity is the "here and now," and not a mere time sequence. To Moreno it is "Man in action, man thrown into action, the moment *not* a part of history but history as a part of the moment" (*Sociometry
and the Science of Man*, p. 60). Because of spontaneity, Moreno feels
that in his therapeutic practices he works forward while the psychoanalyst
works backward.

Spontaneity, or the *s-factor*, is inseparably and strategically linked with
creativity, yet they are distinct. Similarly the s-factor is inextricably mixed
with the process of warming up. In all considerations of spontaneity this
interdependence must not be ignored. Warming up begets spontaneity
which in turn begets creativity. As we shall see later, the resultant condition is the cultural conserve.

Although spontaneity has a degree of novelty, it is far more than a novel response to a new situation. Psychotics are capable of giving a novel response, but the result may be chaotic. The individual who is highly spontaneous, but not at all creative, is what Moreno calls a *spontaneous idiot*. In addition to being novel, the response must be adequate to the situation. To avoid the adequate response which is stereotyped, the s-factor must contain 1. appropriateness to the situation, 2. a degree of competency for a solution to the situation, and 3. immediacy to the here-and-now situation. A genius, Moreno feels, exemplifies at times complete spontaneity.

Importance of Spontaneity. Moreno states that spontaneity and its corollary, creativity, are of such immense importance that they are *the* problem of psychology and of indeed the universe. Without the s-factor, man is reduced to stereotyped behavior which paralyzes the personality. "Robotism is the opposite of spontaneity." The individual or group in any species that insists upon perpetuating the same response to a situation soon faces the problem of extinction. The prehistoric dinosaur perished because he was unable to create spontaneously new modes of behavior to adjust to changing conditions. The quiet vegetablelike imbecile with the stereotyped behavior of banging his head on the floor would soon cease to exist but for the gentle help of others.

Spontaneity releases the latent genius in mankind. Because he can be spontaneous and create new things, man moves off dead center and accumulates the cultural conserves that enable him to be healthier, more productive, and better able to meet new situations. Through spontaneity man exercises the right to a free society. Through group spontaneity society can change some of its conditions through referendum or through the rejection and selection of its elected officials. In a group, the self-initiated capacity, which is Moreno's spontaneity, pushes its leaders forward. Dictatorships quell spontaneity; democracies are founded upon spontaneity and can exist only as long as its constituents spontaneously create new methods to move forward. The American Revolution may be an example of this phenomenon. Gardner Murphy credits Moreno not only for contribution of tele as a personality factor but also for the importance of spontaneity testing and especially spontaneity training as indispensable adjuncts of the human personality.

The importance of spontaneity also rests on the premise that there always exists a certain degree of unpredictability in life. If we know the future, we should not need spontaneity. If the future is unknown or half-known, the individual and/or the human race must possess an adequate degree of flexibility. If the future is known, a fixed pattern of behavior may be worked out to meet the problems of the future; but since it appears the future is not known, it is incumbent upon the collective personality or the singular personality to prepare for the future by acknowledging spontaneity as a key tool to change, and by training as adequately as possible, the capacity to meet changing conditions. Through the avenue of spontaneity training, the individual and the group may better prepare themselves for adjusting to whatever the future may bring. If the above premises are true, then it is mandatory that man appreciate the value and importance of spontaneity as a method of preparing for the unpredictable future.

Development of Spontaneity. Moreno states that fortunately for man birth is not a trauma but a good beginning for spontaneity. The s-factor begins at birth or even before birth through the built-in medium of act-hunger. Even before the infant is born, he moves his foetal body, squirms, and at times causes the mother some discomfort. Thus the genesis of self-initiated behavor is first noticed. Immediately after birth the s-factor begins to expand at a greatly increased rate, as the neonate initiates the demand for food, begins to eliminate urine, and responds to its new environment. Moreno claims the infant could not survive without a built-in s-factor. The obstetrician, the nurse, and the mother can do only so much for the newly emerged human being, and the remaining effort to stay alive is up to him. Later as the neonate develops through infancy and childhood, he continues to exercise the s-factor. Spontaneity training and spontaneity testing are further developed as the human being increases in locomotion, response to parents, siblings and others, and efficiency of its own organic system. "Lack of spontaneity generates anxiety. Anxiety increases as spontaneity decreases."

The development of spontaneity becomes a course in reality testing. To test reality the child makes tentative actions initiated by himself to see if something will work. These reality testings are things which no other can do for him. Gradually the child begins to distinguish between himself and external reality. Although spontaneity is bounded by the institutional setting, there is always room for individual freedom of expression of the spontaneity core. Through the s-factor the human personality learns to differentiate between his psychosomatic roles (eater, sleeper, sex roles), his psychodramatic roles (god, angel, Santa Claus, etc.) and his social roles (father, policeman, doctor, etc.).

Individual differences emerge in the amount of s-factor each human possesses. Starting at birth with his nipple behavior and his ability or lack of ability to relate to his environment, as well as the amount of nature-given inner drive, the human personality reaches adulthood with varying amounts of spontaneity. Consequently the s-factor is distributed unevenly in the human race and probably in all other species. Some of us have a high amount of s-factor while others have little. In addition to the differences in the s-factor that exists between individuals, it is also unevenly distributed during the lifetime of one person. The following summary presents the rise and fall of spontaneity within one person:

Infancy: at birth a great increase proportionately, but low output in general,
Childhood: highest the s-factor will ever be,
Adolescence: high, but fluctuates extremely, due to environmental pressures to conform and also role confusion,
Early adulthood: diminishing,
Adulthood: a true plateau stage, and
Later adulthood: fading and highly stereotyped with little or no s-factor prevalent.

Types of Spontaneity. Moreno finds it useful to differentiate three types of spontaneity. In the first type, he feels there is a novel response to a situation but a response not adequate to the situation. Psychotics, for example, may state that two times two are five, certainly a novel response but hardly one that is adequate. Children also are prone to give novel but inadequate responses. Novelty without adequacy becomes an undisciplined or pathological spontaneity.

The second type is the spontaneous response, which is quite adequate to the situation but lacks sufficient novelty or significant creativity to be fruitful to the situation. Such spontaneity soon descends to a stereotyped response and becomes trite. The comedian's repetitive reaction to a situation soon loses its novelty, and although it may continue to provoke some laughter, it soon ceases to be a spontaneous response. Cultural conserves in the form of art, music, and literature may also lack spontaneity although they may serve as warming up procedures for further spontaneity.

The first two types of spontaneity are false; the third type Moreno considers to be true spontaneity. In this type there is an adequate response always accompanied by characteristics that are both novel and creative. The resulting phenomenon may be in the form of an act or a substantive article such as a poem, story, art object, or piece of machinery. To be truly spontaneous the results must be in some way new, and the results must be useful for some purpose.

Forms of Spontaneity. In somewhat the same fashion as he delineates types of spontaneity, Moreno also postulates three forms of spontaneity. These he calls the *pathological variety,* the *stereotype variety,* and the *high-grade creativity variety.* In the pathological form there is novelty but negligible adequacy and very little creativity. In the stereotype form there is adequacy but negligible novelty and very little creativity. In the high-grade creativity form there is a harmonious combination of novelty and adequacy leading to productive creativity.

Spontaneity–Creativity–Cultural Conserve. Spontaneity does not exist in a vacuum. Spontaneity must be *for* something. As previously intimated the s-factor in its truest form always leads to the creation of something. Creativity may produce a new way of behaving for the individual, a new way of behaving for the group, or a new building, poem, story, oil painting, industry, or form of government. The product of the spontaneity –creativity continuum is called a *cultural conserve.*

The relationship is reciprocal between spontaneity–creativity–cultural conserve. Assume that an artist has gone through the warming up procedures in painting a picture by erecting his easel, mixing the paints, and casting about for an appropriate subject to paint. From this point he utilizes whatever degree of spontaneity he possesses to create the picture. The result of his creative efforts is a cultural conserve. Now the process may be reversed so that the finished painting serves to warm the artist up to do another painting on the same subject using different techniques. In still another way, the completed painting may serve to warm up and cause a degree of spontaneity in a second artist who in turn will create a cultural conserve. Thus the trichotomized concept of spontaneity–creativity–cultural conserve moves back and forth and has done so throughout the history of man.

Moreno makes the plea, however, that a cultural conserve can "freeze" the best efforts of the human personality to be spontaneous and creative. If the resulting cultural conserve becomes too sacred and too immutable in the minds of man, it will serve to thwart his best efforts to create behavioral patterns to meet the changes that time inevitably brings. Old facts are good only in the sense that they can be applied to new, demanding current situations. To worship the old simply for its reliquary value is fruitless, Moreno believes. To illustrate the point, he feels that philosophers can oversell the cultural conserve value of Socrates, Plato, or Aristotle when they are held as sacrosanct idols of the past with no capacity to influence the present. In the same vein man is held back by the provincialisms of the medieval past just as much as by the chauvinistic national fervor of the present—cultural conserves that stultify the future needs of such organizations as the United Nations and its service adjuncts like UNESCO and WHO. The human personality for itself or for its society cannot afford to cling to outmoded cultural conserves which block the spontaneous efforts to create newer things.

Fortunately for mankind, the "mortar" of spontaneity holds together the bricks of the cultural conserve which man has created to build a life and a civilization. To Moreno the Sermon on the Mount is an excellent example of a cultural conserve which can create a better personality if it is not relegated to the past as an untouchable law but is spontaneously used to foster current thinking. "The conserve has done a great deal to encourage the alienation of the self from total self-realization, the technological alienation of Marx is only a small part of it. More than any other single factor the conserve has stimulated the development of the robot."

Creativity Principle

"Creativity is a separate entity from spontaneity and a separate entity from cultural conserve but strategically linked to both," Moreno has said to me.

Moreno considers spontaneity as the chief catalyzer of creativity. Here he means that ideas are brought together by spontaneous action, and, if one is lucky and/or persistently spontaneous about his output, a creative act may occur. As in all catalyzers the spontaneity is not changed. The spontaneity may bubble off in all directions as it does in what he termed the *spontaneous idiot*. Providing, however, that the spontaneous output is genuine and persistent, there usually occurs a creative act. As we shall see later, the resulting creativity may not produce a phenomenal work of art but may be indeed only a new tele relationship between two human personalities. Moreno suggests that creativity can be defined better operationally and pragmatically by its results than by a purely semantic approach. Traditionally, creativity is defined as "bringing something new into being," whether it be an act of behavior or a construct such as a building, work of literature, or a form of government. However one defines the word *creativity*, Moreno feels that the results may be new to the individual but not necessarily to the rest of the world, as we see in a child creating for himself a new relationship to others; or it may be new to the individual and new to the world at large. The crux of creativity to Moreno is not that one discovers anything that man has never known before or that has never to man's knowledge ever existed before, but that in most cases a new relationship has been created which did not exist before.

Importance of Creativity. In Moreno's book *Who Shall Survive?* (1934), the implication is that only the creative man or animal can survive, especially in a world of technocracy. (The student of history may recall that during the depths of the Depression much of the blame for unemployment was directed at machines which were replacing men.) It is readily seen what immense importance Moreno attaches to the creative act. To be creative means more than to be adaptable. The springs in a sofa are adaptable: they depress and adapt to the weight of a person's body. What is of importance here is that the creativity factor leads humanity to respond constructively to new situations rather than merely to adapt to new situations.

Moreno likens the personality that is not creative to the robot. He feels the robot conserves and reacts to situations but cannot create new situations. It is in the treachery of assuming too much from automatons that the personality is likely to defeat itself and fail to survive in a changing world situation. The personality must not only *meet* new situations, but it must *create* new situations, for which it can be prepared.

Creativity is of such importance that Moreno uses the concept to explain how some societies are better able to provide a higher standard of living than are others. He coins the word *creatocracy* to describe the scientific democracy which he feels the United States has become in order to emerge as a world power. Admitting that Americans live in a continent which is blessed with tremendous resources, we still see that they would be unable to use these resources if it were not for their creativity. In contrast, Moreno feels the European nations have held too conservatively to the cultural domains of the past.

Generality of Creativity. The true value of creativity is to be found in daily living, not in the creation of the usual cultural conserves such as operas, best sellers, and huge architectural edifices. Creativity is the central core of human behavior as it is lived from day to day.

Moreno said to me: " 'The future of a culture is finally decided by the creativity of its carriers. If a disease of creative functions, a creativity neurosis, has afflicted the most primary group, the creative men of the human race, then it is of supreme importance that the principle of creativity be redefined and that its perverted forms be compared with creativity in its original states' (*Creativity and the Cultural Conserves*, 1939). There are higher and lower forms of creativity. The highest forms of human creativity are manifest in the lives and works of prophets, poets, saints, and scientists."

It is erroneous, Moreno believes, to assume that only the mentally gifted are capable of being creative. The housewife as she prepares a meal for her family may at times be highly creative in the combinations of foods she serves. The salesman must perforce be creative as he exercises the tele component and social atomic structure in dealing with a tremendous variety of clients' personalities. The schoolteacher employs creativity as she adjusts the curricular material to meet the variant abilities of her students. In fact, it would be difficult to live a normal life without being creative because maintenance of normality requires one to be spontaneous enough to create behavior adequate to the inevitable changes in life. The neurotic and the psychotic may fail to make adjustments because of their noncreative stereotyped behavior. It is true, however, that people of small talent may need longer warming up periods to be creative than the aristocrats of the mind, as Moreno names them.

Creativity is the core of all organic existence. Trees, flowers, vegetables, paramecia, and people must be creative in order to survive. This factor of creativity is general throughout the universe and is general in the daily existence of all living things.

It is for these strongly stated reasons that Moreno emphasizes the therapeutic technique of spontaneity–creativity. If one accepts the assumptions that the more creative the personality, the more problems it can solve, and that the more creative it is the better it can structure and predict the future, then it seems mandatory to Moreno that we must train for creativity.

Forms of Creativity. As with spontaneity Moreno here differentiates three forms of creativity: 1. chance—the type of creative act that happens by pure luck and can rarely be duplicated and which may further cause the person to be unable to appreciate or use what has been created; 2. spontaneous creativity—bringing something new into being from a feeling of spontaneity which is designed to meet an immediate purpose; 3. conservable creativity—wherein the thing created does not necessarily meet an immediate purpose (for example, a painting, poetry); there is very little, if any, feedback in conservable creativity. There always is in the second type.

Cultural Conserve Principle

The last of the triad, spontaneity–creativity–cultural conserve, to be discussed as a principle, is the cultural conserve. Although in a sense, cultural conserve is the end product of the entire process which begins with the warming up period, the flow is not always in one direction.

By definition, a cultural conserve is anything that preserves the values of a particular culture. It is the finished product of the creative process. Normally the cultural conserve is considered to be a material object such as a film, book, building, or musical composition. However, it may also take the form of a stylized ballet, a religious ceremony, or any highly set pattern of behavior. The Viennese salutation "Grüss Gott" is a cultural conserve. Fraternity initiation ceremonies are cultural conserves, as are the inaugural ceremonies for the President of the United States.

Strengths of Cultural Conserves. Cultural conserves perform an important function in the development of the civilization of mankind. Without them man would be reduced to creating spontaneously the same forms to meet the same situations, day after day. Dictionaries, for example, are highly useful cultural conserves. Because of them man does not have to redefine his word every time he wishes to use it.

As a repository of the past, cultural conserves preserve and continue man's creative ego. When they are used properly, as we shall see later, they give continuity to the heritage of human personality. The vestigial qualities of cultural conserves may serve to represent the past power of an organization which holds it together, until newer forms of creativity once again give it the vigor it needs for survival. When actual power or superiority ceases to exist in the human personality, for instance, it may coast on the accumulated strengths of the past until new spontaneous creative behavior begins to take hold. A recently widowed woman may be sustained by the cultural conserves of the past, money, status, and living accommodations, until she gradually warms up to the new role and is able once again to create spontaneously a new role to meet the new situations in which she finds herself.

The proper use of a cultural conserve is that of a springboard for enticing new spontaneity toward creativity. When the pianist interprets "Clair de Lune," for example, he brings to it a modified degree of spontaneity in his playing, which is probably different from the composer's, and thus he creates a new impression upon his audience with each playing of the composition. When an actor portrays the role of Shakespeare's Macbeth, he, too, adds spontaneity and creativity to the well-known characterization. Every cultural conserve has the capacity to arouse new spontaneity and creativity if the new cultural conserve form is not a strict replication. A correct attitude toward a cultural conserve allows all of us to enjoy symphonies, records, fiction, paintings, and ceremonies, and to enjoy them as a boost toward further creativity.

Weaknesses of Cultural Conserves. Moreno states, however, that the world is full of "lovers of conserves" who deliberately or unconsciously freeze the conserve into an untouchable, sacred form. The danger of the cultural conserve lies both in its state of finality and in the abuse of it by mankind. In the first place, once spontaneity and creativity have been conserved in the culture of a people, the twin factors no longer exist as an actuality in the universe. In the second place, the sanctification of conserves is a hard habit to break. The conserve is comforting and maternal. To idealize it is to regress. Weak personalities in particular are prone to seek the security of the conserve and shy from the unpredictability of creating something new from the old. Consequently such valuable conserves as the Bible, great books, great symphonies, and so forth may become objects of worship in themselves, and be ignored for the good they can accomplish as warming up stimuli and spontaneity agents for current creative living.[8]

Forms of Cultural Conserves. Moreno mentions three forms that cultural conserves may take. They are described and illustrated as follows.

1. Burned-out: This is a cultural conserve which has lost its value but continues to be. The pyramids of Egypt, the many-staired Inca temples, old political campaign songs, and stereotyped nineteenth-century portraits are possible examples of the conserve which has lost its ability to create spontaneity. Outdated textbooks may not be ignored in this category, either.

2. Inflammable: The conserve that has the capacity to excite interest and

_____

[8] The student is invited to read Marshall Fishwick on "Robert E. Lee: The Guardian Angel Myth," in the March 4, 1961 issue of *Saturday Review.* Fishwick in no way demeans Lee but postulates that the South has misused Lee in regarding him as a legend to be preserved, rather than as a man to be learned from.

devotees. Examples may be found in current best-seller books; in popular musical comedies like "My Fair Lady" (which came from another cultural conserve that had the capacity to foster spontaneity and creativity, *Pygmalion*); in the political figure with a "new" face and a creative program in the tradition of Franklin Roosevelt in the Depression of the early Thirties; or Winston Churchill during World War II.

3. Eternalized: The Talmud, the Koran, the Bible are examples of this third class of idolized conserve. To be eligible for this classification the conserve must still possess the ability to arouse new enthusiasms, and have the freshness and appeal and vitality to meet current situations.

Although it may appear at this point that cultural conserves may have little or nothing to do with the human personality operating in daily life, quite the opposite is true. The way an individual conducts himself in the pattern of day-to-day living may itself be harmed or helped by the conserve he preserves. Anachronistically dressed U.S. Senators are a cultural conserve of the personal sort. All of us, Moreno asserts, may have hidebound roles which we slavishly play in duplication of the cultural conserve. This conservation of a role may help or harm us in the work our personalities must do in normal living. The scientist who perpetuates his role in sloppy research, the minister who fails to unbend and recognize current issues, the middle-aged woman who frantically and ludicrously tries to preserve an unpreservable youth, and even the perpetual college freshman are all illustrations of the cultural conserve as it applies to the human personality. On the other side of the coin, the conservation of a role may also be quite helpful in stress situations. For examples of this, we may look to the Marine who plays a role of avowed heroism out of a long tradition of heroism in the Marine Corps. As he conserves the role his culture has given to him, he somewhat automatically acts brave whether he feels brave or not. According to his culture the Marine is supposed to act brave in the dangers of a battle. Other examples of the culture conserving a role to benefit the role player and others are the autocratic role for teachers of recalcitrant children, the deterrent effect of the policeman's uniform in riots, the willingness to help the infant, and the quality of humility and fellowship in a devout church congregation.

Group Development Principle

The last three principles (Group Development, Sociogenetic Law, Measurement) that are extracted from Moreno's work by the present author are not as vital as the previous ones but are, nevertheless, basic to an understanding of his system.

In a previous discussion dealing with the social atom the concept of the psychosocial network was presented. The present principle of group development is an extension of the psychosocial network.

Because Moreno is primarily a therapist, the group development principle can be interpreted as a philosophy of adjustment. He feels that his work in psychodrama and sociodrama which center on role play have at last broken the deadlock of secretiveness that has too often surrounded psychotherapy. His techniques are out in the open and, in fact, can only operate with others in an open fashion. In contrast to this the psychoanalyst operates in a sensitive one-to-one relationship that almost defies study by a third party. The student of personality may wonder what place the study of group development has in the study of individual human personality. There is the implication in Moreno's work that weaknesses in society have the same causal factors as weaknesses in the individual personality. Just as individuals have personalities, so also do societies. And, of course, there is the known sociological position that a society, an ethnic group, a culture, are composites of individuals: an obvious fact. Essentially the preceding principle means that a philosophy of adjustment applies equally well to societies as to individuals.

We may now address ourselves to the question Moreno poses: Do societies (and/or individuals within it) change somewhat in the Marxian economic frame of reference, or do they grow and then decline in the tradition of Spengler's or Toynbee's theses? Moreno indicates that both positions are assumptions that may or may not be accurate and that further sound research along the lines of sociodramatic techniques is needed. It may be that societies do both. Certainly, Moreno feels, the individual personality grows from a simple organism into a highly complex and highly differentiated organism. Therefore, if society parallels individuals in their matrices, we may conclude that society has a natural development of growth and decline, and as it develops, it also influences its constituent individuals. Whatever we say of the individual may be an interpretation of his society. Both individuals and groups develop according to the same pattern.

One more introductory theme is needed prior to a basic discussion of the periods, chronology, and characteristics of individuals as they develop into groups and groups as they develop from the effect the individuals have upon them. Using Greek mythology, as he so often does, Moreno employs the gods Eros (god of love), Eris (god of discord), and the lesser known brother of Eros, Anteros who is the god of mutual love, to exemplify the forces of attraction and repulsion among men. As the personality develops in groups, it demonstrates all the capacities of Eros, Eris, and Anteros. Between personalities there is attraction in the form of love, repulsion in the form of hatred, and mutual attraction in the form of reciprocal fellowship, compassion, sympathy, and empathy for one another. Their development is treated in the next section.

Periods of Group Development. The reciprocity of maturing sociability that exists between individuals and their groups follows somewhat the ensuing patterns as Moreno distinguishes them.

Presocialized period: from birth to around 7 or 9 years of age individuals singly and in groups show a diffuse pattern. Most of the action is independent and uncoordinated. Roles are poorly structured. Toward the latter part of the period, strong telic relationships may be found but the incidence of developing attraction, repulsion, and mutual attraction patterns is slow and spasmodic. The social atom structure is probably the strongest factor that exists with the exception of unbridled spontaneity. The value of the warm up and the recognition of strong tele feelings is missing. In short, the child up to the ages of 7 or 9 has a poorly formed personality as does the age group he belongs to.

First socialized period: from 7 to 9 years to around 13 or 14 years of age. There is a rapid increase in both individual and group socialization. The children of this age group are now capable of organizing and operating independent social groups without adult help or interference. Each child now has the capacity to develop and use a telic relationship based on real properties of aversion and affection, and from the tele content strong role structures are being created by their peer society and by themselves.

Second socialized period: the last period that Moreno mentions runs from 13 to 14 years of age into full maturity. Whereas in the first socialization period there was a cleavage between adult and child groups, these differences are now disappearing, especially as the adolescent takes on more and more adult values. At the beginning of the period the sexual cleavages and the racial cleavages are emerging to become, at the adult level, a fully developed cleavage. If a full personality emerges, there is then a full set of principles operating through the Morenian frame of reference:

tele, warm up, role playing, spontaneity–creativity–cultural conserve, and especially the sociogenetic law that will be introduced in a coming section.

Stages of Group Development. Moreno includes these stages as a part of the first socialized group mentioned in the previous paragraphs, but they are discussed separately here for clearer understanding. The period from birth to about the ages of 6 to 8 years is the intersexual stage. The period from 8 to 13 years is the first homosexual stage. From the ages of 13 to 15 Moreno feels there is a parallel set of stages called the second intersexual stage and the second homosexual stage. The meaning is clear that Moreno is not talking about sex *per se,* in the Freudian term of reference, but rather saying that groups are developed with like-sexed or heterosexual emphases. In this case *intersexual* means "between sexes" and *homosexual* means "between the same sex."

Characteristics of Group Development. As previously mentioned, Moreno feels that one of the characteristics of groups as they develop is the cleavage between racial groups. This cleavage is the result of prejudicial attitudes which children get from the adults who surround or control them. Because children wish to meet the approval of their elders, it does not matter if the adults are controlling factors (parents, teachers, etc.) or environmental adult figures with no direct control of the child's behavior. The effect is the same.

Another characteristic of group development is the horizontal and vertical vectors of development. By *horizontal vectors,* Moreno means "interrelatedness in a group with no individual at the top or bottom." By *vertical vectors* he means "a feeling in the group of a hierarchical order from top to bottom in relation to one or more factors." Moreno first began to study this phenomenon by arranging nine babies in a circular position equidistant from each other for about the first year of life. Until approximately the ages of 20 to 28 weeks the infants existed in organic isolation with each infant absorbed in itself. After about 20 to 28 weeks the babies began to react to each other. At this stage psychological distance was highly correlated with physical distance. One baby would respond to the crying or emotional tone of another baby. Moreno gave the name of *horizontal differentiation* to the reciprocity of emotional feeling and felt that it continued to exert an influence on the personality for the remainder of life. At about the 40th to 42nd week the differences in physical strength or mobility and mental alertness began to affect the organization of the group. At this time there began to develop leaders and followers for short periods of time. Moreno called this the *vertical arrangement* in the group organization. It, too, continued to affect the personality for life. Although he did not work with the same group of infants for the entire study, the result with each group studied was that each had within it three types of formations: organic isolates, horizontal and homogenous groupings, and a vertical structure running from the strongest to the weakest, with the strongest exerting strong influences on the behavior of the weaker members of the group.

Out of all of this and innumerable studies with larger and older groups and in a large variety of settings, Moreno evolved something akin to a sociogenetic law which we shall discuss in the next section.

Sociogenetic Law Principle

The sociogenetic law as the previous principle, Group Development, is not a major part of Moreno's theoretical position. Its contribution is strong enough, however, to merit consideration as a contributing factor in molding personality.

The variable personalities in a group do not destroy the entity of the group, Moreno maintains, but rather they seem to create a synthesis. If all personalities were stamped in the same mold, not a group but a monotonous line of robots would emerge. Out of these automatons no spontaneity or creativity could ever be hoped for. What Moreno terms the *criss-crossing of personality currents* or *telic systems* synthesize and produce a dynamic group that makes sense to him.

Similar to biogenetic law, the sociogenetic law states that higher forms of group organizations develop from lower group organizations. The parallel Moreno feels is quite close and quite accurate. Essentially the sociogenetic law states that ontogenetically all groups go through some modifications of form, as did ancient and primeval societies in the historic evolution of man. Basically what Moreno is saying is that there is a law of developmental sequence from simple to complex in the formation of every group. As a basis for supporting his thesis Moreno cites the following:

1. Children and adolescents spontaneously develop groupings from year to year; these groupings get more complex, with rituals and rules as the organization integrates, until such final touches as constitutions and rules of order appear.
2. The above groups always have vestiges of the previous periods of

growth and development. Each stage of growth has both the shades of the past and the portents of the future which can be discerned by careful study of the group in its current form.

3. Retarded adolescents and early school classes are comparable in their groupings.
4. Primitive societies and children's societies are remarkably similar in many of their formal attributes.

The basic importance of the sociogenetic law to personality theorists is threefold. Individual personalities go from simple to complex, thereby providing a parallel kind of study. Individuals comprise groups and are both controlled by the group and control the group. Whatever happens to the singular human personality is of interest to the personality theorist.

Sociodynamic effect. "A distortion of choice distribution in favor of the more chosen as against the less chosen is characteristic of all groupings which have been sociometrically tested" (*Who Shall Survive,* p. 639). "The hypothesis of the sociodynamic effect claims that a number of persons of a group will be persistently left out of a productive contact and communication; the persistent neglect of some individuals is far beneath their aspirations and persistently favors others, out of proportion to their requirements" (Personal note, Spring, 1962).

Measurement Principle

There is no doubt about the fact that an entire text could be written (and has been!) concerning Moreno's measurement principles.

Much of Moreno's work and especially that of the neo-Morenians has been grouped together under the subject of sociometry, which deals primarily with sociograms, spontaneity tests, and sociometric matrices. But actually the measurement principle is not a principle of personality dynamics but a method of measuring these dynamics. Moreno is chiefly noted for sociometry, a method of structuring and graphically portraying group organization. However, as the reader has no doubt observed, Moreno has more to say than how to draw lines from one circle to another. His is a way of thinking about personality and thus becomes a theory of personality.

With his emphasis on graphic presentation of human behavior Moreno has at times been criticized for studying closed systems of societal orders. The renowned anthropologist, Margaret Mead, has felt that sociometry has been guilty of this charge. Moreno's rebuttal is probably best stated by the opening sentence of his book, *Who Shall Survive?*, "A true therapeutic procedure cannot have less an objective than the whole of mankind."

No less a famous figure in psychology's past than E. L. Thorndike has felt that, "Whatever exists at all, exists in some amount,"[9] and practically the entire psychometric world has added, "whatever exists in some amount can be measured directly or indirectly." Along the same line of thinking, but *not* as a direct result of Thorndike's statement, Moreno, too, feels that human behavior can be analyzed structurally. In his sociometric tests, for example, horizontal sociograms reflect little or no reasons for the respondent's choices while the vertical type of sociogram reveals strong reasons for positive or negative choices. This small example of sociograms (the field and its implications are tremendous) reflects something of Moreno's emphasis on the value of graphic presentation. It is interesting if not significant that some of Moreno's followers feel that he predated Lewin in the diagramatic attempt to portray human behavior.

Now, however, the question must be answered: What does measuring personality have to do with the dynamics of personality structure? It is precisely for the reason that personality does have a structure that sociometrists feel they are dealing with the basic stuff of personality. In what appears to be an inversion of cause and effect, they say that personality has dimensions, the social atom, telic sensitivity, role taking, spontaneity testing, creative activity, and cultural conserves and that whatever exists in some amount can be measured. To approach the thesis tangentially, we may say that one cannot measure that which does not exist. The sociometrist can get measurements of the dimensions of personality; *ergo*, personality exists because it can be measured directly or indirectly. It is a way of saying that man has a dynamic personality which does things for him because it can be measured. If this is true, then measurement is part and parcel of man's personality both as that being measured and as that which measures.

DELIMITATIONS

This chapter does not include a discussion of the techniques of psychodrama or sociodrama, nor does it cover the other aspects of therapy. The voluminous literature on sociometry has also been left out of this chapter

[9] *17th Yearbook, NSSE*, Pt. II, p. 16, 1918.

on the dynamics of personality. The author has tried to confine the chapter to Moreno's description of why man does the things he does rather than how we can measure these processes (except, of course, for the short treatment of measurement as a principle).

Other valuable contributions of the sociometric approach which have been omitted are these: act centers and content centers in forgetfulness, dream hunger, first and second universes, psychosocial networks, and the six types of tele. The reasons for omission are twofold: first, although Moreno is highly skilled in theory, therapy, and research, it is only in the theoretical aspects of his work that the current text is interested and, second, many of the ideas listed in the previous sentence are the results of Moreno's followers and not exclusively those of Moreno. As was stated in the beginning of the present text, it is not the purpose here to be an interpreter of an interpreter.

EXPLAINING HUMAN BEHAVIOR VIA MORENO'S SOCIOMETRIC THEORY

No two interpreters of Moreno's work would probably ever agree completely on how to use his theory in explaining certain of man's behavioral problems: marriage, perversions, suicide, lawbreaking, supranatural being, humor, smoking, play and recreation, and psychoses–neuroses. This is not unusual because neo-Freudians, neo-Sullivanians, or neo-Rogerians do not use a theory in accordance with each other's interpretations. In the sections that follow it is not always possible to use Moreno's work directly. Although he is a prolific writer not all the references apply directly to the questions that follow.

Marriage

In an article in *Sociometry*, 1940, 3, 1–23 (later issued as *Psychodrama Monographs*, No. 7, 1945), Moreno discusses the "Psychodramatic Treatment of Marriage Problems." From the point of view of Moreno's role theory he regards roles in marriage as a cluster of roles on many different levels.

We may suppose, because tele is the simplest unit of feeling transmitted from one individual to another, that marriage begins with a telic relationship between the male and the female. Assuming marriage is based upon love, one finds a strong positive current which passes back and forth between the husband and wife. In what Moreno calls *simple tele* there is an unimpeded flow of emotional tone between man and wife. The tele relationship, therefore, is fundamental in understanding a marriage from a Moreno viewpoint.

Prior to marriage, however, the importance of the courtship must be considered. A true courtship may shorten the psychological distance between the interested young man and woman. Fundamentally, courtship and dating are invaluable periods of warming up to each other's tele structure and especially to the roles that must be played in a reciprocal relationship such as marriage. The shorter the engagement, the less chance there is to warm up to each other's role playing capacity. Engagements which run too long are those that lose the capacity for spontaneity. If the couple lose too much spontaneity toward each other, they are then unable to create new roles and new situations to enjoy between themselves. The important aspect in dating, courting, and being engaged is the testing of each other's capacity to sustain a true telic relationship and to delineate the roles each must play. Short engagements may work if they are intense enough to do all of the above. However, we may assume that a reasonable length of time is needed to warm up to the demands of another human personality in so intimate a relationship.

Divorce we may further assume is a complete breakdown in role playing and/or confusion in the roles that marriage requires. The lover, companion, father, economic provider, son-in-law or daughter-in-law, auxiliary ego, partner, and all such roles must be well developed, they must be well accepted, and they must be well played in order for a marriage not to end in divorce or continued disillusionment. Probably most important in an unsuccessful marriage, whether or not it ends in divorce, is the inability of one or both parties to reverse roles. The capacity to see the world from the other person's viewpoint is the foundation stone of marriage or any close human relationship. Age differential, religious differences, socioeconomic imbalance in background, all may be overcome if one person has the ability to reverse his role and see the problem through the eyes and perceptual system of the other.

Looking at marriage in another light according to sociometric theory, we see that it consists of many social atoms of a psychological nature. Marriage patterns itself after other similar social molecular systems. The more social atoms involved the stronger the social molecule, and the stronger the molecular structure the better the participants are able to understand and play their respective roles. The more roles one can play successfully, the more comfortable and adaptable he is in meeting the changing requirements of marriage. From the role of lover during and after the honeymoon, the man, for example, is more successful as a husband if he can also slip comfortably into the role of companion, wage earner, and all the multiple variations of male roles about the house. His success in this may be estimated by the number of comparable roles he has fulfilled in the past and the warming up period he has had to adjust to the variations built upon former roles. Eventually the marriage may result in a psychosocial network as it fits in with the marriages of others in the community. As the marriage moves along, each partner must continue to expand his past roles and to learn new ones.

Children introduce a new role relationship not only toward themselves but between the husband and wife. Occupational success may also call for a stretching of the role structure between man and wife as the husband appears to be going beyond the status of his wife who does not receive the symbols of success that come to him. Apparently a key to the maintenance of a happy marriage is the capacity for each partner to be spontaneous enough toward the other so that boredom and ennui do not result in indifference and incompatability. Spontaneity begets creativity, and the ability to create new things in a marriage may sustain it at a fairly high level of happiness. Apparently, too, sons and daughters of a couple may be considered cultural conserves that can contribute to a successful marriage or cause it to fail. When a child is used as a conserve which creates new forms of energy and effort, the contribution is tremendous; but when a child is looked at and worshipped as an idol, the child deters any spontaneous efforts to sustain the marriage. Parents who spoil their children by casting them in the mold of a cultural conserve that must be served and idolized, with no opportunity for the conserve to exercise its own built-in capacity to stimulate others have created only a monument to themselves. On the other hand, parents who allow their children to stimulate them into new PTA roles, youth organization activity roles, and especially examplary roles to be followed have made the parental parts of their marriage contribute to its success.

Perversions

"Sociometric theory may be applied to the problem of human perversion as considered in the light of a faulty development of the sociogentic law (homosexual cleavage, sociosexual cleavage, ethnic cleavage, etc)," Dr. Moreno wrote to the author. If the human personality does not proceed to higher levels of development from its earliest biological orientation, a form of perversion may result.

In still another frame of reference, homosexuality can easily be considered as basic role confusion. Children who are not brought up to understand and accept their true sex role may indulge in homosexual practices. Unbridled spontaneity of the type that Moreno calls undisciplined or pathological spontaneity (the spontaneous idiot) may be the basis for perverted acts. It is presumed that the tele factor aids and abets a homosexual relationship. Because of infratele the personality may not be able to operate in a warm relationship with socially approved objects such as his parents or siblings, and because of this misunderstanding the individual may project a tele relationship toward a substitute object. Masturbation, for example, may be a substitution of tele toward symbols or objects for tele for people.

Suicide

Suicide may be a collapse of such severe dimensions of the role structure in the personality as to cause the person to destroy all of his roles. Being unable to fulfill any of his role demands, the suicide may decide in a moment of spontaneous idiocy to create an entirely new role: a dead person. He may have the feeling that as a dead person the cultural conserve effect of his passing will have more impact upon society than did his living, role-confused personality. People will feel sorry for him where they did not before; people will belatedly realize his contributions where they ignored them before; and people will elevate him to a role he was never able to achieve in real life (i.e., "Never speak ill of the dead."). All of these he achieves by taking his own life. The importance of warming up may be interpreted as having been ignored by the suicide: if he thought long enough about the consequences of his act (warmed up to the idea), or reversed roles with the survivors, the chances are strong he would forego committing suicide.

Lawbreaking

When the human personality fails to operate within the framework of the laws of his society either by intent or by default, a number of explanations may be given via Moreno's theories.[10] In the case of stealing, there may be an overpowering positive tele for objects which overwhelms

[10] See "Psychodrama of an Adolescent," *Sociatry*, now called *Group Psychotherapy*, Vol. II, 1948.

the counterbalancing tele for people and symbols. The thief wants something so badly that he cares not at all for the consequences of his act upon other humans. This then becomes a case of infra tele or incapability of perceiving the feeling tone of other people.

We may assume that the habitual criminal is playing a stereotyped role. The only spontaneity he employs is the creation of new forms of criminal acts. Possibly the stereotyped role grows out of the criminal's inability to expand his personality beyond the *megalomania normalis* of the child. He deliberately flaunts the laws that society deems necessary because they conflict with his self-centered interests.

Teen-aged gangs and adolescent delinquents are examples of the sociogenetic law undeveloped beyond the primitive forms of society. In addition to the nihilistic behavior of the teen gang its members may be totally unable to structure their confused roles beyond the confines of their particular small closed society. Within the gang the roles are stereotyped, but these roles are completely out of reality to society as a whole. In addition to the adolescent's confusion about his true role in society, he may be unable to expand the dimensions of his role because of the limitations placed upon him by the peer group gang.

Role reversal may be the key explanation in explaining lawbreaking under the tenets of the sociometric theory of Moreno. Whether the crime be embezzling, robbery, rape, murder, petty thievery, traffic violations, each act ignores the feelings of, and consequences to, the victims. If the lawbreaker had the capacity to appreciate how it feels to be victimized in crime, he might be deterred in such crimes. Speedy, reckless, inconsiderate automobile driving, for example, threatens the lives and emotional equilibrium of other drivers. If true role reversal were practiced, the original driver might appeciate what it means to be theatened by the antics of a foolish driver. To some degree the entire value and essence of role reversal may be epitomized in a restatement of the Golden Rule, "Do unto others as you would have them do unto you."

Essentially the type of criminal who takes something that does not properly belong to him ignores the stimulating value of spontaneity–creativity–cultural conserve. In his case the accumulation of the cultural conserve, whether it be money, privileges arising from false status, or any form of property, loses all the value of the cultural conserve's ability to promote greater gains. This line of reasoning implies that gambling is evil not so much for societal reasons but because it robs the gambler of any capacity to do good for himself with the winnings. Not having gone through the thrill of spontaneously creating a cultural conserve, the gambler is inclined to dissipate his winnings in more futile attempts to short cut the true process of producing cultural conserves. From the Moreno frame of reference there is no short cut in creating a cultural conserve. Victory without effort leads to a cheapening of the cultural conserve in the mind of the winner. Thus, not on moral grounds but upon psychological principles, getting something for nothing (no effort) is wrong.

So-called "crimes of passion" may be examples of spontaneous idiocy or pathological spontaneity. This type of lawbreaking ignores the value of warming up. Should the individual warm up to the idea, the contemplation involved in thinking through the criminal act would serve as a deterrent. Thinking about how to commit the act, the consequences of being caught, and especially the chance of realizing a role reversal, all of which are involved in warming up to the act, might cause it never to happen.

Supranatural Being

Moreno has many reasons for explaining why man worships a god figure and why there is a god figure in the universe. "Playing God is a form of psychodramatic behavior." All of the following quotations come from Moreno's writings in the book he edited, *Sociometry and the Science of Man*. We find the phrase, "A central model of the universe . . . ," (p. 103) and later, "We can say with greater certainty than ever that the supreme power ruling the world is Spontaneity–Creativity." A reference from an earlier work (*Words of the Father*, 1920) states, "Creativity is the first and foremost characteristic of the supreme creative Center of the universe" (p. 124). Finally there is this statement: "It is from religious systems that sociometry has drawn its chief inspiration" (p. 186). All of this culminates in a more direct reference to a diety: "God—the Creator, Tao, Brahma, the Supreme Value or whatever name we give to the First Principle . . ." (p. 131). Moreno states also that because God wished to communicate His love, He gave man the world, thereby avoiding the "universal paradox" of having spontaneity and creativity without the natural outcome, a cultural conserve. The earth is God's cultural conserve which He gave to man because He loves man and also because God had to avoid the universal problem of being spontaneous and creative with no conserve as a result. Moreno does not seem unaware of the import of such Biblical phrases as Genesis I:1, "In the beginning God *created* the heaven and the earth," and the cultural conserve connotations of Psalms 24:1, "The earth is the Lord's, and the fulness thereof: the world and they that dwell therein." (Author's italics.)

Moreno's theory may be used to explain participation in a religious form such as Christianity in the western world. The fellowship involved in church participation may be a manifestation of strong tele feelings of an individual for his fellowman as a group. Other individuals may shop around for a minister who can preach to their satisfaction and for whom they have a strong tele feeling. In this case the theological background of the particular church is of minimal importance in relationship to the parishioner's telic feeling for the pastor-preacher. Church service attendance on Sunday morning may be a manifestation of the role the individual wishes to play. If the society of which he is a member considers church attendance an exemplary activity and if he wishes to have the approval of his society, the role playing individual attends church regularly to gain the reputation that society will give him. The doctrines of the church, his belief in them, and their effect upon his behavior are all auxiliary to the role this individual plays. In point of fact, none of the previous considerations is of concern to this individual who attends church solely for the purpose of structuring a role of Christian for himself.

A third explanation of why man has a religion and a relationship to the god figure in it may be reached through an examination of the act of conversion. After a process of warming up, either at the conscious or subconscious level, the convert may spontaneously "make a decision" which leads him to create a role of the "believer," a counterpart of the cultural conserve. As a believer, he may be sustained by his cultural conserve role of believer and go on to create spontaneously new and more reinforcing conserve roles.

Humor

A previous reference has been made to the warming up that a comedian must do in order to be successful in producing laughter. In some cases the entire work of producing humor or a laugh-provoking situation is a neat example of spontaneity–creativity–cultural conserve in its purest form. In what the comedian calls "timing" he is warming up the audience to respond to him. The warming up may take the form of a silly costume, bright and brassy music, or an unexpected gesture. Along with warming up the audience the comedian must appear to produce a novel situation or spontaneity. The higher the degree of novelty the more ridiculous it appears to be to the audience. Suddenly the comedian seems to create a new situation, and thus a joke is born. The joke becomes a cultural conserve as it is repeated to others by the members of the original audience. However, if the cultural conserve does not foster the circular effect of causing new spontaneity and creating a new twist to it, the joke becomes stale as a piece of humor. Comedians who persist in the same comedy situation soon gain the reputation of not being very funny. Television we may assume depletes the comedian's capacity to fulfill the cycle of spontaneity–creativity–cultural conserve, whereas in past days of vaudeville the comedian was able to maintain his reputation for humor because new audiences were available for the clichés of the past. Moreno insists, therefore, that the actor be "deconserved" from clichés in order to free his spontaneity.

Reversing the coin let us now examine humor from the side of the audience and its dynamics. Tele must be considered as the very basis of humor, for it must be remembered that tele is coacting, not reacting. Tickling is an example of reactive laughter. The tickled individual reacts in a laughing way but may not be amused at all. The delight small children have in tickling other children or adults may be a reflection of their inability to coact at a higher level of sophistication. Failing to appreciate or understand what produces genuine humor, the child mistakes the frenetic laughter with which the tickled individual responds as being excruciatingly funny. In turn, the child laughs to make himself enjoy the humor, although he is not sharing the stimulus with his victim. In true humor, the audience coacts with the laugh producer: the comedian. The prerequisites of tele such as intensity (the comedian must project his personality or role in a vivid way), sensitivity (the audience must be paying attention to the activity and be sensitive to its nuances as well as familiar with them), and simple tele (unimpeded flow of emotional tone, i.e., the audience must like the comedian) all help to produce a coactive situation. Once the audience of one or more individuals is coacting with the comedian or joke teller, the three kinds of tele come into play: tele for people, objects, and symbols. Tele for people produces an emotional empathetic basis for the humor; tele for objects represents the content of the props or action employed; and tele for symbols helps us to see ourselves as symbolic forms in the situation. Unless we can recognize the people, objects, and symbols in the humor situation, there can be no acceptance of it as laugh provoking. In short, English humor may escape American audiences because these factors are missing. When the audience and the comedian are coacting, the role the comedian plays becomes very important in the audience's viewpoint. The highest form of humor is one that allows the audience to reverse roles with the comedian at the symbolic tele level: suddenly the audience feels it is as clever as the comedian! If the audience is unable to make such a reversal of roles and to feel it is, in a sense, telling the joke too, the audience may respond by saying, "He's not my type of comedian," or in other words, "I do not wish to be like him." As a consequence, comedians that are hilariously funny to children may leave adults untouched, and adults may enjoy humor which means nothing to the child's tele sensitivity or role reversal capacity.

Moreno's sociometric theory may be involved in still another way in explaining humor. Individuals may accept or even actively seek the role of comedian, fool, or object of ridicule if they pursue a role which is stereotyped. Lacking the capacity to warm up and spontaneously create adequate new roles, an individual may fall back upon the cultural conserve role of comedian hoping to construct a role amicable to his limited talents. The wear and tear of evolving a role in changing situations is eliminated if one adopts and holds a role that is familiar. The warm up time is shortened for this individual. The burden and energy required to be spontaneous and creative then fall upon others who may construct practical jokes or use the person with the stereotyped comedian role to produce humor for themselves.

Smoking

The author's inventiveness is challenged in attempting to use Moreno's theory to explain why man indulges in smoking, which he classifies as a psychosomatic role. However, following the original question, "What good is a theory if it cannot explain man's behavior?" perhaps the reasons following may be acceptable.

In the first place, smoking may be considered as a cultural conserve of the behavioral type. Over the years smoking has become a custom that conserves certain aspects of the culture. From the American Indians' traditional "peace pipe" to the cultural patterns that show certain levels of society chewing tobacco, others smoking cigarettes, wealthy Americans smoking expensive cigars (in Denmark even some women do) and the British male smoking a pipe, we find many examples of smoking as a cultural conserve. It is a stylized behavior widely practiced in many cultures, and, during times of stress and economic instability, tobacco has even become a form of currency.

Cigarette and pipe smoking may also be considered a form of warming up to an activity that will demand spontaneity and creative acts. The use of tobacco may ease the tensions prior to an event that appears to be stressful.

Many users of tobacco play a role of the smoker. Some who smoke do so because others also smoke, and they wish to be identified in the role of a citizen of modern society. Even more true may be the caricature of the college sophomore who holds a pipe in his mouth because it is the prototype of the masculine figure. Even though the pipe is out most of the time and even though his tongue may burn, he holds to the masculine device of a pipe in order to accentuate the manliness of his personality.

Finally we may attempt to explain smoking as a strong tele for objects. The cigarettes, cigars, pipe pouch, and tobacco, plus the instruments to light the tobacco may be replacements for the toys, games, and objects of pleasure that the individual once enjoyed manipulating as a child.

Play and Recreation

There seem to be many clear ideas from the sociometric theory of Moreno that adequately explain why man indulges in games and needs recreation. Within the next paragraphs the following will be applied: role play and role reversal, spontaneity training, cultural conserves, sociogenetic law, group development, and recreation as a form of warming up.

From childhood on, play is an invaluable aid in learning new roles. *Role* in Moreno's theory is associated with the term *play* or *playing*. The relationship is not accidental. Man plays roles in two ways: in an earnest attempt to project his personality to the world and in a loose, informal, trial-and-error way to toy with the changes necessary to create and cast a new role. In either case the connotation of play as being enjoyable is fundamental to role taking. The role must be pleasant, or it collapses as a device to hold the personality intact.

When the human personality indulges in play, it can structure any new kind of role it wishes to enjoy. The rules of play encourage make-believe. The hunter and fisherman are pretending a role of early pioneer, sufficient unto himself; the chess player assumes a role of crafty strategist, pitting his intellect against another. Theater groups give their participants wide latitude in playing all kinds of roles, admirable or reprehensible, with full social approval. Further examples abound: the stamp collector plays the role of preserver of cultural conserves; the golfer in the male foursome plays the boyhood role of yesteryear with his pals; the female bridge players do somewhat the same; the spectator at athletic contests vicariously plays the roles of the participants; the amateur orchestra musician plays the role of spontaneously creating new cultural conserves of the past and possibly covertly assuming the role of a performing professional on the concert stage; the high school or college athlete in interscholastic competition plays the role of potential hero and playmate with his colleagues; and so it seems possibe to see a role relationship in all forms of play in which the played role is different from the individual's actual role in life. Even authors and playwrights may be playing at role taking as they invent the lives of their fictional characters and manipulate them.

Probably the true value in playing games is the ease with which the participants may learn the value of reversing roles. Because the actual role one takes in life is so bounded by rules and regulations and because mistakes in role taking may bring drastic and harmful results in real life, the best way to reverse one's role is in the make-believe characteristics of playing games. It may be assumed that the more opportunity there is in the game to try different roles, the more popular the game. Simple win or lose games such as Tic-Tac-Toe may not be as interesting as Monopoly, where the players may assume vicariously a greater variety of roles. The value of games may be the enjoyment we have in easily slipping from one role to another and being refreshed by the change in viewpoint. The individual who is an academic or occupational failure may be highly sustained by being the victorious hero at table tennis. In this case the short reversal of role may be the counter balance that keeps the personality intact.

As Moreno has stated, untrained spontaneity may be no more than pathological or idiotic spontaneity. It is possible for the child to train his natural ebullience for spontaneous play into something more creative. The simple hammering and pounding of the infant may lead to the actual construction later on of a scooter, house, or toy, created through the avenue of play. Play affords the opportunity to learn by trial and error the fact that the true fruits of spontaneity bring about the creation of some conserve. Play permits mistakes which are not tolerated in actual life situations.

Games, whether they be children's or adults, may be considered as conserves of the culture. Chess, playing school, bridge with its deck of vestigial royal markings, baseball, basketball, are all handed down from one generation to another as a piece of conserved culture of the past.

Sociogenetic law, as stated previously, means that life "proceeds both in its organic and social forms from the simple to the complex." In like manner the play of human beings from the simple forms of the two-year-old to the advanced forms of the twenty-two-year-old follows the precepts of the sociogenetic law as Moreno structured it.

Fortunately for man, he has the opportunity to develop the group through the agency of play. At first the infant plays as a solitary unit. Later on the child indulges in parallel play. After a prolonged period of bickering and violent quarrelling, children gradually learn to play games according to established rules. In adult life the rules of games are often as rigid or more rigid than some of the laws of society. (Men never have men for partners at a social dance, but men may be forgiven for running a stop light.) The total effect of play as it develops in the lives of each individual is to weld him into the group as a contributing member and as a protected member. Hence, play may be essential in group development.

Finally, recreational rest may afford the tired personality a chance to warm up for the next problem that must be faced in life. From a point of exhaustion, for example, the harassed seventh-grade teacher may have lost her capacity to teach effectively when the term ends in June. Throughout the summer she may be able gradually to warm up again to the thrills and satisfactions she has previously felt for her teaching post. The college graduate may be able to restructure his role more satisfactorily from the impact of changing his role of senior student to employee in a large industry by warming up to the idea during the summer vacation. Abrupt change from one all-absorbing activity to another may be so drastic as to create a role lag that is detrimental in assuming the new role. The traditional postwedding honeymoon, if considered as a form of rest and recreation, allows the newly wedded couple to warm up to their untried roles of husband and wife.

It can be seen then that the explanation of play and recreation fits quite comfortably into the framework of the sociometric theories of Jacob Moreno.

Psychoses—Neuroses

Just as Moreno's theory adapted itself readily to an explanation of play and recreation, it also holds many implications for explaining psychotic and neurotic behavior in man.

Most of Moreno's efforts in the field of psychoses and neuroses have been dedicated to the pragmatic problem of easing tensions and stimulating patients to realize and integrate themselves more productively and completely by psychodramatic and sociodramatic therapy. To illustrate Moreno's deep concern for the emotional deviate, the following short bibliography has been prepared. The bibliographical material at the end of this chapter repeats the citations, but this device may help the reader to appreciate Moreno's concern for and his contributions to the field of psychopathology and psychotherapy. It is interesting to note the evolution of his ideas as they are reflected in the titles. The works, of course, are by Jacob Moreno, except where noted.

1. Interpersonal Therapy and the psychopathology of interpersonal relations, *Sociometry*, 1937, *1*, 9–76.
2. Psychodramatic shock therapy: a sociometric approach to the problem of mental disorders, *Sociometry*, 1939, 2, 1–30.
3. Psychodramatic treatment of psychoses, *Sociometry*, 1940, 3, 115–132.
4. Mental catharsis and the psychodrama, *Sociometry*, 1940, 3, 209–244.
5. *Mental Catharsis and the Psychodrama*, N.Y., Beacon House, 1944.
6. A case of paranoia treated through psychodrama, *Sociometry*, 1944, 7, 312–327.
7. Psychodramatic treatment of psychoses, *Psychodrama Monogr.*, no. 15, 1945.
8. Psychodrama and the psychopathology of interpersonal relations, *Psychodrama Monogr.*, No. 16, 1945.
9. *Group Psychotherap.*, Moreno, J. L. (ed.), N.Y., Beacon House, 1946.
10. Psychodrama and group psychotherapy, *Sociometry*, 1946, 9, 249–253.
11. Transference, counter transference, and tele: their relation to group research and group psychotherapy, *Group Psychotherap.*, 1954, 7, 107–117.
12. Interpersonal therapy, group psychotherapy and the function of the unconscious, *Group Psychotherap.*, 1954, 7, 191–204.
13. The significance of the therapeutic format and the place of acting out in psychotherapy, *Group Psychotherap.*, 1955, 8, 7–19.
14. *Progress in Psychotherapy*, F. Fromm-Reichmann, and J. L. Moreno, (eds.), Grune & Stratton, N.Y., 1956.

15. Code of ethics of group psychotherapists, *Group Psychotherap.*, 1957, *10*, 143–144.
16. Psychodrama of Adolph Hitler, *Int. J. Sociometry*, 1957, *1*, 71–80.
17. *Progress in Psychotherapy, Volume II: Anxiety and Therapy*, J. H. Masserman, and J. L. Moreno, (eds.), Grune & Stratton, N.Y., 1957.
18. *The First Book on Group Psychotherapy* (3rd ed.), N.Y., Beacon House, 1957.

There are many surface explanations which can be given concerning the dynamics of emotional disorders. For example, psychotics and neurotics may be truly confused in their roles to the extent of being completely unable to assimilate any properties of the role. The role confusion may be so distorted as to have the psychotic think he is Moses, or a deity, or any person but himself. The evolution of role confusion may stem from faulty early training in spontaneously creating a satisfactory role during childhood. Neurotics as well as psychotics may have inferior tele strengths which have overemphasized tele for objects or symbols, at the expense of the balancing telic relationships. By being unable to coact with his fellow man, the emotionally disturbed person may be reacting through the projective or retrojective qualities of tele. The psychotic state of schizophrenia follows a phantasy role instead of an actual role.

Apparently psychoses stems from a basic misalignment in the structure of the social atom. If this smallest of human relationships is faulty, the personality is unable to build all the requisite superstructure, such as psychosocial networks, enriching telic feelings, membership in the group as it develops, and even a satisfactory role. The task of the therapist is then to unmask the faulty social atomic structure. This is admittedly most difficult because it lies so deeply hidden within the framework of the personality Psychopathic personalities are examples of undeveloped "megalomania normalis" which has been allowed to become ingrained. Role reversal is not possible with the psychopathic personality.

The psychotic behaves as a true case of unbridled, undisciplined, uncooperative spontaneity. The response is novel. The value of warming up is ignored. Pathological spontaneity creates either a rigid sterotyped role that defies change or a spontaneous idiot whose frenetic behavior is pathetic.

PREDICTING HUMAN BEHAVIOR VIA MORENO'S SOCIOMETRIC THEORY

There are some aspects of the sociometric theory that seem to lend themselves admirably to forecasting what the human personality will do. Because Moreno is a therapist first and a theorist second, he operates as all therapists must and indeed do, on the basis that their therapeutic work is going to create some change in the client's behavior and that the change will be in a desired direction. The specific details may not be predictable, but certainly the over-all behavioral pattern is. To assume that therapists do not do this is to level the charge that therapy is completely trial and error manipulation. Any therapist who has no prognostic idea of what he is doing to the client's future had best leave the business. Thus, the emphasis in sociometry with its psychodramatic and sociodramatic techniques of changing human personalities is built around predicting what these techniques will do to the client's future.

Personal Prediction

Many of the ideas represented in this chapter are pragmatically oriented. They are based on ordinary people in ordinary circumstances. Whereas Freud extracted his concepts from deviant individuals and Jung dealt with the entire panoply of human existence from its earliest beginnings to its ultimate teleological end, Moreno works *in situ* (in the life situation where the behavior actually happens) from normal origins or *status nascendi* ("the emerging condition," *statu;* "of things that may be in the unpredictable future," *nascendi;* i.e., the experience is new to the child although not to others, or, the child feels he is creating an experience which is new not only to him but to the world).

Personal prediction, it may be recalled, has two connotations as it is used in this book. One is that no matter what research has indicated or what empirical evidence is at hand, each of us subjectively accepts or rejects the evidence from a personal frame of reference. In short what is predictable proof to Sheldon may be poor evidence to others. We all predict from a personal bias. The second meaning of personal prediction is that the reader is allowed the privilege of using the theory to predict the future of his own life.

On the basis of the second meaning the reader is now invited to test Moreno's theory in predicting his own behavior. For example, it may be a convenient exercise and a fruitful one to take, for a point of referral, the ten propositions as they are considered in the section on explanation. The reader may predict success in his own marriage and in others he knows through a consideration of the roles involved. In a good marriage there must be a strong telic relationship. If the wedded couple cannot reverse roles either symbolically or actually, the marriage may end in divorce, or at best as a very unhappy contract. Children used as idolized cultural conserves will restrict the new roles the husband and wife can play, and there may result a poorly constructed personality for the child. All of these outcomes can be predicted by the reader if he believes in the efficacy of the Moreno theory.

In like manner, perversions may be role confusion, suicide may be collapse of the role structure, and lawbreaking may be role stereotyping accompanied by complete inability to reverse roles. If the *a priori* conditions exist, then we may be able to predict the consequent behavior pattern. One may predict that human personality will always have and worship a supranatural being, that man will always laugh, that he will smoke, that he will play, and finally that he will continue to become neurotic and psychotic.

Scientific or Laboratory Prediction

The literature by Moreno and on Moreno's work is voluminous. However, as is true with most theorists, the bulk of his work concerns itself with therapeutic techniques and devices. Moreno feels he works in the "here and now," which does not, however, make him ignore the future. Predictability, for Moreno, is tied up with constancy. "If there is constancy, then there should also be predictability" (*Sociometry and the Science of Man*, p. 114). From still another viewpoint, spontaneity without the conservability of the cultural conserve will of necessity lead to unpredictability in human behavior. On the other hand we may assure ourselves of predictability if we create and acknowledge the power inherent in the cultural conserve.

Prediction in sociometry is concerned with the role playing situations in psychodrama or sociodrama. Such being the case, prediction is of the greatest importance to Moreno. He feels that low- and middle-range levels of creativity can be adequately predicted in the psychodramatic theater or laboratory if the warming up stage is long enough to cause the spontaneous creation of individual behavior. Plunging an actor in one of his sociodramas into a role before the actor has had sufficient time to warm up to the role will create unpredictable results. Extending this thought out of the laboratory into real life we find that an individual's behavior may be predicted with higher and higher degrees of accuracy if adequate warming up time is provided prior to the spontaneous creativity of a behavioral act. In like manner predictability increases with the knowledge one has of the roles he is expected to play and the amount of experience he has had in playing his actual life roles. If an individual pursues a stereotyped role, we may predict his or her behavior with an extremely high degree of accuracy. The higher the degree of rigidity in playing a stereotyped role the less effect society and other influences have upon behavior. The result is prediction and control of the highest order.

Perhaps the severest criticism of predictability in Moreno's work can be found in Pitirim Sorokin's rebuttal to the theory of spontaneity and creativity, "Remarks on J. L. Moreno's 'Theory of Spontaneity–Creativity'" (*Sociometry and the Science of Man*, pp. 118–126). Although Sorokin is largely in sympathy with Moreno's attempts to define creativity and to study its effects, he departs sharply from the idea of spontaneity as the catalyst for creativity. Because we cannot even predict normal human activities twenty-four hours in advance, Pitirim Sorokin feels that we can hardly expect to predict behavior that creates high forms of art. In a sense, Sorokin is saying prediction belongs to the gods.

Moreno's own reply, which he sent to me, is as follows:

> If you wish to include the criticism of Sorokin . . . it would be only appropriate to include my answer immediately following: "Sorokin has fallen victim to the idolatry of the cultural conserve as have many members of the intelligentsia. The existential circumstances catalyzing his creative work are apparently poorly experienced by him. He draws his inspiration not as much from his own life as from cultural conserves. That may be the reason why his religiously oriented books leave one so cold.—The predictability of behavior cannot rest upon spontaneity, which obviously makes future behavior unpredictable. The bases of predictability of behavior are the cultural conserves.—Sorokin directs his criticism also against the validity of sociometric measurement and its efforts of predicting behavior. Unfortunately, being an academician and not having dedicated his life to organizing social experiments and their follow-up, being mainly concerned with great systems and verbal symposia, his own fads and foibles, he does not see the small things confronting him. That is probably the reason why he sees the creativity of the great scientist and the great saint but does not see the creativity of the little anonymous man." I would suggest you put this in quotation form so all the onus falls upon me.

Much of the voluminous literature that exists about sociometry concerns itself with refining the mechanics of measurement of the results of sociodramatic and psychodramatic techniques. Here again, Sorokin feels that we are living in a "Testomanic Age," which assumes a scientific rigor that does not exist in fact. It is as if the method of conducting research becomes more important than why the research is being conducted, or what the results may indicate. To employ an analogy, baking hundreds of chocolate cakes is more important than why they are being baked. Measuring the flour and mixing the ingredients is an end in itself; not the fact that no one will be eating all the cakes. Moreno is not in disagreement, for he feels that too much is done chiefly because the population is available. The law of diminishing returns may have been met in studying infants because infants are so readily available. We know more about babies than we know what to do with. Moreno pleads for research *in situ* whereby human behavior is studied out of the laboratory and in life situations. (The issue here brings to mind J. Robert Oppenheimer's charge that too much modern research is "stratospheric boondogling.")

———————————◆———————————

SUMMARY

The main theme of Moreno's sociometric theory revolves around the concept of role playing. The actors portrayed in Figure 9 suggest that man plays roles both for himself and for an audience. The social atom is suggested by the proximity of the members of the audience to each other. The feeling of tele also operates between members of the audience and the cast on the stage. The cast on the stage is in a state of flux, as is shown by a member of the audience getting ready to mount the footlights and take part in the drama. In fact, the action of members of the audience in responding to each other is as important as their response to the action on the stage. Children are shown in the theater to suggest an undeveloped group who will eventually stop playing, and, through the sociogenetic law, begin to take the place of the adult figures in the audience as they die and pass out of the theater.

The stage itself represents a cultural conserve just as much as does the play on it. The two actors in this scene (one shown by dotted lines) look alike to indicate role reversal. From the time that the play was first cast

Figure 9. Diagrammatic Summary of Moreno's Theory.

a period of warming up has been going on between the actors and the audience, which had been aware of the play through previous publicity. As each actor enters the scene, engages in action, and leaves the scene at an appropriate time, the full panoply of spontaneity–creativity–cultural conserve is demonstrated. Even if two actors play the same character, they will portray the role differently. The impression an actor leaves of the role he played whether it be the star or a spear carrier can be considered a cultural conserve. Later actors playing the same role may wish to emulate the first one or try desperately to revise the role.

Thus, the quotation which began this chapter is perhaps the best single-sentence summary of Moreno's theory of personality.

> "All the world's a stage,
> And all the men and women merely players:
> They have their exits and their entrances:
> And one man in his time plays many parts."

BIBLIOGRAPHY

PRIMARY SOURCES

BOOKS

Moreno, J. L., *Homo Juvenis,* in *Einladung zu einer Begegnung,* Berlin, G. Kiepenheuer, 1914, 19.

Moreno, J. L., *Das Testament des Vaters,* Berlin, G. Kiepenheuer, 1920.
Trans., *The Words of the Father,* N.Y., Beacon House, 1941.

Moreno, J. L., *Das Stegreiftheater,* Berlin, G. Kiepenheuer, 1923.
Trans., *The Theater of Spontaneity,* N.Y., Beacon House, 1947.

Moreno, J. L., *Who Shall Survive?,* N.Y., Beacon House, 1934.
Also reprinted 2nd ed. and revised in 1953.

Moreno, J. L., *Mental Catharsis and the Psychodrama,* N.Y., Beacon House, 1944.

Moreno, J. L., and F. B. Moreno, *Spontaneity Theory of Child Development,* N.Y., Beacon House, 1944.

Moreno, J. L., *Sociodrama: A Method for the Analysis of Social Conflicts,* N.Y., Beacon House, 1944.

Moreno, J. L. (ed.), *Group Psychotherapy,* N.Y., Beacon House, 1946.

Moreno, J. L., *Psychodrama,* Vol. I, N.Y., Beacon House, 1946.

Moreno, J. L., *A Sociometric Guide for Teachers,* Washington, D.C., Amer. Council on Educ., 1947.

Moreno, J. L., *The Theatre of Spontaneity: An Introduction to Psychodrama,* N.Y., Beacon House, 1947.
See earlier German work in 1923.

Moreno, J. L., *Sociometry: Experimental Method and the Science of Society,* N.Y., Beacon House, 1951.

Moreno, J. L., *Preludes to My Autobiography*, N.Y., Beacon House, 1955.

Moreno, J. L., Psychodrama and sociatry, in A. A. Roback, (ed.), *Presentday Psychology*, N.Y., Philosophical Library, 1955, 679–686.

Moreno, J. L. (ed.), *Sociometry and the Science of Man*, N.Y., Beacon House, 1956.

   Also considered as Vol. 18, No. 4 of *Sociometry*, 1955.

Moreno, J. L. and L. Yablonsky, Progress in psychodrama, in D. Brower, and L. E. Abt, (eds.), *Progress in Clinical Psychology*, Vol. II., N.Y., Grune & Stratton, 1956, 216–222.

Fromm-Reichmann, F., and J. L. Moreno (eds.), *Progress in Psychotherapy*, N.Y., Grune & Stratton, 1956.

Moreno, J. L., in *Personal Problems and Psychological Frontiers*, J. E. Fairchild (ed.), N.Y., Sheridan House, 1957.

Masserman, J. H., and J. L. Moreno, (eds.), *Progress in Psychotherapy: Anxiety and Therapy*, Vol. II., N.Y., Grune & Stratton, 1957.

   Moreno's introduction discusses global psychotherapy and prospects of a therapeutic world order.

Moreno, J. L., *The First Book on Group Psychotherapy* (3rd ed.), N.Y., Beacon House, 1957.

Masserman, J. H., and J. L. Moreno (eds.), *Progress in Psychotherapy: Review and Integration*, Vol. V, N.Y., Grune & Stratton, 1960.

Moreno, J. L., *The Sociometry Reader*, N.Y., Free Press, 1960.

Moreno, J. L., *Code of Ethics for Group Psychotherapy and Psychodrama: Relationship to the Hippocratic Oath*, N.Y., Beacon House, 1962.

   Appeared originally in *Group Psychotherapy*, 1955, 8, 357.

PERIODICALS

Moreno, J. L., Group method and group psychotherapy, *Sociometric Monogr.*, 1932, No. 5.

Moreno, J. L., Who shall survive?, *Nerv. Men. Dis. Monogr.*, 1934, No. 58.

Moreno, J. L., Interpersonal therapy and the psychopathology of interpersonal relations, *Sociometry*, 1937, 1, 9–76.

Moreno, J. L., and H. H. Jennings, Spontaneity training, a method of personality development, *Sociometric Rev.*, 1936.

Moreno, J. L., and H. H. Jennings, Statistics of social configurations, *Sociometry*, 1938, 1, 342–374.

Moreno, J. L., Psychodramatic shock therapy: a sociometric approach to the problem of mental disorders, *Sociometry*, 1939, 2, No. 1, 1–30.

Moreno, J. L., Creativity and cultural conserves with special reference to musical expression, *Sociometry*, 1939, 2, No. 2, 1–30.

Moreno, J. L., Psychodramatic treatment of marriage problems, *Sociometry*, 1940, 3, 1–23.

Moreno, J. L., H. H. Jennings, and J. Sargent, Time as a qualitative index to interpersonal relations, *Sociometry*, 1940, 3, 62–80.

Moreno, J. L., Psychodramatic treatment of psychoses, *Sociometry*, 1940, 3, 115–132.

Moreno, J. L., Mental catharsis and the psychodrama, *Sociometry*, 1940, 3, 209–244.

Moreno, J. L., The prediction and planning of success in marriage, *Marriage Fam. Liv.*, 1941, 3, 83–84.

Moreno, J. L., Foundations of sociometry, an introduction, *Sociometry*, 1941, 4, 15–35.

Moreno, J. L., The philosophy of the moment and the spontaneity theatre, *Sociometry*, 1941, 4, 205–226.

Moreno, J. L., and W. S. Dunkin, The function of the social investigator in experimental psychodrama, *Sociometry*, 1941, 4, 392–417.

Moreno, J. L., and J. K. Fischel, Spontaneity procedures in television broadcasting with special emphasis on interpersonal relation systems, *Sociometry*, 1942, 5, 7–28.

Moreno, J. L., and Z. Toeman, The group approach in psychodrama, *Sociometry*, 1942, 5, 191–195.

Moreno, J. L., Sociometry and the cultural order, *Sociometry*, 1943, 6, 299–344.

Moreno, J. L., The concept of sociodrama, *Sociometry*, 1943, 6, 434–449.

Moreno, J. L., Spontaneity test and spontaneity training, *Psychodrama Monogr.*, No. 4, 1944.

Moreno, J. L., and F. B. Moreno, Spontaneity theory of child development, *Sociometry*, 1944, 7, 89–128.

Moreno, J. L., Psychodrama and therapeutic motion pictures, *Sociometry*, 1944, 7, 230–244.

Moreno, J. L., A case of paranoia treated through psychodrama, *Sociometry*, 1944, 7, 312–327.

Moreno, J. L., and F. B. Moreno, Spontaneity theory in its relation to problems of interpretation and measurement, *Sociometry*, 1944, 7, 339–355.

Moreno, J. L., and H. H. Jennings, Sociometric methods of grouping and regrouping: with reference to authoritative and democratic methods of grouping, *Sociometry*, 1944, 7, 397–414.

Moreno, J. L., Psychodramatic treatment of marriage problems, *Psychodrama Monogr.*, No. 7, 1945.

Moreno, J. L., Psychodrama and therapeutic motion pictures, *Psychodrama Monogr.*, No. 11, 1945.

Moreno, J. L., Psychodramatic treatment of psychoses, *Psychodrama Monogr.*, No. 15, 1945.

Moreno, J. L., Psychodrama and the psychopathology of interpersonal relations, *Psychodrama Monogr.*, No. 16, 1945.

Moreno, F. B., and J. L. Moreno, Role tests and role diagrams of children, *Sociometry*, 1945, 8, 426–431.

Moreno, J. L., Psychodrama and group psychotherapy, *Sociometry*, 1946, 9, 249–253.

Moreno, J. L., Situation test, *Sociometry*, 1946, 9, May–Aug., Nos. 2–3.

Moreno, J. L., Contributions of sociometry to research methodology in sociology, *Amer. Soc. Rev.*, 1947, 12, 287–292.

Moreno, J. L., Discussion of Snyder's "The Present Status of Psychotherapeutic Counseling," *Psychol. Bull.*, 1947, 44, No. 6, 564–567.

Moreno, J. L., and H. H. Jennings, Sociometric control studies of grouping and regrouping, *Sociometry Monogr.*, No. 7, 1947.

Moreno, J. L., How Kurt Lewin's "Research Center for Group Dynamics" started and the question of paternity, *Group Psychotherap.*, 1952, 5, 1–6.

Moreno, J. L., Psychodramatic production techniques, *Group Psychotherap.*, 1952, 5, 243–273.

Moreno, J. L., How Kurt Lewin's "Research Center for Group Dynamics" started, *Sociometry*, 1953, 16, 101–106.

Moreno, J. L., Transference, counter transference, and tele: their relation to group research and group psychotherapy, *Group Psychotherap.*, 1954, 7, 107–117.

Moreno, J. L., Interpersonal therapy, group psychotherapy and the function of the unconscious, *Group Psychotherap.*, 1954, 7, 191–204.

Moreno, J. L., Old and new trends in sociometry: turning points in small group research, *Sociometry*, 1954, 17, 179–193.

Moreno, J. L., Sociometry and experimental sociology, *Sociometry*, 1954, 17, 358–363.

Moreno, J. L., The significance of the therapeutic format and the place of acting out in psychotherapy, *Group Psychotherap.*, 1955, 8, 7–19.

Moreno, J. L., Z. Moreno, and J. Moreno, The discovery of the spontaneous man: with special emphasis upon the technique of role reversal, *Group Psychotherapy*, 1955, 8, 103–129.
      See also *Sociometry*, 1956, 18, 411–438.

Moreno, J. L., First note on the sociometric system, *Sociometry*, 1955, 18, 88–89.

Moreno, J. L., Freud's hundredth birthday, *Group Psychotherap.*, 1956, 9, 251.

Moreno, J. L., The dilemma of existentialism, daseinsanalyse and the psychodrama: with special emphasis upon "existential validation," *Sociometry*, 1956, 1, 55–63.

Moreno, J. L., The sociometric school and the science of man, *Sociometry*, 1956, *18*, 271–279.

Moreno, J. L., American culture-in-transition, *Sociometry*, 1956, *18*, 351–355.

Moreno, J. L., Theory of spontaneity and creativity, *Sociometry*, 1956, *18*, 361–374.

Moreno, J. L., and F. B. Moreno, Spontaneity theory of child development, *Sociometry*, 1956, *18*, 393–411.

Moreno, J. L., Code of ethics of group psychotherapists, *Group Psychotherap.*, 1957, *10*, 143–144.

Moreno, J. L., Ontology of group formation, *Group Psychotherap.*, 1957, *10*, 346–348.

Moreno, J. L., Psychodrama of Adolph Hitler, *Int. J. Sociometry*, 1957, *1*, 71–80.

Moreno, J. L., The role concept, a bridge between psychiatry and sociology, *Amer. J. Psychiat.*, 1961, *118*, 518–523.

FILMS

Moreno, J. L., *Introduction to Psychodrama*, 16 mm, black and white, sound, 10 min., N.Y., Beacon, Therapeutic Film Prod., Inc. 1951.

SUGGESTED READINGS

BOOKS

Mead, G. H., *Mind, Self and Society*, Chicago, Univer. Chicago Press, 1934.

PERIODICALS

Allport, G. W., Comments on: J. L. Moreno, transference, countertransference, and tele—their relation to group research and group psychotherapy, *Group Psychotherap.*, 1954, *7*, 307–308.

Aucilino, J., Critique of Moreno's spontaneity theory, *Group Psychotherap.*, 1954, *7*, 148–158.

Bain, R., Science, art, ethics, and spontaneity, *Sociometry*, 1956, *18*, 296–303.
Creative act is both unique and uniform, and interdependent and interactive.

Borgatta, E. F., Role playing specification, personality and performance, *Sociometry*, 1961, *24*, 218–233.
College students and role playing.

Corsini, R. J., and L. J. Putzey, Bibliography, *Group Psychotherap.*, J. L. Moreno, (ed.), 1956, *9*, 177–249.
1700 items on group psychotherapy published from 1906 through 1955.

Corsini, R., Freud, Rogers, and Moreno: an inquiry into the possible relationship between manifest personality, theory, and the method of some eminent psychotherapists, *Group Psychotherap.*, 1956, *9*, 274–281.

Calls Moreno the man with capacity for immediate action.

Lebovici, S., Psychoanalytical applications of psychodrama, *J. Soc. Ther.*, 1956, *2*, 280–291.

Psychodrama not better than psychoanalysis but both have common goals and principles.

Mann, J. H., Experimental evaluations of role playing, *Psychol. Bull.*, 1956, *53*, 227–234.

Some evidence valid role playing tests can be developed.

Meyer, H. J., The sociometrics of Dr. Moreno, *Sociometry*, 1952, *15*, 354–363.

Munzer, Jean, The effect of analytic therapy groups of the experimental introduction of special "warm-up" procedures during the first five sessions, *Dissert. Abstr.*, 1962, *22*(8), 2896–2897.

Murphy, G., New evaluation of sociometry, *Sociometry*, 1956, *18*, 293–294.

More than technique or technical device but new way of viewing human relationships.

Oeser, O. A., and F. Harary, A mathematical model for structural role theory, *Hum. Relat.*, 1962, *15*(2), 89–109.

Renouvier, P., The group psychotherapy movement and J. L. Moreno its pioneer and founder, *Group Psychotherap.*, 1958, *11*, 69–86.

Sarbin, T. R., and C. D. Hardyck, Conformance in role perception as a personality variable, *J. Consult. Psychol.*, 1955, *19*, 109–111.

Some evidence that normal people and schizophrenics vary in role perception.

Shoobs, N. E., Individual psychology and psychodrama, *Amer. J. Indiv. Psychol.*, 1956, *12*, 46–52.

Using psychodrama and not losing Adlerian status.

Warner, W. J., Sociology and psychiatry, *Brit. J. Social.*, 1954, *5*, 228–237.

A critical appraisal of Moreno's *Who Shall Survive?*

PART IV

GENERAL AND INTEGRATIVE

Carl Rogers, Gordon Allport, and Gardner Murphy seem to have general and integrated approach to personality theory. They comprise the theorists in Part IV.

Rogers, whose personality theory is not fully formulated, stresses the integrative power of the self. To Rogers all things belong to the self, are interpreted by the self, and are integrated by the self. His work has been developed as a full chapter primarily because of his tremendous influence in the field of therapy and also because of the research he has stimulated.

One of the most influential, most quoted, and oldest of personality theories is that of Gordon Allport of Harvard University. Many current theorists begin their own work by citing Allport's 1937 book, *Personality*. Allport specializes in commenting on the general world of personality theory formation. Allport is both a personality theorist and a theorist of theories about personality. His work is also original and integrative.

Gardner Murphy, who has wide influence through his leadership in research and as an educator of many renowned psychologists, has perhaps the most eclectic approach to personality theory of any now extant. From the viewpoint of this text it seems natural and right to conclude the important chapters with Gardner Murphy's eclectic approach to personality theory.

Rogers' interests and talents have a wide scope. He has written for and worked with industry, religion, teaching, (see chap. 9, "Student Centered Teaching," in *Client-Centered Therapy*), and, of course, the field in which he is most noted, psychotherapy. Like Moreno, Rogers has also extended his talents into the field of motion pictures (see the Bibliography).

Although Carl Rogers is primarily known as a therapist, he has not ignored theories of personality. His 1951 book, *Client-Centered Therapy*, culminates at chap. 11 with "A Theory of Personality and Behavior." Rogers wrote the chapter partially to answer charges that his psychotherapeutic methods were based on no clear-cut theory of personality.

Rogers' psychotherapeutic work and theories have never been static; he continues to improve and expand both his therapy and theory. One indication of the movement of his work has been the change in titles given to his therapy: nondirective to client-centered to relationship-centered to "experiencing." Although Rogers is not totally responsible for the change from title to title, it does indicate the movement of his thinking. Whatever the world considers him, Rogers feels that he is, in his practicing of psychotherapy, a "midwife to a new personality."

One of the refreshing things that has come out of Rogers' work is his throwing open the door of the therapist's room to allow others to look and listen. Through the use of films and especially through the extensive use of taped interviews, Rogers has enabled his students and all those interested to see just what it is he is doing. He feels that it is quite necessary to "take a square look at the facts." Until the arrival of Rogers' tape-recorded interviews, the process of therapy was frequently hidden. Only by reading what the therapist may have chosen to write was one able to discover or infer actually what went on in a counseling or clinical situation. No one knows, for example, just exactly what and how Freud spoke, or Jung, or Adler, or any of the early therapists.

In some of his recent work, Rogers has been leaning toward existentialism. He sees certain parallels between the emphasis on existentialism in European psychiatry and the philosophical basis of client-centered therapy. His extremely personal article in 1955 in the *American Psychologist*, "Persons or Science: A Philosophical Question," his dialogue with Martin Buber at Ann Arbor in 1957, and his position on the editorial board of the *Journal of Existential Psychiatry* and the *Review of Existential Psychology and Psychiatry* are indications of this trend.

"For a dozen years Rogers had been working out his method of therapy in his work with children. About 1940 he began to present his point of view as being different from the approaches carried on by others," he has stated. Throughout the years since then, he has felt the need to mold a theory of personality or a theory of behavior which would come out and be compatible with his therapeutic system. Rogers is emphatic in his insistence that theory grows out of therapy. This is much like Freud's experience in which his therapy emerged in a theory. Thus we find Rogers stating in *Client-Centered Therapy* (p. 17), ". . . the fragile flower of theory has grown out of the solid soil of experience." Rogers is strongly opposed to theory building which precedes therapy or what he would refer to as research. Rogers feels that loose theory building not preceded by sound research is extremely hazardous, time consuming, and almost worthless.

Hence, it is almost impossible for anyone to separate the therapeutic aspects from the dynamics of personality which were involved in Rogers' therapeutic program. Theory and therapy are so inextricably interwoven that it is like pulling out the warp from the woof in woven cloth. To do so one is likely to make the theory disintegrate, just as one would cause the cloth to disintegrate into tangled skeins. It is also like trying to make a two-handed person wash only one hand. It can be done but it's most difficult and unnatural. However, as we shall see, there are enough identifiable threads of personality theory running through Rogers' work to make the effort well worthwhile for purposes of this text.

There is an additional difficulty in separating the man Rogers from his total work. There is so much of a highly personal nature in Carl Rogers' contributions that at times it is confusing to know where the personality of the man Rogers ends and where Rogers' personality of man begins. In a beautifully moving first chapter ("This is Me") of his latest book *On Becoming a Person* (1961) the reader wonders at times whether the "becoming" refers to Rogers or to humanity. No other theorist puts his own personality "on the line" so poignantly. He is truly his own theory of personality come to life.

Actually, it is almost too soon to write Rogers' personality theory; he is the first to admit that his theory of personality is still being formulated and that whatever is said now will be sure to change and be behind the times in the near future. At the present time his theory formulation is "full steam ahead."

ROGERS' DESCRIPTION OF HUMAN PERSONALITY

One of Carl Rogers' first efforts to delineate a personality theory or a theory of behavior was made in 1947 (*The American Psychologist*, 2, 35–368). One of his latest efforts has been in the book edited by Koch, *Psychology: A Study of a Science, Volume III: Formulations of the Person in the Social Context*. In this book, Rogers writes one of the chapters, "A theory of therapy, personality, and interpersonal relationships as developed in the client-centered framework." It must be reemphasized that whatever theory of personality Rogers may have at the time is purely a formulating one. Rogers himself does not consider himself to have evolved a definitive theory of personality. Whatever theory he has evolved Rogers feels has been stated in his chapter of Koch's *Psychology: A Study of a Science* (1959). (See footnote, page x of the Preface, in *On Becoming a Person*.)

Although this book is not a book on therapy but on theories of personality, a few words should be said in regard to Rogers' concept of the client-centered therapy. Rogers readily admits that we do not know exactly what is the essential process of therapy. He does feel that therapy is not built upon diagnosis. Psychotherapy, Rogers feels, is the essence of life and should be so understood. In short, Rogers has the feeling that life itself continues to be a therapeutic situation. Whether the individual is in the hands of a clinical psychologist or is pursuing the ordinary course of life, therapeutic incidents are a natural consequence of living. The following, in an abbreviated form, are some of his thoughts on therapy: therapy is internal revolution; client-centered therapy is not a technique, nor must the therapist be considered a "method" actor; the client-centered therapist is probably best described as the subject's "alter ego." Finally, in client-centered therapy the therapist helps the client to experience and live through his problems so that the client himself controls and solves within himself his own psychological difficulty. When Rogers says that client-centered therapy is not a technique, he means that client-centered therapy is a philosophy, a frame of reference, or a belief, dedicated to the idea that the client himself is the main actor who will eventually, with help, speak, write, and act out his own lines.

It has seemed feasible to include the above, although it is incomplete, because of the strong reputation that Rogers has and will continue to have as a successful, seeking, researching, dynamic believer in the process of psychotherapy as an on-going necessary part of all human living. One last word should be added. Rogers, in his early professional life, especially at the Rochester Clinic and prior to that, in his training with Leta Holingworth, held a view almost opposite to the view he presently holds.

In describing man's behavior, Rogers, in contrast to Freud, is an optimist. He feels that humanity is positive, forward-moving, constructive, realistic, and quite trustworthy. Rogers contrasts this with Freud's belief that man may be hostile, anti social, destructive, or even evil, or in pursuit of a life which actually has no solutions. (A note on the nature of man, *J. Counsel. Psychol.*, 1957, 4, 199–203.)

Despite the fact that it may be too soon to write a theory of personality from the work of Carl Rogers, there do seem to be four significant trends in his formulation of a theory of behavior or a theory or personality. The trends, principles, or major themes are these: the self as an experiencing mechanism and the three subsidiary themes of self-actualization, self-maintenance, and self-enhancement. It is the belief of the writer that most of Rogers' major ideas concerning personality can be fitted into the framework of the preceding four themes. In a note to the author, Dr. Rogers said that he hoped that the student would read chap. 11, "A Theory of Personality and Behavior," of *Client-Centered Therapy*, because the author's interpretation departs somewhat from Rogers' own work.

Self Theme

To Rogers, client-centered personality theory is a self-centered theory of personality. We can best examine Rogers' theory of personality by listing the twenty-two propositions which he formulated in 1951 and 1959 in the publication previously mentioned (Koch, *Psychology: A Study of a Science, Volume III: Formulations of the Person in the Social Context.* A theory of therapy, personality, and interpersonal relationships, as developed in the client-centered framework). The first nineteen propositions were formulated in 1951, while the last three were formulated in 1959. Because the self is central to the theme of each of the propositions, it can be readily seen that Rogers' theory of personality revolves about the concept of self. All of the propositions discuss either the individual, the person, or the self. They are not abstractions about society as a whole or theoretical statements about life itself; but somewhat like Gorden Allport's theory, in that each places a primary importance upon the uniqueness of a single human being.

Carl Rogers' Twenty-two Propositions Concerning Personality

Although each one of Roger's propositions stands on its own feet, the writer will add statements wherever it is felt these will clarify the meaning for the student.

Proposition 1. *"Every individual exists in a continually changing world of experience of which he is the center."* We all live in our own private world of experience, in a world that is never the same one day to the next. This viewpoint, of course, stresses introspection. It is called by some, phenomenology. The experience may be conscious or subconscious. When the experience is conscious, it concerns the world of symbols. The individual's private world can be known only to himself.

Proposition 2. *"The organism reacts to the field as it is experienced and perceived."* This perceptual field is, for the individual, "reality." Reality may be abstract to the philosopher or the metaphysician, but to the individual, reality is tested and accepted by his own perceptual system. When the individual has a perceptual system which is consistent for himself, he has a certain degree of predictability upon which he can depend.

Proposition 3. *"The organism reacts as an organized whole to this phenomenal field."* Rogers feels that one of the most basic characteristics of an individual's life is his tendency toward total or organized goal-directed responses. He further feels that he cannot accept any simple S–R type of behavior explanation.

Proposition 4. *"The organism has one basic tendency and striving— to actualize, maintain, and enhance the experiencing organism."* Rogers credits Snygg and Combs for this trichotomized phrasing. We shall have much more to say concerning actualizing, maintaining and enhancing the self in the following section which treats the subsidiary principles of Rogers.

Proposition 5. *"Behavior is basically the goal directed attempt of the organism to satisfy its needs as experienced, in the field as perceived."* Rogers feels that all needs are basically related. Further, reactions are not to reality as others may see them but to the individual's perception of reality. Rogers feels, as does Allport, that motivation exists primarily in the present. There is no behavior except to meet a present need.

Proposition 6. *"Emotion accompanies and in general facilitates such goal directed behavior, the kind of emotion being related to the seeking vs. the consummatory aspects of the behavior, and the intensity of the emotion being related to the perceived significance of the behavior for the maintenance and enhancement of the organism.*" Personality tries to integrate the two kinds of emotions, the unpleasant or excited feelings, and the calm or satisfied emotions. Perception determines the intensity of the emotional reaction.

Proposition 7. "*The best vantage point for understanding behavior is from the internal frame of reference of the individual himself.*" What may seem to be meaningless and strange behavior to an observer may be very purposeful behavior to the individual. There are many drawbacks and immense difficulties in getting at the introspective feeling of any particular individual. Because there are counterparts in our own life to the life of another individual, we may become able to infer introspective behavior. Preconceptions on our part, however, may destroy the ability to see within the skin of another human.

Proposition 8. "*A portion of the total perceptual field gradually becomes differentiated as the self.*" Rogers agrees that how the self develops is extremely difficult to study. We have made, he feels, not too much progress in this area.

Proposition 9. "*As a result of interaction with the environment and particularly as a result of evaluational interaction with others, the structure of self is formed—an organized, fluid, but consistent conceptual pattern of perceptions of characteristics and relationships of the 'I' or the 'me', together with values attached to these concepts.*" Experience with others helps to develop a sense of self. Parental influence is essential at this stage of structuring the self.

Proposition 10. "*The values attached to experiences, and the values which are part of the self structure, in some instances are values experienced directly by the organism, and in some instances are values introjected or taken over from others, but perceived in distorted fashion, as if they had been experienced directly.*" Experiences have values. These values may be direct experiences, gained from others, distorted, but whatever their source, they grow out of experiences.

Proposition 11. "*As experiences occur in the life of the individual, they are either (a) symbolized, perceived, and organized into some relationship to the self, (b) ignored because there is not perceived relationship to the self structure, (c) denied symbolization or given a distorted symbolization because the experience is inconsistent with the structure of the self.*" Again we find the self is the keystone to open perception or to perception which is below the level of consciousness.

Proposition 12.   *"Most of the ways of behaving which are adopted by the organism are those which are consistent with the concept of self."* The self hopes to maintain behavior which is consistent with the picture it has of the self.

Proposition 13.   *"Behavior may, in some instances, be brought about by organic experiences and needs which have not been symbolized."* Such behavior may be inconsistent with the structure of the self, but in such instances the behavior is not "owned" by the individual. When behavior is not controlled, it is regarded as not belonging to the self.

Proposition 14.   *"Psychological maladjustment exists when the organism denies to awareness significant sensory and visceral experiences, which consequently are not symbolized and organized into the gestalt of the self-structure. When this situation exists, there is a basic or potential psychological tension."* The personality cannot actualize itself if the experiences are not true to the real self.

Proposition 15.   *"Psychological adjustment exists when the concept of the self is such that all the sensory and visceral experiences of the organism are, or may be, assimilated on a symbolic level into a consistent relationship with the concept of self."* Inner tension is reduced when the personality has a new feeling about itself.

Proposition 16.   *"Any experience which is inconsistent with the organization or structure of the self may be perceived as a threat, and the more of these perceptions there are, the more rigidly the self structure is organized to maintain itself."* Events which threaten the personality may frequently make the personality stiff and rigid.

Proposition 17.   *"Under certain conditions involving primarily complete absence of any threat to the self-structure, experiences which are inconsistent with it may be perceived, and examined, and the structure of self revised to assimilate and include such experiences."* Change in a personality comes about when the personality can accept a new facet of itself.

Proposition 18.   *"When the individual perceives and accepts into one consistent and integrated system all his sensory and visceral experiences, then he is necessarily more understanding of others and is more accepting of others as separate individuals."* When the personality can develop a consistent self concept, it develops a good interpersonal relationship as a natural result.

Proposition 19.   *"As the individual perceives and accepts into his self-structure more of his organic experiences, he finds that he is replacing his present value system—based so largely upon introjections which have been distortedly symbolized—with a continuing organismic valuing process."* As the individual gains confidence in the valuing process, he finds the old systems unnecessary and no longer threatening.

(The last three propositions are from S. Koch's *Psychology: A Study of a Science,* wherein Rogers presents the latest in his developing theory of personality. These three positions are not as neatly stated as the nineteen positions that Rogers formulated in 1951.)

Proposition 20.   This concerns the personality's desire for social esteem. At times, the desire to be right and praised and esteemed worthy by others in one's society overtakes and overrules the values that the self-organism desires. When it is important for the personality to be considered worthwhile by others, it may overrule the inner functions and inner dynamics of the organismic self.

Proposition 21.   Rogers also finds an extremely strong desire for self-esteem, operating in a parallel system with the desire for social esteem. Because man has this need or desire for self-esteem which grows out of experience, it is possible for the personality to ignore the pressures of society which gave him the desire for social esteem.

Proposition 22.   Because of the forces, desires, and demands of social esteem and self-esteem, there develops an attitude of self-worthiness. The condition of self-worthiness helps the individual in the hurly-burly of every day life. Therefore, the personality's feeling that he is worthy of something helps to buttress his desire for self-esteem and his capacity to obtain the feeling of social esteem.

Even a cursory examination of Rogers' original nineteen propositions and the latest three propositions will give the reader a strong feeling of the value that Rogers places upon the self. The term *self* (or its synonyms, individual or person or organisms) is inherent in each of the twenty-two propositions. Seven other terms are prevalently involved in the formulations of Rogers' theory; indeed it would be impossible to write the propositions without their use: *experienced, perceived, phenomenal, field* or *gestalt, structure of self,* and *symbolized,* or *inner values.* These words are highly important to Rogers' theory of personality or human dynamics. Without them, it appears, Rogers would not be able to construct a theory of personality.

Definition.   At this point, it may occur to the reader that a definition of the word *self* is in order. This is not an easy assignment because Rogers at no point makes a definitive statement in regard to self or defines self

EXPLAINING HUMAN BEHAVIOR VIA ROGERS' SELF THEORY

All explanations are highly hypothetical and heavily loaded with inference. This is especially true of the theory of personality presented by Carl Rogers. Actually, in Rogers' system no one can give an explanation for another because only the introspective self can validly explain an inner mechanism or an inner feeling. The best we can hope to do is to infer an explanation from what another human being shows us of himself. According to Rogers, all stems from an internal frame of reference. In a sense, in this section, the only explanation that is possible is for each of us to explain the nine behavioral phenomena for ourselves. Rogers himself says: "From my own phenomenological point of view, the best explanation of a given behavior comes from permitting the individual to explore his behavior in a safe climate and thus to learn its basis and its explanation."

PREDICTING HUMAN BEHAVIOR VIA ROGERS' SELF THEORY

Personal Prediction

In February, 1961, Carl Rogers published a strongly written paper which has some bearing upon personal prediction (*Personnel and Guidance Journal*, 1961, 39, 442–451). In his ten page article, Rogers is most concerned with a rebuttal to B. F. Skinner's thesis regarding prediction and control of human behavior.[3] The following lengthy quotations best represent Rogers' point of view.

In any scientific endeavor, whether "pure or applied science—there is a prior personal subjective choice of the purpose or the value which that scientific work is perceived as serving."

This subjective value choice, which brings the scientific endeavor into being, must always lie outside of that endeavor, and can never become a part of the science involved in that endeavor.

Science, to be sure, rests on the assumption that behavior is caused—that a specified event is followed by a consequent event. Hence, all is determined, nothing is free, choice is impossible. But, we must recall that science itself in each specific scientific endeavor, each change of course in a scientific research, each interpretation of the meaning of the scientific finding, and each decision as to how the finding shall be applied, rests upon a personal, subjective choice.

[3] B. F. Skinner, Freedom and the Control of Men, *American Scholar*, Winter, 1955–1956, 25, 47–65.

Thus, science in general exists in the same paradoxical situation as does Dr. Skinner. A personal subjective choice made by man sets in motion the operations of science, which in time proclaims that there can be no such thing as a personal subjective choice.[4]

Thus, Rogers is saying, science cannot investigate science (itself); science cannot erect its own goals; science cannot interpret its own findings; only man can do this, and he does this subjectively from his own frame of reference. "Science has its meaning as the objective pursuit of a purpose which has been subjectively chosen by a person or persons" (p. 448).

We find encouragement when such an eminent scientist and psychologist as Dr. Carl Rogers says that, no matter what theory of personality is under consideration, it is always considered from a subjective frame of reference. Rogers espouses the one-sided presentation or single school of thought as a necessary step in scientific formulation. We find the following in Rogers' *Client-Centered Therapy* (p. 8):

It appears to the writer that the somewhat critical attitude which is usually held toward anything which may be defined as a "school of thought" grows out of a lack of appreciation of the way in which science grows. In a new field of investigation which is being opened up to objective study, the school of thought is a necessary cultural step. Where objective evidence is limited, it is almost inevitable that markedly different hypotheses will be developed and offered to explain the phenomena which are observed. The corollaries and ramifications of any such hypotheses constitute a system which is a school of thought. These schools of thought will not be abolished by wishful thinking. The person who attempts to reconcile them by compromise will find himself left with a superficial eclecticism which does not increase objectivity, and which leads nowhere. Truth is not arrived at by concessions from differing schools of thought. The eventual disappearance of such rival formulations comes about either when the issues are settled by research evidence, or when both types of hypotheses are absorbed into some new more penetrating view which sees the problems from a new vantage point, thus, re-defining the issues in a way not hitherto perceived.

It is now the task of the student of the theory of personality to evolve a personality theory of his own. He must make the decision based upon a single source of theory, a multiple source, or a "home-made" theory of personality gained from his own experience. If one follows the Rogerian line of thought, he may defensibly evolve his own self-conceived theory

[4] B. F. Skinner, *Science and Human Behavior*, Macmillan, 1953, p. 447.

of personality. It may be eclectic and gathered from others. Rogers would insist that it is always formulated from a subjective frame of reference.

Scientific or Laboratory Prediction

Rogers feels that prediction actually is an unobtainable goal because we cannot get into another person's full frame of reference (*Client-Centered Therapy*, p. 495).

However, Rogers does feel there is a certain efficiency of prediction in regard to psychotherapy. Thus, we find in a 1956 article, *Teachers College Record*, 1956, 57, 316–322, "Implications of recent advances in prediction and control of behavior," that Rogers does feel a certain optimism toward predicting human behavior, at least in the psychotherapeutic situation. The key to predictability seems to lie in the degree of self-insight that the client is able to evolve through the therapeutic sessions. The more self-insight, the greater one can prognosticate a good adjustment. Toward this end, Rogers has been working upon a process scale. "It is, in other words, a possible tool for prediction of success in therapy" [Brower and Abt, (eds.), *Progress in Clinical Psychology*, Vol. IV, p. 94].

In another sense, Rogers finds prediction toward success as a therapist to consist primarily of the assimilation of attitudes and procedures rather than the use of techniques or tools (*Client-Centered Therapy*, p. 458).

However, the strongest and most generalized feelings in regard to predicting human behavior from laboratory or scientific endeavors appear in the aforementioned article in which Dr. Rogers makes a rebuttal to Dr. Skinner's thesis on the prediction and control of human behavior. Rogers finds six areas in which prediction is possible.

1. We know how to set up the conditions under which many individuals will report as true, judgments which are contrary to the evidence of their senses.

2. We know how to change the opinions of an individual in a selected direction, without his ever becoming aware of the stimuli which changed his opinion.

3. We can predict, from the way individuals perceive the movement of a spot of light in a dark room, whether they tend to be prejudiced or unprejudiced.

4. We know the attitudes which, if provided by a counselor or therapist, will be predictably followed by a certain constructive personality and behavior changes in the client.

5. We know how to provide animals with a most satisfying experience consisting entirely of an electrical stimulation.

6. We know how to provide psychological conditions which will produce vivid halucinations and other abnormal reactions in the thoroughly normal individual in the waking state.[5]

Rogers finds the above six possibilities of prediction to be frightening. He further feels that most psychologists and social scientists have given little thought to what it means to predict and control human behavior. There are four steps by which man may control other men, steps which grow out of a background of the ability to predict human behavior. These four steps are: first, the selection of goals; second, the use of the method of science of controlled experimentation; third, obtaining the power to establish the conditions or use the methods; and fourth, the exposure of the individuals to the previous three steps.

In summary then, we find that Rogers is extremely interested in the prediction which he feels begets control of human behavior.

DELIMITATIONS

As can be seen from the long bibliography at the end of this chapter, there are many things concerning Rogers' theories which have not been covered by the author.

This chapter on the self theory of personality of Carl Rogers is not concerned with the methods of therapy, as rich as his work is in this area. Other than a mention of it, no complete treatment is made of the Process Scale. Other limitations of this chapter in regard to Carl Rogers' work are as follows: his work at the University of Wisconsin on autonomic responses in therapy is not covered; those things which Rogers considers "necessary and sufficient conditions for therapeutic personality change" are also omitted; and we have not included the many contributions toward pastoral psychology and industry, the vast contributions toward educational theory and practice, and Rogers' concern with the training of therapists.

[5] *Personnel and Guidance Journal,* 1961, 39, 442–444 (numbers are mine).

———————————————◆———————————————

SUMMARY

Probably the most conclusive statement one can make about Rogers' theory of personality is that it is not yet in final shape. Rogers' theory is changing and incomplete.

Throughout his work we find one central theme—the self. Whatever Rogers is discussing is always from the self frame of reference. All the ramifications of his work revolve around this concept.

Highly involved in the theory are the terms *self-structure, self-actualization, self-maintenance, self-enhancement, experiencing, phenomenological field,* and *congruence* (bringing together of the self structure and experiencing as perceived by the self).

BIBLIOGRAPHY

PRIMARY SOURCES

BOOKS

Rogers, C., *Measuring Personality Adjustment in Children Nine to Thirteen,* N.Y., Teachers College, Columbia Univer., Bureau of Publications, 1931.

Rogers, C., *A Test of Personality Adjustment,* N.Y., Association Press, 1931.

Rogers, C., *The Clinical Treatment of the Problem Child,* Boston, Houghton Mifflin, 1939.

Rogers, C., *Counseling and Psychotherapy,* Boston, Houghton Mifflin, 1942.

Rogers, C., and J. L. Wallen, *Counseling with Returned Servicemen,* N.Y., McGraw-Hill, 1946.

Rogers, C., Current trends in psychotherapy, in W. Dennis (ed.), *Current Trends in Psychology,* Univer. of Pittsburgh Press, 1947, 109–137.

Rogers, C., The case of Mary Jane Tilden, in W. U. Snyder (ed.), *Casebook of Nondirective Counseling,* Boston, Houghton Mifflin, 1947, 129–203.

Rogers, C., *Dealing with Social Tensions: A Presentation of Client-Centered Counseling as a Means of Handling Interpersonal Conflict,* N.Y., Hines, Hayden and Eldredge, 1948.

　　Also published in *Pastoral Psychol.,* 1952, 3(28), 14–20; 3(29), 37–44.

Rogers, C., Significance of the self-regarding attitudes and perceptions, in M.

L. Reymert (ed.), *Feelings and Emotions*, N.Y., McGraw-Hill, 1950, 374–382.

Also published in L. Gorlow, and W. Katkovsky (eds.), *Readings in the Psychology of Adjustment*, N.Y., McGraw-Hill, 1959.

Rogers, C., *Client-Centered Therapy: Its Current Practice, Implications, and Theory*, Boston, Houghton Mifflin, 1951.

Rogers, C., Perceptual reorganization in client-centered therapy, in R. R. Blake, and G. V. Ramsey (eds.), *Perception: An Approach to Personality*, N.Y., Ronald, 1951, 307–327.

Rogers, C., Some directions and the end points in therapy, in O. H. Mowrer (ed.), *Psychotherapy: Theory and Research*, N.Y., Ronald, 1953, 44–68.

Rogers, C., and R. F. Dymond, *Psychotherapy and Personality Change*, Chicago, Univer. of Chicago Press, 1954.

Rogers, C., Becoming a person, Oberlin College Lecture Series, Oberlin, Oberlin Printing Co., 1954. Reprinted by the Hogg Foundation for Mental Hygiene, Univer. of Texas, 1956, also in *Pastoral Psychol.*, 1956, 7(61), 9–13, and 1956, 7(63), 16–26.

Also published in S. Doniger (ed.), *Healing, Human and Divine*, N.Y., Association Press, 1957, 57–67.

Rogers, C., Client-centered therapy: a current view, in F. Fromm-Reichmann, and J. L. Moreno (eds.), *Progress in Psychotherapy*, N.Y., Grune and Stratton, 1956, 199–209.

Rogers, C., What it means to become a person, in C. E. Moustakas (ed.), *The Self*, N.Y., Harper & Row, 1956, 195–211.

Rogers, C., Training individuals to engage in the therapeutic process, in C. R. Strother (ed.), *Psychology and Mental Health*, Washington, D.C., Amer. Psychological Association, 1957, 76–92.

Rogers, C., Case study, in *Great Cases in Psychoanalysis*, N.Y., Ballantine, 1959.

Rogers, C., A theory of therapy, personality, and interpersonal relationships as developed in the client-centered framework, in S. Koch, (ed.), *Psychology: A Study of a Science*, Vol. III, *Formulations of the Person in the Social Context*, N.Y., McGraw-Hill, 1959, 184–256.

Rogers, C., A tentative scale for the measurement of process in psychotherapy, in E. Rubinstein (ed.), *Research in Psychotherapy*, Washington, D.C., Amer. Psychological Association, 1959, 96–107.

Rogers, C., Comments on Cases, in S. Standal, and R. Corsini (eds.), *Critical Incidents in Psychotherapy*, Englewood Cliffs, N.J., Prentice-Hall, 1959.

Rogers, C., M. Lewis, and J. Shlien, Two cases of time-limited client-centered psychotherapy, in A. Burton (ed.), *Case Studies of Counseling and Psychotherapy*, Englewood Cliffs, N.J., Prentice-Hall, 1959, 309–352.

Rogers, C., Significant trends in the client-centered orientation, in D. Brower, and L. E. Abt (eds.), *Progress in Clinical Psychology,* Vol. IV, N.Y., Grune & Stratton, 1960, 85–99.

Rogers, C., *On Becoming a Person: A Therapist's View of Psychotherapy,* Boston, Houghton-Mifflin, 1961.

Rogers, C., Two divergent trends, in R. May (ed.), *Existential Psychology,* N.Y., Random House, 1961, 85–93.

Rogers, C., A theory of psychotherapy with schizophrenics and a proposal for its empirical investigation, in J. G. Dawson, H. K. Stone, and N. P. Dellis (eds.), *Psychotherapy with Schizophrenics,* Baton Rouge, Louisiana State Univer. Press, 1961, 3–19.

Rogers, C., The meaning of the good life, in A. E. Kuenzli (ed.), *Reconstruction in Religion: a symposium,* Boston, Beacon, 1961.

Rogers, C., Toward becoming a fully functioning person, in A. W. Combs (ed.), *1962 Yearbook,* Washington, D.C., American Society for Curriculum Development.

Rogers, C. R., Actualizing tendency in relation to motives and to consciousness, in M. R. Jones (ed.), *Nebraska Symposium on Motivation, 1963,* Lincoln, Univer. Nebraska Press, 1963.

PERIODICALS

Rogers, C., and C. W. Carson, Intelligence as a factor in camping activities, *Camping Magazine,* 1930, 3(3), 8–11.

Rogers, C., A good foster home: its achievements and limitations, *Men. Hygiene,* 1933, 17, 21–40.
　　Also published in F. Lowry (ed.), *Readings in Social Case Work,* N.Y., Columbia Univer. Press, 1939.

Rogers, C., Three surveys of treatment measures used with children, *Amer. J. Orthopsychiat.,* 1937, 7, 48–57.

Rogers, C., The clinical psychologist's approach to personality problems, *The Family,* 1937, 18, 233–243.

Rogers, C., Needed emphases in the training of clinical psychologists, *J. of Consult. Psychol.,* 1939, 3, 141–143.

Rogers, C., and C. C. Bennett, The clinical significance of problem syndromes, *Amer. J. Orthopsychiat.,* 1941, 11, 222–229.

Rogers, C., The psychologist's contributions to parent, child, and community problems, *J. Consult. Psychol.,* 1942, 6, 8–18.

Rogers, C., A study of the mental health problems in three representative elementary schools, in T. C. Holy, *et al., A Study of Health and Physical Education in Columbus Public Schools,* Ohio State Univer. Bureau of Education Research Monograph, No. 25, 1942, 130–161.

Rogers, C., Mental health problems in three elementary schools, *Educ. Research Bull.,* 1942, 21, 69–79.

Rogers, C., The use of electrically recorded interviews in improving psychotherapeutic techniques, *Amer. J. Orthopsychiat.*, 1942, *12*, 429–434.

Rogers, C., Therapy in guidance clinics, *J. Abnor. Soc. Psychol.*, 1943, *38*, 284–289.

Also published in R. Watson (ed.), *Readings in Clinical Psychology*, N.Y., Harper & Row, 1949, 519–527.

Rogers, C., The development of insight in a counseling relationship, *J. Consult. Psychol.*, 1944, *8*, 331–341.

Also published in A. H. Brayfield (ed.), *Readings on Modern Methods of Counseling*, N.Y., Appleton-Century-Crofts, 1950, 119–132.

Rogers, C., The psychological adjustments of discharged service personnel, *Psychol. Bull.*, 1944, *41*, 689–696.

Rogers, C., The nondirective method as a technique for social research, *Amer. J. Sociol.*, 1945, *50*, 279–283.

Rogers, C., Counseling, *Rev. Educ. Research*, 1945, *15*, 155–163.

Rogers, C., and V. M. Axline, A teacher-therapist deals with a handicapped child, *J. Abnorm. Soc. Psychol.*, 1945, *40*, 119–142.

Rogers, C., R. Dicks, and S. B. Wortis, Current trends in counseling, a symposium, *Marriage Fam. Liv.*, 1945, *7*(4).

Rogers, C., Psychometric tests and client-centered counseling, *Educ. Psychol. Measmt.*, 1946, *6*, 139–144.

Rogers, C., Significant aspects of client-centered therapy, *Amer. Psychol.*, 1946, *1*, 415–422.

Rogers, C., Recent research in nondirective therapy and its implications, *Amer. J. Orthopsychiat.*, 1946, *16*, 581–588.

Muench, G. A., and C. Rogers, Counseling of emotional blocking in an aviator, *J. Abnorm. Soc. Psychol.*, 1946, *41*, 207–216.

Rogers, C., Effective principles for dealing with individual and group tensions and dissatisfactions, *Executive Seminar Series on Industrial Relations*, Session 10, Chicago, Univer. of Chicago Press, 1947.

Rogers, C., Some observations on the organization of personality, *Amer. Psychologist*, 1947, *2*, 358–368.

Also published in A. Kuenzli (ed.), *The Phenomenological Problem*, N.Y., Harper & Row, 1959, 49–75.

Rogers, C., Research in psychotherapy: round table, *Amer. J. Orthopsychiat.*, 1948, *18*, 96–100.

Rogers, C., Divergent trends in methods of improving adjustment, *Harvard Educ. Rev.*, 1948, *18*, 209–219.

Also in *Pastoral Psychol.*, 1950, *1*(8), 11–18.

Rogers, C., Some implications of client-centered counseling for college personnel work, *Educ. Psychol. Measmt.*, 1948, *8*, 540–549.

Also published in *College and University*, 1948, and in *Registrar's Journal*, 1948.

Rogers, C., B. L. Kell, and H. McNeil, The role of self-understanding in the predicition of behavior, *J. Consult. Psychol.*, 1948, *12*, 174–186.

Rogers, C., The attitude and orientation of the counselor in client-centered therapy, *J. Consult. Psychol.*, 1949, *13*, 82–94.

Rogers, C., A coordinated research in psychotherapy: a nonobjective introduction, *J. Consult. Psychol.*, 1949, *13*, 149–153.

Rogers, C., A current formulation of client-centered therapy, *Soc. Ser. Rev.*, 1950, *24*, 442–450.

Rogers, C., What is to be our basic professional relationship?, *Ann. Allergy*, 1950, *8*, 234–239.

Also published in M. H. Krout (ed.), *Psychology, Psychiatry, and the Public Interest*, Minneapolis, Univer. of Minn. Press, 1956, 135–145.

Rogers, C., and R. Becker, A basic orientation for counseling, *Pastoral Psychol.*, 1950, *1*(1), 26–34.

Rogers, C., D. G. Marquis, and E. R. Hilgard, ABEPP policies and procedures, *Amer. Psychologist*, 1950, *5*, 407–408.

Rogers, C., Where are we going in clinical psychology?, *J. Consult. Psychol.*, 1951, *15*, 171–177.

Rogers, C., Client-centered therapy: a helping process, *The Univer. of Chicago Round Table*, 1951, *698*, 12–21.

Rogers, C., Studies in client-centered psychotherapy, III: The case of Mrs. Oak—a research analysis, *Psychol. Serv. Center J.*, 1951, *3*, 47–165.

Also published in C. R. Rogers, and R. F. Dymond (eds.), *Psychotherapy and Personality Change*, Chicago, Univer. of Chicago Press, 1954, 259–348.

Rogers, C., Through the eyes of a client, *Pastoral Psychol.*, 1951, *2*(16), 32–40; (17), 45–50; (18), 26–32.

Rogers, C., T. Gordon, D. L. Grummon, and J. Seeman, Studies in client-centered psychotherapy, I. Developing a program of research in psychotherapy, *Psychol. Serv. Center J.*, 1951, *3*, 3–28.

Also published in C. R. Rogers, and R. F. Dymond (eds.), *Psychotherapy and Personality Change*, Chicago, Univer. of Chicago Press, 1954, 12–34.

Rogers, C., Communication: its blocking and facilitation, *Northwestern Univer. Information*, 1952, *20*, 9–15. Reprinted in *ETC*, 1952, *9*, 83–88; in *Harvard Bus. Rev.*, 1952, *30*, 46–50; in *Human Relations for Management*, C. E. Bursk (ed.), N.Y., Harper & Row, 1956, 150–158.

Rogers, C., A personal formulation of client-centered therapy, *Marriage Fam. Liv.*, 1952, *14*, 341–361.

Also published in C. E. Vincent (ed.), *Readings in Marriage Counseling*, N.Y., Crowell, 1957, 392–423.

Rogers, C., Client-centered psychotherapy, *Scient. American*, 1952, *187*, 66–74.

Rogers, C., A research program in client-centered therapy, *Res. Pub. Ass. Nerv. Ment. Dis.*, 1953, *31*, 106–113.

Rogers, C., The interest in the practice of psychotherapy, *Amer. Psychologist*, 1953, *8*, 48–50.

Rogers, C., G. W. Brooks, R. S. Driver, W. V. Merrihue, P. Pigors, and A. J. Rinella, Removing the obstacles to good employee communications, *Mgmt. Rec.*, 1953, *15*(1), 9–11, 32–40.

Rogers, C., Towards a theory of creativity, *ETC: A Review of General Semantics*, 1954, *11*, 249–260.

   Also published in H. H. Anderson (ed.), *Creativity and Its Cultivation*, N.Y., Harper & Row, 1959, 69–82.

Rogers, C., A personal view of some issues facing psychologists, *Amer. Psychologist*, 1955, *10*, 247–249.

Rogers, C., Personality change in psychotherapy, *The Int. J. Soc. Psychiat.*, 1955, *1*, 31–41.

Rogers, C., Persons or science? A philosophical question, *Amer. Psychologist*, 1955, *10*, 267–278.

   Also published in *Pastoral Psychol.*, 1959, *10* (Nos. 92, 93).

Rogers, C., Implications of recent advances in the prediction and control of behavior, *Teachers Coll. Rec.*, 1956, *57*, 316–322.

   Also published in E. L. Hartley, and R. E. Hartley (eds.), *Outside Readings in Psychology*, N.Y., Crowell, 1957, 3–10.

   Also published in R. S. Daniel (ed.), *Contemporary Readings in General Psychology*, Boston, Houghton Mifflin, 1960.

Rogers, C., A counseling approach to human problems, *Amer. J. Nurs.*, 1956, *56*, 994–997.

Rogers, C., Some issues concerning the control of human behavior, (Symposium with B. F. Skinner), *Science*, Nov. 1956, *124*, No. 3231, 1057–1066.

   Also published in L. Gorlow, and W. Katkovsky (eds.), *Readings in the Psychology of Adjustment*, N.Y., McGraw-Hill, 1959, 500–522.

Rogers, C., and E. J. Shoben, O. H. Mowrer, G. A. Kimble, and J. G. Miller, Behavior theories and a counseling case, *J. Counsel. Psychol.*, 1956, *3*, 107–124.

Rogers, C., The necessary and sufficient conditions of therapeutic personality change, *J. Consult. Psychol.*, 1957, *21*, 95–103.

Rogers, C., Personal thoughts on teaching and learning, *Merrill-Palmer Quart.*, Summer, 1957, *3*, 241–243.

   Also published in *Improving College and University Teaching*, 1958, *6*, 4–5.

Rogers, C., A note on the nature of man, *J. Consult. Psychol.*, 1957, *4*, 199–203.

Also published in *Pastoral Psychol.*, 1960, *11*, No. 104, 23–26.

Rogers, C., A therapist's view of the good life, *The Humanist*, 1957, *17*, 291–300.

Rogers, C., A process conception of psychotherapy, *Amer. Psychologist*, 1958, *13*, 142–149.

Rogers, C., The characteristics of a helping relationship, *Personnel Guid. J.*, 1958, 37, 6–16.

Rogers, C., Significant learning: In therapy and in education, *Educ. Leader.*, 1959, *16*, 232–242.

Rogers, C., The essence of psychotherapy: A client-centered view, *Ann. Psychotherap.*, 1959, *1*, 51–57.

Rogers, C., Lessons I have learned in counseling with individuals, in W. E. Dugan (ed.), *Modern School Practices Series 3, Counseling Points of View*, Minneapolis, Univer. of Minn. Press, 1959, 14–26.

Rogers, C., A. Walker, and R. Rablen, Development of a scale to measure process changes in psychotherapy, *J. Clin. Psychol.*, 1960, *16*, 79–85.

Rogers, C., The process equation of psychotherapy, *Amer. J. Psychotherap.*, 1961, *15*, 27–45.

Rogers, C., The place of the person in the new world of the behavioral sciences, *Personnel Guid. J.*, 1961, *39*, 442–451.

FILMS

Rogers, C., and R. H. Segel, *Client-Centered Therapy: Part I and II*, 16 mm., sound, State College, Penn., Penn. State, Psychological Cinema Register, 1952.

Rogers, C., and R. H. Segel, *Psychotherapy Begins: The Case of Mr. Lin*, 16 mm., sound, State College, Penn., Penn. State, Psychological Cinema Register, 1955.

Rogers, C., and R. H. Segel, *Psychotherapy in Process: The Case of Miss Mun*, 16 mm., sound, State College, Penn., Penn. State, Psychological Cinema Register, 1955.

Rogers, C., *Psychotherapy: The Counselor, and Psychotherapy: The Client*, 16 mm., sound, distributed by Bureau of Audio-Visual Aids, Madison, Wisc., Univer. of Wisc., 1960.

SUGGESTED READINGS

BOOKS

Hall, C. S., and G. Lindzey, *Theories of Personality*, N.Y., Wiley, 1957, 257–295.

Lecky, P., *Self-Consistency*, N.Y., Island Press, 1945.

Mead, G. H., *Mind, Self, and Society*, Chicago, Univer. Chicago Press, 1934.

Seeman, J., Client-centered therapy, in D. Brower, and L. E. Abt (eds.), *Progress in Clinical Psychology II*, N.Y., Grune & Stratton, 1956, 98–113.

Sherif, M., and H. Cantril, *The Psychology of Ego-Involvements*, N.Y., Wiley, 1947.

Snygg, D., and A. W. Combs, *Individual Behavior*, N.Y., Harper & Row, 1949.

Stephenson, W., *The Study of Behavior*, Chicago, Univer. Chicago Press, 1953.

Symonds, P. M., *The Ego and the Self*, N.Y., Appleton-Century-Crofts, 1951.

PERIODICALS

Bertocci, P. A., The psychological self, the ego and personality, *Psychol. Rev.*, 1945, *52*, 91–99.

Chein, I., The awareness of self and the structure of the ego, *Psychol. Rev.*, 1944, *51*, 304–314.

Chodorkoff, B., Self-perception, perceptual defense, and adjustment, *J. Abnorm. Soc. Psychol.*, 1954, *49*, 508–512.

Corsini, R., Freud, Rogers, and Moreno: an inquiry into the possible relationship between manifest personality, theory, and method of some eminent psychotherapists, *Group Psychotherap.*, 1956, *9*, 274–281.

    Calls Freud—man of intellect.

    Calls Rogers—gentle and friendly person.

    Calls Moreno—man who has capacity for immediate action.

Gettering, R. W., Philosophic idealism in Rogerian psychology, *Educ. Theory*, 1955, *5*, 206–214.

Hilgard, E. R., Human motives and the concept of self, *Amer. Psychologist*, 1949, *4*, 374–382.

    Also in H. Brand (ed.), *The Study of Personality*, N.Y., Wiley, 1954, 347–361.

Jessor, R., Phenomenological personality theories and the data language of psychology, *Psychol. Rev.*, 1956, *63*, 173–180.

Lebo, D., The development of client-centered therapy in the writings of Carl Rogers, *Amer. J. Psychiat.*, 1953, *110*, 104–109.

Lundholm, H., Reflections upon the nature of the psychological self, *Psychol. Rev.*, 1940, *47*, 110–127.

Maslow, A. H., Critique of self-actualization, I. Some dangers of being-cognition, *J. Indiv. Psychol.*, 1959, *15*, 24–32.

Nameche, G. F., Two pictures of man, *J. Humanist. Psychol.*, 1961, *1*(1), 70–88.

    Freud and Rogers on man.

Sarbin, T. R., A preface to the psychological analysis of self, *Psychol. Rev.*, 1952, *59*, 11–22.

Schultz, K. V., The psychologically healthy person: A study in identification and prediction, *J. Clin. Psychol.*, 1958, *14*, 112–117.

Theology students self-actualization ratings correlate low but positive.

Smith, D. E. P., Interdisciplinary approach to the genesis of anxiety, *Educ. Theory*, 1956, 6, 222–231.

Compares Freud, Rank, Mowrer, Angyal, Goldstein, Lewin, Rogers, Kierkegaard, and Sullivan on theories of anxiety.

Smith, M. B., The phenomenological approach in personality theory: Some critical remarks, *J. Abnorm. Soc. Psychol.*, 1950, 45, 516–522.

Stock, D., An investigation into the interrelations between self-concept and feelings directed toward other persons and groups, *J. Consult. Psychol.*, 1949, 13, 176–180.

Strupp, H. H., An objective comparison of Rogerian and psychoanalytic techniques, *J. Consult. Psychol.*, 1955, 19, 1–7.

Walker, W. E., Carl Rogers and the nature of man, *J. Consult. Psychol.*, 1956, 3, 89–91.

12

Allport

He is great who is what he is from Nature,
and who never reminds us of others.

RALPH WALDO EMERSON
Representative Men, Uses of Great Men

SOME BIOGRAPHICAL DATA

Gordon Willard Allport was born on November 11, 1897, in Monte-zuma, Indiana.[1] He was one of the four sons of Dr. John Edwards and Nellie Edith (Wise) Allport. Allport received his early education in the public schools of Cleveland, Ohio, and majored in economics and philoso-phy at Harvard, where he was awarded the A.B. degree in 1919. He taught English and sociology at Robert College, Istanbul, Turkey, during the next academic year, 1919–1920. Allport then returned to Harvard and received his A.M. in 1921 and his Ph.D. in psychology a year later. He studied at the University of Berlin and at the University of Hamburg during the school year, 1922–1923, and spent the next year in England at Cambridge University. He again returned to Harvard and taught as an instructor in the Department of Social Ethics for the two following years. Then Allport accepted the position of assistant professor at Dartmouth College and stayed there until 1930, at which time he returned to Har-vard as an assistant professor. He is at present a full Professor of Psy-chology in the Department of Social Relations at Harvard University, a

[1] The author is most grateful to Dr. Allport for his patience and help in refining this chapter.

450

position he has held since 1942. In 1958, Boston University awarded him an honorary L.H.D. degree.

Gordon Allport married the former Ada Lufkin Gould of Lincolnville, Maine, on June 30, 1925. They have one son, Robert Bradlee Allport, a pediatrician.

Allport has held office and membership in a great number of professional and honorary societies. He is a member of both the American Psychological Association (member of the council, 1936–1938; president, 1939) and the Eastern Psychological Association (president, 1943). He is a past member of the National Commission for UNESCO. He is president of the Prospect Union Association, past director of the National Opinion Research Center, and executive secretary of the Ella Lyman Cabot Foundation. In addition, he is a past member of the Social Science Research and National Research councils, a member of the Society of Colonial Wars, and a member of the Harvard Club of New York. He is an honorary fellow of the British Psychological Society and an honorary member of the Deutsche Gesellschaft für Psychologie, the Osterreichische Ärztegesillschaft für Psychotherapie and Société Française de Psychologie. Allport is a member of Phi Beta Kappa. During the period 1937–1949 he served as editor of the Journal of Abnormal and Social Psychology. In 1956 Allport was Visiting Overseas Consultant to the Institute of Social Research, University of Natal, South Africa.

INTRODUCTION

Gordon W. Allport advocates the open approach in considering the problems of personality theory. To him man's personality is not only a self-enclosed entity but is also open to the world in general. Allport feels that psychology has no right to exclude contributions to personality theory, whether they come from the refined methods of science or whether they are the insightful, behavioral descriptions of literature and philosophy.

Allport has the happy faculty of saying and writing provocative thoughts on personality theory without becoming overly controversial. He entertains no bitter recriminations against any man's theory. He does, however, plant very sharp barbs in the hides of zealous workers whose systems and theories seem to him to have proceeded too far in one direction. Such a phrase as "person-destroying psychologists," as well as the following phrases, indicates his capacity to deflate the onesidedness of some psychological efforts: "edifice complex"; "We never seem to solve our problems or exhaust our concepts, we only grow tired of them"; "Personality evaporates in a mist of method"; "human personality . . . is . . . captive into some autistic paradise of methodology," by which Allport means that much is done because it is fit for testing or research, although in essence it has little or nothing to do with human behavior; and "Some of us model man after the pigeon." In advocating "person-centered psychology," Allport also feels that "The greatest failing of the psychologist at the present time is his inability to prove what he knows is true."

To Allport personality theory lives by controversy, and although personality theory itself cannot be cumulative (i.e., a theory built from bits and pieces like beads on a string), research on personality can be cumulative.

ALLPORT'S DESCRIPTION OF HUMAN BEHAVIOR

According to Allport, personality is the "natural subject matter" of psychology. He states, "one of the outstanding events in psychology of the present century has been the discovery of personality" (*Personality and Social Encounter*, p. 146 and p. 5). It is obvious that to Allport the study of personality and the creation of an adequate theory concerning its dynamics are endeavors of the first magnitude for present psychologists. However, because he promotes the open-ended viewpoint of personality study, Allport also firmly believes that an emerging theory of personality must be considered from the viewpoint of, and must come to terms with, literature (Who else can present the most understandable descriptions of behavior?); philosophy (Why ignore the oldest field of personality study?); the natural sciences (Who have so much to contribute to methodology?); and the biological sciences (Is not man an animal?). Allport's rationale is more than an open-ended approach; it is also a plea for a system blended of the work of all who can contribute to the greater understanding of man's personality.

In his *Personality: a Psychological Interpretation* (1937), Allport weaves an interesting history of the word *personality* out of the original Greek word *persona*. He uses the writings of the Roman statesman, orator, and author, Cicero, who found four distinct meanings to the word *persona*:

1. the external appearance but not the true self;
2. the character or role someone plays in life;

3. the collection of highly individual qualities that enables one to live an adequate life;

4. the distinction and dignity with which one fulfills his role in life.

From these four definitions of Cicero, Allport ferrets out fifty definitions to the word *personality*. He ends his list with his own, which is one of the most copied and discussed of all definitions. It is: "Personality is the dynamic organization within the individual of those psychophysical systems that determine his unique adjustments to his environment" (*Personality: a Psychological Interpretation*, 1937, p. 48; changed slightly in *Pattern and Growth in Personality*, 1961, to "characteristic behavior and thought," p. 28.)[2]

The key phrases in Allport's definition are important for an understanding of his conception of the term *personality*.

1. *dynamic organization:* meaning that man's personality is more than a loose collection of behaviors, that it is organized, and further that this organized human is constantly evolving and changing in motivation and self regulation.

2. *psychophysical systems:* meaning that man is both brain and body.

3. *determine:* meaning that "Personality *is* something and *does* something" of and by and for itself which removes personality from being a mere ploy of others.

4. *unique:* meaning that every human being is unique in time, place, person, and adjustment quality, and is unlike any others in these characteristics.

5. *adjustments to his environment:* meaning that "Personality is a mode of survival."

In a later work Allport states that personality has three essential characteristics: locus, uniqueness, and inner congruence. These appear to be an excellent summary of his 1937 definition of personality in *Personality and Social Encounter*, 1960, p. 21.

Before considering the description of human behavior via Allport's system, we may profit from noting his five requirements for an adequate theory of personality. An adequate theory of personality will 1. regard the human personality as integumented, that is, as centered in the organism;

[2] Gordon W. Allport, *Pattern and Growth in Personality*, Holt, Rinehart and Winston, 1961. By permission of Holt, Rinehart and Winston.

"*Pattern and Growth in Personality* changes the definition slightly: not 'unique adjustments to his environment' but 'characteristic behavior and thought' " (Personal letter, March 19, 1962).

2. regard the organism as replete, not empty; 3. regard motivation as normally a fact of present structure and function, not merely as an outgrowth of earlier forces; 4. employ units of analysis capable of living synthesis; and 5. allow adequately for, but not rely exclusively upon, the phenomenon of self-consciousness (*Ibid.,* p. 20).

Like many other theorists, personality and otherwise, Allport continually expands his concepts regarding the personality of the human. His writing style is highly readable and anything but pedantic. He presents his theory of personality primarily in four books: *Personality: A Psychological Interpretation* (1937), *Becoming: Basic Considerations for a Psychology of Personality* (1955), *Personality and Social Encounter* (1960), and a recent revision of his 1937 book, of which he has changed the title to *Pattern and Growth in Personality* (1961).

In this latest revision "The outlook, scope, and emphasis are not greatly changed" (Preface, ix), and the "basic problem remains unchanged" (Preface, x). What has appeared in the newest book is a complete rewriting, citations of current research, and his expanding ideas of cognition, culture, and the self. The greatest change is his delineating more completely the process of functional autonomy.

As a personality theoretician, Allport is basically tender-minded toward the foibles of man. He has a strong, humanitarian orientation toward the behavior of his fellow human beings. Allport does not take an extreme position, as we have seen, and he is eminently fair in considering the value of contributions from all disciplines. Consequently, he is neither pessimistic about man as a species, nor is he unfair to the work of other theoreticians. Allport likes and cares about people, about personality theorists on all continents (his international reputation is excellent and well deserved), and in turn is liked by all who know him and his work.

In many respects Allport talks more about personality theory than he defines what personality theory actually is. Allport seems to cast his role as that of a contemporary judge of personality theories, and in this role he begins to create interpretations which soon become personality theories of his own. This we find is true in his latest work printed in 1961. Here he offers critiques of the motivational concepts of homeostasis, instincts, needs, basic drives, tension reduction, etc. In his critical analysis he finds them wanting because they are unchanging motives. Having judged these theories and found them inadequate, although somewhat helpful, he has developed his own motivational theory of functional autonomy beyond the position that he took in 1937. (See later section.)

Continuing in 1961, Allport still finds his original definition of personality a usable and valuable concept. The term *character,* he feels, can be largely dispensed with since it deals, from his frame of reference, with methods of evaluation of personality and is not directly connected with a definition of personality. As we shall see later, he finds, however, the term *temperament* to be a useful one.

In 1961 Allport was maintaining his "true eclectic" position. He agrees with Gardner Murphy that most of the potentialities of man have never been truly realized by man or by the personality psychologists who study this aspect of man.

Gordon Allport is one of the very, very few American psychologists to acknowledge Asiatic psychology. Within the subject matter of this book, Carl G. Jung is probably the only other personality theorist to pay much attention to the work of Oriental or Asiatic thinking. Allport believes it is inexcusable provincialism for psychologists in our culture to neglect the wisdom of the East. He examines briefly the four central desires of Hindu psychology: pleasure, success, duty, and liberation from the pleasure–success–duty periods of existence (*Pattern and Growth in Personality,* p. 565).

One of the very strong, central themes of Allport is his strong desire to occupy an intermediate position between generalities and individualities about personality. Allport, however, cannot but lean toward the individualistic interpretations of personality. He is like a skier going down hill between two mountains, with successfully maintaining a position in the middle of the valley. But, as the skier may always turn to the right, Allport always turns to the right toward individualism as he comes to the end of the journey.

In his latest book, Allport continues to disagree with Freud although he sees much value in Freud. He feels that Freud "smudged the boundary lines between neurotic and normal mental functioning" (*ibid.,* p. 155). However, he does feel that Freud made a brilliant contribution to the world of psychology in his concept of the ego-defense mechanisms such as repression, denial, rationalization, projection, fixation, regression, and reaction formation.

Allport considers the raw materials of personality to be physique, intelligence, and temperament. Allport gives credit to the work of Sheldon and his work with body types. He feels, too, that there may be a close relationship between body constitution and temperament. Allport feels that the raw material of intelligence is idiographic, that is to say, basically unique to the individual. It is the interplay between the raw materials of physique, intelligence, and temperament that eventually make a personality.

We may now turn our attention to an examination of the seven principles or major themes that the present writer has extracted from the writings of Gordon Allport. The seven principles are: motivation, learning, contemporaneity, uniqueness, ego or self, continuity-discontinuity, and traits–trends–tendencies. (There is a strong inclination at this point to include "becoming" as an eighth principle. It is not included only because the author considers it to be adequately covered in the above seven major themes. It should be stressed, however, that Allport emphasizes the essential nature of man to "be somebody," to become a human being worthy of the self-image in all respects, to achieve a true "life-style" in the fullest Adlerian sense.)

Motivation Principle

According to Allport, "There is no problem in psychology more difficult to handle" than the problem of motivation (*Personality: A Psychological Interpretation*, p. 110). He feels also that motivation theory, including his own, is incomplete: "All theories of motivation fail to provide a full solution" (*Personality and Social Encounter*, p. 144). Allport again repeats this theme in the 1961 book, "The problem of motivation is central to the psychological study of personality" (*Pattern and Growth in Personality*, p. 196).

There appears to be an overemphasis on reactive quality in motivational theory, whereas we need more proactive motivational theory. The "re" has been grossly overplayed at the expense of the dynamics of the "pro" factors in motivation and in fact, in the total picture of psychology.

Motivation is the 'go' of personality, and is, therefore, our most central problem. Psychologists are not agreed in their accounts of what internal conditions induce action and thought. Some say that all conduct is instigated by unchanging instincts or by drives. Such theories stress the reactive side of man's behavior. Severe restrictions must be laid on theories of this order (whether of the psychoanalytic or stimulus-response order). They fail to allow for the extensive transformation in motives from infancy to maturity, or for the extreme diversity of motives that we find in adulthood. Current theories are tending to allow for an additional principle: they claim that competence, self-actualization, and ego autonomy are equally basic features of human motivation. A final theory of motivation will have to admit the truth that lies in all of these views.[3]

Allport holds to the integumented view of motivation in which there is a blending of factors which lead to motivating man. Actually, there are only a few really major motives in any well-integrated personality. These are often "surprisingly well focused and well patterned." The number of motives, "indeed, in a well-integrated adult may be adequately indicated on the fingers of two hands, perhaps one." Thus, in motivation the important factor is the individual's systematized design for living. To understand better the motivational aspects of man's behavior, we must study his private worlds of desire, appreciation, and conscience.

In his latest work of 1961, Allport finds four requirements for an adequate theory of motivation. They are as follows: 1. an acknowledgement of the contemporary nature of motives; 2. allowance for motives of diverse types; 3. allowance for the dynamic forces of cognitive processes, i.e., planning and intention; and 4. constant allowance for the concrete uniqueness of motives.

In this system, traits and motivation are highly similar, although they are, of course, treated separately in the present text. It is those traits which are driving, dynamic, and directional of effort which help to create motivation.

In rebuttal to the learning theorists, Allport feels that all drives are not equally potent for learning, although he feels that many theorists in that field make this assumption. In the latest work Allport has given the name of *quasi-mechanical view* to this type of approach.

Despite the fact that human motivation often strives for goals it has not identified clearly, that it seems to reach hungrily, and that it appears to have "aspirations meshed into no gear," motivation is not Freudian, goal-inhibited sexuality. It is more meaningful to speak of what an individual's intentions are, or what he is trying to do, than of the painful repressions of sexual urges as the mainspring in life. Similarly, the phylogenetic continuity of man and animal appetites for food and shelter is only a fraction of the total motive structure.

[3] *Personality and Social Encounter*, p. 218.

Allport differentiates between activity and participation as behavioral factors in motivation. The student who attends class regularly may not be very motivated because this activity is task involved. It becomes habitual to attend class. The motivation gradient is low. On the other hand, when participation is ego-involved, it usually exists upon much stronger motivational patterns. For example, the college man who goes out for the football team has a large amount of ego-involvement invested in his attempt to make the team. Participation in practice every day and the possibility of playing on the varsity team each Saturday have a tremendous amount of ego involvement. The same individual, however, may have little or no ego involvement invested in the activity of attending classes on the campus. Only as he becomes ego-involved by participating in a class recitation or oral report may we expect more than the minimal amount of motivation to be present. The moral, therefore, is that if the instructor wishes to increase motivation in classrooms, he must involve the student's ego by creating opportunities for full participation in the classwork.

To carry the point further, we see that there are two forms of motivation: one ego-involved and the other not. The latter is called *routine motive* and the former *ego motive*. Routine motives are a result of previously rewarded behavior. They help to maintain self esteem. The father who daily attends his job in order to provide for his family does so under a routine motive. Routine motives may be adequate for lower animals, but they are likely to cause boredom in the human animal. The human being demands new responses in changing goals. As an illustration, we are not likely to repeat successful research, or repeat conversations, or re-play a bridge hand that has ended successfully. To do so is likely to be highly boring. In contrast to the routine motives, ego motives thrive on a degree of frustration. The unmade hand in bridge, the unsold customer in business, and the reciprocation of a new conversation bring forth much more motivation from us than the previous examples cited. Succinctly put, the greater the ego demand, the higher the level of aspirations, and the higher the level of aspirations, the more fully are we motivated. Repeated success brings boredom and little motivation. Continuous challenge to the ego brings stimulation and high motivation. In this capacity, Allport maintains, we are different from the lower forms of living things. On this score as well as some others, does he find fault with the work of the comparative and stimulus–object–response research psychologist.

Finally, Allport feels that "all units of motivation are at the same time units of personality, but not all units of personality are simultaneously units of motivation" (*Personality and Social Encounter*, p. 118). Thus, although motivation is an essential characteristic of human behavior, it is by no means all of the story of man's personality.

Normal–Abnormal Motives. There is a difference in the motivational patterns between children and adults and between emotionally stable and emotionally unstable people. The character of motives changes from infancy to maturity. Adult motives supplant infant motives. As an infant the human being is motivated by organic demands of food, body warmth, elimination. As an adult the human being goes far, far beyond these elemental motives and indeed may deny himself food in order to diet, may dress his body only for style and suffer lack of warmth or too much warmth, and may regulate his elimination functions to fit social demands to the point of considerable visceral discomfort. Beyond these extensions of former motivating mechanisms are the mature motives that regulate the adult's existence.

There is also a discontinuity between the motivations of normal and abnormal people. Motivation which is simple tension reduction is pathological. The ordinary human wants much more than to return to mere *status quo*. He may sentimentally regard the "good old days," but he wants more to have and own the newer things in life: automobiles, job advancement, travel to new lands, success for his children. Parents who are motivated to keep their children at an infantile *status quo* level are pathological. It is the neurotic and the psychotic who strive for complete homeostasis in life. The normal personality is vigorous and dynamic enough to want and demand change at ever higher levels.

Contemporaneity in Motives. Allport feels certain that motivation is always a contemporary process. An individual's current self image is far more important than whatever he has been in the past (except for pathological cases, as previously discussed). No central motive, even for the abnormal personality, is ever totally independent of the contemporary ego structure. The most withdrawn catatonic will, upon recovery, speak of events which occurred and to which he attempted to respond, although unable to do so, even during the deepest states of his catatonic condition.

Not only are motivational processes current in their dynamics, but most of them can be taken at their face value. Allport mentions, for example, that if we were to ask a hundred individuals who had raided the icebox for a midnight snack why they did so, they would quite truthfully answer, "Because I was hungry." Only one person out of the one hundred snackers might be guilty of compulsive oral regression in the Freudian sense. Why then, Allport asks, do so many theorists base motivational processes on the one case. Because one person does have an unconsciously operating motive, it is false to assume that all the others have an unconscious desire for oral regression, especially with the further assumption that all one needs to do is dig around deep enough to uncover the repression. It seems to Allport that the rationale is erroneous which states that a condition exists universally despite the fact that it can be found true in only a few of the species. It is erroneous to state, "It is there all right, only we cannot find it." Along this line, Allport makes some devastating comments in regard to the overuse of, and overdependency upon, the projective type of clinical psycho-diagnostic tests. In 1961, Allport stated strongly and directly, "Motivation is always contemporary" (*Pattern and Growth in Personality*, p. 227).

Functional Autonomy.   One cannot consider motivation from an Allportian frame of reference without special consideration of the term he coined: *functional autonomy.* This theme has caught the interest of many theorists. Functional autonomy has been criticized, examined, discussed widely, and above all been highly associated with the name of Allport as a personality theorist.

He feels that *functional autonomy* is a shorthand phrase that represents the present "go" of interests and tendencies that initiate and sustain current behavior. As most customarily defined, it means a strong tendency for a motive system to develop which becomes highly independent of the primary drive which first originated the action. Thus, a given activity may become an end or goal itself, or we may continue to pursue an activity for the love of the activity for its own sake.

The traditional example from Allport is that of the employee who prides himself on his high quality of workmanship. Originally it was necessary for him to learn a skill in order to obtain the position. In the years that follow, he has been doing quite satisfactory work, but the autonomous (ruling) nature of the function may dictate that he is compelled to do clean-cut work of the highest standards because he enjoys doing it that way. The actual job demands may be far less than his self-imposed standard. Further illustrations may be found in 1. the behavior of maternal sentiment which began as a necessary task to keep the child alive, but which is continued for the sheer enjoyment of motherhood, long after the child needs protection and nurturance; or 2. the sailor who has spent his working years on the sea and who enjoys his retirement near the sea; or 3. an original hunger drive which becomes a motive of acquisition for objects completely unrelated to hunger. It is interesting to note that within the dynamics of functional autonomy, college students may take a course for the credit alone, but through participation where there is ego-involvement rather than mere attendance of lecturers with routine motivation, the student comes to learn for the sheer pleasure and curiosity of knowing something new. Few activities in life have an *a priori* built-in motivation from the initial point. Motivation comes out of participation where the ego is involved.

Allport distinguishes between two types of functional autonomy. *Perseverative functional autonomy* is a closed or almost-closed system which continues primarily under its own power with little or no outside reinforcement. This is a self-sustaining circuit mechanism and is of a lower order than the next type.

Propriate functional autonomy is an open system which presupposes the view that the individual is bombarded with stimuli in the world that surrounds him. Although both types are essential to motivation, it is this second type which is the most important. Because of the open system, the personality is led to achieve progressively higher levels of behavior.

Perseverative funtional autonomy gives consistency and coherence to man's personality, while propriate functional autonomy brings him to respond appropriately to life's challenges so that he can produce greater and greater things.

In summary, the following Allport statement helps to express all of the facets of functional autonomy. "The doctrine in a functional autonomy helps to express the uniqueness of motives that confer distinctiveness to a person's characteristic adjustments" (*Personality and Social Encounter,* p. 146). In this book, Allport expands the concept of functional autonomy but leaves the core essentially untouched. The reader of Allport's work gains the impression that he continues to answer the critics of his concept of functional autonomy even though some of the criticisms were made as far back as 1940.[4] This particular reference occurs and reoccurs in all of the books Allport has written since the 1937 edition.

In *Pattern and Growth in Personality* (1961), Allport buttressed his

[4] P. A. Bertocci, Critique of Gordon W. Allport's Theory of Motivation, *Psychol. Rev.,* 1940, 47, 501–532.

argument in support of functional autonomy. "We turn now to one general law of motivation that allows fully for the concrete uniqueness of personal motives, and observes all other criteria for an adequate theory of motivation" (p. 226). However, Allport does not claim that the concept of functional autonomy is the only valid principle to developing human motives nor that it explains all of the motivational aspects of man. What he does add to his theory is a rebuttal to the critics and a further development of the processes which are not functionally autonomous.

In regard to the latter statement, Allport suggests eight processes which are *not* functionally autonomous. These are as follows:

1. Biological drives: air, sleep, hunger, elimination.
2. Reflex action: eye blink and the knee jerk.
3. Constitutional equipment: raw materials of physique, intelligence and temperament.
4. Habits: since habits are motivational in Allport's view.
5. Primary reinforcement: behavior that stops after the goal is gained.
6. Infantalisms and fixations: "behavior due to repressed infantile motives in the Freudian sense when and where these actually occur (which is seldom)." [Allport's note to author.]
7. Some neuroses: those in which therapy, by going backward, traces the original causal behavior to create a cure.
8. Sublimation: "if a primary drive or early fixation is being sublimated it is not a case of functional autonomy (but this too is a rare situation)." [Note to author.]

In regard to the eight processes above, Allport feels that it is a question of degrees of yes or no and not an either/or proposition.

There are two major methods in which functional autonomy may be created in the personality pattern of the human. The first is the quasi-mechanical, and the second way is the propriate. In regard to the first way of the quasi-mechanical, functional autonomy may grow out in a gradual sense from stimulus–object–response or from the learning theory methods. Functional autonomy may also come about through propriate means in which the self attempts to enhance itself. In this case, the self image demands a continuation of ego-involvement.

Most of the transformations from basic drives, basic needs, basic motives, as usually considered by many theorists, to the Allport concept of functional autonomy, are very gradual. Only in rare cases such as traumatic (sudden and painful) events may we find a transformation from basic drives to functional autonomy to be sudden, highly emotional, and dramatic.

Learning Principle

In keeping with the general trend of emphasizing learning and therapeutic work, Allport follows this trend, but only to emphasize learning as a personality development factor.

Allport finds that learning is highly involved as a mode of motivation. Self-actualization (the philosophical term is *teleological functions of mankind*) helps to advance man toward his goals. Although the dual pathways of 1. mechanical determinism and 2. self-actualization ("becoming") may appear to be contradictory, man learns to do things and to create a personality because of these two factors. By mechanical determinism Allport refers to the stimulus–response, conditioning, and reinforcement theories of learning. By "becoming" he is referring not to the philosophical definition but rather to the psychologically oriented definition of an advance toward goals. As man advances and learns how to have a personality, he does so through the avenues of differentiation and integration. The serious student of personality theory will see a relevance here to the theory of Gardner Murphy.

"How personality develops is basically a problem in learning" (*ibid.,* p. 108). It is evident, then, that man gains a sense of self by learning. In his first two years of life, man employs essentially the "quasi-mechanical ways (condition, reinforcement, and repetition)."

Allport, however, makes strongest use of the term *proprium* as the principle source of learning about the self and finding one's own personality. The *proprium* has become uniquely an Allport word, meaning "the aspects of personality which together seem singularly one's own." These aspects taken together make for individuality and inward unity. In other words, one seeks goals to develop what he wants to be and does not necessarily wait on circumstances to develop goals for him. The personality creates and seeks conditions in life which are favorable to its own purposes.

Not only does man learn how to have a personality and how to use personality, he must also learn the roles which he finds compatible in society and the roles which he finds society has given or made for him. The human personality must learn how, when, and why to play the roles of life.

Cognition. Cognition, mental set, and perception as well as the term *procept* seem to fit most comfortably into this major theme of learning.

In *Pattern and Growth of Personality* (1961), Allport recognizes the voluminous research which has been done approximately in the area of perception. Such heavy current emphasis has been placed upon the concept of perception, that he has found well over three hundred studies done in this area in the decade 1946–1956. Nearly all of these more than three hundred studies seem to indicate that personality influences perception. It seems, therefore, to Allport to be worthy of some consideration in his latest work.

Despite the emphasis on perception, Allport makes use of the term *procept* as a wider and more valuable concept in personality study. He feels that perception is uniquely tied in with sensory processes. However, *procept* connotes the sensory processes plus the past, present, future, as well as the imagery, judgment, reason, remembering, forgetting, and reporting that all are on-going activities of any human personality.

Personality, it is said, is an individual's unique way of perceiving his environment, including himself.

This definition has the merit of raising cognitive operations to a level of primary importance. It counteracts the common misconception of higher mental processes as mere shadows (servants and rationalizations) of underlying motives. There is nothing secondary about cognition. The hunger to know, to comprehend our environment, is a basic motive in life.

It would be still more accurate to say that all motives are an inextricable blend of feeling and cognition. The root factor in both is a 'set' or 'tendency' (both cognitive and affective). The most important sets are personal traits which are basic modes of striving—and—thinking. These sets direct our perceptions, images, judgments (in short our proceptions) of our personal world.

There results for each individual a 'cognitive style.' To some extent culture slants this style, thus accounting for much of uniformity in people's thought and behavior. But, in the last analysis, each person is unique in the way he blends veridicality, culture, and his own personal existence.[5]

Contemporaneity Principle

Allport firmly believes that man lives and thinks in the present and not the past. Just as we have seen in the previous section, motivation is always contemporary. What the individual intends for the future (immediate or distant) is best explained by his behavior in the present. The links between past and present are historical not functional. For example, the

[5] *Ibid.*, p. 274.

human personality does not strive for a goal successfully achieved any more than a student who earns an "A" grade in a course wants to repeat the course, nor does the individual who successfully solves a puzzle want to repeat the puzzle. Although Allport does not deny a continuity at all times with the past, the past is most inadequate to explain present drives. For illustration, Allport admits a modern city is historically related to its past (the buildings, streets, facilities did not spring up overnight) but it is naive to assume that the modern city is not living for the present day's activities and planning for the future activities.

Whereas to Freud and his followers the terms *preconscious, unconscious* or *subconscious* were of extreme importance, Allport feels that the unconscious has been grossly overplayed and overestimated as a dynamic factor in life. Although there may be archaisms of past infantilisms, the unconscious mental states are primarily malfunctions of the abnormal personality. Normal human beings are not prisoners of the past. The picture of the fully mature adult is one who operates from traits that are rational, conscious, and appropriate.

Therapists in particular are highly prone to exaggerate the client's past, according to Allport. Too often the psychologist and his subject for therapy face in different directions. Whereas the psychologist as a therapist looks back, the individual with a problem looks forward with fond hopes for a happy future. One is oriented toward the past, and the other is interested only in his future. There has been an excessive dependence on geneticism in all its forms, contrary to the feeling of Allport that man has subjective values and not only reactive tendencies. He feels the most important question that anyone can ask a client is, "What do you want to be doing five years from now?"

Allport continues this theme: "Adult motives are infinitely varied, self-sustaining, contemporary systems. They are not fossils" (*ibid.*, p. 211). It will be remembered from the aforementioned requirements for an adequate theory of motivation that the first requirement is to acknowledge the contemporaneity of motives. There can be no doubt that Gordon Allport feels that man lives in the present and looks to the future and is not bound to the past in the Freudian sense.

Uniqueness Principle

Some personality theorists consider the study of single humans as the fruitful way of learning more about man's personality. Allport feels very strongly about this and bases much of his work on the unique aspects of each human personality. The uniqueness of each human is a cornerstone in his theoretical framework of personality.

He feels that personality is never general in nature but must always be particular to a single human. Consequently, whatever work the behaviorist psychologist may do in experimenting with animals such as rats, hamsters, or rhesus monkeys will have very little, if anything, to do with any human being. In another sense, Allport maintains that the affective units of personality are peculiar only to an individual. Percentile scores, standard deviations, and the like are extremely poor units of description for the human personality. The intelligence quotient may also be considered in the same light.

Allport advocates the use of traits for descriptive purposes, (see Traits–Trends–Tendency–Temperament Principle later in this chapter). Each individual can be described by a different cluster of traits. No cluster would hold true for more than one person, and thus a universal cluster for all people of even a few traits such as self-preservation and desire for love would be an impossibility. Traits are Allport's favorite descriptive tool because he feels they are enduring, meaningful, and lend themselves to accurate personal description. Thus, if psychology deals only with universals (i.e., general laws of learning or behavior) and not with particulars, it cannot be dealing adequately with the human personality. So strongly does Allport feel about uniqueness of personality that he levels his strongest criticism upon the studies of human behavior which he calls a "particular hash" of all the participants in the study. The study has little to do with any single person. As important as it may be to measure a group's total amalgamated response, the study should never be utilized to measure the individual. The individual is lost the moment he becomes a statistic in the total data, and he can never be extracted from the data or meaningfully compared to the total result of the group. At this point it should be obvious that Allport has little use for many of the measures of personality that are nonprojective. His attitude toward projective techniques, which is equally critical, will be discussed in a later section.

In his defense of his use of traits as descriptive devices, Allport says that most adjectives used in the current psychological world cut across people rather than within the single person. The novelist, the poet, and the biographer frequently are much superior to the psychologist in using meaningful, descriptive language for human behavior. In short, all too frequently we know more about a person after reading a passage from the biographer's page than we do after studying a Rorschach analysis or the traditional case study used in the guidance clinic. All too often the recipient of the information wonders, "Yes, I know, but what is he really like?"

Allport likens his position that no two human beings may have the same set of traits to that of the ancient Greek philosopher Heraclitus, who said we cannot step into the same river twice. Although the banks of the river, the bottom of the river, and the surrounding area may be very similar with each step, the river is different from what it was before. It is the same with individuals. Although they may be surrounded by many identical things, each person is different from another.

Allport makes wide use of the terms *idiographic* and *nomothetic*. These two terms he credits to Windelband, a German writer who first used the terms in 1904. Allport is very much in favor of the term *idiographic* to describe man's personality. Idiographic means one's own. Nomothetic means seeking universal laws.[6]

Allport does believe there are similarities between personalities. However, he feels these similarities are due to species, culture, differing stages of development, climatic conditions, and so on. Although these factors may reveal some resemblances, the resemblances are mere approximations and do not constitute one-to-one general laws of behavior for mankind.

Whatever we are in the way of personality, Allport feels, we must always be considered as peculiar to our own selves. The laws of behavior that interest Allport are the laws that are possible within one given person.

[6] Allport writes: "I now prefer the term 'morphogenic' (because people misuse and misspell 'idiographic'). I introduce the term occasionally in *P & G* (especially preface and last paragraph. Am sending a more recent paper that makes use of it. . . . An improved version of this paper will appear in the Septembr, 1962 number of the *J. Personality*, probably under the above title. See, *Image of Man, Proceedings of the 1961 Summer Conference*, Vol. 14, Western Washington State College, Bellingham, Washington, December, 1961, especially page 26 as follows, 'The science of molecular biology shows us that life-substances are identical across species. The building blocks of life—vegetable and animal—turn out to be strikingly uniform in terms of nucleic acids, protein molecules, and enzymatic reactions. Yet an antelope differs from an ash tree, a man from an antelope, and one man is very unlike another. The challenge of morphogenesis (accounting for pattern) grows more acute as we discover the commonalities of life.'" [Personal communication to the author, March 19, 1962.]

Allport frequently uses the terms *personal nexus* or *patterned personality* or *person centered* as the most important consideration for a theory of personality.

Repeatedly Allport says that there is far too much research of an exclusively nomothetic nature. He especially berates factor analysis, which attempts to extract characteristics of man's personality which are poorly defined and may not have existed in the original person in the first place. Some of his sharpest questions are directed at factor-analysis-minded personality theorists who, he feels, cannot take out of their statistical data any more than was put in in its original form. Measuring instruments for personality are also considered to be nomothetic. Allport makes a plea for the use of case records, life histories, and biographical data, facts which concern the singular human being. Only as these instruments may be perfected may we have more valuable predictive tools for purposes of helping mankind. The psychologist who is interested in personality research should also direct his efforts at "the pattern of events within the single personality."

Allport likens some aspects of personality to the molecular theory of chemistry. Although common molecules may exist in trees, animals, clouds, he feels that it is obviously an error to assume that all of these things are the same. Similarly, common properties or molecules of human behavior which may exist from one human being to another do not necessarily make human beings alike. Hydrogen and oxygen may exist in many forms of organic matter. The commonalities between the organic matter, however, are far apart. It is just as ridiculous to Allport to assume that commonalities such as courage and other traitlike attributes of human behavior, although they may be found in many individuals, can necessarily lead to the conclusion that these individuals will be very much alike. He feels it is nomothetic fantasy to find common units which alone make common personalities.

Having stated this position in 1937, Allport repeats the plea for individuality or uniqueness twenty-four years later in *Pattern and Growth in Personality*. In both he quotes Goethe, "Nature seems to have staked everything on individuality" (p. 7). Innumerable times he comes to the conclusion that the major dilemma which haunts the house of clinical psychology is the uniqueness of man. Every time the clinic psychologist feels he has a strong theme running through human behavior, he meets client after client who defies classification. Although, as we shall see later,

Allport does entertain the concept of *traits*, he does so in a highly idiographic manner. Allport admits some limited value in a psychogram, but he feels that too few psychologists acknowledge the overwhelming limitations of profiling an individual's strengths and weaknesses. One limitation is that it gives us only a diagram of the things we chose to investigate. It tells us nothing beyond what questions we have asked of the client. A second and even stronger limitation, he feels, is that it gives nothing of the inner organization and dynamics of any individual. A profile is nothing more than a silhouette. All we can see of the human being is a dark outline against a white background which tells us little more than a rough outline of what the human being is like. He summarizes, "the fact of the matter is that psychography *cannot* synthesize. It can only string beads" (*ibid.*, p. 16).

The strong insistence by Allport that man must always be considered as a unique individual has grown stronger through the years.

Ego or Self Principle

In many ways Allport uses the term *ego* as synonomous with the term *self*. Allport admits that the consideration of the subjective, or feeling about oneself or one's own person, is most difficult. However, personality theorists, he feels, cannot shelve this difficult problem.

Allport feels that there may be an overemphasis on the self. He hazards a guess that many people go through an entire day without being aware of self at all. As each of us pursues his daily chores, he may do so in a somewhat automated way. Consequently, he goes about the duties of the day and does not spend many reflective moments upon who he is, what he is, why he is, where he is, and how he got there in the first place. His life consists of minutiae.

Allport admits that despite the difficulty of describing the nature of self, the concept of self is essential in the study of personality. Historically this may be attributed to the strong influence of the work of Sigmund Freud. Allport feels that Freud died before completing fully his theory of the ego. Allport's concept is that the ego has within itself a dynamic process of great positive power rather than the Freudian concept of the ego as a "rider on a horse." It may be remembered by the reader that in the Freudian sense, the ego sits upon the id and tries to control it as the executor or administrator of id impulses. In Allport's terms, the ego and/or the self is the unifying force or mastic for all the habits, traits, attitudes, sentiments, and tendencies of a human being.

Historically, psychology has gone from the soul to the self to the ego. The current emphasis seems to be upon ego involvement, wherein the ego serves as the knower, organizer, observer, status-seeker, or the socialized being, or, as is most often true, a combination of all five of the previous forces. Beyond this, whenever the ego is involved in human behavior, it affects the confidence, judgment, memory, frame of reference, learning aptitude, and all of the motivational aspects of any human being. It is essential, then, Allport feels, in studying anyone, to study the ego structure. Where the ego is involved, there is usually a total participation of the self. Ego involvement or the absence of ego involvement makes a critical difference in human behavior.

Allport feels that if democracy is ever to be a success, it is essential that its constituents be ego involved. It will be recalled that ego involvement was an important factor in motivation in the previous section.

The self-image leads to the ego ideal. However, the ego ideal does not automatically allow the self to be a mover, motivator, or agent toward further action. Primarily the self-image is only the individual as he is known to himself. The self-image may at many times be completely inaccessible to any other human. Although self-images grow out of good intentions and intentions are important in the theory of Allport, we cannot say that intentions will necessarily motivate, or lead to, changed behavior.

Allport considers that there are eight historical conceptions which have led toward the concept of the ego. All of these eight conceptions have three things in common: 1. that the ego is never the entire personality; 2. that one must always consider ego involvement in degrees; 3. that whatever one considers about the ego, it is always operating in the present and is highly preoccupied with the future.

Eight Historical Concepts Toward Ego Formation

1. Ego as the knower.
2. Ego as the object of knowledge.
3. Ego as a source of primitive selfishness.
4. Ego as the prime dominant drive.
5. Ego as the passive organizer of mental processes.
6. Ego as "fighter for ends" (purposive and forceful).
7. Ego as the variable set of forces which lead to a behavioral system.
8. Ego as the subjective organizer of culture (social values).

Proprium. Much of Allport's discussion of the ego or self culminates in the proprium. The proprium is more than a style of life; it is the understanding that man wants to become something for himself and not just to survive on a tension reduction basis. Allport adroitly presents the view that man wants to become something in his *Becoming: Basic Considerations for a Psychology of Personality* (1955). The proprium includes all of the collected aspects of an individual's personality that are uniquely his own. All of these collective aspects of personality make the individual different from all other individuals and give the individual some inward unity. The proprium includes bodily sense, rational thinking, propriate striving, and the concepts of self-image, self-identity, self-extension, and self-esteem. The proprium does not develop automatically, nor does it develop very quickly. At least partially Allport agrees with Jung that man does not have a fully developed sense of self or ego until he reaches the middle years and is able to develop all of the above characteristics. The proprium initially develops through the usual consideration of the laws of learning. From an infant on, man develops his proprium through conditioning, reinforcement, habits, and other aspects of learning. However, in full adulthood man needs to develop and learn a self-image, a great deal of cognitive insight, a true identification of self and closure (bringing together the figure of himself and the background into a unity). Allport considers the mature adult to be a true extension of all the self concepts he has gained in achieving adulthood. The mature adult is also able to objectify himself in the world scene. Allport considers two components to be highly important in objectifying the self. These components are insight and humor. To be able to see oneself in the true position one occupies in life and, further, to have the ability or the sense of ridiculous to see oneself as not overpoweringly important in the world order of things are key components to objectifying, or seeing oneself objectively.

Pattern and Growth in Personality discusses the steps which lead up to a development of the proprium. There are seven aspects of behavior which evolve a sense of self in the individual.

1. The first aspect is developing a sense of one's own body and organic and physiological systems.
2. The second aspect has to do with continuing the sense of self-identity, that is to say, who one is, the relationship of an individual to others, and the position one holds in life.
3. The next step is fulfilling a sense of pride in one's self, or a feeling of

self-esteem. (Aspects 1, 2, and 3 are the first three years of life.)

4. At this period of life, Allport feels, one begins to extend the limits of the self. This comes from being out more in the world, meeting more people, and experiencing deeper levels of contact with things and people.

5. Following this we find the individual gradually gaining a greater self-image. (Aspects 4 and 5 are ages four to six.)

6. Beginning with approximately the age of six, the individual develops his self as a rational "coper." The self as a coper hopes to find solutions and hopes to cope with life's problems as they occur at this age level. (Ages 6–12.)

7. The last aspect to develop out of the beginnings of life is the one which occurs at the adolescent level.[7] Allport feels these seven steps are necessary before the proprium is fully developed at the adulthood level.

In a final word, the proprium may develop ineffectively providing two subjective conditions occur. These conditions are feelings of inferiority and deeply involved feelings of conscience. Providing these two feelings are present in the concept of the self, Allport feels that such subjective conditions affect negatively all of the functioning and especially all of the structuring of the personality.

Roles. Being a true eclectic, Allport does not ignore the value of roles in the development of the personality. He follows somewhat the accepted conception of roles as structured modes of indulging in the social life. ". . . it is what society expects of an individual occupying a given position in a group" (*ibid.*, p. 181). Although Allport feels one cannot question the importance of roles, he does feel that they are all too frequently over-emphasized by the social psychologist.

There is considerable latitude in the way each person conducts his roles. "We cannot agree that personality is a mere colligation of roles" (*ibid.*, p. 185).

Four factors are involved in the consideration of roles. First, there are the roles that one is expected to take. These constitute "the rules of the game" and are what are expected of us from society. Second, much depends upon how each of us conceives the role that society may want to ascribe to us. We all define our role from our own perceptual system. Consequently, two fathers or two college-aged sons may not conceive of their roles in exactly the same way. As a matter of fact, it is highly un-

---

[7] Allport states further: "One does not strive for a proprium. His ego-involved functional autonomous interests are 'propriate striving'." [Note to author.]

likely that two fathers conceive of their father role in an identical manner. Third, there is the factor of the degree to which each one of us decides to accept the roles that society has determined for us, and which we see in differing ways. It is quite possible, thinks Allport, that radical people are inclined not to accept roles which they find untenable, whereas conservative people are more likely to accept their socially assigned roles. Fourth, the performance of each one of us in the roles that face us varies tremendously. This is another manifestation of the uniqueness of personality. It is obvious to Allport, as it is to many others, that the levels of ability from one individual to another are so varied that the performance of any so-called equal roles will never produce equal results. Thus, the captain of one football team can never be compared in his performance of that role to the captain of the same football team for the second game of the season. Each of us can play the role only to the best of our ability—a quality that must differ from person to person.

Allport asks this provocative question and spends considerable time discussing it: What is the fully developed self or what may we call a mature personality? (chap. 12, "The Mature Personality," *Pattern and Growth in Personality*, p. 307). He admits that neither he nor any other psychologist can tell us completely what normal, or healthy, or mature personalities are. However, there is a practical aspect which in our western culture he feels does lead to considerable agreement as to what can be considered the mature personality or the fully developed self. Allport finds six criteria that all of us may agree upon. "The mature personality will 1. have a widely extended sense of self; 2. be able to relate himself warmly to others in both intimate and nonintimate contacts; 3. possess a fundamental emotional security and accept himself; 4. perceive, think, and act with zest in accordance with outer reality; 5. be capable of self-objectification, of insight in humor; 6. live in harmony with a unifying philosophy of life." Allport makes no claim to originality for the six criteria, but does feel that too often psychotherapy and counseling ignore these factors and overstress one or two. Also involved, and not too well-handled, are our habits and developmental techniques in training children to become adults. It is the well-rounded individual who can meet the above six criteria.

Continuity—Discontinuity Principle

In this principle, as interpreted by the writer, Allport appears to run counter to the generally accepted current practice of assuming that all behavior exists on a continuum basis. Gordon Allport presents a case which states approximately that many aspects of life are not on a continuum basis, or in other words, that what we do is not always a matter of degree, but a difference in kind.

Allport feels that there is confusion between symptoms and processes. Where there appears to be a continuum, it is a continuum of symptoms and not processes. Appearances may be deceiving. When persons judge an individual or measure outward appearances by response to a psychological test, these appearances (performances) may very well distribute themselves along a continuum basis. But, he strongly maintains that the underlying basis which brings about appearances (performances) are definitely not continuous. The dynamics or processes in mechanisms are frequently polar in nature.

Allport feels there is a great gulf between the lives of different human beings. Each human being is not a continuum toward the next human being but must be considered as an entity of and by himself. As we have stated before, he rejects Freud's idea of tying all adult motivations to infant biological ones. The personality that is normal does not drag its infantile expressions around but leaves them behind, grows out of them. Allport agrees that there may be some instinctive behavior in the infant or some reflexive form of behavior throughout life. However, the developed mature personality is essentially a post-instinctive behavior pattern. The tiny infant is a creature of heredity, motivated primarily by primitive drives, and has a high degree of reflex existence. As such, the infant is a biological model. The adult is also a biological model plus a sociological member of society plus a fully integrated ego culminating in the aspect of functional autonomy. Allport almost suggests a discontinuity between the child and adult motivational structure, which creates approximately two theories of personality. The theory of personality for the child is based on tension reduction, avoidance of pain and seeking of pleasure, and a biological model. The adult personality operates from a matrix or radix of organized and highly focused traits. The adult, then, no longer derives his power from organic, primitive sources but from the functional autonomy motivating system. Allport repeats this theme again in 1961, having first posited it in his 1937 book. In one section (p. 196) he uses the phrase, *the adult vs. the infant*. It is almost as if there were two kinds of worlds, a childhood world and an adult world. The theme is a recurrent one that normal people are not prisoners of the past (*Personality and Social Encounter*, p. 145).

In still another sense, Allport approaches the problem of continuity *vs.* discontinuity by quoting from Julian Huxley, "Man stands alone." It is partially for this reason that Allport questions the value of using rats or primates as models to study personality. Although he readily admits that mice and monkeys are not used directly in personality studies, he objects primarily to the extension of research data on animals for human beings.

As we have previously stated, Allport feels that Freud "smudged" the boundary lines between the behavior of a neurotic and a normal human being, stating that ". . . there is, in a restricted sense, a discontinuity between normal and abnormal motivation, and that we need a theory that will recognize this fact. Discontinuities are distinctly unpopular in psychological science" (*ibid.*, p. 105). There is a difference between the normal and the abnormal human being. Allport is willing to admit border line cases or a linear continuum in behavior. He is also willing to admit a relative shifting from culture to culture in man's behavior and some abnormal behavior. However, he insists there is a vast difference in the motivational structure, in the perceptual systems, and in the behavioral processes between a normal and a psychotic human being. In 1937, Allport delineated some of the characteristics he felt to be possesed by normally behaving people. In a sense, he is, therefore, saying that the abnormal person or the psychotic acts differently from these behavioral processes. (See especially p. 154 in *Pattern and Growth in Personality*.) The normal human being is able to do at least some or all of the following three things: 1. There is a capacity to make an ego extension beyond the self. To be interested in more than the self is a normal behavioral activity. 2. Self-objectification, which includes the capacity for self-insight and also the capacity for humor or laughter about oneself, is also in the normal behavioral pattern but not in the abnormal one. 3. The normal individual almost always has a unifying philosophy of life. By this, Allport means there is a frame of meaning and a feeling of responsibility as a human being. In 1958, he added three more factors which he felt the normal human being possessed. They are: "The capacity for a warm, profound relationship of oneself to other people; the possession of realistic skills, realistic abilities," and a realistic perceptual system for solving the practical problems of every day living; and "a compassionate regard for all living creatures" (*Personality and Social Encounter*, p. 162).

The process of going from normality to abnormality is not continuous. There is a difference between a preponderant anabolic process which the normal human being builds, or attempts to build for the future, and a catabolic process in which the abnormal human being is attempting to destroy or forestall a forward motion.

Allport feels there is a need for something like a moral philosophy in determining continuity and discontinuity in human behavior. This again reflects his willingness to admit all fields as valuable aspects of personality study. Allport does not profess to have settled the issue of continuity–discontinuity but he feels strongly that psychologists and philosophers working together may come much closer than we are at present.

Allport entertains the idea that there may be two ways to divide the normal from the abnormal: statistical and ethical. The ethical quality obviously belongs to the psychologist-philosopher. Currently he feels that we have not progressed far enough in admitting an ethical standpoint in delineating normality from abnormality, that there may be a basis for considering behavior as either right or wrong. It is, however, the statistical approach which he feels creates many more problems than it possibly solves. Psychologists are too much in love with the beauty of the normal distribution curve. The normal distribution curve fails psychology in the field of personality study because the curve is only a label. Whenever one works with numbers or quantified data, the scales and the test scores automatically distribute continuously. This creates a situation in which measurement dictates the behavior of man, bimodal data not being possible because of the instrument used. Scores on a single instrument which measures personality will fall on a continuum basis. It might be far better to use a number of measurement devices and compare the results of the devices to find out what dichotomies may exist. Despite the fact that traits, even though intercorrelated positively, may fall on a continuum within a single testing instrument, Allport feels that traits nonetheless are distinct from each other. Studies of averages among differing subjects which must be treated statistically often lead to creating false continua. Allport does not deny the value of statistics and quantitative measurement. His point is that in use of such techniques their weakness must be acknowledged. It is a weakness to measure human beings and allow the measuring instrument to determine the quality of human behavior.

Another tool that Allport finds which does not support the theory of continuity in behavior is his tool of functional autonomy. If one accepts the concept of functional autonomy, he must realize that it permits a relative divorce from the person's past. Thus, "as the individual matures, the bond with the past is broken" (*Pattern and Growth in Personality*, p. 227).

Traits—Trends—Tendency—Temperament Principle

This principle reflects a high degree of evolution in the thinking of Allport. The primary theme of this principle is, however, that of traits. The terms *traits, trends, tendency,* and *temperament* are not intentionally alliterative. The alliteration uniquely represents the evolution in Allport's thinking. Not represented in the title but contained in the body of this principle, however, is another word beginning with "t," types. As we shall see later, Allport does not use this concept of types.

In studying the human personality, Allport asks quite sensibly which units shall we use? In his 1958 essay (pp. 111–129) Allport discusses ten current possibilities as units of study.

1. Intellectual capacities. Measuring and analyzing intellectual ability, Allport feels, may some day be a fruitful approach. However, he feels that at the present the field is not well enough developed to give many cues to motivation and personality.

2. Syndromes of temperament. Allport feels that the work of Sheldon, Thurstone, Cattell, Guilford and others, has made a valuable contribution to personality theory.

3. Unconscious motives. This is the dimension with the Freudian flavor in the study of personality.

4. Social attitudes. This is a method of personality study primarily practiced by the social psychologist.

5. Ideational schemata. Personality study is conducted through generalizing the forms of thought.

6. Interests and values. Personality is studied through the structuring of motives such as those measured by the Allport-Vernon-Lindzey Study of Values Test.

7. Expressive traits. Primarily postures, but also gestures, and possibly graphology are studied.

8. Stylistic traits. This is a field which Allport feels is not too well studied but which considers those behavioral traits which lie on the surface of human behavior.

9. Pathological Trends. This field or unit of study of personality has received wide emphasis. Such tests as the MMPI and many others like it are instruments of measure for the pathological trends. (Unit of study for personality.)

10. Factorial clusters. In this, Allport includes all of the current work of Cattell, Eysenck, and others who use primarily a statistical approach as a unit of study of personality. In regard to the last unit of study, factorial clusters, Allport feels "psychology cannot synthesise. It can only string beads," by which Allport means that the factorial analysis unit of study may not derive true units of human behavior (*ibid.,* p. 16).

Allport has repeated the question, "What unit shall we use?" especially in his *Pattern and Growth in Personality*. After much consideration of the value as a unit of study of the terms *trait, trend, tendency, temperament,* or *type,* Allport seems to hold the strongest argument for the concept of trait. It is "the only approach possible if we wish to compare people" (*ibid.,* p. 360). He does not deny the value of tendency, or trends, which he later develops as personal dispositions. Temperament, he feels, has a strong hereditary flavor. The use of types as a unit of study does not seem feasible because types are assigned by others, and the individual loses his unique characteristics. The type is more a classification system than a unit of study.

In addition to the five kinds of units of study mentioned above, Allport also considers attitudes and character as units of study. Character is difficult to cope with as a unit of study because of the judgment of moral rightness and wrongness involved. On the other hand, attitudes, he feels, are a disposition to an object or toward an object of value. There may be in this sense a retraction or a repulsion for the object. Also involved is an emotional response from the very narrow range of stimuli toward the object of value. Attitude also evaluates, while a trait does not evaluate but simply exists within the individual. Attitudes also are very changeable, a fact which makes attitude difficult to work with as a unit of measurement. As we shall see later, Allport considers attitude also as a somewhat difficult unit of study. He eventually employs the term *values* as a unit of study for the unique individual. (See Allport-Vernon-Lindzey, *A Study of Values,* rev. ed., Houghton Mifflin, 1960.)

In his 1961 work, Allport still finds it difficult to discover the fundamental units that psychology may use in studying personalities. Historically, we have progressed in the following manner:

A. Units of the Humors:	(black bile—melancholic)
	(yellow bile—sanguine)
	(red bile—choleric)
	(white bile—phlegmatic)
B. Faculties:	(powers of the mind)
C. Instincts:	(Freud and McDougall)
D. Drives:	(behaviorists)
E. Needs:	(H. A. Murray)
F. Current themes:	(habits, S–R, value–vectors, sentiments, syndromes, ergs, personal constructs, dimensions, schemata, and factors)

Having considered the struggles Allport has had with adopting a comfortable and profitable unit of study, we shall now review the most tenable units that Allport has found to date. These are presented not in order of importance or chronological development but simply as a pedagogical method. They are, as the title of this principal or major theme indicates, traits, trends, tendency, and temperament.

Traits. Allport's consideration of the term *traits* as a unit of study for personality has continued for many years. He writes, "My first paper on trait was, 'What is a trait of personality?' published in 1931 (as you show in your bibliography). Actually this paper was given at the International Congress in 1929 (at Yale). So my interest dates back over thirty years" [note to author]. In that time he has not changed his essential position but has simply added more and more detail to the picture. In fact, Allport's treatment of this term has so much depth that it will be the device of the writer to enumerate some but not all of the considerations Allport makes for the term *trait*.

Eight criteria to define trait: 1. A trait has more than nominal existence (habits of a complex order). 2. A trait is more generalized than a habit (two or more habits which are organized and coherent). 3. A trait is dynamic, or at least determinative (plays a motivating role in each act). 4. The existence of a trait may be established empirically or statistically (evidence of repeated reactions or statistical treatment). 5. Traits are only relatively independent of each other (usually correlate positively to some degree with each other). 6. A trait of personality, psychologically considered, is not the same as moral quality (may or may not coincide with conventional social concept). 7. Acts and even habits that are inconsistent with a trait are not proof of the nonexistence of the trait (may be contradictory traits in the same personality—neatness and carelessness—plus behavior acts under stress which temporarily belie the trait). 8. A trait may be viewed either in the light of the personality that contains it or in the light of its distribution in the population at large (traits are unique and traits are universal).

The following list covers some, but certainly not all, of the considerations that Allport sees in trait as a comfortable and meaningful unit of study for personality.

1. Traits have the capacity to motivate, inhibit, or select appropriate human behavior. A trait is a combination of motives and habits.

2. Mutually interdependent traits are the main elements in behavior.

3. Traits help to explain the consistencies that we find in personality. Although, as we have stated, traits are highly interdependent and highly consistent, they are not completely interdependent nor consistent.

4. Traits are not directly observable but must be inferred. As such, traits are very difficult to classify.

5. A trait begins with a neuro-psychic system.

6. There are two kinds of traits: individual and common. The individual trait is a true trait, while the common trait is simply a measure of a number of individual traits as found in a number of people. Allport adds: ". . . might add to 'individual trait' (called in 1961 'personal disposition'). It is just a shift in terms because no one fully understood the sharp difference between my conceptions (1937) of 'common' and 'individual' trait" [Note to author.]

7. As we have stated, a trait is a combination of two or more habits. However, habits no longer have the capacity to dominate traits, but traits may force a creation of new habits. These new habits, then, must be compatible to the trait. Traits may be considered as stylistic and dynamic. The stylistic trait tells how one goes about behaving, while the dynamic trait tells why one behaves as he does. The first gives style, whereas the second gives motivating factors.

8. Traits may drive as well as direct. They may push as well as dictate the path. Traits guide and initiate behavior.

9. Traits have a strong connotation of contemporaneity or a state of being and a "nowness" of things. Traits do not exist directly from the past.

10. The question of what to call traits or the names to give to them is very interesting. Allport and Odbert (1936), for example, made a search of the dictionary and other works and found 17,953 trait names! So there are literally thousands of traits. In his 1937 book, Allport gives four solid columns of trait names, divided approximately into true dispositions, present activities, evaluative terms, metaphorical, and other trait names. The following are obviously only a few, a very few, of the names for true traits: *punctuality, aggressiveness, cheerfulness, competitiveness, fancifulness, gregariousness, vigor,* etc.

11. Despite the fact that there are many, many hundreds of traits, Allport makes a rough classification of traits for a given individual into cardinal, central, and secondary traits. The cardinal traits are all-pervasive and are few. Cardinal traits are the dominant traits and become almost "ruling passions." Central traits are the "building blocks of personality." These traits bring focus to the primary aspects of the individual's behavior. The third kind of trait is the secondary trait. This is minor and less important in the scheme as Allport sees it. Secondary traits are not as evident to others, and one must study an individual quite thoroughly in order to delineate what the secondary traits are.

12. Each existing trait may not have an opposite trait. For example, the absence of a trait may not guarantee the presence of its opposite. Allport, in short, does not believe in the polarity of behavior.

13. The value of common traits helps all of us to compare approximate modes of adjustment of similar individuals in similar societies. A secondary value of common traits is to help train young psychologists in a common language and to give them training in analytical procedures with common factors.

14. Clusters of traits are often called *syndromes* by Allport.

15. Expressive traits and stylistic traits are two of the units which are often sought in personality assessment in a clinical situation. Expressive traits, for example, are extraversion, persistence, and traits which denote degrees of sociability. On the other hand, stylistic traits center on manners of behaving, such as politeness or hesitancy.

16. In an essay derived from a symposium in which Allport participated in 1946, he argues strongly that acquired traits may become primary motivational units. This is an introduction in a sense to his concept of functional autonomy. It is also a rebuttal to the Freudian concept of the ego being the executor of the id. Allport prefers to consider the ego as

having a "go" of its very own and not having to be responsible to the id for primary moving forces (*Personality and Social Encounter*, pp. 137–151).

Harking back to much of his previous work, Allport still finds a tremendous value in the concept of traits. He continues to pursue this trait system idea in his 1961 book. Here he asks the question, "Are traits veridical (really true to the individual) or are traits fictional (made up for convenience sake)?" He answers this question for himself by saying, "We have voted in favor of the veridical view of traits" (*Pattern and Growth in Personality*, p. 337).

Allport emphasizes the common traits as a necessary aspect in studying human behavior to the point where he defines the term and then gives two other statements which, in a sense, are redefinitions and reinforcements of the original definition. They are as follows:

Common traits are, then, those aspects of personality in respect to which most people within a given culture can be profitably compared.

A common trait is a category for classifying functionally equivalent forms of behavior in a general population of people. Though influenced by nominal and artifactual considerations, a common trait to some extent reflects veridical and comparable dispositions in many personalities who, because of a common human nature and common culture, develop similar modes of adjusting to their environments, though to varying degrees.[8]

Finally, Allport gives a simpler though less precise definition of a common trait as, *"generalized disposition in respect to which people can be profitably compared"* (*ibid.*, p. 349).

Allport himself is not satisfied with the common trait approach. He feels it creates many ambiguities, and the difficulties we have are necessary ones because we are forced to use them. We have nothing better at the moment than common traits. As we have said, Allport feels that the trait approach is the only sensible one if we are to compare one individual to another.

Personal Dispositions. This term Allport finds much more comfortable than the term individual traits. He often calls it by the initials "PD". A personal disposition is defined as ". . . a generalized neuropsychic structure (peculiar to the individual), with the capacity to render many stimuli

[8] *Ibid.*, pp. 340 and 349.

functionally equivalent, and to initiate and guide consistent (equivalent) forms of adaptive and stylistic behavior" (*ibid.*, p. 373).

Borrowing the terms *phenotypical* and *genotypical* from Lewin, Allport finds them convenient in distinguishing between personal dispositions. Phenotypical personal dispositions attempt to describe behavior in terms of the present or current ongoing behavior. Genotypical personal dispositions are of much the deeper nature. It is the genotypical with which the psychoanalyst wishes to deal. Because the genotypical personal disposition is so difficult to get at, it is possible that the therapist may be dealing with psuedo-traits.

Carrying over his former discussion of cardinal, central, and secondary traits, Allport also uses these three classifications in regard to personal dispositions. The definitions and explanation for these three is essentially the same as that given for traits in the above section.

Purely in a hypothetical manner, Allport asks the question, "How many dispositions has a person?"

"When psychology develops adequate diagnostic methods for discovering the major lines along which a particular personality is organized (personal dispositions), it may turn out that the number of such foci will normally vary between five and ten. We state this proposition as a hypothesis subject to eventual scientific testing" (*ibid.*, p. 367).

We now end our major consideration of traits as a behavioral phenomenon or descriptive or comparative phenomenon of human behavior. Allport has worked with these traits over the past twenty-four years, weaving in and out, clarifying a little more closely what his concept of the trait system in personality theory is. We now turn our attention to a short discussion of trends as a necessary part of personality structure.

Trends. The question of trends in human behavior is somewhat synonomous with style of life or the tendency to action, or, as Allport has finally worked it out, the personal dispositions of each individual. Gordon Allport's brother, Floyd H. Allport, now retired from the Maxwell School for Citizenship, Syracuse University, is credited with the principle of life purposes or teleonomic trends. The idea here is that principal themes or trends or constructs are highly involved in any given life. Gordon Allport feels that probably the best solution to what units may be profitably used in studying personality lies in identifying the unique dynamic *trends* peculiar to the structure of each individual life (*Personality and Social Encounter*, p. 111).

Tendency. The term *tendency* also occurs frequently in the thinking of Allport. It is almost synonomous with trends and both of these terms, *trends* and *tendency*, ultimately become the personal dispositions which Allport has created in his latest work of 1961. The term *tendency* appears to mean a long range mental set toward behavior, or some kind of a disposition for readiness to act, and in a certain prescribed way.

Both the terms, *trend* and *tendency*, appear to be overtures of the prologue to the current theme of personal dispositions as Allport treats it.

Temperament. Allport finds the term *temperament* useful and defines it in the following way.

Temperament refers to the characteristic phenomena of an individual's emotional nature, including his susceptibility to emotional stimulation, his customary strength and speed of response, the quality of his prevailing mood, and all peculiarities of fluctuation and intensity in mood, these phenomena being regarded as dependent upon constitutional makeup, and therefore largely hereditary in origin.[9]

Allport finds temperament, intelligence, and physique to be the "raw materials" from which personality is fashioned.

Temperament as a hereditary factor cannot be ignored although it is changeable as are all the considerations of Allport concerning personality. It will be remembered that Allport's is an open-ended system of personality theory.

We have now covered the primary themes or principles, as they are called in this book, of Gordon Allport's theory of personality as he has considered it primarily through the years 1937 to 1961, the date of issue of his latest book, *Pattern and Growth in Personality*. These seven principles around which we find it most convenient to group the ideas of Allport are motivation, learning, contemporaneity, uniqueness, ego or self, continuity–discontinuity, and traits–trends–tendency–temperament.

DELIMITATION

As must be true with all eclectic personality theorists, there is much of Allport's theory or considerations regarding personality which is not covered in this chapter. This is unavoidable in any attempt to condense the writings of well over twenty years and the thinking of an active and intellectually curious mind such as that of Gordon Allport.

[9] *Pattern and Growth in Personality*, p. 34.

This chapter does not cover, except as an introduction, the fascinating development of how to approach personality theory through the interdisciplinary approach of literature and psychology, philosophy and psychology, religion or ethics, and psychology, for instance; and many others of Allport's valuable contributions. The primary reason for not including the approach theory is that it seems to concern *how* to consider personality rather than the dynamics of *why* man behaves as he does.

Also missing in this chapter is Allport's discussion of morale as a dynamic force.

Although much more could be said, because Allport is a prolific and exciting writer, in the final analysis some of his writing is, of course, not directly applicable to personality theory as it is covered in the present text.

Any student deeply interested in the work of Allport is urged to make a thorough study of the Allport-Vernon-Lindzey *Study of Values Test*. This has been previously mentioned in the body of the chapter. The six values measured by this test are theoretical values, economic values, aesthetic values, social values, political values, and religious values.

Also missing from this book is Allport's excellent discussion of the various methods of assessment. (Chapters 17 and 18 in his *Pattern and Growth in Personality*.)

For good fun in reading and stirring exposition, the student is urged to try at least one work of Gordon Allport (see bibliography at end of chapter).

EXPLAINING HUMAN BEHAVIOR VIA ALLPORT'S THEORY

Once again we come to that section of the theorist's work in which we test by extrapolation how well the theory can answer or explain certain phenomenon in life. As may be expected we find the work of Gordon Allport and his personality theory to be eclectic in explaining why man does the following things: gets married, commits perversions, commits suicide, breaks laws, believes in a supranatural being or practices a religious custom, has a degree of humor or laughs, indulges in smoking any form of tobacco, indulges in play or the pursuit of some recreational activity, and succumbs to psychotic or neurotic behavioral patterns.

One might assume that in Allport's frame of reference all explanations would consider the uniqueness of man, that is, there would be as many explanations for behavior as there are people. However, as we shall see in later sections, Allport's work is more complete than that of other theorists.

In contrast to many of the theorists in this text, Allport gives very full explanations for the behavior of man as we consider the nine phenomenon mentioned above. This is a tribute to the thoroughness and the eclectic quality of Allport's theory of personality.

Marriage

Allport does not directly deal with marriage in his theory; however, he feels that psychology sidesteps a consideration and examination of the concept of love. Finding that many psychologists operating in the modern scene are fleeing from anything which appears to be sentimental or tender or denotes the capacity of love from one human being for another, he uses the term from Ian Suttie called *Flight from Tenderness.*

At times Allport uses the word *affiliation* as practically a synonym for the word *love.* His feeling concerning affiliation is that it is one of the strongest desires, and is almost inescapable as one considers the groundwork of human life. In contrast to modern psychology, which he condemns as ignoring the facet of man's capacity to love or to be loved, Allport devotes an entire chapter to a consideration of this subject. (Chapter 13, "A Basic Psychology of Love and Hate," *Personality and Social Encounter,* pp. 199–219.) Love, or the feeling of affiliation toward another individual, is a post-instinctive phenomenon. As man progresses through life, he develops a system of positive attachment toward objects or primarily toward people, but he is not born with this feeling.

As man develops from infancy through childhood, adolescence and on into adulthood, love becomes an extension of himself. He finds then an esteem toward other people who in turn bring to him feelings of security, happiness, and trust. Allport calls this extension of self and a feeling of esteem toward other people the *affiliative thrust.* It is possible, however, for this affiliative thrust to turn to feelings of deep hatred. In this we find some of the polarity of Freud in the love–hate dichotomy.

"It is the nature of human life to crave affiliation and love, providing such attachments are not inimical to one's sense of personal security and self-esteem" (*Personality and Social Encounter,* pp. 214–215). Allport is saying by this that there is a tremendous drive toward affiliation and love in almost every human being. However, he does feel that the sense of self-esteem, or the feeling of worthiness for self, preceeds the feeling of affiliation, or love toward another human.

In *Pattern and Growth* Allport feels that the self-image may be highly involved in the act of falling in love and in the subsequent marriage that may result. In a sense, falling in love and getting married may be a way of testing the self image and of giving support to the self image. It is assumed that a deep affiliation and attachment to another human would help to create for the individual a better feeling of his own image. Somebody loves him and he cares about somebody.

Perversions

As we have seen before, Allport does not feel that much of man's behavior is "goal inhibited sexuality." In this disagreement with Freud, Allport feels that if all motivation were goal inhibited sexuality, we should expect that all of the species of man would have it. Allport cannot find it plausible that the human animal is a repressed pervert. Rather he feels that any kind of perversion may be an inappropriate proprium in the motivational pattern. In short, there has been a faulty functional autonomy.

There is in Allport's writing a strong feeling that perverted forms of behavior growing out of sexual aberration have received much more attention than they warrant. It should be stressed, Allport feels, that man is more of a cooperative animal than a sexually perverted animal. In addition to this, Allport feels there should be much more warrant to acknowledge the rightness and wrongness in immoral behavior. He finds it faulty and tiresome to have behavior excused as nothing more than an irrepressible id. He feels many of the theorists run away from the issue of immoral behavior.

Despite the fact that Allport makes some criticisms of Freud, he does feel there is "residual truth" in some of Freud's formulations. He feels that the sex drive cannot always be considered as a uniform need, and central and demanding upon the personality even though "sex is intricately fused with all manner of acquired beliefs, tastes, habits, and inhibitions" because the nervous system does not conveniently keep sex impulses separated.

To say, for example, that a certain man or woman is *homosexual* is by no means to characterize his or her motivation. There are myriad forms of homosexuality: overt, covert, active, passive, compulsive, sublimated, diffuse, specific, altruistic, gentle, sadistic, protective, adulatory, superficial, repressed, peripheral, central, temporary, lasting, esthetic, intellectual—ultimately, as many forms as there are individuals whose *need Sex* has been 'cathected' toward their own sex— and think of the many other ways this abstract need can be affected. Concretely, then, it seems artificial to a high degree to say that sex takes the same form or has the same significance in any two personalities. Each lives with his own particular pattern. Although we may learn something of the nature of these patterns by studying the common biological foundation, it would be a mistake to assume that the abstracted sex capacity is itself a separable unit of motivation.[10]

Allport does agree with the Freudians and neo-Freudians that abnormal motivation probably comes from the unconscious; therefore, we do not know much about perverted forms of behavior. "Much motivation, we repeat, is unconscious, infantile, and hidden from one's self. The important point however is that *some* motivation is functionally autonomous, especially in personalities that we consider normal, mature, sound" (*ibid.*, p. 217). Allport is saying perhaps that we simply do not know enough about the unconscious, preconscious characteristics of man's behavior.

Suicide

Loss of self-image and the loss of the sense of ego may be the causal factors for suicide, although Allport makes no direct references to suicide in his writings. Essentially, when a person commits suicide, the entire motivational pattern is twisted and contorted out of reality. It is possible to consider suicide as the ultimate in the defense mechanism of repression. In wishing to escape in using the ego defense mechanism of repression, an individual may repress his life to the ultimate point of losing it. Inadequate personalities who commit suicide may have forgotten completely their value systems and the commitments they have made toward themselves and toward others.

Lawbreaking

The habitual criminal may have a very faulty system of traits which he has gained through an inadequate functional autonomous system. In this individual the personal disposition to break the law overemphasizes the egocentric self-image pattern.

Allport feels that lawbreaking or criminality is a question of morality and religion as well as a question of the dynamics of behavior.

Allport acknowledges, especially from the Gluecks' study, that there may be some tendency to uphold Sheldon's somatotyping. He finds some of the Gluecks' work promising but rather imperfect evidence to date.

[10] *Pattern and Growth in Personality*, p. 371.

People who break laws, but are not necessarily following the life of a criminal, are unable to "internalize" an obedience into the self and have been unable to develop a true conscience. In this sense, there is a pathology of conscience. No inner control exists but only obedience to outer control. Where the outer control, such as police or other restraining force, is weak or not present, the individual without an inner conscience cannot preconceive the consequence of the act and thus breaks laws whenever he wishes to do so. In the adult conscience, there is a feeling of obligation toward others, an obligation to uphold laws that the representatives of the people have made. Robbery, however, cannot be felt to have achieved an adult level or proprium. Because the conscience takes a long time to develop through childhood and adolescence into adulthood, the childhood obligation of "must" is unable at times to evolve into the adult concept of "ought." It is only when the human being can internalize his feelings of obligation toward others that a conscience can develop. It is only when a conscience develops that we may expect human beings to follow the laws of the land.

In the final analysis, lawbreaking may be an illustration of continuity–discontinuity since normal distribution is lacking in criminal activity. It is considered that one does or does not break a law. He does not half-break or half-maintain a law.

Supranatural Being

Unlike many theorists, Allport has a great deal to say about man's worshipping a supranatural being or indulging in a religious activity.

Allport feels that much of psychology overreacts against religion and love. Allport does not wish to evade the issue of religion or belief in a supreme being. For example, in 1960, Allport gave the Ingraham Lectures in philosophy and religion in Colby College, Waterville, Maine. His topic for that lecture was "Psychology and Religion." This has since been published in *The Student Seeks an Answer*. [J. Clark (ed.), Colby College Press, 1960.][11]

Although Allport has much to say about religion, it is not necessarily directed toward why man believes in a supreme being but is a discussion of religion itself as a practice of man's behavior.

Allport speaks of two forms of "religiosity": extrinsic and intrinsic. He

[11] See also G. W. Allport, *The Individual and His Religion*, N. Y., Macmillan, 1950.

finds brotherhood and bigotry very much intertwined in all religions. "*Extrinsic* religion is a self-serving, utilitarian, self-protective form of religious outlook, which provides the believer with comfort and salvation at the expense of out-groups. *Intrinsic* religion marks the life that has interiorized the total creed of his faith without reservations, including the commandment to love one's neighbor. A person of this sort is more intent on serving his religion than on making it serve him. In many lives, both strands are found; the result is inner conflict, with prejudice and tolerance competing for the upper hand." The above quotation comes from the Ratcliff lecture at Tufts University, April, 1959. (*Personality and Social Encounter,* p. 257.)

In a delightfully perceptive section Allport reiterates the statement of the golden rule "Love thy neighbor as thy self." He finds this an excellent statement but a very difficult one for the citizen of the modern world to understand or implement. It is difficult for example, to know who is your neighbor. He asks, is it the man next door, is it the man in Africa, is it the individual you have never seen, or is it all of man all over the world living at the present moment? In such instances, the object of love is removed two or three times through such agencies as UNESCO, Red Cross, or any philanthropic organization designed to help less fortunate people. Consequently, this is not love but obligation toward the betterment of fellow man. Allport believes, then, that it is difficult for modern man to know what to do when he is admonished to love his neighbor as himself.

In the practice of any religion, Allport feels there is a deep security in the "in-group" of the church itself.

The more one's religious life is ego involved, the more enriching it can be. If religious practice involves the ego, it further involves the deeper sentiments and feelings and personal dispositions of the individual. He is inclined to be more dedicated and more active in the work of his own church.

One reason why religion is an almost universal attachment of mankind is that religion maintains the basic love relationship of the individual with some embracing principle. The major religions represent not only a free, indestructible attachment to one's Creator, but likewise the unattained ideal of the brotherhood of man.[12]

[12] *Ibid.,* p. 205.

Although the psychologists and the social scientists have overreacted against theology, Allport feels it is high time that both pay some attention to this unique and emphatic characteristic of human behavior. Allport finds in his fellow social scientists a feeling that it is more sophisticated to be tough-minded rather than to approach a study of human brotherliness and compassion. This, he feels, is actually an unsophisticated approach to man's behavior. Religious sentiment may confer intelligible and meaningfulness to life as a whole. It should be noted that in Allport's measurement device "A Study of Values" he has included religion as a value worth measuring.

Following Spranger's concept of religion as a unity, Allport feels that one relates the self to the cosmos as a whole. By thus doing so, we are able to embrace totality. On the other hand, Allport also finds that "religious sentiment" may be practised by many who are immature. This is "a holdover from childhood." Consequently, religion is not always a unifying philosophy of life, but may instead promote feelings of prejudice. Here it is of the extrinsic quality mentioned previously. The intrinsic type of religion may, however, give conclusive solutions to life's puzzles in the light of an intelligible theory. In this way, an intrinsic religious feeling can be comprehensive, it can be integrative, and it can be a highly motivating force in man's behavior. If the religious feelings of an intrinsic quality are so, they may lead to much good, and to new perspectives in the life of any personality.

In the final analysis, Allport feels, as, of course, do many, that actually we do not know much about religion. However, in contrast to almost all theorists, he feels there should be much research and study by psychologists in this area. Allport admits this is definitely not popular in the psychological world of today. He urges, however, there is a need for something like "a science of morals."

As we can see from the above, Allport has much more to say concerning religion than do any of the other theorists, except perhaps Jung.

Humor

Allport makes an excellent comparison between, oddly enough, humor and religion. "We may joke and pray about the same disturbing events in life, but never at the same time" (*Pattern and Growth in Personality*, p. 301).

While religion gives congruity to life, humor gives incongruity to life.

While religion gives the "best fit" for unity in life, humor, work, or the desire to know and understand may also be unifying sentiments.

In his 1961 book, Allport treats humor as being the correlate of insight. He makes a very sharp distinction between a sense of humor and what he calls *the cruder sense of the comic*. Almost all people feel that they have a sense of humor, but it is actually a sense of the comic which they share. If one were to ask a group, "Do you have a sense of humor?" he might meet almost unanimous agreement that they do. It is not this factor that Allport is talking about. All of us think that we have a sense of humor, but we may be unable to have that kind of humor—self-objectification or the capacity to laugh at oneself—which Allport regards very highly. The ability to see incongruities or absurdities in oneself or others, or in situations, is a valuable adjunct of life. In one study, Allport mentions students who were asked if they had a sense of humor and to estimate this sense of humor. Ninety-four percent felt that they had a good or better than average sense of humor.

Allport admits that as of now psychologists have had very little success in measuring a sense of humor. Actually he feels that humor and insight deal with a very subtle depth in personality. In summary, humor appears to be, from the Allport frame of reference, the ability to objectify self, to see self from other than a purely subjective viewpoint. The individual who can do this has a valuable contribution in combating the vicissitudes of life. When he can laugh at others and essentially laugh at himself, he has then a proper sense of proportion between that which is real and that which is not real.

The sense of the comic, often mistaken for a sense of humor, he feels, consists of the absurdities of life or the degradation of some imagined opponent. Aggressive impulses are very slightly disguised, and it is the sudden glory of one's own ego over the ego of another individual which may bring him to sudden laughter. Aggressive wit which derides one human being at the expense of another may be expressed in displaced aggression or through a sexual theme. This, it must be remembered, is what Allport calls the *comic,* and it has nothing directly to do with the sense of humor.

One other apparent manifestation of humor is that of smiling, or the happy countenance. Allport treats this as a product of social encounter. He considers it a gesture in which we signify that we understand society, that we belong together, and that we have agreed upon some basis for being together. It does not however, have anything directly to do with humor or the capacity to laugh. It is a socialized method of gestural response to others whom we wish to please. Therefore, one whom we may sometimes mistakenly take for a humorous person because he is smiling may have no sense of humor as treated above. He is merely trying to be liked or to gain favor with his society. He may even be slightly miserable although he dons the role of a "humorous person."

Smoking

Smoking may be a secondary trait. As such, it is not cardinal, "all pervasive," or central in the behavior of man, but is rather a peripheral activity in man's behavior. Smoking is also, of course, to be considered in the sense of uniqueness according to Allport.

There are no direct references to smoking in Allport's work, but there are references to the use of tobacco or a "craving for tobacco" which is treated as a possible function of the perseverative functional autonomy. Smoking might be considered one of the best examples of perseverative functional autonomy. Whatever started the individual in smoking has long since ceased to motivate the individual to continue to smoke. Thus, functional autonomy—behaving from new and acquired motives which are not directly connected with initial motives—gives an excellent reason why man continues to smoke, if not why man began to smoke in the first place. It is assumed that man first began to smoke or indulge in tobacco as a form of imitative behavior or identification with some individual who appeared favorable.

Smoking may also be considered as an illustration of conformity to social behavior. As such, it still continues to operate as a perseverative functional autonomy. One has long ceased to enjoy particularly the use of tobacco but indulges in tobacco forms because all the others in the group do the same thing.

Play and Recreation

A number of interesting things emerge when one extrapolates Allport's theory to explain play and recreation.

There are two ways of looking at play and recreation, from a child's and from an adult's viewpoint. We may assume that as the child first pursues play and recreational activities, he finds satisfaction in these activities and is encouraged by pleasure rewards to continue them. They are fun. Play and recreation, then, in the adult are a product of learned responses.

However, in the child we may consider play and recreation, random sort of play, as purely organic, visceral, and muscular activities. The child goes from one type of play activity to another in a very spasmodic manner, whereas in the adult, the play and recreational activities are quite formalized towards certain structured activities. Thus, there may be a strong continuity–discontinuity in explaining play and recreation from a childhood or an adulthood point of view.

It must be admitted that, for Allport, there may be as many explanations for play and recreation as there are individuals who play and who indulge in recreation.

Allport rejects the concept of *psychological hedonism* as a total explanation of play. He feels that to seek happiness and avoid pain is an inadequate explanation for play. He finds that duty and conscience may seriously impede play or any kind of totally hedonistic life. Psychological hedonism may, however, be a partial explanation for play and recreation.

If one accepts the Hindu psychological view of man's existence which Allport finds valuable, as being a trichotomized pleasure–success–duty kind of existence, then it must be assumed that pleasure is primarily an early life phenomenon and decreases with age. Under this theory, we might expect play and recreation to hold less and less a role in the life of an individual as his age increases until in the later part of life or during senility, we find the older personality indulging in very little play but a great deal of introspection concerning the duty of the individual in conducting his life. Life passes, then, from play and recreation in its earlier years to a philosophical frame of reference in its later years. In this scheme of things, play may be considered as a developmental aspect of man rather than as a main stream of activity throughout life. Children play more than adolescents, adolescents play more than middle-aged adults and middle-aged adults play more than older adults.

It is possible that pleasure-bound people may have strong over-riding personal dispositions toward this goal of play.

In extending Allport's writing to explain play and recreation, one sees that ego-involvement is the most dedicated form of play. By this we mean that an individual does not indulge in play unless his ego is highly involved. We may further assume that because his ego is involved, it receives some satisfaction or strength in the play activity.

Psychoses–Neuroses

Allport does not write much directly concerning psychoses. Most of his remarks concern neuroses. This may be natural because Allport does not work in a clinical setting or a mental hospital. There are, however, some references to schizophrenia, and in general, Allport's approach to explanations of psychoses and neuroses follows very much a straight academic line. Most of Allport's writings concerning deviant behavior grows out of his discussion of what normality is. In a sense, then, what normality is not is what is to be considered abnormal. Despite the above limitations, there is a rich amount of explanation, more so than in some of the other theorists.

Probably the main concept is that abnormality is a process, not a symptom. All of us may possess symptoms of abnormality, even at the deep level of psychoses, from time to time. It is the process by which we solve problems, however, rather than the symptoms of our behavior as judged by others which delineates the normal from the abnormal human being. All of us can appear neurotic at times, but it is how we handle some or all of the following types of processes which delineates normality from abnormality in human behavior. 1. The neurotic–psychotic lives to escape. He may do that through fantasy or autistic thinking. 2. There is an ineffective effort to repress painful past experiences by the psychotic and the neurotic. Whereas the normal human being can successfully repress and keep repressed the painful past, the psychotic or neurotic is unable to do so or is ineffective in this repression. 3. The neurotic especially is an artist at self-deception. At no time does he wish to indulge in true insight. His main rationale is to deceive himself, although it may be quite apparent that he deceives no one else. 4. There is a true disintegration, in the sociological sense, of the personality, especially in the psychotic. It is as if the personality completely falls apart and cannot integrate or coordinate all of the aspects of the personality. Being the only individual who can pick up the pieces and being so disintegrated as not to have the capacity to pick up pieces, the psychotic is unable to cure himself. He needs a helping hand to identify for him the parts that go together in his personality, to hand him these parts, and to tell him where they go. 5. Both the psychotic and the neurotic narrow their thinking to very isolated facts. For example, the neurotic may have compulsions or obsessions regarding very singular events and be unable to see the total picture. 6. The abnormal personality is completely unable to control impulsive actions. Whereas the normal human being may recognize and hold down his impulsive actions, the neurotic and especially the psychotic is totally unable to do this. 7. There is, in the final sense, a strong fixation at the infantile or juvenile level of expression. All of these, according to Allport, are not merely symptoms but ways of thinking, or processes of the mind. It is this process that Allport maintains that is discontinuous from the normal to the abnormal human being. Thus, we find the dichotomy existing.

Infantilism and fixation are only partially perseverative functional autonomies. If a neurosis cannot be cured—for example, if the therapist is unable to "dislodge it"—then the neurosis becomes the Adlerian "life style." On the other hand, psychosis is much the same as perseverative functional autonomy. The difference between the neurotic and the psychotic is that the psychotic is totally unable to handle problems of existence, whereas, of course, the neurotic may operate in society even though at a limited level. Because the psychotic cannot exist in society, he has, then, a perseverative functional autonomy.

Allport calls the neurotic a "cognitive cripple" (*ibid.*, p. 271). "Moral stupidity" is the best definition for the psychopathic personality. This human being is unable to benefit by any type of interior conscience. Thus he is morally stupid although he may be quite bright intellectually.

Allport feels there may be some promise in the Kretschmer and Sheldonian doctrine of somatotypes. However, he feels that much remains to be done in better research than has been conducted up to this point. However, he does not ignore or deny the value of any contribution. It will be remembered that Allport's is the open-ended and integumented theory of personality.

"True neuroses, we know, are best defined as stubborn self-centeredness" (*Personality and Social Encounter*, p. 173). Allport repeats the theme in his 1961 book: "The truest and most general statement about the neuroses seems to be that they are a reflection of uncontrolled self-centeredness" (*Pattern and Growth in Personality*, p. 151). In agreement with Freud, Allport feels that the true neurotic is largely dominated by the unconscious, whereas in disagreement with Freud he feels that the normal or nonneurotic, nonpsychotic human being is dominated very much by conscious motivations. The abnormal human being, therefore, cannot coordinate the preconscious with the conscious levels of behavior.

Allport admits that catastrophic social change, trauma, brain washing-menticide, cannot be ignored in explaining neurotic–psychotic behaviors. In these instances, as previously stated, the personality disintegrates.

Once again the reader is urged to discover explanations in the work of each theorist and again now in Allport, in trying to explain the nine behavioral phenomenon posited in this chapter. The writer makes no claim to having exhausted the possibilities of explanation. There is again, of course, the inevitable extrapolation of the theory.

PREDICTING HUMAN BEHAVIOR VIA ALLPORT'S THEORY

Personal Prediction

It is evident that no two readers will read the same book in the same manner or with the same understanding. So it is with the prediction of each one's personal life. We come now to that aspect of Allport's theory which invites the individual reader to predict the course of his own life. The theme of this book, it will be remembered, is an attempt to lead each student of the theory of personality to construct a theory of his own. No matter how shrewd, clever, or interesting, any of the preceding theories are, it eventually is the task of the reader to evolve his own personality theory. It is our contention that the student will do this with or without study. The job, then, is to help the student to arrive at the most defensible, the most meaningful, and the most fruitful theory of personality possible for his own purposes, be it experimental, or clinically oriented.

Hadley Cantril (once a coworker with Allport) said, "The aim of science is often defined as the attempt to increase the accuracy of our *predictions*. While the accuracy of predictions is clearly a most important criterion of progress in scientific formulation, emphasis on prediction alone can easily obscure the more fundamental aim of science covered by the word *understanding*."[13]

Allport himself feels that *self-confrontation* is necessary in psychological thinking. But he feels that it is barely beginning to be applied to the productions of psychology. Thus, the student is invited through self-confrontation to examine his own predictions regarding his own behavior from the framework of Allport's theory of personality. "It is a good idea to invite students to apply the theories to their own lives, and see which theories are the 'best fit'." [Note to author.]

Is it true that the primary or one of the primary motivational aspects of behavior for ourselves is based on functional autonomy? Have we gone beyond the basic needs and drives of organic life and yet continued to be

[13] *Perspectives in Personality Theory*, H. P. David, and H. Von Bracken (eds.), Basic Books, 1957, p. 198.

motivated by things far beyond original causes? This is the key question of functional autonomy. We must further decide whether propriate functional autonomy, or the open-ended system, continues to operate in our life or whether our motivational pattern is highly interconnected with the infantile past. Further involved is the consideration of our behavior as either homeostatic, or wishing to maintain a balance, or as motivated by contemporary and future goals. Probably it appeals to our own egos to be considered as having different processes than the abnormal individual as we strive for unity in our own life. We must decide for ourselves, again, whether we are primarily reactive to situations or proactive, looking for the future. Probably none of us would disagree with Allport that the problem of motivation is central to the study of personality, especially our own personalities. For if we know why we do what we do, we have gone a long way toward understanding ourselves. Consequently, if we are to predict our own behavior, it is necessary that we understand how we learn to develop a personality, for this is central to the theme of Allport's theory of personality.

If we accept Allport's ideas of self-love and pride as being universal in the nature of man, we may find it easier to predict our own behavior, providing we have self-love and pride. "My statement is that although self-love and pride are universal, they *need not be sovereign* in a life. This qualification is very important." [Note to author.]

And finally we must decide for ourselves, because no one else can decide for us, whether the traits, the trends, the temperaments, the tendencies, and particularly the personal dispositions that each of us have will help in predicting something of what we are going to do in the future.

Scientific or Laboratory Predictions

Allport feels that whenever prediction is involved it can probably be done better idiographically than nomothetically. "In short, successful scientific prediction requires knowledge of the essential relations that comprise the unique ego-structure of the individual" (*Personality and Social Encounter*, p. 148). Allport agrees that one of the aims of science is prediction. He asks if it is possible to foretell a later personality from a study of the infant years. He agrees, further, that one cannot foresee all the environmental influences that lie ahead. However, he does feel that in regard to prediction, the pattern of later personality is somewhat discernible in infancy. There is consistency to a personality. There is some truth in the statement that the child is father of the man. There is some predictive validity in the raw materials of personality: physique, temperament, and intelligence. Allport states in *Pattern and Growth in Personality*, p. 82

Research shows that some broad predictions can be made in infancy concerning the style of personality that will develop. The success of these predictions is not great enough to justify the belief that personality is firmly fixed in the early years. The process of becoming continues one's whole life through.

In another dimension, Allport discusses the "extraordinary continuity and sameness of individual personalities" which he found to hold true in the inmates of Nazi prisons during Hitler's era. It was almost as if one could predict the personality pattern of an individual prior to imprisonment, during imprisonment, and definitely after imprisonment in the German Nazi concentration camps. He discusses the cases of people who were colorless before imprisonment and emerged after imprisonment as colorless. It is to be supposed that, similarly, a sparkling individual might well go through imprisonment and emerge as a sparkling individual. Allport cautions, however, that no individual can permanently withstand complete collapse in a brainwashing environment.

Allport feels that, certainly at the present time, whatever prediction success can be achieved must be reached in miniature or controlled life situation experiments. It is not possible now and may be quite impossible in the near future to predict any kind of human behavior from a true life situation *in situ*. Probably the most accurate predictions which can be made regard the field of prejudice. Allport has written and studied and thought about prejudicial behavior probably as much as any other psychologist. He finds that given a certain set of circumstances, one may predict a prejudicial set toward another group with a great degree of accuracy.

SUMMARY

Figure 10 is an attempt by use of a diagram to summarize the major themes of Gordon Allport's theory of personality. One note of caution should be added. There is no attempt to consider Allport's theory as atom-

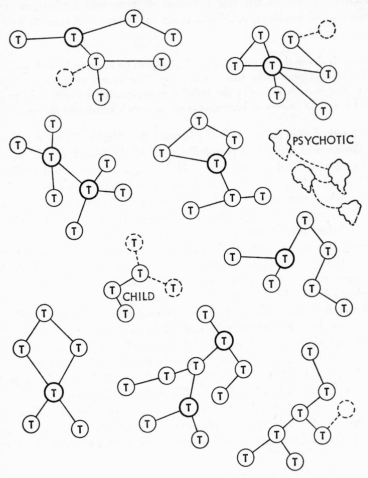

Figure 10. Diagrammatic Summary of Allport's Theory.

istic. Although the structures are atomic structures, they are used as a convenience in highlighting his theory.

The outstanding feature of all of the models is that no one is like the other. This is a portrayal of the uniqueness of man. Again we find that the traits are very few in number in each individual. Some traits can be seen linked to other traits. These would be cardinal traits. Some traits are central and have other traits attached to them, while still other traits are out by themselves and become secondary traits. Children, it will be seen, do not have very many traits, and those that they do should be considered as instinctual or drive-need traits, whereas adults have more traits because they have learned more things. Clusters of traits can be considered to be the style of life.

It should be noticed that no two traits blend with each other. There is a continuity–discontinuity between the individual "chemical compounds" as represented in the drawing. Some traits which are in the background and can hardly be seen, could be considered as the unconscious or preconscious dynamics of behavior, while others are more nearly on the surface or closer to the reader's eye. If the personalities as represented by the chemical compounds in Figure 10 do not possess an adequate perseverative or propriate functional autonomy, they can be seen to have fallen apart: i.e., they are the psychotics or neurotics.

Psychology is truly itself only when it can deal with individuality. . . . We study the human person most fully when we take him as an individual. He is more than a bundle of habits, more than a point of intersection of abstract dimensions. He is more than a representative of his species, more than a citizen of the State, more than an incident in the movements of mankind. He transcends them all. The individual, striving ever for integrity and fulfillment, has existed under all forms of social life—forms as varied as the nomadic and feudal, capitalistic and Communistic. No society holds together for long without the respect man shows to man. The individual today struggles on even under oppression, always hoping and planning for a more perfect democracy where the dignity and growth of each personality will be prized above all else.[14]

Allport finds it refreshing that psychologists are beginning to ask some kinds of philosophical questions and equally that philosophers are beginning to ask questions of a psychological nature. Only as all the arts and sciences work together can we really have a true dimension and a true theory of personality.

[14] *Ibid.*, p. 573.

BIBLIOGRAPHY

PRIMARY SOURCES

BOOKS

Allport, G. W., and F. H. Allport, *A–S Reaction Study*, rev. ed., [1928] Boston, Houghton Mifflin, 1949.

Allport, G. W., and P. E. Vernon, *A Study of Values* [1931], rev. ed. (with G. Lindzey, 1951, 3rd ed., 1960, Boston, Houghton Mifflin.

Allport, G. W., and Vernon, P. E., *Studies in Expressive Movement*, N.Y., Macmillan, 1933.

Allport, G. W., and H. Cantril, *The Psychology of Radio*, N.Y., Harper & Row, 1935.

Allport, G. W., Attitudes, in C. C. Murchison, (ed.), *A Handbook of Social Psychology*, Worcester, Mass., Clark Univer. Press, 1935. Chap. 17.

Allport, G. W., *Personality: A Psychological Interpretation*, N.Y., Holt, Rinehart and Winston, 1937.

Allport, G. W., Dewey's individual and social psychology, in P. A. Schilpp (ed.), *The Philosophy of John Dewey*, Evanston, Ill., Northwestern Univer. Press, 1939, Chap. 9.

Allport, G. W., *The Use of Personal Documents in Psychological Science*, N.Y., Social Science Research Council, 1942, Bull. 49.

Allport, G. W., The nature of democratic morale, in G. Watson, (ed.), *Civilian Morale*, Boston, Houghton Mifflin, 1942, Chap. 1.

Allport, G. W. (ed., and author of Foreward), ABC's of scapegoating, Central YWCA College, Chicago, 1944, (rev. ed.), *Freedom Pamphlet Series*, N.Y., Anti-Defamation League of B'nai B'rith, 1948, (rev.) 1959.

Allport, G. W., and Postman, L., *The Psychology of Rumor*, N.Y., Holt, Rinehart and Winston, 1947.

Allport, G. W., Psychology, in *College Reading and Religion*, New Haven, Conn. Yale Univer. Press, 1948, Chap. 3.

Allport, G. W., *The Individual and His Religion*, N.Y., Macmillan, 1950.

Allport, G. W., *The Nature of Personality: Selected Papers*, Cambridge, Mass., Addison-Wesley, 1950.

Allport, G. W., How shall we evaluate teaching? in B. B. Cronkhite, (ed.), *A Handbook for College Teachers*, Cambridge, Mass., Harvard Univer. Press, 1950, Chap. 3.

Allport, G. W., The role of expectancy, in H. Cantril, (ed.), *Tensions that Cause Wars*, Urbana, Ill., Univer. of Illinois Press, 1950.

Allport, G. W., A psychological approach to the study of love and hate, in

P. A. Sorokin, (ed.), *Explorations in Altruistic Love and Behavior*, Boston, 1950, Beacon Press, Chap. 5.

Allport, G. W., The situation we face: A psychological analysis, in A. W. Loos, (ed.), *Religious Faith and World Culture*, Englewood Cliffs, N.J., Prentice-Hall, 1951, 35–48.

Also in *New Outlook*, 1955, 8, 82–87.

Allport, G. W. Basic principles in improving human relations, in K. W. Bigelow (ed.), *Cultural Groups and Human Relations*, N.Y., Teachers College, Columbia Univer., 1951, Chap. 2.

Allport, G. W., An evaluation of AFSC volunteer work service camps in Germany, in H. W. Riecken (ed.), *The Volunteer Work Camp: A Psychological Evaluation*, Cambridge, Mass., Addison-Wesley, 1952, Append. A, 185–220.

Allport, G. W., Resolving intergroup tensions, an appraisal of methods, in L. A. Cook (ed.), *Toward Better Human Relations*, Detroit, Wayne Univer. Press, 1952, Chap. 3.

Allport, G. W., Reading the nature of prejudice, Claremont, Calif., *Claremont College Reading Conference, Seventeenth Yearbook*, 1952, 51–64.

Allport, G. W., *The Nature of Prejudice*, Cambridge, Mass., Addison-Wesley, 1954; Boston, Beacon Press (abr. ed.), Garden City, N.Y., Doubleday (Anchor), 1958.

Allport, G. W., Techniques for reducing group prejudice, in P. A. Sorokin (ed.), *Forms and Techniques of Altruistic and Spiritual Growth*, Boston, Beacon Press, 1954, Chap. 24.

Allport, G. W., The historical background of modern social psychology, in G. Lindzey (ed.), *Handbook of Social Psychology*, Cambridge, Mass., Addison-Wesley, 1954, 1, Chap. 1.

Allport, G. W., *Becoming: Basic Considerations for a Psychology of Personality*, New Haven, Conn., Yale Univer. Press, 1955.

Allport, G. W., and J. M. Gillespie, *Youth's Outlook on the Future*, Doubleday, Doubleday Papers in Psychology, N.Y., (distributed by Random House), 1955.

Allport, G. W., The limits of social service, in J. E. Russell (ed.), *National Policies for Education, Health and Social Services*, Garden City, N.Y., Doubleday, 1955, 194–213.

Allport, G. W., Prejudice in modern perspective, *The Hoernle Memorial Lecture*, The South African Institute of Race Relations, Durban, South Africa, 1956.

Allport, G. W., The participant citizen, *The Sixth Annual George Denny Lecture*, Natal Technical College, Durban, South Africa, 1956.

Allport, G. W., European and American theories of personality, in H. P. David, and H. von Bracken (eds.), *Perspectives in Personality Theory*, N.Y., Basic Books, 1957, Chap. 1.

Allport, G. W., What units shall we employ?, in G. Lindzey (ed.), *Assessment of Human Motives*, N.Y., Holt, Rinehart and Winston, 1958, Chap. 9. (Reprinted as paperback, N.Y., Grove Press, 1960.)

Allport, G. W., Normative compatibility in the light of social science, in A. H. Maslow (ed.), *New Knowledge in Human Values*, N.Y., Harper & Row, 1959, 137–150.

> Also in *Religious Education*, 1958, 53, 62–68.

Allport, G. W., Preface to V. E. Frankl (trans.) *From Death-Camp to Existentialism*, Boston, Beacon Press, 1959.

Allport, G. W. *Personality and Social Encounter*, Boston, Beacon Press, 1960.

Allport, G. W., Uniqueness in students, in W. D. Weatherford Jr. (ed.), *The Goals of Higher Education*, Cambridge, Mass., Harvard Univer. Press, 1960, 57–75.

Allport, G. W., Psychology and religion, in J. Clark (ed.), *The Student Seeks an Answer*, Ingraham Lectures in Philosophy and Religion, Waterville, Me., Colby College Press, 1960, Chap. 2.

Allport, G. W., *Pattern and Growth in Personality*, N.Y., Holt, Rinehart and Winston, 1961.

Allport, G., Foreword, in N. L. Farberow (ed.), *Taboo Topics*, N.Y., Atherton Press, 1963.

PERIODICALS

Allport, G. W., and F. H. Allport, Personality traits: Their classification and measurement, *J. Abnorm. Soc. Psychol.*, 1921, 16, 6–40.

Allport, G. W., Personality and character, *Psychol. Bull.*, 1921, 18, 441–455.

Allport, G. W., Germany's state of mind, *New Republic*, 1923, 34, 63–65.

Allport, G. W., The Leipzig Congress of Psychology, *Amer. J. Psychol.*, 1923, 34, 612–615.

Allport, G. W., The study of the undivided personality, *J. Abnorm. Soc. Psychol.*, 1924, 19, 132–41.

Allport, G. W., Eidetic imagery, *Brit. J. Psychol.*, 1924, 15, 99–120.

Allport, G. W., The standpoint of Gestalt psychology, *Psyche*, 1924, 4, 354–61.

Allport, G. W., Concepts of trait and personality, *Psychol. Bull.*, 1927, 24, 284–93.

Allport, G. W., The eidetic image and the after-image, *Amer. J. Psychol.*, 1928, 40, 418–425.

Allport, G. W., A test for ascendance-submission, *J. Abnorm. Soc. Psychol.*, 1928, 23, 118–136.

Allport, G. W., The study of personality by the intuitive method: An experiment in teaching from *The locomotive god, J. Abnorm. Soc. Psychol.*, 1929, *24,* 14–27.

Allport, G. W., The composition of political attitudes, *Amer. J. Sociol.,* 1929, *35,* 220–238.

Allport, G. W., Some guiding principles in understanding personality, *The Family,* June 1930, 124–128.

Allport, G. W., The neurotic personality and traits of self-expression, *J. Soc. Psychol.,* 1930, *1,* 524–527.

Allport, G. W., and P. E. Vernon, The field of personality, *Psychol. Bull.,* 1930, *27,* 677–730.

Allport, G. W., Change and decay in the visual memory image, *Brit. J. Psychol.,* 1930, *21,* 133–148.

Allport, G. W., What is a trait of personality? *J. Abnorm. Soc. Psychol.,* 1931, *25,* 368–372.

Allport, G. W., and P. E. Vernon, A test for personal values, *J. Abnorm. Soc. Psychol.,* 1931, *26,* 231–48.

Allport, G. W., The study of personality by the experimental method, *Char. Pers.,* 1933, *1,* 259–264.

Allport, G. W., H. Cantril, and H. A. Rand, The determination of personal interests by psychological and graphological methods, *Char. Pers.,* 1933, *2,* 134–151.

Allport, G. W., and H. Cantril, Recent applications of the study of values, *J. Abnorm. Soc. Psychol.,* 1933, *28,* 259–73.

Allport, G. W., and H. Cantril, Judging personality from voice, *J. Soc. Psychol.,* 1934, *5,* 37–55.

Allport, G. W., The radio as a stimulus situation, *ACTA Psychol.,* 1935, *1,* 1–6.

Allport, G. W., The nature of motivation, *Understanding the Child,* Jan. 1935, 3–6.

Allport, G. W., and H. S. Odbert, Trait-Names: A Psycho-Lexical Study, *Psychological Monogr.,* 1936, *47,* No. 211.

Allport, G. W., and R. L. Schanck, Are attitudes biological or cultural in origin?, *Char. Pers.,* 1936, *4,* 195–205.

Allport, G. W., The functional autonomy of motives, *Amer. J. Psychol.,* 1937, *50,* 141–156.

Allport, G. W., The personalistic psychology of William Stern, *Char. Pers.,* 1937, *5,* 231–246.

Allport, G. W., The Journal of Abnormal and Social Psychology: An editorial, in *J. Abnorm. Soc. Psychol.,* 1938, *33,* 3–13.

Allport, G. W., William Stern: 1871–1938, *Amer. J. Psychol.,* 1938, *51,* 770–774.

Allport, G. W., and R. Ruggles, Recent applications of the A–S Reaction Study, *J. Abnorm. Soc. Psychol.*, 1939, 34, 518–28.

Allport, G. W., The education of a teacher, *The Harvard Progressive*, 1939, 4, 7–9.

Allport, G. W., The psychologist's frame of reference, *Psychol. Bull.*, 1940, 37, 1–28.

Allport, G. W., and J. S. Bruner, Fifty years of change in American psychology, *Psychol. Bull.*, 1940, 37, 757–776.

Allport, G. W., and J. M. Faden, The psychology of newspapers: Five tentative laws, *Publ. Opin. Quart.*, 1940, 4, 687–703.

Allport, G. W., Motivation in personality: Reply to Mr. Bertocci, *Psychol. Rev.*, 1940, 47, 533–554.

Allport, G. W., Liberalism and the motives of men, *Frontiers of Democracy*, 1940, 6, 136–137.

Allport, G. W., Liabilities and assets in civilian morale, *Ann. Amer. Acad. Pol. Soc. Sci.*, 1941, 216, 88–94.

Allport, G. W., Psychological service for civilian morale, *J. Consult. Psychol.*, 1941, 5, 235–239.

Allport, G. W., J. S. Bruner, and E. M. Jandorf, Personality under social catastrophe: Ninety life-histories of the Nazi Revolution, *Char. Pers.*, 1941, 10, 1–22.

Allport, G. W., Morale: American style, *Christian Science Monitor*, (weekly magazine section), April 26, 1941, 1–2, 13.

Allport, G. W., Defense seminars for morale study and morale building, *J. Soc. Psychol.*, SPSSI Bull., 1942, 15, 399–401.

Allport, G. W., Morale and its measurement, *Public Policy*, Cambridge, Mass., Littauer School of Public Administration, 1942, 3, 3–17.

Allport, G. W., The productive paradoxes of William James, *Psychol. Rev.*, 1943, 50, 95–120.

Allport, G. W., Test tube for rumors, *Coronet*, 1943, 14, 136–40.

Allport, G. W., Psychological considerations in making the peace: Editorial note, *J. Abnorm. Soc. Psychol.*, 1943, 38, 131.

Allport, G. W., This clinical supplement: Editorial note, *J. Abnorm. Soc. Psychol.*, 1943, 38, 3–5.

Allport, G. W., and E. C. Winship, Do rosy headlines sell newspapers?, *Publ. Opin. Quart.*, 1943, 7, 205–10.

Allport, G. W., and H. R. Veltfort, Social psychology and the civilian war effort, *J. Soc. Psychol.*, SPSSI Bull., 1943, 18, 165–233.

Allport, G. W., The ego in contemporary psychology, *Psychol. Rev.*, 1943, 50, 451–478.

Also published in C. L. Stacey, and M. F. DeMartino (eds.), *Understand-*

ing Human Motivation, Cleveland, Howard Allen, 1958, 140–158.

Allport, G. W., and G. R. Schmeidler, Morale research and its clearing, *Psychol. Bull.,* 1943, *40,* 65–68.

Allport, G. W., Restoring morale in occupied territory, *Publ. Opin. Quart.,* 1943, *7,* 606–617.

Allport, G. W., This clinical number: Editorial, *J. Abnorm. Soc. Psychol.,* 1944, *39,* 147–149.

Allport, G. W., and G. R. Schmeidler, Social psychology and the civilian war effort, *J. Soc. Psychol., SPSSI Bull.,* 1944, *20,* 145–180.

Allport, G. W., The bigot in our midst, *Commonweal,* 1944, *25,* 582–586.
  Also published in *The Catholic Digest,* 1944, *9,* 93–96.

Allport, G. W., The psychology of participation, *Psychol. Rev.,* 1945, *52,* 117–132.

Allport, G. W., Human nature and the peace, *Psychol. Bull.,* 1945, *42,* 376–378.

Allport, G. W., Is intergroup education possible?, *Harv. Educ. Rev.,* 1945, *15,* 83–86.

Allport, G. W., Catharsis and the reduction of prejudice, *J. Soc. Issues,* 1945, *1,* 1–8.

Allport, G. W., and L. Postman, The basic psychology of rumor, *Trans New York Acad. Sci.,* Section of Psychology, 1945, *8,* 61–81.
  Also published in G. E. Swanson, T. M. Newcomb, and E. L. Hartley (eds.), *Readings in Social Psychology* (rev. ed.), N.Y., Holt, Rinehart and Winston, 1952, Pt. IIb, 160–171; in D. Katz, D. Cartwright, S. Eldersveld, and A. McG. Lee, *Public Opinion and Propaganda,* N.Y., Holt, Rinehart and Winston, 1954, 394–404.

Allport, G. W., Personalistic psychology as science: A reply, *Psychol. Rev.,* 1946, *53,* 132–135.

Allport, G. W., Controlling group prejudice, (ed. and author of Foreward), *Ann. Amer. Acad. Pol. Soc. Sci.,* 1946, *244.*

Allport, G. W., and E. G. Boring, Psychology and social relations at Harvard University, *Amer. Psychologist.,* 1946, *1,* 119–122.

Allport, G. W., and B. M. Kramer, Some roots of prejudice, *J. Psychol.,* 1946, *22,* 9–39; rev. ed., *Roots of Prejudice,* New York American Jewish Congress, Pamphlet Series, *Jewish Affairs,* 1946, *1,* 13.

Allport, G. W., Geneticism versus ego-structure in theories of personality, *Brit. J. Educ. Psychol.,* 1946, *16,* 57–68.

Allport, G. W., Effect: a secondary principle of learning, *Psychol. Rev.,* 1946, *53,* 335–347.

Allport, G. W., The priest and the psychologist, *Bull. Gen. Theol. Sem.,* Sept., 1946.

Allport, G. W., and L. Postman, An analysis of rumor, *Publ. Opin. Quart.*, 1946–47, *10*, 501–17.

Also published in *Science Digest*, 1947, 22, 58–61.

Allport, G. W., Guidelines for research in international cooperation, *J. Soc. Issues*, 1947, 3, 21–37.

Also in T. H. Pear (ed.), *Psychological Factors of Peace and War*, London, Hutchinson, 1950, Chap. 7.

Allport, G. W., The genius of Kurt Lewin, *J. Person.*, 1947, *16*, 1–10.

Also in *J. Soc. Issues*, 1948, *4*, 14–21, Suppl. Series I.

Allport, G. W., Scientific models and human morals, *Psychol. Rev.*, 1947, *54*, 182–192.

Allport, G. W., J. M. Gillespie, and J. Young, The religion of the post-war college student, *J. Psychol.*, 1948, *25*, 3–33.

Also in J. Seidman (ed.), *The Adolescent: A Book of Readings*, N.Y., Holt, Rinehart and Winston, 1953.

Allport, G. W., Psychology and the fourth R, *New Republic*, Oct. 17, 1949, 23–26.

Allport, G. W., Prejudice: A problem in psychological and social causation, (Kurt Lewin Memorial Lecture), *J. Soc. Issues*, 1950, Suppl. Series.

Also in T. Parsons, and E. A. Shils (eds.), *Toward a General Theory of Action*, Cambridge, Mass., Harvard Univer. Press, 1951, Pt. 4, Chap. 1.

Allport, G. W., The individual and his religion, *The Andover Newton Bull.*, 1952, 44, 3–10.

Allport, G. W., The resolution of intergroup tensions, *Intergroup Educ. Pamphlet*, N.Y., National Conference of Christians and Jews, 1952.

Allport, G. W., The mature personality, *Pastoral Psychol.*, 1952, 2, 19–24.

Allport, G. W., What is in the student's mind?, proceedings of the Thirtieth Annual Meeting, *Amer. College Health Ass.*, Bull. No. 32, Stanford Univ. Press, Stanford, 1952.

Allport, G. W., Why do people join?, interview in *Adult Leadership*, 1952, *1*, 10–12.

Allport, G. W., The trend in motivational theory, *Amer. J. Orthopsychiat.*, 1953, *25*, 107–119.

Allport, G. W., The teaching-learning situation, *Publ. Hlth. Rep.*, 1953, 68, 875–79.

Allport, G. W., The psychological nature of personality, *The Personalist*, 1953, 34, 347–357.

Allport, G. W., A psychologist views the Supreme Court ruling on segregation, *Nieman Reports*, 1954, 8, 12–13.

Allport, G. W., Comments on: J. L. Moreno, Transference, countertransference and tele: their relation to group research and group psychotherapy,

Group Psychother., 1954, 7, 307–308.

Allport, G. W., and T. F. Pettigrew, Cultural influence on the perception of movement: The trapezoidal illusion among Zulus, *J. Abnorm. Soc. Psychol.*, 1957, 55, 104–113.

Allport G. W., Perception and public health, *Hlth. Educ. Monogr.*, Oakland, Calif., Society of Health Educators, 1958, No. 2, 2–15.

Allport, G. W., T. F. Pettigrew, and E. O. Barnett, Binocular resolution and perception of race in South Africa, *Brit. J. Psychol.*, 1958, 49, 265–278, Pt. IV.

Allport, G. W., Personality: normal and abnormal, *Sociol. Rev.*, 1958, 6, 167–180.

Allport, G. W., Religion and prejudice, *The Crane Rev.*, 1959, 2, 1–10.

Allport, G. W., The open system in personality theory, *J. Abnorm. Soc. Psychol.*, 1960, 60, No. 5.

Allport, G. W., Values and our youth, *Teachers Coll. Rec.*, 1961, 63, 211–219.

Allport, G. W., Prejudice: is it societal or personal? *J. Soc. Issues*, 1962, 18(2), 120–134.

TAPE RECORDINGS

Allport, G. W., *Motivation Theory and Psychodynamics*, (G. W. Kisker, ed.) No. 132, Cincinnati, Ohio, Sound Seminars.

SUGGESTED READINGS

BOOKS

Allport, F. H., *Theories of Perception and the Concept of Structure*, N.Y., Wiley, 1955.

Hall, C. S., and G. Lindzey, *Theories of Personality*, N.Y., Wiley, 1957, 257–295.

Wolff, W., *The Expression of Personality*, N.Y., Harper & Row, 1943.

PERIODICALS

Baldwin, A. L., Personal structure analysis: A statistical method for investigating the single personality, *J. Abnorm. Soc. Psychol.*, 1942, 37, 163–183.

Baldwin, A. L., Statistical problems in the treatment of case histories, *J. Clin. Psychol.*, 1950, 6, 6–12.

Bertocci, P. A., Critique of Gordon W. Allport's theory of motivation, *Psychol. Rev.*, 1940, 47, 501–532.

Kaul, J. H., How autonomous is functional autonomy?, *J. Educ. Psychol.*, Baroda, 1959, 16, 481–491.

Allport is a good writer but theory is premature—evidence is anecdotal.

King, W. A., Communication theory and the Allport concept of structure,

Audiovis. Commun. Rev., 1961, 9(2), 119–128.

Use of Allport to support communication theory.

Long, L. M. K., Alfred Adler and Gordon Allport: A comparison on certain topics in personality theory, *Amer. J. Indiv. Psychol.*, 1952–53, *10*, 43–53.

Lundy, R. M., Assimilative projection and accuracy of prediction in interpersonal perceptions, *J. Abnorm. Soc. Psychol.*, 1956, *52*, 33–38.

McCreary, J. K., The problem of personality definition, *J. Gen. Psychol.*, 1960, *63*, 107–111.

Reviews definitions by Allport, Lewin, Murray and Murphy.

O'Connell, D. C., Idiographic knowledge, *J. Gen. Psychol.*, 1958, *59*, 21–33.

A critique of Allport's idiographic approach.

Oppenheimer, O., A behavioral theory of traits, *Educ. Theory*, 1957, *7*, 112–121.

In contrast to Allport the author contends traits exist. Action is not inferred from personality.

Seward, J. P., The sign of a symbol: A reply to Professor Allport, *Psychol. Rev.*, 1948, *55*, 277–296.

Skaggs, E. B., Personalistic psychology as science, *Psychol. Rev.*, 1945, *52*, 234–238.

Steer, H. O., Allport's concept of structure, *Canad. J. Psychol.*, 1957, *11*, 75–78.

Use of Allport's theories in conducting research.

Steward, N. S., Attitudes toward literary characters as related to factors in personality, *Dissertation Abst.*, 1955, *15*, 2301.

13

Murphy

Every habit and faculty is preserved and increased
by corresponding actions,—as the habit of walking,
by walking; or running, by running.

EPICTETUS
How the Semblances of Things Are to be Combated

SOME BIOGRAPHICAL DATA

Gardner Murphy was born in Chillicothe, Ohio, on July 8, 1895. He was the son of Edgar Gardner Murphy, an Episcopal minister, and Maud (King) Murphy. He attended Hotchkiss School in Lakeville, Connecticut, from 1910 to 1912, received his B.A. from Yale in 1916, his M.A. from Harvard in 1917, and his Ph.D. from Columbia in 1923. During World War I he served with the American Expeditionary Forces in France. In 1921 Murphy began his teaching career at Columbia, where he taught until 1940. He taught in the capacity of a lecturer from 1921 to 1925, as an instructor from 1925 to 1929, and as an assistant professor from 1929 to 1940. He then left Columbia to accept the position of professor of psychology at City College of New York where he remained until accepting his present position, Director of Research at the Menninger Foundation in Topeka, Kansas. Murphy was married to the former Lois Barclay on November 27, 1926 and has two children, Alpen Gardner and Margaret. In 1932, for his studies in the field of experimental social psychology, Columbia University awarded Murphy the Butler Medal. He is a member of the American Psychological Association and a past member of the Eastern Psychological Association, serving as president of the former in 1943–1944 and the latter in 1941–1942. Also he is a member of the American Association for the Advancement of Science and of the Society for the Psychological Study of Social Issues of which he was president in 1938. In 1950 Murphy and his wife visited India on a UNESCO mission to study the cause of social tensions. From this resulted the book, *In the Minds of Men* (1953), a nontechnical interpretation of his impressions and of the research reports of eight Indian social scientists. Since Murphy has not sought to popularize psychology, his largest portion of writing is serious scholarship. He is a specialist in personality theory and is also interested in social psychology. In addition, Murphy has been interested in the field of parapsychology, which considers the phenomena of clairvoyance and telepathy, and he has served as president of the London Society for Psychical Research. Murphy continues to be a prolific contributor to the psychological world.

INTRODUCTION

In a way it is most fitting that the theories of Gardner Murphy are treated as the last full chapter in this book. Not because Murphy has the last word nor the most definitive treatment on personality theory (indeed, he would be the strongest disclaimer of such a title) but because his theory is the most eclectic. Murphy invents, but he also picks, chooses, interprets, and reemphasizes the work of many others. His interests are catholic; his interpretations are concise; his integrations of theories are comprehensive.

Murphy has an inheritance of ideas from the works of William James, McDougall, Allport, Woodworth, and others. Perhaps the strongest influence of another theorist upon Murphy has been the field theory emphasis of the late Kurt Lewin.

Murphy is a widely read and influential scholar of man's behavior. At many times in his career he has appeared to be out of the mainstream of psychological thought. Possibly one reason for Murphy's wide range of psychological interests has been his increasing desire for interaction between all fields of human endeavor. Parapsychology, for example, is not popular in the current world of psychological thinking. Gardner Murphy dares to write what he thinks about a psychological field that the majority of psychologists are inclined to back away from in favor of more tried and true research areas and publishable fields. In like manner he is equally at home with the older psychologists such as James, McDougall, Thorndike, Woodworth, and others who are inclined to be neglected because their dates of publishing predate the second world war. The older names are not only psychological history to Murphy but still hold current interest to be studied and used.

The following list of some of his major publications is an indication of the wide talents this psychologist displays.

General psychology
> *General Psychology*, 1933
> *Introduction to Psychology*, 1951

History of Psychology
> *Historical Introduction to Modern Psychology*, 1929, revised 1949

Applied psychology
> *Public Opinion and the Individual*, 1938 (with Rensis Likert)
> *Human Nature and Enduring Peace*, 1945 (edited for the Society for the Psychological Study of Social Issues)
> *In the Minds of Men: the Study of Human Behavior and Social Tensions in India*, 1953

Social psychology
> *Experimental Social Psychology*, 1931 (with his wife Lois Barclay Murphy), 1937, (a revised edition with an additional author, Theodore Newcomb)

Parapsychology
> *William James on Psychical Research* edited by Gardner Murphy and Robert O. Ballou, 1960
> *Challenge of Psychical Research: a Primer of Parapsychology* in collaboration with Laura A. Dale, 1961

Personality
> *Approaches to Personality*, 1932 (with Friedrich Jensen)
> *Personality: a Biosocial Approach to Origins and Structure*, 1947
> *Human Potentialities*, 1958

Education
> *Freeing Intelligence Through Teaching*, 1961

The everpresent main theme of Gardner Murphy's personality theory is that man is both a biological phenomenon and a social phenomenon, and that these two aspects of man must be brought together in a third phenomenon, that of integration. Thus, when he states that ". . . your hunger is different from my hunger . . . " (*Personality*, p. 143), he means that man branches from a basic need for food toward the multiple kinds of aversions and appetites which man learns through the social order he lives in. Beyond that, however, is the highly important aspect of integrating the biological and social sides of man. Two further quotations are necessary to advance the major theme of integration. It is apparent that although eleven years separate the quoted material, Murphy has maintained the same idea. From his definitive work of 1947, *Personality,* we find, "But personality study is an art and an engineering enterprise as well as a science, and at the present stage in its development the three often flow together and refuse to be separated" (p. 14). In the philosophically and ethically oriented book of 1958, *Human Potentialities,* we find, "But I have believed for a long time that human nature is a reciprocity of what is inside the skin and what is outside; that it is definitely not 'rolled up inside us' but our way of being one with our fellows and our world. I call this field theory . . ." (p. viii).

Murphy has a strong tendency to think in characteristics of three. By no means, however, does he confine thoughts within a triadic framework. Nonetheless so strong and clear is his penchant for threeness that the following list is offered. Two purposes may be served by this list of thirty-three examples of ideas in threes: the list itself approximates a summary of many of Murphy's theories and it surprises one with the scope of concepts which can be phrased in triadic form.

The first nineteen examples in abbreviated form are taken from his *Personality: a Biosocial Approach to Origins and Structure* (1947). The remaining fourteen examples are taken from Murphy's latest work *Human Potentialities,* published in 1958.

1. The "threads" from three fields, biology, clinical experience, and social sciences, should be brought together in an attempt to define how personality grows (p. 26).

2. There are three levels of complexity in studying personality problems: personality as an object, a chrysalis, and a continuously changing field view (pp. 3–5).

3. There are three ways in which man refuses to cooperate in studying the whole man: traits express intangibles, "some of the phases of this inner structure are hidden, pocketed off . . ." and he reacts in the present to situations which we do not understand (pp. 5–6).

4. Three major research tools are suggested: genetic—both in the developmental and longitudinal sense—comparative, and experimental (p. 15 ff.).

5. Murphy suggests at least three types of evolutionary forces in

process these days: recombinations of germinal tendencies, differential birth rates, and cultural forces which redefine the significance of biological traits (pp. 45–46).

6. There are three ways in which the endocrine system relates to personality syndromes: endocrine products in the blood stream may lower the thresholds for muscular reaction patterns, endocrine products may intensify muscular reaction patterns, and endocrine products may stabilize and coordinate patterns already at work (p. 77).

7. Individual differences in motivation may be studied in three ways: directly through organic processes, indirectly by inference of verbal and gestural external behavior, and still more indirectly through inferential testimony of observers (p. 118).

8. Organic traits may be of three types: broad characteristics of tissue response, persistency in modes of reaction of individual tissues, and persistent interaction between tissues (p. 133).

9. Anatomical clues, such as Sheldon uses to study personality, indirectly may be valuable in three ways: anatomical traits may limit or control conduct, long-time trait effects may produce expressive behavior or may affect appearance, and physical appearance may have an effect upon others (p. 150).

10. Murphy suggests three ways of measuring laboratory conditioning situations: measuring the number of stimulations, the intensity of established responses, or the number of repetitions needed for extinction (p. 194).

11. ". . . we may say that genuine individuality or personality in verbal expression depends first upon the asocial physiognomic response of the child; second, upon its antithesis, the stereotyping and freezing of formal linguistic structure; third, synthetically, upon the capacity to transcend both asociality and sociality in individual expression" (p. 268).

12. Most of the previous trichotomized ideas are an outgrowth of the major theses of "three principles" which govern much of what personality is: the original constitution, the early canalizations and conditioning, and the field of organism-environment interaction (p. 294).

13. There are three levels at which graphologists work: global, characteristics, and integrative (p. 692).

14. Usually there are three forms of response to frustration although a fourth may be involved: aggression, resignation, reality distortion, and displaced aggression (p. 322).

15. Perceptual development proceeds in three stages: the "blur" stage,

the differentiation stage, and the integration stage (p. 342).

16. Capital punishment has three aspects: expiation, protection, and reassertion of the conscience against hostile impulses (p. 388).

17. At least three factors contribute to genius: affective, intellectual, and motor (p. 457).

18. Loss of selfhood may be induced in three ways: by organic changes, by self-obliteration, and by reconstituting the self to find a new person (pp. 519–521).

19. ". . . economic determinism is valuable as an avenue of approach to personality. Three points must be stressed:

> (1) The economic situation can limit the possibilities of personality growth in particular directions. . . .
>
> (2) . . . The economic situation will indicate the likely directions in which the various social patterns will evolve. . . .
>
> (3) In defining the role of the economic arts, we shall use a principle well described by Margaret Mead: the same geographic problems may take entirely different forms by virtue of different social attitudes, different ways of 'phrasing the situation.' . . . If, then, we look closely at economic determinism, we find that it is not a question of the economic *situation,* but a question of the economic *behavior* of the group. Economic behavior does not result solely from the economic situation, but from a complex which includes non-economic factors. It would consequently be meaningless to say that the economic *situation* alone determines the personality pattern; the economic situation is one of several factors that shape the personalities who express and are expressed in the culture . . ." (pp. 775–776).

(NOTE: Eleven years after this quoted material Gardner Murphy continued in his *Human Potentialities* (1958) to trichotomize his material.)

20. Gardner Murphy organizes *Human Potentialities* around the concept of three kinds of human nature as follows:

> 1st Human Nature: modifiable biological individuality;
>
> 2nd Human Nature: cultural forces;
>
> 3rd Human Nature: creative thrust to understand.

Around these three, Murphy groups the seventeen chapters of the book (p. 16).

21. There are three specifications our animal ancestors were equipped

to meet: physical warmth, response to others for interdependent living, and specific responses to the opposite sex (p. 27).

22. The three core qualities of humanness are the intense or slightly diffuse needs that are met biologically, the diffuse demands for activity such as rhythm, manipulation of objects or exercise, and the need and capacity to learn (p. 37).

23. How does human individuality come about? Approximately in three different ways: (1) cognitive experiences—exploring the world; (2) affective experiences—feeling about the world; (3) impulse experiences—acting toward the world (p. 58).

24. The heart of the "great periods" of creativity in art depend upon three things: canalizations, ego involvement, and reciprocity between master and pupil (p. 148).

NOTE: Lest the reader at this point become convinced that Murphy phrases all of his ideas in three, the following brief list may add perspective to the list of 33 triadic concepts. All of them are taken from *Human Potentialities*. The list in no way exhausts the nontrichotomized concepts.

Four human needs (p. 61).

Six common kinds of learning (p. 64).

Two types of studies in sociology (p. 105).

"Thought, like perception, is bipolar" (p. 117).

Four specific steps to how wishes guide perceiving, remembering, and thinking (p. 116).

Four stages in creative thinking (p. 129).

25. Creativeness is encouraged or freed by three steps: increase sensitiveness, build strong canalizations especially of the self as a creator, and allow freedom to move from fantasy to controlled thinking (p. 164).

26. Murphy speaks of the "three-fold basis for craving to know and understand": visceral drives (instinctual), love of order (formal), and resonance to the nature and structure of that which surrounds us—excitement about reality and the capacity to respond to it (sensory) (p. 179).

27. Human potentialities are withheld from fulfillment by three current crises: huge power systems are in conflict, the systems we have evolved such as governments, industries, and social rules now control us more than we control them, and biological changes in man through nuclear accidents may make man unfit for his environment (p. 198).

28. There are three viewpoints as to the biological changes in man:

rapid changes of a physical type, the increase and decrease of certain diseases, and the fact that evolution is still going on (pp. 218–221).

29. Homogamy, or developing similar traits, is sensitive to three social factors: vertical mobility, horizontal mobility, and change of habitat (pp. 231–232).

30. The boundaries between the person and the world are the physical and/or biological, the psychological, and the social boundaries (p. 288).

31. Out of the psychological boundaries mentioned in No. 30 come three possible approaches to studying the relationships of man to his world: the Gestalt concept, the concept of Functional Interdependence, and the Lewinian Field Theory concept (p. 290).

32. Murphy feels that there are three directions towards which new research should be pushed: greater understanding of the physical world through astronomy, greater understanding of man through social psychology, and a greater understanding of the immediate environment through organic chemistry (p. 269).

33. The last of the triads to be outlined here is actually a triad upon a triad. After discussing the world that might be in the future, he assumes "there will soon be a world scientific–technical–political system (a triad) in which the question of the independence of sovereign states is less important than it seems today." If this system is to be created and is to survive chaos, three higher components must come into interaction with one another. The first is curiosity about man and his environment in which scientists may become a group apart in the service of humanity as a whole. The second is the development of something like "super-executives" or a "power elite" whose job it will be to use the inventions and social interactions that are developing. The third and, in a sense, the most important component is a genuine vertical communication system between all of the integrated parts of the scientific-technical-political world system (p. 264).

The strong passion for humanistic interpretations of man's foibles that runs through all of the works of Murphy is probably best indicated by his statement, "The castigation of one's fellows for their limited or warped outlook is comparable with the castigation of the heart for beating" (*Human Potentialities*, p. 57).

In somewhat the same vein as Gordon Allport, Murphy feels that the study of personality dynamics has been neglected by the psychologists of today. He feels that psychology fails to appreciate personality because it lacks the rigors of the so-called scientific approach. As previously stated, personality study is more than a science or an engineering project, it is also an art.

A unique eulogy of Gardner Murphy was prepared by his former students and coworkers. This eulogy is in the form of a book entitled, *Festschrift for Gardner Murphy,* published in 1960 and edited by Eugene L. Hartley and John G. Peatman. The book avoids the cultism frequently found in such works although a play on the initials of Gardner Murphy —G.M.—as "Great Man" is apparent. With the exception of the first two chapters the book deals solidly with psychological material and research findings.

MURPHY'S DESCRIPTION OF HUMAN BEHAVIOR

Because Murphy writes extensively on varied topics, it is not possible to treat his work within the framework of principles, as has been done with the previous theorists. The author has chosen to present Gardner Murphy's ideas as four major themes rather than as principles. Murphy himself feels that the study of personality is a particular kind of "general psychology." The four major themes are the following: the biological personality, the emerging, integrating personality, the socialized personality, and human potentialities or new perspectives.

An indication of the vastness of Gardner Murphy's treatment of the dynamics of personality is best shown by a listing of the 41 chapter headings in his major work, *Personality* (1947):

1. The Approach
2. The Organism
3. Heredity and Individual Growth
4. The Individual Constitution
5. The Elementary Biology of Motivation
6. The Biology of Motive Patterns
7. Organic Traits and Their Measurement
8. Canalization
9. Conditioning
10. The Hierarchy of Conditionings
11. The World of Symbols
12. The World of Values
13. Conflict
14. The Perceiver
15. Autism
16. Imagination and Thought
17. The Dreamer
18. Multiple Personality
19. Creativeness
20. The Origins of the Self
21. The Evolution of the Self
22. Enhancement and Defense of the Self
23. Psychoanalytic Mechanisms
24. Compensation for Inferiority
25. Extroversion-Introversion
26. Personality Structure

What follows, then, approximates a book review. The wide dimensions and the total coverage of personality theory may all be found in the 1947 treatise. The strong eclectic approach of Murphy is no better illustrated than in the above listing of chapters.

Murphy does not sit in judgment on the material he uses from the research and work of others. Rather it is his desire to describe personality. However, he feels there is no "danger in this century" of anyone completely describing or understanding the human personality.

To Murphy personality theory is synonymous with motivation theory. His primary quest is to answer the question, *"Why* does man do the things he does?" To him "every aspect of personality is conceived of in terms of motives."

To Hall and Lindzey, whose 1957 book added so much to personality theory, "The dimensions of his [Murphy's] theory are practically the same as those of the whole science of psychology." The techniques of outlining will be employed in presenting the theory of Gardner Murphy since a discursive treatment of his theory is only to do poorly what Murphy does well. As with all the theorists discussed herein, one must read the theorist in the original if a *full* understanding is what the reader desires. The present work only hopes to sketch out the primary features for the beginning student of personality theory and then pass them on to the masters themselves.

The Biological Personality Theme

General Concepts. "The first definition of personality is therefore in terms of a biochemical system" (*Personality,* p. 31). With these words we may begin to describe man's personality as Murphy sees it.

One of the difficulties in dealing with the human personality is the biological nature of the physical and chemical properties which are highly involved in man's behavior, since neither of these properties wants to adjust to social pressures. Thus nature ignores our artificial distinctions between man and his environment.

The organic system is a tension system which operates in a complex hierarchy of interdependent parts. The biological personality is therefore to be considered as part of the field theory. A *field* in this case means "the distribution of energy in space and time." Because man is biological, the concept of homeostasis is important. But because man is also social and operates in an uncontrollable and changing environment, homeostasis can render him incapable of changing to meet changing times. If he returns only to a state of equilibrium, he is forever going back, reactionary, to situations which no longer exist. This, Murphy feels, is a dilemma of human personality brought about by its biological basis. "It is the development, the differentiation, the integration (a triad again!) of these individual motive patterns that constitute the first great biological clue to personality" (*Personality*, p. 124).

Murphy feels strongly, as does the present author, the lack of value in pursuing the nature–nurture controversy. "There is no room, *ever*, for special pleading for heredity any more than for environment" (*ibid.*, p. 73).

The relationship of personality to anatomy may be studied in three ways. First, by studying indirectly the role the body plays in limiting and controlling conduct, we may gain valuable information about an individual's personality. Second, an advantage may be gained by studying the continuing effect expressive behavior has upon body appearance, an effect illustrated by Abraham Lincoln's quip that a man is responsible for his face after the age of forty. Third, the effect of one's physical appearance on others may afford a valuable clue to the relationship of anatomy to personality.

Organization. Four functions are involved in the organization of that part of man which is organic:

1. Energy is transmitted from one region of the body to another.
2. The transmission is simultaneous as energy flows in various directions and always in a highly interdependent fashion.
3. A degree of adjustment and regulation of each part to another is involved.

4. Each of the separate organic parts is responsive to "out of the skin" stimulation which in turn may create sympathetic responses of other organs.

Individual Constitution. The matter of individual differences springs, according to Murphy, from a constitutional fact which is indisputable. The fact that no two human bodies are exactly the same is hardly a new or startling revelation. All theorists acknowledge this fact. However, it is Murphy's use of individual differences which introduces an interesting aspect to personality theories. Only because man has differing organic systems within himself and because his individual organic system differs from all others is man able to fulfill a tremendously important function of integration. Integration, the functional interdependence of parts or the amalgamation of differing parts of any organism, is the crux of growth and development. If all the parts of a system were exactly alike, complete homeostasis would exist, and with complete homeostasis no action occurs. Action is essential to any kind of forward movement. Let us examine further this phenomenon of differences creating progress.

Keeping in mind that differences are extremely important because of the third factor which involves the interdependence of parts to each other, we may begin with a further study of constitutional differences. Beginning with the original state of organic existence within the single individual, the personality arises from the discontinuities of the tissue system such as receptors and effectors, ducts and ductless glands, and central and autonomic nervous systems. The interplay and interdependence of these dual systems help to create a personality. To Murphy "nothing is more certain than discontinuities." There exist, therefore, not only differences of degree but also differences of kind. An example is that certain species of animals cannot be mated to each other due to chromosomic differences. Even the mating of the horse with the donkey results in a sterile offspring, a mule. Murphy employs these illustrations to demonstrate that life and personality are more than points on a continuous scale.

Moving to the realm of social differences or discontinuities, he talks of quales and nodal points. A *quale* is "any characteristic which is distinct in an individual and which operates entirely independent of other forces." A *nodal point* (a term from the field of optics), as used by field theorists, is "any emanating point which has very complex and strong pervasive influences upon the field in which it operates." Murphy, following the tradition of the Gestaltists, denies that man's personality, both organic and social, has qualic characteristics. He prefers rather to postulate a personality theory on the nodality of life forces, whether they be biological or sociological. Nodal points may have high or low energy concentration. Man is a nodal point in the field of society.

The above discussion reveals the importance of individual differences in constitution. They are the backbone of further differences in individual nodality in society, but both kinds of differences are unimportant in themselves. The important idea is that the third force brings these differences together to be played off against each other and then to be integrated. The individual's constitutional makeup merely serves as an original ingredient of an emerging personality.

Development. The child begins to individualize his personality through his use of his five senses. These teach him through thresholds of receptivity to make affective judgments of hot–cold, sour–sweet, and so on. The sensory apparatus develops unequally in time. Taste and touch may develop before sight and sound. The interplay of these senses may be important as an affective quality. Also, what the child does about the things which affect him brings about the effector qualities in developing his personality. The child initially develops a personality from the organic senses which affect him and by the effect he makes upon his own body in adjusting.

Murphy pays respect to Herbert Spencer and Heinz Werner in discussing the three developmental levels he feels are involved in the biological aspects of man and his personality. The first level is the global and undifferentiated mass activity of the new organism at birth. This may be traced back as far as the cellular division of the human in the embryonic stage. The second developmental level concerns the organic parts as they begin to act individually in performing the duties for which they were formed. The third and most important developmental level concerns the integrated action of each part with all the other organic parts and especially the interdependence of the parts. Thus, the heart, the visceral organs, the neural fibers, the skeletal structure, the musculature, and all the portions of the body must depend upon and act in concert with each other. To fail to do so is to fail to function properly, and death results.

Needs. Four inborn organic needs are assumed to be part of the biological nature of man's personality. They are as follows:

1. Visceral needs: food, water, air, etc.
2. Activity needs: exploration and manipulation.
3. Sensory needs: perceptual clarity in color, tone, rhythm, and orientation.
4. Preservation needs: avoidance of pain, death, threat, shocks, etc.

Motivation. The theme of motivation runs strongly and pervasively through all of Murphy's writings. It is treated here as it applies to the biological orientation of personality. The motivating theme will reoccur in later sections. For a fully adequate understanding of motivation in Murphy's work the reader is urged to study especially chap. 5 and 6 of *Personality*. For the present we must content ourselves with an outline treatment. By outline we may replicate the work without losing any of the essential features.

1. Every single cell in man's body has the capacity to initiate behavior.

2. "Motivation never 'starts' or 'stops'," but there are tension gradients which produce degrees of motivation.

3. Because motivation depends upon the interdependence of outer and inner pressures of the organism against each other, it is a fusion of parts and not a simple arithmetical addition of pressures.

4. Because "sheer readiness is the same thing as motivation," we may expect to find that studying the human personality is the same thing as studying his preparatory responses. (for explanation of preparatory responses see canalizations)

5. The factor of discontinuity or individual differences also applies to motivation: "one man's motivation . . . can never be the duplicate of anothers."

6. As seen from a motivational viewpoint, personality is as much a "way of becoming sensitive" as it is a "way of reacting upon the environment." Thus, man is as much inner directed as outer pushed.

7. It is only because there is a discontinuity in motivation that integration can possibly take place. In other words with no discontinuity there is nothing to integrate, and with nothing to integrate there can be no motivation. As previously mentioned, it is the discontinuous parts of man which, because they must be integrated, lead to getting off dead center. A completely homeostatic, in-balance system is not prompted to do anything.

8. When motivation originates, it is not specifically aware of its goals. In the beginning, it more than less tries to integrate its bivariant parts. Only later in life does "purposivism" come into play. Then the personality knows what it is struggling for. Purposivism is a late-developing, derived, learned, special experience. It is not essential to motivation as motivation originates.

9. There are three ways to study individual differences in motivation:
   (a.) by measuring visceral or organic or physiological differences,
   (b.) by measuring external behavior which is an indirect method of
       studying individual differences in motivation,
   (c.) and, the most indirect study method of all, which is via the testi-
       mony of trained observers.

It is apparent that motivation begins with the biological aspects of
man but that much more is involved, as we shall see in the main section
on emerging integrating personality and also in the socialized personality.

Traits. Murphy begins his discussion of traits in the consideration of
the biological aspects of human personality. To him traits are only surface
indicators of the highly dynamic interdependence of inner organic parts.
Traits have their earliest beginnings as organic phenomena which consist
of specific tissue tensions. These organic traits are frequently highly complex systems of functional relations between body tissues and the specific
environment in which they operate. Out of this basic fabric of ideas
Murphy finds his term: *biosocial.*

Man begins life with organic traits. These can be measured only in a
very limited way. But organic traits help to explain the single person's
unique self, different from all other selves on earth. Organic traits give
him physiological strengths and weakness, strengths of drives, tendencies
to relaxation or excitement, and the very important factor of his prone-
ness to success or failure in physiological interaction.

There are three kinds of organic traits: the broad characteristics of
tissue response and needs, the persistent modes of individual reaction of
tissues, and the persistent modes of interaction between tissues.

In a much later statement made eleven years after the above thesis was
first developed, Murphy states in *Human Potentialities,* "The more
meaningful a trait is for social living, the further it is from simple
determination through any single genetic factor" (p. 224). Thus, the more
socially usable a trait is, the less directly traceable it is to a single organic
factor. Social traits, therefore, are infinitely complex patterns of interdependent basic organic traits; consequently, they defy direct measurement. In this, Murphy is in contradiction to the trait theories of H. A.
Murray. For example, Murphy feels that the primary mental abilities
theory of Louis Thurstone consists of complicated, interwoven, primary
organic traits which are most difficult to measure, if they can be measured at all.

The final word on traits can be found in the work cited above (p. 231) in which the degree of homogamy (inbreeding) of traits is sensitive to three social factors: vertical mobility, horizontal mobility, and acute changes in habitat.

Future. Murphy asks the sensible question, "What about the future of man as a biological specimen in the universe?" To this question, he poses three possible points of view, not answers. The first consideration, which constitutes more of a change than a threat, is the rapid changes one finds in physical types when they are compared with man of no more than a century ago. He cites the increased stature of the Japanese people or of American youth as examples which cannot be ignored. How far man will continue to change in physiological structure is a fair question to pose. These changes are, of course, not genetic.

Secondly, he finds a marked increase and also decrease in the prevalence of certain diseases. Cancer, for example, seems to be a more general problem in the present than in the past, even when one considers inadequate record systems in past centuries. Tuberculosis, on the other hand, seems to have a decreasing effect on the physical welfare of man.

In the third place, he finds the most important of all changes taking place. In what Murphy refers to as the "gene pool" that man has available, the changes have been extremely slow in the past thousands of years. Now however, he finds three considerations which must be acknowledged. Using Sewell Wright's words, "Human evolution is still going on," Murphy notes that we seem to be manipulating and increasing changes in human evolution much more rapidly than we may be able to assimilate the changes in the behavioral world of society. The first consideration is found in the field of genetic research. One illustration is the refined techniques which now bring us to the realization that man does not have 48 chromosomes but 46. Genetic research itself may show us means of rapidly changing human structure, just as it has in the field of hybridizing corn. As a second illustration, he refers to the papal discussion of positive and negative eugenics which was proclaimed in 1953. To this we must add the non-Catholic emphasis upon birth control which may or may not change the relative numbers of racial groups. One step beyond this is the consideration of amalgamating races through interracial marriages. Will we finally in the centuries to come evolve a single-colored people throughout the world? But it is to the third consideration of changes in man's biological makeup that Gardner Murphy directs most of his pertinent thoughts: the transmutation of genetic structure by accident or through atomic radiation. This, he feels, may change the human race beyond all recognizable features. Being a realist, Murphy does not automatically assume that change will be all bad. It may be perfectly possible that man can strengthen his biological structure through genetic manipulation via radiation. Until we know much more about it, however, he joins most of the world in fearing the evils which may come out of accidental radiation.

On this note, then, we leave the discussion of the biological personality as one factor in man's makeup and take up the dynamics of man's personality as it emerges through integration of its biological and social parts. The trail is long and involved, and hence we may turn again to frequent, outlined categories to cover Murphy's wide wide range of interests that constitute personality study. Once again, personality study is almost the total field of psychological study in Gardner Murphy's system.

The Emerging and Integrating Personality Theme

Following the previous theme of the biological foundations of personality, let us now turn our attention to the second major theme of man in his personality as both an emerging and as an integrating mechanism. Once again we find that Murphy is capable of covering the entire panorama of psychological concepts, using wisely, and choosing well, the ideas of others, as well as incorporating his own original thinking. Murphy uses the ideas of the big three, Freud, Adler, and Jung, in his own personality theory formation. From Freud rises a vast discussion of the psychoanalytic mechanisms, from Adler a discussion of inferiority and of positional psychology, and from Jung a discussion of introversion and extroversion. To these three, Murphy devotes a chapter each in his 1947 book, *Personality*. There are also touches of Gordon Allport's idea of *functional autonomy* as shown in the following sentence from Murphy's *Human Potentialities*: "The very process of learning and thinking may in themselves become satisfying." Also there are some overtones of Murray's personality theory in this quotation, also from *Human Potentialities*: "We have, then, a tremendous range of human motives which are organized around the central nervous system and its processes." However, we find some reluctance to speculate on the work of Sheldon in this section: "We should prefer not to speculate much about the matter of body types" (p. 41).

Another illustration of the wide range of Murphy's work is his treatment of such concepts as feeling, will power, autism, and the place of mood in personality formulation. In regard to feeling, which to Murphy connotes desire and will power, or the power to act in any given or desired direction, he feels that man can and does change conditions. He may change them through canalizations, conflict, his perceptual system, or through the symbols he uses. In regard to autism, Murphy says, *"The best is the norm."* Murphy very cleverly shows the duplicity of man by this quotation; all of us as we play golf, bowl, or participate in any kind of activity are inclined to think that our best golf shot or our strike in bowling is actually our average game, and that all the other not so successful scores, fish, or games are really below our usual performance. In regard to mood, Murphy states, "Personality is first of all a drive system of which mood is a prominent aspect." We may see from the three illustrations above the vast range of Murphy as he treats man's personality.

Possibly the best illustration, however, of the total strength, breadth, and complication of the personality structure itself can be gained from the following lengthy quotation (*Personality*, 1947, p. 641. Italics as in the original).

. . . the ultimate elements in personality structure are the needs or tensions, *and they are interrelated by means of the functional connections between regions which permit the spread of these tensions.* The result is a *tension system* whose lawful structure is expressed in terms of the relative strengths of tensions and the relative rigidity of barriers to their diffusion. Our hypothesis therefore claims that *the organism's tension system is organized,* in the sense that each event is limited and controlled by the relations between elements, as in homeostasis. There is organization at every moment in time, in the form of a 'static' system. There is also temporal or dynamic organization, each tension or group of tensions initiating changes which eventually bring the organism to a new balance, or restore it to the first. Of special importance is Weiss' concept of the *development of a system that retains its organization.* This may be achieved through the gradual complication of individual parts, the overall relation between the parts remaining unchanged. Such phases of personality development as 'kinetics,' 'style,' 'individual rhythm,' etc., are of this type. The organism is a physiological gradient system. Jacobson's relaxation experiments indicate that muscular tension in one region spreads gradient-fashion to other muscle groups; similarly, the reduction of tension in one region spreads until the tension is reduced in the functionally correlated muscle groups, the process in all probability continuing until most or all of the muscle groups are involved. Considerable other evidence tends to the same direction; and the principle holds for neural and biochemical tensions as well.

We now consider in more detail those aspects of the personality which are attempting to integrate and emerge into the full stature of man as a living human being. The following six terms, it is thought, adequately cover this second theme. They are: canalization, conditioning, conflict, perception, symbols, and self.

Canalization. Two approaches may be taken in defining the term *canalization.* This term Gardner Murphy has used extensively but it has not been generally adopted by the psychological world. The first definition, which is also the traditional definition, is as follows: "Establishing and progressively strengthening a preference for one among several potential ways of satisfying a drive or the established preference itself" (English and English, *A Comprehensive Dictionary of Psychological and Psychoanalytical Terms,* Longmans, 1958. (Courtesy David McKay Co.) p. 75). The second attempt to define the word is an excerpt from Gardner Murphy's *Personality* (p. 162).

This process by which general motives (which are first rather nonspecifically related to a class of stimuli) tend, upon repeated experience, to become more easily satisfied through the action of the specific satisfier than of others of the same general class, has been known so long that it would be impossible to name its discoverer. But good names are a great convenience, and Janet's term *canalization* is a good name for this process. The energies awaiting an outlet break through the barrier at a given spot, are channeled or canalized in the process, and, as the barrier weakens, tend more and more to focus their pressure upon it.

Because the original treatment of canalization by Gardner Murphy is voluminous, the following outline may help the student of personality to glimpse some of the highlights or main points of the term canalization and Murphy's use and emphasis of it.

1. The first canalizations center around the body itself in all the aspects of bodily or organic growth. This, according to Murphy, is the first great center for canalizations. Following the capacity of the body to individualize the differing sensations or senses, the first canalizations are upon specific things, as far as a child can discriminate among specific things. However, since the child first learns about the outside world through his body, it is the canalizations of the body which are the initial ones. In this

initial state the intensity of the gratification that the object, the body, or the child receives strengthens the individual response. As each individual response is strengthened, the initial strength grows or gains in response as it receives further gratifications. This process continues until a canalization or a strongly channeled response results. In this developmental stage the frequency of certain responses which become canalized is of much importance.

2. Not all canalizations need be pleasant; some may be avoidant or unpleasant canalizations. Hence, Murphy's theory is not a hedonistically oriented theory.

3. Usually, a canalization can be broken only by other more powerful canalizations or more powerful responses. It is possible to destroy one canalization if another more potent behavior or behavioral tendency competes with it in a manner powerful enough to prevent the original physiological expression. However, it should be remembered that canalizations are in general autonomous and free of interference from one another.

4. "Canalizations, then, are not, so far as we know, subject to extinction whether by disuse or by displacement of other canalizations" (*ibid.*, p. 169). It is not too far-fetched to use the analogy of a river as it wanders about, channeling its course. If one can imagine a river as it flows, then meets a blockage and creates a new channel, but always remains with some vestige of the former channel, we can gain an idea of the effect of canalizations upon the behavior of man.

5. As long as some degree, even though small, of actual satisfaction of the drive occurs, a canalization of fixation will follow. In all major types of motivation, canalization occurs.

6. When there is a choice to be made in action and the contrast between alternatives is great, canalized choices, it is assumed, will be made more quickly.

7. Canalizations are dependent upon major interests, as well as upon bodily activity, as causal factors. The body may produce or the body may do certain things which, having once done, it does not care to repeat, for example, a sneeze.

8. The rate of the canalization process depends to a degree upon the ascendance of one satisfaction over another. That is to say, the higher the degree of satisfaction, the faster the rate of developing a canalization.

9. Murphy considers that the process of the canalization formation is never ended but continues throughout life.

10. One of the most important clues that the personologist may look for or work toward is the concept of the canalization upon the self, or *self-canalization* (Murphy's terms). He feels that the closer one gets in experimentation and research to discovering the roots of self-canalization, the closer one comes to discovering the inner structure of the human personality.

11. In the same light, Murphy feels that self-love, or the love and respect of self, is probably the most powerful form of canalization that we may find. Although Murphy never ignores the effect and the strength of the environment upon the single human personality, he does feel that constitutional differences and especially the intensification of the needs of each individual constitution or body may account for the individuality among people. Because there seems to him a quantitative difference in canalizations between one person and another, we may find that one individual has very few canalizations and that these few may be deeply imbedded, while in another person we may find many canalizations, only some of which are deeply imbedded.

12. The more complex a person has become, the more canalizations he is likely to have. This does not necessarily mean that the older one is, the more canalizations he will have, but it does mean that the more experiences an individual receives and undergoes, the more canalizations he is likely to have. Consequently, the individual living in a very quiet, rural environment is not likely to gain as many canalizations, although they may be deeper, than the individual who lives in a complicated, metropolitan area. Murphy feels that canalizations can be found in much of the language of modern man. In fact, he believes it is harder to avoid references to canalizations than it is to find examples of them. He gives as examples, "Take the boy out of the country but not the country out of the boy," or the longing for "My Old Kentucky Home." These and many more he feels abound in the literature and in the language of all people.

13. Murphy feels that each society maintains a system of associated canalizations, by which phrase he is referring to stereotype or similar canalizations within a society or ethnic group. As each society finds canalizations valuable, they are handed forward to the next generation.

In a sense, then, there is a biological and cultural inheritance of canalizations, but not, however, in the Jungian sense. Because society is reluctant
to give up associated canalizations which have been valuable, we have
such phenomenon as the cultural lag, affecting, for example, the stability
of the family unit.

Murphy makes a strong distinction between conditioning and canalization. For example, he feels that conditioning is subject to extinction, that
the experimenter may extinguish any conditioned response, whereas a
canalization, as far as he knows, is not capable of being extinguished but
survives in some residual form throughout the course of life. The major
difference between conditioning and canalization responses in the human
being is whether the stimulus itself, the thing that causes the action,
starts a consummatory response or a preparatory response. By *consummatory response* is meant the thing achieved is achieved for itself alone
and is then consumed for the value inherent in the activity itself. The
preparatory response, as it is found in canalization, always assumes that
the individual is preparing for another activity beyond the impact of the
original stimulus. For example, a canalization which centers around
thrift will be inclined, where money is the stimulus, to lead to the response of saving money in preparation for further use or further saving.

The following listing may help one to see the differences that Murphy
finds between his term *canalization* and the term generally accepted in
psychology, *conditioning*.

Canalizations	*Conditioning*
1. Irreversible	1. Can be reversed
2. Stimulus is the satisfier	2. Symbol is the satisfier[1]
3. Nonextinctive	3. Can be extinguished
4. Consummatory response	4. Satisfying response

Conditioning. A second factor in how the human personality emerges
from its organic and bodily conditions and how it integrates its inner and
outer forces is found in Murphy's treatment of the word *conditioning*. He
begins chapter 9 in *Personality* with the following quotation: "Most
learning springs from struggle. The motivated individual strives, blindly
or intelligently, to find the means of satisfaction. As he strives, he dis-

---

[1] ". . . the second criterion of conditioning, 'symbol is the satisfier', is quite likely
to be misunderstood. Ordinarily the symbol would not be a satisfier but only a signal.
The metronome beat, for example, does not satisfy the dog's hunger as the meat
powder would." [Note to author.]

covers things and activities that bring him into contact with the source of satisfaction. These things and activities come to elicit, in their own right, part (or sometimes all) of the responses made to the satisfier itself. In this very broad sense, the term conditioning will be used. But from the present point of view, conditioning occurs only because motivation is present in the first place" (p. 192). Hence to Gardner Murphy, "Personality is grounded in the experience of satisfaction and frustration; it is not capriciously extensible in all directions" (p. 216).

It is now obvious that not only canalizations but conditioning are absolutely essential to the emergence of any kind of human personality, and, although conditioning is commonplace and essential to human behavior, the failure to be conditioned is also commonplace. This factor, Murphy feels, is often ignored or forgotten in the psychological work concerning personality and personality theory research. It is too often assumed, he feels, that conditioning is automatic because it happens to be so commonplace.

Emerging out of the concept of conditioning of the human personality are a number of factors, such as that of individual difference. In *Personality*, (p. 193) Murphy states,

As a simple physiological principle, then, it is permissible to say that a given response originally aroused by one or only a few stimuli can in time, as a result of experience, be aroused by a wide range of stimuli, many of which bear no similarity whatever to the original stimulus and are connected with it only by close association with it. Since each individual encounters different patterns of stimulation and acquires different conditioned responses, personality may be conceived to consist in the system of conditionings which distinguishes one man from another.

Murphy pays a great deal of attention to the principle of *dominance,* which he feels is sufficient to explain the acquisition and the loss of any conditioned responses. Certain conditioned responses are far more dominant than others. We have, then, a sort of hierarchy or "pecking order" of conditioned, dominant, and less dominant responses within the individual. Thus, when any dominant conditioned response is brought into activation, it inhibits numbers of other conditioned responses, putting the less dominant conditioned responses in a lower order in controlling human behavior. In like manner, the spontaneous recovery of a conditioned response is due to its dominance over other less conditioned responses.

Thus, dominance and submission in conditioning are of vital importance to the emerging personality as it attempts to integrate the numerous forces that are "in the skin and out of the skin," one of Murphy's favorite terms.

As we have seen before, the problem of transfer or generalization of stimuli comes from established conditionings, which occur when there are similarities between the stimulus situations. Since, "All conditionings, as far as we know, are subject to transfer," the problem of transfer or generalization between established conditioned responses is of utmost importance in the study of human personality. In addition to this, and on the assumption that all conditioning leads to transfer, it is true, therefore, that when stimuli vary we may expect all conditionings to lead to differentiation between responses. In a sense, intellectual processes, are due to the value of, and the ability to make, differentiations; as these differentiations are made, they become further compartmentalized. The inability to compartmentalize differentiations, it would seem, is the problem of the less intelligent human being. The greater the intelligence, we may then assume, the greater the ability to differentiate and compartmentalize conditioned responses.

There are three mechanisms which, under the rubric of conditioning, especially conditioning around cultural norms, have an important role in the early stylizing of behavior. These three mechanisms are *suggestibility, imitation,* and *sympathy.* Out of these three mechanisms a fourth factor emerges, that of *attitudes,* which are in themselves, according to Murphy, also conditioned responses. These attitudes, then, help to determine what responses, especially cultural norm responses, may later be conditioned. Conditionings of those aspects where the culture and society are involved in the emerging and integrating personality are to patterns and not to isolated stimuli. This, of course, is much in the tradition of Kurt Lewin.

Conflict. In Murphy's treatment of conflict in human behavior, one is reminded somewhat of Adler's work on inferiority to superiority as a goal, or pathway, of emerging human behavior. Murphy gives a large place to the contribution that conflict can make to the human individual. He feels, for example, that most learning actually springs out of struggle or, to put it in other words, "Choice means conflict" (*Human Potentialities,* p. 79). Without getting into the question of whether man has free will, Murphy finds that because man does have some choices in life, he must be cognizant that these choices will lead to conflict. Without choice there can be no conflict; everything would be automatic. In short, choice begets conflict. This phenomenon begins with the earliest emergence of the human being as a living organism in which physiological balance and imbalance are to be considered normal and commonplace. However, Murphy feels that physiological conflict is not true conflict since this conflict can resolve itself. In other words, the imbalance between eating or starving to death, although not normal and commonplace, is not a true conflict since the body either is fed and survives or is not fed and dies. True conflict actually comes, for example, when one has to choose between a number of items on a menu or in the cafeteria line. Although death obviously is not imminent in this case, true conflict may come about through the inability to decide what one wants to eat at that particular moment.

Psychological conflict in contrast to physiological conflict is genuine, especially when the signals given to the integrating self are ambiguous. Ambiguous signals are those for things which have varying values or about which we must make decisions or in which the pathways are obscure. He uses, for example, Pavlov's dogs in their inability to distinguish the differences between circles and ellipses. It was not that Pavlov's dogs were starving that caused the conflict of a genuine psychological nature; it was their inability to identify an ellipse, which is very like a circle.

Frustration comes from any blocking of an outlet. When the outlet is blocked, the energy inherent in the system is dammed up and seeks a release of energy through canalized drives. Following the exposition previously given of the biological personality, one can see that there is a high degree of individualization always present in the frustration. This tolerance to frustration is intrahuman and interhuman. That is, the degree of difference within the human, the single human, may vary from time to time. Tolerance may be higher in the morning than in the evening after one has had a tiring day. Also involved are the degrees of difference between two people, or interhuman toleration. Murphy feels that conflict is not the result of organic *vs.* functional, or body *vs.* mind dichotomies; the process of conflict, he believed, is far more involved than a conflict between two opposing forces. What is involved is the integration and hierarchy of dominance traits. There are many, many factors involved in any true psychological conflict, and as we recall, psychological conflict is the only true kind of conflict. One does not lead a life of struggle, therefore, between the mind and the body, both wanting to do different things. It is the integration of the mind and the body in relationship to the outside or cultural world, plus degrees in canalizations and dominance in conditionings, which are involved.

Murphy finds three forms of response to Freud's frustration, which comes out of psychological conflict. These three forms of response are: 1. aggression; 2. resignation; and 3. self-deception. An example of aggression is any direct or frontal attack upon the person or situation which causes the frustration. The "death feint" is an example of a resignation form of response to frustration. Self-deception as a form of response is of three different types, as given by Murphy. It is, first, the distant self-image, a self with tremendous gifts and powers which would overcome any frustration. A second is deception of self by imagining a fantasy world which would provide a conflict-free life. In the third type of self-deception one conceives of oneself as a superior being, above any kind of threat, in a somewhat psychotic withdrawal syndrome. Murphy also sees a place for a fourth form of response to frustration in the activity of displaced aggression.

It can be seen then that Murphy considers conflict as an essential, not only to the existence of man but also to the progression of man beyond his simple biological organic self. It is, therefore, within the framework of the emerging and integrating personality, the second of the four major themes, we are treating the work of Gardner Murphy.

Perception. Murphy feels that we do not really "see" with our eyes or "hear" with our ears. The sound of an automobile horn is perceived differently by all of us; even though the sound, the decibel content, the intensity, the timber of the automobile horn, remain the same, each of us has a different way of hearing it. To some of us, it may be annoying, while to others it may herald a future activity and to still others it may mean that an awaited friend has arrived and an enjoyable social engagement is soon to begin. Similarly, a mountain may mean to some of us a thing to be climbed or an obstacle which lies in our path or simply a thing of grandeur and beauty. Thus, to Murphy, we do not really see with our eyes or hear with our ears; all depends upon the perceptual system of each individual. This is, of course, not unlike the concept of perception within the general world of psychology.

Perception first begins in the human animal by self-reference, or in the Piaget sense, it is egocentric. Continuing from this, Murphy finds the process of perceptual development involving three activities: identification, reaction, and differentiation. First, we must identify through our past experience any phenomenon which occurs to us. Upon identifying the phenomenon as pleasant or unpleasant, we respond to it with a favorable or unfavorable reaction. After having identified or reacted to the phenomenon, we then differentiate it further. The fourth process of integrating the stimulus or phenomenon lags far behind the first three processes of identification, reaction, and differentiation. Murphy feels that perception like motor-learning and maturation develops in three stages. The first stage is the blur stage. The second stage is the differentiation stage, and the third stage is the integration stage. It is only after these three stages have been reached in that order that one develops a fully successful or efficient perceptual system.

One of the valuable aspects of a perceptual system is that it solidifies human behavior and helps to resist change through the activity of canalization. It is canalization which keeps man from floating about like a leaf or a loose feather in the air. There is, of course, the difficulty in changing human behavior as perceptual systems canalize and resist change; however, Murphy also feels that this is a saving grace in man's behavior. Man does not have to learn new methods of canalizing his behavior each morning as he arises to begin a new day.

Other factors regarding perception interest Murphy very much. He feels, for example, that much of perception is intuitive or, using the Freudian term, is in the unconscious. Perception is not directly identifiable in the conscious processes, either by the person who perceives something or by the individual who studies a person who is perceiving. Murphy finds, also, that perception is quite satisfying to the self-system in that perception is a tension reducing process. The ability to achieve adequate perception for living is fundamental.

"*Needs keep ahead of percepts.*" This often quoted statement of Murphy's from his book, *Personality* (p. 378), means essentially that needs control the perceptual systems, or that, in a sense, they give the orders to the perceptual systems. We see what we want to see and not what actually exists. Thus, the things we need, the things we want, the things that motivate us, are always ahead of our perceptual systems, and our perceptual systems are guided by the need systems in each human being.

According to Murphy, there are two principles under which our perception is organized. The first is the regularity of the experience which arouses an expectation. The second principle is the relevance or meaningfulness of the object to our desires or fears. Following these two principles of regularity of experience and relevance of the object, our perceptual system is organized.

Learning. Murphy feels that the ability to learn entails five processes in the following order: 1. the capacity to form simple associations; 2. the ability to develop sound and gestures which enable one to communicate with oneself and with other humans; 3. the ability to use symbols and in using symbols to think abstractly; 4. the capacity to invest personal feelings in stable and in specific objects; 5. the capacity to systematize and classify objects, feelings, and symbols so that one is able to share them socially with the world.

All five of the processes result in a consolidation of ways of perceiving. One cannot learn unless one is able to perceive. Murphy also feels that learning and, in a sense thinking, can be done only under the pressure of wants. In short, one does not learn, nor does one think, unless he has a desire or a pressure which creates or helps to create that capacity within his neurological system.

In *Human Potentialities,* Murphy speaks of six kinds or six common kinds of learning as follows:

1. Pavlovian: classical conditioning (stimulus–response behavior).
2. Skinnerian: operant conditioning (rewarding and reinforcing correct responses).
3. Associative linkage: correlations (phenomenon such as the natural phenomenon of thunder which occurs with lightning).
4. Reorganization of perception: insight (sudden resolution of a problem).
5. Reorganization of totality: Gestalt (use of all facilities—physical and mental—to reorient by way of feeling, cognition, emotions, etc.).
6. Canalization: channelling consummatory behavior habits (nonextinguishable direct satisfaction of a need by a specific want if no symbols necessarily involved).

Thus, we find that canalization, conditioning, perception, and learning all have integral places in the emerging and integrating personality.

Symbols.   Symbol, to Gardner Murphy, has a wide range of meaning. It means essentially any stimulus which can stand for another stimulus. One word can stand for another word, one gesture can stand for or mean another gesture, and so on. The following outline will give some of the highpoints of the importance of symbols in the personality theory of Gardner Murphy.

1. Differences in personality are due in a large measure to differing responses to the world of symbols. In other words, Murphy feels that the way man responds to a symbolic world is in a large way the factor which makes individual differences possible.

2. As a human being acquires a language, it is completely socially controlled and has no relationship (other than speech pathology) to any organic condition. This Murphy feels is true in every stage of language acquisition or, in other words, in the learning of symbols.

3. Frequently, he feels, in the field of research, that what often passes as higher order conditioning is nothing more than first order verbal conditioning or symbolic manipulation.

4. Although man has language and uses language to conceal his thoughts, the fact of having language and symbols also helps man to liberate his thoughts and to put thoughts into actions.

5. The world of symbols actually comes from the world of action and returns constantly to a world of action in which man frequently does something physically because of his use or others' use of symbols.

6. Harking back to William James's phrase "stream of thought," Murphy feels that this innerspeech is a method in which man is forever signalling to himself. Murphy feels that if only the researcher could know what the stream of thought is and could understand it, he would know everything that need be known about any given personality.

7. Man lives, dreams, hopes, and plans in a purely symbolic world.

8. Because symbols are inner cues to action, one may study the tension systems of any human personality by studying the symbol content of that personality.

9. An important factor in the shaping of any human personality and its organization for the future can be action which is solely symbolic. Thus, in counseling, in clinical work, in psychotherapy, much of what is done is done to the symbolic actions of the client. In short, we do not feed him differently, clothe him differently, or treat him differently, physically, in this realm of therapy, but simply use symbols or words.

10. It is possible that a symbolic cue may set the stage or create a kind of behavior which will persist long after the particular symbols have been removed. For example, someone may use a word which angers us very much. Long after that word has been used, we still continue to be angry.

In other words, the symbol has been removed, but the behavior caused by that symbol persists, sometimes for a long period.

11. As stated previously, Murphy does not feel that symbols are restricted to language alone. Clothing, gestures, pictorial forms of art, all may be classified as symbols. However, he does feel that language is one of the richest clues to an individual's personality that a researcher may work with.

12. As the human being develops, the individual characteristics of his speech patterns become highly stable. This is a form, of course, in the Murphy terminology, of canalizations. These highly stable speech patterns are quite set and firm regardless of outer pressures. Any speech pathologist or speech correctionist is certainly aware of the difficulties of altering a stuttering pattern of speech.

13. Murphy sees a valuable area of research in the relationship between symbols and value systems. When canalizations in the symbolic world become fully established, he feels they may be called *values*. ". . . the central fact about values is that they arise from definite wants, of all types . . ." (*Personality*, p. 272). Most values of the individual, Murphy feels are "anchored deep within the skin." This is, in a sense, Murphy's way of dealing with the unconscious. Murphy sees a value in long periods of immaturity because the longer the period of immaturity, the more plastic or fluid is the organism. The more fluid the organism, the greater the number of values it can form. Those organisms which are "set" at an early age are unable to gather many more values. It is the individual who keeps an open mind who is likely to gain a great breadth or depth of value systems. This long period of plasticity or immaturity has benefit to both the individual and society. It would be difficult to build a value system in a human being, or for that human being to experiment with the value system, were he to reach a level of maturity which would close off feeding in any further values. "There are many values partly because it takes so long to grow up" (*ibid.*, p. 284).

14. The world of symbols and the world of attitudes are also involved in the personality theory of Murphy. Whereas values arise from definite wants within and without the system and are integrated by the personality, attitudes, Murphy feels, are present dispositions toward action or toward setting up values. The relationship between symbols and attitudes is the result of a long and complex process. Equally involved is the relationship between attitudes and values. Attitudes are motivated. They

are adjustments to present situations and remind us of values. The more closely we regard attitudes, the more difficult it is to find any essential differences between attitudes and values. Attitudes are defined by some as a value expression. Whereas Murphy feels value is inner or inner-centered, an attitude expresses a value via verbal symbols. "Value and attitude can be distinguished only by a convenient surgical separation whose utility is subject to doubt" (*ibid.*, p. 286). Social attitudes in the main are triggered by symbolic stimuli. These social attitudes are then expressed in symbolic form. Murphy feels that the human personality never has entirely a specific attitude and on the other hand never has entirely a general attitude.

15. Each individual personality has a symbol system integrated within itself. It is therefore not possible for another individual to make any integrated response to the symbol system of another human being prior to that person's integration of his own symbol system. In other words, it is not possible for an adult to respond to a child's symbolic value system of honesty or fair play before that child can have created or integrated within himself such a system.

16. Murphy feels that much of personality as we know it is organized through the symbols that the personality acknowledges and has integrated within itself. However, no system of symbols overrides the wisdom of the body; it is the integration of a symbolic world and an organic world within the human being that sets the limits to which symbols can aspire.

17. Despite the implications of the above statement, it is possible in a neurotic or highly psychotic disorder, that the human personality can live almost absolutely in a symbolic world, ignoring demands for food, clothing, shelter, and any organic needs.

Self. All of the preceding discussion regarding canalization, conditioning, conflict, perception, and symbols culminates in the emerging and integration of a self for each individual human personality. In dealing with the material concerning the concept of self, we may divide it roughly into three categories; the canalization of self, the enhancement of self, and the defense of the self. This is reminiscent of the work of Carl Rogers. The concept of self plays such a large part in Murphy's theory that he believes that much of what is personality, as it behaves in everyday living, is self-oriented or self-determined.

The canalization of self begins at a very early age when it centers on the body and the mouth. In the beginning then, the self grows out of a complex of indefinite feelings which exist at the first perceptual level. The feelings we have about ourselves from infancy on gradually come into being as the result of a process of differentiation which goes on within the perceptual field. In Murphy's words, "Our thesis is, then, the perceptual activities and motor activities are at first utterly selfless; that as one perceptual object, the body, becomes defined, other objects are related to it in context; and, similarly, that motor responses which are at first rather independent activities become activities oriented to or serving the self. Unconscious dispositions maintain the self-reference of our activities, and these dispositions have become associated with selfhood through a nexus of associative processes similar to those in operation elsewhere" (ibid., p. 502).

The second of the considerations concerning self is self-enhancement. Because the self is a perceived object, it follows all the laws of perception. In its efforts to enhance itself, the self depends a great deal upon the process of identification in a truly active way. This process includes strong feelings of autism. Also involved in the emerging self concept are the activities of projection and introjection. Murphy feels that whatever the self is, it becomes the center, the focal point, and a standard of comparison to ultimate reality. This leads inevitably to having the self take its place as a supreme value for any human personality. Thus, the self moves from a feeling of body awareness to one of prestige and power. All of this is designed to enhance the self of any human being. As the self tries to enhance itself, it becomes less and less a purely perceptual object and moves more and more into the realm of being a conceptual trait system.

Eventually the self, through trying to enhance its value system, achieves the level of ego-structure. However, the self depends not so much upon who a person is, but what he is, and what value he has in life. Whether the self is a direct physical object, such as the body, or a type of abstraction; whether the self is very loosely organized or well structured, the thing of primary importance is the ego. Murphy advances four hypotheses which are individual factors in determining selfhood. The first hypothesis is that education seems to have a bearing upon whether one considers himself as a physical object or as a system of high abstraction. The second hypothesis is that one tends to use verbal symbols to a great degree in attempting to integrate one's picture of the self. The third hypothesis is that one evaluates or esteems himself to a degree that the culture in which he lives promotes a respect for the self. The fourth hypothesis depends upon parental approval; we are inclined to value or undervalue ourselves in line with the amount of parental approval we receive. The more approval from parents, the higher the degree of value we place upon the self. Murphy is careful to point out that these are hypotheses which could lend themselves quite readily to clinical types of research.

After the self has evolved from a loosely disorganized, unintegrated beginning and is attempting to enhance its position, self-defending tendencies appear. Murphy feels it is not possible to enhance or defend oneself without possibly encroaching on the self-defense and self-enhancement of others. Defense itself, he feels, is a primary concept in the study of human personality. Man cannot but feel that he is, like the spider at the center of a web, the being in which all things of value begin and end. In short, instead of all roads leading to Rome, all things lead to the self. This self-centeredness not only enhances man but helps him to defend himself. Man has the ability to canalize his feelings, and this canalization tends to increase the rigidity in which he conceives of himself and the rigidity of the self within a place in society. Thus, egocentrism and sociocentrism are natural, parallel developments.

However, man has some difficulties in delineating where the self begins and where the self ends as he tries to enhance and defend himself. Consequently, where the human personality is attempting to identify with two individuals, the canalizations that result from this are inclined to create for one human personality two or more incomplete diverging selves. Such divergences can, and, in a sense almost must, lead to neurotic or psychotic involvement. Somewhat similar to this, Murphy feels, are the degrees of independence of the self from the nonself. Although in the early organic stages, the child has some difficulty with this concept, he is on fairly safe ground. Either the self ends with the skin or does not end with the skin. However, after a time, *symbolization* and *canalization* by *identification* toward others (parents and other ego objects) become blurred. The delineation between the self and nonself becomes indistinct. Murphy feels that this particular area of study between self and nonself can be a rich and rewarding one for the research oriented psychologist. Murphy tentatively states that it is possible the study of telepathy may provide new clues.

In summary, then, Murphy feels that as we learn to accept our place in the world and the way our selves, or self-system, fit within this complex, we may better realize the nature of our own self-system.

The Socialized Personality Theme

The socialized personality is the third of the four major themes in the present author's treatment of the work of Gardner Murphy. Man begins as a biological being and as he later integrates his biological and cultural milieu, he reaches the third level of a socialized human being, one capable of living in harmony with other human beings. Whether this is called culture, society, or family, this is a necessary step in the total concept of human personality.

According to Murphy it is impossible to consider a human personality without considering the social process in which that personality operates, for as he feels, even among the protozoa, we find that one individual protozoan is sensitized to another. Again, because Murphy's work is voluminous and all inclusive, we find it profitable to enumerate some of the factors which he considers to be components of the socialized personality.

1. All personalities are interdependent. It is not possible to consider personalities as independent building stones in a social world.

2. Personalities, however, are not the sole components of a group or social life. One must consider weather, climate, the fertility of the soil, and economic life, which also help to make up the totality of what we call a culture.

3. Man is not entirely passive in his relationship to the pressures of a group life. It is possible that he may accept, reject, compromise, or integrate the various pressures that are brought upon him by the world in which he lives. For example, at times we may consider a child as being unable to manipulate his environment. Murphy feels, however, that the child does wield influence upon his environment, and as he does so, he does it in his own individual way. The mother or father may be much manipulated by the child.

4. It is important to keep in mind that any individual reacts, not to the culture at large, but only to specific aspects of the culture which his perceptual system recognizes. Much as the soldier in Stephen Crane's *The Red Badge of Courage* could know only that part of the battle which he could see, so it is that man can know only that part of the world which he can feel or perceive. Even though he may read in news magazines and newspapers of international events, it is not possible for him to be too greatly moved by that which is not a specific aspect of his social world.

5. Murphy makes good use of the research of Linton, Mead, Ruth Benedict, Kardiner, Bateson, Fromm, Horney, the Lynds, the Gluecks, and Moreno in his treatment of the social world of man. In regard to economic determinism (any system of thought in which main outlines of social life are derived from economic organization of the group) Murphy feels that this is too often a neglected area of study in regard to personalities. There are three ways in which economic determinism may be used as an approach to personality study. The first is that man's economic life may restrict his activities. This is certainly evident in the experience of Karen Horney or in the writings of Fromm. The second way is that economic determinism may so strongly direct human behavior as to highly affect the individual and his personality. A third way in which economic determinism is a factor in personality formation is as a part of the total economic environment in which his employment, his chances for success, and his chances for gaining superiority over others are influenced or even controlled. Economic determinism means both situation, that is, the resources that are available, and institutions such as banks, guilds, unions, and others.

6. Murphy feels that the value of mores have been underestimated in personality study. Mores, he feels, add vitality and love to social institutions. These institutions play an important part in the formation of individual and collective personalities. Murphy divides them into four valuable kinds of groups, as follows: (1.) self-maintenance, farming, manufacturing, forestry; (2.) self-perpetuation, marriage, family, courtship; (3.) self-gratification, amusements, culinary arts, painting, literature, and music; and (4.) self-regulation, police, courts of law, the constitution, etc. These four groups of institutions are able to aid the human flow of the history of man.

7. Murphy does not de-emphasize or ignore the value of social roles in the formation of a personality. He feels that roles serve to mold personality. The two most clearly defined bases for roles are age and sex. Resemblances which may occur between parents and children are partially due to the child's carrying forward the roles that he learns from parents. Much in the same tradition as Karen Horney, Murphy feels that economic factors strongly influence a personal outlook, which, in turn, determines role acceptance or role rejection by any given person. Murphy strongly denies the rigid adherance to cultural relativism. (All cultures are equally well adapted to human nature, or, human nature can take on any shape

with equal ease.) He feels that cultural relativism denies and even ignores the strong, common biological bases of human adaptation although there are many deviates or nonconformists in any given culture.

In summary of our thesis regarding roles, we have attempted to show (1) that society, with its system of mores, and with the self maintenance mores more or less central in the pattern, does not merely "mold" people, but requires from them the enactment of specific roles in accordance with their place in the system; (2) that not all roles are easily accepted, but that many require effort, and indeed frequently put a strain upon the individual; (3) that a given person must enact several different roles (sex, class, etc.) at once, and that their integration is no obvious or mechanical matter; (4) that roles derive not merely from primary obligations, but also in response to the roles of others (there is not only melody but counterpoint); (5) that in consequence of all this the individual develops balancing or complementary roles, so that he is a complement both to others and to himself; and (6) that it is thus a long way from the simplest economic determinism to a realistic role psychology based ultimately upon the recognition of self-maintenance factors.[2]

8. The family, as an agent of personality formation, acts very strongly as the mediator and as the canalization agent of culture. For it is through the parents that the personality socializes itself and learns the standards by which it must operate. Secondly, the family as a unit acts as a small society or unique culture in which it is less expensive for the emerging socializing personality to use trial and error in formulating its own personality.

9. Murphy feels that, given a changed situation which is total and powerful, it is quite likely that one may change roles and that consequently a changed personality, in the social sense, may emerge. Situationism may further determine differences we find between persons, which are fundamentally those of the roles which they must enact. For example, from the work of Hartshorne and May, *Character Education Inquiry*, he finds that honesty consists of what others are doing, not necessarily that honesty is an integral part of any given human being. That is to say, we act honestly or dishonestly at a gradient level, which gradient is affected by the others who are around us. If others are highly honest, we are inclined to be highly honest; if others are somewhat dishonest, we follow that pattern. Thus, situationism has a strong effect upon the socialized personality. Situationism applies mainly to everyday personality

[2] *Ibid.*, p. 794.

changes. He feels that personality must be free to select its own environment and its own situational content. Only in this way may personality truly unfold. In the final analysis, situationism becomes actually a field theory in the traditional sense of the Lewinian Gestalt approach.

10. When attitudes affect behavior, they may do so in dichotomized ways. We may expect a normal distribution of attitudes when they are viewed impersonally or in a quantified way. However, any personal viewpoint of attitudes in which stress or decisions are forced creates a bi-modal distribution. By this Murphy means that we are forced through attitudinal sets to be either for or against something. On the other hand, in measuring a group and their attitudes, we can create a continuum from very high to very low attitudinal sets regarding any phenomenon.

11. Murphy finds that society may mold personality through social pressure in four different ways. (1.) The individual may very effectively be molded by being sensitized to the symbols which any society finds valuable. Even though he, the individual, is not aware of these symbols, they do determine and mold his behavior. (2.) Because of canalizations of a social nature and a stereotyped structure, the individual is molded by that which society considers to be satisfactory. Thus, his satisfactions are reinforced and deepened by competitive exposure. Science, art, music are all examples of this phenomenon. (3.) Drives and needs such as those for food preferences may actually determine the level, amount, and direction of hunger of a given human being. (4.) The predominant feeling tone of a given individual or in short, the ethos, is highly dependent upon the cultural process through which the individual goes as he develops in life into a socialized creature. However, Murphy feels that "the cultural relativists" do not accept the wide patterns of human conduct and that man is not merely the product of his environment.

Murphy makes an interesting comparison between the assets and liabilities of our Western culture and those of the Soviet culture as we know it to be. He finds assets and liabilities in each culture. The assets of the Western culture are these: (1.) we have a high level of moral and legal recognition of the importance of the individual; (2.) we have a deep recognition and acceptance of individual differences both in our educational systems and in our social customs; (3.) we have had, since the Bill of Rights, a continuing sense of freedom to think, talk, and read what we want; and (4.) we have an abiding faith in the continuity of progress.

The liabilities of our Western culture are these: (1.) because our ego needs become frustrated and our needs for status and prestige are difficult to fulfil in a complex society, there is an accompanying feeling of pathological insecurity among most people; (2.) because family ties are becoming looser and there is great mobility both geographically and socially, there is a pronounced loss of group identification; (3.) because of the multiple kinds of conflict we have between ourselves and the value systems of others, there is too often an overriding feeling of conflict with our culture; and (4.) because of the impersonality of much that happens to us, we too often feel a lack of support and a feeling of loneliness despite the crowded circumstances that frequently surround the metropolitan citizen.

In a brief comparison with the Soviet Union, Murphy finds roughly three assets of the Soviet Union's style of life. The first is a strong feeling of identification with the group. It seems to him that citizens of the Soviet Union have little doubt in their mind that they belong to that particular type of society which we call Communist. A second positive attribute that Murphy finds in the Soviet system is a freedom from the insecurity of joblessness. Despite the Soviet Union claims that all people are equal within their system of government, there is wide latitude and much structuring of each person's role within that society. In a third sense, after these security needs are met and one feels secure in his position in society, he may then turn his thoughts toward art, music, and the drama. Perhaps this might explain the strong interests of Russian peoples in the Bolshoi Ballet.

Just as there are assets in the Soviet system, Murphy feels that from the standpoint of personality needs there are very strong liabilities. The first liability, he feels, is coercion. The individual human personality has no freedom in the highly structured, tightly administered plan of life which is laid out for him and which he must accept regardless of his feeling toward it. Another liability is the difficulty in knowing with which group to identify. In the history of the Soviet system, citizens have passed from an identification with Lenin or Trotsky to Stalin, who was followed by Malenkov, and now, of course, to Khrushchev. A third negative factor is the complete lack of recognition of individual differences. In general, the Soviet system follows Lysenko, in whose viewpoint heredity is considered to be equal for all peoples, while the environmental factors help determine how an individual personality will succeed or fail. The Russian system considers, then, that it can make "a silk purse out of a sow's ear."

In the long run it would seem that the Soviet style of life is bound to fail because it ignores the fundamental, psychological dynamics of human personality. On the other hand, our own society must attempt to alleviate or correct some of its own liabilities. Although both of the systems mentioned previously are Occidental in nature, we must assume that there will be a deep assimilation from the Oriental cultures.

Murphy thinks that if it is possible to destroy a society, and such possibility does not seem remote, it may not mean the complete cessation of a special form of life. It is possible that a phenomenal, strong, overriding personality will be able to reorganize and reorient and restructure a new society which will be built to meet the new demands with a new image. In the history of man, there have always been immense figures or "men of destiny" who seem to have the capacity to meet the needs of a new order.

With the publication of *Human Potentialities* in 1958, Murphy continued a discussion of the future of man. The main rationale is that man always has had a changing body and that man always has been a changing social animal trying to avoid annihilation. He feels it is, therefore, important that we look at new insights into the future.

Individual differences which are caused by culture are of three types:

1. Cognitive Differences: these are differences caused by ways of exploring the world.
2. Affective Differences: these are ways in which each individual begins to feel about the world in which he lives.
3. Impulse Differences: these are ways in which each individual is taught how to act toward the world about him which would include his biological, organic, geographical, climatic and social worlds.

Human Potentialities or New Perspectives Theme

The fourth major theme of Gardner Murphy's theory of personality is obtained almost entirely from *Human Potentialities*. In this book, Murphy outlines three human natures: biological (man meets intense and diffuse organic needs); cultural (man becomes fixed and standardized); and creative thrust (man attempts the creative thrust to understand himself, the world in which he lives and from a philosophical frame of reference, why he is in the world).

There is inherent in this book a strong touch of Jungianism. Murphy broadens his perspective and is willing to admit that "man is a part of the sweep of the cosmos."

Barriers to Fulfillment. If man tries to reach the fullest potentialities of the full or good life, he will find many barriers to this achievement. In a sense the entire book is about one of life's problems, the gaining of new horizons to combat the rigidity of present society. At the present time because the Russians are the most rigid society, and our society is the least rigid, we are made to look the weaker. This weakness may in the long run be our strongest asset because we may be better able to adapt to changing conditions.

Industrialization with its strong emphasis on automation and synchronized parts has a strong influence on the increase of rigidity within our own society.

Following the work of David Riesman, Murphy finds another barrier to fulfilling the huge potential of mankind. Murphy finds, as does Riesman, too much outer-directed instead of inner-directed behavior. Although rigidity and ossification seem to characterize our twentieth century more and more, historically and personally we have always been a flexible and creative nation. In trying to break the rigidity of outer-directed behavior, our culture must be stimulated to strive for greater flexibility and creativeness. For as Murphy feels "Creation is in itself satisfying," beyond the actual results and benefits of any created object or social system.

It is necessary that all of us realize there has been almost a geometrical increase in social change and creativeness. We now invent in ten years what formerly may have taken as much as one hundred years.

One of the barriers to the fulfillment of the potential that lies within mankind is our unwillingness to accept new dimensions in society and in science as additional factors toward a better life. It is our inclination to force or squeeze the newer dimensions into the forms of the old society and culture. In no way, however, does Murphy ignore the strength of a conservative position. After all, his concept of canalization indicates the benefits of a conservative or stylized position. However, complete adherence to a stylized, conservative frame of reference, he feels, is destructive because it cannot meet the challenges of change. Change is an inevitable concept of life.

One of the greatest problems in releasing human potentials is the transfer of the "fires" of an infant's enthusiasm into structured and disciplined creativeness. All too frequently this "precious freshness" of response is stifled or distorted in further development.

One of the tragedies in attempts to fulfill the human potential in mankind is that none of the systems, political or social, has a true long-range system of development. It is possible, of course, to agree that the Soviet Republics do have a long-range system of conquering the world, a plan which makes them appear stronger and more directed in their efforts than the other cultures, ethnic groups or political systems. As a consequence, it affects other social systems, as they attempt to bend to the winds of varying pressures. The dilemma is difficult to resolve. On the one hand come the necessary adjustments which must be made in order not to be too rigid in policy. On the other hand, a too rigid system of thought which makes one appear strong and oriented toward direct goals denies the flexibility and creativity that appear to be necessary in any social order.

At the present time, there seems to be a threefold crisis in fulfilling the human potentiality within mankind. In the first place, we have huge power systems that are locked in struggle in an attempt to gain superiority or at least a favorable position over the competing system. Russia and the United States are current examples. In the second place, as shown in the thinking of Erich Fromm, man has evolved and created social systems, political systems, and economic systems which control man more than he controls them. In the third place, there is a biological unfitness in the organic structure of man to meet the changes in future environment. Medical science has made huge advances in the protection of man's life which have caused man to live longer but not necessarily to adjust to differing or future environments, of which the current emphasis on interplanetary existence is an example.

Despite this rather dismal situation, Murphy feels that all is not lost. There are short and long range possibilities to eliminate some of the crises that exist at the present time.

Murphy sees four possibilities to alleviate or eliminate the current crisis of failure to fulfill the potentialities of mankind.

1. The present crisis may be ended in short order by a conquest through technical advances. It is true these technical advances may come either through the efforts of the U.S.A. or the U.S.S.R. Either social order or political system which is able to make the most technical advances can win the struggle.

2. Another short range possibility to end the crisis is, of course, one of which all society lives in fear. A total, annihilating war could, obviously, end the crisis.

3. The third possibility is the one to which the United Nations is directing most of its efforts. That is a disarmament program which may begin by short steps but eventuate in a reduction or elimination of machines and power to make total war. This step may be taken by all nations, either by achieving an atomic method of waging war or by going in the opposite direction: creating a device to make atomic war impossible.

4. The fourth short range possibility comes closer to the present situation in the world today—that is, a long period of garrison life. This would be somewhat like medieval times in which small groups lived a garrison existence in fortified castles. Murphy considers this garrisonlike existence, one nation walling up against the other, quite unlikely to endure for long because man is so interrelated in his economic and social systems.

The long range possibilities for ending the current crisis are quite interesting as Murphy presents them.

1. Murphy admits that it may take a very long time to create an international, authoritarian system with full police powers. This would be a possibility for not only ending the crisis but maintaining some sort of peace.

2. In addition to an international state which might grow out of the United Nations organization, Murphy feels that an extremely high degree of centralization of scientific investigation, in which there is immediate feedback of research findings, could mean that no nation could gain a superiority of the other. Whatever is created or invented would be immediately available to all the peoples of the world.

3. It is unlikely, but possible, that a world society under a very loose political unity, something like the United Nations, might be based on a competition of ideas. It would be essential that information be readily available but that the ideas would extend beyond the scientific fields and would include art, music, educational systems, literature, etc.

4. The fourth possibility is dismal but one which Murphy feels cannot be ignored in the present state of chaos. If all political systems disintegrate or break down, man may end the current crisis in the long range view of things by existing in an ant hill or leaderless, machinelike system. This would approximate the type of tribal organization or living which existed in world civilization in the distant past.

In considering the short and the long range possibilities of ending the current crisis and bringing about a richer fulfillment of mankind, Murphy sees three kinds of social order. In the first place, he has very strong convictions that "a world system, there must be." His second point is that there should be "a loose-jointed Authoritaria." The third suggestion is for democratic group-planning in most areas of the world in which there would be controls by those who are to be influenced by the plans. This, of course, is very much in the democratic tradition of the United States.

Murphy asks the pertinent question, "Can the three human natures which (Gardner Murphy proposes) be entirely fulfilled?" He admits that the three human natures are and will be in conflict at most times. In answer to his question, Murphy gives a qualified affirmative with four reasons. (It will be remembered that the three human natures mentioned are the biological, the cultural, and the creative thrust to understand.)

1. Heredity or environment alone is impotent. Consequently, interdependence of these two factors may lead to a fulfillment of all three human natures.

2. Man has always been a beautiful example of "adaptive radiation." No matter what man came from in the past he has always been able to change in response to new environments. Murphy sees no reason that man, given enough time, cannot continue to change and adjust to his environmental differences.

3. Another favorable aspect of the fulfillment of the three natures of a human being is that both extrapolation (projection into the future) and especially the emergence of new skills can work toward the fulfillment of man. However, he feels that the underlying structure of human behavior must be better known than we know it at the present.

4. The last condition that gives hope to the fulfillment of man is a decentralization of democratic procedures for better control of new scientific data. This is Murphy's way of saying that scientific research should be given a free hand and not be controlled by a central authority.

The last of the barriers to fulfilling the three basic human natures of man is the boundaries that lie between the individual and his world. There are three such boundaries as considered by Murphy.

1. There has been, is now, and always will be a definite barrier between the inner skin and the outer skin, that is, between the physical or biological self and all that surrounds it.

2. A second condition is the psychological boundary between one

human being and another. This is inevitable, though it may not always be so. Despite the deep and intense knowledge one human being may have of another human being it is never possible to have a total exchange of personalities. It is not possible to be completely within the psychological framework of another human.

3. The third boundary between the person and his world is a social boundary. This boundary is not easily defined and is more nebulous than the boundaries of the physical or the psychological nature.

Future. Murphy feels ". . . we cannot set limits upon human potentials or tell what can or cannot come into existence. . . ." He feels the predispositions within the cosmic structure are unpredictable. However, ". . . the potential self-fulfillments lie scattered there beyond the horizon; and man with all the wisdom he can marshall, must strive to define them —and then to choose among them" (*Human Potentialities,* p. 301).

Later on in "Human Natures of the Future" which began as a lecture for the Lewin Memorial address given to the Society for the Psychological Study of Social Issues in 1953, Murphy again introduces the keystone of much of his theoretical position on the personality: interaction.

Let us begin with the fact, already noted, that nothing is inherited, nothing acquired; everything is the realization through the environment of a specific potentiality permitted by the genes; or, if you prefer, the realization by the genes of a potentiality permitted by the environment.

Let us go on from this to the self-evident, yet shocking fact that in my experience nothing springs from *me* and nothing from my environment, but everything from the interaction, the "life space" in which I, as a person, navigate (*ibid,* p. 303).

Science of Human Potentialities. Murphy suggests four steps in the fulfillment of the field science of human potentialities: 1. quantitative (the measureable attributes of personality); 2. qualitative (changes in richness and new dimensions as the personality grows); 3. addition–infusion (recognition of new elements); and 4. configurational (recombining and reorganizing the familiar and the newly known into new forms).

Five Theoretical Principles to Evolving Individual Potentialities. Murphy considers two negative and three positive principles that are involved in discovering what the individual potentialities are in the total fulfillment of human nature.

1. The first principle is not to provide easy conflict resolution for any

human being. On the basis that a homeostatic existence leads to nothing or leads to no future growth, Murphy feels as does Adler, that the pampered existence is to be avoided.

2. A second principle is to avoid overemphasis on competition. This may lead to deep ego involvement and consequently may ignore the best avenues of fulfillment through overemphasis on victory at all costs.

3. The third theoretical principle is the need for studying progressively richer human experiences rather than a repetitive study of the past.

4. The only avenue to self-fulfillment is active effort on the part of all concerned. Although there is room for passive, reflective efforts, this will not, however, fulfill the human natures of man until some active participation is attempted, even though it may be of a trial and error nature.

5. Murphy concludes with a plea to ". . . express the humaneness of the movement in the direction of integration—fluid, sensitive, ever-changing integration as a step toward further integration" (*ibid.*, p. 322).

Murphy ends on a note of optimism, for he feels that fulfillment is never ending, that the entire history of the world and of the cosmic nature of things is to be more and more fulfilled and less destructive. There almost seems to be built into the natural order of all things a progressive desire for fulfillment beyond the present state.

Summary

We have now examined the four major themes involved, as this author sees them, in the personality theory of Gardner Murphy. These four themes are the biological personality, the emerging–integrating personality, the socialized personality, and the potentialities that the human has for full, integrated fulfillment. Probably the most outstanding strain is that of the interaction between the three kinds of human nature. The word *interaction* is very valuable to Murphy's theoretical position on personality. Much of the richness of Murphy's theory must necessarily be lost in any attempt to summarize his work. The student of personality theory, therefore, is urged to make reading excursions into the work of this well-known and beloved personality theorist.

EXPLAINING HUMAN BEHAVIOR VIA MURPHY'S THEORY

Once again, we put each theory to the test in an attempt to see if it can explain why man does certain things. The difficulty with Murphy's theory lies not in its failure to explain the dynamics of human behavior but in one's choice of the many, many possible answers. The nine behavioral phenomena used in all the chapters are as follows: marriage, perversions, suicide, law breaking, supranatural being, humor, smoking, play and recreation, and psychoses and neuroses.

Although it does not do justice to the theory of Murphy, it is possible to explain human behavior by using only six or seven of the principle points in his theory. For example, we may explain law breaking, marriage or smoking or any of the other nine behavior patterns by stating that an individual fails, for example, to pursue life and ends in suicide, or fails to reach emotional stability through psychoses or neuroses, because he has failed to integrate the three characteristics of his personality. Still another all inclusive explanation may be gained from nodal behavior or perseveration or projection. Finally, we may turn to the four human needs, visceral needs, activity needs, sensory needs, and the need to avoid or escape attack, injury or threat, in attempting to explain why man does the things that he does. However, in justice to the theory but still in an incomplete way, the present author will attempt to explain more definitely man's behavior by extrapolating Murphy's theory.

Marriage

One possible explanation for marriage is found in the fact that most children are brought up in a family which consists of a mother and father who are married. Since this is such a large and vital part of the child's environment, he becomes canalized toward the idea of getting married himself some day. The greater the depth of love between the mother and father in the relationship of marriage as the child perceives it, the greater the depth of love he may carry to his own marriage relationship. Children who come from homes in which there is a divorce or separation may, therefore, not be able to create or maintain as deep a canalization towards marriage as those whose homes were surrounded by warm, affectionate relationships between the mother and father.

A second explanation may be found in the desire for the engaged couple to come to a full integration of the love that they feel for each other. Society affords them this avenue of full integration through the ritual of marriage and the continuance of living together as man and wife. This culminates, then, in a full, integrated, love of one human being for another.

Although in this next passage Murphy is talking about the love a child has for his parents, it is possible that the following selection also describes somewhat adequately the relationship of marriage as it exists in our society.

Long before the advent of the lawgiver, and long indeed before the appearance of the super-ego, life has been structured in terms of a satisfying system of love objects. Love has been exercised, strengthened, articulated; the real world is made up largely of love objects. Autisms have given the loved objects positions of anchorage in the figure-ground relations of the world, and everything is set to make human nature the continuing fulfillment of an affectional system.[3]

Because Murphy is equally at ease in the world of the sociologist, he probably could make an even stronger case for marriage from that viewpoint. Marriage is the acquiring of a satisfying role as husband or wife. In addition to this, it gives to the man or the woman the status of an adult, as he marries and takes on the role of husband or wife and later of a mother or father. Gardner Murphy is equally willing to entertain other sociological concepts which would not necessarily fit Western culture. Although he does not speak of it directly, it is assumed that Murphy accepts the idea of the sociological pressures that are brought to bear on an arranged marriage in the Oriental or Asiatic customs. Mores also can play a part in the arranging of a marriage. Since it is against the customs or mores of most cultures to live in "sin," the institution of marriage provides for an arrangement whereby man and woman live together in close harmony.

In the final analysis, Gardner Murphy entertains the possibility that there are reasons for marriage in all cultures rising from the strength and benefits of family membership. "Family membership is a primary reality for personality." Possibly it is because family membership is so important in all cultures that the institution of marriage has been instigated to protect the role of the family in the formation of a personality. Society, through its mores and customs, prefers to have a stabilized relationship between a man and a woman who are begetting children. It is necessary, therefore, to institute a relationship with both legal and religious manifestations to hold together this union of man and woman in a mother–father role.

[3] *Personality*, p. 555.

Perversions

Much of what Gardner Murphy has to say in regard to the causal factor of perversions follows a Freudian and Jungian and neo-Freudian line of thinking. Murphy uses the term *lopsidedness* to describe the social aspects of perverted behavior.

In the main, however, Gardner Murphy eschews much discussion of the deviant behavior known as perversion. One of the reasons for this is possibly that Murphy is not and has not been directly involved in clinical therapy, either as a clinical psychologist or a psychiatrist. Even though he has been very much involved with the Menninger Clinic, it has been chiefly in the role of a research psychologist with that organization.

Suicide

Once again it is necessary to extend the remarks of Gardner Murphy in order to attempt an explanation of the various behavioral phenomenon. The rank extension of Gardner Murphy's work is not necessary, not because the information is missing but rather because Gardner Murphy's personality theory covers so much that practically all of psychological thought is in some way involved.

One reason for suicide might be an utter lack of ability to integrate all of the forces that impinge upon one's personality. The individual who cannot bring together and integrate all of the forces in his life is inclined to want to give up and to cease an existence which to him is most painful.

Another reason for suicide might be found in the complete loss of a self-image. The individual has so lost his own image of self that to destroy himself does not necessarily mean to him that he is going to hurt himself. In his delusionary system, therefore, he is destroying a self or an individual that he does not even recognize as himself.

Murphy speaks frequently of aggression, both indirect and direct, physical and symbolic. Suicide may be considered to be, therefore, a direct physical aggression against the self.

Suicide may also be considered as an utter rejection of the society in which an individual lives. This rejection might occur as a result of one's being totally engulfed by societal pressures.

Gardner Murphy speaks frequently of Alfred Adler's work. Suicide may be the ultimate in inferiority feeling. If the inferiority feeling is allowed to continue until it becomes canalized as a mode of life or style of life, it is then possible that the human being descends in levels of inferiority, never gaining superiority, until he gives up life itself. In this case death is a *node* or a nodal method of living.

The dynamics of suicide are not directly accessible from the writings of Gardner Murphy. One must assume that some or all of the above explanations would be within the framework of his theory of personality.

Lawbreaking

Murphy finds no simple direct one-to-one causal relationship between human behavior and criminal activities.

The following can be considered to be some of the reasons why man breaks laws, which man, of course, has made in concert with other men.

1. Ostensibly there is a breakdown in the relationship between man and his environment when he breaks the laws that he himself has helped to make.

2. Whether, in minor breaches of the law, one breaks a moral law or a strictly legalistic one, *autism*, that is, thinking only of oneself, seems to be involved. Here we have an individual who is so involved in thinking about himself that he does not or is unable to think of the effect upon others.

3. In the behavior of an habitual criminal (one who continues to pursue a life of crime despite the penalties that the courts may deal out to him) we may assume that the value system has total negative connotations. This individual has lost sight of the fact that "rightness is a mutual consideration of needs" (*Personality*, p. 386). The habitual criminal has "a conception of self as the lawgiver" (*ibid.*, p. 857).

4. People who consider law as being something which can be broken at their own will or at their own convenience may have had a wrong canalization of the conscience during their formative years.

5. Lawbreaking may also be considered as an example of aggressive behavior. This may be especially true in the inconsiderate driving habits of some motorists who feel their rights denied by the driving habits of other motorists.

6. One of the few direct references that Murphy makes to this kind of behavior may be appropriate. (Author's italics.)

The aggressiveness of the delinquent is not just protest against restrictions or crowded streets or a poor biological environment; it is not just exuberance or getting even or showing off. It is to some degree the product of the elemental recognition that power can be achieved only by cutting loose from the power systems established by others, and by setting up, arbitrarily or capriciously, a limited power system of one's own. *The robbing of a shop* and happy participation in a club or junior republic may have a great deal in common psychologically.[4]

Supranatural Being

A belief in a supranatural being or the practice of religion as a social activity, although they are not exactly the same, are somewhat difficult to explain from the frame of reference of Murphy's work.

Actively being involved in a religious practice may be an imitation of the culture pattern. It is possible that the practice grows out of an identification with one's parents.

In some ways, religious practice may be an accumulation of the culture habits through the past by any social group. It becomes traditional and part of the mores to worship a supranatural being. In addition to this may be the ethical or moral codes involved with the religious practice. Murphy calls this type of group activity self-maintenance mores.

In one short section (*Personality*, p. 729) Murphy talks about religious conversion as being an example of the continuity/discontinuity of the personality. In a religious conversion the old self has lost its equilibrium, and the new self emerges. This creates a traumatic and intense experience for the convertee. He must restructure a new personality and recondition old responses.

Humor

Although humor appears to be an ever-present behavioral activity in all cultures, there are no direct references to humor, or why man laughs or thinks certain things are funny, in the work of Murphy. Some, all, or none of the following explanation may apply to why man laughs, from the viewpoint of Murphy.

Laughter may be the sudden inflation of the ego. The inflation of the ego comes, it is assumed, from no effort on the part of the individual.

Symbols appear to be involved in the humor content of man's activity. Symbols may be used to resolve conflicts which cannot be resolved in actual practice.

We may also assume that with Murphy, as with the other theorists,

[4] *Ibid.*, p. 558.

humor is the resolvement of a problem or the reduction in tension of everyday living problems.

It is also possible that humor may be used by authoritarian individuals or others as a motivating device. In this example one attempts to get others to laugh and relax and respond to the humor of the situation in order to control the group's behavior toward a second but real goal.

Humor may be promoted by simple organic well being or organic pleasure. When the body has been well fed, bathed, and thoroughly relaxed, it may be more receptive to humor. Examples such as a small baby smiling illustrate this organic explanation of humor.

Since man is a social animal, we may assume that some kinds of humor are infectious. We laugh because we are in a "laughing" environment. Although the situation may not seem funny to us, it gains a humorous aspect because those around us, with whom we wish to be identified, are laughing. Therefore, we feel it necessary to laugh.

A final explanation of why man laughs or why man exercises humor may be found in the enhancement of the self-portrait. This explanation borders on autism. Here we have the human being who makes himself feel good by his capacity to laugh at others whom he considers less fortunate than himself.

Smoking

Three explanations for smoking may be found in the work of Murphy. 1. Smoking may be an example of identification with an individual we wish to imitate who also smokes. This is an example of imitation and suggestibility. It is assumed that one would not smoke if he were not surrounded by others who smoked. That is to say, if one were the only individual in the entire society who smoked, it is not likely that the habit would be pursued. 2. Once the habit of smoking is established, it may be considered as a perfect example of canalization. It is evident that many, many people who smoke cigars, cigarettes or pipes are unable to stop this habit. 3. Without doing too much injustice to Murphy's theory, we may find an explanation of why man smokes in the Freudian concept of oral regression. Man returns to the early labial pleasures which he once knew when he first ingested food from the mother's breast or the nipple of a bottle. From the framework of Murphy's work, however, there appear to be more things involved than simple oral regression. The concept of Gestalt may be also involved. Smoking, in the Gestalt sense, includes being with others who smoke, the manipulative pleasures of taking out the cigarette, tamping it, lighting it, inhaling, exhaling, and the whole process that is involved in smoking any form of tobacco.

Play and Recreation

There are numerous reasons why man plays and indulges in recreational activities that one may extrapolate from Murphy's theory. Actually, because there are many types of play and recreation, it is possible that an explanation may fit one type of play but not another. Any one or all of the following may be adequate explanations of why man plays and why man indulges in recreational activities.

1. Play and recreation may simply be a halt in the struggle for existence. The explanation may be no more complicated than that the human being wishes to relax and enjoy life at his own pace after having worked at some occupation. Involved in play and recreation in this case would be the freedom of choice of the escape from the regimentation of the occupation or the mores and taboos of any particular society.

2. The games man indulges in as he plays may be an important way to gain the self-enhancement which he cannot get in his normal role in life.

3. Recreational pastimes, particularly creative hobbies, may be a manifestation of man's curiosity. The individual who works at a monotonous job in an automated industry may find himself able to express a creative urge through the hobby or recreation which he pursues.

4. Play, especially the more physically active forms of play, may be sheer physical exuberance. This exuberance meets the sensory needs which Murphy talks about. As the individual grows from childhood to adulthood, specific forms of play may become conditioned or canalized. The individual who enjoyed the outdoors in a rural environment where he could fish and hunt as a natural pastime, may pursue the same activities in his adult years with considerable expenditures of time, money, and effort.

5. Some forms of play and recreation may give the personality a free rein to indulge in fantasy and autisms which are not possible in the normal pattern of life. Feelings of aggression may take societally approved forms of play and recreation. The killing of fish or animals, the struggle against an opponent, as for example, in hitting back a served ball, may become forms of direct aggression of which society approves.

6. Some forms of play may be regressions to childhood experiences.

Camping may be a recapitulation of an earlier remembered pleasure of Boy Scouts or Girl Scouts and the organized camping that one enjoyed so much as a child.

7. It is possible to consider some forms of recreation as simply a method of social behavior. We may indulge in a recreational activity simply because our friends do it and we wish to be with our friends. We may play bridge, for example, not because we like to play bridge but because to be with our friends we must indulge in this form of card playing.

8. Play, especially the play of children, may be society's way of teaching a child how to play the roles which will be demanded of him in his adult years. Children who play school or who mother dolls are examples of this. Thus, we may learn to integrate our various roles and our pressures and desires at a time when failure to play the role correctly carries not too harsh a penalty.

As can be seen by the above, there are many reasons which we can extrapolate from the work of Murphy for why man plays. One difficulty in giving explanations lies in the multiple forms of play and recreation throughout society. It is possible that there are as many explanations for play as there are games or as there are people who play.

Psychoses–Neuroses

Despite the fact that Gardner Murphy has been highly involved in the work of therapeutic agencies such as the Menninger Clinic, there are no full explanations for psychoses and neuroses in his personality theory. Perhaps this is because, as previously stated, Murphy's major role in these organizations and in his teaching has been as a research-oriented psychologist.

One overall explanation may be given for man's deviant behavior as a psychotic or neurotic. Such behavior may be caused by the failure of a human personality to integrate the three human natures with which he is endowed. (It must be assumed that in this section, as in all previous sections of explanation for each of the theorists, we are dealing primarily with the functional psychoses and not the organic psychoses.)

Another blanket explanation may be found, according to Murphy, when the human personality proceeds along faulty lines of canalization. These become deeper and deeper and almost cannot be remedied.

Another explanation of psychotic–neurotic behavior may be found in the inability of the human personality to proceed through the three developmental levels, the first developmental level being that of global and undifferentiated mass activity. Consequently, some psychotic behavior is truly a regression to this developmental level. The second level, a level of differentiating parts in which each part acts more or less autonomously, can be found in the typical behavior of the schizophrenic. Some neurotic behaviors are also parallel behaviors which are acting in an autonomous sense. (The third level of development, which is the top level of integrating the action of all the parts and recognizing and utilizing the interdependence of the parts, would ostensibly be nonpsychotic, nonneurotic and very much at the normal level of behavior.)

Along with emphasizing the difficulties involved in canalization of a true selfhood, Murphy also entertains the bipolar ideas found in Jungian and Freudian theories. He speaks of the conflict which comes out of "opposed perceptual habits," "opposed canalization," "opposed conditionings."

In his discussion of the ego, Murphy says ". . . neurotic conflict is quite literally a question of keeping a perenially beautiful self-picture before the eyes. It is because the *picture* rather than the person is besmirched or mutilated that neurotic breakdown occurs" (*Personality*, p. 561). Murphy underlines the word picture because he is discussing the ego as a grammatical illusion. "The ego is indeed a grammatical illusion because of the tendency to confuse three things: 1. the self, 2. the self-enhancing and self-defending mechanisms, and 3. the whole organism of which the first two are aspects" (*ibid.*, p. 561).

Work of Freud, Adler, and Jung (the former greats), as well as of the neo-Freudians, is well represented in the explanations that Gardner Murphy gives in discussing the aberrant (though not necessarily neurotic or psychotic) behavior of man. For example, Murphy makes liberal use of the Freudian terms of *cathexis* and the ego-defense methods of *introjection, rationalization, regression, identification, repression,* and *displacement.*

Murphy also uses liberally the words of Adler on inferiority, the work of Horney on cultural pressures, and the work of Jung on the extraversion–introversion aspects of man's behavior.

The total effect, therefore, of using Murphy's work in explaining psychoses and neuroses is to abuse his ideas, because these two subjects are so inextricably interwoven in the warp and woof of his entire theory. One must almost beg the question in trying to seek only the highlights of the psychotic and neurotic patterns of behavior.[5] We find, then, that Gardner Murphy explains neurotic–psychotic behavior in the human personality with the eclectic broadness of the entire field.

PREDICTING HUMAN BEHAVIOR VIA MURPHY'S THEORY

Personal Prediction

It is now the privilege of the individual reader to decide how valuable Gardner Murphy's theory is in predicting his own behavior.

Some of the factors involved in this personal prediction are as follows:

1. It appears that psychology as we know it at the present time continues to change and will be changing. Psychology is a new science, a thrilling science, and a changing science. Because of this, the individual may find it difficult to extract material which helps him to make a personal prediction for himself from the field of psychology.

2. Much of Murphy's book, *Human Potentialities*, concerns itself with the future of mankind. The title itself indicates that. Consequently, in striving for a prediction of personal self, one must read and digest practically all of this work.

3. Whatever psychology has to say, Murphy has used. One of the greatest strengths of Murphy's work lies in his capacity to fortify strongly his position with good research.

Scientific or Laboratory Prediction

Murphy has some significant things to say regarding prediction. In some ways prediction is more important in Murphy than in the work of any other theorist. Almost all the rationale of *Human Potentialities* concerns itself with the prediction or prognostication of human behavior, either of an individual or of a social group. He feels that "the human personality can never be so defined as to permit precise prediction in new situations" (*Personality*, p. 73).

Murphy deals with the concept of prediction by using the general principle of "soft determinism." This is in contrast to "hard determinism"

---

[5] Murphy writes on this topic: "One might almost get the idea that I had intended the book to be used in the study of psychoses and neuroses. It will be very evident at the beginning of my book that I had no such applications in mind. It is certainly not true that I explain psychotic-neurotic behavior, or that I think myself capable of doing this."

in which particular developmental laws may be precisely followed in knowing what the future will bring.

But as science and philosophy stand today, we cannot evade the question whether prediction is possible or not. We would say that it is in general possible to a far greater degree than was the case a generation ago. As matters stand now, we must on the one hand use the physicists principle of uncertainty, considerably extended; and on the other hand we must adopt the principle of 'soft' determinism—the participation of the person as cause—as one of the most valuable working concepts available.[6]

Murphy often pays sincere homage to the work of Kurt Lewin. He feels that Lewin's topology is one valuable key in predicting human behavior. "The present approach [Lewin's] is relevant to the ever-recurring question of *predicting* behavior from the clinical interview or the test profile. The field theorist now considers himself sure enough of his ground to say that the usefulness of the prediction will depend largely upon the care with which the situation pressing upon the individual is studied . . ." (*ibid.*, p. 891). In other words, Murphy is saying that one must know the field and all of the surrounding, impinging factors which play upon any individual or any group before one may attempt any kind of valuable prediction.

Most of the discussion in regard to predicting behavior can be found in Murphy's *Human Potentialities* (1958). Murphy feels that the reciprocity of man to man everywhere in the world must be thoroughly recognized and adequately studied. The keystone lies in the word *reciprocity*, "which must be used in an effort at prediction" (*ibid.*, p. 24).

In his chap. 17 of that text, "The Human Natures of the Future," Murphy states that prediction is more than mere extrapolation. It is always, to Murphy, the interaction of changing bodies whether they be organic and social or organic to organic or social to social.

Creative errors may have "time-trends"; only in this sense of denoting trends may one extrapolate the information he now possesses.

Murphy deals directly with predictions in a short section in *Human Potentialities* (pp. 256–260) in "the logic of predictions."

The reason why the mystery of predicting an emergence ordinarily remains is that we do not know enough about the underlying structure of events. From this it would follow only that the emergence is baffling, not that it is inacces-

---

[6] *Ibid.*, p. 645.

sible to scientific prediction. It is baffling just because the specific subject matters have not been mastered. It is not an instance of a truly unknowable, a true shift to another plane about which no conclusions can be made at an earlier stage or at a lower level. It is possible to predict the emergent expressions of human potentialities, whether at the biological or the cultural level, insofar as one knows enough concretely about the changes going on at either level, and how the various biological changes are likely to interact, and how the various social changes are likely to interact, in new emergent forms at specified periods of development.

---◆---

SUMMARY

Gardner Murphy's theory of personality is the result of long years of labor. Into his theory he has put all the richness and depth of his own research, and that of many others. Murphy is an eclectic in his approach to personality theory. He does not neglect a contribution to a more thorough understanding of man regardless of the source of the contribution. Gardner Murphy uses, and knows how to use, the endeavors of biologists, psychologists, and sociologists in building a theory about personality dynamics. He uses all three fields well.

This chapter is an attempt to highlight some of the major themes of personality theory as found in his published works. We are using four themes: the biological personality, the emerging and integrating personality, the socialized personality, and human potentialities or new perspectives. These four themes by no means exhaust the material in his theory.

In the biological personality theme we have indicated that man is first of all a biological creature and from this basic nature stems much of the mastic with which his personality will be constructed. Essential to man's biological self is the fundamental interdependence of the inner organic parts. Nothing in man's body functions by and for itself. Each part is important because it is different from other parts and because of this difference it can function with other organic parts.

The second theme concerns itself with the emergence of physiological, psychological, and sociological aspects of man's behavior and how these three aspects emerge into a human personality. Included in this section are discussions of canalization, conditioning, conflict, perception, learning, symbols, and self.

Man begins life as a biological being and, as he later integrates his biological and cultural forces, he achieves a third level—the socialized personality. This is the third theme in this chapter.

In the final and fourth theme we have summarized the concepts of Murphy's *Human Potentialities* (1958). The theme here is that Murphy outlines three human natures: biological (man meets intense and diffuse organic needs), cultural (man becomes fixed and standardized), and creative thrust (man attempts the creative thrust to understand himself, the world in which he lives, and from a philosophical frame of reference, why he is in the world and what to do about his future).

Throughout Gardner Murphy's theory of personality there seems to be a pervasive, binding, pivotal idea: the universe is comprised of differing objects and these differences *must* interact, *must* be interdependent, *must* be integrated.

The author has found many ideas of Murphy's to be expressed in triadic form. This threeness of things has been used as a device to present some of his theoretical considerations.

In final consideration, to study Murphy's work is to study the field of psychology as we know it today. It is exciting, challenging, and worthwhile.

BIBLIOGRAPHY

PRIMARY SOURCES

BOOKS

Murphy, G., *Historical Introduction to Modern Psychology* (rev. ed. 1949), N.Y., Harcourt, Brace & World, 1929.

Murphy, G., and L. B. Murphy, *Experimental Social Psychology*, N.Y., Harper & Row, 1931.

Murphy, G., and F. Jensen, *Approaches to Personality*, N.Y., Coward-McCann, 1932.

Murphy, G., *General Psychology*, N.Y., Harper & Row, 1933.

Murphy, G., and T. M. Newcomb, *Experimental Social Psychology* [1931], (rev. 2nd ed.), N.Y., Harper & Row, 1937.

Murphy, G., and R. Likert, *Public Opinion and the Individual*, N.Y., Harper & Row, 1938.

Murphy, G. (ed.), *Human Nature and Enduring Peace*, Boston, Houghton Mifflin, 1945.

Murphy, G., *Personality: A Biosocial Approach to Origins and Structure*, N.Y., Harper & Row, 1947.

Murphy, G., *Historical Introduction to Modern Psychology*, (2nd ed.), N.Y., Harcourt, Brace & World, 1949.

Murphy, G., *Introduction to Psychology*, N.Y., Harper & Row, 1951.

Murphy, G., *In the Minds of Men: The Study of Human Behavior and Social Tensions in India*, N.Y., Basic Books, 1953.

Murphy, G., Some relations of perception to motivation, in G. H. Seward, and J. P. Seward (eds.), *Current Psychological Issues: Essays in honor of Robert S. Woodworth*, N.Y., Holt, Rinehart and Winston, 1958.

Murphy, G., *Human Potentialities*, N.Y., Basic Books, 1958.

Murphy, G. and R. O. Ballou (eds.), *William James on Psychical Research*, N.Y., Viking, 1960.

Solley, C. M., and G. Murphy, *Development of the Perceptual World*, N.Y., Basic Books, 1960.

Murphy, G. (with collaboration of Laura A. Dale), *Challenge of Psychical Research: A Primer of Parapsychology*, Vol. XXVI in the *World Perspectives* Series, N.Y., Harper & Row, 1961.

Murphy, G., *Freeing Intelligence Through Teaching*, N.Y., Harper & Row, 1961.

Murphy, G., Parapsychology, in N. L. Farberow (ed.), *Taboo Topics*, N.Y., Atherton Press, 1963.

PERIODICALS

Levine, R., I. Chein, and G. Murphy, The relation of the intensity of a need to the amount of perceptual distortion: A preliminary report, *J. Psychol.*, 1942, *13*, 283–293.

Proshansky, H., and G. Murphy, The effects of reward and punishment on perception, *J. Psychol.*, 1942, *13*, 295–305.

Murphy, G., Psychology and the post-war world, *Psychol. Rev.*, 1942, *49*, 298–318.

Murphy, G., Spontaneous telepathy and the problem of survival, *J. Parapsychol.*, 1943, *7*, 50–60.

Levine, J. M., and G. Murphy, The learning and forgetting of controversial material, *J. Abnorm. Soc. Psychol.*, 1943, *38*, 506–517.

Postman, L., and G. Murphy, The factor of attitude in associative memory, *J. Exp. Psychol.*, 1943, *33*, 228–238.

Schafer, R., and G. Murphy, The role of autism in a visual figure-ground relationship, *J. Exp. Psychol.*, 1943, 32, 335–343.

Murphy, G., Field theory and survival, *J. Amer. Sociol. Psychol. Res.*, 1945, 39, 181–209.

Schmeidler, G. R., and G. Murphy, The influence of belief and disbelief in ESP upon individual scoring levels, *J. Exp. Psychol.*, 1946, 36, 271–276.

Murphy, G., Psychical research and personality, *Proc. Soc. Psychol. Res.*, 1949, London, 49, 1–15.

Murphy, G., and J. Hochberg, Perceptual development: Some tentative hypothesis, *Psychol. Rev.*, 1951, 58, 332–349.

Chein, I., R. Levine, G. Murphy, H. Proshansky, and R. Schafer, Need as a determinant of perception: A reply to Pastore, *J. Psychol.*, 1951, 31, 129–136.

Murphy, G., Affect and perceptual learning, *Psychol. Rev.*, 1956, 63, 1–15.

Murphy, G., Concepts of personality—then and now, *Proc. 1956 Inv. Conf. on Testing Prob.*, Princeton, N.Y., 1956, 41–47.

Murphy, G., The boundaries between the person and the world, *Brit. J. Psychol.*, 1956, 47, 88–94.

Murphy, G., The current impact of Freud upon psychology, *Amer. Psychologist*, 1956, 11, 663–672.

Murphy, G., Progress in parapsychology, *J. Parapsychol.*, 1958, 22, 229–236.

Murphy, G., Trends in the study of extrasensory perception, *Amer. Psychologist*, 1958, 13, 69–75.

Murphy, G., Self-realization and mental health, *Bull. Menninger Clin.*, 1959, 23, 81–84.

Murphy, G., New knowledge about family dynamics, *Soc. Casework*, 1959, 40, 363–370.

Santos, J. F. and Murphy, G., An odyssey in perceptual learning, *Bull. Menninger Clin.*, 1960, 24, 6–17.

Murphy, G., Psychoanalysis as a unified theory of human behavior, *Psychiatry*, 1960, 23, 341, 346.

Murphy, G., Four conceptions of research in clinical psychology, *Bull. Menninger Clinic*, 1961, 25(6), 290–295.

Murphy, G., Toward a field theory of communication, *J. Commun.*, 1961, 11, 196–201.

Murphy, G., Testing the limits of man, *J. Soc. Issues*, 1961, 17, 5–14.

Murphy, G., New vistas in personality research, *Personnel Guid. J.*, 1961, 40, 114–122.

Murphy, G., Robert Sessions Woodworth, 1869–1962, *Amer. Psychologist*, 1963, 18, 131–133.

TAPE RECORDINGS

Murphy, G., *Introduciton to Parapsychology*, (G. W. Kisker ed.), No. 124, Cincinnati, Ohio, Sound Seminars.

Murphy, G., *The Boundaries Between the Individual and His World*, (G. W. Kisker ed.), No. 174, Cincinnati, Ohio, Sound Seminars.

SUGGESTED READINGS

BOOKS

Blake, R. R., and G. V. Ramsey (eds.), *Perception: An Approach to Personality*, N.Y., Ronald, 1951.

Bruner, J. S., and D. Krech (eds.), *Perception and Personality*, Durham, N.C., Duke Univer. Press, 1950.

Hall, C. S., and G. Lindzey, *Theories of Personality*, N.Y., Wiley, 1957, 503–537.

Hartshorne, H., and M. May, *Studies in Deceit*, N.Y., Macmillan, 1928.

Peatman, J. G., and E. L. Hartley (eds.), *Festschrift for Gardner Murphy*, N.Y., Harper & Row, 1960.

Articles in honor of Murphy's sixty-fifth birthday.

Sherif, M., *The Psychology of Social Norms*, N.Y., Harper & Row, 1936.

PERIODICALS

Collier, R. M., Independence: an overlooked implication of the open system concept, *J. Indiv. Psychol.*, 1962, *18*(2), 103–113.

Living tissue integrates but is also independent.

McCreary, J. K., The problem of personality definition, *J. Gen. Psychol.*, 1960, *63*, 107–111.

Reviews definitions by Allport, Lewin, Murray, and Murphy.

Smith, M. B., Murphy's *Novum Organum*, *Cont. Psychol.*, 1959, *4*, 161–164.

An ambivalent review of Murphy's *Human Potentialities*.

Williams, R. J., Biochemical approach to the study of personality, *Psychiat. Res. Rep.*, 1955, No. 2, 31–33.

CONTRIBUTIONS OF OTHER THEORISTS

Part V is an attempt to include some of the contributions of other theorists. The first half of Chapter 14, Symbolical-Mathematical-Learning, includes the work of Lewin, Cattell, and Eysenck. The latter half of Chapter 14 covers Mowrer's theory, which revolves around the learning concept. In Chapter 15 of Part V, the theorists are arranged as follows: the Holistic approach, which includes the work of Goldstein; the Holistic-Integrative approach, which includes the work of Maslow; and the Social-Interaction theory, which is presented in the framework of Erich Fromm.

Those theorists who have been included seem to have a truer theory or a better way of measuring and talking about theory than do those who have not been included. The dynamics of man's behavior or "why man behaves as he does" seem better handled by those theorists included than by those omitted. For example, one could have included Angyal, Hilgard, Hull, Kelly, McClelland, Meyer, Nuttin, Rotter, Sears, Selye. Probably the most eligible for inclusion would be Miller and Dollard, and especially Skinner. The omission of some of the theorists does not mean they are completely lacking in factors which pertain to personality.

It will be noticed that the theorists included in Chapters 14 and 15 are not treated as were the previous theorists, that is, within a framework of description, explanation and prediction. Again, the limitations of space do not allow a sufficiently elaborated treatment. There is no intention of creating a connotation of major and minor prophets even though some of the theorists have full chapters devoted to their work while the others have been treated in a more truncated manner.

This text gives a framework for an approach to the study of any kind of personality theory. The author has included bibliographies at the end of each section to help the student who wants to know more. Let us hope that there are many who do.

14

Contributions of Other Theorists: Symbolical, Mathematical, Learning

SYMBOLICAL [Lewin]

She saw every personal relationship as a pair
of intersecting circles. . . . Probably perfection
is reached when the area of the two outer
crescents, added together is exactly equal to that
of the leaf-shaped piece in the middle. On
paper there must be some neat, mathematical formula
for arriving at this: in life, none.

JAN STRUTHER
Mrs. Miniver

SOME BIOGRAPHICAL DATA

Kurt Lewin was born in Mongilno, Germany on September 9, 1890. He attended the University of Freiburg in 1908, the University of Munich in 1909, and spent the next five years at the University of Berlin where he received the Ph.D. in 1914. From 1914–1918 he served in the German Army, first as private, then as lieutenant. Lewin was married to Gertrud Weiss in October, 1928. They had four children: Esther, Reuven, Miriam, and David. In 1921 he returned to the University of Berlin Psychological Institute as an assistant. He later became professor of philosophy and psychology at the University of Berlin, 1926–1933. In 1933 he taught at Stanford University as visiting professor and became professor of psychology at Cornell University, 1933–1935. He spent the years from 1935 to 1944 at the Child Welfare Station at the University of Iowa as a professor of child psychology and directed the Research Center for Group Dynamics at M.I.T. from 1944 until his death in 1947. He was a member of the American Psychological Association, the Midwest Psychological Association, the Society for the Psychological Study of Social Issues, the Psychometric Society, A.A.A.S., Phi Epsilon Pi, and Sigma Xi.

INTRODUCTION

Kurt Lewin had a strong affinity for mathematical symbols. Lewin's question was not whether to use mathematics but which kind of mathematics to use. He decided that geometry with its topological dimensions best fitted the language of space in which he liked to talk. Lewin's work utilized nonmetrical symbols, that is, the size and distances of the geometric drawings or designs were not important. Lewin's devotion to using symbols almost made him a victim of his own system. Lewin did not consider himself to be a mathemetician, to which statement most mathemeticians would agree. Lewin, however, hoped that some good mathemetician would come along some day and do what he could not do, that is to prove functionally his theory. Most of Lewin's ideas about levels of aspirations, group dynamics, regression, recall in tension, satiation, and others can probably be explained without topology.

One large difficulty in writing an explanation or interpretation of Kurt Lewin's work is that one can explain what he does but cannot demonstrate it without repeating his experimental work in its entirety. (One can describe dancing or football with diagrams without actually being able to *see* it in person or on film; admittedly, much is lost with only a printed, diagrammatical description.)

Lewin felt, as many of us do, that using words to describe human behavior only obfuscates the issue of man's behavior. Many times to use a word requires then that man use two more words to explain the first.

Because "words inevitably lead to using more words" Lewin substituted one kind of symbol, mathematical, for another kind of symbol, verbal. However, when one studies diagrams in lieu of words, he encounters another difficulty in interpreting Lewin's theory. The mathematical symbol by itself is usually quite meaningless; we must use words to explain the symbol, which brings us then to using words to explain symbols when the symbols were originally employed to do away with words!

This is like having a home so highly mechanized with labor-saving devices that one is constantly laboring to service the machines which are designed to save labor.

A third difficulty presents itself in the use of diagrams to explain human behavior. Lewin always considered his diagrams to be momentary, or what Mark Twain called a photograph: "A moment of petrified truth." Thus, in a diagram we have a frozen moment of human behavior but are unable to indicate the past or the present behavior from it.

Essentially, Kurt Lewin's topological system was a "means of communication." It became one man's language. This system of symbols, which Lewin himself felt was not real mathematics, grew out his use of the blackboard in teaching his classes. There is a short and interesting account which Lewin made of this metamorphosis from the use of a pedagogical tool (the use of the blackboard) to the sudden realization that he was dealing actually not with a pedagogical tool but a true theory of personality (see *Principals of Topological Psychology*, p. vii).

Lewin did not go much beyond stages of definition or graphic presentation; he did not establish rules of mathematical operations with his diagrams.

Through his diagrams Lewin was trying to introduce into psychology a shift of interest from objects or people, as such, to processes between people and from the state of being to the changes that occur in behavior.

Lewin approached the study of human personality at the level of methodology. He appeals greatly to research and method-minded psychologists. Lewin developed theory construction to a high degree of sophistication for his time. He was most ingenious at contriving experiments with all the controls and variables accounted for. Through his emphasis upon action research, Lewin made possibly his greatest contribution in scientific methodology. His experimental methods have been more widely accepted than have his theoretical views. He impressed the world of psychology as a brilliant research methodologist. Lewin's emphasis upon action research meant essentially changing social conditions. This has sometimes been misjudged as changing the objectives of research as one proceeds with the research design.

Lewin took motivation studies out of the clinic and the rat laboratory and placed them in a more natural setting. He was highly interested and involved in group dynamics causation and group dynamics research. Because of his experiences, Lewin considered psychology to be essentially a social science which he based on Gestalt or social physical situations. Actually, Kurt Lewin's theory is largely unformulated. His untimely death in 1947 occurred before he had a real chance to extend and refine his theory.

Shortly before his death, Lewin became associated with Norbert Wiener and others, among them, Margaret Mead, in an approach which hoped to use cybernetics as a communication system which would include feedback and information theory.

Lewin firmly believed in the value of theory. Although he has been noted for saying, "Nothing is more practical than a good theory," this phrase actually was first stated at the turn of the century and should be credited to Dorpfeld (see Chapter 1). Lewin did not feel, however, that theory should be left to the theorist but should always be applied in a research situation which was as near a true life situation as was possible.

THE SYSTEM, THEORY, OR ESSENTIAL FEATURES

General Considerations

Lewin felt that the foundations in developing any kind of science and especially the science of psychology as a social science went through three stages: the speculative, the descriptive, and the constructive.

Speculative. The speculations of Plato and Aristotle about earth, fire, and water are examples of this type of scientific development. Lewin felt speculative considerations must be seen in the light of their historical perspectives. He was, however, a harsh critic of modern scientists who employ this type of reasoning. He considered it absolutely unproductive for any kind of work in today's scientific world.

Descriptive. The next step in the development of science, according to Lewin, was a descriptive one in which classification or taxonomic endeavors were primary. Lewin thought that, although this was a necessary step, it should not be considered the final one.

Constructive. The work of Galileo is probably the best historical example of the constructive foundation in developing a scientific point of view. Lewin felt that there can be a comfortable use of empirical theories or laws. These may be based upon one case and may not necessarily use statistics. The primary purpose of the constructive effort is to discover laws of behavior and especially to predict behavior in individual cases. Lewin preferred the genotypic approach which concerns itself with individuals rather than the phenotypic approach which concerns itself with statistical averages.

Lewin postulated that behavioral events revolve around three principles as follows:

Relatedness—One fact alone cannot cause a behavioral event. A behavioral event must have two or more facts which are related to each other and toward the eventual behavioral pattern.

Concreteness—Behavioral events are not caused by potential facts or potential considerations which may or may not happen. Only solid facts that actually exist in the here and now and have a concrete quality may be considered in the principles of behavior.

Contemporaneity—It was very important to Lewin that only present facts can cause present behavior. The causal factors of human behavior are contemporary, and facts which no longer exist cannot be considered to be a part of the behavioral scene.

Specific Considerations

What follows now is a list of terms and concepts which Lewin found it necessary to use in describing man's personality. The list is by no means complete but does give the reader a strong idea of the work of Kurt Lewin.

Mathematical Constructs. Lewin's work was couched in mathematical terms but was not necessarily applicable to mathematical computational systems or mathematical verification. He used primarily the signs and symbols of geometry but did not associate numbers with them. Thus, it is not possible to add, subtract, multiply, or divide in the Lewinian diagram system. The outstanding feature of Lewin's mathematical constructs is the drawing of circles, squares, triangles, walls or membranes, arrows of force, and all types of geometrical designs both from original mathematical systems and from those which Lewin invented in order to present his theory without being bound by the use of words.

Topology. Lewin used the term *topology* as a model for describing psychological or behavioral phenomena. Behavior was classified and described in terms of geometrical functions, which did not, however, use direct mathematical manipulations. A human being could be shown as a circle or a square or an elliptical shape. The human being was represented as being within the figure. All that which existed outside of the figure belonged to some other phenomena, such as environmental forces or life space.

Hodology. Lewin invented this term which he found necessary in drawing the circles, elliptical shapes, and pathways of behavior. *Hodology* may be considered to be a special type of geometry of paths of energy where the shortest distance between two points is the path of least resistance, which is not necessarily the Euclidian concept of the least distance actually traveled. In hodology, a line between points A and B is not necessarily a straight line. It may be a tangential line because of forces which lie directly in the path from A to B. In hodology, the direction toward or away from an object or force is important. Hodology can be construed as a tri-dimensional rather than a two-dimensional theory. That is to say, although Lewin was held to the drawings he could make on a blackboard or a sheet of paper, he did not consider that it would be impossible to go over or under an object as well as around it. To dimensions of length and breadth, the science of hodology or the science of paths of forces would also add depth.

Life Space. Assuming that one has drawn a circle, triangle, or any enclosed figure, all of the area surrounding the figure is considered the life space. The figure is to be considered as the human personality. In the life space are all of the forces that impinge upon a person and that determine his behavior. The forces include everything which is known and unknown at the conscious level of the individual. Inherent in the life space is the interaction between a person and the environment. The life space is the total aspect of every possible event or thing that could influence the behavior of the individual. Life space may be considered as the past, present, and future; however, it must always be *seen in the present.* Consequently, Lewin did not deny that man has a past or that he is going to have a future (he is not going to drop dead at the moment of action), but Lewin did insist that a human's behavior can only be *seen* in its present context.

Regions. Regions are the additional areas within any enclosed space which represent an individual or which represent parts of his environment. The environmental parts of a region are limited in number. All regions are momentary as previously stated. There are seven kinds of regions, as follows:

1. Connected regions: Any activity or behavior that goes on inside a region and does not affect another region is a connected region. In other words, connected regions are autonomous and are simply connected with no interplay between them. 2. Incident regions: Any activity which can go from one region to another region without entering a third region is considered to be a incident region. Obviously, the two incident regions are adjacent within the diagram. 3. Motoric region: The motoric region concerns itself with overt responses and outward appearances. Sometimes it is called the executive portion of the person because it gets things done. The motoric region always comes between the inner personal life space and the psychological environment. It is at the periphery of the life space beyond which is the psychological environment. 4. Motor-perceptual regions: Any region that forms a boundary between the environment or the area outside of the circle and the inner personal regions is a motor-perceptual region. It is a boundary which must be passed through and may approximate a barrier. It does not, however, have the drive or the executive portions of the motor regions mentioned previously. 5. Neighboring region: Any two regions that touch each other within the life space can be considered neighboring regions. Unlike incident regions, these neighboring regions have somewhat common properties. 6. Psychological region: This is a group of regions which have similar attributes which are different from those of any other group of regions. 7. Private regions: Within the shape that one has drawn to indicate the human being, those regions which lie closest to the inner core of the shape (or person) and are most difficult to observe by others are called private regions.

$B = F(PE)$. In this oft-quoted formula of Lewin's, the letter B means behavior, the letter F means function or law, the letter P means person, and the letter E means total environment. Unfortunately, one must use many words in order to make this formula meaningful. Another way of considering Lewin's formula of $B = F(PE)$ in human behavior consists of examining the function of the relationship between the person and his environment. The parentheses signify the relationship function operating as a law or condition. Environment means the total environment, which again connotes the past, present, and future although the behavior is always seen in the present tense. This formula is a nonmathematical formula. It can neither be added, subtracted, multiplied or divided. It consists of symbols which to Lewin expressed human behavior or were his shorthand methods of indicating behavior which includes the person, his environment, and the interaction between them.

Vectors. Vectors and/or vector analysis is a force which proceeds in a given direction. Any line that has force or psychological energy behind or in it and which is outside of the person in a vector. Thus, as Lewin drew his diagrams, the length of the line, the thickness of the line, and especially the point where the front of the line in the shape of an arrow head met the individual were considered to be quite important.

Valence. Lewin borrowed the term *valence* from chemistry but used it in his theory in a non-scientific way. There are two kinds of valences, one which has a positive value and one which has a negative value. Anything which satisfies the need of the human personality has positive valence, and any object or force which threatens the human personality has a negative valence.

Need. Lewin defined *need* as "any desire for object possession or any desire to achieve a goal." Needs are primarily prompted by organic conditions. There may be many needs that direct their forces through the valences upon the human personality.

Tensions. Tensions are defined "as any emotional states that go with, or are accompanied by, needs." We may assume that if no emotion is aroused, there is no true need structure. All the tensions are within the person and do not come from the environment. Tensions are also of a temporary nature.

Differentiation. We may define this in Lewinian terms as "the depth and richness of experience." Intelligence and variety of experiences help an individual to differentiate. It is assumed here that the more one is able to differentiate between the forces and vectors in his life space, the better personality he has. From the word root of differentiation Kurt Lewin introduced the term *de-differentiation,* which means that "the parts within a system lose their differences and return to a state of homogeneity." Balance in the personality is achieved when de-differentiation is in effect. In addition to differentiation and de-differentiation, Lewin also introduced the term *un-differentiation.* This refers to states where there is no difference between the parts of a system. In this case there is no tension, no force, no movement. It is not a return from differentiation as in the term *de-differentiation* but is meant primarily to indicate that no differentiation, tension, or differences in parts are found in the beginning states of the organism. As an example, we may assume that a new born baby is un-differentiated in contrast to adults who are highly differentiated.

Equilibrium and Disequilibrium. According to Lewin, the individual or human personality wants to be in a state of equilibrium. Needs, however, arouse a state of disequilibrium. It is the job of the human personality to win its way back into a state of equilibrium between the regions that are contained within the personality.

Regression and Retrogression. Lewin takes the Freudian terms of *regression* and *retrogression* and treats them somewhat differently. Regression means "any behavior which is primitive behavior that has not been in the past experience of the person." Thus, to act savagely is a regression form of behavior in the person who has never before acted in a savage-like way. The term *retrogression,* however, means "a return to a previous behavior which has once been experienced by that person."

Barriers and Blockages. If we were to draw an area of any shape or size and draw within that area a perpendicular line of any thickness, this would represent a barrier, or a blockage. A barrier is a membrane or obstruction between the person and the goal he wishes to obtain. Thick barriers create frustration. Overly thick and impenetrable barriers create a true blockage and create apathy if the person cannot pass through them. Barriers which lie between the person and goal he wishes to obtain also may enhance the positive valence or allure of an object or a goal. "We want what we cannot have." Barriers in this sense may be a part of motivation. The very fact that a barrier exists may make it attractive to surmount or to penetrate.

Locomotion. As the personality moves from one region to another within the life space, or changes his position within the life space, the motive force which comes from within the person is considered to be the locomotion. Locomotion may be fast or slow depending upon individual talents.

Fluidity. *Fluidity* is the ease of locomotion between parts, between a part to the whole, or between regions.

Conflict. Partially, from the work of others, Lewin drew three basic types of conflict: approach–approach, avoidance–avoidance, and approach–avoidance. In approach–approach conflicts, the personality desires two things and has a difficult time choosing between them. An example of this would be trying to decide which of two kinds of delicious chocolate bonbons one would like to consume. In the avoidance–avoidance type of conflict, the individual does not want to do either of two alternatives but cannot avoid them. An example of this would be the unhappy husband who neither wants a divorce nor wants to continue living with a wife with whom he is unhappy. In the approach–avoidance type of conflict, there is a desire to achieve a goal, but in order to achieve this goal one must go through a painful period. The traditional example is that of the individual with a toothache who wants to go to the dentist in order to have the tooth fixed and whose approach is to visit the dentist; however, he wishes to avoid the dentist because the dentist also may inflict pain. Thus, he has an approach–avoidance conflict.

Level of Aspiration. Lewin used this term which was originated by Tamara Dembo in 1931. Lewin utilized the term *level of aspiration* in a sense as a prediction of a future goal which will satisfy the person *at the present moment*. Lewin felt that the attainment of a future goal, however, may not guarantee satisfaction. Within this rubric, Lewin considered two kinds of goals: action goals and ideal goals. The action goal is what actually will be accomplished. The ideal goal is the value one derives from doing well and being praised for doing well.

Summary

Kurt Lewin has been an important force in American psychology primarily because of his methodology. He employed the extensive use of geometric forms of mathematics to illustrate his concepts without the full use of the mathematical procedures.

DELIMITATION

The present treatment of Kurt Lewin's work is extremely short. Among the many things which have not been covered are the excellent experiments Lewin did with Ovsiankina, Zeigarnik, and with Lippitt and White at the Iowa Child Welfare Station. Some commentators of the psychological scene consider the Lewin-Lippett-White studies of social climates to be more of a study of types of leadership than of social climates or of personality formation.

We also have not covered the study that Lewin did of large groups, particularly the differences he found in pre-World War II German and

American populations. Also omitted are Lewin's learning theory formulations.

Undoubtedly the greatest omission of this section is the innumerable drawings and diagrams and arrows and penciled lines—which descriptive devices, however, often lose the essence of Lewin's theory on the drawing board. Lewinian diagrams need explanatory words. It is hoped this novel approach retains the essence of an interesting theory even without the "do-it-yourself" mechanics of drawing.

BIBLIOGRAPHY

Primary Sources

BOOKS

Lewin, K., Environmental forces, in C. Murchison (ed.), *Handbook of Child Psychology,* Worcester, Mass., Clark Univer. Press, 1934.

Lewin, K., *A Dynamic Theory of Personality,* N.Y., McGraw-Hill, 1935. Also in paperback edition.

Lewin, K., *Principles of Topological Psychology,* N.Y., McGraw-Hill, 1936.

Lewin, K., T. Dembo, L. Festinger, and P. S. Sears, Level of aspiration, in J. McV. Hunt (ed.), *Personality and the Behavior Disorders,* N.Y., Ronald, 1944, chap. 10.

Lewin, K., Behavior and development as a function of total situations, in L. Carmichael (ed.), *Manual of Child Psychology,* N.Y., Wiley, 1946, chap. 16.

Lewin, K., Group decision and social change, in T. Newcomb and E. Hartley (eds.), *Readings in Social Psychology,* N.Y., Holt, Rinehart and Winston, 1947.

Lewin, K., *Resolving Social Conflicts: Selected Papers on Group Dynamics,* G. W. Lewin (ed.), N.Y., Harper & Row, 1948. Foreword by G. W. Allport.

Lewin, K., Cassirer's philosophy of science and the social sciences, in P. A. Schilpp, (ed.), *The Philosophy of Ernst Cassirer,* Evanston, Ill., Living Philosophies, 1949.

Lewin, K., Will and need, in W. D. Ellis (ed.), *A Source Book of Gestalt Psychology,* N.Y., Humanities Press, 1950.

Lewin, K., *Field Theory in Social Science,* D. Cartwright (ed.), N.Y., Harper & Row, 1951.

PERIODICALS

Lewin, K., Vectors, cognitive processes, and Mr. Tolman's criticism, *J. Gen. Psychol.*, 1933, 8, 318–345.

Lewin, K., Psycho-sociological problems of a minority group, *Char. Person.*, 1935, 3, 175–187.

Lewin, K., Some social-psychological differences between the United States and Germany, *Char. Person.*, 1936, 4, 265–293.

Lewin, K., The conceptual representation and measurement of psychological forces, in *Cont. Psychol. Theory*, Durham, N.C., Duke Univer. Press, 1938, 1, No. 4.

   Also in *Univ. Iowa Contr. Psychol. Theory*, 1938, 1, No. 4, 1–247.

Lewin, K., R. Lippitt, and R. K. White, Patterns of aggressive behavior in experimentally created "social climates," *J. Soc. Psychol.*, 1939, 10, 271–299.

Lewin, K., Formalization and progress in psychology, *Univ. of Iowa Studies in Child Welfare*, 1940, 16, No. 3, 9–42.

Barker, R., T. Dembo, and K. Lewin, Frustration and regression: An experiment with young children, *Univ. Iowa Studies in Child Welfare*, 1941, 18, No. 1.

Lewin, K., Field theory of learning, in *41st Yearbook NSSE*, 1942, 41, (Pt. II), 215–242.

Bavelas, A., and K. Lewin, Training in democratic leadership, *J. Abnorm. Soc. Psychol.*, 1942, 37, 115–119.

Lewin, K., The special case of Germany, *Publ. Opin. Quart.*, 1943, 7, 555–566.

Lewin, K., Defining the "field at a given time," *Psychol. Rev.*, 1943, 50, 292–310.

Lewin, K., Forces behind food habits and methods of change, *The Prob. of Changing Food Habits, Nat. Res. Council Bull.*, 1943, No. 108.

Lewin, K., Constructs in psychology and psychological ecology, *Univ. Iowa Studies in Child Welfare*, 1944, 20, 1–29.

Lewin, K., Action research and minority problems, *J. Soc. Issues*, 1946, 2, 34–46.

Lewin, K., Frontiers in group dynamics: II. channels of group life—social planning and action research, *Hum. Relat.*, 1947, 1, 143–153.

SUGGESTED READINGS

BOOKS

Adams, D. K., *The Anatomy of Personality*, Garden City, N.Y., Doubleday, 1954.

   Personality studied via field theory.

Escalona, S., The influence of topological and vector psychology upon current research in child development: An addendum, in L. Carmichael (ed.), *Manual of Child Psychology*, N.Y., Wiley, 1954.

Hall, C. S., and G. Lindzey, *Theories of Personality*, N.Y., Wiley, 1957, 206–256.

Excellent discussion on how to draw diagrams.

Leeper, R. W., *Lewin's Topological and Vector Psychology: A Digest and Critique*, Eugene, Ore., Univer. Oregon Press, 1943.

Lippitt, P., and R. White, The "social climate" of children's groups, in R. G. Barker, J. S. Kounin, and H. F. Wright (eds.), *Child Behavior and Development*, N.Y., McGraw-Hill, 1943.

Wolman, B. B., *Contemporary Theories and Systems in Psychology*, N.Y., Harper & Row, 1960.

See especially chap. 13, Field Theory.

PERIODICALS

Allport, G. W., The genius of Kurt Lewin, *J. Person.*, 1947, *16*, 1–10.

Also published in *J. Soc. Issues*, 1948, *4*, 14–21, Suppl. Series I.

Berelson, B., The state of communication research, *Publ. Opin. Quart.*, 1959, 23(1), 1–6.

Lewin's "small groups approach" is one of the major influences.

Brolyer, C. R., Review of Kurt Lewin's, *Principles of Topological Psychology*, *Char. Person.*, 1936-37, *5*, 255–272.

Cantril, H., Review of Lewin's *Dynamic Theory of Personality*, *J. Abnorm. Soc. Psychol.*, 1935, *30*, 534–537.

Freud, A., The contribution of psychoanalysis to genetic psychology, *Amer. J. Orthopsychiat.*, 1951, *21*, 476–497.

Anna Freud criticizes the Barker, Dembo, and Lewin frustration experiment.

Garrett, H. E., Lewin's "topological" psychology: An evaluation, *Psychol. Rev.*, 1939, *46*, 517–524.

Hearn, G., Kurt Lewin on adolescence, *Group*, 1954, *17*(2), 9–15.

Heider, F., On Lewin's methods and theory, *Soc. Issues*, 1959, Suppl. 13.

Koriel, H. S., Democracy unlimited: Kurt Lewin's theory, *Amer. J. Sociol.*, 1956, *62*, 680–689.

Lindzey, G., Review of Lewin's *Field Theory in Social Science*, *J. Abnorm. Soc. Psychol.*, 1952, 47, 132–133.

Lippitt, R., Field theory and experiment in social psychology: autocratic and democratic group atmospheres, *Amer. J. Sociol.*, 1939, *45*, 26–49.

London, I. O., Psychologists' misuse of the auxiliary concepts of physics and mathematics, *Psychol. Rev.*, 1944, *51*, 266–291.

McCall, S.H.A., A comparative study of the systems of Lewin and Koffka with specific reference to memory phenomena, *Contr. Psychol. Theory*, Duke Univer. Press, 1939, 2, No. 1.

McCreary, J. K., The problem of personality definition, *J. Gen. Psychol.*, 1960, 63, 107–111.

> Reviews definitions by Allport, Lewin, Murray, and Murphy.

Moreno, J. L., How Kurt Lewin's "Research Center for Group Dynamics" started and the question of paternity, *Group Psychotherap.*, 1952, 5, 1–6.

Moreno, J. L., How Kurt Lewin's "Research Center for Group Dynamics" started, *Sociometry*, 1953, 16, 101–106.

Smith, D.E.P., Interdisciplinary approach to the genesis of anxiety, *Educ. Theory*, 1956, 6, 222–231.

> Compares Freud, Rank, Mowrer, Angyal, Goldstein, Lewin, Rogers, Kierkegaard, and Sullivan on theories of anxiety.

Tolman, E. C., Kurt Lewin: 1890–1947, *Psychol. Rev.*, 1948, 55, 1–4.

White, R. K., The case for the Tolman-Lewin interpretation of learning, *Psychol. Rev.*, 1943, 50, 157–186.

MATHEMATICAL [Cattell]

Science moves but slowly, slowly,
creeping on from point to point.

TENNYSON
Locksley Hall, Line 134[1]

SOME BIOGRAPHICAL DATA

Raymond B. Cattell was born in Staffordshire, England, in 1905. He received his B.S., M.A., Ph.D., and D.Sc. at Kings College, University of London. He married Monica Rogers on December 1, 1930. They have one son, Hereward Seagrieve, a surgeon. He was married again on April 2, 1946 to Alberta Karen Schuettler. They have four children: Mary, Heather, Roderic, and Elaine. Cattell was lecturer at the University of Exeter, 1927–1932; director at the City of Leicester Child Guidance Clinic, 1932–37; Research Associate to E. L. Thorndike, 1937–1938, and

---

[1] The author is most grateful to Dr. Cattell for suggesting this couplet from Tennyson and also for his meticulous reading of this chapter.

G. Stanley Hall professor of genetic psychology, 1938–1941. In 1941 he went to Harvard where he served in the capacity of lecturer in psychology until 1944, and after war service, left for the University of Illinois where he has been research professor in psychology ever since. Cattell was awarded the Darwin Research Fellowship in 1935 and he wrote the Wenner-Gren Prize Essay on Research in 1953. He is a fellow of the British Psychological Society and a member of the American Psychological Association. Furthermore, he is a member of the Eugenics Society and of the Human Genetics Society. He is a member of Sigma Xi. Cattell also serves as a civilian consultant on personal research at the Adjutant General's Office of the War Department.

INTRODUCTION

Raymond Cattell is a very creatively active and talented psychologist. He, along with Eysenck, is probably one of the most productive psychologists in the current psychological world. Like Eysenck, Raymond Cattell writes a fantastic number of articles. Also like Gardner Murphy, Cattell writes on a wide variety of psychological and technical areas. In the past, Cattell has written textbooks and numerous articles on general psychology, social psychology, experimental psychology, statistical methods, mental testing, and personality theories, and he is also the creator of a number of personality tests.

Raymond Cattell publishes internationally. He has published in American, British, Australian journals and has been translated into French psychological journals. So vast is his output that he has averaged about ten articles per year through the period 1950 to 1960. In point of fact, the present text deals with only about one half of Cattell's writing.

Cattell is fascinated with the quantitative aspects of personality measurement. He uses factor analysis as one of his favorite tools to discover personality traits.

He has a wide variety of talents which he seems to have put to use in many fields. Even a cursory examination of the voluminous bibliography for Cattell brings out his interest in music, his interest in national differences, his interest in organic tests, the culture-free intelligence tests that he was worked on, and, of course, his extremely sophisticated work as a statistician.

As one might expect because of his training in English universities, and his interest in factor analysis and his voluminous publications, Cattell is a personal friend of Eysenck and Sir Cyril Burt.

THE SYSTEM, THEORY, ESSENTIAL FEATURES

General Considerations

According to Cattell, the goal of psychology and personality theory is to formulate laws which enable us to predict behavior under many conditions. His definition of personality is not surprising in that it is based on prediction. *"Personality is that which permits a prediction of what a person will do in a given situation"* (Personality: A Systematic, Theoretical, and Factual Study, 1950, p. 2).

Cattell emphasizes that there are many motivational variables which must be carefully spelled out. His feeling is that personality theory is still in transition or being formed. Cattell believes this generation has neglected the hereditary aspects of human personality, and his emphasis is on the structure of personality, both in regard to biological background, and social determiners. His workshop is in fact called "The Laboratory of Personality Assessment and Group Behavior," and has published much on group dimensions and roles as well as physiological aspects. All of Cattell's interest in personality theory and the dynamics of personality have grown out of the findings of continuous research rather than speculative writings.

Raymond Cattell feels very strongly that if personality cannot be demonstrated, measured, and quantified, it should be called *philosophy* and not *personality theory* in psychology.

However, Cattell does not mean by experiment "only brass instrument laboratory experiments," as he explained to me in a letter. He remarked in the *Kentucky Symposium* (p. 109), "We let events happen in life as they will and tease out by statistical finesse what cannot be handled by brute experimental control." His theory is based, therefore, on controlled experimentation with the independent variables carefully considered. It resembles the type of experimentation done in the field of physics. In the same symposium, Cattell argued that psychology must answer the small questions before attempting the global answers. He feels that the clinic may be the best place to study personality but that it may not be the best place to verify hypotheses that predict behavior change, for its methods are weak until measurement, control and subtle statistical analysis are introduced. There is a difference in personality theory between what is socially acceptable in a "popular" subject and what is scientifically respectable. Thus, change that may occur through therapy might be quite acceptable to society yet not be demonstrable with any scientific reliability. Feeling that personality Theory—with a capital "T"—in the present day has much "semantic nonsense," he likens it to Oscar Wilde's definition of history: "An account of things that never should have happened." Cattell advocates a concentrated study of personality which should be done in the life situation. After the facts have been gathered, they should be treated statistically and not philosophically.

Cattell proposes that we measure and statistically treat covariance or similarities in togetherness. This "going-togetherness" needs demonstration by correlation coefficients and factor analytic treatment; "A statistical method of arriving at a definition of similarity" is far superior to the normal scientific idea of what goes together.

In a 1957 article, "A Universal Index for Psychological Factors," Cattell pleads strongly for standardized symbols for describing psychological data while concepts are being developed. These, he feels, could be accomplished by a committee to create standards for international research and to publish these standards so that all who work on the common factors of personality are working within the same framework. In contrast to this he feels that the current research done in personality is done with so many kinds of measurement techniques and so many variant terms that no cross reference or comparison is possible.

Because of his heavy emphasis upon sound and powerful statistical approaches to the study of personality, some of the current observers have the perhaps erroneous impression that Cattell's contribution is more to methodology than to personality theory *per se*.

Specific Considerations

Much of Cattell's work has been done in the delineation of traits. Cattell started out with the 1937 list of 17,953 trait names that Allport suggested. He reduced this list through factor analysis to 160 trait names. To this list he added 11 more that he felt were essential or important, making a total of 171 trait names. As we shall see, he reduced this list to fewer source traits, eleven of which are listed later in this section.

Cattell feels that determining trait structure and structural concepts is the necessary basis for studying personality. In this, he parallels statistically the nonstatistical writings of Gordon Allport. Traits are patterns generating covariant behavior acts, giving consistency to behavior, and hence enabling us to predict. Cattell looks for the consistency in behavior that can be observed and/or measured directly or indirectly.

In his work Cattell finds two major kinds of traits: source traits and surface traits. Surface traits are clusters of observable, behavioral events; they are less stable and merely descriptive, and therefore, less important in Cattell's viewpoint. On the other hand he feels that source traits are the genuine influences that help to determine and explain human behavior. Source traits are the underlying influences that help to determine surface traits. Source traits are stable, extremely important and are the major material which the personality psychologist should be studying.

Source traits may be divided into constitutional traits and environmental-mold traits. The former are internal or within the skin and have some basis in heredity. Environmental-mold traits come from the environment and are molded by events which occur outside the skin.

Through statistical techniques, Cattell has identified or confirmed some sixteen to twenty source traits. The traits are arranged somewhat in the polarity of Freud. Cattell feels that naming traits is extremely misleading. He prefers to use code numbers. However, the goal toward which the human being aspires usually gives the trait its name. The following double list exemplifies a few of the source traits that Cattell has found in ratings and in questionnaire responses. The letter to the left of the number in parenthesis is Cattell's preferred symbol.

A (1)	Cyclothymia	vs.	Schizothymia (Constitutional trait)
B (2)	Mental capacity	vs.	Mental defect
C (3)	Ego strength	vs.	Ego weakness
E (4)	Dominance	vs.	Submissiveness
F (5)	Surgency	vs.	Desurgency
G (6)	Superego strength	vs.	Superego weakness
H (7)	Adventurus cyclothymia	vs.	Withdrawn cyclothymia
I (8)	Premsia	vs.	Harria
K (9)	Socialized mind	vs.	Boorish mind (Environmental-mold)
M (10)	Bohemian freeness	vs.	Conventional rigidity
Q (11)	High ergic tension	vs.	Low ergic tension

Cattell advocates a method of analyzing quantitatively the goals or the incentives that motivate the human personality in action in a natural setting. This he calls the *dynamic calculus*. Attitudes and responses of all kinds are considered to come from dynamic source traits, of two kinds. The first is the erg and the second is the sentiment. An erg is almost like an instinct. The term *erg* comes from the field of physics and in its simplest definition is considered to be a unit of energy. An erg is defined as, "An innate psychophysical disposition which permits its possessors to acquire reactivity to certain classes of objects more readily than do others, to experience a specific emotion in regard to them, and to start on a course of action which ceases more completely at a specific goal activity than at any other."[2] Cattell feels he has identified at least nine of these ergs, including sex, fear, parental protectiveness, assertion, curiosity, etc. Cattell prefers the term *ergs* to get away from what he calls the "semantic confusion" that is usually involved in the mixing of drive with instincts. A *sentiment*, on the other hand, is "a motivational source trait which comes out of environmental influences" such as the religious sentiment, sentiment to home, sentiment to the self, and so on.

His investigation of dynamic structure has been possible only through advances in the objective measurement of motivation strength. By measuring attitudes, Cattell has been able to demonstrate, through these objective devices, the presence of basic motivational source factors. The atomic attitudes follow this pattern: "Under these conditions I wish (so much) to do this with that," and thus each contains the characteristics of the incentive or situational conditions, the organism, the intensity (which is to be measured), the goal directed activity, and the goal objects.

His objective motivation tests utilize experimental principles, many of which have been well studied by other investigators in the area of motivation, such as: differential information, selective memory, autism, projection, selective perception, and selective attention. A large number of new measurement devices have been demonstrated to be related to motivation measured in this way. Over sixty objective device methods have been established and studied intensely for directly measuring the manifested change within the organism which can be attributed to the introduction of incentive stimulation. The analysis of these measures has shown that basic patterns of motivational expression exist which are relatively uniform, regardless of the specific characteristics of the goal object. Seven factors of devices which measure the same way have been found. These can be considered to be made up of motivational behaviors and fall into the general patterns of the id, ego, superego and some other components of motivation not proposed by Freud. The value of having a theoretical framework which permits measurement of motivation on different

[2] H. B. English and A. C. English, *A Comprehensive Dictionary of Psychological and Psychoanalytical Terms*, Longmans, 1958, p. 185. (Courtesy David McKay Co.)

levels is of great importance, and sets his theory and experimental procedures on a different plane from the other monotonic measures being used.

He refers to the motivational structures of related goal directions as "dynamic factors", as an acknowledgment of their sensitivity to environmental presses and incentive conditions. A list of these "ergs" and "sentiments" would sound not too different from McDougall's "instincts" or Murray's "needs." The real difference lies in the fact that these are dimensions which are empirically discovered and repeatedly measurable. For example, the pugnacity erg found in both adults and children contributes major variance to such attitudes as "I want the United States to beat its enemies", "I want to beat-up other kids who cause me trouble" or "I want to see more gangster movies."

By means of factor analysis, eighteen replicable ergs and sentiments have been found in children and thirteen in adults. The ergs seem to be more primary and to be more directly related to the actual goal activity such as eating, sleeping, fighting, and so forth. The sentiment structures are made up of attitudes having the same institution or goal object which has seemingly proved useful over a long period of time for the satisfaction of many varied primary motives. These primary motives include religion, patriotism, sweetheart, self, parents, and mass amusement. Thus, some have compared sentiments to instrumentalities and ergs to more basic needs.

It is very easy to become involved in a morass of conflicting terminology in this area. This is a special reason that Cattell has purposely delineated his system from others seeking to systematize motivation. He feels that if his "protective erg" measures the same variance found by Murray's "nurturance need" then the path of science will be made easier, but that this is not necessary for the measurement of both concepts in their present systems.

This fundamental work in motivation is now opening new vistas for measurement, central to the needs of clinical and industrial psychology. Areas of repression, motivational conflict, intrafamilial attitudes, as well as vocational motives, are all in various stages of systematization.[3]

Formally, Cattell proceeds to divide traits into three *modalities:* temperament, dynamics, and ability. Temperament traits are often tied to constitutional bodily characteristics. Dynamic traits concern themselves with getting started or initiating any behavioral act. Ability traits, in a way, measure or express the efficiency of the personality in behavior directed to solving cognitive problems.

The manner in which one dynamic trait is linked with another in

---

[3] This section has been prepared almost exclusively by a close associate of Cattell's, Professor Arthur Sweney. I am obligated to both Professor Sweney and Dr. Cattell for permission to use it.

trying to achieve a goal is called subsidiation. The term *subsidiation* originated largely from the work of Murray, who felt that there should be more goal levels or a hierarchy of goals. Subsidiation concerns itself primarily with the innumerable interrelated and highly complex pathways that an individual may take to a final goal. In other words, an individual may have to go through many minor goals or subgoals in order to achieve the final goal state. The intermediate steps are frequently highly involved. Factor analyses is one way of discovering these ergic subsidiations.

Like almost all contemporary theorists, Raymond Cattell gives an important place to the aspects of self. He speaks of the self sentiment which gives stability and a high degree of organization to the source traits. Cattell divides his consideration of the total self into three parts: self-sentiment, real self, and ideal self. *Self-sentiment* means "the concern which one has about his conceived self." The *real self* is, as one might expect, "actually the personality." The *ideal self* is what "one would like to be, granted all things and all power."

Cattell considers that there are essentially three ways to measure personality. 1. Objective test: create a situation and observe an individual's behavior. 2. Self-rating: may or may not be accurate because of the possibility of falsification by the subject. 3. Life record: is the best at discovering the primary source traits. It means measuring day to day behavior by events or by the ratings of others. The ratings of others such as school teachers, members of the family, and experienced clinicians can be of extreme value. Cattell has used all three of these methods of measuring personality in systematic interrelation.

Cattell and co-workers have worked together to make available to psychologists who are not factor analysts, the means of measuring and experimenting with the factors they have found. In the questionnaire realm, the 16 Personality Factor Questionnaire (16 PF Test), the High School Personality Questionnaire (HSPQ), (the PQ) and others, systematically measure the same factor for developmental purposes over the child and adult age range. Along with the objective test factors theme are Objective-Analytic (O-A) batteries, also for adults and children. These batteries have already yielded valid results where previous personality tests were too insensitive, for example, in clinical diagnoses and prognosis and in industrial selection.

In relating group and family to individual personality, Cattell has introduced the concept of group syntality. Briefly, *syntality* means "the relevant characteristics of an entire group which leads to consistent behavior by that group, thereby leading to possible prediction of group performance." It is the factor of syntality, or the sociocultural pressures, as it influences the behavior of the individual that Cattell has examined at some length. He finds there are three ways that social institutions may influence the behavior of the individual. This individual behavior may be influenced by the deliberate inculcation of social values into the individual, by situations which are purely happenstance, and by the reaction of the individual to the above two factors. Thus, the individual's family or the cultural milieu are significantly important to the personality formation of the individual. In studying the phenomenon of syntality, one responds to pressures inside and outside of the family.

Cattell postulates seventeen laws of personality formation in his 1950 book, *Personality: A Systematic, Theoretical and Factual Study* (p. 664). The seventeen laws are as follows:

1. The Law of Innate Goal Tension Patterns.
2. The Law of Satisfaction in Rigidity.
3. The Law of Dispersion with Excitement and Deprivation.
4. The Law of Dynamic Effect.
5. The Law of Alternating Expression in Naive Conflict.
6. The Law of Suppressive Mechanisms in Permanent Conflict.
7. The Law of the Nature of Conditions of Repression in Permanent Conflict.
8. The Law of Consequences of Repression.
9. The Law of Combined Expression.
10. The Law of Deflection Strain.
11. The Law of Cognitive-Dynamic Investment Strain.
12. The Law of Short-Circuiting.
13. The Law of Integration by the Contemplated Self.
14. The Law of Persisting Dissociations from the Ego.
15. The Law of Subsidiation and Integration of the Dual-Self Concepts in the Self-Sentiment.
16. The Law of Ergic and General Regression.
17. The Law of Superpersonal Context and Limitation of Prediction.

Since much of the foregoing discussion has centered on these seventeen laws, no attempt is made to follow the long discourse that Cattell presents in defining and explaining his seventeen laws of personality formation.

In measuring personality, Cattell employs two units: normative and ipsative. Normative units concern themselves with the amount an individual will vary from other individuals. The ipsative unit is the amount of variation that is found within the individual himself, for example, in anxiety and other states, dynamic conditions, etc.

Following the above lead, Cattell employs two types of factor analysis techniques, one which he calls the P technique—"the factoring of the unique structure of the single person"—and the other, the R technique. The primary distinction between the two is that the P technique is an ipsative technique and can reveal causal sequences, while the R technique is a normative unit technique. He points out that a vast area of clinical use of P-technique is at present unexplored.

Finally, we may get some flavor of the thinking of Cattell by quoting his remarks at the Educational Testing Service Invitational Conference of 1951 where he stated, "The educational psychologist is unduly obsessed with items, item analysis and scaling, so that he suffers from delusions that personality is paper. If any personality test I am designing falls into itemizable and atomizable form, that is generally the sheerest accident. . . . So long as personality testing is conceived only within the cramped perspective of juggling with what are essentially fragments of scholastic examinations called 'items' it remains an unimaginative and trivial creature, unweaned from attainment and ability tests and psychologically impotent" (p. 82).

Summary

Cattell is dedicated to developing personality theory out of multivariate experimental methods, i.e., from the application of complex statistical analyses to manipulated (laboratory) and naturally occurring behavior. He has been and continues to be a prolific contributor in many psychological journals both here and abroad, concerned with the systematic development of multivariate experiment. The result may be described as a system of complex interactions of patterns of traits and patterns of environment—the Gestalt and trait and stimulus response concepts integrated in mathematical models.

DELIMITATION

The outstanding omission in this chapter concerning Raymond Cattell's work is the work he has done in factor analysis methods and the problems of measurement.

BIBLIOGRAPHY

Primary Sources

BOOKS

Cattell, R. B., *A Guide to Mental Testing for Psychological Clinics, Schools, and Industrial Psychologists*, Bickly, Kent, Eng., London Press, 1936, rev. ed. 1948.

3rd rev. ed. 1953, London, Univer. of London Press.

Cattell, R. B., *General Psychology*, Cambridge, Mass., Sci-Art, 1941.

Cattell, R. B., *The Factors of the Mind*, N.Y., Macmillan, 1941.

Cattell, R. B., *The Culture Free Test of Intelligence*, Champaign, Ill., Inst. Person. and Ability Testing, 1944.

Cattell, R. B., *Description and Measurement of Personality*, N.Y., Harcourt, Brace & World, 1946.

Cattell, R. B., *An Introduction to Personality Study*, London, Hutchinson, 1950.

Cattell, R. B., *Personality: A Systematic Theoretical and Factual Study*, N.Y., McGraw-Hill, 1950.

Cattell, R. B., D. R. Saunders, and G. F. Stice, *The 16 Personality Factor Questionnaire*, Champaign, Ill., Inst. Person. and Ability Testing, 1950.

Cattell, R. B., Personality structure and personality measurement, in *ETS, 1951, Invitational Conference on Testing Problems*, Princeton, N.Y., 1952, 82–88.

Cattell, R. B., *Factor Analysis: An Introduction and Manual for the Psychologist and Social Scientist*, N.Y., Harper & Row, 1952.

Cattell, R. B., Personality structures as learning and motivation patterns—a theme for the integration of methodologies, in *Learning Theory, Personality Theory and Clinical Research: The Kentucky Symposium*, N.Y., Wiley, 1954, 91–113.

Cattell, R. B., J. E. King, and A. K. Schuettler, *Personality Factor Series* (series of 3 tests), (the O-A Personality Test Battery), Champaign, Ill., Inst. Person. and Ability Testing, 1954.

Cattell, R. B., Personality and motivation theory based on structural measurement, in J. L. McCary (ed.), *Psychology of Personality: Six Modern Approaches*, N.Y., Logos Press, 1956.

Cattell, R. B., *Personality and Motivation Structure and Measurement*, N.Y., Harcourt, Brace & World, 1957.

Cattell, R. B., H. Beloff, and R. Coan, *IPAT High School Personality Questionnaire (HSPQ)*, Champaign, Ill., Inst. Person. and Ability Testing, 1958.

Cattell, R. B., *The I.P.A.T. Anxiety Scale,* Champaign, Ill., Inst. Person. and Ability Testing, 1958.

Cattell, R. B., The dynamic calculus: Concepts and crucial experiments, in M. R. Jones, (ed.), *Nebraska Symposium on Motivation, 1959,* 84–134, Lincoln, Nebr., Univer. Nebraska Press, 1959.

Cattell, R. B., Personality theory growing from multivariate quantitative research, in S. Koch (ed.), *Psychology: A Study of a Science,* Vol. III. *Formulations of the Person and the Social Context,* N.Y., McGraw-Hill, 1959.

Cattell, R. B. and I. H. Scheier, *The meaning and measurement of neuroticism and anxiety,* N.Y., Ronald, 1961.

Cattell, R. B., Group theory, personality and role: a model for experimental researches, in F. Geldard (ed.), *Defence Psychology,* London, Pergamon, 1962.

PERIODICALS

Cattell, R. B., and J. L. Willston, Contributions concerning mental inheritance: I. of intelligence, *Brit. J. Educ. Psychol.,* 1938, 8, 129–149.

Cattell, R. B., and E. J. Molteno, Contributions concerning mental inheritance: II. temperament, *J. Genet. Psychol.,* 1940, 57, 31–47.

Cattell, R. B., The description of personality: basic traits resolved into clusters, *J. Abnorm. Soc. Psychol.,* 1943, 38, 476–506.

Cattell, R. B., An objective test of character temperament, *J. Soc. Psychol.,* 1944, *19,* 99–114.

Cattell, R. B., The cultural functions of social stratification: I. regarding the genetic basis of society, *J. Soc. Psychol.,* 1945, *21,* 3–23.

Cattell, R. B., The riddle of perseveration, *J. Person.,* 1946, *14,* 229–267.

Cattell, R. B., and L. G. Wispe, The dimensions of syntality in small groups, *J. Soc. Psychol.,* 1948, *28,* 57–78.

Cattell, R. B., Concepts and methods in the measurement of group syntality, *Psychol. Rev.,* 1948, *55,* 48–63.

Cattell, R. B., The dimensions of culture patterns by factorization of national character, *J. Abnorm. Soc. Psychol.,* 1949, *44,* 443–469.

Cattell, R. B., and L. G. Tiner, The varieties of structural rigidity, *J. Person.,* 1949, *17,* 321–341.

Cattell, R. B., and L. Luborsky, P-technique demonstrated as a new clinical method for determining personality and symptom structure, *J. Gen. Psychol.,* 1950, *42,* 3–24.

Cattell, R. B., The main personality factors in questionnaire, self-estimate material, *J. Soc. Psychol.,* 1950, *31,* 3–38.

Cattell, R. B., and D. R. Saunders, Interrelation and matching of personality factors from behavior rating, questionnaire, and objective test data, *J. Soc. Psychol.,* 1950, *31,* 243–260.

Cattell, R. B., H. Breul, and H. P. Hartman, An attempt at more refined definition of the cultural dimensions of syntality in modern nations, *Amer. Soc. Rev.*, 1952, *17*, 408–421.

Cattell, R. B., and K. P. Cross, Comparison of ergic and self-sentiment structures found in dynamic traits by R- and P-techniques, *J. Person.*, 1952, *21*, 250–271.

Cattell, R. B., The three basic factor-analytic research designs—their inter-relations and derivatives, *Psychol. Bull.*, 1952, *49*, 499–520.

Cattell, R. B., Research designs in psychological genetics with special reference to the multiple variance method, *Amer. J. Hum. Genet.*, 1953, *5*, 76–93.

Cattell, R. B., and J. C. Anderson, The measurement of personality and behavior disorders by the IPAT Music Preference Test, *J. App. Psychol.*, 1953, *37*, 446–454.

Cattell, R. B., The personality factor structuring of 11-year-old children in terms of behavior rating data, *J. Clin. Psychol.*, 1953, *9*, 256–266.

Cattell, R. B., and H. Beloff, Research origin and construction of the IPAT Juniors Personality Quiz, *J. Consult. Psychol.*, 1953, *17*, 436–442.

Cattell, R. B., and W. Gruen, The primary personality factors in the questionnaire medium for children 10–14 years old, *Educ. Psychol. Measmt.*, 1954, *14*, 50–76.

Cattell, R. B., and G. F. Stice, Four formulae for selecting leaders on the basis of personality, *Hum. Relat.*, 1954, *7*, 493–507.

Cattell, R. B., S. S. Dubin, and D. R. Saunders, Personality structure in psychotics by factorization of objective clinical tests, *J. Ment. Sci.*, 1954, *100*, 154–176.

Cattell, R. B., Musical preferences and personality diagnosis, *J. Soc. Psychol.*, 1954, *39*, 3–24.

Cattell, R. B., D. B. Blewett, and J. R. Beloff, The inheritance of personality: A multiple variance analysis determination of approximate nature-nurture ratios for primary personality factors in Q-data, *Amer. J. Hum. Genet.*, 1955, *7*, 122–146.

Cattell, R. B., and J. E. Drevdahl, A comparison of the personality profile (16 P.F.) of eminent researchers with that of eminent teachers and administrators and of the general population, *Brit. J. Psychol.*, 1955, *46*, 248–261.

Cattell, R. B., The principle replicated factors discovered in objective personality tests, *J. Abnorm. Soc. Psychol.*, 1955, *50*, 291314.

Cattell, R. B., The chief invariant psychological and psycho–physical functional unities found by P-technique, *J. Clin. Psychol.*, 1955, *11*, 319–343.

Cattell, R. B., and W. Gruen, The primary personality factors in 11-year-old children, by objective tests, *J. Person.*, 1955, *23*, 460–478.

Cattell, R. B., Validation and intensification of the Sixteen Personality Factor

Questionnaire, *J. Clin. Psychol.*, 1956, *12*, 205–214.

Cattell, R. B., Second-order personality factors in the questionnaire realm, *J. Consult. Psychol.*, 1956, *20*, 411–418.

Cattell, R. B., and A. R. Baggaley, The objective measurement of attitude motivation: Development and evaluation of principles and devices, *J. Person.*, 1956, *24*, 401–423.

Cattell, R. B., A shortened "Basic English" version (Form C) of the 16 PF Questionnaire, *J. Soc. Psychol.*, 1956, *44*, 257–278.

Cattell, R. B., and R. W. Coan, Personality factors in middle childhood as revealed in parents ratings, *Child Develpm.*, 28, 439–458.

Cattell, R. B., Formulae and table for obtaining validities and reliabilities of extended factor scales, *Educ. Psychol. Measmt.*, *17*, 491–498.

Cattell, R. B., G. F. Stice, and N. F. Kristy, A first approximation to nature-nurture ratios for eleven primary personality factors in objective tests, *J. Abnorm. Soc. Psychol.*, 1957, *54*, 143–159.

Cattell, R. B., The conceptual and test distinction of neuroticism and anxiety, *J. Clin. Psychol.*, 1957, *13*, 221–223.

Cattell, R. B., A universal index for psychological factors, *Psychologia*, 1957, *1*, 74–85.

Cattell, R. B. and I. H. Scheier, Clinical validities by analyzing the psychiatrist exemplified in relation to anxiety diagnoses, *Amer. J. Orthopsychiat.*, 1958, *28*, 699–713.

Cattell, R. B., and A. R. Baggaley, A confirmation of ergic and engram structures in attitudes objectively measured, *Australian J. Psychol.*, 1958, *10*, 289–318.

Cattell, R. B., and R. W. Coan, Personality dimensions in the questionnaire responses of six- and seven-year-olds, *Brit. J. Educ. Psychol.*, 1958, 28, 232–242.

Cattell, R. B., Extracting the correct number of factors in factor analysis, *Educ. Psychol. Measmt.*, 1958, *18*, 791–838.

Drevdahl, J. E., and R. B. Cattell, Personality and creativity in artists and writers, *J. Clin. Psychol.*, 1958, *14*, 107–111.

Cattell, R. B., and R. W. Coan, Child personality structure as revealed in teacher's behavior ratings, *J. Clin. Psychol.*, 1957, *13*, 315–327.

Coan, R. W., and R. B. Cattell, Reproducible personality factors in middle childhood, *J. Clin. Psychol.*, 1958, *14*, 339–345.

Peterson, D. R., and R. B. Cattell, Personality factors in nursery school children as derived from parent ratings, *J. Clin. Psychol.*, 1958, *14*, 346–355.

Cattell, R. B., What is "objective" in "objective personality tests"?, *J. Counsel. Psychol.*, 1958, *5*, 285–289.

Cattell, R. B., R. W. Coan, and H. Beloff, A reexamination of personality structure in late childhood, and development of the High School Personality Questionnaire, *J. Exp. Educ.*, 1958, *27*, 73–88.

Scheier, I. H., and R. B. Cattell, Confirmation of objective test factors and assessment of their relation to questionnaire factors: A factor analysis of 113 ratings, questionnaire and objective test measurements of personality, *J. Ment. Sci.*, 1958, *104*, 608–624.

Cattell, R. B., A need for alertness to multivariate experimental findings in integrative surveys, *Psychol. Bull.*, 1958, *55*, 253–256.

Cattell, R. B., and I. H. Scheier, The nature of anxiety: A review of thirteen multivariate analysis comprising 814 variables, *Psychol. Rep.*, 1958, *4*, 351–388.

Cattell, R. B., and R. W. Coan, Objective test assessment of the primary personality dimensions in middle childhood, *Brit. J. Psychol.*, 1959, *50*, 235–252.

Cattell, R. B. and D. R. Peterson, Personality structure in four- and five-year-olds in terms of objective tests, *J. Clin. Psychol.*, 1959, *15*, 355–369.

Peterson, D. R., and R. B. Cattell, Personality factors in nursery school children as derived from teacher's ratings, *J. Consult. Psychol.*, 1959, *23*, 562.

Coan, R. W., and R. B. Cattell, The development of the early school personality questionnaire, *J. Exp. Educ.*, 1959, *28*, 143–152.

Cattell, R. B., and I. H. Scheier, Extension of meaning of objective test personality factors: Especially into anxiety neuroticism, questionnaire, and physical factors, *J. Gen. Psychol.*, 1959, *61*, 287–315.

Cattell, R. B., and A. R. Baggaley, The salient variable similarity index for factor matching, *Brit. J. Statist. Psychol.*, 1960, *13*, 33–46.

Cattell, R. B., and J. L. Muerle, The "max plane" program for factor rotation to oblique simple structure, *Educ. Psychol. Measmt.*, 1960, *20*, 569–590.

Cattell, R. B., and I. H. Scheier, Stimuli related to stress, neuroticism, excitation, and anxiety response patterns: Illustrating a new multivariate experimental design, *J. Abnorm. Soc. Psychol.*, 1960, *60*, 195–204.

Scheier, I. H., R. B. Cattell, and J. L. Horn, Objective test factor V. I. 23: its measurement and its relation to clinically-judged neuroticism, *J. Clin. Psychol.*, 1960, *16*, 134–145.

Cattell, R. B., and R. B. McMichael, Clinical diagnosis by the IPAT music preference test, *J. Consult. Psychol.*, 1960, *24*, 333–341.

Cattell, R. B., A. B. Sweney, and J. A. Radcliffe, The objective measurement of motivation structure in children, *J. Clin. Psychol.*, 1960, *16*, 227–232.

Cattell, R. B., Evaluating interaction and non-linear relations by factor analysis, *Psychol. Rep.*, 1960, *7*, 69–70.

Cattell, R. B. and F. W. Warburton, A cross cultural comparison of patterns of extraversion and anxiety, *Brit. J. Psychol.*, 1961, *52*, 3–15.

Cattell, R. B., The theory of situational, instrument, second order, and refraction factors in personality structure research, *Psychol. Bull.*, 1961, 58, 160–174, 176.

A rebuttal to Becker's challenge (see *Psychol. Bull.*, 1960, 57, 201–212).

Cattell, R. B., R. R. Knapp, and I. H. Scheier, Second-order personality factor structure in the objective test realm, *J. Consult. Psychol.*, 1961, 25(4), 345–352.

Cattell, R. B., and W. Sullivan, The scientific nature of factors: a demonstration by cups of coffee, *Behav. Sci.*, 1962, 7(2), 184–193.

Factor analysis and cups of coffee as the model.

Cattell, R. B., J. Horn and H. J. Butcher, The dynamic structure of attitudes in adults, *Brit. J. Psychol.*, 1962, 53, 57–69.

Research on ergs, sentiments and motivation.

Cattell, R. B., and E. D. Lawson, Sex differences in small group performance, *J. Soc. Psychol.*, 1962, 58(1), 141–145.

Hurley, J. R., and R. B. Cattell, The Procrustes Program: producing direct rotation to test a hypothesized factor structure, *Behav. Sci.*, 1962, 7(2), 258–262.

Sweney, A. B., and R. B. Cattell, Relationships between integrated and unintegrated motivation structure examined by objective tests, *J. Soc. Psychol.*, 1962, 57, 217–226.

TAPE RECORDINGS

Cattell, R. B., *Theory and Method in Personality Research*, (G. W. Kisker, ed.) No. 143, Cincinnati, Ohio, Sound Seminars.

Cattell, R. B., *Measuring Personality by Structurally Defined Factors*, (G. W. Kisker, ed.) No. 144, Cincinnati, Ohio, Sound Seminars.

Cattell, R. B., *The Dynamic Calculus of Personality*, (G. W. Kisker, ed.) No. 145, Cincinnati, Ohio, Sound Seminars.

Cattell, R. B., *Group Dynamics and the Measurement of Group Characters*, (G. W. Kisker, ed.) No. 146, Cincinnati, Ohio, Sound Seminars.

Cattell, R. B., *The Psychological Measurement of Culture Patterns*, (G. W. Kisker, ed.) No. 147, Cincinnati, Ohio, Sound Seminars.

Suggested Readings

BOOKS

Chaplin, J. P., and T. S. Krawiec, *Systems and Theories of Psychology*, Holt, Rinehart and Winston, N.Y., 1960, 424–431.

Hall, C. S., and G. Lindzey, *Theories of Personality*, N.Y. Wiley, 1957, 393–417.

Harsh, C. M., and H. G. Schrickel, *Personality: Development and Assessment*,

(2nd ed.), N.Y., Ronald, 1959, 456–466.

French, J. W., The description of personality measurements in terms of rotated factors, *E.T.S. Bull.*, Princeton, N.J., 1953.

Spearman, C., *Abilities of Man*, N.Y., Macmillan, 1927.

Thomson, G. H., *The Factorial Analysis of Human Ability* (5th ed.), Boston, Houghton Mifflin, 1951.

Thurstone, L. L., *Multiple Factor Analysis: A Development and Expansion of the Vectors of the Mind*, Chicago, Univer. Chicago Press, 1947.

Tomkins, S., A discussion of "personality structure and personality measurement" of R. B. Cattell, in *E.T.S., 1951, Invitational Conference*, Princeton, N.J., 1952, 97–107.

    A sharp critique of Cattell's comments.

PERIODICALS

Becker, W. C., The matching of behavior rating and questionnaire personality factors, *Psychol. Bull.*, 1960, 57, 201–212.

    Challenges some of Cattell's methods.

Bensberg, G. J., and W. Sloan, The use of the Cattell Culture-Free Test with mental defectives, *Amer. J. Ment. Defic.*, 1955, 59, 499–503.

    Fail to find evidence of culture-free aspects.

Cavanaugh, M. C., I. Cohen, D. Dunphy, E. A. Ringwell, and I. D. Goldberg, Prediction from the Cattell infant intelligence scale, *J. Consult. Psychol.*, 1957, 21, 33–37.

Dowdy, C. D., An experimental test of Eysenck's and Cattell's theories of extroversion–introversion, *Dissertation Abstr.*, 1960, 20, 3376.

Eysenck, H. J., The nature of anxiety and the factorial method, *Psychol. Rep.*, 1958, 4, 453–454.

    Cattell's work is a "landmark in the development of personality theory" —but—it has its statistical weaknesses.

Guilford, J. P., When not to factor analyze, *Psychol. Bull.*, 1952, 49, 26–37.

Sells, S. B., Structured measurement of personality and motivation: A review of contributions of Raymond B. Cattell, *J. Clin. Psychol.*, 1959, 15, 3–21.

    Broad critical review of Cattell's work.

Spearman, C., General intelligence objectively determined and measured, *Amer. J. Psychol.*, 1904, 15, 201–293.

Thurstone, L. L., Psychological implications of factor analysis, *Amer. Psychologist*, 1948, 3, 402–408.

MATHEMATICAL [Eysenck]

It is as fatal as it is cowardly to blink
facts because they are not to our taste.

JOHN TYNDALL
Science and Man

SOME BIOGRAPHICAL DATA

Hans Jurgen Eysenck was born in Germany on March 4, 1916. He was educated in Germany, France, and England and received his Ph.D. in psychology at the University of London in 1940. From 1942 to 1946 Eysenck was at the Mill Hill Emergency Hospital as senior research psychologist. In 1949–1950 he came to the United States as visiting professor at the University of Pennsylvania and in 1954 he taught at the University of California. He has been professor of psychology at the Institute of Psychiatry at the University of London since 1955 and director of the psychology department at Maudsley Hospital since 1946. Eysenck has published some 200 articles in British, American, German, and French journals of psychology.

INTRODUCTION

The volume of work that Hans Jurgen Eysenck turns out is truly gigantic.[1] Not only is the volume of his publications tremendous, but he has much wider interests than are usually considered. At one time or another Eysenck has studied and written about body types, handwriting, psychotic–neurotic behavior, the effects of heredity in twin studies, tranquilizing drugs, and also jokes and cartoons. Much of the above breadth of his interest can be found in his books, *The Structure of Human Personality* (1960, 2nd ed.), *The Dynamics of Anxiety and Hysteria* (1957), *Experiments in Personality* (ed.) (1959), *Behavior Therapy and the Neuroses* (ed.) (1960), and *Handbook of Abnormal Psychology* (ed.) (1961).

[1] The kindness and generosity of Professor Eysenck in reviewing and commenting on this section is greatly appreciated. I am also grateful for his hospitality during my visit to Maudsley Hospital, London, in the fall of 1959.

With the exception of Sigmund Freud, Hans Eysenck may be the most controversial figure to appear in this book. Eysenck is attacked and freely attacks in return. He scorns nonempirical research and he invites controversy in his outspoken statements. However, as Gordon Allport has said, "controversy is the *sine qua non* of psychological progress."

At one time or another, Hans Eysenck has crossed swords with the following: Beezhold, Albino, Luborsky, Hamilton, Karon, Saunders, Rosenzweig, Mowrer, Sheldon, Rokeach, Christie, Wellek, Wyatt, and Else Frenkel-Brunswik. In most of the cases Eysenck's rebuttal has been as sharp as the original attack upon him.

Eysenck's criticisms have centered primarily about projective tests, psychiatrists, Sheldon, nonscientific formulations, psychotherapy, and especially the entire procedure of psychoanalysis. For example, in his attack upon Sheldon (see *J. Ment. Sci.*, 1959, *105*, 1053–1058.), he finds that Sheldon's system is "Unnecessarily complicated, statistically inadequate, and theoretically not well founded." His strong criticism, with an almost passionate emotional appeal that psychotherapy needs methodology, has been repeated a number of times. Eysenck states categorically that psychotherapy is not a science but a loose art form. He feels that acceptable statements about personality must be scientifically established and that if they are not, they are to be relegated to the fields of literature, philosophy, or religion. His criticism of Freudian psychoanalysis is that even if it were able to explain everything, it could predict nothing. In one of the rebuttals to Eysenck's comments, Wyatt, in *Perspectives in Personality Theory* (p. 350) accuses Eysenck of being against psychoanalysis but somehow quite dependent upon it for his original ideas.

Eysenck, like Cattell, also publishes internationally. His work has also been translated into foreign psychological journals. At times, one gains the impression that Eysenck and Cattell seem to be in a race to publish articles. Eysenck has managed to publish approximately ten articles per year in the period from 1950 to 1960. The bibliography which is at the end of this section covers approximately half of his work. Eysenck has visited Cattell at Cattell's laboratory at the University of Illinois. In some ways, because of their statistical interest, the two theorists may be considered to be somewhat alike.

Eysenck through his persistent efforts to create good replicable research has given a refreshing impetus to investigations in the field of personality study. There appears to be an emerging interest in his work, primarily from the statistically oriented psychologists of this country. To date, the primary effect has been in the increase of citations found in texts on personality. With very few exceptions the newer references are highly favorable.

Eysenck considers himself to be a "cautious psychologist" unwilling and unable to make statements unless they are the results of replicable research, statistically controlled, and openly reported.

THE SYSTEM, THEORY, OR ESSENTIAL FEATURES

General Considerations

Eysenck states that it is much too early to have a meaningful, sensible, testable, researchable theory of personality. In his own work he makes no claims to having a full-fledged theory of personality. He also feels that all other workers in this field are premature or faulty in their own theory of personality formation. Eysenck considers the present state of personality theory formulation in general to be primarily descriptive more than concerned with the basic dynamics of human behavior. His own theory, therefore, has been in the descriptive or classification stage.

However, Eysenck has become more and more concerned with the causal or dynamic aspects of behavior in his more recent work. This is especially true in his 1957 book, *The Dynamics of Anxiety and Hysteria* which contains his concepts of learning theory and its application to psychotherapy. As Eysenck wrote to me, ". . . [I] not only abjure Freud and all his works, but have tried to put a *rational* method of diagnosis and treatment in the place of psychoanalysis—i.e., Behavior Therapy. This is an important part of my system."

Eysenck has been influenced by Jung's typology of introversion and extraversion, and also the work of Kretschmer and body or constitutional dimensions. Eysenck is strongly against the proliferation of components in a personality theory. He much favors the parsimonious practicality in theory construction. In any case, theory must always be buttressed by replicable research. To talk about the "whole man" is vague and overly philosophical. He is not against philosophy but does not feel that philosophically couched terms should be called "psychology" or "scientific." There is a need, therefore, to find the dimensions of personality before a theory can be constructed. In working with these dimensions, one must use factor analysis, even though factor analysis may be weak, because no other method appears to be practicable. It is necessary to quantify fundamental facts in the behavioral sciences. Eysenck also wrote to me: "I think you make too much of the factor analytic method in our work; in recent years we have repeated it all using multiple discriminant functions. It has been very welcome to see that this much more respectable method gives very similar results."

In his own work with personality theory, Eysenck insists upon as many variables as it is possible to obtain. Variables such as ratings by self and others, body measurements, galvanometric measurements, biographical data, historical data, and observational reports are all quite necessary to fill out the picture of personality for any one being. In addition to including as many variables as possible in studying personality, Eysenck always tries to get a criterion or a control group that does not have these quantities, or differs from them to a measurable and discrete degree. Then, he feels, one can do research. Consequently, Eysenck almost always works with two groups which are dichotomous in any category such as honesty, dishonesty, cowardice, and courage, which he happens to be studying.

From the above, it is easy to see that Eysenck very much favors the team approach to narrow down the data by the "'hypothetico-deductive" method. He prefers to study personality founded on a hypothetical structure and then, through deductive testing and the use of statistical methods, to arrive at a defensible position with as few components as possible.

Eysenck's definition of personality revolves around four behavior patterns: the cognitive (intelligence), the conative (character), the affective (temperament), and the somatic (constitution). Thus, to Eysenck, personality is "The sum total of the actual or potential behavior-patterns of the organism, as determined by heredity and environment; it originates and develops through the functional interaction of the forming sectors into which these behavior patterns are organized . . ." (*Dimensions of Personality*, p. 25). In the past Eysenck has also considered Allport's famous and oft-repeated definition which Eysenck accepted in his 1953 work, *Structure of Human Personality*. He has also utilized Roback's definition of personality as found in Warren's dictionary (1934): "The integrated organization of all the cognitive, affective, conative, and physical characteristics of an individual as it manifests itself in focal distinctness to others." Inherent in this definition of personality by Eysenck is his belief in the continuity of behavior.

In regard to the idiographic (individual) *vs.* the nomothetic (discovering general laws of behavior), Eysenck states strongly that if personality study is to be a science, it must by its very nature be nomothetic.

Specific Considerations

Whereas Cattell emphasizes traits, Eysenck emphasizes types. Much of the goal of his work has been to identify these types. At times, the types have been defined by what we have generally considered descriptions of traits.

Three Primary Dimensions of Personality. In his work so far, Hans Eysenck has identified three primary dimensions of personality:

Introversion (superego)	Extraversion (id)
Neuroticism	Non-neuroticism
Psychoticism	Non-psychoticism

In most personality systems which deal with deviant behavior the general concept is that of the Gaussian curve or Bell shaped curve. By this device normal subjects distribute themselves at the center with neurotics and psychotics being indicated as the opposite sides. Thus we have a situation as follows.

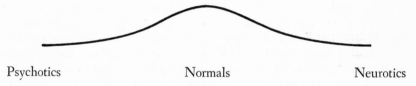

Psychotics   Normals   Neurotics

Other attempts to delineate the differences between psychotics, neurotics, and normals assume a dichotomy in which the normal individual deviates either as a psychotic *or* neurotic in the following manner.

Out of his vast experience and experimentation, Eysenck suggests an original third method of viewing the differences among people who are normal or neurotic or psychotic. The following is a schematic 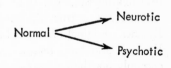 presentation somewhat adapted from the orthogonal concepts first proposed by Eysenck in his *The Scientific Study of Personality* (1952) and later presented in his Maudsley Monograph Number Two, *Perceptual Processes and Mental Illness* (1957, with Granger and Brengelmann).

Thus we see from the preceding that the human personality can move from normal to neurotic, normal to psychotic, and normal to a mixed psychotic–neurotic behavior pattern. Movement can also take place from neurotic through the mixed psychotic–neurotic area and then into straight psychotic behavior without entering the area of normal behavior. The reverse of any of the above movements is, of course, equally possible. Eysenck feels that mixed cases of psychoticism–neuroticism are far more likely to occur than pure psychotic or neurotic behaviors. He feels, as do

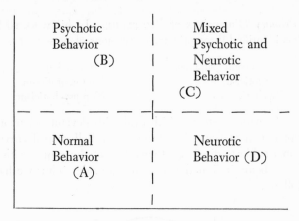

others, that the preponderance of mixed cases "agrees well with clinical experience." Eysenck feels his data now indicate that the "either . . . or" classification method is passé. Rather, an individual is placed on the plane which comes nearest to his true emotional self. Referring once again to the schematic presentation above we can see that person (A) is normal, (B) is psychotic but close to the limits of being a mixed type, (C) is very much at the borderline of being mixed psychotic-neurotic but also close to the outer fringes of normalcy, while (D) is far to the right in the area of true neuroticism. Admittedly the above schema is only a device and not operationally a true phenomena. It does, however, closely approximate Eysenck's original orthogonal relationships drawn from his factorial work. Eysenck also feels that the above three dimensions of personality are certainly not the only possibilities. Further research will certainly uncover more of them. He credits Cattell with the skill to "prospect" for more dimensions.

Other considerations of the three dimensions of personality (introversion–extraversion, psychoticism, and neuroticism) are as follows:

1. Introverts condition better than extraverts via a Hullian or Pavlovian method.

2. All three dimensions of personality are highly resistant to extinction.

3. "I consider introversion–extraversion to be just as much constitutionally determined as neuroticism." [Note to author.]

4. Some of Eysenck's recent studies with drugs (meprobamate, chlorpromazine, dextro-amphetamine, and sodium amytal) support the postulate that, "Depressant drugs increase cortical inhibition, decrease cortical excitation and thereby produce extraverted behavior patterns," while conversely "Stimulant drugs decrease cortical inhibition, increase cortical excitation and thereby produce introverted behavior patterns" (*Dynamics of Anxiety and Hysteria*, p. 31).

5. Despite the opinion Eysenck strongly holds that much of the research in drug effects on behavior is loose, divergent, and incompetent, he does feel that there may be worth-while results in studying the hypothesis that a stimulant drug will increase neuroticism while a depressant drug will decrease neuroticism. In line with some studies Eysenck is also interested in the hypothesis that tranquilizers will have a "depsychoticizing action." He feels much work is to be done in this area before any true results can be recognized.

Primarily through the study of identical twins, Eysenck concludes that neuroticism may have a constitutional basis or may be based upon heredity as a factor. For example, using self-devised instruments and tests for measuring neuroticism, Eysenck found a correlation of .85 between neurotic behavior and nonneurotic behavior in identical twins, while in fraternal twins the correlation was only .21.

The outline that follows is a very short summary of some of the factor analysis and type and trait work which Eysenck has been pursuing in the past ten to fifteen years.

Eysenck's Factors	*Personality Factors*	*Political Correlates*
General factor (high importance)	Type (constellation of traits)	Ideology
Group factor	Traits (consistent habits)	Attitude
Specific factor	Habitual responses (reoccur in similar circumstances)	Habitual opinion
Error factor (low importance)	Specific responses (one single act)	Specific opinion

On the left side of the above outline are Eysenck's categories, drawn from factor analysis and employing somewhat the work of C. L. Burt in *Factors of the Mind*. Eysenck has discovered four kinds of factors through his factor analysis work: the general, the group, the specific, and the error factors. In the center of the outline above are the four comparable personality factors. The personality types grew out of his general factors. It may be remembered that the personality types were introversion–extroversion, neuroticism–non-neuroticism, and psychoticism–non-psychoticism. Traits grew out of the group factors. Eysenck makes a strong point that traits must be operationally defined and capable of being measured. He finds that traits are approximate to consistent habits of behavior. Specific factors grow out of habitual responses which are behavioral acts and which reoccur in similar circumstances. Error factors that he finds in his work which are the lowest in importance grow out of specific responses to any single act and cannot be used with a great degree of accuracy in the discussion of personality or personality theory.

One of Eysenck's most recent interests, among many interests, is to link learning theory with what he has called *behavior therapy*. In the *Behavior Therapy and the Neuroses* (1960), which he edited and supplied with two chapters, "Learning theory and behavior therapy," and "Modern learning theory" Eysenck interestingly enough dedicates the book, "To the memory of J. B. Watson." The gist of Eysenck's position is that "neurotic symptoms are *learned patterns of behavior*" which apparently become "*unadaptive;*" but it may be possible to uncondition that which was once conditioned: neurotic symptoms. He feels compelled to utilize learning theory in restructuring human behavior because psychotherapeutic techniques, whether Freudian or neo-Freudian, have long since come to a blind alley, despite 50 or more years of trial. Because Freudianism is inconsistent, generates no testable deductions, he feels it is time to examine human behavior and its derivations within the full framework of learning theory. As his theoretical models he uses the theories of Pavlov, Thorndike, Tolman, Guthrie, and Hull. Eysenck also pays tribute to the work of Miller and Mowrer, Spence, Wolpe, and pays a special tribute to Watson. In summary, then, we find that Eysenck states: "Once we are agreed that learning and conditioning are instrumental in determining the different kinds of reaction we may wake to environmental stimulation, we will find it very difficult to deny that neurotic reactions, like all others, are *learned* reactions and must obey the laws of learning" (*ibid.*, p. 5. Italics in the original). And again at the end of this book, "We have, then, the beginnings of a genuinely scientific system of learning theory from which we can deduce certain methods of treatment for behavioral disorders" (*ibid.*, p. 466).

In *The Psychology of Politics* (1954) Eysenck stated that he had found political correlates in the four kinds of factors growing out of his work. The general factor seemed to him to be an ideology, the group factor an attitude, the specific factor an habitual opinion, and the error factor any kind of specific opinion, regarding a political situation.

Summary

Eysenck, like Cattell, makes frequent use of the statistical technique of factor analysis. However, he does not feel it is too strong a tool. Eysenck denies the crucial significance of individuality in favor of a nomothetic approach. He feels self should not be considered as overly important in the study of personality. He also gives a heavy emphasis to the role of heredity because of his study of fraternal and identical twins. There are relatively few motivational concepts in Eysenck's theory, because he prefers the parsimonious approach. In the last analysis, Eysenck is a tremendous generator of research on his own theory. He does not consider a theory of personality to have emerged yet from his own work or the work of anyone else.

DELIMITATION

The reader has but to look at the enormous bibliography, only parts of which are included in this book, to discover that much has been omitted in the work of Hans Eysenck. Among the many things omitted are his work on the Maudsley Medical Questionnaire, the Rees-Eysenck Body Index, all of his many contributions to the factor analytic methods of measuring personality through criterion analysis, and a number of his interesting rebuttals and counterrebuttals on the work of others.

BIBLIOGRAPHY

Primary Sources

BOOKS

Eysenck, H. J., *Dimensions of Personality*, London, Routledge, 1947.

Eysenck, H. J., *The Scientific Study of Personality*, N.Y., Macmillan, 1952. Sequel to *Dimensions of Personality*, 1947.

Eysenck, H. J., *Uses and Abuses of Psychology*, Baltimore, Md., Penguin, 1953.

Eysenck, H. J., *The Structure of Human Personality*, N.Y., Wiley, 1953.

Eysenck, H. J., *The Psychology of Politics*, London, Routledge, 1954. Also published by N.Y., Frederick A. Praeger, 1955.

Eysenck, H. J., *Psychology and the Foundations of Psychiatry*, London, H. K. Lewis & Co., 1955.

Eysenck, H. J., *Sense and Nonsense in Psychology*, Baltimore, Md., Penguin, 1957.

Eysenck, H. J., Characterology, stratification theory and psychotherapy: An evaluation, in H. P. David, and H. von Bracken (eds.), *Perspectives in Personality Theory*, N.Y., Basic Books, 1957, 323–335.

Eysenck, H. J., *The Dynamics of Anxiety and Hysteria: An Experimental Application of Modern Learning Theory to Psychiatry*, N.Y., Frederick A. Praeger, 1957.

Eysenck, H. J., E. W. Granger, and J. C. Brengelmann, *Perceptual Processes in Mental Illness*, N.Y., Basic Books, 1957.

Eysenck, H. J., Personality Tests: 1950–1959, in G. W. T. H. Fleming, and A. Walk (eds.), *Recent Progress in Psychiatry, Vol. III*, N.Y., Grove Press, 1959.

Eysenck, H. J. (ed.), *Experiments in Personality*, 2 Vols., London, Routledge, 1959.

Eysenck, H. J., A rational system of diagnosis and therapy in mental illness, in L. E. Abt, and B. F. Riess (eds.), *Progress in Clinical Psychology, Vol. IV*, N.Y., Grune and Stratton, 1960.

Eysenck, H. J. (ed.), *Behavior Therapy and the Neuroses*, London, Pergamon, 1960.

Eysenck, H. J., Drug postulates, theoretical deductions, and methodological considerations, in L. Uhr, and J. G. Miller (eds.), *Drugs and Behavior*, N.Y., Wiley, 1960.

Eysenck, H. J. (ed.), *Handbook of Abnormal Psychology: An Experimental Approach*, N.Y., Basic Books, 1961.

PERIODICALS

Eysenck, H. J., Type-factors in aesthetic judgment, *Brit. J. Psychol.*, 1941, *31*, 262–270.

Eysenck, H. J., Some factors in the appreciation of poetry and their relation to temperamental qualities, *Char. & Pers.*, 1941, *9*, 160–167.

Eysenck, H. J., Suggestibility and hysteria, *J. Neurol. Psychiat.*, 1943, *6*, 22–31.

Eysenck, H. J., Suggestibility and hypnosis—an experimental analysis, *Proc. Royal Soc. Med.*, 1943, *36*, 349–354.

Eysenck, H. J., States of high suggestibility and the neuroses, *Amer. J. Psychol.*, 1944, *57*, 406–411.

Himmelweit, H. T., and H. J. Eysenck, An experimental analysis of the mosaic projection test, *Brit. J. Med. Psychol.*, 1945, *20*, 283–294.

Eysenck, H. J., Graphological analysis and psychiatry: An experimental study, *Brit. J. Psychol.*, 1945, *35*, 70–81.

Eysenck, H. J., and W. D. Furneaux, Primary and secondary suggestibility: and experimental and statistical study, *J. Exp. Psychol.*, 1945, *35*, 485–502.

Eysenck, H. J., and W. L. Rees, States of heightened suggestibility: narcosis, *J. Ment. Sci.*, 1945, *91*, 301–310.

Eysenck, H. J., Primary social attitudes: I. the organization and measurement of social attitudes, *Int. J. Opin. Attitude Res.*, 1947, *1*, 49–84.

Eysenck, H. J., 'Neuroticism' and handwriting, *J. Abnorm. Soc. Psychol.*, 1948, *43*, 94–96.

Eysenck, H. J., Schizothymia–Cyclothymia as a dimension of personality: I. Historical, *J. Person.*, 1950, *19*, 123–152.

Eysenck, H. J., Criterion analysis: An application of the hypothetico–deductive method to factor analysis, *Psychol. Rev.*, 1950, *57*, 38–53.

Eysenck, H. J., Psychology Department, Institute of Psychiatry (Maudsley Hospital), University of London, *Acta. Psychol.*, 1951, *8*, 63–68.

Eysenck, H. J., Neuroticism in twins, *Eugen. Rev.*, 1951, *43*, 79–82.

Eysenck, H. J., and D. B. Prell, The inheritance of neuroticism: An experimental study, *J. Ment. Sci.*, 1951, *97*, 441–465.

Eysenck, H. J., Personality, *Ann. Rev. Psychol.*, 1952, *3*, 151–174.

Eysenck, H. J., The effects of psychotherapy: An evaluation, *J. Consult. Psychol.*, 1952, *16*, 319–324.

Eysenck, H. J., The organization of personality, *J. Person.*, 1952, *20*, 101–118.

Eysenck, H. J., Schizothymia–cyclothymia as a dimension of personality: II. Experimental, *J. Pers.*, 1952, *20*, 345–384.

Eysenck, H. J., The logical basis of factor analysis, *Amer. Psychologist*, 1953, *8*, 105–114.

Eysenck, H. J., The application of factor analysis to the study of personality:

A reply, *Brit. J. Psychol.*, 1953, *44*, 169–172.

Eysenck, H. J., A reply to Luborsky's note, *Brit. J. Psychol.*, 1954, *45*, 132–133.

Eysenck, H. J., The science of personality: Nomothetic!, *Psychol. Rev.*, 1954, *61*, 339–342.

Eysenck, H. J., Cortical inhibition, figural after-effect, and theory of personality, *J. Abnorm. Soc. Psychol.*, 1955, *51*, 94–106.

Eysenck, H. J., The effects of psychotherapy: A reply, *J. Abnorm. Soc. Psychol.*, 1955, *50*, 147–148.

Eysenck, H. J., A dynamic theory of anxiety and hysteria, *J. Ment. Sci.*, 1955, *101*, 28–51.

Eysenck, H. J., Psychology, philosophy, and psychoanalysis, *Manasi*, 1955, *2*, 1–6.

Eysenck, H. J., Psychiatric diagnosis as a psychological and statistical problem, *Psychol. Rep.*, 1955, *1*, 3–17.

Eysenck, H. J., The inheritance of extraversion–introversion, *Acta Psychol.*, 1956, *12*, 95–110.

Eysenck, H. J., The inheritance and nature of extraversion, *Eugen. Rev.*, 1956, *48*, 23–30.

Eysenck, H. J., Reminiscence, drive, and personality theory, *J. Abnorm. Soc. Psychol.*, 1956, *53*, 328–333.

Eysenck, H. J., The psychology of politics: A reply, *Psychol. Bull.*, 1956, *53*, 177–182.

Eysenck, H. J., The psychology of politics and personality: Similarities between fascists and communists, *Psychol. Bull.*, 1956, *53*, 431–438.

Eysenck, H. J., Diagnosis and measurement: A reply to Loevinger, *Psychol. Rep.*, 1956, *2*, 117–118.

Eysenck, H. J., Drugs and personality: I. Theory and methodology, *J. Ment. Sci.*, 1957, *103*, 119–131.

Eysenck, H. J., S. Casey, and D. S. Trouton, Drugs and personality: II. The effect of stimulant and depressant drugs on continuous work, *J. Ment. Sci.*, 1957, *103*, 645–649.

Eysenck, H. J., H. Holland, and D. S. Trouton, Drugs and personality: III. the effects of depressant and stimulant drugs on visual aftereffects, *J. Ment. Sci.*, 1957, *103*, 650–655.

Eysenck, H. J., H. Holland, and D. S. Trouton, Drugs and personality: IV. The effects of stimulant and depressant drugs on the rate of fluctuation of a reversible perspective figure, *J. Ment. Sci.*, 1957, *103*, 656–660.

Eysenck, H. J., and S. Aiba, Drugs and personality: V. The effects of stimulant and depressant drugs on the suppression of the primary visual stimulus, *J. Ment. Sci.*, 1957, *103*, 661–665.

Eysenck, H. J., and P. Slater, Effects of practice and rest on fluctuations in the Müller-Lyer illusion, *Brit. J. Psychol.*, 1958, *49*, 246–256.

Eysenck, H. J., Hysterics and dysthymics as criterion groups in the study of introversion–extraversion: A reply, *J. Abnorm. Soc. Psychol.*, 1958, *57*, 250–252.

Eysenck, H. J., A short questionnaire for the measurement of two dimensions of personality, *J. Appl. Psychol.*, 1958, *42*, 14–17.

Eysenck, H. J., The continuity of abnormal and normal behavior, *Psychol. Bull.*, 1958, *55*, 429–432.

Eysenck, H. J., The nature of anxiety and the factorial method, *Psychol. Rep.*, 1958, *4*, 453–454.

Eysenck, H. J., Anxiety and hysteria: A reply to Vernon Hamilton, *Brit. J. Psychol.*, 1959, *50*, 64–69.

Eysenck, H. J., The differentiation between normal and various neurotic groups on the Maudsley Personality Inventory, *Brit. J. Psychol.*, 1959, *50*, 176–177.

Eysenck, H. J., Serial position effects in nonsense syllable learning as a function of interlist rest pauses, *Brit. J. Psychol.*, 1959, *50*, 360–362.

Eysenck, H. J., Learning theory and behavior therapy, *J. Ment. Sci.*, 1959, *105*, 61–75.

Eysenck, H. J., The inheritance of neuroticism: A reply, *J. Ment. Sci.*, 1959, *105*, 76–80.

Eysenck, H. J., Some recent criticisms of the dimensional analysis of personality, *J. Ment. Sci.*, 1959, *105*, 220–223.

Eysenck, H. J., The Rees-Eysenck body index and Sheldon's somatotype system, *J. Ment. Sci.*, 1959, *105*, 1053–1058.

Eysenck, H. J., Personality and the dimension of time, *Percept. Mont. Skills*, 1959, *9*, 405–406.

Eysenck, H. J., Personality and problem solving, *Psychol. Rep.*, 1959, *5*, 592.

Eysenck, H. J., Levels of personality, constitutional factors, and social influences: an experimental approach, *Int. J. Soc. Psychiat.*, 1960, *6*, 12–24.

Singh, S. D., and H. J. Eysenck, Conditioned emotional response in the rat: III. Drug antagonism, *J. Gen. Psychol.*, 1960, *63*, 275–285.

Eysenck, S. B. G., H. J. Eysenck, and G. Claridge, Dimensions of personality, psychiatric syndromes, and mathematical models, *J. Ment. Sci.*, 1960, *106*, 581–589.

Eysenck, H. J. and J. A. Easterbrook, Drugs and personality: VI–XI, *J. Ment. Sci.*, 1960, *106*, 831–857.

Eysenck, H. J., Reminiscence, extraversion, and neuroticism, *Percept, Mot. Skills*, 1960, *11*, 21–22.

Eysenck, H. J., Reminiscence as a function of rest, practice and personality, *Percept. Mot. Skills*, 1960, *11*, 91–94.

Eysenck, H. J., and H. Holland, Length of spiral after-effect as a function of drive, *Percept. Mot. Skills*, 1960, *11*, 129–130.

Eysenck, H. J., Reminsicence and post-rest increment after massed practice, *Percept. Mot. Skills*, 1960, *11*, 221–222.

Holland, H., and H. J. Eysenck, Spiral after-effects as a function of length of stimulation, *Percept. Mot. Skills*, 1960, *11*, 228.

Eysenck, H. J., The concept of statistical significance and the controversy about one-tailed tests, *Psychol. Rev.*, 1960, *67*, 269–271.

Eysenck, H. J., Psychosis, drive and inhibition: a theoretical and experimental account, *Am. J. Psychiat.*, 1961, *118*, 198–204.

Eysenck, H. J., and A. E. Maxwell, Reminiscence as a function drive, *Brit. J. Psychol.*, 1961, *52*, 43–52.

Eysenck, H. J., A note on "Impulse Repression and Emotional Adjustment," *J. Consult. Psychol.*, 1961, *25*(4), 362–363.
 Critique of Grater's work with morals and the MMPI in 1960 (see *Psych. Abst., 34*, 8202).

Eysenck, H. J., The measurement of motivation through the use of objective indices, *J. Ment. Sci.*, 1961, *107*, 961–968.

Eysenck, H. J., Personality and social attitudes, *J. Soc. Psychol.*, 1961, *53*, 243–248.

Lynn, R., and H. J. Eysenck, Tolerance for pain, extraversion, and neuroticism, *Percept. Mot. Skills*, 1961, *12*, 161–162.

Costello, C. G., and H. J. Eysenck, Persistence, personality, and motivation, *Percept. Mot. Skills*, 1961, *12*, 169–170.

Eysenck, H. J., Conditioning and personality, *Brit. J. Psychol.*, 1962, *53*(3), 299–305.
 Defends self against criticisms by Champion.

Eysenck, H. J., Response set, authoritarianism and personality questionnaires, *Brit. J. Soc. Clin. Psychol.*, 1962, *1*(1), 20–24.

Eysenck, H. J., Reminiscence, drive and personality: revision and extension of a theory, *Brit. J. Soc. Clin. Psychol.*, 1962, *1*(2), 127–140.
 Summary of 20 studies on extraversion and introversion.

Eysenck, H. J., and G. Claridge, The position of hysterics and dysthymics in a two-dimensional framework of personality description, *J. Abnorm. Soc. Psychol.*, 1962, *64*, 46–55.
 Statistical proof of his theory.

Willett, R. A., and H. J. Eysenck, Experimentally induced drive and difficulty level in serial rote learning, *Brit. J. Psychol.*, 1962, *53*, 35–39.

Eysenck, S. B. G. and H. J. Eysenck, Rigidity as a function of introversion and neuroticism: a study of unmarried mothers, *Int. J. Soc. Psychiat.*, 1962, *8*(3), 180–184.

Eysenck, H. J., Behavior therapy, extinction, and relapse in neurosis, *Brit. J. Psychiat.*, 1963, *109*, 12–18.

Eysenck, H. J., Psychoticism or ten psychotic syndromes? *J. Consult. Psychol.*, 1963, *27*(2), 179.

SUGGESTED READINGS

BOOKS

Burt, C. L., *Factors of the Mind*, N.Y., Macmillan, 1941.

Bonner, H., *Psychology of Personality*, N.Y., Ronald, 1961.

Guilford, J. P., *Personality*, N.Y., McGraw-Hill, 1959.

    The factor analytic approach to personality.

Hall, C. S., and Lindzey, G., *Theories of Personality*, N.Y., Wiley, 1957, 381–393.

PERIODICALS

Albino, R. C., Some criterion of the application of factor analysis to the study of personality, *Brit. J. Psychol.*, 1953, *44*, 164–168.

Biggs, J. B., The relation of neuroticism and extraversion to intelligence and educational attainment, *Brit. J. Educ. Psychol.*, 1962, *32*(2), 188–195.

    Criticizes Eysenck's theory of conditionability.

Carrigan, P. M., Extraversion–introversion as a dimension of personality: a reappraisal, *Psychol. Bull.*, 1960, *57*, 329–360.

Christie, R., Eysenck's treatment of the personality of communists, *Psychol. Bull.*, 1956, *53*, 411–430.

Christie, R., Some abuses of psychology, *Psychol. Bull.*, 1956, *53*, 439–451.

    Eysenck is guilty.

Dowdy, C. D., An experimental test of Eysenck's and Cattell's theories of extraversion–introversion, *Dissertation Abst.*, 1960, *20*, 3376, (abstract).

Granger, E. W., Eysenck's theory of anxiety and hysteria and the results of visual adaptation experiments, *Acta Psychol.*, 1957, *3*, 98–126.

Guilford, J. P., When not to factor analyze, *Psychol. Bull.*, 1952, *49*, 26–37.

Jensen, A. R., The Maudsley Personality Inventory, *Acta Psychol.*, 1958, *4*, 314–325.

    Good questionnaire for intro-extraversion and neuroticism.

Jones, H. G., Inhibition: a symposium, IV. Individual differences in inhibitory potential, *Brit. J. Psychol.*, 1960, *51*, 220–225.

    Eysenck's theory may have to be modified.

Luborsky, L., A note on Eysenck's article, "The effects of psychotherapy: An evaluation," *Brit. J. Psychol.*, 1954, *45*, 129–131.

Lynn, R., Comments on the article by J. B. Biggs, *Brit. J. Educ. Psychol.*, 1962, *32*(2), 196–199.

    States that Biggs misunderstands Eysenck's theory.

Lynn, R., and J. Butler, Introversion and the arousal jag, *Brit. J. Soc. Clin. Psychol.*, 1962, *1*, 150–151.
> Supports Eysenck's theory.

Lynn, R., and I. E. Gordon, The relation of neuroticism and extraversion to intelligence and educational attainment, *Brit. J. Educ. Psychol.*, 1961, *31*, 194–203.
> Five of Eysenck's predictions statistically significant.

McDonell, C. R., and J. Inglis, Verbal conditioning and personality, *Psychol. Rep.*, 1962, *10*(2), 374.
> Fails to support Eysenck's theory.

Parnell, R. W., The Rees-Eysenck body index of individual somatotypes, *J. Ment. Sci.*, 1957, *103*, 209–213.

Rokeach, M., and C. Hanley, Eysenck's tendermindedness dimension: A critique, *Psychol. Bull.*, 1956, *53*, 169–176.

Rosenzweig, S., A transvaluation of psychotherapy: A reply to Hans Eysenck, *J. Abnorm. Soc. Psychol.*, 1954, *49*, 298–304.

Wells, W. D., H. E. Egeth, and N. P. Wray, An American application of Eysenck's short neuroticism and extraversion scales, *J. Appl. Psychol.*, 1961, *45*, 271–272.
> Scales were uncorrelated when applied to 180 American housewives.

---◆---

LEARNING [Mowrer]

*An imperfectly denatured animal intermittently
subject to the unpredictable reactions of an
unlocated, spiritual area.*

RUDYARD KIPLING
Surgeons and the Soul (Definition of Man)

SOME BIOGRAPHICAL DATA[1]

Orval Hobart Mowrer was born on January 23, 1907 in Unionville, Missouri. He received his A.B. from the University of Missouri in 1929 and his Ph.D. from Johns Hopkins University in 1932. On September 9,

[1] I am grateful to Dr. Mowrer for his suggestions regarding the preparation of this chapter.

1931, he married Willie Mae Cook. They have three children: Linda, Kathryn and Todd. Mowrer was a National Research Fellow at both Northwestern (1932–1933) and Princeton (1933–1934). He spent the years from 1934 to 1940 at Yale as a Sterling Fellow (1934–1936) and as an instructor in psychology and a member of the staff at the Institute of Human Relations (1936–1940). From 1940 to 1948 he was assistant professor, then associate professor of education at Harvard. Since leaving Harvard in 1948 he has been research professor at the University of Illinois. Mowrer is a fellow of the American Orthopsychiatric Association, the American Psychology Association (president, 1953–1954), and the A.A.A.S. He is a member of the American Academy of Psychotherapists, the Linguistic Society of America, the American Association of University Professors, and Sigma Xi. Mowrer was the recipient of the Certificate of Merit from the University of Missouri. He has served as clinical psychologist for the O.S.S. and acts as special consultant at the USPHS. While at Harvard he edited the *Harvard Educational Review*.

INTRODUCTION

As we have previously stated, there are many excellent learning theorists whose theories could be included in this section. We have chosen to use Mowrer's work because it seems to be more general in nature and possibly more adaptable to a general theory of behavior than are the others.

O. Hobart Mowrer is an original thinker. Some of his work is in the vein of Miller-Dollard. The versatility of Mowrer can be seen in his rat work, his work on enuresis, psychoanalysis, anthropology and culture, language, his primary work in learning theory, and his current work in religion and morality. Mowrer is also a product of Yale University's Institute of Human Relations. Mowrer is not the only learning theorist who has left laboratory work with animals to work with people. However, Mowrer seems to have extended his theories further than have some of the others.

THE SYSTEM, THEORY, OR ESSENTIAL FEATURES

General Considerations

Mowrer began, as did many learning theorists, primarily within the framework of reinforcement theory and secondary drives. However, as early as 1947, he moved over into a two factor theory which he considered to be integrative or dualistic. In Mowrer's own words he gave up trying to "squeeze" all behavior into one system. Essentially his learning theory is mediated by states of hope and fear within the organism. Originally his learning theory work was approximately in the tradition of the associationist theoretical school.

Almost all of Mowrer's work is empirically oriented. There is not much that is allied to many previous theories. Although Mowrer was a former Hullian, he deviates considerably from the Hullian position. Also after his early experience with analysis, Mowrer deviated from the Freudian concepts of pleasure principle and reality principle. However, Mowrer has taken a genuine research interest in proving or disproving Freud's pleasure principle and reality principle in the framework of an empirical approach.

Mowrer's definition of personality grows out of three areas of endeavor: 1. learning theory; 2. social anthropology or cultural differences; and 3. psychoanalysis. Probably the best definition comes from the chapter of Mowrer and Kluckhohn, A Dynamic Theory of Personality (in J. Mc-Vickers Hunt's, *Personality and the Behavior Disorders, Vol. I.*, 1944) The coauthors used four criteria in defining *personality*. The four criteria must be considered to be integrated in the action of any individual. They are as follows: "(1) The meaning or *function*, which an individual's actions have for him, (2) the *conflicts* which exist between his various habit systems, (3) The environment or *field* to which he is accustomed, and (4) The more or less unique way in which he is held together, or *integrated*. These four criteria, derived from the four basic assumptions of dynamic theory, thus provide a comprehensive scheme for defining 'personality' in general and for identifying any 'personality' in particular" (p. 77).

Out of this framework, as we shall see later, Mowrer defines a two-factor learning theory which concerns itself with solution learning and sign learning. These he feels have a strong bearing upon personality and upon an individual's behavior.

Mowrer also considers that an individual's personality may continue and even grow for years after his death. This obviously would be carried over as a reputation and does not mean an interacting personality. He cites, for example, painters, poets, writers, others who are being discovered and rediscovered, whose personalities in the interpersonal sense, continue to grow and develop despite the individual's death.

As previously stated, Mowrer has extended some of Freud's ideas. For example, he finds that in neurotic behavior, the id is equivalent to primary drives, the ego equivalent to solution learning, and the superego equivalent to sign learning.

Specific Considerations

Mowrer's learning theory, which he finds adaptable to personality study, involves both reinforcement and contiguity. Reinforcement has and probably will continue to have innumerable meanings, but generally it means "a strengthening of a response, whether the response is positive or negative." *Contiguity* means to Mowrer "a nearness of two objects in time or space," but it also means "a nearness of two experiences for the same organism or the human personality."

The following outline is an attempt to summarize some of the more pertinent and outstanding features in Mowrer's two-factor learning theory.

SOLUTION LEARNING	SIGN LEARNING
1. Problem solving	1. Problem making
2. Drive reducing	2. Creates expectation or predispositions or a belief or set to act
3. Pleasure giving	3. Secondary drives and emotions—relate or connect to new objects—so new problems exist to be solved which were not in the original organism.
4. Autonomic nervous system involved (contiguity)	4. Central nervous system involved (Law of Effect)
5. Closely allied to instrumental learning	5. Goes beyond S–R bonds into cognition or learning meanings, attitudes, and sets.
6. Relates to reinforcement	6. Relates to contiguity
7. Requires reward or pleasure	7. Does not require rewards but relates to higher processes (language and symbolic learning, for example)
8. Life in the past or present	8. Life in the present or future

In some of his recent work, Mowrer has reintroduced the concept of habit into his two-factor theory (see especially chap. 7, "Revised two-factor theory and the concept of habit," in *Learning Theory and Behavior*, 1960). The sequel to this tome is his 1960 work, *Learning Theory and the*

Symbolic Processes. In actuality each book is a companion piece to the other and could almost be read concurrently.

Essentially Mowrer is saying that the human language (symbolic processes) is learned much in the same manner as the responses of primary-drive reduction. Thus, producing responses is equally as important in personality formation as reducing primary drives. The former concept (response production) relies heavily upon hope and fear within the organism. This extension of the former two-factor theory involves a newer viewpoint of the age-old concept of habit. In regard to synaptic connections Mowrer goes on to say, " . . . revised two-factor theory assumes that so-called habit formulation involves a strengthening of synapses between the neurones' *connecting stimuli produced by some behavioral act and the emotion of hope* and that punishment involves a similar conditioning of fear": i.e., you (the organism) hope to gain the reward or hope to avoid pain (*Learning Theory and Behavior*, p. 220 ff. Italics in the original). In this way the neural connections involved in a habit formulation are not inflexible and set. In summary, then, we find Mowrer stating after precautionary recognition, "In advancing a feedback conception of both response inhibition (punishment) and response facilitation (habit), we have emancipated behavior theory from what may be called the 'bondage' of Thorndike's scheme and also liberated it from the crass reflexology of Pavlov" (*ibid.*, p. 251).

In his book, *The Crisis in Psychiatry and Religion* (1961), O. Hobart Mowrer makes an extremely intriguing side trip into the area of abnormal behavior and religious values. The book is a collection of published papers and lectures. Although Mowrer acknowledges a "major objective" in this collection as being an attempt to delineate the religious from the psychiatric, so that each can proceed at its own task, there is no major thesis or thread in the book. The following represents merely a random selection of salient points.

1. Biological adaptation and survival do not help us much in solving problems of psychological survival; or, how can the body best serve the mind?

2. Psychoanalysis (which Mowrer feels is on the way out as a therapy and a personality theory) and its approach to psychoneurosis implies no sense of moral responsibility. At some point, we must abandon mental "sickness" as a pessimistic approach and think also about deviant behavior and responsibility for self-action as "sin" on account of its implication

of promise and hope. (Needless to say this idea has created a thundering chorus of denial and rebuttal in the American psychological world. It is *not* popular to use the word "sin" in this country.)

3. Guilt (not just guilt feelings) is a real aspect of disturbed persons. They "are not 'disturbed' for nothing."

4. The pastoral counseling movement usurped its peripheral function and took over the whole show mainly through the overzealous acceptance of psychoanalysis and nondirective frames of reference. Theology took a back seat to therapy in seminary and in pastoral duties.

The above four points are only a small sampling of Mowrer's text, advancing the hypothesis that mental illness has a moral basis.

Summary

In summarizing the work of O. Hobart Mowrer, we find his theory not as complete as some of the others. The theory does branch out from the two-factor learning theory with Freudian and cultural overtones. The main theme seems to be in solution learning and sign learning, and in revising his two-factor learning theory to include the states of hope and fear within the organism in an expansion of the Thorndikian habit position. The solution and sign learning systems appear to be basically different from each other. However, they are both involved in any single human being. We also find that Mowrer has moved from laboratory work with animals to people, language, and, especially currently, morals.

DELIMITATION

The current treatment of Mowrer's work omits much of his work which was done with rats. Also his work on enuresis and language as "tension indexes" and especially his experiences in psychoanalysis have been omitted. We also have not mentioned the work that Mowrer and Sears and many others did in 1939 on frustration leading toward aggression. Mowrer continues, however, to expand his theory primarily from the framework of the learning theorist.

BIBLIOGRAPHY

PRIMARY SOURCES

BOOKS

Dollard, J., L. W. Doob, N. E. Miller, O. H. Mowrer, and R. R. Sears, *Frustration and Aggression*, New Haven, Conn., Yale Univer. Press, 1939.

Mowrer, O. H., and C. Kluckhohn, Dynamic theory of personality, in J. McV. Hunt (ed.), *Personality and the Behavior Disorders*, N.Y., Ronald, 1944, Chap. 3.

Mowrer, O. H., *Learning Theory and Personality Dynamics*, N.Y., Ronald, 1950.

Mowrer, O. H., Neurosis and its treatment as learning phenomena, in D. Brower, and L. E. Abt (eds.), *Progress in Clinical Psychology*, Vol. I, N.Y., Grune and Stratton, 1952, 312–323.
Neurosis is essentially a problem of moral failure.

Kluckhohn, C., and O. H. Mowrer, Determinants and components of personality, in A. Weider, (ed.), *Contributions Toward Medical Psychology*, N.Y., Ronald, 1953.

Mowrer, O. H., Motivation and neurosis, in J. S. Brown, and others, *Current Theory and Research in Motivation: A Symposium*, Lincoln, Nebr., Univer. Nebraska Press, 1953, 162–164.

Mowrer, O. H. (ed.), *Psychotherapy: Theory and Research*, N.Y., Ronald, 1953.

Mowrer, O. H., Emerging conceptions of neurosis and normality, in L. K. Hsu (ed.), *Aspects of Culture and Personality*, N.Y., Abelard-Schuman, 1954, 119–138.

Mowrer, O. H., Ego psychology, cybernetics, and learning theory, *Learning Theory, Personality Theory and Clinical Research: Kentucky Symposium*, N.Y., Wiley, 1954, 81–90.

Mowrer, O. H., Symposium remarks on re-evaluation in the social sciences, in *Academy of Religion* and *Mental Health Religion, Science and Mental Health*, N.Y., N.Y. Univer. Press, 1959.

Mowrer, O. H., *Learning Theory and Behavior*, N.Y., Wiley, 1960.

Mowrer, O. H., *Learning Theory and the Symbolic Processes*, N.Y., Wiley, 1960.

Mowrer, O. H., Footnotes to a theory of psychopathology, in L. E. Abt, and B. F. Riess (eds.), *Progress in Clinical Psychology*, Vol. IV, N.Y., Grune & Stratton, 1960.

Mowrer, O. H., *The Crisis in Psychiatry and Religion*, N.J., Van Nostrand, 1961.

Mowrer, O. H., in *Reinforcement: An Enduring Problem in Psychology—Selected Readings*, in R. C. Birney, and R. C. Teevan (eds.), N.J., Van Nostrand, 1961.

Mowrer, O. H., *The New Group Therapy*, N.J., Van Nostrand, 1963.

PERIODICALS

Mowrer, O. H., and W. M. Mowrer, Enuresis—a method for its study and treatment, *Amer. J. Orthopsychiat.*, 1938, 8, 436–459.

Mowrer, O. H., Apparatus for the study and treatment of enuresis, *Amer. J. Psychol.*, 1938, 51, 163–165.

Mowrer, O. H., A stimulus-response analysis of anxiety and its role as a reinforcing agent, *Psychol. Rev.*, 1939, 46, 553–565.

Mowrer, O. H., An experimental analogue of "regression" with incidental observations on "reaction formation," *J. Abnorm. Soc. Psychol.*, 1940, 35, 56–87.

Mowrer, O. H., Anxiety reduction and learning, *J. Exp. Psychol.*, 1940, 27, 497–516.

Mowrer, O. H., and R. R. Lamoreaux, Avoidance conditioning and signal duration: A study of secondary motivation and reward, *Psychol. Monogr.*, 1942, 54, No. 5.

Mowrer, O. H., and H. Jones, Extinction and behavior variability as a function of the effortfulness of task, *J. Exp. Psychol.*, 1943, 33, 369–386.

Whiting, J. W. M., and O. H. Mowrer, Habit progression and regression: A laboratory study of some factors relevant to human socialization, *J. Comp. Psychol.*, 1943, 36, 229–253.

Mowrer, O. H., and C. Kluckhohn, Personality and culture: A conceptual scheme, *Amer. Anthrop.*, 1944, 46, 1–29.

Mowrer, O. H., and P. Viek, Language and learning: An experimental paradigm, *Harv. Educ. Rev.*, 1945, 15, 35–48.

Mowrer, O. H., The law of effect and ego psychology, *Psychol. Rev.*, 1946, 53, 321–334.

Mowrer, O. H., and R. R. Lamoreaux, Fear as an intervening variable in avoidance conditioning, *J. Comp. Psychol.*, 1946, 39, 29–50.

Dollard, J., and O. H. Mowrer, A method of measuring tension in written documents, *J. Abnorm. Soc. Psychol.*, 1947, 42, 3–32.

Mowrer, O. H., On the dual nature of learning: A reinterpretation of "conditioning" and "problem solving," *Harv. Educ. Rev.*, 1947, 17, 102–148.

Mowrer, O. H., Learning theory and the neurotic paradox, *Amer. J. Orthopsychiat.*, 1948, 18, 571–610.

Mowrer, O. H., Biological versus moral "frustration" in personality disturbances, *Progressive Educ.*, 1949, 26, 65–69.

Mowrer, O. H., Two-factor learning theory: Summary and comment, *Psychol. Rev.*, 1951, 58, 350–354.

Mowrer, O. H., Speech development in the young child: I. The autism theory of speech development and some clinical applications, *J. Speech Disorders*, 1952, 17, 263–268.

Mowrer, O. H., The therapeutic process: III. Learning theory and the neurotic fallacy, *Amer. J. Orthopsychiat.*, 1952, 22, 679–689.

Mowrer, O. H., Neurosis: A disorder of conditioning or problem solving, *Ann. N. Y. Acad. Sci.*, 1953, 56, 273–288.

Mowrer, O. H., Some philosophical problems in mental disorder and its treatment, *Harv. Educ. Rev.*, 1953, 23, 117–127.

Mowrer, O. H., The psychologist looks at language, *Amer. Psychologist*, 1954, 9, 660–694.
  APA presidential address.

Mowrer, O. H., Learning theory and identification: I. Introduction, *J. Genet. Psychol.*, 1954, 84, 197–199.

Mowrer, O. H., Learning theory: Historical review and re-interpretation, *Harv. Educ. Rev.*, 1954, 24, 37–58.

Mowrer, O. H., Neo-analytic theory, *J. Counsel. Psychol.*, 1956, 3, 108–111.

Mowrer, O. H., Two-factor learning theory reconsidered with special references to secondary reinforcement and the concept of habit, *Psychol. Rev.*, 1956, 63, 114–128.

Mowrer, O. H., Some philosophical problems in psychological counseling, *J. Counsel. Psychol.*, 1957, 4, 103–111.

Donitz, J. R., D. J. Mason, O. H. Mowrer, and P. Viek, Conditioning of fear: A function of the delay of reinforcement, *Amer. J. Psychol.*, 1957, 70, 69–74.

Mowrer, O. H., and J. D. Keehn, How are intertrial "avoidance" responses reinforced?, *Psychol. Rev.*, 1958, 65, 209–221.

Mowrer, O. H., Hearing and speaking: An analysis of language learning, *J. Speech Disorders*, 1958, 23, 143–152.

Mowrer, O. H., Symposium on relationships between religion and mental health: Discussion, *Amer. Psychologist*, 1958, 13, 577–579.

Mowrer, O. H., Changing conceptions of the unconscious, *J. Nerv. Ment. Dis.*, 1959, 129, 222–234.

Mowrer, O. H., Comments on Trude Weiss-Rosmarin's "Adler's psychology and the Jewish tradition," *J. Indiv. Psychol.*, 1959, 15, 128–129.

Mowrer, O. H., Judgment and suffering: Contrasting views, *Faculty Forum*, 10, 1959.

Mowrer, O. H., "Sin"; The lesser of two evils, *Amer. Psychologist,* 1960, *15,* 301–304.

Mowrer, O. H., Basic research methods, statistics, and decision theory, *Amer. J. Occup. Ther.,* 1960, *4,* 199–205.

Mowrer, O. H., Some constructive features of the concept of sin, *J. Counsel. Psychol.,* 1960, *7,* 185–188.
Also in *The Crisis in Psychiatry and Religion.*

Mowrer, O. H., Payment or repayment: the problem of private practice, *Amer. Psychologist,* 1963, *18,* 577–580.

Mowrer, O. H., Cognitive dissonance or counterconditioning?: A reappraisal of certain behavioral "paradoxes," *Psychol. Rec.,* 1963, *13(2),* 197–211.

SUGGESTED READINGS

BOOKS

Hall, C. S., and G. Lindzey, *Theories of Personality,* N.Y., Wiley, 1957, 456–465.

Lundin, R. W., *Personality: An Experimental Approach,* N.Y., MacMillan, 1961.
Personality is a valid subject for scientific study.

McClelland, D. C., *Personality,* N.Y., Holt, Rinehart and Winston 1951. (Reissued as a Holt-Dryden book in 1958.)

Wolman, B. B., *Contemporary Theories and Systems,* N.Y., Harper & Row, 1960, 170–172.

PERIODICALS

Eysenck, H. J., A dynamic theory of anxiety and hysteria, *J. Ment. Sci.,* 1955, *101,* 28–51.
Criticizes Mowrer's theory as being more introversion–extroversion than neuroses theory.

Funk, M. F., Moral judgements and neurosis, *Dissert. Abstr.,* 1962, *22(10),* 3740–3741.

Szasz, T. S., The myth of mental illness, *Amer. Psychologist,* 1960, *15,* 113–118.

Smith, D. E. P., Interdisciplinary approach to the genesis of anxiety, *Educ. Theory,* 1956, *6,* 222–231.
Compares Freud, Rank, Mowrer, Angyal, Goldstein, Lewin, Rogers, Kierkegaard, and Sullivan on theories of anxiety.

15

Contributions of Other Theorists: Holistic, Holistic-Integrative, Social Interaction

HOLISTIC APPROACH [Goldstein]

They found that even the Belly, in its dull quiet way, was doing necessary work for the Body, and that all must work together or the Body will go to pieces.

AESOP
The Belly and the Members

SOME BIOGRAPHICAL DATA

Kurt Goldstein was born on November 6, 1878 in Kattowitz, Germany. He received his M.D. degree at the University of Breslau in 1903. During the period 1912–1930 he was professor of neurology and psychiatry at the Universities of Koenigsberg and Frankfurt am Main, Germany. In 1933 he came to the United States, working first as Chief of the Neuro-psychiatric laboratory of Montefiore Hospital of New York City from 1936 to 1940. In 1938 he was invited to give the William James lecture at Harvard University. In 1940 he became head of the neurological laboratory of the Boston Dispensary. He served as clinical professor of neurology at Taft Medical School from 1940 to 1946; later he was at Brandeis University as professor of psychology, then at the New School for Social Research of New York until 1958. He is a member of the American Neurological Association, the American Psychiatric Association, Association for Research in Nervous and Mental Disease, American Psychological Association, member of the Association for the Advancement of Psychotherapy, member of the American Academy of Arts and Sciences, and a member of the New York Academy of Science.

INTRODUCTION*

Most of Kurt Goldstein's work has been as neurologist and psychiatrist particularly concerned with brain damage of veterans of World War I [3]. He has also done considerable work in speech disturbances, primarily again with brain damaged individuals. Like Gordon Allport, Goldstein favors an extremely intensive study of one personality over an extremely long period. During that time, he feels, one should use every available means for studying the personality [3]. Some of his subjects Goldstein has studied for at least ten years; only in this way does he feel that one can thoroughly understand an individual's personality. He feels that much of personality theory, as it exists today, is "beadstringing." Rather than defending his use as subjects of individuals who are sick, Goldstein positively advocates the study of sick individuals on the grounds that it may be easier to ascertain the facts about their behavior.

The highlights of the behavioral patterns of a sick human being are readily seen. Goldstein also feels that work in a laboratory should be done only to control the phenomena found in observations of patients in life situations. Therefore, most of his tests concern such situations. The laboratory procedure is based mainly on the observation of isolated phenomena studied with the atomistic method, while his studies are made from the organismic approach, that is, from the consideration of each phenomenon as it relates to the total organismic functioning.

* Note that the superior numbers in this chapter refer to the reference section at the end.

ESSENTIAL FEATURES

General Considerations

Goldstein's theory of personality is an organismic one with a flavoring of Gestaltism (*1*). Actually, however, his theory is more holistic than Gestalt. The Gestalt viewpoint considered each phenomenon related to the Gestalt to which it belongs. The organismic theory puts the relation of the Gestalt to the total organism in the foreground, each in their significance and meaning for the organism (1, p. 371).

There is only one central theme in his personality theory: self-actualization. (1, p. 303) All human motivation arises from the one motive of trying to actualize the self, the personality. *Self-actualization* can be defined as: the fulfilling of one's capacities or potentialities in the best possible way under a given condition. The theory is in opposition to all theories which assume different drives or instincts.

The following outline presents the primary features of Goldstein's singular theory of personality in which all of the considerations are directed toward self-actualization.

1. The only motive in human existence is the trend to actualize oneself (2). Self-actualization occurs in the process of coming to terms with the world. The individual tries to find an adequacy between his own potentialities and the demands of the outer world. If he does not achieve adequacy and order, he comes to a state of disorder which is called *catastrophe,* in which he is not able to act. He experiences anxiety. Anxiety is the subjective experience in this state of disorder which goes along with the danger to the individual's existence. The individual is not aware of the cause of this danger. In the situation of an emotion similar to anxiety which is called *fear,* the individual is aware of the cause which produces the emotion and, insofar as he is able, may deliberate how to eliminate the danger. This distinction between anxiety and fear is an essential point for the understanding of human behavior in patients and in normal individuals in great distress.

2. The condition of the organism changes continually in relation to the stimuli. This change must be replaced by the normal condition, which is accomplished by the process of equalization which brings the organism back to the threshold which corresponds to his nature. This process concerns each activity of the organism and is fundamental to the normal activity of the organism. The change of the organism finds its ex-

pression in tension which is necessary for life. Therefore, according to Goldstein, it is normal that we feel a certain amount of tension.

3. The essential key to understanding personality is to find out what the personality prefers (preferred performance). Self-realization is based on preferred behavior forms.

4. For understanding behavior, Goldstein employs the concept of Figure-Ground, which characterizes the structure of any ordered performance, and the explanation of which is that under normal conditions, those activities come to the fore which correspond to the best form of self-realization in the moment.

5. The self-actualization process which any personality uses is not entirely at the mercy of environmental winds or pressures. According to Goldstein, the *organism* (his term for *personality*) has a very strong desire to maintain a strong behavior pattern, and the organism also wishes to retain its own sense of identity. "We carry ourselves with us." We do not wait for or bend with each pressure that comes along.

6. A normal personality may even enjoy an increased tension by trying new things, may become excited by newness, by travel, by meeting different situations that are out of the monotonous routine. Goldstein feels there is a zest or appetite for life and all of the life tension states which are necessary to the best self-actualization. He does not feel, in contrast to the Freudian concept, that tension should always be avoided and eliminated as much as possible. Goldstein does not feel that life is entirely repetitive and that man is driven by an instinct of death. Goldstein does not feel, as does Freud, that life is determined by the so-called pleasure principle, that means the elimination of pain. Because we do not live alone, it is incumbent upon us to endure some restriction: what we have to do in the interests of the "other." The possibility for the self-realization of the "other" is the presupposition of our own self-realization. This mutual self-restriction, has to be experienced with the feeling of necessity and taken without resentment. It guarantees the highest fulfillment of man.

7. The normal individual has the urge to reduce the anxiety which occurs in his trying to come to terms with the difficulties of life. We are not always able to do so and we try then to find a protection against the advent of anxiety. As an expression of the seeking for protection we find the tendency toward order, norms, and so on—in general, the organization of what we call *civilization*. The individual's behavior may oscillate

between the effect of the two tendencies: protection and reduction of anxiety. Individuals differ as to how much anxiety they can bear. The capacity of bearing anxiety is a manifestation of genuine courage, an affirmative answer to the shock of existence which belongs to man's nature.

Specific Considerations

There are three kinds of organismic behavior according to Goldstein: processes, performances, and attitudes. Performances are conscious, purposeful voluntary acts. Processes are biological-physiological functions of which we are not directly aware. Attitudes are moods, emotions, deeply inward urges, likings, dislikings, etc. All the three kinds of behavior are involved in a voluntary performance, which means the usual performance of man.

According to Goldstein, behavior has four symptomatic patterns. These patterns gain their names according to how they originate in the personality. Behavior originates (1) directly or (2) indirectly and is determined by the outer world in an adequate way, which means it is adequate to the situation or as a protective mechanism against catastrophe. Each performance has to be considered in the light of how much it is determined by (3) fatigue or (4) perseveration, which may hinder the normal fulfillment of goal.

In behavior, we have to distinguish, according to Goldstein, two modes: abstract behavior and concrete behavior. In abstract behavior the individual thinks about the consequences of the moment for the self-realization and reacts in the best possible way. In this category belongs symbolic behavior. In concrete behavior, the organism reacts directly to the stimulus, without any reflection. This reaction will occur correctly only if the situation is organized by the abstract attitude in a corresponding way. These concepts were developed by Goldstein and Gelb many years ago and helped them to understand the behavior of patients and to treat them in a correct way. It is necessary for understanding any kind of behavior to find out whether the individual acts in a concrete or an abstract way. Goldstein and Scheerer have worked out a number of tests to determine whether the individual is able to react in an abstract way or only concretely. The abstract behavior belongs to a higher function of the mind. A defect of abstract behavior due to a damage of the brain shows in all performance fields. The abstract behavior is damaged earlier in the brain than the concrete one.

Summary

Goldstein demands that we study the entire personality. Behavior is a unitary thing and the personality can be understood in a total sense. The primary feature of Goldstein's theory is that all behavior is self-actualization and that it is the trend of the organism or the personality to come to terms with the world in the given moment. If the trend is fulfilled, the individual emerges as a real self. Goldstein assumes also that the organism desires to remain constant, despite continuous changes in the environment. Beyond that, however, the real personality that can self-actualize itself must be able to bear pressures and tensions if he wants to rise to the higher level of existence which belongs to man. The individual who doesn't achieve this level exists in a state of mere self-preservation, not of self-realization of the total personality. This limited state occurs in the brain-injured, neurotics, or psychotics, and in other sicknesses, and in times of great distress in normal people. In a final analysis, we find Goldstein's theory relatively simple in its advocacy of the singular theme of self-actualization.

DELIMITATION

As in all the descriptions of the theorists in Chapters 14 and 15, this presentation of Kurt Goldstein omits some of his work. We have not included, for example, his work with aphasics, his excellent work with language as such, tests on abstract impairment behavior, his work on emotions, smiling, disease and health in schizophrenia and his theory of biologic knowledge, which presents a particularly difficult problem.

BIBLIOGRAPHY

PRIMARY SOURCES

BOOKS

1. Goldstein, K., *The Organism: A Holistic Approach to Biology Derived from Pathological Data in Man*, N.Y., American Book, 1939.
2. Goldstein, K., *Human Nature in the Light of Psychopathology*, Cambridge, Mass., Harv. Univer. Press, 1940.

3. Goldstein, K., *After-Effects of Brain Injuries in War*, N.Y., Grune & Stratton, 1942.

4. Goldstein, K., *Language and Language Disturbances*, N.Y., Grune & Stratton, 1948.

5. Goldstein, K., and M. Scheerer, Tests of abstract and concrete thinking. Tests of abstract and concrete behavior, in A. Weider (ed.), *Contributions Toward Medical Psychology*, N.Y., Ronald, 1953.

6. Goldstein, K., New ideas on mental health, in J. E. Fairchild (ed.), *Personal Problems and Psychological Frontiers*, N.Y., Sheridan House, 1957.

7. Goldstein, K., Health as value, in A. H. Maslow (ed.), *New Knowledge in Human Values*, N.Y., Harper & Row, 1959.

7a. Goldstein, K., Organismic approach to aphasia, in *Psychological and Psychiatric Aspects of Speech and Hearing*, D. A. Barbara (ed.), Springfield, Ill., Thomas Publishing, 1960.

PERIODICALS

8. Goldstein, K., Clinical and theoretical aspects of lesions of the frontal lobes, *Arch. Neurol. Psychiat.*, 1939, *41*, 856–867.

9. Goldstein, K., and M. Scheerer, Abstract and concrete behavior: An experimental study with special tests, *Psychol. Monogr.*, 1941, *53*, No. 2.

10. Hanfmann, E., M. Rickers-Ovsiankina, and K. Goldstein, Case Lanuti, *Psychol. Monogr.*, 1944, *57*, 51–65.

11. Scheerer, M., E. Rothman, and K. Goldstein, A case of "idiot savant": An experimental study of personality organization, *Psychol. Monogr.*, 1945, *58*, No. 4.

12. Goldstein, K., Organismic approach to the problem of motivation, *Trans. N. Y. Acad. Sci.*, 1947, *9*, 218–230.

13. Goldstein, K., Frontal lobotomy and impairment of abstraction, *J. Nerv. Ment. Dis.*, 1949, *110*, No. 2.

14. Goldstein, K., On emotions: Considerations from the organismic point of view, *J. Psychol.*, 1951, *31*, 37–49.

15. Goldstein, K., The effect of brain damage on the personality, *Psychiatry*, 1952, *15*, 245–260.

16. Goldstein, K., The concept of health, disease, and therapy: Basic ideas for an organismic psychotherapy, *Amer. J. Psychother.*, 1954, *8*, 745–764.

17. Goldstein, K., The smiling of the infant and the problem of understanding the "other," *J. Psychol.*, 1957, *44*, 175–191.

18. Goldstein, K., Concerning the concreteness in schizophrenia, *J. Abnorm. Soc. Psychol.*, 1959, *59*, 146–148.

19. Goldstein, K., Abnormal mental conditions in infancy, *J. Nerv. Ment. Dis.*, 1959, *128*, 538–557.

FILMS

Goldstein, K., and M. Scheerer, *Impairment of the Abstract Attitude as Shown in the Cube (Stick) Test,* 2 motion picture films on brain-impaired subjects, 1950, Psychological Cinema Register, State College, Penn., Penn. State, 1950.

TAPE RECORDINGS

Goldstein, K., *The Nature of Anxiety* (G. W. Kisker, ed.), No. 131, Cincinnati, Ohio, Sound Seminars.

Suggested Readings

BOOKS

Chaplin, J. P., and T. S. Krawiec, *Systems and Theories of Psychology,* Holt, Rinehart and Winston, N.Y., 1960.

Hall, C. S., and G. Lindzey, *Theories of Personality,* N.Y., Wiley, 1957, chap. 8.

Wolman, B. B., *Contemporary Theories and Systems in Psychology,* N.Y., Harper & Row, 1960, Chap. 5.

PERIODICALS

Adler, A., The concept of compensation and over-compensation in Alfred Adler's and Kurt Goldstein's Theories, *J. Indiv. Psychol.,* 1959, *15, J. Indiv. Psychol.,* Kurt Goldstein's 80th Anniversary Issue, 1959, *15.*

Freiman, I. S., Kurt Goldstein—an appreciation, *Amer. J. Psychotherap.,* 1954, *8,* 3–10.

Katsoff, L. O., Review of K. Goldstein's *Human Nature in the Light of Psychopathology, J. Gen. Psychol.,* 1942, *26,* 187–194.

Kelman, H., Kurt Goldstein's influence on psychoanalytic thought, *Amer. J. Psychoanal.,* 1959, *19,* 149–156.

Pankow, G., Dynamic structurization and Goldstein's concept of the organism, *Amer. J. Psychoanal.,* 1959, *19,* 157–160.

Piotrowski, Z., Basic human motives according to Kurt Goldstein, *Amer. J. Psychotherap.,* 1959, *13,* 553–560.

Porter, L. W., Job attitudes in management: perceived deficiencies in need fulfillment as a function of job level, *J. Appl. Psychol.,* 1962, *46*(6), 375–384.

Self actualization was the highest need.

Skinner, B. F., Review of K. Goldstein's *The Organism, J. Abnorm. Soc. Psychol.,* 1940, *35,* 462–465.

Smith, D. E. P., Interdisciplinary approach to the genesis of anxiety, *Educ. Theory,* 1956, *6,* 222–231.

Compares Freud, Rank, Mowrer, Angyal, Goldstein, Lewin, Rogers, Kierkegaard, and Sullivan on theories of anxiety.

Tillich, P., The significance of Kurt Goldstein for philosophy of religion, *J. Indiv. Psychol.*, 1959, *15*, 20–23.

Weiss, F. A., Kurt Goldstein and his concept of human nature, *Amer. J. Psychoanal.*, 1959, *19*, 143–148.

◆

HOLISTIC-INTEGRATIVE [Maslow]

What you cannot as you would achieve,
You must perforce accomplish as you may.

WILLIAM SHAKESPEARE
Titus Andronicus, II, 1

SOME BIOGRAPHICAL DATA[1]

Abraham Harold Maslow was born in Brooklyn on April 1, 1908. He was educated at the University of Wisconsin, receiving his B.A. in 1930, his M.A. in 1931 and his Ph.D. in 1934. He married Bertha Goodman on December 31, 1928. They have two children, Ann and Ellen. Prior to his appointment at Brandeis in 1951, Dr. Maslow served on the faculty of the University of Wisconsin as Research Assistant in Social Psychology (1929–1930), Assistant Instructor in Psychology (1930–1934), and Teaching Fellow in Psychology (1934–1935). After serving as a Carnegie Fellow at Columbia University from 1935–1937, he joined the faculty of Brooklyn College to serve as Associate Professor until 1951. He served as plant manager at the Maslow Cooperage Corporation from 1947 to 1949. Since 1951 he has been associate professor, professor, and chairman of the department of psychology at Brandeis University. Dr. Maslow is a member and officer of a number of learned societies. He was President of the Massachusetts State Psychological Association and served on the coun-

[1] The cooperation of Professor Maslow in reviewing this section and supplying additional comments is gratefully acknowledged.

cil of the Society of Psychological Study of Social Issues. A member of the American Psychological Association, he was elected a Fellow of both the Association's Division of Abnormal and Clinical Psychology and the Division of Personality and Social Psychology of which he was president. He also served as president of the Division of Esthetics. A former Fellow of the New York Academy of Sciences, he is a member of Phi Beta Kappa and Sigma Xi.

INTRODUCTION

Abraham H. Maslow is a realistically oriented personality theorist. From the factual material of his studies he finds both optimistic and some pessimistic characteristics in human behavior.

Maslow has studied with and been personal friends with some of the greatest names in psychology. He freely acknowledges his debt to his many teachers and his friends. At some time in the past, Maslow has studied under or worked with the following: Goldstein, Sheldon, Harlow, David M. Levy, Wertheimer, Koffka, Kardiner, Fromm, Horney, Adler, Ruth Benedict, Thorndike, Mittelmann, Ralph Linton, Else Frenkel-Brunswik, Tolman, Allport, and Murphy. As can be seen, the list is a veritable, "Who's Who" of psychology.

Some students of personality theory consider Maslow as having "done some of the best writing on motivation" (Bonner, *Psychology of Personality*, p. 267).

Maslow's theory of personality is based on a limited number of cases. Like many other theorists, he started working with primates and has ended by working with people.

THE SYSTEM, THEORY, OR ESSENTIAL FEATURES

General Considerations

Maslow's theory concerns itself primarily with growth motivation which he feels can be gained through self-actualization. Another name given to it is *meta motivation theory*. Thus, Maslow feels man is most interested in need-gratification rather than in need-frustration. He believes that man can be essentially and innately good. The badness in man's behavior comes out of a bad environment rather than an inherent rottenness. In other words, man is more than just an animal; he is a special kind of animal.

Consequently, any true motivation study concerns people, not animals only. The inner nature of self-actualization is "weak, delicate and subtle." This thin thread of the inner nature of man's self-actualization may be overcome by poor culture, bad parents, or faulty habits. But it never fully disappears. "It persists underground forever pressing for actualization" [*The Self,* Moustakas, (ed.), 1956, p. 233].

Maslow emphasizes growth motivation and not just deficiency motivation. Man's behavior is more than homeostasis. The human personality wants not just food but variety and differences in food. He finds, for example, that happier people are oriented to growth motivation while neurotics are oriented toward deficiency motivation. In this sense, the neurotic or unadjusted human is trying to satisfy only his basic drives and to maintain a *status quo.*

Maslow's is a unified organismic theory. He freely credits the Adlerians with understanding need structure. Much of his work is well summarized in his chief book, *Motivation and Personality* (1954), in which he makes a synthesis of the three approaches: holistic, dynamic or motivational, and cultural.

In every self-actualizing personality there is a hierarchy of need priority. These are degrees of psychological health in which one must successfully achieve the first degree in order to go on to the second degree. Maslow does not use the word *instinct* but coins the word *instinctoid*. We may assume from this that it is an innate or inborn capacity within the structure of man's organism.

Degrees of Psychological Health. Maslow proposes approximately six degrees of need priority which lead to psychological health. The first and second are of the lower order and are most potent. If these first two, physiological needs and safety needs, are not met, the following four cannot be met either. Thus, belongingness, love, self-esteem, and self-actualization are considered to be of a higher nature.

1. Physiological needs. These are needs for air, food, water, and physical comfort, which must be met before the next needs can be approached.

2. Safety needs. Using children for an example, Maslow finds that they have a desire for freedom from fear and insecurity. Safety needs are needs in which one wants to avoid harmful or painful incidents.

3. Belongingness. Belongingness needs begin the higher order needs. By this, Maslow means that the human personality wants security. The human being wants to be somebody even though it is in a small group.

Because man is brought up by his fellowmen, it is almost natural that he has a feeling of wanting to belong to that group of human beings that helped to rear him.

4. Love needs. Man has had, now has, and always will have the desire to love someone else and be loved in return.

5. Self-esteem needs. In this need man wants to feel that he is worthwhile, that he can master something of his own environment, that he has a competence and an independence and a freedom and a feeling of being recognized for some type of endeavor.

6. Self-actualization needs. These are the highest needs, as Maslow considers them. They involve the needs for cognition and for aesthetic reality. Man has a strong desire and a need to know and understand not only himself but the world about him. In addition to this cognitive need man does not want to live in a stark, unbeautiful world, but needs to have beauty and art, to appreciate and to create things of an aesthetic nature.

In explaining the six needs above, Maslow feels that achieving one level drives a person on to the next highest level. However, an unsatisfied need at the lower end of the structure will dominate the higher human need: "Bread before Bach." The physiological and safety needs are certainly of a lower order. As we have seen, neurotics have not had these needs met to a satisfactory point. He feels the first two levels have been highly overemphasized by most personality theorists. The ultimate and achievable nature of man is to operate at the upper levels and especially the self-actualization level. It may be that at times society inhibits man's strivings to actualize himself. One of the most important points that Maslow makes is that human behavior is *not* a question of normality or dichotomy between good and bad behavior, but is essentially a question of self-fulfillment. Thus, what is normal is not a comparative thing; what is normal is an inner ability to make oneself the best and fullest possible personality that he is able to create.

Specific Considerations

In order to study the hierarchy of need structure as Maslow proposes it, he has conducted a unique type of research. Maslow began with the concept that to study abnormal personalities is bound to prove or produce an abnormally oriented theory of personality. It would be onesided. His next step, then, was to find a group that he considered to be composed of actualized, successful people. *Successful* here meant possessing the ability to discover their own deepest roots of personality. From this framework, Maslow came up with forty-nine people, from public and private life. The list included personalities from history and those living whom he considered to meet the characteristics of good, psychological health. About two-thirds of this group of forty-nine people were truly self-actualizing personalities. Among the group were Lincoln, Jefferson, Walt Whitman, Thoreau, Eleanor Roosevelt, Albert Einstein, Albert Schweitzer, and a number of Maslow's friends and acquaintances. The bulk of his findings were published in 1950 in his study "Self-Actualizing People." In order to understand better what made these individuals truly self-actualizing, we must now look at the characteristics that Maslow felt were contained in them.

Outstanding characteristics of self-actualized people. We have chosen to summarize in fifteen items the main characteristics of a fully self-actualized personality. They are as follows:

1. Oriented realistically, efficient perception, good judge of others, quick to judge them.
2. Accept selves and others and the world for what they actually are, not what they wish they would be, not hypocritical.
3. High degree of spontaneity, unaffected in behavior, act natural, may appear unconventional.
4. Problem-centered not self-centered, work on problem not self, not very introspective.
5. Inclined to be detached, great need for privacy at times, not entirely dependent on others, can amuse self, can detach self and concentrate alone, may appear aloof to others.
6. Autonomous within self and independent, dependent on self, serene.
7. Fresh appreciation of people and world, not dulled—not "I've been there before," but "Every sunset is as beautiful as the first," "Ten thousandth baby as miraculous as the first."
8. Somewhat mystical or profound inner experiences, seem out of this world at times.
9. Identify strongly with fellow man, but not join in empathetic way, have older brother personality, want to help, truly interested in the welfare of man.
10. Deep and intimate relationship with only very few, have special

friends or small circle of friends, highly selective in friends, give absolutely to them, easily touched and moved by children.

11. Strong democratically oriented values, can relate and learn from rich or poor, acquaintance's class or race or position not important.

12. Understand difference between means to achieve a goal and the rightful ends to be achieved, strongly ethical and highly moral, though may differ with popular idea of right and wrong, focus on ends and purposes.

13. Philosophical and whimsical inner-motivated sense of humor, not laugh at cruelty, strong sense of incongruity, do not tell jokes as jokester but rather see jokes in everyday things spontaneously.

14. Tremendous capacity to be creative, one of *most* universal capacities in all self-actualized people, not special talent but new touches to life, creativeness of child, fresh way of doing things.

15. Swim against mainstream, very open to new experiences, resistant to conformity.[2]

Maslow does not feel that one has to be highly intelligent to do the above fifteen things. Intelligence or intellect may help in some of the aspects but it is not essential. Neither does he feel that one must be perfect and follow the scout code (loyal, faithful, reverent, obedient, etc.). Many of the subjects he studied who he felt were self-actualized were prideful, prejudiced, vain, and indeed had some sort of "surgical coldness." That is to say, they were not overly sentimental after the death of a loved one. They also had fears and doubts but did recover well from their fears and doubts. The self-actualized man is not competely happy or successful or extremely well adjusted. He has simply self-actualized his own personality to the best of his ability.

In keeping with much of the newer thinking about personality theory, Maslow's latest work (*Toward a Psychology of Being*) also emphasizes the desire to integrate our results within a scientific framework. Maslow's refreshing and non-pedantic style is probably best seen in the above book. In some ways he almost comes out as one of the "new" voices in personality theory. He readily admits that his position is structured out of "pilot researches, bits of evidence, on personal observation, on theoretical de-

[2] The student is encouraged to read a further extension of this list in 43 "propositions" which enhances these 15 characteristics. (See chap. 14, "Some basic propositions of a growth and self-actualization psychology," *Toward a Psychology of Being*, pp. 177–200.)

duction, and on sheer hunch" (*ibid.*, p. v). However, it must not be presumed that Maslow is against the scientific approach because, "Science is the only way we have of shoving truth down the reluctant throat." And, "Only science can progress."

Maslow finds that human personality is far from dichotomized but that it is an integrated and integrating entity. He sees loyalty to a set position whether it be pro- or anti-Freudian, for example, as just "plain silly." In his newer work Maslow re-emphasizes the value of reconciling: Being-cognition (B-psychology) with Deficiency-cognition (D-psychology), "i.e., the perfect with the imperfect, the ideal with the actual, the eupsychian with the extant, the timeless with the temporal, end-psychology with means-psychology" (*ibid.*). Some of these reconciliations may be our true "peak experiences."

Summary

In Maslow we find an optimistic personality theorist who desires to study normal people. Much of what he feels comes out of the degrees of psychological health begin with an "instinctoid depth." The hierarchy of the need priority is physiological, safety, belongingness, love, self-esteem and self-actualization needs. He feels that personality theory should concern itself with growth motivations and not deficiency motivations. Toward this end he studied 49 people and continues to study others to see how closely they come to being fully self-actualized and, if they are self-actualized, how they achieved this state.

DELIMITATION

We have omitted the research Abraham Maslow did on photographs of faces, good teaching, and his Security–Insecurity Test. Also because many of the studies have been in the past, we have not included his work with hunger in animals and primates while he was studying motivation. His views on expressive behavior and coping behavior, as well as his work in writing in abnormal psychology, have not been included.

BIBLIOGRAPHY

PRIMARY SOURCES

BOOKS

Maslow, A. H., Personality and patterns of culture, in R. Stagner, *Psychology of Personality*, N.Y., McGraw-Hill, 1937.
> Also in S. Britt (ed.) *Selected Readings in Social Psychology*, N.Y., Holt, Rinehart and Winston, 1950.

Maslow, A. H., and B. Mittelmann, *Principles of Abnormal Psychology* [1941], N.Y., Harper & Row, rev. ed., 1951.
> Recorded as a talking book for the blind.

Maslow, A. H., Conflict, frustration and the theory of threat, in S. S. Tomkins, (ed.), *Contemporary Psychopathology*, Cambridge, Mass., Harv. Univer. Press, 1943.

Maslow, A. H., Theory of motivation, in P. L. Harriman (ed.), *Twentieth Century Psychology*, N.Y., Philosophical Library, 1946, 22–48.

Maslow, A. H., Self-actualizing people: A study of psychological health, *Personality Symposium*, No. 1, April, 1950, in W. Wolff (ed.), *Values in Personality Research*, N.Y., Grune & Stratton, 1950, 11–34.
> Also in Maslow's *Motivation and Personality*, 1954, 199–234.
> Also in C. E. Moustakas (ed.), *The Self*, N.Y., Harper & Row, 1956.

MacKinnon, D. W., and A. H. Maslow, Personality, in H. Nelson (ed.), *Theoretical Foundations of Psychology*, N.Y., Van Nostrand, 1951, 602–655.

Maslow, A. H., Human motivation in relation to social theory, in M. Shore (ed.), *Twentieth Century Mental Hygiene*, N.Y., Social Science Research Council, 1951.
> Also in K. Zerfoss (ed.), *Readings in Counseling*, N.Y., Association Press, 1952.

Maslow, A. H., *The S–I (Security–Insecurity) Test*, Stanford, Calif., Stanford Univer. Press, 1953.

Maslow, A. H., Love in healthy people, in M. F. A. Montagu (ed.), *The Meaning of Love*, N.Y., Julian Press, 1953.

Maslow, A. H., *Motivation and Personality*, N.Y., Harper & Row, 1954.

Maslow, A. H., Deficiency motivation and growth motivation, in M. Jones (ed.), *Nebraska Symposium on Motivation*, Lincoln, Nebr., Univer. Nebr. Press, 1955, 1–39.
> Also in Coleman, J. C., *Personality Dynamics and Effective Behavior*, Chicago, Scott Foresman, 1960, 475–485.

Maslow, A. H., Personality problems and personality growth, in C. E. Mousta-kas, *The Self*, N.Y., Harper & Row, 1956.

Maslow, A. H., Power relationships and patterns of personal development, in A. Kornhauser (ed.), *Problems of Power in American Democracy*, Detroit, Wayne State Univer. Press, 1957.

Maslow, A. H. (ed.), *New Knowledge in Human Values*, N.Y., Harper & Row, 1959.

Maslow, A. H., Creativity in self-actualizing people, in H. E. Anderson (ed.), *Creativity and Its Cultivation*, N.Y., Harper & Row, 1959.

Maslow, A. H., Symposium remarks on investigating "our best human beings," in *Academy of Religion and Mental Health, Religion, Science, and Mental Health*, N.Y., N.Y. Univer. Press, 1959.

Maslow, A. H., and R. Diaz-Guerrero, Delinquency as a value disturbance, in J. G. Peatman, and E. L. Hartley (eds.), *Festschrift for Gardner Murphy*, N.Y., Harper & Row, 1960, 228–249.

Maslow, A. H., Resistance to being rubricized, in B. Kaplan, and S. Wapner (eds.), *Perspectives in Psychological Theory*, N.Y., Internat. Univer. Press, 1960.

Maslow, A. H., Some frontier problems in mental health, in *Personality Theory and Counseling Practice*, A. Combs (ed.), Coral Gables, Univ. of Florida Press, 1961.

Maslow, A. H., Existential psychology—What's in it for us?, in R. May (ed.), *Existential Psychology*, N.Y., Random House, 1961.

Maslow, A. H., *Toward a Psychology of Being*, Princeton, N.J., Van Nostrand (Insight Books), 1962.

PERIODICALS

Maslow, A. H., with H. Harlow, and H. Uehling; Delayed reaction tests on primates from the lemur to the orangoutan. *J. Comp. Psychol.*, 1932, *13*, 313–343.

Maslow, A. H., with H. Harlow, Delayed reaction tests on primates at Bronx Park Zoo. *J. Comp. Psychol.*, 1932, *14*, 97–107.

Maslow, A. H., The "emotion" of disgust in dogs, *J. Comp. Psychol.*, 1932, *14*, 401–407.

Maslow, A. H., Food preferences of primates, *J. Comp. Psychol.*, 1933, *16*, 187–197.

Maslow, A. H., and E. Groshong, Influence of differential motivation on de-layed reactions in monkeys, *J. Comp. Psychol.*, 1934, *18*, 75–83.

Maslow, A. H., The effect of varying external conditions on learning, retention and reproduction, *J. Exp. Psychol.*, 1934, *17*, 36–47.

Maslow, A. H., The effect of varying time intervals between acts of learning with a note on proactive inhibition. *J. Exp. Psychol.*, 1934, *17*, 141–144.

Maslow, A. H., Individual psychology and the social behavior of monkeys and apes, *Int. J. Indiv. Psychol.*, 1935, *1*, 47–59.

Maslow, A. H., Appetites and hungers in animal motivation, *J. Comp. Psychol.*, 1935, *20*, 75–83.

Maslow, A. H., The dominance drive as a determiner of the social and sexual behavior of infra-human primates, I–IV, *J. Genet. Psychol.*, 1936, *48*, 261–338, *49*, 161–198.

Maslow, A. H., with W. Grether, An experimental study of insight in monkeys. *J. Comp. Psychol.*, 1937, *24*, 127–134.

Maslow, A. H., The influence of familiarization on preference, *J. Exp. Psychol.*, 1937, *21*, 162–180.

Maslow, A. H., Dominance–feeling, behavior, and status, *Psychol. Rev.*, 1937, *44*, 404–429.

Maslow, A. H., The comparative approach to social behavior, *Social Forces*, 1937, *15*, 487–490.

Maslow, A. H., Dominance–feeling, personality and social behavior in women, *J. Soc. Psychol.*, 1939, *10*, 3–39.

Maslow, A. H., Dominance–quality and social behavior in infra-human primates, *J. Soc. Psychol.*, 1940, *11*, 313–324.

Maslow, A. H., A test for dominance-feeling (self-esteem) in college women, *J. Soc. Psychol.*, 1940, *12*, 255–270.

Maslow, A. H., Deprivation, threat and frustration, *Psychol. Rev.*, 1941, *48*, 364–366.

    Also in T. Newcomb, and E. Hartley, (eds.), *Readings in Social Psychology*, N.Y., Holt, Rinehart and Winston, 1947.

    Also in M. Marx, *Psychological Theory: Contemporary Readings*, N.Y., Macmillan, 1951.

    Also in C. Stacey, and M. DeMartino, (eds.), *Understanding Human Motivation*, N.Y., Howard Allen Publishers, 1958.

Maslow, A. H., The dynamics of psychological security–insecurity, *Char. Person.*, 1942, *10*, 331–344.

Maslow, A. H., Liberal leadership and personality, *Freedom*, 1942, *2*, 27–30.

Maslow, A. H., Self-esteem (dominance-feeling) and sexuality in women, *J. Soc. Psychol.*, 1942, *16*, 259–294.

Maslow, A. H., A comparative approach to the problem of destructiveness, *Psychiatry*, 1942, *5*, 517–522.

Maslow, A. H., The authoritarian character structure, *J. Soc. Psychol.*, 1943, *18*, 401–411.

    Also in P. Harriman, (ed.), *Twentieth Century Psychology: Recent Developments in Psychology*, N.Y., Philosophical Library, 1946.

Maslow A. H., Conflict, frustration and the theory of threat, *J. Abnorm. Soc. Psychol.*, 1943, 38, 81–86.

Also in S. Tomkins, (ed.), *Contemporary Psychopathology; A Sourcebook*, Cambridge, Mass., Harvard Univer. Press, 1943.

Maslow, A. H., Preface to motivation theory, *Psychosom. Med.*, 1943, 5, 85–92.

Maslow, A. H., A theory of human motivation, *Psychol. Rev.*, 1943, 50, 370–396.

Also in P. Harriman (ed.) *Twentieth Century Psychology*, N.Y., Philosophical Library, 1946.

Also in H. Remmer *et al.* (eds.), *Growth, Teaching and Learning*, N.Y., Harper & Row, 1957.

Also in C. Stacey, and M. DeMartino (eds.), *Understanding Human Motivation*, N.Y., Howard Allen Publishers, 1958.

Also in Lazer, W. and E. Kelley (eds.), *Managerial Marketing*, Homewood, Ill., Irwin, 1958.

Also in W. Baller, *Readings in Psychology of Human Growth and Development*, N.Y., Holt, Rinehart and Winston, 1962.

Also in J. Seidman (ed.), N.Y., *The Child*, Holt, Rinehart & Winston, 1958.

Also in L. Gorlow, and W. Katkovsky (eds.), *Readings in the Psychology of Adjustment*, N.Y., McGraw-Hill, 1959.

Maslow, A. H., Dynamics of personality organization I, II, *Psychol. Rev.*, 1943, 50, 514–539, 544–558.

Maslow, A. H., What intelligence tests mean, *J. Gen. Psychol.*, 1944, 31, 85–93.

Maslow, A. H., Experimentalizing the clinical method, *J. Clin. Psychol.*, 1945, 1, 241–243.

Maslow, A. H., E. Birsh, M. Stein, and I. Honigman, A clinically derived test for measuring psychological security–insecurity, *J. Gen. Psychol.*, 1945, 33, 21–41.

Maslow, A. H., A suggested improvement in semantic usage, *Psychol. Rev.*, 1945, 239–240, 53.

Maslow, A. H., and I. Szilagyi-Kessler, Security and breast feeding, *J. Abnorm. Soc. Psychol.*, 1946, 41, 83–85.

Maslow, A. H., Problem-centering vs. means-centering in science, *Phil. Sci.*, 1946, 13, 326–331.

Maslow, A. H., A symbol for holistic thinking, *Persona.*, 1947, 1, 24–25.

Maslow, A. H., Some theoretical consequences of basic-need gratification, *J. Person.*, 1948, 16, 402–416.

Maslow, A. H., "Higher" and "lower" needs, *J. Psychol.*, 1948, 25, 433–436.
Also in C. Stacey, and M. DeMartino (eds.), *Understanding Human Motivation*, N.Y., Howard Allen Publishers, 1958.
Also in K. Schultz (ed.), *Applied Dynamic Psychology*, Berkeley, Calif., Univer. Calif. Press, 1958.

Maslow, A. H., Cognition of the particular and of the generic, *Psychol. Rev.*, 1948, 55, 22–40.

Maslow, A. H., Our maligned animal nature, *J. Psychol.*, 1949, 28, 273–278.
Also in S. Koenig, *et al.* (eds.), *Sociology: A book of Readings*, Englewood Cliffs, N.J., Prentice-Hall, 1953.

Maslow, A. H., The expressive component in behavior, *Psychol. Rev.*, 1949, 56, 261–272.
Also in H. Brand, *The Study of Personality: A book of readings*, N.Y., Wiley, 1954.

Maslow, A. H., Higher needs and personality, *Dialectica*, 1951, 5, 257–265.

Maslow, A. H., (ed.), American culture and personality, *J. Soc. Issues*, 1951, 7(4), 1–49.

Maslow, A. H., and J. M. Sakoda, Volunteer-error in the Kinsey study, *J. Abnorm. Soc. Psychol.*, 1952, 47, 259–262.

Maslow, A. H., and W. Zimmerman, College teaching ability, scholarly activity, and personality, *J. Educ. Psychol.*, 1953, 47, 185–189.

Maslow, A. H., The instinctoid nature of basic needs, *J. Person.*, 1954, 22, 326–347.

Maslow, A. H., Normality, health and values, *Main Currents*, 1954, 10, 75–81.

Maslow, A. H., and N. L. Mintz, Effects of esthetic surroundings: I, Initial effects of three esthetic conditions upon perceiving "energy" and "well-being" in faces, *J. Psychol.*, 1956, 41, 247–254.

Maslow, A. H., A Philosophy of Psychology, *Main Currents*, 1956, 13, 27–32.
Also in *Etc.*, 1957, 14, 10–22.
Also in J. Fairchild (ed.), *Personal Problems and Psychological Frontiers*, N.Y., Sheridan Press, 1957.
Also in S. I. Hayakawa (ed.), *Our Language and Our World*, N.Y., Harper & Row, 1959.

Maslow, A. H., *Defense and Growth*, Merrill-Palmer Quart., 1956, 3, 36–37.

Maslow, A. H. and J. Bossom, Security of judges as a factor in impressions of warmth in others, *J. Abnorm. Soc. Psychol.*, 1957, 55, 147–148.

Maslow, A. H., Emotional blocks to creativity, *J. Indiv. Psychol.*, 1958, 14, 51–56.
Also in *The Humanist*, 1958, 18, 325–332.

Also in *Best Articles and Stories*, 1959, 3, 23–35.

Also in H. Harding, and S. Parnes (eds.), *Creative Problem Solving*, N.Y., Scribner, 1962.

Maslow, A. H., The mission of the psychologist, *Manas*, 1958, *11*, (No. 17, 18), 1–8.

Maslow, A. H., Cognition of being in the peak experiences, *J. Genet. Psychol.*, 1959, *94*, 43–66.

Maslow, A. H., Critique of self-actualization: I, Some dangers of being-cognition, *J. Indiv. Psychol.*, 1959, *15*, 24–32.

Maslow, A. H., Remarks on existentialism and psychology, *Existential Inquiry*, 1960, *1*, 1–14.

Also in *Religious Inquiry*, 1960, No. 28, 4–7.

Also in Rollo May (ed.), *Existential Psychology*, N.Y., Random House, 1961.

Maslow, A. H., H. Rand, and S. Newman, Some parallels between sexual and dominance behavior of infrahuman primates and the fantasies of patients in psychotherapy, *J. Nerv. Ment. Dis.*, 1960, *131*, 202–212.

Maslow, A. H., Peak experiences as acute identity experiences, *Amer. J. Psychoanal.*, 1961, *21*, 254–262.

Maslow, A. H., Are our publications and conventions suitable for the Personal Sciences? *Amer. Psychologist*, 1961, *16*, 318–319.

Maslow, A. H., Health as transcendance of the environment, *J. Humanistic Psychol.*, 1961, *1*, 1–7.

Maslow, A. H., Comments on Skinner's attitude to science, *Daedalus*, 1961, *90*, 572–573.

Maslow, A. H., Was Adler a disciple of Freud? A note, *J. Indiv. Psychol.*, 1962, *18*(2), 125.

Maslow says Adler said no.

Maslow, A. H., The need to know and the fear of knowing, *J. Gen. Psychol.*, 1963, *68*, 111–125.

Excellent and readable on why we need to know things. A must for undergraduate psychology majors.

SUGGESTED READINGS

BOOKS

Bonner, H., *Psychology of Personality*, N.Y., Ronald, 1961, 70–73, 97–102, 350–352.

Coleman, J. C., *Personality Dynamics and Effective Behavior*, Chicago, Scott, Foresman, 1960, 475–485.

Hall, C. S., and Lindzey, G., *Theories of Personality*, N.Y., Wiley, 1957, 324–327.

McClelland, D. C., *Personality* [1951] N.Y., Holt, Rinehart and Winston, rev. ed. 1958, 370–396, 402–416.

Woodworth, R., *Dynamics of Behavior*, N.Y., Holt, Rinehart and Winston, 1958.
Good for motivation theory.

PERIODICALS

Gourevitch, V., and H. Melvin, A study of motivational development, *J. Genet. Psychol.*, 1962, *100*(2), 361–375.
Research on Maslow's hierarchy of motives with results confirming the theory.

Mathews, W., Successful adjustment: a frame of reference, *Amer. J. Orthopsychiat.*, 1960, *30*, 667–675.

Porter, L. W., Job attitudes in management: perceived deficiencies in need fulfillment as a function of job level, *J. Appl. Psychol.*, 1962, *46*(6), 375–384.
Self actualization was the highest need.

White, R., Motivation reconsidered: the concept of competence, *Psychol. Rev.*, 1959, *66*, 297–333.

◆

SOCIAL INTERACTION [Fromm]

He who knows nothing, loves nothing. He who can do nothing understands nothing. He who understands nothing is worthless. But he who understands also loves, notices, sees. . . . The more knowledge is inherent in a thing, the greater the love. . . . Anyone who imagines that all fruits ripen at the same time as strawberries, knows nothing about grapes.

PARACELSUS

SOME BIOGRAPHICAL DATA

Erich Fromm was born in Frankfurt, Germany, on March 23, 1900. The University of Heidelberg awarded him the Ph.D. in 1922. He married Frieda Reichmann on June 16, 1926. After being divorced from her he was married to Henny Gurland on July 24, 1944. Following her death, he married Annis Freeman on December 18, 1953. After receiving his degree from the University of Heidelberg he studied at the University of Munich and later at the Psychoanalytic Institute in Berlin. He served as lecturer at the Psychoanalytic Institute of Frankfurt, the Institute for Social Research, and the University of Frankfurt during the period from 1929 to 1932. In 1934 he went to the International Institute for Social Research in New York City and stayed until 1939. Fromm was guest lecturer at Columbia during the years 1940–1941, was a member of the faculty at Bennington College (1941–1950), and delivered the Terry Lectures at Yale in 1949. He was a fellow on the faculty at the William Alanson White Institute of Psychiatry in New York. Fromm has been Professor National at the University of Mexico since 1951 and has also been on the staff at Michigan State University since 1957. He is a Fellow of the New York Academy of Science and a member of the Washington Psychoanalytical Society and of the Mexican National Academy of Medicine.

INTRODUCTION

Erich Fromm is a "socio-psychoanalyst." He is well trained as an analyst. Fromm has had an optimistic approach to the human personality. He feels that all men are ultimately idealists and hope for a life beyond pure physical satisfaction. However, Fromm is not a dreamer. In the latest book he has written (*May Man Prevail?* 1961), Erich Fromm reveals a tremendous sense of urgency about the atomic-nuclear threat. Although he is not directly against current psychological research, he does wonder if it will do any good in saving mankind. While the comparative psychologists and the factor analysts crank out their new data, he feels the world may blow apart around them.

Individual behavior is shaped by society. But counter to the Freudians he feels that there is hope because man has the capacity to solve his own problems. Since man has created most of his problems beyond those of weather and natural phenomenon, he feels that man can solve these problems. In short, man can unwind what he has wound up, but it will take just as long to unwind his problems as it took to wind them up. Consequently, Erich Fromm does not look for quick solutions.

Since his arrival in the United States, Fromm has been an exceedingly popular symposium speaker. He has at different times spoken on creativity, appeared at many APA meetings, discussed Zen Buddhism, and psychoanalysis. He is in wide demand as a platform speaker.

Fromm considers man to be an animal, but with certain differences. "Man is the only animal who finds his own existence a problem which he has to solve and from which he cannot escape. In the same sense man is the only animal who knows he must die" (*The Sane Society*, p. 23–24).

THE SYSTEM, THEORY, OR ESSENTIAL FEATURES

General Considerations

Erich Fromm thinks in broad, historical terms, as did Jung. He uses human history as a laboratory in his own study of human personality. He feels that man is a history-made animal. Man is primarily the product of social influences. In contrast to Freud, who believed that personalities make society, Fromm feels that society in general makes the personality. He thus reverses the causal order of Freud. Fromm sees the differences in man's personality as being due to social processes. All men must eat, drink, breathe, defecate, sleep, rest, and exercise, but society molds basic behavior into different forms. The most beautiful and ugly of man's actions do not spring from his biological system but emerge from his environmental forces. As a consequence of all this, man has transformed himself into a thing. He now worships the products of his own hand. Erich Fromm feels that this is the idolatry of materialism. Man even worships the mechanisms of war that he has created, such as the atomic bomb. Quoting Emerson, who felt that "Things are in the saddle and ride mankind," Fromm thinks we can still put man back in the saddle and let him decide his own destiny.

In regard to democratic order, Erich Fromm feels we have mistaken democracy and equality as "sameness" rather than "one-ness" (*The Art of Loving*, p. 15). Fromm does not believe that because man has a democratic way of living, we must homogenize humanity, but rather that each variant human being can be directed toward the same goal but not always along the same path.

Man is not instinctual even though he may have a general or uniform mode of behavior. Also, man does not satisfy his physiological needs in an animal like way. He cooks his meat, he does not eat it raw. The higher the species, the better developed is the brain, the less instinctual, therefore, is the behavior. Thus, it is possible that more learning, reasoning, and adaptable behavior can be and have been achieved by the human animal. The development of each human personality, as the human being goes through childhood, Fromm believes, somewhat recapitulates what the human race has gone through. Out of experience with his fellowmen, through the prime psychological agent of the family, the child emerges into adulthood and has a social character. Fromm believes the family is an overpowering and extremely strong force in the formation of any personality.

Specific Considerations

Dichotomies of Existence. Erich Fromm feels that man is surrounded by contradictions which are of a polar nature. These contradictions are man-made, and because they are man-made, they can be man-solved. Thus, except for one problem, our problems in life are not insoluble. One, which he feels has no solution, is called *existential dichotomies*. Fromm is referring primarily to religion. Some of the dichotomies of existence are these: man lives but he must die; man is part of nature but he also transcends it; man loves peace but wages war; in some societies man has abundance, but through inequality of wealth, many people face starvation; man has a future, but he cannot achieve his future personally (he must do it through a social order); man wants freedom but he also wants security; and man likes to believe that he behaves rationally but he is also unreasonable, immoral, and has a strong urge to behave emotionally. Other dichotomies of existence are that man wishes both to submit and to dominate others. Man wants to be alone but he has an inexpressible urge to be with others. Man denies his identity with nature as a natural animal, but he is part of nature, and always will be. Man wants governmental protection, but he chafes under governmental restrictions. Man wants to be fully individualized and be himself, but he also wants strongly to be socialized and to be like everyone else. Therefore, there is a strong dichotomy in man's existence and a split between the intellect and the emotions. Erich Fromm has taken considerable trouble to spell out his ideas in his well-known book, *Escape from Freedom.* Man now has a portion of negative freedom. Man is "free from" certain things, but he is definitely not "free to" do as he wishes. In the progress of human society mankind has developed a "marketing orientation" or "what he is worth," but he also wants a "productive orientation." Man should create out of his own individual capacities a productive way of life. Unfortunately man strives for "what he is worth" rather than "what he can do." The pleasure of satiation is not differentiated from the pleasure of production. Man finds himself gluttonous rather than creative.

Fromm feels that humanity's problems may be resolved by restoring the unity of man to nature. Man needs an orientation, a devotion, and ideals which are beyond his own selfish purposes. Without an aim, an objective, an ideal, man will continue to be lost in the dichotomies of existence. Looking back at the history of man, Fromm feels that nature is a continuing process, and it has always involved a creative activity. Thus he feels that man may still continue to emerge and resolve his dichotomies because he has continued throughout the hundreds of years to emerge beyond a pure animal state.

The name Fromm gives to the total social order which may achieve the resolvement of the dichotomies is Humanistic Communitarian Socialism. Fromm is not referring to any political party by this label nor even any national structure. He refers rather to a total world order which uses the humanistic approach, shares in a communal way, produces in a socialistic order, and will thus achieve the best possible state of existence for the human race.

Mechanisms of Escape.   There are four mechanisms of escape from the dichotomies of existence. The first is sadism toward others who are dependent upon one. He may destroy them or try to swallow up all of his problems. The second mechanism is masochism. In masochism the single personality gives up or submits to another stronger personality or another stronger group and in so doing tries to escape loneliness. The lonely masochistic personality may even ignore the bestiality of the group in order to belong to a strong group, have it engulf him, and identify with its strength, even though it hurts him in the process. The third mechanism is one of wanton destructiveness. The human personality may try to escape the feeling of powerlessness by crushing any outside force. The adolescent delinquent who perpetrates senseless destruction of property is an example of this form of escape mechanism. The fourth mechanism of escape which many people follow is automaton conformity. The automaton personality simply has a blind acceptance of all of the dichotomies of life. He has a feeling that if he can't beat them, he must join them. He totally lacks any kind of spontaneity and has no true experience of what is really his own life. In a social group he is full of meaningless chatter. This meaningless chatter which carries over to much of his thinking takes the place of true communication with his fellow men.

Temperament and Character. Fromm believes that all therapy and all of life, too, must stand on moral issues. Ultimately value judgments always determine action. There are problems of right and wrong in personality dynamics, in life itself, in religion, in any ethical consideration of behavior. Fromm does not believe there are good and bad people, but there are people who do good and bad things. The human personality is made up of temperament and character. The temperament of man's personality is the basic constitutional organic stuff with which he is born. Character, however, is formed through social pressures and influence. Character may have and usually does have two parts or halves: the individual character and the social character. The individual character comes primarily out of man's innate biological makeup plus the valuable things his famiy may or may not do for him. The social character is molded by society, and man shares this social character with society. The considerations of temperament and character may be much like Adler's style of life. In man's orientation to the world he may follow the primary path of assimilation, or being oriented toward things. The second kind of orientation would be that of socialization, or being oriented toward people. This is another example of the dichotomy of existence.

Love. In the final analysis of man's troubled existence, Fromm fervently feels that the answer to the problem is the manner and capacity of man to love. He feels that all of humanity is starved for love but that being loved is no more important than loving someone. The need to love and be loved is reciprocal. Fromm feels that love is a faculty or a function of behavior, not an object cathexis. We do not speak of true love, therefore, if we speak of a love object as if something were possessed. He also feels that love is an art and must be practiced and mastered like an art. In any art form, the artist must do two things: master the theory of his art and master the practice of it. Of all of the potentials and dynamics in man's behavior, love is probably the most active power in man and will continue to be so.

Fromm mentions four basic elements to love. They are care, responsibility, respect, and knowledge. All four of these basic elements must be mutually interdependent. None is more important than the other.

In his powerfully written book, *The Art of Loving,* Fromm proposes five types of love. They are described below:

Brotherly love is the most fundamental, the most powerful and the most underlying kind of love. It is a love between equals.

Motherly love is the love and care for the helpless, the wanting to make them strong and independent; the greatest test of motherly love is the capacity to let go or to wean; it is a love between unequals.

Erotic love is usually allied with sexual experience, a "craving for complete fusion," and is what is usually considered by most as the only kind of love. It is exclusive and inclined toward jealousy. (Fromm doubts it has anything to do with true love, because love is not basically a phenomenon of sexual satisfaction or discharge but of intimacy.) It is a love between equals.

Self-love is the care, responsibility, respect, and knowledge of self (not sinful as often assumed because of Calvinistic rigidity). Self love and love for others are not mutually exclusive; one must love self in order to be able to love others. Selfish people are not capable of self-love, but only of vanity.

Love of God has the highest value, is the most desirable good, and emphasizes care, respect, responsibility, and especially knowledge. It must be remembered that love is an act or a function, and not an object cathexis. It is essential to human existence because man must have something perfect to aspire to. Fromm quotes Miester Eckhart, "By knowing God I take him to myself. By loving God, I penetrate him" (*Art of Loving*, p. 81).

Five Human Needs. Erich Fromm recommends that there are at least five human needs which must be met in order for man to fulfill completely a true personality. They are as follows:

Transcendance: to go above being just an animal, to improve and learn, to increase in material things.

Identity: knowing one's true self, being able to identify with others.

Rootedness: return to nature or a natural way of existence and not artificial symbols, gaining satisfaction from work and not just working for money.

Frame of orientation: a consistent, good way of life, to be creative and aware and respond, live a reasonable life in a reasoning world.

Relatedness: feeling a oneness with fellowmen and with self.

Summary

Erich Fromm is a trained psychoanalyst who uses history for his psychological data. He feels that personality begins out of organic nature which very soon merges with, and is organized and molded by, society. Because man so highly prizes security, he has given up some of his freedom, so that he now has freedom from pain and threat but has lost the greater freedom to do things as he wishes. Fromm places extreme importance on the capacity to love and be loved. He feels that without love a personality cannot exist satisfactorily. And in the final analysis, Fromm continues to be an optimist. He feels man has inherent in his own personality and in the social systems he organized the capacity to solve the problems he himself has created.

DELIMITATIONS

There are no gross omissions from Fromm's work, except that Fromm's writing and thinking and speaking have been extremely abbreviated in the above treatment.

BIBLIOGRAPHY

PRIMARY SOURCES

BOOKS

Fromm, E., *Escape from Freedom,* N.Y., Holt, Rinehart and Winston, 1941.

Fromm, E., Hitler and the Nazi Authoritarian character structure, in T. M. Newcomb, and E. S. Hartley (eds.), *Readings in Social Psychology,* N.Y., Holt, Rinehart and Winston, 1947.

Fromm, E., *Man for Himself: An Inquiry Into the Psychology of Ethics,* N.Y., Holt, Rinehart and Winston, 1947.

Fromm, E., The Oedipus Complex and the Oedipus myth, in R. N. Anshen (ed.), *The Family: Its Functions and Destiny,* N.Y., Harper & Row, 1948, 334–358.

Fromm, E., Individual and social origins in neurosis, in C. Kluckhohn, and H. A. Murray (eds.), *Personality in Nature, Society and Culture,* N.Y., Knopf, 1948 and 1953.

Fromm, E., Psychoanalytic characterology and its application to the understanding of culture, in S. S. Sargent, and M. W. Smith (eds.), *Culture and Personality,* N.Y., Viking, 1949.

Fromm, E., *Psychoanalysis and Religion,* New Haven, Conn., Yale Univer. Press, 1950.

Fromm, E., *The Forgotten Language*, N.Y., Holt, Rinehart and Winston, 1951.

Fromm, E., Man-woman, in M. M. Hughes (ed.), *The People in Your Life*, N.Y., Knopf, 1951, 3–27.

Fromm, E., *The Sane Society*, N.Y., Holt, Rinehart and Winston, 1955.

Fromm, E., *The Art of Loving*, N.Y., Harper & Row, 1956.

Fromm, E., *Sigmund Freud's Mission: An Analysis of His Personality and Influence*, N.Y., Harper & Row, 1959.

Fromm, E., Values, psychology, and human existence, in A. H. Maslow (ed.), *New Knowledge in Human Values*, N.Y., Harper & Row, 1959, 151–164.
Also in J. C. Coleman, *Personality Dynamics and Effective Behavior*, Chicago, Scott, Foresman, 1960, 522–527.

Fromm, E., D. T. Suzuki, and R. DeMartino, *Zen Buddhism and Psychoanalysis*, N.Y., Harper & Row, 1960.

Fromm, E., *May Man Prevail?: An Inquiry into the Facts and Fiction of Foreign Policy*, Garden City, N.Y., Doubleday, 1961.
Also published in hardback and paperback editions.

Fromm, E., Rational and Irrational Faith, in A. E. Kuenzli (ed.), *Reconstruction in Religion: a symposium*, Boston, Beacon, 1961.

PERIODICALS

Fromm, E., Sex and character, *Psychiatry*, 1943, 6, 21–31.

Fromm, E., Individual and social origins of neurosis, *Amer. Sociol. Rev.*, 1944, 9, 380–384.

Fromm, E., The contribution of social sciences to mental hygiene, *Proc. 4th Int. Congr. Ment. Health*, 1951, 38–42.

Fromm, E., Remarks on the problem of free association, *Psychiat. Res. Rep.*, 1955, 2, 1–6.

Fromm, E., Love and its disintegration, *Pastoral Psychol.*, 1956, 7(68), 37–44.

SUGGESTED READINGS

BOOKS

Brown, I.A.C., *Freud and the Post-Freudians*, Baltimore, Penguin, 1961.
Horney, Fromm, and Sullivan also included.

Coleman, J. C., *Personality Dynamics and Effective Behavior*, Chicago, Scott, Foresman, 1960.

Munroe, R. L., *Schools of Psychoanalytic Thought*, N.Y., Holt, Rinehart and Winston, 1955.
Analysis and integration of Freud, Adler, Jung, Rank, Fromm, Horney, Sullivan, *et al.*

Schaar, J. H., *Escape from Authority: The perspectives of Erich Fromm*, N.Y., Basic Books, 1961.

PERIODICALS

Arieti, S., The double methodology in the study of personality and its disorders, *Amer. J. Psychother.*, 1957, *11*, 532–547.
  Fromm and Sullivan on the idiographic–historical and nomothetic–scientific approaches to personality study.

de la Fuente-Muniz, R., Fromm's approach to the study of personality, *Psychiat. Res. Rep.*, 1955, *2*, 7–14.

James, W. T., Karen Horney and Erich Fromm in relation to Alfred Adler, *Indiv. Psychol. Bull.*, 1947, *6*, 105–116.

Yonker, H. J., Ambiguities of love: an inquiry into the psychology of Erich Fromm, *Dissert. Abstr.*, 1961, *22*(4), 1245.

PART VI

FINAL THOUGHTS
AND RECONSIDERATIONS

Rightly or wrongly, students develop theories of personality of their own. It seems most sensible, therefore, not to ignore this natural bent but to use it. The creation of a sensible and usable theory of personality is the rationale of this book. It is obvious that the theories will be imperfect. This is not necessarily bad. All the theories in the present book are in a sense imperfect. Students develop theories of personality because they need them. They need them in teaching, counseling, therapy, and practically all pursuits of life where one human being touches another. Students also need an emerging theory of personality specifically to understand themselves, whether they operate within a psychological frame of reference in an occupation, as a student preparing for an occupation, or whether they operate in a life situation not directly allied with the psychological field.

As we said in the beginning, the question usually asked by a student taking a course in theories of personality is, "Why can't we have one inclusive theory of personality to settle all of this?" The question is premature but sensible. It, therefore, requires some kind of answer. Possibly, one of the best answers is that psychology does not have a single over-all theory of personality primarily because the psychology of personality has not had the full benefits and the contributions of rigid experimental research that other psychological fields have had. Such fields as learning and perception have long been worked over and have been able to produce more definitive statements than has the field of theories of personality. The conventional techniques that have been so valuable and have contributed so much to other fields are not applicable to research in personality as yet. We are still wondering *how* to proceed rather than *what to report* in the field of personality study.

Hall and Lindzey in their *Theories of Personality* (pp. 555–557) also attempt to answer the question of why we have no over-all theory at this point in psychological history. They feel that a synthesistic harmony is not the healthiest thing now. Theories of personality are also not clearly enough stated; the conflicts emerging from the divergent theories are not yet resolvable; and at the present time, all theories are not important contributions to the field.

The final chapter of this text, Chapter 16, contains no summary or conclusions. It is the strong conviction of the present author that summarization and conclusions are the job of the student, with the aid and guidance of the instructor.

16

Recapitulations

INTRODUCTION

Chapter 16 has been divided into five sections: Summarizing Personality Theories, Evaluating Personality Theories, The Use and Abuse of Personal Personality Theories, A Personal Theory of Personality, and The Future of Personality Theories. It is hoped that these five sections will help the instructor and the student to arrive at comfortable conclusions and a summary of the work contained in the present text.

SUMMARIZING PERSONALITY THEORIES

To repeat the theme introduced before, the present author contends that summarization is the province of the instructor and especially his students. Too much "cooking" can be done for the reader.

Various methods may be employed in summarizing the work of the preceding theorists. One method is listing the principles, which has been done in the following outline. Having listed the principles, we must ask ourselves, "Are all the principles listed equally important?"

Freud: Pleasure, Reality, Tension-Reduction, Polarity, Repetition-Compulsion (5).

Sheldon: Body-Temperament, Continuous Variable, Inductive–Empirical, Objective Measurement, Consistency of Somatotype, Behavioral Environment (6).

Murray: Regnancy, Motivation, Longitudinal, Physiological Processes, Abstract, Uniqueness, Role (7).

Jung: Polarity, Equivalence, Entropy, Self-Actualization, Unconscious States, Teleology (6).

Adler: Inferiority, Superiority, Style of Life, Creative Self, Conscious Self, Fictional Goals, Social Interest (7).

Sullivan: Interpersonal Relations, Tension System, Anxiety, Dynamism, Personification, Cognitive Experiences (6).

Horney: Optimism–Positivism, Society–Culture, Character Structure, Self Concept, Complementation–Conflict, Self-Analysis (6).

Moreno: Social Atom, Tele, Warming Up, Role Playing, Spontaneity, Creativity, Cultural Conserve, Group Development, Sociogenetic Law, Measurement (10).

Rogers: Self, Self-Actualization, Self-Preservation, Self-Enhancement (4).

Allport: Motivation, Learning, Contemporaneity, Uniqueness, Ego or Self, Continuity–Discontinuity, Traits–Trends–Tendency–Temperament (7).

Murphy: (Themes) Biological Personality, Emerging and Integrating Personality, Socialized Personality, Human Potentialities or New Perspectives (4).

The student of personality theory may now summarize these sixty-eight principles according to their importance, their necessity, or the completeness with which they treat each personality theory.

A second method of summarizing personality theories may be by suggesting explanations of behavioral phenomena which are not handled in the explanation section of each of these chapters. For example, thumb sucking, stuttering, forgetting, anger, thrift, amnesia, shame, dancing, singing may all be explained by these theories. In addition to creating new explanations, the student may find it of further profit to extract different explanations then has the present author for the nine behavioral activities as they have been treated in this text: marriage, perversions, suicide, law-breaking, supranatural being, humor, smoking, play and recreation, and functional psychoses–neuroses. It would be interesting to conjecture whether the student would give the same explanations that have been given in this text.

A third method of summarizing personality theories as they are contained in this book would be to rearrange the theories from the most significant to the least significant on a number of criteria. The author suggests that one may rearrange the theories as to their importance concerning hereditary influence on personality development. Another method may be to decide the influence of early development, such as the Freudians advocate, in personality formation. Following Allport's suggestion, we may rearrange or decide the importance of the theories in their treatment of the uniqueness of each personality. The self concept as handled by Gold-stein, Rogers, and others may be a fourth method of determining the significance of each theory. Social and cultural determinants may also be a method. Undoubtedly, the undergraduate student has already considered or can be led to consider the theories from the viewpoint of the easiest to the most difficult to understand. The author, in teaching his own classes in personality theory, has frequently had the students attempt to study the theories in a different sequence, putting Freud last, for example, rather than first, or rearranging the theories in some other order which seems meaningful to the student. However, probably the most meaning-ful method of summarizing personality theories is from the viewpoint of those which have produced or seem to stimulate the most research.

A fourth approach to summarizing personality theories is to look for the common use of terms such as *ego, self, homeostasis, polarity, unique-ness,* or other terms which repeatedly occur, although treated differently in each of the theories.

One of the best ways of summarizing the personality theories is to read the original work and compare it with the present treatment in this text. What agreements and what discrepancies are found? For example, does the student find more or fewer principles? Having read all of the works of Moreno, does the student find ten principles, as there are in this book, or does he find more or fewer?

Evaluating Personality Theories

Evaluating personality theories, whether it be one's own or the theory of another individual, is much like summarizing theories, for in sum-marizing we often find ourselves evaluating them at least through the position which they should hold. Hall and Lindzey in their *Theories of Personality* (chap. 14) employ six criteria for evaluating a personality theory: which theories possess the ability to generate or stimulate research, that is, which have the better methodology; which theories are prone to have too much literary brilliance and not enough research utility; which theories are highly creative and radical but also need to be critically evaluated; which theories depart from customary preconceptions; which theory works better; and which theory, while condemning all others, is itself trivial?

Wolman in his *Contemporary Theories and Systems in Psychology* evaluates theories on a five-point basis. Does the theory have an inner consistency, that is, does it contradict itself; is the theory testable in the situation by controlled experimentation; is the theory useful; is the theory simple enough in language and in dynamics to be workable; and, especially, does the theory lead to some kind of prediction?

Another method of evaluating a theory is to use Allport's five requirements as they are found in this book. Personality should be centered in the person. Personality theory should be full of meaning. Motivation should be central to any personality theory. Personality theories should use units that are capable of being coordinated or synthesized. Personality theories should allow for self-consciousness in behavior.

Yet another method of evaluating personality theories is that of Sears, in which he discusses five dimensions or properties that should be inherent in a personality theory.[1] Sears states that a personality theory should have a basic reference to behavior in terms of action; it should integrate monadic and dyadic events; it should explain action and learning rather than rely on learning alone to explain all human behavior; it should describe the human being in terms of potentials to act; and as human behavior changes, it should have some chance to predict the changes.

We suggested in Chapter 1 that personality theories should be evaluated according to their use of simple and clear language; their usefulness; their orderliness and organization; their ability to clarify and explain human behavior; and their capacity to predict human behavior.

The semantic device used in each chapter of this book may lend itself in another way to evaluating personality theories. Description, explanation, and prediction of human behavior may be used. In short, how well does the theory describe man's behavior? How well can we explain reasons for what a human being does by using the theory? How well does the theory predict, either on a personal basis or a scientific and laboratory basis, the future outcome of human behavior for the individual or for society?

The student of personality theory is strongly urged not to ignore any new approach. It is best to listen and learn first, and only then to add a strong dose of healthy skepticism. Skepticism in the beginning is premature. It closes off the mind and erects a prejudicial block which prevents one's progress. The student is cautioned not to be overwhelmed by the language of a theory. Some theories appear more pedantic than they actually are because of the words used.

[1] See Sears's excellent article in Parson and Shil's, *Toward A General Theory of Action* (pp. 465–476).

In the *Kentucky Symposium,* Ammons presents (pp. 139–141) some interesting comments in regard to his own experience with graduate students in theory-making and creating postulates, the assuming or seeking of principles. Ammons finds theory-making or postulating to be very hard work for his students. Careful and logical thinking is rigorous exercise, which many of his students try to avoid, only to end by begging the question. Students will say, "I don't know enough to postulate a system of personality theories." Whether or not this be rationalization to avoid the hard work of thinking, the excuse becomes more pointed when the rewards of personality theory formation are seen by the student not to be immediate.

The writer is strongly influenced toward one method of evaluating any or all personality theories—that is, that the best way is to construct a research design and so test the theory. It is hoped that the student will attempt some research in personality theory.

The Use and Abuse of Personal Personality Theories

Hard work is required to create a theory about human behavior. There is a benefit to be gained in thinking about the world of ideas. There is a further benefit gained in knowing where and how an individual gets his ideas.

While one is working in the field of personality theories, whether or not they are acknowledged as real theories, one finds that they often influence one's way of behaving. It may be true that the theory evolves out of trial and error, which is not an unusual process in the course of living. It must further be admitted that a theory may often be a disguise for a prejudice, attitude, conviction, or conditioned mode of behavior.

The importance of personality theories has been stressed throughout this book. It seems important to know why man behaves as he does, why he does the things that he does, and the significance of his behavior in all realms of living. This has been emphasized especially in Chapters 1 and 2.

Much danger lies in creating a theory of one's own that is meaningful. Armchair theorizing can create confusion. It is not our intention to encourage a student of personality to proliferate theories. However, only by creating, especially from the fabric of others, can we hope to forward the efforts of all. It is possible that if enough workers are involved, we may be able to test these theories in practice, as well as in the hoped-for, refined research that is so badly needed in this field.

A Personal Theory of Personality

It is possible, but improbable, to create a theory of one's own with no trace of other theories. The theories considered in this book cover almost every conceivable approach. Therefore, in constructing his own theory, the student is bound to select from aspects of theories that have been studied, and then to add his own unique touch.

A number of benefits in creating a personal theory of personality are advanced. Limited as is the field of personality theory, it is almost incumbent on all students that they do what they can in their own realm to advance the field. This is not unlike other phenomena in life for which all of us have personal theories, in regard to voting for political candidates, purchasing goods, the raising of our children, our occupational endeavors, or most human behavioral acts. Having to undergo the extremely hard work and advanced thinking demanded in creating a theory of personality may help us, of course, in understanding ourselves. It follows from this that we may have better contacts and better understanding with others, be they parents, friends, teachers, employers, or employees. The strongest benefit, however, would seem to be in the direction of research. At the present time it seems that the knowing *how to proceed* or *how to create tools* to study personality can be as important as the results that one may get.

When a student is forced to create a personal theory of personality, he must come to grips with some definition of personality. Although his definition may be fairly loose and disorganized, it may still have tremendous value if it comes from himself. There is, of course, the problem of communication in that the language one uses does not always communicate his thoughts to others. For example, the use of symbols or mathematical formulations does not necessarily reduce the problem of communication. Symbols may cause the theory to be confined or compressed into a symbolic device. Then, if we find that behavior does not fit the symbol, we must reinterpret the behavior to fit, or we must create more symbols, which only adds to the confusion.

It is the strongest conviction of the author that research or testability is the essential feature of psychological progress. To find the laws of human behavior is an essential problem that cannot be solved without research. Actually, personality theories are easily constructed, as are projective tests. Finding out, however, how worthwhile the theories are is no simple matter. Research is the key, the material from which good theories are constructed.

The writer feels compelled to caution the student not to take himself too seriously. There is always some room for the sense of the ridiculous in one's own theory or the theory of others.

With emphasis upon the word *good*, we may best end with Dorpfeld's dictum: "There is nothing more practical than a *good* theory."

Future of Personality Theories

It should seem evident to any reader of this book that personality theories will become more and more important in the field of psychology. Many have called them the central problem in psychology. At the present time we may predict that at least two things will happen in the field of personality theories: It will continue to change, and it seems inevitable that errors will be made and that these errors will be corrected.

There is progress in psychology. There is excitement in psychology. There is movement in psychology. The student of human behavior is invited to join the progress and the excitement.

BIBLIOGRAPHY

SUGGESTED READINGS

BOOKS

Adams, D. K., *The Anatomy of Personality*, Garden City, N.Y., Doubleday, 1954.

Bandura, A., and R. H. Walters, *Social Learning and Personality Development*, N.Y., Holt, Rinehart and Winston, 1963.
  Social variables and social learning theories.

Blum, G. S., *Psychoanalytic Theories of Personality*, N.Y., McGraw-Hill, 1953.
  A classic on Freud and the neo-Freudians.

Bonner, H., *Psychology of Personality*, N.Y., Ronald, 1961.

Brand, H., *The Study of Personality: A Book of Readings*, N.Y., Wiley, 1954.

Bronfenbrenner, U., Toward an integrated theory of personality, in R. R. Blake, and G. V. Ramsey (eds.), *Perception: An Approach to Personality*, N.Y., Ronald, 1951, Chap. 9.

Coleman, J. C., *Personality Dynamics and Effective Behavior*, Chicago, Scott, Foresman, 1960.

Based on the premise that man has "inborn capacity for responsible self-direction."

David, H. P., and H. von Bracken (eds.), *Perspectives in Personality Theory,* N.Y., Basic Books, 1957.

The international touch—22 authors from 10 countries.

Diamond, S., *Personality and Temperament,* N.Y., Harper & Row, 1957.

Development of individuality in the normal person.

Dollard, J., and N. E. Miller, *Personality and Psychotherapy,* N.Y., McGraw-Hill, 1950.

Dreger, R. M., *Fundamentals of Personality,* N.Y., Lippincott, 1962.

Grinker, R. R. (ed.), *Toward a Unified Theory of Human Behavior,* N.Y., Basic Books, 1956.

Excellent source.

Guilford, J. P., *Personality,* N.Y., McGraw-Hill, 1959.

Heavy emphasis on factor analytic approach to personality study.

Hall, C. S., and G. Lindzey, *Theories of Personality,* N.Y., Wiley, 1957.

One of the best overall treatments of personality theory for resource purposes.

Harsh, C. M., and H. G. Schrickel, *Personality: Development and Assessment* [1950], (2nd ed.), N.Y., Ronald, 1959.

Johnson, P. E., *Personality and Religion,* N.Y., Abingdon, 1957.

Uses Freud, Lewin, Sullivan, and Allport views in studying a girl's development.

Kentucky Symposium, *Learning Theory, Personality Theory, and Clinical Research,* N.Y., Wiley, 1954.

Eleven lectures at Univer. of Kentucky, March, 1953, by such notables as Cattell, Harlow, Mowrer, Snygg, Spence, and Wickens.

Klein, G. S., and D. Krech, *Theoretical Models and Personality Theory,* Durham, N.C., Duke Univer. Press, 1952.

Personality theory must be unified and explanatory.

Kluckhohn, C., H. A. Murray, and D. M. Schneider (eds.), *Personality in Nature, Society and Culture,* (2nd ed.), N.Y., Knopf, 1953.

A compilation of all the approaches.

Leary, T., *Interpersonal Diagnosis of Personality: A Functional Theory and Methodology for Personality Evaluation,* N.Y., Ronald, 1957.

Interpersonal behavior and personality theory in the therapeutic setting.

Leeper, R., Theories of personality, in W. Dennis, (ed.), *Current Trends in Psychological Theory,* Pittsburgh, Pa., Univer. Pittsburgh Press, 1951.

Lundin, R. W., *Personality: An Experimental Approach,* N.Y., Macmillan, 1961.

Experiments, many of them animal, on personality.

McClelland, D. C., Toward a science of personality psychology, in H. P. David, and H. von Bracken (eds.), *Perspectives in Personality Theory*, N.Y., Basic Books, 1957.

Highly recommended for the student of personality theory who is discouraged or confused–so are others.

McClelland, D. C., *Personality*, N.Y., Holt, Rinehart and Winston, 1951, (reissued, 1958).

Intensive study of one personality.

McCrary, J. L. (ed.), *Psychology of Personality: Six Modern Approaches*, N.Y., Logos Press, 1956.

Symposium Univer. of Houston, 1954.

McCurdy, H. G., *The Personal World: An Introduction to the Study of Personality*, N.Y., Harcourt, Brace & World, 1961.

An undergraduate text.

Mednick, M. T., and S. A. Mednick, *Research in Personality*, N.Y., Holt, Rinehart and Winston, 1963.

Nielson, G. (ed.), Personality Research, *Proceedings of the Fourteenth International Congress of Applied Psychology*, Vol. 2, Copenhagen, Denmark, Munskgaard, 1962.

Notcutt, B., *The Psychology of Personality*, N.Y., Philosophical Library, 1953.

Nuttin, J., *Psychoanalysis and Personality: A Dynamic Theory of Normal Personality*, N.Y., Sheed, 1953.

Father Nuttin, a Belgian, in a refreshing approach.

Roback, A. A., *Personality in Theory and Practice*, Cambridge, Mass., Sci-Art, 1950.

Roback, A. A., Personality study at crossroads, in A. A. Roback (ed.), *Present Day Psychology*, N.Y., *Philosophical Library*, 1955, 189–238.

Rotter, J. B., *Social Learning and Clinical Psychology*, Englewood Cliffs, N. J., Prentice-Hall, 1954.

Systematic theory for clinical psychologists.

Sarnoff, I., *Personality Dynamics and Development*, N.Y., Wiley, 1962.

Integrates psychoanalytic theory and research for normal individuals.

Saul, L. J., *The Development and Dynamics of Personality: Emotional Maturity* (2nd ed.), Phila., Pa., Lippincott, 1960.

A developmental theory of personality–based on psychoanalysis–combines biological, psychological and sociological.

Sears, R. R., Social behavior and personality development, in T. Parsons, and E. A. Shils (eds.), *Toward a General Theory of Action*, Cambridge, Mass., Harvard Univer. Press, 1951, 465–476.

Snygg, D., and A. W. Combs, *Individual Behavior*, N.Y., Harper & Row, 1949.

A much-quoted classic in its field.

Thorpe, L. P., and A. M. Schmuller, *Personality: An Interdisciplinary Approach*, Princeton, N.J., Van Nostrand, 1958.

A "patterned eclecticism" is the rationale.

Wallace, A.F.C., *Culture and Personality*, N.Y., Random House, 1961.

Analysis of personality research and personality theory.

White, R. W., *Lives in Progress: A Study of the Natural Growth of Personality*, N.Y., Holt, Rinehart and Winston, 1952.

Highly readable, interesting account of three lives: a physician, businessman, and housewife.

Wolman, B. J., *Contemporary Theories and Systems in Psychology*, N.Y., Harper & Row, 1960.

Excellent source book—almost encyclopaedic.

Young, K., *Personality and Problems of Adjustment* (2nd ed.), N.Y., Appleton-Century-Crofts, 1952.

A traditional author in the field of sociology.

PERIODICALS

Allen, D. A., Aptitudes and personality, *Harv. Educ. Rev.*, 1956, 26, 17–23.

Aptitudes emerge from personality factors.

Beck, S. J., Personality research and theories of personality structure: Some convergences, *J. Proj. Tech.*, 1955, 19, 361–371.

Jackson's neurological theories, Freud's psychological, and Rorschach's theory are compatible, consistent and logical.

Falk, J. L., Issues distinguishing idiographic from nomothetic approaches to personality theory, *Psychol. Rev.*, 1956, 63, 53–62.

Freides, D., Toward the elimination of the concept of normality, *J. Consult. Psychol.*, 1960, 24, 128–133.

Normality in personality theory is criticized.

Gilbert, A. R., Intentionalism, *J. Psychol.*, 1959, 48, 181–190.

The author attempts for a "unified theory of personality" to avoid "small package theories."

Greenspoon, J., Perspectives in psychology: XIX. Private experience revisited, *Psychol. Rec.*, 1961, 11, 373–381.

Private experience is a false point of departure—start with behavior.

Hayakawa, S. I., The fully functioning personality, *ETC Rev. Gen. Semant.*, 1956, 13, 169–181.

Uses Rogers, Maslow, D. H. Lawrence, and Korzybski in discussing the healthy personality.

Helson, H., An experimental approach to personality, *Psychiat. Res. Rep.*, 1955, 2, 89–99.

Personality and perception viewed in the same light.

Kanner, L., Centripetal forces in personality development, *Amer. J. Psychoanal.*, 1959, *19*, 123–133.

Freud is to integrate centrifugal (internal) and centripetal (external) forces.

Kelly, E. L., Consistency of the adult personality, *Amer. Psychologist*, 1955, *10*, 659–681.

Test of 600 persons, ages 16–18 and retested later—showing people don't give up—"adults may hope for continued psychological growth."

McGriegan, F. J., Confirmation of theories in psychology, *Psychol. Rev.*, 1956, *63*, 98–104.

Maier, N. R. F., Maier's Law, *Amer. Psychologist*, 1960, *15*, 208–212.

Any theory that cannot be quantified is inadequate, even if it works.

Mailloux, N., The contribution of clinical research to personality theory, *Canad. J. Psychol.*, 1955, *9*, 133–143.

Restricted interpretation of method has delayed theory development. Methodologists are stopping ideas before they get started.

Milner, E., New frontiers in personality theory, *J. Nat. Ass. Deans Wom.*, 1954, (Mar.) 105–119.

Advocates the cross-discipline approach.

Roby, T. B., An opinion on the construction of behavior theory, *Amer. Psychologist*, 1959, *14*, 129–134.

Natural sciences are ahead of the behavioral sciences—the latter is far from satisfactory.

Sears, R. R., Personality theory: the next forty years, *Monogr. Soc. Res. Child Develpm.*, 1959, *24*, 37–48.

Secord, P. F., and C. W. Backman, Personality theory and the problem of stability change in individual behavior: an interpersonal approach, *Psychol. Rev.*, 1961, *68*(1), 21–32.

Three components: subject, object, and their interaction.

Shaklee, A. B., Optional stopping and theory making, *Psychol. Rep.*, 1958, *4*, 17.

The value of terminating observations in theory construction.

Van Kaam, A., Existential psychology as a comprehensive theory of personality, *Rev. Existent. Psychol. Psychiat.*, 1963, *3*(1), 11–26.

Because it is so complex, existential psychology is valuable as a personality theory.

Winthrop, H., Scientism in psychology, *J. Indiv. Psychol.*, 1959, *15*, 112–120.

Because methods and assumptions work in the physical sciences does not mean they will, can, or should, in psychology.

Index of Names

[Italicized numbers indicate pages on which reference works appear.]

Index of Subjects

137
B62i

19220   19220

Bischof

Interpreting personality theories